Policy, Pedagogy, and Professional Practice in the AI-Enabled University

Caroline M. Crawford
https://orcid.org/0009-0006-6507-1960
University of Houston-Clear Lake, USA

IGI Global
Scientific Publishing
Publishing Tomorrow's Research Today

Vice President of Editorial	Melissa Wagner
Director of Acquisitions	Mikaela Felty
Director of Book Development	Jocelynn Hessler
Production Manager	Mike Brehm
Cover Design	Jose Rosado

Published in the United States of America by
IGI Global Scientific Publishing
701 East Chocolate Avenue
Hershey, PA, 17033, USA
Tel: 717-533-8845 | Fax: 717-533-7115
Website: https://www.igi-global.com E-mail: cust@igi-global.com

Library of Congress Cataloging-in-Publication Data

LCCN: 2026032300 (CIP Data Pending)
ISBN13: 9798260028117
Isbn13Softcover: 9798260028124
EISBN13: 9798260028131

British Cataloguing in Publication Data
A Cataloguing in Publication record for this book is available from the British Library.

Editorial Advisory Board

Table of Contents

Detailed Table of Contents

The paper presents the results of exploration of the use of AI within the field of software engineering with particular attention to AI support for the tasks of requirements engineering, coding, code reviews, testing and debugging, deployment and maintenance, and software project management. Within this broader topic, the paper discusses current AI tools for software development, the limitations, risks, and strengths of AI in software development, as well as issues of bias, hallucinations, error injection and the juxtaposition of these risks versus productivity gain. The paper and its references together provide an introduction to the current state of AI for assisting with software engineering educators and researchers.

AI use in education is becoming more prevalent every day and the particular research subfield of AI in education is commonly abbreviated as AIEd. AI in higher education is particularly getting research attention; there are several survey papers published on this topic. On the other hand, trustworthy AI is an important research problem that emerged due to the need to address the topics of fairness, privacy, accountability, explainability, bias, and ethics when deploying and using AI applications and tools. In this book chapter, we focus on trustworthy AI and nursing education, based on recent related papers. First, we cover those studies on AI use in higher education, and next we analyze research papers and review papers on the use of AI systems in nursing education, with a particular emphasis on trustworthy AI concepts and principles. We conclude our chapter with a compilation of relevant insights on the topic and also outline future research directions.

A strength of higher education is the ability to engage teaching, research, and service for greater good. With the growing worldwide demand for seafood, aquaculture has emerged as an essential element of nutritional security and sustainability. In this context, automatic monitoring and feeding have become indispensable tools for improving aquaculture performance. In this paper, we developed an intelligent system for real-time monitoring and automatic food distribution in aquaculture. The system combines sensors, electronic devices, and data processing algorithms to monitor fish health, analyze environmental conditions, and distribute feed in a precise and controlled way. The main goal is to increase productivity and profitability while ensuring the welfare of the fish. By detecting signs of disease, stress, or abnormal behavior, the system enables rapid intervention to prevent health issues and reduce losses. Furthermore, by adjusting the amount and frequency of feed according to the specific needs of the fish, the system minimizes food waste and supports healthy, consistent growth.

AI-powered teaching support has reshaped financial market prediction by capturing non-linear relationships, complex features, and hidden structures in data. Improved computing power and advanced algorithms have raised hopes of overcoming earlier forecasting limits. Yet, financial markets tend to absorb information quickly, reducing the scope for consistent predictability. Although these models can detect patterns, their stability over time remains doubtful. Market data often show non-stationarity,

This chapter examines the transformative role of Large Language Models (LLMs) in AI-powered automation within higher education, highlighting strategic opportunities and emerging risks across teaching, research, and academic service. The purpose of this chapter per the authors is to evaluate how LLMs support pedagogical innovation, personalised learning, curriculum design, research productivity, and administrative efficiency, while addressing challenges related to academic integrity, bias, data governance, epistemic reliability, and potential deskilling. Drawing on recent theoretical and empirical developments, the discussion situates LLM adoption within ethical AI, quality assurance, and institutional governance frameworks. Emphasis is placed on human-centred integration that balances automation with academic oversight. The chapter concludes by proposing a governance-oriented model to guide responsible and sustainable LLM deployment in higher education ecosystems.

Artificial Intelligence has emerged as a lifestyle adaptation technology posing novel challenges to existing legal and ethical frameworks. Such frameworks are required to ensure that AI systems are developed with safety, transparency, and alignment with human values and ethics in mind. The evolving and ever-changing characteristics of AI make it difficult to regulate or govern. This chapter focuses on three broad aspects. Firstly, we try to define characteristics that make AI governance a unique endeavour. Secondly, we examine prevalent frameworks that are adopted worldwide by various organisations/ nations. Thereafter, we concentrate on five policy frameworks that

Preface

INTRODUCTION

Artificial intelligence (AI), agentic artificial intelligence (agentic AI), and large language models (LLMs) have realized significant growth at a global scale, with significant impact upon societal and cultural realms. Equally impactful is the impact of AI, agentic AI, and LLMs, on higher education. The recognition of policy, pedagogy, and professional practice that equally includes the realms of scholarly research and service, recognizing the current shifts and earthquakes occurring do necessitate a thoughtful and elastic response to the ever-changing experience and impact of AI, agentic AI, and LLMs upon higher education. Specifically at the university level, the response to these influential resources affects and collides with the more traditional teaching, scholarly research, and service that occurs within and throughout higher education. The question raised through this current impact, is how does higher education respond as the evolution into an AI-enabled university evolve and embrace an evolution of policy, pedagogy, and professional practice within this new landscape.

The primary objective of this edited volume is to explore the current and potential impact of AI, agentic AI, and LLMs upon the policy, pedagogy, and professional practice of a higher education institution within which AI-powered automation is in the midst of its evolution and the potential impact from a short-term consideration as well as a long-term strategic understanding. This timely publication has the potential to capture a snapshot of the current understanding of higher education as it evolves to embrace AI-enabled resources. This evolution may have a significant impact on policy within the current bounds of higher education. Specific focus upon policy as it guides and impacts teaching, scholarly research, and teaching as aspects of professional practice are inherent within the understanding of AI as offering potential support for the learning process as well as scholarly research and service opportunities, while recognizing the potential for AI-enhanced structures to directly impact the creative aspects of higher education, including higher order thinking skills that equally includes a focus upon critical thinking and wisdom, while consistently reflecting upon the potential impact upon the ever-evolving knowledge base of each specialization area. The shifts and changes that are currently in progress may directly evolve into an impact upon faculty careers within higher education realms.

ORGANIZATION OF THE BOOK

The book is organized into thirteen chapters, within three distinct sections. The sections are:

- AI Impact Upon Higher Education Policy
- AI Impact Upon Areas of Specialization
- Technology as an Innovation

A brief description of each of the chapters follows.

Chapter 1 is titled *Harnessing Context-Aware AI to Strengthen Teaching Practices in Higher Education* by Archana Tamizharasan and Yamuna Devi. This chapter outlines how Context-Aware Artificial Intelligence (AI) enhances teaching and learning in higher education. By analyzing learner behavior, existing knowledge, engagement patterns, and performance data. AI enables early risk detection, adaptive content delivery, personalized support and real-time assessment feedback. This chapter observes how AI based analytics, intelligent tutoring systems, and contextualized assessment reshape learning assessment and support student practices. It also highlights the key implementation considerations, including ethical governance, faculty digital skills, and unified system integration. Finally, it outlines future directions such as active learning environments and AI-supported teaching assistants, then the context-aware AI is positioned as a strategic tool for advancing instructional quality and student success.

Chapter 2 is titled *Context-Aware AI in Teaching: Balancing Efficiency, Authenticity, and Academic Honesty* by Vivit Rosmayanti and Hasnawati Hasnawati. This chapter is focused on explaining how context-aware AI technologies have transformed the opportunities and challenges of post-secondary education. AI teaches the flexibility of methods and how automation can improve instruction efficiency. However, concerns about AI and automation can lead to a loss of teaching and learning human touch. This chapter also touches on human agency, the ethics of AI policies, and the role of sustainability. In relation to AI and teaching, the author introduces a three-pillar system. Sustainability in AI and teaching can come through transparent instructional design, policy integration to ensure a balance of teaching integrity, academic integrity, and the adoption of technology, and continuous training of teaching staff.

Chapter 3 is titled *Cognitive AI Agents and Natural Language Processing Transforming Higher Education* by Ayesha Farooqi. High-level education, in its entirety, is undergoing a paradigm shift with the integration of cognitive AI agents and natural language processing regarding how teaching, research and academic services are provided. Autonomous reasoning, adaptation, and decision-making are possible with the help of cognitive AI agents, and meaningful interaction with written and spoken academic texts can be done with the help of NLP. This chapter discusses the technology of basis and use of cognitive AI and language processing in higher education, and its impact on intelligent tutoring, customized education, research robotics, and intelligent institutional services. It is also critical about the problems of algorithm bias, transparency, ethical governance, and the connection between humans and AI. Offering an interdisciplinary and detailed view, the chapter provides information on how AI agents of cognitive agents and NLP can contribute to the innovative and inclusive and responsible changes in higher education ecosystems.

Chapter 4 is titled *Exploring Opportunities, Risks, and Policy Implications of Artificial Intelligence in Higher Education and Research* by Rampelli Manojkumar. Artificial intelligence is rapidly becoming part of the everyday fabric of higher education, influencing how universities teach, conduct research, and manage institutional operations. This chapter examines AI not as a neutral technological upgrade, but as a transformative force that reshapes academic practices, professional roles, and ethical responsibilities. In teaching and learning, AI enables personalization and accessibility while raising concerns about autonomy, surveillance, bias, and trust. In research, AI tools enhance productivity and analytical capacity but challenge long-standing norms of authorship, originality, and responsibility. The chapter argues that responsible AI adoption requires strategic collaboration, clear and adaptive policies, and strong ethical foundations. By aligning technological innovation with academic values, universities can leverage AI's benefits while safeguarding integrity, accountability, and social responsibility.

Chapter 5 is titled *AI in Software Engineering: Overview, Tools, Limitations, Risks and Strengths* by Sharon K Andrews. The paper presents the results of exploration of the use of AI within the field of software engineering with particular attention to AI support for the tasks of requirements engineering, coding, code reviews, testing and debugging, deployment and maintenance, and software project management. Within this broader topic, the paper discusses current AI tools for software development, the limitations, risks, and strengths of AI in software development, as well as issues of bias, hallucinations, error injection and the juxtaposition of these risks versus productivity gain. The paper and its references together provide an introduction to the current state of AI for assisting with software engineering educators and researchers.

Chapter 6 is titled *Trustworthy AI and Nursing Education* by Emine Ela Küçük and Dilek Küçük. AI use in education is becoming more prevalent every day and the particular research subfield of AI in education is commonly abbreviated as AIEd. AI in higher education is particularly getting research attention; there are several survey papers published on this topic. On the other hand, trustworthy AI is an important research problem that emerged due to the need to address the topics of fairness, privacy, accountability, explainability, bias, and ethics when deploying and using AI applications and tools. In this book chapter, we focus on trustworthy AI and nursing education, based on recent related papers. First, we cover those studies on AI use in higher education, and next we analyze research papers and review papers on the use of AI systems in nursing education, with a particular emphasis on trustwor-thy AI concepts and principles. We conclude our chapter with a compilation of relevant insights on the topic and also outline future research directions.

Chapter 7 is titled *Teaching, Research, and Service Through Smart Aquaculture in the Age of AI-Powered Automation: An IoT System for Automatic Feeding and Monitoring* by Balkis Tej, Soulef Bouaafia, Mohamed Ali Hajjaji, and Abdellatif Mtibaa. A strength of higher education is the ability to engage teaching, research, and service for greater good. With the growing worldwide demand for seafood, aquaculture has emerged as an essential element of nutritional security and sustainability. In this context, automatic monitoring and feeding have become indispensable tools for improving aquaculture performance. In this paper, we developed an intelligent system for real-time monitoring and automatic food distribution in aquaculture. The system combines sensors, electronic devices, and data processing algorithms to monitor fish health, analyze environmental conditions, and distribute feed in a precise and controlled way. The main goal is to increase productivity and profitability while ensuring the welfare of the fish. By detecting signs of disease, stress, or abnormal behavior, the system enables rapid intervention to prevent health issues and reduce losses. Furthermore, by adjusting the amount and frequency of feed according to the specific needs of the fish, the system minimizes food waste and supports healthy, consistent growth.

Chapter 8 is titled *Higher Education Instruction Through AI-Powered Automation with Machine Learning in Financial Market Prediction: Algorithmic Trading, Structural Limits, and Economic Realities* by Mohammad Irfan, Bhanu Pratap Singh, Saurabh Kumar, and Rashi Malik. AI-powered teaching support has reshaped financial market prediction by capturing non-linear relationships, complex features, and hidden structures in data. Improved computing power and advanced algorithms have raised hopes of overcoming earlier forecasting limits. Yet, financial markets tend to absorb information quickly, reducing the scope for consistent predictability.

Although these models can detect patterns, their stability over time remains doubtful. Market data often show non-stationarity, volatility clustering, and structural changes, making predictions less reliable. In addition, as market participants adapt, widely known patterns lose their advantage. Challenges such as overfitting, data leakage, and weak signal strength further affect model outcomes. Studies also show that better statistical results do not always lead to real economic benefits once costs and risks are considered. Therefore, the limits of prediction are largely economic in nature, and machine learning is better viewed as a support tool for decision-making rather than a guaranteed source of excess returns.

Chapter 9 is titled *The AI-Enhanced Classroom A Blueprint for Collaborative Intelligence* by Seema Mishra and Devender Kumar. The widespread release of the generative AI towards the end of 2022 has not only been a technological disruption, but it has triggered a major epistemological crisis in the field of higher education. Schools of higher education all over the world have reacted in a fairly familiar pattern of panic, reactive policymaking, and existential panic that revolves around detection, banning, and policing of academic honesty. This chapter claims that this kind of defensive posture, though it may be explainable, is a misdiagnostic of the situation that we are in. It is not whether artificial intelligence will be present in our classrooms but whether we have the vision to help make it so, with the purpose of humanistic educational goals.

Chapter 10 is titled *Large Language Models (LLMs)* by Nizirwan Anwar, Abdul Rakhim Nanda, Muhammad Faisal, Irmawati Irmawati, Muhammad Syafaat S. Kuba, Muh. Fajri Raharjo, Nurnawaty Nurnawaty, Alex Gufron, Ida Lestari, and Nina Nurhasanah. This chapter examines the transformative role of Large Language Models (LLMs) in AI-powered automation within higher education, highlighting strategic opportunities and emerging risks across teaching, research, and academic service. The purpose of this chapter per the authors is to evaluate how LLMs support pedagogical innovation, personalised learning, curriculum design, research productivity, and administrative efficiency, while addressing challenges related to academic integrity, bias, data governance, epistemic reliability, and potential deskilling. Drawing on recent theoretical and empirical developments, the discussion situates LLM adoption within ethical AI, quality assurance, and institutional governance frameworks. Emphasis is placed on human-centred integration that balances automation with academic oversight. The chapter concludes by proposing a governance-oriented model to guide responsible and sustainable LLM deployment in higher education ecosystems.

Chapter 11 is titled *Navigating Artificial Intelligence Policy and Governance Frontiers: Applying Established Policy Frameworks* by Anand R Navaratna and Deepak Saxena. Artificial Intelligence has emerged as a lifestyle adaptation technology posing novel challenges to existing legal and ethical frameworks. Such frameworks are required to ensure that AI systems are developed with safety, transparency, and alignment with human values and ethics in mind. The evolving and ever-changing characteristics of AI make it difficult to regulate or govern. This chapter focuses on three broad aspects. Firstly, we try to define characteristics that make AI governance a unique endeavour. Secondly, we examine prevalent frameworks that are adopted worldwide by various organisations/ nations. Thereafter, we concentrate on five policy frameworks that can be used by academics, policymakers, and practitioners to design, govern, and regulate AI in the education field. Finally, we apply one of the frameworks, multiple streams framework to the application of AI in education.

Chapter 12 is titled *Navigating Job Displacement in the Circular Economy: Ethical AI and the Future of Work* by Sharad kumar, Aditya Jadeja, and Supriya Singh. The chapter starts from risk identification and proceeds to analyse the strategic and ethical and policy-based solutions that US and Asian and African case studies offer. The analysis considers various critical levers which encompass ethical AI development practices and workforce reskilling and algorithmic transparency and inclusive labour policy frameworks. The multi-stakeholder ethical model agenda requires involvement from policymakers and businesses and technologists and educators to achieve equitable transitions in the AI-driven economy. The chapter investigates how human people and intelligent technologies exchange "agreement" about controlling human agency and maintaining human dignity and providing human access to an AI-driven environment.

Chapter 13 is titled *Large Language Models as Adaptive and Context Aware Partners in Knowledge Creation* by Ashutosh Bhardwaj. The concept of Large Language Models (LLMs) has become the innovative technologies that can transform the existing knowledge creation processes due to the capability to act as adaptive and context-sensitive partners instead of passive computational mechanisms. With the use of modern architectures, contextual reasoning, and lifelong learning, LLMs have the ability to dynamically comprehend user intent, domain knowledge and situational context to ideate, analyze and synthesize information. The chapter discusses theoretical principles of LLMs, their use in human-AI collaborative knowledge creation, and their uses in academia, education, industry, and policy making. It also seeks to critically point out with their application to ethical, governance and reliability issues. Placing LLMs as co-producers in a human-centered system of knowledge offers a direction in future research and stresses on the necessity of responsible, transparent, and trustful application of such models into the practice of knowledge-intensive activities.

CONCLUSION

This edited book is intended for higher education policy makers, administrators, faculty and scholarly researchers within higher education institutions, professional organizations, and professional academic journals, as well as the professional academic publishing houses that are trying to deal with the rise of AI in manuscript submissions. Equally important and with an intention towards supporting statesmen and politicians who are charged with overseeing higher education. The long-term welfare and viability of higher education is currently in the midst of significant changes as well as significant attacks, some of which are well-deserved and may evolve higher education into a different age of understanding throughout this revolutionary period in time. The breadth and depth of AI as an impactful innovation highlights this rare opportunity to evolve an edited book with the intention to offer a snapshot of the policy, pedagogy, and professional practice currently inherent within the AI-enabled higher education institution.

Caroline M. Crawford
University of Houston-Clear Lake, USA

Section 1
AI Impact Upon Higher Education Policy

Chapter 1
Harnessing Context-Aware AI to Strengthen Teaching Practices in Higher Education

Archana Tamizharasan
http://orcid.org/0000-0003-1202-7836
VIT University, Vellore, India

Yamuna Devi
VIT University, Vellore, India

ABSTRACT

This chapter outlines how Context-Aware Artificial Intelligence (AI) enhances teaching and learning in higher education. By analyzing learner behavior, existing knowledge, engagement patterns, and performance data. AI enables early risk detection, adaptive content delivery, personalized support and real-time assessment feedback. This chapter observes how AI based analytics, intelligent tutoring systems, and contextualized assessment reshape learning assessment and support student practices. It also highlights the key implementation considerations, including ethical governance, faculty digital skills, and unified system integration. Finally, it outlines future directions such as active learning environments and AI-supported teaching assistants, then the context-aware AI is positioned as a strategic tool for advancing instructional quality and student success.

DOI: 10.4018/979-8-2600-2811-7.ch001

I. INTRODUCTION

Higher education is experiencing a rapid change due to digital transformation, large class sizes, and various learners. Currently, students enter colleges with different levels of prior knowledge, learning preferences and technologies explored. The modern changes challenge the educator who needs to maintain academic quality and support diverse learning requests for the learner. In traditional teaching methods such as uniform education, manual monitoring and periodic assessments are no longer enough to ensure continuous engagement or identify learners who need additional support. AI enables early identification of learning risks and supports timely intervention. Unlike static systems, context-aware AI continuously understands the learner's situation and adapts to new strategies automatically. Context-aware AI enables more responsive and personalized learning experiences.

Behavioural indicators such as less participation, irregular attention to course materials and repeated errors in assessments which can be detected early through predictive models and allow educators to offer the assistance, support plans and personalized resources that can improve students' academic success. AI also supports adaptive learning by adjusting content based on student needs. AI-driven systems can motivate students to increase their academic interest by suggesting materials, resources, reminders, and study techniques based on behaviour and academic profiles. Context-aware AI must be guided by responsible governance, ethical practices and education goals because academic institutions significantly adopt context-aware AI. Implementing AI features in the current LMS would need suitable technical facilities and educators' digital knowledge.

Overall, context-aware AI represents a transformation from a conventional way to an individual learning environment. AI serves as a tool of improvement that can raise the level of education, students' interest, and decision-making rather than replacing educator. The chapter covers the various changes happening in AI by studying its roles in teaching, student support, assessment, and continuous improvement in higher education. Specifically, this chapter aims at giving a full context-aware decision-making framework that integrates learning analytics, adaptive learning, intelligent tutoring, and contextualized assessment into one outstanding decision-making process. Major contributions include a well-organized five-stage framework, critically reviewing existing AI methods, and offering practical implementation advice to higher education institutions.

II. NEED FOR CONTEXT-AWARE AI IN MODERN HIGHER EDUCATION

Higher education institutions now work in a complex environment with different learners who can adopt technologies faster and expectations for personalized learning. Modern universities must support students with various academic backgrounds, learning behaviours, digital skills, and strengths. The modern change has created a need for a teaching system that can dynamically understand and respond to each student's needs instead of a manual teaching process.

One of the biggest challenges faced in higher education is massive student enrollment, which results in hundreds of learners by one educator. This becomes difficult to continue checking on student engagement, performance and progress without automated support. Context-aware AI addresses this drawback by continuously analyzing learner data and offering early insights into academic and behavioural patterns. The digital transformation of higher education has increased the use of online learning platforms and hybrid classrooms and has further strengthened the need for Intelligent Tutoring Systems (ITS). LMS generates vast amounts of data like patterns, timestamps, resource usage, status of activity and quiz attempts. Context-aware AI can support by automating monitoring and assessment procedures. The increasing need for data-driven decision-making (DDDM), the rising faculty workload and changing leaner expectations together highlights the importance of context-aware AI in higher education. Educators alone cannot understand students' needs and supports, when several roles of teaching, advising, assessment and administration expected at scale. On other hand, Institutions rely on data-driven insights to improve retention, learner satisfaction, and academic outcomes. Besides all these, just like finding digital platforms, learners expect personalized and adaptive learning experiences.

Context-aware AI solves the above problem by enabling constant data analysis, offering predictive insights and give personalized interventions, thereby supporting both efficiency of instructional and learner engagement. The context-aware AI enables risk identification, predictive modelling and performance prediction to help the institutions to allocate resources more effectively and support students for their success. When compared to traditional systems, context-aware AI enables proactive identification of intervention before academic decline occurs. This chapter discusses the idea of a complete context-aware framework that combines analytics, assessment, and intervention that bridge gaps that exist.

Critical Analysis of Existing Literature

Existing research on AI in higher education has already proved considerable progress in multiple areas. Research on learning analytics has demonstrated that it is possible to predict very accurately students who are at-risk based on their behaviour and performance records. The models have achieved such high levels of precision that they can find the students at most risk with a prominent degree of accuracy (Romero & Ventura, 2020). At the same time, adaptive learning systems have shown their capacity to increase student engagement and the quality of learning by way of personalizing content and pacing (Koedinger et al., 2013). ITS are computer programs that provide customized instruction through one-on-one interaction. They have been shown to be as effective as human tutoring at least in some subject areas by delivering feedback and guidance in real-time (VanLehn, 2011).

Despite these advancements, some approaches reveal limitations when considered in isolation. Learning analytics models, although powerful prediction tools, fundamentally depend on historical data and in most cases, act in a reactive way, that is, they only detect risk behaviour once it has already started. On the other hand, while adaptive learning systems make it possible to personalize proactively and individually, they are still quite dependent on continuous data channels and a heavy computational infrastructure, which may ultimately limit their scalability across a wide range of institutional environments. Intelligent tutoring systems offer in-depth, on-the-spot instructional support; however, they are often limited in their deployment by this complexity of domain modeling and their ability to scale across disciplines and large student populations is challenging.

The differences above illustrate that the current AI methods only solve individual aspects and therefore, do not form an integrated decision-making system. Therefore, implementations remain fragmented, limiting their effectiveness in higher education where integrated, end-to-end support is necessary. Also, extreme issues like algorithmic bias, scalability constraints, data dependency and faculty adoption challenges are often overlooked in many existing papers, thus lowering their practical utility at an institutional level.

Research Gap and Contribution

This chapter has determined a specific gap in the research: no integrated, context-aware framework combining data analysis, adaptive intervention and instructional decision-making into a continuous and iterative process has been developed so far. Current methods are fragmented and do not offer an effective system for linking prediction, personalization and action in real-time.

To fill this gap, a context-aware decision framework is put forward in this chapter as the main tool that unifies and scales the processes of learning analytics, adaptive learning, intelligent tutoring systems and assessment. This unified system differs from previous approaches as it not only enables decision-making in real time but also intervention with personalization and continuous feedback refinement. It also builds on the major concepts of Educational Data Mining (EDM) and Learning Analytics (LA), turning them from mere analysis tools into decision-making, context-driven processes. Incorporating several AI features into a single framework, this paper offers a more workable and higher education institution-oriented solution for teaching, learning, and student support enhancement. Learning analytics (LA) was established as one major strand of data-supported education by Siemens (2013) who is also the author of LA concept. Still, majority of existing methods still focus on analysis rather than on real-time, context-aware decision making.

III. FOUNDATIONS OF CONTEXT-AWARE AI SYSTEMS

Context-aware artificial intelligence stands for an intelligent system that is designed to sense, interpret and respond to a situation based on the learner's behaviour, environment, and academic progress. The intelligent systems differ from traditional tools because they integrate data from multiple sources and adjust their outputs accordingly in real time. By forming a deep understanding of what students do, how they learn and where they struggle, it helps the systems to support responsive and effective teaching strategies.

Understanding Context in Educational AI

In terms of educational technology, the word *'context'* refers to any information that can influence the learning process, including learners' existing knowledge, learners' preparedness, motivation, and cognitive characteristics. Performance indicators also contribute to context by including the grades, grasp levels, error patterns, and progress histories. Context-aware AI brings these varied elements together to produce a complete representation of the learner's state, which can enable the system to interpret the needs and challenges more accurately than standard models.

Key Components of Context-Aware AI Systems

A context-aware AI system naturally functions through several interconnected components. The first component is the context acquisition layer where raw data is collected from the LMS online platforms, assessment tools, communication channels, and sometimes physical classroom information from sensors. The data collection helps the system to understand the learner better and organizes the next layer, context modeling, into a meaningful learner profile or a behavioral model using a technique such as semantic mapping and feature extraction. The system identifies the relevant patterns and helps to describe the learner's evolving state. Next, the reasoning and interface layer forms an analytical system by applying Machine Learning (ML), statistical modeling, and rule-based logic to interpret the contextual information. Finally, the adaptation layer executes the personalized action such as recommending resources, adjusting content, triggering alerts, and guiding faculty decisions. Altogether, these components create a continuous cycle of observation, response and analysis that is illustrated in Figure 1.

Figure 1. Architecture of a context-aware AI system for higher education

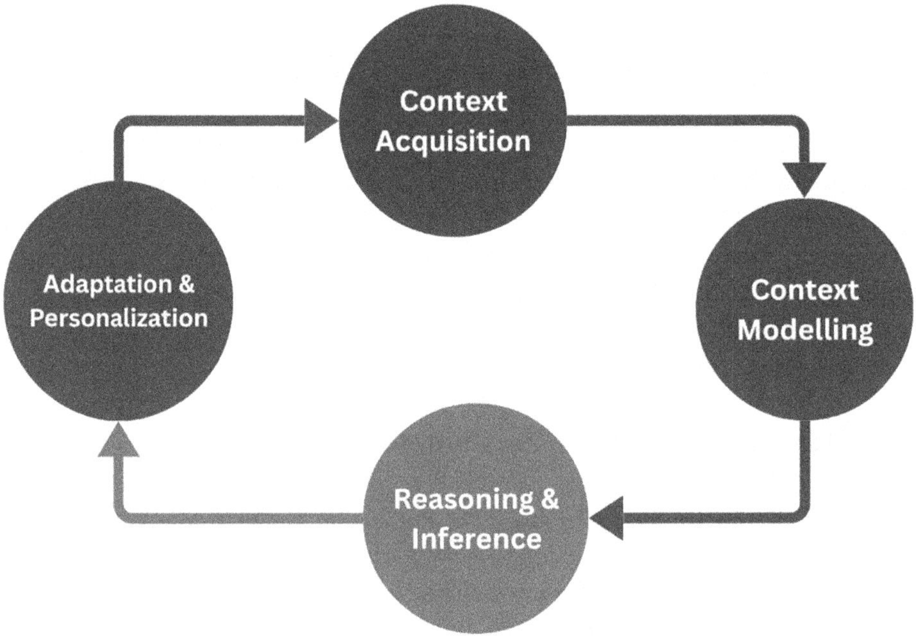

Data Sources

In context-aware AI, the data source is generated through student interaction with digital platforms and other sources. The behavioral data, such as navigation patterns, time spent on each course's materials and access logs, help to indicate how the learners are involved in studies. The performance data from assignments, quizzes and assessments provide an insight into academics and areas of difficulty. Text data sources from messages, forums and written submissions expose the levels of understanding, sentiment, and misconceptions. Temporal data resources indicate when and how often the students interact with coursework, while the environmental data highlights the circumstances of study. When available and effective information such as stress indicators adds depth and must be handled with ethical caution. Overall, these data sources strengthen the system's ability to identify the hidden or difficult pattern.

Techniques Behind Contextual Intelligence

Context-aware AI includes a wide variety of techniques that help the systems to adjust to learners' needs and environments. Predictive analytics is the major approach that uses learner's historical academic data to recognize learning risks and predict student performance. Based on the analysis of the learner's past behaviors and outcome, the models assist in timely intervention and personalized support.

Besides that, Natural Language Processing (NLP) methods are used for analyzing the textual data that is generated during learner interactions, for example in discussion forums, messages, and written submissions. NLP helps in the detection of sentiment, finding misconceptions, and understanding learning gaps, thus empowering the system's capability to respond in a smart way.

Knowledge tracing is yet another major technique. The idea is to keep track of learner behavior continuously so that through estimated learner's knowledge the mastery of various concepts is judged. These models keep on updating the learner knowledge state, resulting in the possibility of providing more accurate and suitable learning experiences. Besides that, recommendation systems are important to the extent that they help in providing the right learning resources which fit well with individual learner profiles according to their taste, performance, and engagement patterns.

Ethical and Responsible AI Practices

Using context-aware AI in education means collecting and managing very personal data of students, which opens major ethical issues. It is important to think through how to protect students' data, be open about it, and keep things fair. Institutions have a big role in protecting student data, keeping things confidential, and making sure that decisions made with the help of AI are fair and can be explained. Defining solid ethical principles and setting up governance structures are necessary steps in gaining trust and ensuring that system uses such technologies in a responsible way.

Institutional System Integration

Seamlessly integrating with institutional technologies is a matter of life and death for the proliferation of context-aware AI in education. LMSs, analytics dashboards, assessment platforms, among others, establish the backbone of modern educational infrastructures (Muñoz et al., 2014). To be effective, AI solutions must be integrated properly so that they serve as enhancements and complements of existing workflows instead of disrupting them. When aligned with the institutional practices, context-aware AI can generate valuable insights and assist in decision-making without sacrificing efficiency.

A Context-Aware Decision Framework for Higher Education

While the existing research discusses context-aware systems, adaptive learning, learning analytics and early alert mechanisms separately still their real effect in higher education depends on how well they are combined into a single and coordinated decision-making process. To address this gap, this chapter uses a context-aware decision framework that explains how AI-generated insights can be transformed into practical and effective educational actions. The framework follows a cyclic and iterative structure that consists of five organized stages: context acquisition, context interpretation, decision generation, intervention execution, and feedback refinement. Instead of introducing new algorithms, this framework brings together unified existing AI techniques in higher education and explains how they can be applied in real-time.

Figure 2. The framework is a continuous cycle of data analysis, decision-making, and personalised intervention in education

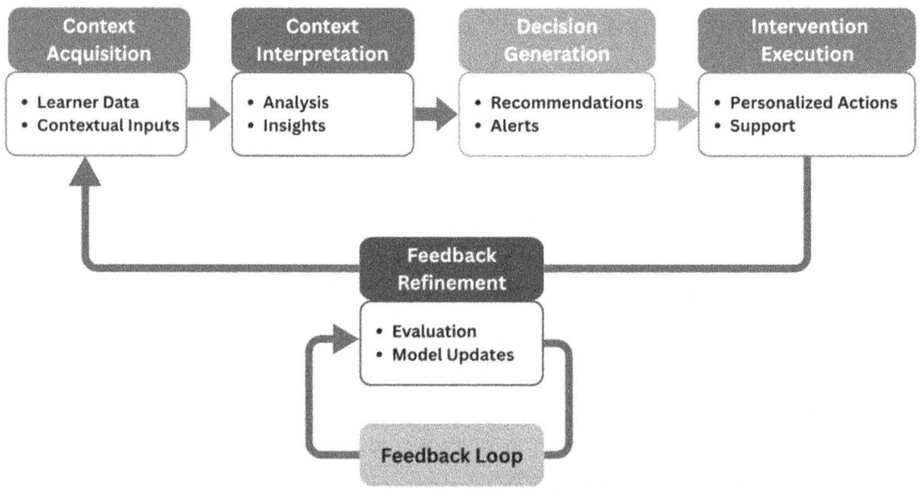

Context acquisition is the first stage that collects learner-generated data from multiple sources, including LMS, assessments, forums, and digital learning tools.

The data captures behavioural patterns, temporal activity, performance trends, and interactive histories, which together form a raw input for context. Next, in the context interpretation stage, artificial intelligence techniques such as ML, NLP, predictive analytics and knowledge tracing are used to transform raw data from acquisition into meaningful insights. This stage identifies learning gaps, engagement levels, progression patterns, and academic risks. The decision generation stage uses the interpretation stage context to support instructional and institutional decision-making, including identifying at-risk students, early alerts, recommending adaptive content and selecting suitable assessments. Decisions generated at this stage are probabilistic and recommended rather than deterministic, which supports human judgment rather than replacing it. After decisions are generated, the intervention execution stage may deliver targeted actions involving personalized feedback, adaptive learning resources, tutoring support, and academic advising notifications. The last stage, feedback refinement, is a closed loop that evaluates the outcomes of interventions, and the flow is presented in Figure 2. Learner responses, constant challenges, and performance improvements are the feedback shared with the system that allows models and recommendation systems to improve over time.

Evaluation Metrics for the Framework

The effectiveness of the proposed context-aware decision framework can be evaluated using specific performance metrics that are aligned with each phase of the cycle. Table 1 below summarizes key evaluation criteria:

Table 1. Framework stages

Framework Stage	Evaluation Metrics
Context Acquisition	Data quality, completeness, and consistency
Context Interpretation	Prediction accuracy, model performance (typically 75–85% in learning analytics)
Decision Generation	Relevance and accuracy of recommendations
Intervention Execution	Success rate and improvement in student engagement
Feedback Refinement	Learning outcome gains, retention improvement (typically 10–15%), system adaptability

Metrics enable both technical progress and educational impact assessment of the framework. While technical measures evaluate system performance and outcomes-based metrics such as engagement, academic improvement and retention. Table 2 summarizes Mapping of AI techniques to Higher education

Table 2. Mapping of AI techniques to educational applications

AI Technique	Primary Educational Application	Key Functionality	Typical Data Used	Impact on Teaching and Learning
Predictive Analytics	At-risk student detection	Identifies early warning signals and dropout risk through pattern analysis	LMS logs, grades, attendance, engagement metrics	Enables early intervention, improves retention and academic success
Knowledge Tracing	Mastery estimation and progress tracking	Models concept-level knowledge acquisition over time	Quiz responses, problem-solving attempts, assessment history	Supports adaptive pacing and targeted remediation
Natural Language Processing (NLP)	Feedback generation and assessment	Analyses textual responses, discussion posts, and written assignments	Essays, forum posts, short-answer responses	Provides personalised feedback and scalable evaluation
Reinforcement Learning	Adaptive content delivery	Optimises learning pathways based on learner responses and rewards	Interaction history, performance feedback	Enhances engagement through personalised sequencing
Recommendation Systems	Resource and content recommendation	Suggests learning materials based on learner profiles and behaviour	Clickstream data, resource usage, preferences	Improves learning efficiency and motivation
Clustering Algorithms	Learner profiling and segmentation	Groups students based on behaviour or performance similarities	Engagement patterns, performance metrics	Supports differentiated instruction and group interventions
Classification Models	Academic performance prediction	Categorises learners into performance or risk groups	Assessment data, behavioural indicators	Assists instructors in targeted decision-making
Sentiment Analysis	Engagement and affect detection	Identifies emotional and motivational cues from learner text	Discussion posts, feedback comments	Supports affect-aware interventions and learner well-being
Bayesian Models	Uncertainty-aware learning estimation	Handles incomplete or noisy educational data	Assessment outcomes, learning trajectories	Improves robustness of mastery and risk estimation
Deep Learning Models	Complex pattern recognition	Captures non-linear relationships in large-scale educational data	Multimodal LMS data, temporal sequences	Enables scalable and accurate learning analytics

IV. KEY APPLICATIONS

Identifying and Supporting At-Risk Students

Traditional approaches heavily rely on continuing assessments, manual monitoring and instructor insight, which are often unable to detect the early issues for effective intervention. Context-aware Artificial Intelligence (AI) addresses this by continuously analyzing learners' data, recognizing developing risk patterns, and enabling institutions to provide targeted and timely support to at-risk students.

At-risk students are learners who show signs of struggle in academics, inconsistent performance, and declining activities. Students may miss deadlines, struggle with foundational concepts, or disengage from learning activities. The students' interaction patterns in digital learning platform reveal valuable information about the engagement and motivation of students (Knobloch et al., 2018).

Figure 3. AI-driven framework for early detection and support of at-risk students

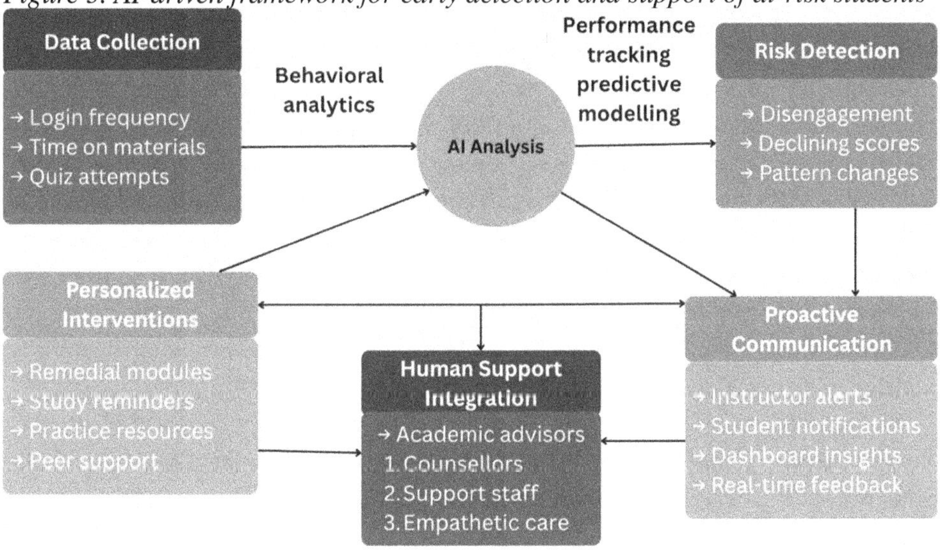

In addition to behavioural indicators, analytical performance data plays an important role in identifying at-risk students. Context-aware AI tracks quiz result, error rates, assignment patterns and grasp level of a student over time to uncover whether there is any development in their academic performance. Falling behind, consistently making errors on certain topics, or struggling to get to a level of mastery can be some of the earliest indicators of academic difficulties (Weber et al., 2015). Besides predictive modeling, another significant way in which AI can be used to help students at risk. By studying large past data collections of students, ML models detect patterns of behaviour, academic performance, and demographic factors linked to dropout or learning difficulties of learners.

After at-risk students have been identified, context-aware AI generates a customized intervention plan for the student. AI systems recommend personalized actions for each student based on their activities rather than generic advice. Learners who are struggling with fundamental concepts may be directed toward remedial modules, brief explanation resources, and additional practice. While students with low motivation or engagement may receive study reminders, time-management strategies, or peer support sessions. In addition to personalized recommendations, context-aware AI also helps facilitate communication between students and teachers. Automated early-warning systems can alert instructors when a student's engagement level drops below a certain point or when there is a major change in the student's performance. This notification method helps educators to extend their support and make students more aware even in very large classes. In fact, in many educational institutions, AI-based tools are combined with student support services to provide comprehensive assistance. Academic advisors, counselors, and support staff access analytics dashboards that highlight behavioural, academic, and emotional risk indicators. By integrating AI-generated insights with the understanding of human experts, educational institutions can establish complication support systems that confront academic as well as personal issues. Figure 3 shows the process of using behavioral and performance data for analyzing student disengagement and academic risk through AI modeling. To implement early risk identification and targeted student support, the context-aware AI systems combine multiple analytical resources that function at different stages of the intervention process. Table 3 summarizes the key AI capabilities used to support at-risk students and highlights how each capability contributes to early detection of students.

Illustrative scenarios show how context-aware AI can support early identification of at-risk students and help in their timely support (Pecuchova & Drlik, 2024). However, automated risk predictions must coordinate with human judgment and continuous monitoring to ensure accuracy and fairness. Even the best predictive models are not 100% accurate and can make errors in classification, such as giving a positive analysis to a student who is not really at risk or failing to identify those at risk. Furthermore, the use of historical data can lead to biases, especially when the training data reflects the inequalities that already exist in the education system.

Table 3. AI-driven framework for early detection and support of at-risk students

AI Capability	Primary Role in At-Risk Student Support	Key Indicators Analysed	Typical Interventions Enabled
Behavioural Analytics	Detect disengagement patterns	Login frequency, time on materials, participation trends	Engagement nudges, study reminders, peer interaction prompts
Performance Analytics	Identify learning gaps and decline	Quiz scores, assignment outcomes, error patterns	Remedial content, adaptive practice, instructor feedback
Predictive Modelling	Estimate dropout and failure risk	Historical performance, behavioural trajectories, cohort data	Early-risk classification, advisor escalation
Early Alert Systems	Trigger timely academic interventions	Threshold-based risk scores, sudden behaviour changes	Automated alerts to instructors and students
Context-Aware Recommendation Systems	Personalise support strategies	Learner profile, mastery level, engagement context	Tailored learning resources and pathways
Temporal Pattern Analysis	Monitor progression trends over time	Submission delays, inactivity periods	Time-management support, pacing adjustments
Natural Language Processing (NLP)	Analyse sentiment and communication cues	Discussion posts, feedback text, student messages	Emotional support prompts, counsellor referrals
Human-in-the-Loop AI	Enable contextual and ethical decision-making	AI-generated insights with human validation	Academic advising, mentoring, empathetic interventions
Learning Analytics Dashboards	Provide holistic risk visibility	Integrated behavioural and performance metrics	Data-driven instructional and institutional decisions

To illustrate this, consider a hypothetical scenario in which a big public university implements a context-aware AI-based early warning system within its LMS to reduce dropout rates among first-year undergraduate students. The system focused on analyzing behavioural indicators such as irregular login patterns, late assignment submissions, a fall in assessment scores, and reduced participation in discussion forums during the first six weeks of the semester. One of the tools that the system uses is predictive learning analytics models to calculate the likelihood of a person being at risk and only academic advisors and student support teams are given access to this information via a secure dashboard. Importantly, the system did not make decisions automatically, but it was utilized as a decision-support tool to guide human intervention. According to the information provided, the advisors can provide measures of support like academic counselling sessions, study workshops and personalized mentoring plans.

The following examples are just imagined situations and illustrations of how the proposed framework can be put into practice. They should not be considered as specific cases of institutional implementation. This example demonstrates how context-aware AI can support student retention technique by identifying early signs of disengagement while maintaining ethical oversight and human judgement. Even though the above example is fictional, comparable results are what real studies have shown too. To mention a few investigations, the research done on early alert systems suggest that through using such systems the retention rate can be increased by around 10-15% in similar types of institutions (Bhat & Jayaram, 2023; Al Hashmi et al., 2025). Also, research within the field of educational data mining has demonstrated prediction accuracies of ~75%-85% in forecasting student performance measures (Kotsiantis et al., 2004). Very recent learning analytics illustrate predictive accuracies of at least 80% but the actual figure depends on a particular context and dataset (Baker & Inventado, 2014). Having detected students at-risk, it is time to, first of all, address the delivery of customized and tailored instructional support by means of adaptive learning systems.

AI-Driven Personalization of Dynamic Lesson planning

Adaptive learning has become one of the most transformative applications of context-aware AI in higher education. Unlike traditional method, the real classrooms reveal different varieties in learning speed, motivation, cognitive ability, and background preparation of students. Address the issue, adaptive learning systems use AI to adjust learning resources, content and study plans to match every individual student's requirement. The system continuously adapts based on real-time learning data of learners, which ensures all the students receive learning experiences according to their abilities and progress on time (Yekollu et al., 2024; Abrar et al., 2025). For example, if a student is having difficulty with a certain topic, the system might suggest simpler explanations, extra exercises, or a remedial session to help the student understand better. A student who demonstrates a high level of knowledge might be given advanced or challenging activities to help further enhance their abilities. Based on the analysis, the system determines which activities, content or assessments are more suitable for a learner at any given time (Conati & Kardan, 2013). As a result, the learners' activities are continuously adjusted by the personalized learning pathways that lead to the development of the system.

In traditional classrooms, students move into the next topic without understanding the foundational concepts, which leads to collective learning difficulties. With the help of adaptive learning systems, one can detect students' lack of conceptual knowledge at early stages and suggest learning plans to tackle learning difficulties experienced towards the end of the course. The learning plans may include repeated practice, focused review modules, or targeted feedback to strengthen weaker concept areas. Such personalized measures ensure the learner builds strong foundational knowledge before advancing to mastery. Adaptive learning is further supported by Knowledge Tracing (KT) models, which track how well the student levels up in a specific concept over time. Bayesian Knowledge Tracing (BKT) and Deep Knowledge Tracing (DKT) analyze the probabilities to estimate knowledge level from correct and incorrect patterns of response. These models help to determine whether a student is ready to progress to the next level of the learning process. Otherwise, student requires additional support by continuously monitoring the current levels and guiding personalized learning paths. Table 4 summarizes the core adaptive learning system and their corresponding educational impact.

Context-aware AI also supports continuous lesson planning through real-time analytics. Instructors often do not have real-time vision to find students difficult, or which concepts require further reinforcement. Adaptive learning systems solve this by generating analytical dashboards that summarize overall class learning patterns, highlight commonly misunderstood topics and identify areas that need additional support.

Table 4. Adaptive learning mechanisms and educational impact

AI Mechanism	Learner Data Used	Adaptation Strategy	Educational Benefit
Knowledge tracing	Quiz responses, mastery history	Concept-level pacing	Improved mastery
Learner profiling	Engagement, performance trends	Personalised pathways	Reduced learning gaps
Recommendation systems	Error patterns, progress	Resource suggestion	Faster remediation
Enrichment logic	Early mastery indicators	Advanced content	Learner motivation

Many modern learning platforms combine adaptive technology systems such as Knewton Alta, Carnegie Learning's cognitive tutors, Coursera's adaptive pathways, and ALEKS to personalize the content and track learner mastery level, as demonstrated in documented implementations of adaptive learning systems (Ranasinghe, 2025). Fairness is promoted by ensuring the learners with diverse backgrounds and learning styles will receive proper support through adaptive learning. Despite its benefits, adaptive learning also presents a challenge such as transparency and over-personalization. Where an excessive adaptation may limit the exposure to wider learning experiences, educators must balance personalization with shared learning outcomes to ensure that all students meet essential academic standards. Transparency is essential; if a learner or an instructor is not clear about why certain materials are suggested, they may not trust the system. As an illustrative example, take a research-focused university that implements a context-aware adaptive learning system in its LMS to support large numbers of students taking STEM (Science, Technology, Engineering, and Mathematics) courses. The AI system continuously evaluates time spent on tasks, quiz results and the student's overall progress to adjust the learning paths in terms of concepts. Those learners who revealed confusion are automatically given more concise explanations, illustrations, and exercises.

In contrast, the learners who achieved early mastery receive advanced problems and materials. Instructors accessed analytics dashboards that displayed topic-level mastery gaps across student groups. This helps to redesign and target classroom instruction. The case example demonstrates how adaptive learning systems enhance theoretical understanding and teaching efficiency by adjusting content difficulty according to student sequencing with individual learner progress. This scenario reflects implementation patterns documented in adaptive learning research (Koedinger et al., 2013; Ranasinghe et al., 2025). Adaptive learning focuses on delivering personalized content. However, assessment plays a crucial role in evaluating students' growth and deciding on the next steps in teaching. An AI that understands context goes beyond that by altering how content is delivered.

Contextualized Assessment generation aligned to learning outcomes.

Assessment is a critical component of the teaching and learning process, as it provides an insight into student learning, supports instructional changes, and influences academic progress. The traditional assessment is time-consuming to design, evaluate and provide delayed feedback, which is not effective in large classrooms. Moreover, in traditional classrooms, assessments are set by faculty, and the same set of questions is available for all the students. The outcome of the results is focused on entire classroom, not on an individual. Address this challenge, context-awareness AI helps by transforming traditional assessment methods into a more effective, personalized, and adaptive process that can support both the learners and instructors (Moonsamy & Lotriet, 2026). Artificial intelligence in assessments significantly helps the educator to automate the generating of questions. The AI-powered tools can create a variety of assessment methods such as multiple-choice questions, short-answer prompts, scenario-based activities, and problem-solving tasks on course content and objectives. NLP analyzes the instructional materials, then identifies key concepts to generate questions with different levels of reasoning complexity. This reduces faculty workload in creating and analyzing the assessment and ensures the assessments remain aligned with the learning outcomes of students (Johnson et al.,

2024). Automating question generation for assessments increases the variety of assessments and helps focus deeper learning rather than memorization of the concept.

AI also plays a role in automating grading and evaluation, where ML models can accurately grade the assessment, such as quizzes and multiple-choice tests. More advanced NLP-based systems can evaluate essays, coding submissions, and mathematical proofs. AI tools help reduce the time needed and ensure that students receive timely feedback. For faculty, this type of automatic generation is a great support for managing many assessment activities without loss of quality and consistency. Innovation enabled by AI is the development of adaptive assessment systems that can adjust question difficulty according to individual performance in real-time. Instead of distributing the same question set to all students, the adaptive assessments will change the kind of question as well as the judgment depending on the students' level. When a student answers correctly for most of the questions, the system may provide more challenging levels. Similarly, if the student is wrong, the system offers questions that are simpler or are at the level of the foundation. This method leads to a more accurate comprehension of the student's ability, lessens the negative aspects of the test, motivates the students, and makes sure that the assessments are suitable.

Context-aware AI system enhances the assessment by integrating real-time feedback loops. The modern assessment method responds and gives reason for correct or wrong answers which point to improvement, lead to personal reflection, or provide targeted learning materials. Immediate feedback helps students figure out their mistakes, control their learning, and timely make changes by self-managing their actions. For example, when a student answers a question, instead of the system just telling the student the answer is wrong, it may give the reason and suggest remedial activities or foundational lectures related to previous difficulties. This personalization system increases the relevance and effectiveness of feedback and supports deeper understanding. The learning analytics dashboard provides faculty detailed insights into student performance trends of assessment. Educators can use such insights for recognizing students' weaknesses, changing teaching strategies, and helping a low-performing student. Analytics-based teaching employs assessments as a tool of guiding educational decisions and not merely as a measure of outcomes. In addition, context-aware AI helps evaluate skills and higher-order thinking beyond traditional academic tests. Tools like digital simulations, ITS, and virtual laboratories allow students to show practical skills through interactive activities (Thomas et al., 2024).

AI-based assessment must be designed carefully to ensure fairness and avoid bias, supported by continuous monitoring and human oversight. Despite these benefits, AI-driven assessment requires careful execution because over-relying on automation systems may reduce opportunities for human feedback mainly in complex or creative tasks. Educators must balance AI support with human judgement to ensure academic integrity remains neutral. In this way, AI can be a tool for supporting fairness and transparency in assessment practices. Apart from assessment and feedback, providing continuous academic support is crucial in improving learning outcomes. ITS can take this a step further by providing real-time, personalized help and individualized learning support.

To use a hypothetical example, think of an online program that provides the LMS with a context-aware AI feedback system for the dual purpose of boosting the quality of assessment and enabling the students to regulate their learning. The system, by analyzing student responses, errors, and previous performances in quizzes and assessments, can understand the student-conditioned output. The university integrated an AI-based feedback system into its LMS. The system generated immediate personalized feedback that explains misconceptions, highlight errors, and recommend targeted learning resources. At the same time, instructors received a report summary of common misunderstanding trends that allowed them to refine assessment design and explanations. The case demonstrates how AI-driven feedback systems can transform assessment into a continuous learning and self-regulation process.

Intelligent Tutoring System (ITS)

ITS are among the most advanced applications of context-aware artificial intelligence in higher education. Recent studies comparing context-aware AI tutors with multipurpose AI chatbots show that the system that controls learner context provides more meaningful learning support and improved educational outcomes (Bassner et al., 2025). ITS provides personalized, one-on-one learning support based on student needs. ITS contributes significantly to improving learning outcomes, especially for the students who need continuous attention and individual assistance.

An ITS begins by building a detailed learner model which represents the student's intellectual understanding, skills, knowledge gaps, and learning preferences. The model keeps on updating the system as the learner engages in quizzes, problem-solving tasks, hints, and other activities, enabling ITS to adjust its teaching responses appropriately. For example, student continually making errors in a specific point, the system then recognizes the patterns, diagnoses the misunderstandings, and chooses a solution for the student to get better. ITS depends on domain modeling, which explains how the subject is organized. The model divides the subject into related concepts, skills and learning goals to help the system understand how different topics are interconnected. It explains how mastering one concept supports learning another concept. Domain modeling allows ITS to guide learners through content in a logical order to ensure a strong understanding of core concepts.

The next critical component of ITS is the tutorial model which administrates how the system interacts with learners and includes approaches for presenting instructions, offering hints, prompting learners, and delivering feedback. The tutorial model is basically the blueprint of how the computer talks to the student to give instructions, hints, and feedback by first checking the complex task and behavior of the student. Feedback helps the students to correct errors on the spot and leads to faster learning and greater retention. ITS platforms also integrate metacognitive support that can help the students to become aware of their own learning processes and level to improve academic performance. Some systems guide the learners to set their own goals, work on their mistakes, monitor their progress and develop self-regulation strategies.

There are quite a few real-life examples of how ITS is being used in different fields. A cognitive tutor from Carnegie Mellon University, for instance, has made a very positive impact on the students' understanding of mathematics by guiding their problem-solving process step by step (Aleven et al., 2017). Language learning applications like Duolingo use AI-powered teaching technique to track mastery, personalize the lessons and adjust difficulty actively. Together, the examples supported by recent reviews show how ITS can deliver high-quality personalized support at a large scale (Létourneau et al., 2025).

In addition to academic content, ITS can also include an affective tutoring system that replies to the students about their emotional states by analyzing the indicators such as engagement behaviour or learning patterns. Although effective tutoring requires careful ethical handling because emotional data is sensitive and it can enhance personalized learning by supporting students' well-being. ITS also enhances collective learning by peer interactions; few systems can allot learners to collaborative problem-solving groups based on their progress levels. Some ITS platforms support collaborative learning by grouping students and monitoring participation patterns. This feature helps institutions to support teamwork, communication, and social learning, which are increasingly important in higher education. From an instructional perspective, ITS provides insights through analytics dashboards. The dashboards highlight how students interact with the system and in which concepts they struggle with and what strategies lead to improving their performance. Using the dashboard information exacted instructors can refine their teaching approaches, adjust course content, and support targeted interventions.

One of the main concerns of ITS is how much content should be developed for it to be a valid domain model since it is a very knowledge intensive domain that requires detailed and accurate knowledge of the domain. Firstly, it is vital that these systems provide guidance and at the same time promote the learner's independence. Secondly, if schools or other educational institutions become dependent on automated tutoring, the amount of human interaction is likely to decrease; therefore, ITS should be considered only as a supporting tool in a human, AI collaboration model. Besides technical implementation, ethics-related issues such as privacy and fairness are among some of the considerations. In conclusion, ITS are quite a remarkable tool for personalized learning. However, their effectiveness depends on the correct institutional implementation, scalability issues and ethical concerns.

Strategic Continuous Improvement teaching model

Learning analytics has become a key pillar of digital transformation in higher education, including collection, analysis, measurement, and interpretation of data. The generated data helps in improving teaching, learning, and institutional decision-making. Vast amounts of behavioural and performance data are generated through LMS, digital resources, virtual classrooms and assessment tools (Romero & Ventura, 2020). Context-aware AI enhances the role of learning analytics by making the data streams predictive, personalized, and actionable.

Table 5. Learning analytics functions supporting continuous improvement

Analytics Type	Data Source	Decision Supported
Performance analytics	Grades, assessments	Curriculum redesign
Engagement analytics	LMS logs	Early intervention
Error analysis	Assessment attempts	Concept reinforcement
Predictive analytics	Historical trends	Retention planning
Prescriptive analytics	Risk indicators	Targeted actions

Table 5 outlines key learning analytics functions and the types of decisions they enable (Papamitsiou & Economides, 2014). Every time students log into an LMS they generate data, and they can engage with a resource, take a quiz, do a task, and chat in a forum. AI systems analyze this result data to identify patterns that humans may fail to notice. One of the most useful applications of learning analytics is analyzing the performance trends. AI systems track individual students and entire classes over time to see whether learning is improving, declining in certain areas, or being still stable. The long-term view helps the instructors to evaluate the success of their teaching methods and identify where changes are required. Research shows that student retention has been improved by 10%-25% due to learning analytics, and the accuracy of the predictive models is often more than 80% (Siemens, 2013; Gašević et al., 2015).

In tracking performance trends, the learning analytics help in analyzing error patterns by examining what type of mistakes students make and how often they occur. AI can combine these mistakes together, show common misunderstandings and emphasize the gaps in learning. For example, if many students repeatedly make the same mistake in a coding problem, AI shows the concept was not explained properly and the educators can use this information to improve their lessons. In this way, error analysis turns simple assessment scoring tools into valuable support for deeper learning. Context-aware AI also improves learning analytics by analyzing the student engagement in digital learning environments. Engagement indicators include how much time the students spend on tasks, how often they interact with materials, their participation in discussions and their use of multimedia content.

Learning analytics also supports institutional-level decision-making through predictive modelling. The model analyzes historical datasets, and AI is used to predict future outcomes such as graduation rates, course completion likelihood, or departmental performance trends. These predictions inform resource allocation, program planning, and staffing. For instance, if predictive analytics indicate a particular course consistently shows high dropout rates, the academic managers can inspect the causes and target the improvements. Predictive models not only function as academic support tools but also as strategic planning instruments. For example, predictive analytics may identify a student at risk of failing a course, but prescriptive analytics can go a step further by recommending intervention measures such as a tutor, offering more detailed feedback, or organizing extra sessions to support the student's learning.

Learning analytics dashboards provide an understandable and user-friendly interface that makes non-technical users to grasp the key metrics easy such as student performance, mastery progression, risk indicators and engagement levels. This is done through visuals and features that are extremely easy to use. Educators can not only use the dashboard insights for their teaching purposes but also to change their methods very easily (Gutiérrez et al., 2020; Susnjak et al., 2022). Academic advisors can also rely on these analytics dashboards to guide students more effectively and support academic decision-making. As higher education gradually evolves, learning analytics will remain an important driver of innovation and strengthen both academic and institutional success. However, predictive analytics models are not trusted to generate accurate predictions, mainly if the data is incomplete or biased. Besides, analytics results could mislead if the interpretation is wrong, particularly when there is a lack of teacher's professional input. The use of context-aware AI brings major advantages, and their success depends on careful consideration of ethical, technical, and institutional factors.

V. IMPLEMENTATION

Feasibility and Challenges

The implementation of context-aware AI systems in higher education involves challenges related to cost, infrastructure and scalability. Utilizing AI-driven systems needs data storage, processing capabilities, and fitting with the current platform, which might be the cause of the financial and technical barriers for small institutions. The requirement for an initial investment and ongoing expenditure on maintenance could be limitations to the widespread adoption of the product. Despite their positive changes, AI implementations in education often face challenges. Faculty resistance is one of the barriers, the educators sometimes do not believe the automated predictions or see them as threatening their professional judgment (Nguyen et al., 2021). Algorithmic drift is another limitation which reduces model accuracy over time and requiring constant retraining (Romero & Ventura, 2020). Early alert systems may generate high false positive rates, which can cause the alert systems to overload and thereby limit proper intervention. These issues have demonstrated that without the institutional capacity, predictive accuracy alone is not enough.

Similarly, adaptive learning systems that are successful in limited course settings may struggle to reach the level of whole university due to differences in course content, data availability, and faculty engagement, these indicate that it is both technical and organizational issues. For under-resourced institutions, these obstacles are more severe due to lack of technical expertise, infrastructure, and financial capacity. These risks spread the gap between well-resourced and under-resourced institutions. Solving this requires policy support, open-source tools, and shared data frameworks.

Looking at the cost and benefits is very necessary for assisting with the decision to use AI. Before implementing, institutions should weigh the need for AI against the benefits such as reduced workload, improved retention and more efficiency assessment. An implementation by phases approach, starting with pilot deployments, allows institutions to assess effectiveness before scaling. Modular and cloud-based solutions also facilitate the gradual adoption.

Practical Constraints in challenges

The real adoption of context-aware AI in higher education is influenced by several active and institutional limitations. Table 6 summarizes key challenges and their implications across different institutional contexts.

Table 6. Implementation challenges of context-aware AI in higher education

Challenge	Description	Impact on Institutions
Infrastructure Requirements	Context-aware AI systems require high-performance computing, secure data storage, and integration with LMS platforms.	Institutions with limited IT infrastructure may face difficulties in deploying real-time analytics systems.
Cost and Resource Constraints	Implementation involves costs related to system development, cloud services, data management, and maintenance.	High initial investment may limit adoption, especially in public or underfunded institutions.
Scalability Issues	AI models must handle large volumes of student data across courses and departments.	Systems may perform well in pilot studies but face challenges when scaled institution wide.
Adoption in Small Institutions	Smaller institutions often lack technical expertise, data infrastructure, and funding.	May require simplified or phased adoption strategies such as cloud-based or shared AI services.

Ethics, Governance, and LMS Integration

The successful implementation of context-aware Artificial Intelligence (AI) in higher education requires careful consideration on ethics, governance, policy, infrastructure, and system integration (Floridi et al., 2018). Since these systems depend on processing huge amounts of student data, institutions must pay extra attention to transparency, data protection and fairness. Following the laws like the General Data Protection Regulation (GDPR) and institutional data policies is also important (Slade & Prinsloo, 2013).

The urgency of these considerations is reflected in recent institutional data. A 2025 UNESCO global survey (UNESCO, 2025) shows that although about two-thirds of higher education institutions have or are developing guidance on AI use, only 19% have a formal AI policy. This clearly indicates that governance frameworks are significantly behind the pace of adoption. In a 2024 survey of 445 faculty and administrators from over 330 institutions in the United States and Canada, it was found that concerns about algorithmic bias went up from 36% in 2023 to 49% in 2024. The problem related to data privacy and security increases from 50% to 59% over the same period (Ellucian, 2024). In addition, another survey that was done in 2024 by American Association of Colleges and Universities amongst higher education leaders and revealed that faculty lack of familiarity with or resistance to AI tools was one of the major barriers cited for institutional AI adoption apart from distrust of AI outputs and fear of reduced student learning outcomes (AAC&U, 2025). Research evidence also points towards this scenario: Cervantes et al. (2024) found out that 42% of the faculty members who knew about AI tools had never used them, which shows that just having them available does not automatically result in their being used. The above-mentioned patterns further highlight that ethical management, transparency and gaining the trust of the instructional staff are not the only secondary concerns but, in fact, the major factors for a long-lasting embedding of AI in the higher education sector.

Effective data governance models should define in detail not only the ways of data collecting, data storage and data access but also the data usage policies. Prevent data breaches and misuse, Institutions must implement security measures like encryption, access control and secure storage. Equally important is transparency, institutions required to explain students about how their data were collected and used to support learning.

Bias and fairness in AI systems is another major concern (Chinta et al., 2024). As AI models are trained on historical data, they may unintentionally reinforce existing biases if not carefully managed. Hence, Institutions not only regularly audit but also apply fairness-aware evaluation methods. Human oversight is vital to confirm that AI-generated insights support decisions rather than replacing them.

In fact, tangible bias reducing approaches include fairness-aware model training, disaggregated performance evaluation of different student groups (e.g., by gender, socioeconomic status, or ethnicity), and the use of counterfactual fairness testing before deployment. Apart from that, it is also advisable to periodically re-audit the model results against the institutional equity aims to find and rectify any emerging biases (Chinta et al., 2024).

The initial step in implementing content-aware AI in universities is to have a well- structured governance (Nguyen et al., 2021). Institutions can establish AI administration committees or set up special task forces that are responsible for setting ethical standards, monitoring system performance and guiding adoption. These committees include members from academic departments, student services, IT teams, legal offices, and administrative leadership. Besides that, transparent policies should clearly define roles, decision-making processes, responsibilities etc., to ensure the AI adoption is accountable and sustainable.

Faculty Readiness and Training for AI-Enhanced Teaching

Effective integration of content-aware AI tools in higher education not only has technical challenges but also factors like faculty readiness and digital literacy can make a huge difference. One of the studies emphasizes the level of this problem: 83% of educators in higher education who surveyed in 2025 recognized faculty training as the key resource needed for successful adoption of AI (Ellucian, 2025). Educators without proper training will not be able to understand AI-generated insights. Besides, even the most perfectly designed AI tools may be used inappropriately.

So, it makes sense that institutions come up with training plans that acquaint faculty members with the main functions of AI-powered LMS platforms. Importantly, the training should not only focus on technical operation but should also address the ethical side responsibilities of educators. Technically proficient and ethically knowledgeable faculty will make a significant difference in serving higher education as a collaborative tool.

Apart from faculty readiness and training, the implementation of context-aware AI tools in higher education depends on institutional readiness and digital capacity. Universities require dependable infrastructure, like LMS, cloud-based storage, and capabilities for real-time data processing. Proper integration with LMS platforms such as Canvas, Moodle, and Blackboard is vital for ensuring smooth data flow and minimizing disruption to existing academic workflows. Student trust is also a premise for implementation success. Learners may feel uncomfortable with continuous monitoring or automated decision-making. Therefore, giving students more control over their data (for instance, the chance to review or debate AI-generated results) is a way to get their trust and illustrate AI as a tool that helps rather than a device that observes.

Future Directions: Proactive Learning Environments and Evolving Faculty Roles

Context-aware artificial intelligence continues to evolve, as the higher education is expected to move toward more initiative-taking, learner-centered needs and adaptive educational environments. Instead of just responding to learner disengagement or a drop in performance, AI systems will interpret their behaviour patterns and use historical data to offer early advice that helps to decrease academic risks and improve learning progression quickly and effectively. Personalization can be further improved by incorporating data from digital interactions, engagement signals and even emotions through multimodal learning analytics. Besides that, AI teaching assistants will be so integrated within the curricula that they will help with daily academic tasks, offer support to learners and guide individuals in a personalized way. Thereby, AI teaching assistants allow faculty to focus on mentoring, curriculum design, high-impact teaching practices.

Future learning platforms will gradually support collaborative and long-term learning techniques. AI systems will help in creating student groups, motivating students to learn from one another and monitoring how they collaborate. Meanwhile, collecting data over time about students will make it possible to personalize one's learning path through different courses and semesters. These systems can adjust learning experiences to match individual strengths, career goals, and interests. Thus, instead of focusing on day-to-day tasks, the educators can focus on guiding students, planning lessons and designing learning activities. Administrative tasks will be reduced through automation while AI-based tools will provide insights that help teachers make informed decisions.

Besides that, technologies such as AI-powered adaptive learning, lifelong learning platforms and immersive AR/VR (augmented reality/virtual reality) technologies expand education to new possibilities as well as help in institutional decision making. When ethical governance and policies lay the foundation for these new innovations, then higher education will become a more versatile, comprehensive, and future-aligned system. Hence, new technologies can be a force both in enhancing human capability and student success.

VI. CONCLUSION

This chapter proposes an integrated, iterative and unified context-aware decision framework that includes learning analytics, ITS, adaptive learning, and contextualized assessment. While most previous papers treat these components separately, the proposed framework sees context-aware AI as a continuous and dynamic decision-making cycle, which makes it suitable for different higher education environments on a large scale.

In addition, the chapter offers a structured basis for teachers, academic leaders, and tech experts to implement responsibly and effectively AI-driven educational practices. Thus, closing the gap between AI theoretical abilities and the practice of institutional implementation. This is achieved by giving the importance to ethical or moral considerations, including data confidentiality, educators' preparedness, algorithmic impartiality and LMS integration, as the very first steps for sustainability of the system.

Looking forward, context-aware AI has the potential to enable practical, learner-centered educational ecosystems supported by AI teaching assistants, personalized learning pathways and multimodal analytics. Importantly, this work reinforces the role of AI as a tool of augmentation that improves human judgments instead of switching human educators. Overall, this framework enables higher education institutions to use context-aware AI in a new, ethically responsible and integrated way that works both on the technical and ethical levels. Also, it serves as a practical way to enhance student engagement, student retention and the overall educational quality.

REFERENCES

Abrar, M., Aboraya, W., Subramanian, K. P., Abdulghafor, R., Al Husaini, Y., & Al Husaini, M. (2025). Adaptive intelligence: AI-powered personalized learning and dynamic assessments. In *Proceedings of the 2025 International Conference on Electrical, Communication and Computer Engineering (ICECCE)* (pp. 1–7). IEEE. DOI: 10.1109/ICECCE67514.2025.11257877

Al Hashmi, R. A., Ozturk, I., & Elmehdi, H. M. (2025). Early detection of at-risk health sciences students: A machine learning-based predictive study using midterm grades. *BMC Medical Education*, *25*(1), 1651. DOI: 10.1186/s12909-025-08192-6 PMID: 41299422

Aleven, V., McLaughlin, E. A., Glenn, R. A., & Koedinger, K. R. (2017). Instruction based on adaptive learning technologies. In Mayer, R. E., & Alexander, P. A. (Eds.), *Handbook of research on learning and instruction* (pp. 522–560). Routledge.

American Association of Colleges and Universities (AAC&U). (2025). *Higher education leaders navigate AI disruption: Leading through disruption survey report*. AAC&U & Elon University. https://www.aacu.org/newsroom/higher-education-leaders-navigate-ai-disruption

Baker, R. S., & Inventado, P. S. (2014). Educational data mining and learning analytics. In Larusson, J. A., & White, B. (Eds.), *Learning analytics: From research to practice* (pp. 61–75). Springer. DOI: 10.1007/978-1-4614-3305-7_4

Bassner, P., Lottner, A., & Krusche, S. (2025). Towards understanding the impact of context-aware AI tutors and general-purpose AI chatbots on student learning. In *Proceedings of the 25th Koli Calling International Conference on Computing Education Research* (pp. 1–11). ACM. DOI: 10.1145/3769994.3770025

Bhat, J., & Jayaram, Y. (2023). Predictive analytics for student retention and success using AI/ML. *International Journal of Artificial Intelligence, Data Science, and Machine Learning*, *4*(4), 121–131. DOI: 10.63282/3050-9262.IJAIDSML-V4I4P114

Cervantes, J., Garcia-Lamont, F., Rodríguez-Mazahua, L., & Lopez, A. (2024). Faculty perceptions and adoption of artificial intelligence tools in higher education. *Frontiers in Education*, *9*, 1360300. DOI: 10.3389/feduc.2024.1360300

Chinta, S. V., Wang, Z., Yin, Z., Hoang, N., Gonzalez, M., Quy, T. L., & Zhang, W. (2024). FairAIED: Navigating fairness, bias, and ethics in educational AI applications. *arXiv*. https://arxiv.org/abs/2407.18745

Conati, C., & Kardan, S. (2013). Student modeling: Supporting personalized instruction from problem solving to exploratory open-ended activities. *AI Magazine*, *34*(3), 13–26. DOI: 10.1609/aimag.v34i3.2483

Ellucian. (2024). *AI in higher education: Annual survey report* (2nd ed.). Ellucian. https://www.ellucian.com/newsroom/ellucians-ai-survey-higher-education-professionals-reveals-surge-ai-adoption-despite

Ellucian. (2025). *AI in higher education: Annual survey report* (3rd ed.). Ellucian. https://www.ellucian.com/newsroom/ellucians-3rd-annual-higher-education-ai-survey-signals-shift-individual-ai-use

Floridi, L., Cowls, J., Beltrametti, M., Chatila, R., Chazerand, P., Dignum, V., Luetge, C., Madelin, R., Pagallo, U., Rossi, F., Schafer, B., Valcke, P., & Vayena, E. (2018). AI4People—An ethical framework for a good AI society: Opportunities, risks, principles, and recommendations. *Minds and Machines*, *28*(4), 689–707. DOI: 10.1007/s11023-018-9482-5 PMID: 30930541

Gutiérrez, F., Seipp, K., Ochoa, X., Chiluiza, K., De Laet, T., & Verbert, K. (2020). LADA: A learning analytics dashboard for academic advising. *Computers in Human Behavior*, *107*, 105826. DOI: 10.1016/j.chb.2018.12.004

Johnson, H. L., Cruthirds, D. F., Taylor, L. A., Suszan, L. T., Owen, R. P., Trautmann, J. L., & Seibert, D. C. (2024). Redefining faculty workload metrics: A data-driven approach. *Journal of Professional Nursing : Official Journal of the American Association of Colleges of Nursing*, *55*, 112–118. DOI: 10.1016/j.profnurs.2024.08.006 PMID: 39667876

Knobloch, J., Kaltenbach, J., & Bruegge, B. (2018). Increasing student engagement in higher education using a context-aware Q&A teaching framework. In *Proceedings of the 40th International Conference on Software Engineering: Software Engineering Education and Training* (pp. 136–145). ACM. DOI: 10.1145/3183377.3183389

Koedinger, K. R., Booth, J. L., & Klahr, D. (2013). Instructional complexity and the science to constrain it. *Science*, *342*(6161), 935–937. DOI: 10.1126/science.1238056 PMID: 24264979

Kotsiantis, S., Pierrakeas, C., & Pintelas, P. (2004). PREDICTING STUDENTS'PERFORMANCE IN DISTANCE LEARNING USING MACHINE LEARNING TECHNIQUES. *Applied Artificial Intelligence*, *18*(5), 411–426. DOI: 10.1080/08839510490442058

Létourneau, A., Deslandes Martineau, M., Charland, P., Karran, J. A., Boasen, J., & Léger, P. M. (2025). A systematic review of AI-driven intelligent tutoring systems in K–12 education. *npj Science of Learning, 10*(1), 29.

Moonsamy, W., & Lotriet, H. (2026). Contextualization, assessment, and generative AI. In *ICT Education: 54th Annual Conference of the Southern African Computer Lecturers' Association (SACLA 2025), Revised Selected Papers* (p. 17). Springer.

Muñoz, A., Lasheras, J., Capel, A., García-Valverde, T., & Caballero, A. (2014). On adapting LMS for recommendation and personalization based on context-aware technologies. In *EDULEARN14 Proceedings* (pp. 5694–5701). IATED.

Nguyen, A., Tuunanen, T., Gardner, L., & Sheridan, D. (2021). Design principles for learning analytics information systems in higher education. *European Journal of Information Systems, 30*(5), 541–568. DOI: 10.1080/0960085X.2020.1816144

Papamitsiou, Z., & Economides, A. A. (2014). Learning analytics and educational data mining in practice: A systematic literature review of empirical evidence. *Journal of Educational Technology & Society, 17*(4), 49–64.

Pecuchova, J., & Drlik, M. (2024). Enhancing the early student dropout prediction model through clustering analysis of students' digital traces. *IEEE Access : Practical Innovations, Open Solutions, 12*, 159336–159367. DOI: 10.1109/ACCESS.2024.3486762

Ranasinghe, A., Gresham, T., Newsome, S., & Wijesinghe, D. (2025). Work in progress: Adaptive learning technologies in higher education—Measuring impact on student engagement and academic performance. In *ICERI2025 Proceedings* (pp. 2103–2109). IATED.

Romero, C., & Ventura, S. (2020). Educational data mining and learning analytics: An updated survey. *Wiley Interdisciplinary Reviews. Data Mining and Knowledge Discovery, 10*(3), e1355. DOI: 10.1002/widm.1355

Siemens, G. (2013). Learning analytics: The emergence of a discipline. *The American Behavioral Scientist, 57*(10), 1380–1400. DOI: 10.1177/0002764213498851

Slade, S., & Prinsloo, P. (2013). Learning analytics: Ethical issues and dilemmas. *The American Behavioral Scientist, 57*(10), 1510–1529. DOI: 10.1177/0002764213479366

Susnjak, T., Ramaswami, G. S., & Mathrani, A. (2022). Learning analytics dashboard: A tool for providing actionable insights to learners. *International Journal of Educational Technology in Higher Education, 19*(1), 12. DOI: 10.1186/s41239-021-00313-7 PMID: 35194560

Thomas, D. R., Gatz, E., Gupta, S., Lin, J., Tipper, C., & Koedinger, K. R. (2024). Using generative AI to provide feedback to adult tutors in training and assess real-life performance. In *Proceedings of the Learning Ideas Conference* (pp. 204–214). Springer. DOI: 10.1007/978-3-031-73427-4_21

UNESCO. (2025). *UNESCO survey: Two-thirds of higher education institutions have or are developing guidance on AI use*. UNESCO. https://www.unesco.org/en/articles/unesco-survey-two-thirds-higher-education-institutions-have-or-are-developing-guidance-ai-use

VanLehn, K. (2011). The relative effectiveness of human tutoring, intelligent tutoring systems, and other tutoring systems. *Educational Psychologist*, *46*(4), 197–221. DOI: 10.1080/00461520.2011.611369

Weber, C., Truong, H. M., & Vas, R. (2015). Context-aware self-assessment in higher education. In *EDULEARN15 Proceedings* (pp. 5910–5920). IATED.

Yekollu, R. K., Bhimraj Ghuge, T., Sunil Biradar, S., Haldikar, S. V., & Farook Mohideen Abdul Kader, O. (2024). AI-driven personalized learning paths: Enhancing education through adaptive systems. In *Proceedings of the International Conference on Smart Data Intelligence* (pp. 507–517). Springer. DOI: 10.1007/978-981-97-3191-6_38

Chapter 2
Context-Aware AI in Teaching:
Balancing Efficiency, Authenticity, and Academic Honesty

Vivit Rosmayanti
http://orcid.org/0000-0002-3648-9878
Universitas Negeri Makassar, Indonesia

Hasnawati Hasnawati
STIKES Datu Kamanre, Indonesia

ABSTRACT

This chapter is focused on explaining how context-aware AI technologies have transformed the opportunities and challenges of post-secondary education. AI teaches the flexibility of methods and how automation can improve instruction efficiency. However, concerns about AI and automation can lead to a loss of teaching and learning human touch. This chapter also touches on human agency, the ethics of AI policies, and the role of sustainability. In relation to AI and teaching, the author introduces a three-pillar system. Sustainability in AI and teaching can come through transparent instructional design, policy integration to ensure a balance of teaching integrity, academic integrity, and the adoption of technology, and continuous training of teaching staff.

INTRODUCTION

The proliferation of artificial intelligence in higher education has profoundly impacted learning practices. The launch of ChatGPT and the emergence of agentic

DOI: 10.4018/979-8-2600-2811-7.ch002

AI and large language models have disrupted learning practices by integrating advanced technologies. As AI tools are being adopted at an unprecedented rate, there is a growing concern for the ethical use, misuse, and abuse of these technologies and their impacts on authentic learning (Oh & Sanfilippo, 2024; Tzoneva, 2023). The academic community has to grapple with this paradoxical situation in which efficiency gains and technological pragmatism are at odds with the principles of authenticity in education and academic integrity.

Context-aware AI systems are instructional partners with capabilities to dynamically adapt to the needs of individual learners and personalize their educational experiences. These systems are created with the purpose of optimizing learning through the analysis of learner interactions, preferences, and performance. The use of these AI systems is beneficial to learning and can promote an engaging educational experience (Ivanytska et al., 2024). The concern of the erosion of authentic learning as a result of the over-reliance on AI is justified.

If AI technologies are implemented such that students are assisted or even entirely substituted for AI in tasks like assignments or comprehension exercises, concerns emerge regarding ownership of the work and whether students are developing true critical thinking skills. (Ivanytska et al., 2024; Alrayes et al., 2024). Positively, AI has the potential to streamline administrative tasks, improve student engagement through adaptive learning, and improve access to learning materials (Tzoneva, 2023; Aghaee et al, 2024). However, with these enhancements, significant ethical issues arise. AI's misuse can lead to biased automated content generation, academic dishonesty, and erode the value of teaching. This situation warrants a balance between the benefits of AI in education and the risk of ethics in policy-making. Universities have to establish guidelines to enable the ethical use of AI without compromising academic integrity and student participation in learning (Oh & Sanfilippo, 2024; Aghaee et al, 2024).

AI in higher education has a far-reaching impact on teaching responsibilities and student learning outcomes. The responsibilities of faculty members seem to be straddling the line between the adoption of AI technologies and the commitment to the sustainment of academic integrity. They must integrate AI into the curricula. They must also promote the culture of critique and ethical use of the technology. Not to mention, educators must ensure that the students are equipped with the very skills that are needed to illegally engage with AI (Oh & Sanfilippo, 2024; Alrayes et al., 2024). Evidently, the pedagogical frameworks that aim at constructing the digital literacy and ethical reasoning of the students are most needed, particularly as the institutions of learning are faced with the evolving challenges posed by the emergent AI tools.

The primary focus of the chapter will be to examine the complex realities of contextually aware AI in teaching, with particular reference to the thin line between the possible productivity, efficacy, and potential of AI, and the necessary/ desirability of educational integrity and honesty. It will deal with the impact of these technologies on the institutional frameworks in relation to the faculty obligations and the student learning experience. Recognizing the intersection of these elements is critical for improving the learning process, but more importantly, for developing an ethical structure that navigates the complexities of a technologically advanced learning environment.

Additionally, this chapter will evaluate the body of literature and disparate case studies that show the tightrope walk of the effective utilization of AI while still preserving the fundamental principles of academic integrity. This discussion will incorporate the perspectives of educators, administrators, and students in order to advocate for the constructive engagement that will be required to adequately balance the policy-making process in order to capture the benefits of AI and address the detrimental impacts of the technology. The following sections will outline a continuum that begins with the assessment of the prevailing models of AI practice and ends with the recommendation for fostering an ethically focused educational climate in the face of AI technology.

UNDERSTANDING CONTEXT-AWARE AI IN HIGHER EDUCATION

Definition and Key Characteristics

Context-aware technologies are beginning to innovate in the field of educational technology. Incorporating the ability to sense, process, and respond to contextual information of the coming AI solutions, educational technology will be radically transformed. Empathic technologies will sense the context and emotions of individuals in a learning situation and respond in a manner appropriate to the educational situation. A context-aware AI system will be able to process and combine history, learner, and discourse models simultaneously and provide the learner with the needed and appropriate guidance (Hu & Zhang, 2025; Gurung & KC, 2023). One of the key aspects of context-aware artificial intelligence in higher education is context interpretation. Context-aware AI systems utilize learner profiles comprising various elements of the learner, including demographics, previous knowledge, and learning behavior, in order to help systems understand the individual needs of each learner (Wang & Wu, 2025). In task design, AI incorporates variables such as assignment type, task objectives, and goals determined by the professors/customers, and therefore, AI can guide effective teaching strategies based on those factors. Additionally, the analysis of discourse cues means AI systems can evaluate student interactions and adjust learning experiences to improve active learning by refining AI responses to better meet the requirements of teaching and the attitudes of the students. For instance, context-aware systems can adjust the learning activities and teaching approach to help students better understand a concept (Al-Shallakh, 2024; Wang & Wu, 2025).

Adaptive decision-making is yet another feature of context-aware AI, which makes it an effective partner in creating individualized learning experiences. Such programs use a reinforced learning model in which real-time data about users' interactions and performance is collected to create changes in instructional materials and aids promptly. (Gurung & KC, 2023; Mukooyo & Kasse, 2024). An example is an AI system that can appropriately determine an optimal amount of scaffolding based on a student's real-time performance and provide guidance on how to do more difficult activities. This capacity to adapt is imperative to improving and sustaining student motivation and engagement, particularly in the diverse learning situations typical of higher education.

When context-aware AI systems become fully integrated, personalization will become a real outcome of such systems. Personalizing the teaching and learning processes will undoubtedly improve the effectiveness of teaching and subsequently the learning processes. Considerable improvement will take place because the AI systems will be able to customize and personalize processes to meet individual student needs. Different language learning applications, for instance, use context-aware AI to improve students' pronunciation by providing them with feedback tailored to their specific needs based on their input and performance data (Al-Shallakh, 2024). Such a level of customization will reinforce the learning experience because the AI system will target the specific needs of the learner and provide interventions that are relevant to and based on the learner's real needs.

In addition, context-aware AI exhibits automated support that can refine teaching and learning, and this support can include proactive resource suggestions, content summaries, and the use of game-oriented feedback to improve learner engagement (Wang & Wu, 2025). Automated systems like this facilitate students' ability to control their learning pathways, and in turn, create learner agency and the possibility to self-regulate their learning process (Hu & Zhang, 2025). This learner and AI interaction prompts and creates a space for learner exploration and inquiry, and enables students to pursue their interests without traditional limitations, with AI as a support and guide to their learning, not just another traditional information resource.

As mentioned earlier, context-aware AI for higher education encompasses multiple cutting-edge features that positively impact learning. With a focus on contextual understanding, adaptive decision-making, personalization, and automated support, there are opportunities and obstacles all higher education institutions must address. Increased application of AI technologies in education means that the impact and function of context-aware AI must be understood by all teachers, learners, and decision-makers in the education sector. The combination of AI and education will continue to rapidly evolve, while also evolving the goals and objectives of educational systems, the teaching and learning activities, and the policies that ensure educational systems retain their integrity and effectiveness.

Underlying Technologies

It's important to comprehend the driving technologies behind context-aware AI for its future possibilities in pedagogy. One of the most revolutionary aspects of this emerging technology is large language models (LLMs), which serve as the backbone for the next generation of agentic AI and autonomous agents. Deep-learning-based LLMs possess the ability to synthesize and comprehend text in a manner comparable to humans. They are central to the creation of agentic AI, which can engage in autonomous interaction with learners in a context-sensitive manner by providing personalized responses, explanations, and suggestions (Catalano, 2025; Al-Saadawi & Daş, 2024).

The autonomous agents of agentic AI are also able to perform functions with little to no human involvement and can revise their methodologies based on the changing conditions of a learning system. This is particularly useful in environments where the learning requirements of the students are in a constant state of flux (Catalano, 2025; Zhang et al., 2023). For example, in a system where these agents are able to create adaptive personalized learning pathways by modifying the complexity of learning materials based on students' demonstrated understanding, engagement, and comprehension are likely to be improved significantly, and a more robust learning outcome is likely to be realized.

Multimodal context recognition is equally important as it enhances the educational interface by processing varied data types, not just textual data, but also data generated through the students' behaviors and the surrounding environment. This results in a more comprehensive perspective about the student. It is also known as a recognition system, and it is a system that can collect data from different streams, including but not limited to, behavioral data, data from the students' body and their environment, and from that data, the system can determine the cognitive state and preferences of the learner (Al-Saadawi & Daş, 2024; Kumar & Martin, 2024). Behavioral cues, for instance, can be used by AI systems to determine when a student is losing concentration or when the student is cognitively overloaded with the material being presented so that the system can assist or support the student in achieving their educational goals through adaptive interventions.

The use of new technologies integrated into Learning Management Systems (LMSs), e-learning tools, and assessment systems needs to be further developed to be fully useful in higher education. By incorporating context-aware AI systems into their tools, models, and systems, universities will be able to significantly reshape the learning experience. Catalano (2025) notes that, for example, LMS platforms powered by LLMs will be able not only to automate grading but, in addition, to offer students real-time, tailored feedback. The quality and speed of the provision of education will be greatly improved. In the same way, e-learning systems that use context-aware systems will be able to modify and allocate learning materials in real time, thus catering to different learning styles and paces, and hence creating a more equitable learning experience (Zhang et al., 2023; Liu et al., 2023).

In addition, assessment systems that incorporate contextual AI are revolutionizing traditional assessment systems. Context-aware assessment systems are able to study how students interact with their learning materials and assess their level of participation and engagement. In this way, they assess not only the academic performance of the student but also the emotional and cognitive states of the learner. All of this information can guide educators in designing learning activities that meet the needs of students (Kumar & Martin, 2024; Liu et al., 2023).

Educational institutions face ethical questions regarding the integration of AI technologies that protect academic integrity and the responsible use of AI technology. The rapidly changing environment creates an opportunity and concerns that continue research and policy frameworks regarding context-sensitive AI and education. The priority should focus on the creation of environments where technology fosters learning and increases engagement and adaptability while assuring the technology does not overshadow the essential elements of education. This approach will enhance the learning experience.

EFFICIENCY GAINS IN TEACHING THROUGH CONTEXT-AWARE AI

Automation of Teaching Tasks

The automated teaching task nature of context-aware artificial intelligence (AI) for higher education instruction is changing how teaching is done. This change includes automated lesson planning, automated curriculum mapping, automated instructional materials generation, and automated assignment feedback. Investing in teaching technologies allows instructors to engage more in teaching and promote teaching and learning productivity.

An emerging context-aware AI technology is automating lesson planning and curriculum mapping, as AI tools utilizing Large Language Models (LLMs) can generate lesson plans that satisfy certain learning objectives and curriculum standards

(Datta, 2025), and in addition, these sophisticated systems are capable of accessing various educational databases to produce teaching materials for a variety of learning situations. For example, an AI system can assemble and organize teaching materials, such as articles, videos, and exercises, according to topics, and therefore, teachers do not need to do this task (Pedró, 2020). The automation of lesson planning not only provides teachers with more time to focus on other educational activities, but also improves the quality of educational materials by making them up-to-date and context-based; in other words, educational materials are aligned to the National or State Learning Standards.

Shan 2025 notes that context-aware AI can also generate AI-based teaching materials and adaptive content. Adaptive content can change based on various criteria-student level, student interests, or learning preferences. Mehta et al. 2025 gives the example of AI platforms that offer tailored learning experiences that create different paths based on the learner's history of interactions and performance data. Over the history of learning, different pieces of content can be presented in vastly different ways, such as a video, a quiz, or in written form. Adaptive features like these help teachers account for the wide range of different abilities in their classrooms and invite more engagement from learners. Mehta et al. 2025 also notes that the ability to automatically create different types of resources at the right time helps teachers offer new materials that can support learning on more intricate subjects.

Context-aware AI has also developed the function of providing real-time feedback on assignments. Feedback from teachers can be a long process, creating a feedback loop for everyone involved in the learning process (Pernaa et al., 2023). In contrast, AI can evaluate the submission itself and provide feedback on the submission's accuracy, the areas that need improvement, and additional resources for improvement. AI in assessment provides feedback based on additional areas, including the individual's improvement and learning trajectory. Feedback is often the most beneficial when given at the moment of the student's need. AI can also provide feedback on the responses to open-ended questions while using a grading rubric that assesses the quality of response on a range of issues, structure, argument, and relevance (Pedró, 2020).

Automated teaching with context-aware AI has far-reaching effects. Teaching automated areas also increases the teaching professional's impact on the educational process. With the administrative tasks supplemented by AI, the teachers can spend almost all of their time in the classroom, fostering higher-order thinking, creativity, and social skills in the students. In addition to this, automated learning feedback systems bolster formative assessment cycles of the learning outcomes, creating higher levels of educational agility in the class (Datta, 2025; Mehta et al., 2025).

However, the challenges related to the automation of teaching tasks need to be addressed. Issues regarding the privacy of data, bias in algorithms, and the need for instructors to review AI materials are primary challenges to consider (Pernaa et al., 2023). It will be vital to protect the integrity of the educational process while maximizing the advantages that come with innovations in automation to assist educational sectors with the integration of AI technologies.

Optimizing Student Support

The use of context-aware AI in improving student assistance in higher education is becoming more prominent in teaching innovations. Some of the most important uses of sophisticated AI technologies include personalized tutoring and scaffolding, predictive learning analytics that identify emerging difficulties of the learner, and personalized recommendations based on specific learner data. These technologies aim to improve academic engagement and support systems to nurture diverse student needs.

Context-aware AI personalized tutoring and scaffolding solutions represent a significant technological advancement. Learning analytics, psychological insights, and interaction improvement data enable them to personalize support and resources (Powell & Courchesne, 2024; Isiaku et al., 2024). For instance, tutoring systems provide personalized scaffolding for students to incrementally master a skill, and (ii) flexibly alter a problem and its guiding questions based on the students' understanding, alleviating the difficulties associated with traditional tutoring systems that are not responsive to the students' differing learning trajectories. For instance, the personalization of tutoring has consistently fostered a higher level of student engagement and achievement in the challenging disciplines of mathematics and science (Karpouzis et al., 2024; Costa et al., 2024). On top of this, gathering millions of interaction data points allows the AI systems to recognize and track students' misconceptions and offer assisting interventions that are purposefully designed to improve the learning experience by addressing the students' needs promptly.

Additionally, AI technologies can be integrated with learning analytics for the early diagnosis of learning challenges. AI with contextual understanding can detect potential learning problems by understanding the changes in metrics related to student performance and engagement, and can even assist in preventing the further deterioration of students' academic situations (Brummelen & Lin, 2020). With the help of predictive analytics, AI can perform diagnosis of learning challenges and assist in determining the content/skill areas in which the student has deficiencies, thus aiding the instructor in providing the appropriate support at the right time. Assessment and measurement of the learning task engagement and performance (including time and scores on quizzes, etc.) empower the instructors to better support students. This shift moves support for students from a reactionary manner to a proactive state where instructors provide appropriate support to students before deficiencies become a significant issue (Costa et al., 2024; Isiaku et al., 2024). For example, learning analytics in modern educational institutions can assist instructors in understanding and exploring the learning challenges of various student cohorts, and provide individualized learning support (including workshops and learning materials) to help the students in overcoming their specific learning challenges, thus improving the overall performance of the students and the institution.

AI-powered education support systems are enhanced with the ability to generate specific recommendations for students based on their individual profiles. AI systems can provide personalized study aids, study strategies, and peer collaboration recommendations based on student data, learning patterns, and prior academic records (Powell & Courchesne, 2024; Karpouzis et al., 2024). Personalization advances the educational system from a singular approach model to an educational environment where students can determine the educational path and the resources that will help them to answer their educational questions. Students value the resources that are available to help them to answer specific educational questions and to resolve academic-related problems.

While implementing context-aware artificial intelligence in student support systems raises several intricate issues, particularly from an ethical standpoint, numerous advantages are evident in relation to personalized tutoring, the ability to detect problems early on, and the inclusion of recommendations to aid students. However, numerous ethical concerns must be addressed, including privacy issues, bias in algorithmic decision-making, and the transparency of support systems (Isiaku et al., 2024). The protection of the student body's personally identifiable information and sensitive academic information requires the application of ethical standards in the use of artificial intelligence (AI) technologies. Nevertheless, while the integration of AI may streamline operational tasks taken on by instructional staff, it is critical to maintain the human aspect of education so that students receive the instructional support that is warranted (Isiaku et al., 2024).

PRESERVING AUTHENTICITY IN TEACHING AND LEARNING

Risks to Authentic Learning

The escalating use of context-aware artificial intelligence (AI) in higher education offers both novel pedagogical possibilities and threats to authentic learning. This part of the study addresses several issues, including concerns about human pedagogy being diminished due to the over-automation of teaching tools, the potentially damaging pedagogical over-reliance of students on AI, and difficulties associated with the preservation of meaningful, inquiry-driven learning.

The substantial risk that AI tools generate in teaching and education is the automated learning process, where human pedagogy is diminished. Although AI may improve the efficiency of educators' lesson planning, content creation, and assessment, the opposite problem of over-reliance on AI instruments may shift the balance of the learning process to the negative role of the learning process's facilitator (Noviaristanti & Hanifan, 2022). The role of the educator is not restricted to the provision of learning content. Educators are also essential in facilitating the development of students' critical thinking and emotional intelligence by fostering positive learning relationships (Navarro et al., 2021). Depersonalized educational experiences where human interaction is over automated erodes the educational foundation of empathy, critical inquiry, and collaboration. The instructor-student relationship is likely to decline, reducing formative learning feedback, mentorship, and substantive discussion that are essential for the development of authentic learning experiences (Xhafaj et al., 2022).

Reliance on AI tools can lead to problems with users' intellectual growth and users' academic honesty. AI tools provide answers to questions, and this causes users not think about the problem. Critical and engagement thinking will decline (Ter, 2025). When students use AI to write papers and to solve difficult problems, they will lose the ability with independent thinking and analyze (Alaidi et al. 2020). This dependence not only affects their learning outcomes/ ability, but students will lose the ability to solve their own problems because of the complacent behavior. Many students cannot solve problems because they rely on external problems and do not solve problems internally. This creates an AI problem because they help students to cheat on their homework, and this creates problems with honesty in schools (Ter, 2025).

Finally, the rapid advancement of AI technology makes it increasingly difficult to maintain meaningful, inquiry-facilitated learning experiences. Learning through inquiry fosters the exploration of questions, critical thinking, authentic engagement, and collaboration with learners and educators (Xhafaj et al., 2022). The use of automated AI tools can diminish the spirit of inquiry. Students may be drawn to AI-produced answers rather than conducting research or developing a hypothesis (Noviaristanti & Hanifan, 2022). Students may also become reliant on AI for instant gratification in obtaining answers. This can hinder their development of questions, analytical skills to synthesize, and information processing. The described dynamics can lead to an unwillingness to explore the complex nature of inquiry, as it is academics, inut is the nature of inquiry. Instead, the dynamics described foremost learning focus on the use of inquiry in the learning process.

Maintaining Human-Centered Pedagogy

As the educational world embraces context-aware AI, it's crucial to keep the focus on human-centered pedagogy. Careful integration of AI and teaching methods such as PjBL, inquiry-based studies, and reflective practices, as well as the creation of genuine assessments and human-AI co-teaching partnerships, can enable us to nurture the human aspects of teaching and learning while making the best use of AI to improve educational experiences.

Additionally, the potential for instituting AI in Pedagogical practices and PjBL and inquiry-based learning exemplifies the strength of AI-enhanced student engagement. AI in learning technologies is beneficial in developing project frameworks and resources that stem student interest (Kasneci et al 2023; Kiran 2025). For example, AI educational resources analyze project results and facilitate personalized learning by offering exploration and critical thinking, purposeful resources to encourage student engagement. AI can help teachers discover new ways to engage students in challenging reflective practices that result in learning.

Evaluations designed while keeping a human-centered approach to education show how important student-centered assessments are when using artificial intelligence to help create assessments and evaluate student performance. Evaluations should go beyond measuring knowledge to include both critical and creative thinking as well as problem-solving skills (Parnin, 2025; Vikram et al., 2025). Authentic assessments, i.e., evaluations that demonstrate real-world application of knowledge, skills, and abilities, allow students to go beyond knowledge. Using AI to create assessments helps educators improve the quality of assessments while also keeping the assessments aligned to the purpose of the assessments, i.e., quality, integrity, and student-centered engagement. (Kasneci et al., 2023). Design assessments that incorporate AI while also using Authentic Assessment principles to create a well-rounded experience.

Human-AI co-teaching frameworks highlight the importance of integrating human aspects in AI-supported educational frameworks, especially with regard to balancing the roles of humans and AI in the educational process. For example, teachers can use the AI system to take care of routine educational administrative work and, as a result, spend more quality time interacting with students. On the other hand, AI can help personalize pathways to students by offering immediate feedback and tailored educational resources (Vikram et al., 2025; Kiran, 2025). Human-AI collaboration upholds that educational processes can be more dependent on human observation, empathy, and cultural appropriateness, and address students' individual needs by utilizing the effectiveness of AI.

Incorporating AI into education raises several important ethical issues that need to be addressed as these technologies continue to evolve. For AI to be integrated successfully into education, teachers need AI literacy that prompts critical thinking around AI, including limitations, biases, and ethical issues related to students' interactions with AI (Kasneci et al., 2023). AI discussions, critical thinking around, and evaluation of the reliability of AI outputs should guide educators in preparing students to be responsible technology users.

Designing Authentic Learning Experiences with AI

For educators, the most important challenge when engaging students in higher education is designing authentic learning activities that thoughtfully employ the context-sensitive AI technologies. Authentic learning activities can be AI-enhanced, rationally integrated learning activities while maintaining the authentic learning concept.

Contextualized learning activities that are AI-supported are authentic learning activities that create rich educational experiences and help students recognize the relevance of learning activities in their real-life situations. Personalized learning pathways, actionable insights, and real-time adaptive recommendations are some of the ways AI can support Project-based Learning (PjBL) (Goyal, 2025; Kaddouri et al., 2025). With the help of AI, educators can develop and facilitate real-world learning activities and encourage students to address and solve contemporary societal problems. Designing and developing learning activities that stimulate student interests and collaborative learning is possible by leveraging AI to evaluate students' strengths and weaknesses. These activities encourage students to bridge the gap between theoretical and practical knowledge.

Furthermore, AI fosters development in higher-order cognitive skills by nurturing critical thinking, personal reflection, and self-assessment skills. AI-focused education technologies create the opportunity to provide individual differentiated instructional feedback and reflection activities that prompt learners to critically evaluate their problem-solving strategies (Goyal, 2025; Anselmo et al., 2025). The incorporation of AI and educators' prompts that direct AI learners' inquiries and self-assessment reflection to the cognitive stage about their thinking functional (process) of thinking and cognitive functions levels, and boosts the recognition of their own learned patterns and cognitive distortions (Jia & Tu, 2024; Tohir et al., 2025). The most effective instructional approach encourages metacognitive skills, cognitive development, and AI technologies. By maintaining the balance of AI technologies and metacognitive skills, learners sustain the accountability for learning and active engagement (as opposed to passive consumption) of learning material knowledge.

AI assistance can also implement culturally responsive and inclusive pedagogy. AI can support inclusivity by presenting different adaptive learning pathways (Jia & Tu, 2024; Kaddouri et al., 2025). Educators can also use AI to create culturally and socially equitable, inclusive instructional materials so all students feel represented. Besides creating adaptive learning pathways, AI can also identify gaps in student representation and assist in building an engagement strategy, as well as help teachers identify and close gaps in their approach to teaching inclusively.

Even with setbacks, AI won't deter learning experiences; Educators, however, must navigate the use of AI carefully. Students must always come first in their approach. The need to focus on student-centered learning must always overrule the desire to build technology and cut out instructor support (Tohir et al., 2025). Educators must navigate AI thoughtfully and with intentional focus toward the potential algorithm biases homogenizing the educational content. Educators must focus their gaze to limit the risk of homogenizing the learning experiences. It is important to keep the learning experiences as varied as possible to minimize the overreliance on a single AI. It is the responsibility of the teacher to use their students' experiences to diversify the AI, not to focus on the technology. This is the first step in breaking down student-centered learning technology to create a varied educational toolbox. It is the first step to promoting technology as a significant educational component. It may support student-centered learning, but a big part of technology must be an instructor's vision. Overall, the use of technology should not be in place of the teaching.

Developing a system where AI supplements human insight nurtures an ecosystem that supports deep learning, equity, and cultural relevance. When educational stakeholders use AI in purposeful ways, they create genuine learning opportunities that help students think and act, like engaged and responsible global citizens.

ACADEMIC HONESTY IN THE ERA OF CONTEXT-AWARE AI

The rise of contextual artificial intelligence (AI) presents new and exciting possibilities for education, but significant challenges persist, particularly in regards to maintaining integrity in academic pursuits. Most of the challenges are driven by the volume of work-generating AI, whose capabilities may include the production of essays, translations, solutions, and even computer code. Educators are worried about the impossibility of establishing the degree of AI involvement with respect to the student submissions. This ambiguity inspires students to claim authorship of AI-generated content and exacerbates the problems of authorship and ownership of the content. The continual evolution of AI technologies and their impact on the definitions of plagiarism, originality, and collaboration will be of greater relevance to Tzoneva (2023), Perkins & Roe (2023), and other authors. New and emergent technologies will expand the challenges for educators and educational institutions to adjust their definitions of academic integrity in the face of evolving AI technologies.

Because of AI integration, academic honesty has many challenges as a result of institutional policy gaps. There are many higher education institutions without a single set of guidelines concerning the ethical use of AI for students and faculty, as a result, leading to differing expectations as a result of departmental and journal academic divides. Lacking policy, educators are left to sort through policy gaps, and with little support from the institution, these gaps are often filled with unilateral and arbitrary solutions which are fair, and even, less effective (Babalola et al., 2024), and unclear gaps are policy, authorship, and disclosure standards, which lead to misunderstandings, and miscommunication regarding how AI should, and can, be used in academics to compromise integrity in scholarship.

As a response to the challenges to integrity, consider combining different ethical and pedagogical methods. One practical option for educators and institutions is to include AI acknowledgment statements in student submissions. These statements would explain the AI's involvement in the creation of the assignment. While students would be instructed not plagiarize, and to create an engagement, AI would still be embraced as an assistive tool (Krueger et al., 2025). In addition, AI education will be the first step in understanding academic integrity. Students who are taught the ethical use of AI are more likely to have academic integrity. Students can use AI tools to help, but not to do all the work for them (Michel-Villarreal et al., 2023; Rosmayanti, 2025).

As a newly emerging strategy in the age of context-based AI, developing assessments that defend against dishonest academic behaviors is critical. Oral assessments, process-based assignments, and drafts with specific annotations enable teachers to evaluate student comprehension in totality and encourage students to interact with the content more meaningfully. In shifting focus to the learning process, instead of concentrating on the end product, teachers are able to create a more honest academic environment, thereby ensuring assessments are a true reflection of student understanding and skills. In doing so, teachers create a culture in which learning is more important than simply doing the bare minimum (Perkins & Roe, 2023).

BALANCING THE THREE PILLARS: A FRAMEWORK FOR SUSTAINABLE AI INTEGRATION

A solid structure that supports all three of the pillars of the triad model (the balance of paradoxes of context-aware artificial intelligence (AI) in higher education) will be strongly needed for the increasing presence of context-aware AI in higher education. Each of the pillars encapsulates the various paradoxes that exist in educational settings. When trying to attain educational efficiency through the use of technology, there often is the opposing need to provide real educational opportunities for the preservation of authentic learning in order to maintain the sanctity of academic honesty. The educational community will continue to need to focus on this type of equilibrium in order to ensure that AI technologies are appropriately applied to educational systems without negative ramifications on educational values.

Course instructor strategies are essential for the responsible and effective integration of AI tools. Azevedo et al. (2025) notes that setting boundaries on the appropriate uses of AI within a course helps students understand the ethics and responsible uses of AI within the course. Educators can promote human–AI blended workflows in which students view AI as a useful tool for the project rather than a resource that eliminates the need for their own thinking or work. Teachers can scaffold assignments that include specific uses of AI so that students are encouraged to adopt AI tools for responsible and constructive purposes, along with real human thinking. This modeling leaves the students with a real-world sense of entitlement and accountability in the use of AI.

Institutional policy development and policy harmonization relating to the use of AI in education are critical priorities. Institutions need single policies with an ethical dimension, best practices, and a framework for policy transparency around student and faculty use of AI (Khoury et al., 2024). Different policies cause confusion regarding expectations across departments and disciplines in a university. Faculty development and training are also important because they help faculty understand the issues related to the use of AI and teach them to integrate cultural and ethical dimensions into their pedagogy. Finally, strong policies around AI are important for transparency and bias and ethics transparency frameworks around AI (Lāma & Lastovska, 2025).

The adoption of ethical measures is of utmost importance when evaluating the impact of AI on the integrity of academia. Measures that prompt AI use acknowledgment, like statements included in student AI use acknowledgment statements, promote transparency and foster honesty about AI use in assignments and create an environment where students are encouraged to think critically about the AI technologies at their disposal (Krueger et al., 2025; Sukmawati et al., 2025). Furthermore, AI educational literacy helps form the basis of responsible and ethical use of technology as well as a culture of integrity within academia. Educators are encouraged to develop resilience to AI assignments, integrate oral assignments, process-oriented assignments, and draft assignments. The process shifts students' reflections and their thinking to the desired direction, trust, integrity, and honesty in academia, and minimizes the incidence of academic dishonesty.

CONCLUSION

The use of context-aware artificial intelligence (A) in education provides opportunities to change how we teach and how we learn. This chapter presented the primary arguments of the complexity of AI and how it can improve the process of learning; how it affects the realness of learning experiences; and the importance of upholding integrity in learning in these emerging situations. As AI grows, it is even more important to keep the balance among these three pillars so educational institutions can manage technology and preserve the real essence of education.

Balancing efficiency with authenticity and academic integrity is key to a sustainable framework for integrating AI into instruction and AI's ethical and responsible use in education. AI integration's instructional framework needs exact parameters and workable guidelines for both students and teachers. Setting AI usage limits, along with human-guided AI blended workflows, can advance education. Educators' roles will be essential in demonstrating responsible AI use to students and developing the analytical skills necessary to critique AI's output to avoid AI-dependency in their academic endeavors.

AI-related PD for faculty can be the launchpad for equity in teaching and learning at the classroom level. For integration to be effective, decision-making authority, ethics, and the control of AI application to collaborate with education pedagogical practices are necessary. AI's ethical use amidst the integration challenges and complexity can be addressed with policies and practices that build an integrity-centric culture.

RECOMMENDATION

Higher education institutions should implement context-aware AI through a policy framework that balances instructional efficiency, learning authenticity, and academic honesty. Universities need to formulate clear regulations regarding permitted and prohibited uses of AI in teaching, learning, assessment, and research. These regulations should include provisions on AI acknowledgment, authorship, data privacy, algorithmic bias, and student accountability. Consistent institutional guidelines can reduce differences in interpretation among lecturers and students regarding acceptable AI use.

Lecturers should position AI as a pedagogical support tool rather than as a substitute for students' reasoning and teachers' judgment. AI can support lesson planning, provide feedback, offer personalized tutoring, and learning recommend resource resources. However, lecturers need to retain responsibility for instructional decisions, assessment design, and ethical supervision. Learning activities should require students to demonstrate reasoning, reflection, problem-solving, creativity, and contextual understanding through observable academic tasks.

Students need structured AI literacy training across relevant courses. This training should develop students' ability to use AI tools responsibly, evaluate AI-generated content, identify potential bias, protect personal data, and avoid excessive dependence on automated outputs. AI literacy should also include discussion of authorship, citation, disclosure, and academic integrity. Course-based integration can help students understand AI use as part of scholarly practice rather than as an external shortcut.

Assessment practices should emphasize learning processes as well as final products. Lecturers can use process-based assignments, oral presentations, annotated drafts, reflective journals, project-based learning, and revision logs to examine students' understanding and intellectual contribution. Institutions should also provide continuous professional development for lecturers on ethical AI integration, assessment redesign, and human-centered pedagogy. This approach allows AI to support teaching efficiency while maintaining student agency, academic responsibility, and the educational value of higher education.

REFERENCES

Aghaee, N., Vrågård, J., & Brorsson, F. (2024). Generative AI in Higher Education: Educators' Perspectives on Academic Learning and Integrity. European Conference on E-Learning, 23(1), 406-414. DOI: 10.34190/ecel.23.1.3090

Al-Saadawi, H., & Daş, R. (2024). Multimodal Emotion Recognition Using Bi-LG-GCN for MELD Dataset. *Balkan Journal of Electrical and Computer Engineering*, *12*(1), 36–46. DOI: 10.17694/bajece.1372107

Al-Shallakh, M. (2024). Embedding Artificial Intelligent Applications in Higher Educational Institutions to Improve Students' Pronunciation Performance. *Theory and Practice in Language Studies*, *14*(6), 1897–1906. DOI: 10.17507/tpls.1406.31

Alaidi, A., Yahya, O., & Alrikabi, H. T. H. S. (2020). Using Modern Education Technique in Wasit University. *International Journal of Interactive Mobile Technologies (Ijim)*, *14*(06), 82. DOI: 10.3991/ijim.v14i06.11539

Alrayes, A., Henari, T., & Ahmed, D. (2024). ChatGPT in Education – Understanding the Bahraini Academics Perspective. *Electronic Journal of e-Learning*, *22*(2), 112–134. DOI: 10.34190/ejel.22.2.3250

Anselmo, C., Bete-Liban, A., Ollero, J., Baui, D., Pascua, J., & Sario, Y. (2025). Role of AI in Enhancing Critical Thinking in Science Education: Challenges and Opportunities for Science Instructor. *International Journal of Multidisciplinary Applied Business and Education Research*, *6*(8), 3877–3891. DOI: 10.11594/ijmaber.06.08.12

Azevedo, L., Robles, P., Best, E., & Mallinson, D. J. (2025). Institutional Policies on Artificial Intelligence in Higher Education: Frameworks and Best Practices for Faculty. *New Directions for Adult and Continuing Education*, *2025*(188), 70–78. DOI: 10.1002/ace.70013

Babalola, D., Adedoyin, A., Ogundipe, F., Folorunso, A., & Nwatu, C. (2024). Policy framework for Cloud Computing: AI, governance, compliance and management. *Global Journal of Engineering and Technology Advances*, *21*(2), 114–126. DOI: 10.30574/gjeta.2024.21.2.0212

Brummelen, J., & Lin, P. (2020). Engaging Teachers to Co-Design Integrated AI Curriculum for K-12 Classrooms. https://doi.org//arxiv.2009.11100DOI: 10.48550

Catalano, I. (2025). Rearing condition affects behavioral response to cross-modal expectancy violation paradigm in zebra finches. DOI: 10.1101/2025.10.10.681716

Costa, G., Júnior, W., Mombelli, M., & Júnior, G. (2024). Revisiting a Teaching Sequence on the Topic of Electrolysis: A Comparative Study with the Use of Artificial Intelligence. *Journal of Chemical Education*, *101*(8), 3255–3263. DOI: 10.1021/acs.jchemed.4c00247

Datta, S. (2025). Agentic AI Security: Threats, Defenses, Evaluation, and Open Challenges. https://doi.org//arxiv.2510.23883DOI: 10.48550

Goyal, A. (2025). AI as a Cognitive Partner: A Systematic Review of the Influence of AI on Metacognition and Self-Reflection in Critical Thinking. International Journal of Innovative Science and Research Techno, 1231-1238. DOI: 10.38124/ijisrt/25mar1427

Gurung, L., & Kc, A. (2023). Considerations of Artificial Intelligence for Higher Education and Implications of ChatGPT for Teaching and Learning. *The Journal of Educational Research*, *13*(1), 1–7. DOI: 10.51474/jer.v13i1.660

Hu, X., & Zhang, H. (2025). Exploring AI-Assisted Self-Regulated Learning Profiles and the Predictive Role of Academic Appraisals: A Control-Value Perspective on Chinese EFL University Students. *European Journal of Education*, *60*(4), e70249. Advance online publication. DOI: 10.1111/ejed.70249

Isiaku, L., Muhammad, A., Kefas, H., & Ukaegbu, F. (2024). Enhancing technological sustainability in academia: Leveraging ChatGPT for teaching, learning and evaluation. *QEA*, *1*(1), 385–416. DOI: 10.1108/QEA-07-2024-0055

Ivanytska, N., Vasylivna, K., Kovalevska, T., Matsera, O., & Tetiana, T. (2024). Analyzing the Possibilities of Implementation of AI and Social Networks in Teaching Foreign Language Students: Ukrainian Universities Case Study. https://doi.org/DOI: 10.31235/osf.io/gn7s8

Jia, X., & Tu, J. (2024). Towards a New Conceptual Model of AI-Enhanced Learning for College Students: The Roles of Artificial Intelligence Capabilities, General Self-Efficacy, Learning Motivation, and Critical Thinking Awareness. *Systems*, *12*(3), 74. DOI: 10.3390/systems12030074

Kaddouri, M., Chniete, I., Mhamdi, K., Bouamri, A., & Atmani, K. (2025). Critical Thinking Skills and Artificial Intelligence (AI)., 337-376. DOI: 10.4018/979-8-3373-4576-5.ch010

Karpouzis, K., Pantazatos, D., Taouki, J., & Meli, K. (2024). Tailoring Education with GenAI: A New Horizon in Lesson Planning. DOI: 10.1109/EDUCON60312.2024.10578690

Kasneci, E., Seßler, K., Küchemann, S., Bannert, M., Dementieva, D., Fischer, F., & Kasneci, G. (2023). ChatGPT for Good? On Opportunities and Challenges of Large Language Models for Education. https://doi.org/DOI: 10.35542/osf.io/5er8f

Khoury, Z., Ferguson, A., Price, J., Sultan, A., & Wang, R. (2024). Responsible artificial intelligence for addressing equity in oral healthcare. *Frontiers in Oral Health*, *5*, 1408867. Advance online publication. DOI: 10.3389/froh.2024.1408867 PMID: 39092200

Kiran, A. (2025). Applications and impact of AI tools in Education. DOI: 10.47716/978-93-92090-38-7

Krueger, L., Clemenson, S., Johnson, E., & Schwarz, L. (2025). ChatGPT in Higher Education: Practical Ideas for Addressing Artificial Intelligence in Nursing Education. *The Journal of Nursing Education*, *64*(5), 323–326. DOI: 10.3928/01484834-20240424-02 PMID: 39038826

Kumar, H., & Martin, A. (2024). Cross-Modal Harmony: Low-Rank Fusion for Enhanced Artificial Emotion Recognition. *Interantional Journal of Scientific Research in Engineering and Management*, *08*(10), 1–5. DOI: 10.55041/IJSREM37976

Lāma, G., & Lastovska, A. (2025). AI competence and sentiment: A mixed-methods study of attitudes and open-ended reflections. *Frontiers in Artificial Intelligence*, *8*, 1658791. Advance online publication. DOI: 10.3389/frai.2025.1658791 PMID: 41069933

Liu, X., Wei, F., Jiang, W., Zheng, Q., Qiao, Y., Liu, J., Niu, L., Chen, Z., & Dong, H. (2023). MTR-SAM: Visual Multimodal Text Recognition and Sentiment Analysis in Public Opinion Analysis on the Internet. *Applied Sciences (Basel, Switzerland)*, *13*(12), 7307. DOI: 10.3390/app13127307

Mehta, V., Sharma, C., & Thiyagarajan, K. (2025). Large Language Models and 3D Vision for Intelligent Robotic Perception and Autonomy. *Sensors (Basel)*, *25*(20), 6394. DOI: 10.3390/s25206394 PMID: 41157446

Michel-Villarreal, R., Vilalta-perdomo, E., Salinas-Navarro, D., Thierry-Aguilera, R., & Gerardou, F. (2023). Challenges and Opportunities of Generative AI for Higher Education as Explained by ChatGPT. *Education Sciences*, *13*(9), 856. DOI: 10.3390/educsci13090856

Mukooyo, H., & Kasse, J. (2024). Towards Sustainable Education: A Machine Learning Model for Early Student Dropout Prediction in Higher Education Institutions. *UHERJ*, *11*(2), 57–68. DOI: 10.58653/nche.v11i2.5

Navarro, M., Prasetyo, Y., Young, M., Nadlifatin, R., & Redi, A. (2021). The Perceived Satisfaction in Utilizing Learning Management System among Engineering Students during the COVID-19 Pandemic: Integrating Task Technology Fit and Extended Technology Acceptance Model. *Sustainability (Basel), 13*(19), 10669. DOI: 10.3390/su131910669

Noviaristanti, S. and Hanifan, H. (2022). Factor Analysis of Learning Management System Acceptance.. DOI: 10.46254/EU05.20220464

Oh, S., & Sanfilippo, M. (2024). University Governance for Responsible AI. *Proceedings of the Alise Annual Conference*. DOI: 10.21900/j.alise.2024.1706

Parnin, C. (2025). Revolutionizing Education through AI with Tailored Learning Experiences and Dynamic Assessments, 10-18. DOI: 10.34293/ICAICM-25.ch002

Pedró, F. (2020). Applications of Artificial Intelligence to higher education: Possibilities, evidence, and challenges. *Iul Research, 1*(1), 61–76. DOI: 10.57568/iulres.v1i1.43

Perkins, M., & Roe, J. (2023). Decoding Academic Integrity Policies: A Corpus Linguistics Investigation of AI and Other Technological Threats. *Higher Education Policy, 37*(3), 633–653. DOI: 10.1057/s41307-023-00323-2

Pernaa, J., Ikävalko, T., Takala, A., Vuorio, E., Pesonen, R., & Haatainen, O. (2023). Artificial Intelligence Chatbots in Chemical Information Seeking: Educational Insights through a SWOT analysis. DOI: 10.20944/preprints202312.1066.v1

Powell, W., & Courchesne, S. (2024). Opportunities and risks involved in using ChatGPT to create first grade science lesson plans. *PLoS One, 19*(6), e0305337. DOI: 10.1371/journal.pone.0305337 PMID: 38885244

Rosmayanti, V. (2025). Eco-Linguistics and Digital Learning: Integrating Environmental Awareness in Language Education. In *Nexus of Environmental Quality and Technology Innovation* (pp. 71-96). IGI Global Scientific Publishing. DOI: 10.4018/979-8-3373-1822-6.ch004

Shan, S. (2025). Reflexive Evidence-Based Multimodal Learning for Clean Energy Transitions: Causal Insights on Cooking Fuel Access, Urbanization, and Carbon Emissions. https://doi.org//arxiv.2511.15342DOI: 10.48550

Sukmawati, R., Rosmayanti, V., & Amin, S. (2025). Blending Technology and Tradition: PjBL in ELT to Foster Self-Directed Learning. *International Journal of Language Education, 9*(2), 356–376. DOI: 10.26858/ijole.v1i2.75114

Ter, K. (2025). Taxonomy and Trends in Reinforcement Learning for Robotics and Control Systems: A Structured Review. https://doi.org//arxiv.2510.21758DOI: 10.48550

Tohir, A., Muslim, S., & Situmorang, R. (2025). Integration of Technology in Learning: Enhancing Higher Order Thinking Skills (HOTS) in Secondary School Students. *International Journal of Computational and Experimental Science and Engineering*, *11*(3). Advance online publication. DOI: 10.22399/ijcesen.3474

Tzoneva, I. (2023). Benefits and challenges in using AI-powered educational tools. DOI: 10.36315/2023v2end079

Vikram, E., Kalaivani, K., Praanesh, M., & Surya, M. (2025). GEN AI Based Personalized AI Tutor. *Interantional Journal of Scientific Research in Engineering and Management*, *09*(10), 1–9. DOI: 10.55041/IJSREM52545

Wang, A., & Wu, X. (2025). Building a triadic model of technology, motivation, and engagement: A mixed-methods study of AI teaching assistants in design theory education. *Frontiers in Psychology*, *16*, 1624182. Advance online publication. DOI: 10.3389/fpsyg.2025.1624182 PMID: 40672855

Xhafaj, E., Qendraj, D., Xhafaj, A., & Gjikaj, N. (2022). A Hybrid Integration of PLS-SEM, AHP, and FAHP Methods to Evaluate the Factors That Influence the Use of an LMS. *International Journal of Decision Support System Technology*, *14*(1), 1–17. DOI: 10.4018/IJDSST.286697

Zhang, S., Yang, Y., Sun, F., & Fang, B. (2023). Application of Image Sensing System in Mineral/Rock Identification: Sensing Mode and Information Process. *Advanced Intelligent Systems*, *5*(11), 2300206. Advance online publication. DOI: 10.1002/aisy.202300206

Chapter 3

Cognitive AI Agents and Natural Language Processing Transforming Higher Education

Ayesha Farooqi
http://orcid.org/0009-0000-4556-4211
Poornima University, Jaipur, India

ABSTRACT

High-level education, in its entirety, is undergoing a paradigm shift with the integration of cognitive AI agents and natural language processing regarding how teaching, research and academic services are provided. Autonomous reasoning, adaptation, and decision-making are possible with the help of cognitive AI agents, and meaningful interaction with written and spoken academic texts can be done with the help of NLP. This chapter discusses the technology of basis and use of cognitive AI and language processing in higher education, and its impact on intelligent tutoring, customized education, research robotics, and intelligent institutional services. It is also critical about the problems of algorithm bias, transparency, ethical governance, and the connection between humans and AI. Offering an interdisciplinary and detailed view, the chapter provides information on how AI agents of cognitive agents and NLP can contribute to the innovative and inclusive and responsible changes in higher education ecosystems.

DOI: 10.4018/979-8-2600-2811-7.ch003

1. INTRODUCTION

1.1 Evolution of AI Agents in Academic Environments

There have been several shifts in technological advancement in higher education: the initial stage of computer-assisted instructions has been evolving into the modern data-driven digital learning environment. Within the past few years, the advent of the cognitive AI agents has brought a major change in the conceptualization and application of artificial intelligence in scholarly circles. However, in contrast to the more traditional rule based or narrowly focused AI systems, the cognitive AI agents are created to feel, reason, learn and adapt automatically in the more complicated and dynamic environments. Such features allow making them active participants in academic eco systems, and not passive equipment, which affect teaching practice, research processes, and services of the institutions.

The development of AI in higher education has been prompted by the development of machine learning, cognitive computing, and human-computer interaction. The initial AI education systems were predominantly interested in automating disjointed activities like grading or content suggestiveness. By comparison, Cognitive AI agents combine several functions, such as situational knowledge, goal-oriented action and high-level decision making. This integration will enable them to facilitate higher functions in academics like diagnosing the needs of learners, support inquiry-based learning and helping the researchers in the synthesis of knowledge. With the growth of the digital platform in universities, cognitive AI agents are being integrated into learning management systems, research infrastructure, and administrative processes (Abbas et al., 2022).

This development is a larger trend toward smart academic services, commonly referred to as intelligent or digital universities. AI agents in those settings can cross institutional borders and engage with the students, faculty, and administrators via numerous channels. Their increased independence and agency pose significant concerns associated with the production, review, and control of knowledge in advanced learning. The interpretation of this development is critical to placing the transformative role of cognitive AI agent in modern scholarly systems.

1.2 Application of Natural Language Processing in Education Transformation

The processing aspect of natural language is critical to facilitating the work of cognitive AI agents in the areas of higher education. School settings are, essentially, language-based including lectures, discussions, reading, tasks, and academic communication. The NLP technologies enable the AI systems to read, comprehend, and write human language, which helps in balancing the concept of computational intelligence and scholarly speaking. By using NLP, AI agents will be able to conduct meaningful dialogue with the learners and educators, read vast amounts of academic content, and contribute to the creation and sharing of knowledge.

Introduction of NLP in AI systems of education has revolutionized the process of teaching and learning through mediation. NLP-based conversational interfaces are used to support intelligent tutoring systems, virtual teaching assistants, and automatic feedback systems, which interrelate with learners using a natural language. Such systems may react to the questions of students, explain, and adjust support to instructions according to language signals. NLP can also be used to analyze student writing and discussion posts automatically, providing feedback into the student learning progress and conceptual knowledge. These capabilities have extended the scope of individual learning as well as bringing significant concerns of equity, openness, and linguistic differences (Adamopoulou & Moussiades, 2020).

In addition to teaching and learning, NLP is transforming the academic research and the operations of the institutions. NLP based resources can help researchers in literature review, thematic analysis and discovery in knowledge through deriving patterns and insights with large scholarly corpora. NLP can be used in the administrative environment to automatically process student questions, policy documents, and messages sent by the institution. This widespread use of NLP in educational environments supports the idea that it is a background technology to enhance the influence of neural AI agents in tertiary education.

1.3 Cognitive AI and NLP as Systems Changers

The intersection of cognitive AI agents and NLP is not merely an increment in technological advancement, but an indication of the systemic change in higher education. The combination of these technologies facilitates the use of autonomous and semi-autonomous systems with the ability to grasp the academic context, make informed decisions and learn through interaction. This intersection causes AI agents to leave using specific scripts and interact dynamically within the intricate academic procedures, including making curriculum strategies, collaborating in research, and advising learners (Kumari et al., 2026).

The latter is a type of systemic change manifested in the transition of the fixed digital platforms to well-adjusting academic ecosystems. The NLP-enabled cognitive AI agent can analyze language data constantly in classrooms, research work, and internal communications to make decisions. As an example, AI agents can determine the new trends in research, recognize learning challenges in a cohort or allocate resources in a university in optimal way. These abilities present novel types of intelligence to the academic governance and change the way in which institutions react to change and uncertainty.

Figure 1. Conceptual integration of cognitive AI agents and natural language processing in higher education

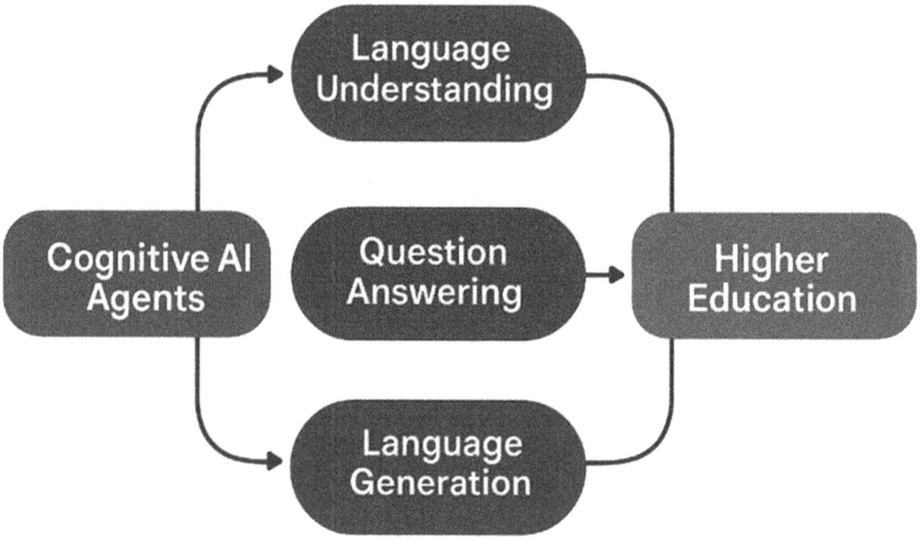

Nevertheless, systematic change also brings in new bonds and hazards. With cognitive AI and NLP starting to form an integral part of the fundamental operations of academic institutions, universities and colleges are faced with the issue of trust, responsibility, and humanity. The prospect that AI agents manipulate pedagogical and research choices creates the importance of critical thinking about the way that authority and responsibility are shared between human and machine. These opportunities and challenges are framed in this introductory section establishing the context on which further analysis can be done in future sections.

1.4 Driving forces and critical problems in AI-driven higher education framing

Significant ethical, pedagogical, and institutional issues have been observed to be associated with the transformational potential of cognitive AI agents and NLP in the context of higher education. On the one hand, the technologies provide a possibility to increase accessibility, efficiency, and personalization of teaching, research, and services. They are able to serve different learners, facilitate learning faster and simplify management procedures. Conversely, their growing independence and dependence on language data creates the issue of algorithmic bias, transparency, and academic values conservation.

Interestingly, AI systems that focus on languages are especially vulnerable to bias and exclusion since they tend to take the dominating linguistic standards imprinted in the training data. On college campuses, where language diversity and freedom of speech are the key principles, discriminatory NLP systems can obstruct the voice of some individuals or support the unfair practices. Furthermore, automated decisions may be hard to challenge or comprehend by educators and the administration due to the obscurity of complicated AI models. These concerns present the necessity of ethical development and regulation of the cognitive AI systems (Alkaissi & McFarlane, 2023).

The section forms the conceptual basis of the chapter placing cognitive AI agents and NLP in the context of the larger change of higher education. It emphasises the duality of the technologies as the drivers of innovation, and the origin of novelties. The parts that follow based on this premise discuss how technology works, how it has been applied in teaching and research, institutional services, and the ethical and governance practices that may be necessary to realize that AI-driven change is in concert with the mission the institution should focus on.

2. FOUNDATIONS OF COGNITIVE AI AGENTS AND NLP TECHNOLOGIES

2.1 Cognitive Architectures and Agent-Based Intelligence

Cognitive AI agents are made to be similar to human cognition in terms of perceptions, reasoning, learning, and decision-making. Cognitive agents are able to work in dynamic environments unlike traditional AI systems which perform fixed tasks or functions and can adjust their behaviour according to the goals or situation and past experiences. These agents can be seen in the context of higher education as intelligent agents that are able to assist complex academic processes including personalized instruction, assisting research and making decisions on the part of the institution. Their performance relies on cognitive architectures that combine various elements such as representation of knowledge, inference processes and learning modules.

Autonomy, proactive, and social interaction are some of the characteristics of agent-based intelligence. The autonomous agents are able to engage in making actions without direct human intervention and proactive behavior enables them to foresee the needs to react to changing academic contexts. Through social interaction, agents are able to exchange messages with the users and other systems which is especially crucial in the educational setting where teamwork and discussion are put at the center. The structural design of cognitive architectures is what makes such behavior possible and can thus enable such agents to organize perception and reasoning and act in a consistent way (Allouch et al., 2021).

Within the academic context, cognitive AI agents are typically used as a component of multi-agent systems, where multiple intelligent agents cooperate in finding the solution to the institutional goals. As an example, one agent can be devoted to learner modeling, another one to content adaptation, and the third, to assessment analytics. The agents share information as well as image the actions so as to form a distributed intelligence which is more complex like the higher education ecosystems. It is important to be educated on cognitive architectures and agent-based intelligence in order to value how AI systems are being deployed to go beyond specific applications to enable comprehensive academic change (Kumari & Goyal, 2026).

2.2 NLP Basics Techniques of Educational Uses

The linguistic features of Natural language processing furnish cognitive AI agents with the abilities necessary to work in higher education. The basic NLP methods are text preprocessing, syntactical and semantic processing, discourse modeling and language generation. These methods enable the AI systems to read, listen to academic texts and extract meaning of the intricate texts and generate contextually appropriate responses. Another application of NLP in the learning field is as a way of human interaction with AI agents.

Recent developments in machine learning and deep learning have greatly improved the NLP performance, especially in speech recognition, machine translation, and text summarization. These capabilities can be used in the context of higher education, which can be associated with automated essay assessment, chat-based tutoring, and academic search. NLP systems can be used to analyze student writing and detect missing concepts, evaluate argument organization and make specific feedback. Equally, NLP that works with speech also facilitates an interactive learning experience by use of voice-activated assistants and discussion facilitating programs (Ayedoun et al., 2019).

Nevertheless, NLP methods are not neutral despite such developments. They are projections of the language skills and suppositions of both training material and model creation. Language used in education is very specific and heterogeneous as it includes disciplinary jargon and the multilingual mode of expression and different rhetorical modes. Systems that do not take this diversity into consideration can lead to biased or incorrect results of NLP systems. It is also important to learn technical roots and constraints of the NLP techniques in order to use them in higher education responsibly (Ba et al., 2021).

2.3 Cognitive AI and NLP integration into Academic Systems

The cognitive AI agent combined with the NLP technologies brings about the transformational effects of AI in higher education. The reasoning and decision-making facilities are offered by cognitive architectures and meaningful academic language communication is made possible by NLP. The combination of them creates intelligent systems that are able to read between the lines, talk, and adjust to the needs of the user. This combination enables AI agents to work in various fields in academics, such as teaching and learning to research and administration.

The language input may be linked to action and cognitive processing by networked AI systems. As an example, a student query written using natural language can be put through NLP modules to remove intent and meaning which are relayed to the cognition parts where they can be reasoned and responses generated. The output of the system is then structured in natural language thus providing a natural interaction process. Examples of such pipelines are how cognitive AI and NLP collaborate to facilitate academic interactions of a complex nature (Sharma et al., 2026).

Integration in an institutional setting is not limited to the specific systems but a general digital infrastructure. An example is where cognitive AI agents can access learning management systems, research databases, and administrative systems and synthesize information using NLP to help navigate the websites. This interconnection allows comprehensive support of academic activities at the expense of enhancing the complexity of the system. To be able to integrate effectively, the design has to be well thought of to be interoperable, reliable, and in line with educational objectives (Bavaresco et al., 2020).

2.4 Learning, Adaptation and context Awareness

One of the most distinguishing characteristics of the cognitive AI agents is that they are able to learn and evolve. Machine learning allows agents to optimize their models as a result of interacted data thereby enhancing performance in the long-term basis. The adaptative ability of AI systems can support personalized learning in higher education, meaning are changing the content, learning pace, and encouraging feedback, depending on individual learner profiles. NLP helps in this flexibility as it gives information about the language behavior of learners, in terms of question patterns, writing style as well as level of engagement (Bickmore et al., 2016).

Context awareness is mentioned in close relation to adaptation and it is paramount to allowing meaningful AI support in academic contexts. Cognitive AI agents need to take into consideration the context-related factors like disciplinary standards, learning goals and institutional policies. The NLP methods allow the agents to read the context within language use making them respond on a more personalized manner. Indicatively, interpretation of a student question can be based on course material, previous interactions as well as testing schedules.

Nonetheless, adaptive and context-aware systems also facilitate transparency and control issues. With the development and learning of AIs, there exist the chances that they will act in a more unpredictable manner, and that their actions become hard to comprehend and control by an educator. To make learning and adaption consistent with pedagogical values, there is a need to have a clear governance system along with human control. This part captures the essence of the need to base the technical innovation with the principles of education as the prelude to other parts, which explore the application, ethical considerations, and the system of governance (Farooqi et al., 2026).

3. AI-DRIVEN TEACHING AND LEARNING INNOVATIONS

3.1 Intelligent Tutoring Systems and Conversational AI

Intelligent tutoring systems have greatly evolved through cognitive AI agents that are incorporated with the natural language processing in higher education. In contrast to the old-fashioned computer-based instruction, modern AI-based tutors can be used to involve learners in interactive dialogues, adjust the teaching methods on the fly and react to the needs of specific learners. These systems can be made to understand student queries, explanations and reflections that are based on natural language applications through NLP which facilitates more authentic and learner centered interaction. Consequently, intelligent tutoring system comes out to be more and more like human tutor in terms of scaffolding learning and offering contextual support (Briel, 2021).

The primary role of conversational AI in this change is based on the ability to experience ongoing, dialogue-based learning. Chatbots and virtual teaching assistants powered by AI will be able to answer the questions related to courses, explain the concepts, and assist the students in the complex procedures of resolving the problems. Such systems are used on digital platforms, which serve the learners outside the classroom. Conversational tutors are especially useful in high education as in large or online classes where an instructor might not have the time to provide individual attention to students. Through the application of NLP, these agents are able to generate coherence over the prolonged interactions and modify the responses in regards to the learner input and previous interactions (Carayannopoulos, 2018).

Nevertheless, the use of conversational AI in education provokes pedagogical issues as well. Although AI tutors could offer timely feedback regularly, they are not as judicious and understanding as human instructors. The intelligent tutoring systems should be carefully integrated into the curriculums to ensure that they do not supplant human teaching. This equilibrium is critical towards up keeping the relational and reflective aspects of higher education.

3.2 Individual Learning and Adaptive Instruction

One of the most evident opportunities of cognitive AI and NLP in higher education is the personalized learning. Cognitive artificial intelligence representatives can convert personal learning features, including prior knowledge, learning styles, engagement patterns, etc., into customized learning content and directions. NLP provides its contribution through the analysis of linguistic data on the basis of student interaction, written work and other input on the discussion board, and allows pinpointing the knowledge of the learners. Combined, such technologies facilitate adaptive learning which develops as learners do (Goyal et al., 2026).

Adaptive learning systems are able to dynamically update the difficulty levels, recommend resources, and give specific feedback of real-time analysis. As an example, an AI can detect false beliefs based on the student responses to questions and modify the instructions. The reflective writing or discussion posts can be analyzed using NLP and the gaps in concepts that cannot be identified in the conventional evaluation can be identified. Such a degree of individualization can have a positive effect on learning and can help lessen attrition by meeting the needs of learners in advance.

Although these advantages exist, personalized learning systems also have issues on equity and transparency. The adaptive algorithms can unwillingly propagate the existing inequalities in the cases when they are based on biased data or limited performance metrics. Furthermore, the decision-making process of personalization might not be very visible to students and educators. To solve these concerns, it is necessary to design adaptive systems that are explicable, inclusive and pedagogically oriented (Chang et al., 2022).

3.3 automatic evaluation and NLP based Feedback

Automated assessment is one of the major fields of innovation that NLP and cognitive AI agents allow. Assessment is resource intensive and central in the development of an academic in higher education. NLP-based systems have the potential to considered written submissions, short answers and even oral feedback, which presents the feedback in a massively scalable manner. Such systems examine the language characteristics of coherence, argument structure, and use of terminologies and provide more than just correctness.

Formative assessment using the NLP-based feedback systems helps learners to improve by pointing them in the right direction, instead of having them graded. The cognitive agents of AI have the ability to contextualize feedback depending on learning goals and previous performance, and so the student knows not only what is wrong but why. It is a feature that improves the instructing value of assessment and promotes self-managed learning. Automated feedback can be used to supplement instructor feedback in subjects where writing and argumentation play a large part (Chen et al., 2022).

Nonetheless, automated assessment does present some risks with regard to both fairness and validity as well. NLP systems can also give preference or bias against non-standard expression and, therefore, divergent learners. The assessment models must be properly calibrated to ensure fairness and their effects should also be evaluated regularly. The role of human supervision is vital to justify expert judgments and to resolve issues when the evaluation, conducted by algorithms, can be inadequate (Goyal et al., 2026).

3.4 Knowledge Construction and Learning Collaboratively

NLP and cognitive AI agents are another aspect that involves collaboration in learning and constructing knowledge in higher learning institutions. Education is a collaborative process and AI systems are becoming more and more facilitative of group communication, discussion and peer-reviewing. With NLP, discourse patterns in online forums, collaborative documents, and group chats can be analyzed, which will allow gaining an insight into the dynamics of participation and conceptual development. This information may be used by cognitive agents to engage in further debate, point out the unanswered questions, or relate ideas (Diederich et al., 2022).

In the collaborative environments, AI agents can act as facilitators instead of instructors and promote thoughts and discussion among the learners. As an illustration, an artificial intelligence application can either provide a summary of salient points in a discussion board or propose relationships between contributions made by students. This can be positively achieved through such interventions that boost group knowledge and promote non-discrimination. The analysis based on NLP is able to isolate the voices that can be sidelined during a group interaction thus providing personalized support.

Meanwhile, the introduction of AI in a group learning environment circumvents agency and authenticity. Strong dependence on AI facilitation could affect the ways students interact with each other or the course of discussion. When it comes to designing AI systems that facilitate effective and not dominating collaborative learning, one has to take a pedagogical intent and ethical considerations very seriously (Fidan & Gencel, 2022).

3.5 Implications to Teaching Practice and Faculty Roles

Teaching using cognitive AI and NLP will transform the faculty role in colleges. Instead of substituting instructors, AI-motivated teaching tools redefine faculty roles and neo-faculty as a designer, facilitator and mentor. Teachers put more emphasis on more advanced pedagogical activities like curricular design, critical discourse, and differentiated instruction, whereas AI machines undertake low-level or scalable tasks.

Figure 2. Applications of generative AI in teaching, research, and academic services in higher education

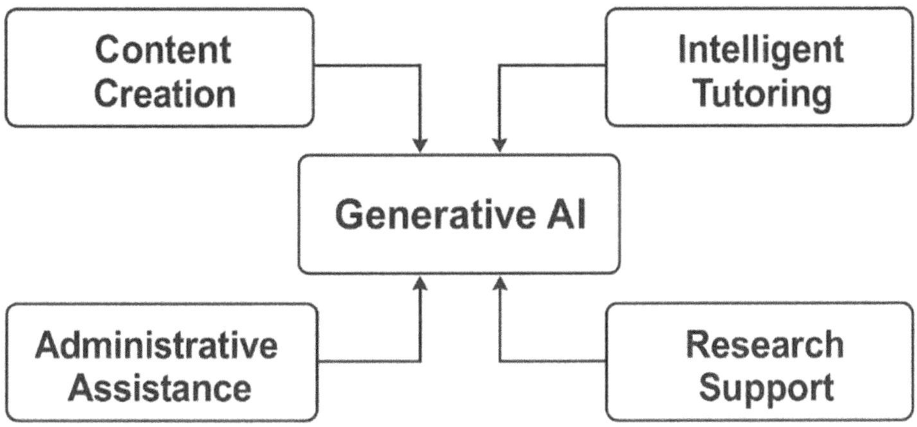

The change has a consequence to the institution culture and faculty development. The teachers will have to learn new skills that will enable them to include AI in the classroom instruction and to analyze the results correctly. Colleges and universities should also help faculty to overcome the ethical and pedagogical issues related to AI-based teaching. The understanding of the complementary functions of human expertise and machine intelligence is an important element in achieving the advantages of AI-based teaching innovations.

4. TRANSFORMING ACADEMIC RESEARCH THROUGH COGNITIVE AI AND NLP

4.1 AI-Assisted Literature Analysis and Knowledge Discovery

The proliferation of scholarly writings is so high that researchers in higher education find it more difficult to conduct Comprehensive literature analysis. AI agents with natural language processing provide sophisticated solutions to dealing with such a complexity by automating parts of literature review and knowledge discovery. Text mining, topic modeling and semantic analysis represent NLP methods which allow the AI system to consume large volumes of scholarly literature and discern themes, trends and other relationships that might not be readily detectable by humans reading this same literature (Dandotiya et al., 2026).

The literature analysis using AI aids in reducing the cognitive and temporal load of the traditional review process, which is also associated with researchers. The cognitive AI agents have the capabilities of summarizing research articles, grouping similar studies, and underlining the often-impactful works in a domain. The abilities enable scholars to get a high level of vision of research landscapes and interim gaps or highlighting direction. The analysis based on AI is especially effective in interdisciplinary research, when the literature of interest cuts across disciplines and promotes integrative research.

Although these can be seen as benefits, AI-aided literature analysis creates the question of epistemic bias and interpretive authority. NLP systems are also based on a set of training data and algorithmic assumptions that could favour some research paradigms, publication outlets or language styles. Scientists need to learn to approach AI-generated information critically, as supplements and not as replacements of academic judgment. To guarantee academic rigor, it is vital to ascertain, in terms of the above, that AI systems identify and prioritize knowledge in a transparent manner.

4.2 Perspectives on Research Automation and Writing in Support of Scholarly writing

In addition to literature analysis, cognitive AI and NLP are also applied to facilitate the automation of research and academic writing. The tools that are controlled by NLP aid in creating outlines, polishing language, reviewing flow coherence, and compliance with academic grammar. Cognitive AI agents have the ability to read research manuscripts giving suggestions on structure, clarity and flow of the argument to assist in better conveying of ideas by the researchers.

The tools are especially important in the field of higher education where research dissemination and evaluation mainly revolve around writing. In multilingual scholars and at the beginning of their career, NLP-based writing support might reduce publication barriers by providing language, style feedback. Cognitive artificial intelligence agents also have the potential to support citation management, plagiarism detection, and formatting which makes the administrative side of academic work easier. Through the automaticity of the routine tasks, the ideas of the AI systems can enable researchers devote additional time to conceptual growth and methodological rigor (González et al., 2022).

Nevertheless, AI use in a research paper also has normative ethical considerations regarding the credibility and authorship of the writing and the originality of knowledge in the research. The contribution of AI-generated text can undermine the role of a human in the production of text, and the classical idea of scholarly authorship. Learning institutions should thus put up distinct principles on the responsible utilization of AI writing tools so that they can back the principles of academic research rather than erode them.

4.3 Data Analysis and Interdisciplinary Research Support

The use of cognitive AI agents and NLP also play a part in sophisticated data analysis as an academic field, especially where the methods involve qualitative or mixed methods. NLP can be used to perform automated coded process, sentiment analysis, and thematic extraction of interviews transcripts, survey responses sponsored by study any point open about open-ended data. Cognitive AI agents have the potential to combine such analyses with numerical data, which contributes to the holistic interpretation and interdisciplinary research (Gupta & Chen, 2022).

Interdisciplinary research is becoming popular in the field of higher education in order to resolve complex challenges facing society. Collaboration across disciplines is aided by the use of AI systems that are capable of analyzing different types of data and languages of disciplines. An AI agent can, as an example, contribute to the combination of social science interview findings with scientific reports or policy papers. This ability allows the scalability and reproducibility of qualitative research and provides novel directions in which data can be used to inquire.

Meanwhile, automatic data analysis comes with the risk of oversimplification and the contextual blurry. The qualitative data may have hidden meanings, cultural elements, or moral aspects that may be overlooked by NLP-based analysis. The researchers should be careful of these drawbacks, and the technology of AI as an enhancement of, not substitution to interpretative sophistication. Transparency and reflexivity in the methodology are essential in incorporating AI into the research processes (Kumari et al., 2026).

4.4 Knowledge Management and Research Cooperation

The use of cognitive AI agents is also increasing as an agent to support research collaboration and knowledge management in institutions of higher learning. Implying the use of NLP, researchers are able to structure the results of their work, monitor collaboration networks, and accelerate the exchange between scientists. AI agents can also suggest possible partners according to the research interests, research funding possibilities, or track project advancement within teams.

Institutional research capacity and innovation would not be possible without effective management of knowledge. It is possible to ask cognitive AI systems to manage institutional repositories, terminate duplication of activity, and point at interdepartmental synergies. NLP helps such systems to process unstructured research data, including project reports and grant proposals, which makes the institutional knowledge more available and practical. The capability is useful in resource allocation and strategic research planning (Hamzah et al., 2021).

Nevertheless, AI-mediated collaboration makes issues of data privacy, intellectual property and power relations as well. Robotically suggested recommendations and analytics can affect research agendas and patterns of collaboration in relationships that are not visible and even-handed. Academic institutions should make sure that knowledge management systems deployed with the help of AI should protect academic autonomy and foster inclusive collaboration. The process of responsible usage of AI needs guidance by systems of governance in the research coordination area.

4.5 Re-defining the Relationship between the Researcher and AI

The relationship between researchers and technology is being redefined due to the introduction of cognitive AI and NLP in academic research work. AI agents do not operate as instruments of passivity but become research partners as they provide suggestions, insights, and automation. The change problematizes the idea of scholarly expertise and agency. To successfully work with AI systems, researchers should create new versions of digital literacy to ensure that it does not restrict themselves.

The relationship between the researcher and AI also needs to be redefined in order to solve the problem of trust and accountability. Since AI systems contribute to research choices and outputs, issues that are left to be answered include what may happen in terms of errors or bias. It is necessary to separate the sphere of human judgment and the assistance of machines to ensure academic research and its integrity. This section brings out the point of AI attentive incorporation to research practice, balancing technological advancement with ethical and epistemic accountability (Hayashi, 2020).

5. AI-ENABLED ACADEMIC AND ADMINISTRATIVE SERVICES

5.1 Smart Student Support and Advisory Systems

Artificial intelligent agents that are cognitive and ones that include natural language processing are steadily reshaping student services and advisory services in higher education, in particular. Universities are faced with complex interactions with their students in the area of admissions, enrolment, academic advising, mental healthcare, and career preparation. Conventionally, they are human-intensive services that have little or no availability and scalability. Another option is AI-powered advisory systems that are intended to help individuals with ongoing, one-on-one, and responsive assistance based on conversational input and smart decision-making (Kumari et al., 2026).

The use of chatbots with NLP and virtual advisors will be able to attract students to chat with it using natural language and answer their questions related to the choice of courses, degree requirements, deadlines, and institutional policies. These interactions are boosted with the help of cognitive AI agents that keep contextual awareness of the academic history of a student, his or her goals, and performances. This makes it possible to have recommended advisory systems replace the generic response and provide individualized recommendation. In case students have to follow complicated academic routes, these systems may lessen the level of disorientation and enhance access to relevant information at the opportune moment.

In spite of their benefits, AI based advisory systems have to be thoughtfully constructed to prevent over-robotisation and fake news. The decision to advise will often be a delicate one; it is often emotional and may touch upon certain personal issues and/or problems with learning. Although AI systems are capable of giving a starting direction and triage, when complex or of high stakes, human advisors will be necessary. It then follows that the implementation process needs hybrid models of service that combine efficiency of AI with human expertise (Hsu et al., 2021).

5.2 NLP-Based Institutional Service automation

In addition to serving students, cognitive AI and NLP are transforming institutional services, as well as administrative functions, in higher education. Universities produce and process data in textual forms in large amounts such as policy documents, emails, reports, and compliance records. Following automation through NLP, the institutions are now able to handle this information more effectively by identifying the meaningful content, categorizing documents, and producing summaries. These processes can be coordinated by cognitive AI agents, which can help in making decisions quicker and eliminate the administrative load.

In other parts of the organization, including admissions processing, financial aid management, and human resources, AI can be used to provide analysis of applications as well as inquiries that are made using natural language. These systems are capable of the interpretation of intent and prioritization of tasks through NLP, and it is the work of cognitive agents to apply institutional rules and contextual knowledge. This integration reduces workflow and enhances responsiveness, especially in a large institution that has different stakeholder needs. Automation also drives uniformity in service provision, which eliminates variability due to manual handling (Kuhail et al., 2023).

Nevertheless, the automatization of administration raises the issue of both transparency, accountability and favoritism. Intelligent systems based on NLP can reproduce historical injustices, or misunderstand unusual language. Such mistakes, in an institutional context, may be very important to the access to education and employment. It is imperative that fairness and accuracy be thoroughly checked, as well as, human rights be evaluated as well as appeal and corrective mechanisms. Through automation, there should be greater institutional effectiveness without equity or trust being undermined.

5.3 Spartan Campus Management and Operational Intelligence

Smart campus management also involves the use of cognitive AI agents and NLP whereby academic services are used together with operational intelligence. Universities are becoming even more complex socio-technical systems, which can be described by physical facilities, digital space, and people. AI agents can be utilized to facilitate the work of the campus by processing text and sensor information about maintenance requests, safety reports, and sustainability efforts. NLP facilitates unstructured report and feedback interpretation and cognitive reasoning provides priorities and coordination (Sheikh et al., 2026).

As an example, AI systems will be able to handle maintenance requests expressed in natural language, detect common mistakes, and suggest preventative measures. The energy management and policy development can be informed in sustainability efforts through the NLP-driven analysis of institutional reports and communications. Those applications exemplify that AI-enabled applications can be used in any domain outside of academic functions and assist the entire institutional management. Individually, universities can work more efficiently and resiliently by incorporating operational intelligence with priorities of the university.

Simultaneously, intelligent campus systems provoke the issue of data governance and data surveillance. The gathering and the processing of textual data surrounding campus activity should adhere to the privacy and ethical boundaries. Companies have to create explicit policies that regulate data usage and make sure that AI-based operational intelligence does not conflict with the values held by institutions. The key to keeping the smart campus initiatives trustworthy is transparency and involvement of stakeholders (Kumar, 2021).

5.4 Quality of Service, Fairness, and Consumer experience

The effectiveness and fairness of AI-based academic services are defined by the extent of cognitive AI and NLP systems to consider the many forms and experiences of users. Colleges cater to diverse groups of heterogeneous students who have different language, culture, and technology backgrounds. Inadvertently, some groups might be left out or disadvantaged by AI-driven services, which have not identified this diversity. Specifically, NLP systems should withstand the linguistic diversity and be available to users with dissimilar communication preferences.

The truth is that user experience is a very serious consideration in adoption and effectiveness of AI enabled services. The interface used in conversations is to be user-friendly, open, and friendly without authoritative or obscure interactions. The limits and human support should be communicated with AIs of the cognitive type and lead to a human support where necessary. The principles of inclusivity and usability design make sure that AI services improve access to instantiated resources other than making it difficult (Lahav et al., 2020).

Equities are also applied to the decision-making processes and communication. Any AI-powered offerings that offer suggestions or autopilot results should also provide explanations to be comprehended and disputed by its user. This is particularly significant in the academic and administrative areas where judgments have implications on the advancement of the student or the job. On the one hand, it is necessary to incorporate into the service design explainability and accountability, which would ensure fairness and institutional legitimacy.

5.5 Institutional Capacity and Organization Change

The implementation of cognitive AI and NLP in academic and administrative services requires organizational change in institutions of higher learning. One of the requirements of the implementation of AI-enabled services, as an entity, is the presence of technical infrastructure, data governance framework, and qualified staff capable of managing and judging AI systems. To make sure that AI projects will be in line with strategic objectives and ethical practices, institutions should make investments in personnel development and cross-disciplinary interaction (Latorre-Navarro, & Harris, 2015).

The organizational culture is also an important factor which helps to influence the success of the AI-enabled services. Their only condition may be resistance due to the fear of being replaced, losing control, or trust in automated systems. To tackle these issues, one is going to need an open communication channel, consultative design efforts, and articulating the complementary functions of human beings and AI. To embrace AI as an enhancing aspect, as opposed to a displacing one, is what can aid more positive adoption.

6. GOVERNANCE CHALLENGES IN AI-DRIVEN HIGHER EDUCATION

6.1 Algorithmic Bias and Fairness in Cognitive AI and NLP Systems

As cognitive AI agents and natural language processing are integrated into the teaching, research, and academic services, the issue of algorithmic bias and fairness come to the forefront as the major areas of concern. NLP models learn NLP-processed texts in significant amounts which usually echo the hegemony of linguistic patterns, cultural expectations, and the historic injustices. These biases may take place in automated assessment, student support system, and research analytics when put in practice in higher education, which puts a disadvantage to learners and scholars who have linguistic or cultural backgrounds different (Neumann et al., 2021).

The issue of algorithmic bias in the education sphere is particularly concerning since the academic choices carry both short- and long-term consequences of the educational results, advancement, and career opportunities. The use of cognitive AI agents reinforces narratives of deficit by relying on biased NLP models, except where they misunderstand studio language and rely on non-standard academic language and expression, which is undermined. The issues put the principles of equity and inclusion in higher education to the test. Combating bias does not need just technical measures, including various training data and equitable-based modeling, but also institutional devotion to non-discriminatory teaching ethos.

Social-technical, not computational, fairness in AI-driven higher education should be interpreted. The development of cognitive AI agents takes place in institutional setting and policy contexts that influence decision-making process and interpretation of the decisions. Fairness therefore requires the harmonization of the technological design and the values of education, which is sustained by monitoring and assessment.

6.2 Transparency, Explainability and Trust

To gain trust in AI-driven academic systems, transparency and explainability are key to achieving trust. Complex models with a complicated decision-making process are frequently used by cognitive AI agents, especially when it applies to deep learning models and large language models. The use of opaque AI systems in orchestrating academic judgment and accountability in higher education can create a sense of mistrust in students, university staff and administrators.

Explainable AI is a method aimed at rendering algorithms transparent enough to be interpretable by human users and, therefore, allow its stakeholders to explain the results and even dispute their decisions on an exceptional basis. Explainability can be used in teaching and evaluation by enabling an educator to contextualize AI generated feedback and verify that it aligns with the learning goals. Transparency has applications in research and administrative services as it fosters good judgment in decision making and institutional accountability. AI-based recommendations can be taken at face value or disregarded without explanations because of the lack of trust in them (Pérez et al., 2020).

User agency is related closely to trust in AI systems. Both students and faculty need to be encouraged to ask questions of AI outputs and demand human intervention on the same. Effective development of AI systems that convey the uncertainty, insufficiency and explain why a decision was taken is crucial towards developing informed trust and not blind trust. Transparency therefore, is an ethical obligation as well as a pragmatic demand to sustainable use of AI in higher institutions of learning.

6.3 Data Privacy and Academic Autonomy

Working of language processing systems and cognitive agents of AI requires a large amount of data, such as student interactions and academic records as well as the research output and institutional communications. This dependency provokes great concerns regarding the privacy of data and academic freedom. The higher institutions of learning need to strike a compromise between the advantages of smart use of data and the requirement to safeguard confidential information and uphold the rights of people.

In the teaching and student services, NLP systems process personal and academic language information and this can involve sensitive information regarding learning difficulties or personal situations. The ethical practice must include informed consent, safe data storage, and restricted data utilization. The use of AI in academic research has to honor the intellectual property rights and should not exploit unpublished or owned data (Rodrigues et al., 2022).

Another problem is that academic independence is threatened when AI is used to make decisions on the curriculum, research concentration, or performance ratings. The excessive use of algorithmic suggestions can limit intellectual differences and innovations. The systems of governance should then ensure that the human judgment and academic freedom is preserved and the AI systems can supplement and not determine the decision-making processes in an institution.

6.4 Frameworks of institutional Governance and Accountability

The ethical and operational issues with cognitive AI and NLP in higher education are critical to control by means of effective governance. The governance frameworks specify the roles, responsibilities and accountability mechanisms of deployment and usage of AI. They can offer the advice on what should be done and what should not be done, risk management, and adherence to the legal and ethical standards (Rodríguez et al., 2021).

The multidisciplinary approach to the institution governance should be provided with the inclusion of educators, technologists, ethicists, and representatives of students. This kind of collaboration will see AI projects equipped with diversity of values and considerations of stakeholders. Consistency and accountability of the AI systems can only be achieved through clear policies concerning procurement, evaluation and lifecycle management of the systems.

The distributed nature of AI systems that reimagines outside vendors and complicated infrastructures must also have accountability mechanisms. The institutions are to put in place systems of auditing the AI performance, dealing with grievances and dealing with unintended consequences. Through institutional practice approaches, such as infusing governance, universities will be able to make choices amidst support or resistance of an AI-driven transformation and maintain social responsibility and academic integrity (Valdivieso & Luzón, 2021).

6.5 Towards responsible and human centric AI in higher education

The ethical issues that accompany the aspect of cognitive AI agents as well as NLP emphasize the necessity of humanistic use of AI in post-secondary education. This would allow AI to be more of an additive concept, making it complementary and aiding human ability and decision-making. Human-centered design emphasizes inclusivity, accessibility, and according to the educational values so that AI systems can benefit the needs of the diverse representatives of the academic communities (Villegas-Ch et al., 2021).

Higher education needs responsible AI to be constantly reflected and continually adjusted. With the emerging technologies, it is time to reconsider rules of ethics in institutions, their governance, and methods of teaching. Discussion with students and faculty about the use of AI will help build common understanding and joint ownership over the technological change. Finally, subject adoption of cognitive AI and NLP requires technical innovation coupled with ethical future and institutional responsible management (Zhou et al., 2022).

CONCLUSION

Intelligent cognitive AI agents and natural language processing are transforming higher education by bringing new intelligence to teaching, research and academic services. These technologies allow personalized learning, research automation, intelligent support services, and data-driven institutional decision-making as it has been shown in this chapter. Their understanding and ability to produce academic language dynamic makes them a strong force in the modern academic ecosystems and they can be used to increase efficiency, access and innovation.

Simultaneously, there are ethical, pedagogical and governance concerns that emerge due to the integration of cognitive AI and NLP. Algorithms bias, transparency, privacy of data and academic autonomy all present issues that indicate that the mentioned issue should be carefully and responsibly implemented. Higher education facilities have to overcome these obstacles by balancing between technology design and values in education, maintaining human control, and developing confidence in the stakeholders. The transformation being proposed by AI cannot be seen only as the position of the technical effort; it is the socio-institutional process that reinvigorates the power, responsibility, and production of knowledge.

In the future, it is up to the current decisions of institutions to determine the sustainability of cognitive AI and NLP in the sphere of higher education. Universities will be able to leverage technological innovation, protect equity, academic freedom, and institutional integrity by implementing human-centered, ethically sound, as well as well-managed AI systems. By so doing, the higher education will become an smarter and more interactive ecosystem that will assist with learning, discovery, and service in a more complex digital environment.

REFERENCES

Abbas, N., Whitfield, J., Atwell, E., Bowman, H., Pickard, T., & Walker, A. (2022). Online chat and chatbots to enhance mature student engagement in higher education. *International Journal of Lifelong Education, 41*(3), 308–326. DOI: 10.1080/02601370.2022.2066213

Adamopoulou, E., & Moussiades, L. (2020). Chatbots: History, technology, and applications. *Machine Learning with Applications, 2*, 100006. Advance online publication. DOI: 10.1016/j.mlwa.2020.100006

Alkaissi, H., & McFarlane, S. (2023). Artificial hallucinations in ChatGPT: Implications in scientific writing. *Cureus*. Advance online publication. DOI: 10.7759/cureus.35179

Allouch, M., Azaria, A., & Azoulay, R. (2021). Conversational agents: Goals, technologies, vision and challenges. *Sensors (Basel), 21*(24), 8448. Advance online publication. DOI: 10.3390/s21248448

Ayedoun, E., Hayashi, Y., & Seta, K. (2019). Adding communicative and affective strategies to an embodied conversational agent to enhance second language learners' willingness to communicate. *International Journal of Artificial Intelligence in Education, 29*(1), 29–57. DOI: 10.1007/s40593-018-0171-6

Ba, S., Stein, D., Liu, Q., Long, T., Xie, K., & Wu, L. (2021). Examining the effects of a pedagogical agent with dual-channel emotional cues on learner emotions, cognitive load, and Knowledge transfer performance. *Journal of Educational Computing Research, 59*(6), 1114–1134. DOI: 10.1177/0735633121992421

Bavaresco, R., Silveira, D., Reis, E., Barbosa, J., Righi, R., Costa, C., Antunes, R., Gomes, M., Gatti, C., Vanzin, M., Junior, S. C., Silva, E., & Moreira, C. (2020). Conversational agents in business: A systematic literature review and future research directions. *Computer Science Review, 36*, 100239. DOI: 10.1016/j.cosrev.2020.100239

Bickmore, T., Trinh, H., Hoppmann, M., & Asadi, R. (2016). Virtual agents in the classroom: Experience fielding a co-presenter agent in University courses. [Springer International Publishing.]. *Lecture Notes in Computer Science, 10011*, 154–163. DOI: 10.1007/978-3-319-47665-0_14

Briel, A. (2021). Toward an eclectic and malleable multiagent educational assistant. *Computer Applications in Engineering Education*, cae.22449. Advance online publication. DOI: 10.1002/cae.22449

Carayannopoulos, S. (2018). Using chatbots to aid transition. *International Journal of Information and Learning Technology, 35*(2), 118–129. DOI: 10.1108/IJILT-10-2017-0097

Chang, C. Y., Hwang, G. J., & Gau, M. L. (2022). Promoting students' learning achievement and self-efficacy: A mobile chatbot approach for nursing training. *British Journal of Educational Technology, 53*(1), 171–188. DOI: 10.1111/bjet.13158

Chen, Y., Jensen, S., Albert, L. J., Gupta, S., & Lee, T. (2022). Artificial intelligence (AI) student assistants in the classroom: Designing chatbots to support student success. *Information Systems Frontiers*. Advance online publication. DOI: 10.1007/s10796-022-10291-4

Dandotiya, M., Goyal, N. K., Yadav, P., Sankhla, K., & Kumari, M. (2026). GENALYTICS: A Deep Dive Into Real-Time Insights via Generative AI. In Elbaghazaoui, B., Amnai, M., & Gherabi, N. (Eds.), *Generative AI-Powered Data Architectures: From Governance to Autonomous Analytics* (pp. 105–134). IGI Global Scientific Publishing., DOI: 10.4018/979-8-3373-5616-7.ch005

Diederich, S., Brendel, A. B., Morana, S., & Kolbe, L. (2022). On the design of and interaction with conversational agents: An organizing and assessing review of human-computer interaction research. *Journal of the Association for Information Systems, 23*(1), 96–138. DOI: 10.17705/1jais.00724

Farooqi, A., Das, D., Tripathi, M., Dutta, R., Goyal, N. K., & Sheikh, M. F. (2026). Navigating Ethical Frontiers in AI-Driven Geriatric Care. In Stolakis, K., & Efthymiou, I. (Eds.), *AI for Geriatric Care in an Aging Society: Ethical, Clinical, and Policy Challenges* (pp. 243–266). IGI Global Scientific Publishing., DOI: 10.4018/979-8-3373-5462-0.ch009

Fidan, M., & Gencel, N. (2022). Supporting the instructional videos with chatbot and peer feedback mechanisms in online learning: The effects on learning performance and intrinsic motivation. *Journal of Educational Computing Research, 60*(7), 1716–1741. Advance online publication. DOI: 10.1177/07356331221077901

González, L. A., Neyem, A., Contreras-Mckay, I., & Molina, D. (2022). Improving learning experiences in software engineering capstone courses using artificial intelligence virtual assistants. *Computer Applications in Engineering Education, 30*(5), 1370–1389. DOI: 10.1002/cae.22526

Goyal, N. K., Goyal, N. K., Kumar, S., Dutta, R., Kothari, V., & Sinha, S. K. (2026). Empowering Elderly Care Through Artificial Intelligence. In Stolakis, K., & Efthymiou, I. (Eds.), *AI for Geriatric Care in an Aging Society: Ethical, Clinical, and Policy Challenges* (pp. 1–28). IGI Global Scientific Publishing., DOI: 10.4018/979-8-3373-5462-0.ch001

Gupta, S., & Chen, Y. (2022). Supporting inclusive learning using chatbots? A chatbot-led interview study. *Journal of Information Systems Education and Information Technologies, 33*(1), 98–108.

Hamzah, W. M. A. F. W., Ismail, I., Yusof, M. K., Saany, S. I. M., & Yacob, A. (2021). Using learning analytics to explore responses from student conversations with chatbot for education. [iJEP]. *International Journal of Engineering Pedagogy, 11*(6), 70–84. DOI: 10.3991/ijep.v11i6.23475

Hayashi, Y. (2020). Gaze awareness and metacognitive suggestions by a pedagogical conversational agent. *International Journal of Computer-Supported Collaborative Learning, 15*(4), 469–498. DOI: 10.1007/s11412-020-09333-3

Hsu, M.-H., Chen, P.-S., & Yu, C.-S. (2021). Proposing a task-oriented chatbot system for EFL learners speaking practice. *Interactive Learning Environments*. Advance online publication. DOI: 10.1080/10494820.2021.1960864

Kuhail, M. A., Alturki, N., Alramlawi, S., & Alhejori, K. (2023). Interacting with educational chatbots: A systematic review. *Education and Information Technologies, 28*(1), 973–1018. DOI: 10.1007/s10639-022-11177-3

Kumar, J. A. (2021). Educational chatbots for project-based learning. *International Journal of Educational Technology in Higher Education, 18*(1), 65. Advance online publication. DOI: 10.1186/s41239-021-00302-w

Kumari, M., & Goyal, N. K. (2026). Artificial Intelligence in the Cryptocurrency Ecosystem: Crime Mechanisms, Detection Strategies, and Legal Perspectives. In Lin, L. (Ed.), *Innovations in Cryptocrime and Financial Fraud* (pp. 245–282). IGI Global Scientific Publishing., DOI: 10.4018/979-8-3373-0675-9.ch007

Kumari, M., Kumawat, R., Tripathi, M., Suganthi, K., Goyal, N. K., & Sheikh, M. F. (2026). Blockchain for Transparency and Traceability in Supply Chains. In Khan, M., Mehmood, T., & Rao, M. (Eds.), *Maximizing Operational Efficiency at the Intersection of Supply Chain Management and Marketing* (pp. 35–64). IGI Global Scientific Publishing., DOI: 10.4018/979-8-3373-3109-6.ch002

Lahav, O., Talis, V., Cinamon, R. G., & Rizzo, A. (2020). Virtual interactive consulting agent to support freshman students in transition to higher education. *Journal of Computing in Higher Education, 32*(2), 330–364. DOI: 10.1007/s12528-019-09237-8

Latorre-Navarro, E. M., & Harris, J. G. (2015). An intelligent natural language conversational system for academic advising. *International Journal of Advanced Computer Science and Applications, 6*(1). Advance online publication. DOI: 10.14569/IJACSA.2015.060116

Neumann, A. T., Arndt, T., Köbis, L., Meissner, R., Martin, A., de Lange, P., Pengel, N., Klamma, R., & Wollersheim, H.-W. (2021). Chatbots as a tool to scale mentoring processes. *Frontiers in Artificial Intelligence, 4*, 668220. Advance online publication. DOI: 10.3389/frai.2021.668220

Pérez, J. Q., Daradoumis, T., & Puig, J. M. M. (2020). Rediscovering the use of chatbots in education: A systematic literature review. *Computer Applications in Engineering Education, 28*(6), 1549–1565. DOI: 10.1002/cae.22326

Rodrigues, C., Reis, A., Pereira, R., Martins, P., Sousa, J., & Pinto, T. (2022). *A review of conversational agents in education technology and innovation in learning teaching and education*. Springer.

Rodríguez, J. A., Santana, M. G., Perera, V. A., & Pulido, J. R. (2021). *Embodied conversational agents: Artificial intelligence for autonomous learning*. Pixel-Bit Revista de Medios y Educación., DOI: 10.12795/pixelbit.86171

Sharma, P., Kumawat, R., Jain, G., Keswani, G., Goyal, N. K., & Sheikh, M. F. (2026). Machine Learning-Based Intrusion Detection Systems for Healthcare Internet of Things (HIoT). In Shieh, C., Goel, P., Horng, M., & Pandey, H. (Eds.), *Resilient Healthcare Internet of Things Systems: Architectures, Security, and Trust* (pp. 185–214). IGI Global Scientific Publishing., DOI: 10.4018/979-8-3373-7610-3.ch007

Sheikh, M. F. A., Kapoor, S. K., Goyal, N. K., & Tuba, E. rao, A. (2026). Enhancing Healthcare Security with Fog Computing and Blockchain Technology. In: Nayak, R., Mittal, N., Khunteta, A., Kumar, M. (eds) Recent Advancements in Artificial Intelligence. ICRAAI 2025. Lecture Notes in Networks and Systems, vol 1468. Springer, Singapore. DOI: 10.1007/978-981-96-7760-3_38

. Valdivieso, P. Á. C., & Luzón, M. D. C. A. (2021). The use of chatbot as an element of tutorial action in university teaching. Revista electrónica de investigación Docencia Creativa ReiDoCrea. DOI: 10.30827/Digibug.69299

Villegas-Ch, W., García-Ortiz, J., Mullo-Ca, K., Sánchez-Viteri, S., & Roman-Cañizares, M. (2021). Implementation of a virtual assistant for the academic management of a university with the use of artificial intelligence. *Future Internet*, *13*(4), 97. DOI: 10.3390/fi13040097

Zhou, L., Gao, J., Li, D., & Shum, H.-Y. (2022). The Design and implementation of xiaoice, an empathetic social chatbot. *Computational Linguistics*, *46*(1), 53–93. DOI: 10.1162/coli_a_00368

Chapter 4

Exploring Opportunities, Risks, and Policy Implications of Artificial Intelligence in Higher Education and Research

Rampelli Manojkumar
http://orcid.org/0000-0002-8141-0321
BVRIT HYDERABAD College of Engineering for Women, India

ABSTRACT

Artificial intelligence is rapidly becoming part of the everyday fabric of higher education, influencing how universities teach, conduct research, and manage institutional operations. This chapter examines AI not as a neutral technological upgrade, but as a transformative force that reshapes academic practices, professional roles, and ethical responsibilities. In teaching and learning, AI enables personalization and accessibility while raising concerns about autonomy, surveillance, bias, and trust. In research, AI tools enhance productivity and analytical capacity but challenge long-standing norms of authorship, originality, and responsibility. The chapter argues that responsible AI adoption requires strategic collaboration, clear and adaptive policies, and strong ethical foundations. By aligning technological innovation with academic values, universities can leverage AI's benefits while safeguarding integrity, accountability, and social responsibility.

DOI: 10.4018/979-8-2600-2811-7.ch004

INTRODUCTION

Artificial intelligence (AI) has become a defining feature of contemporary higher education, reshaping how universities teach, conduct research, and manage institutional operations. Over the past decade, AI has moved beyond experimental applications and niche innovations to become embedded in everyday academic practices. Learning management systems increasingly rely on predictive analytics, research workflows are supported by AI-driven data analysis and text generation tools, and institutional decision-making is informed by automated systems that process vast amounts of educational data. This growing integration has intensified scholarly, professional, and policy-oriented debates about the role AI should play in shaping the future of academia.

The literature suggests that higher education is currently situated in a transitional phase of AI adoption. Crompton and Burke (2023) characterize the field as rapidly expanding yet uneven, with institutions experimenting with AI in diverse ways but often lacking coherent, institution-wide strategies. While some universities have developed structured approaches to AI integration, many continue to adopt tools in a fragmented manner, driven by immediate needs rather than long-term planning. This unevenness reflects broader uncertainties about the pedagogical value, ethical implications, and organizational consequences of AI in academic contexts. Early discussions of AI in higher education often emphasized its transformative potential. Bates et al. (2020) argue that AI could fundamentally alter teaching and learning by enabling personalization at scale, improving access, and supporting more flexible educational pathways. From this perspective, AI is viewed as a catalyst for addressing long-standing challenges such as massification, resource constraints, and diverse learner needs. However, these optimistic narratives are increasingly tempered by critical perspectives that question whether technological adoption alone can resolve structural issues within higher education systems.

A significant body of recent scholarship highlights that AI is not a neutral or purely technical intervention. Bearman et al. (2023), in their critical review of AI discourses in higher education, identify contrasting narratives that frame AI either as an inevitable solution to institutional inefficiencies or as a threat to academic values such as autonomy, collegiality, and professional judgment. These discourses influence how AI is interpreted and implemented, often shaping institutional priorities and policy decisions. Rather than being driven solely by pedagogical or research considerations, AI adoption is frequently intertwined with managerial logics, performance measurement, and broader agendas of digital transformation.

The emergence of generative AI has further intensified these debates. Tools capable of generating coherent text, synthesizing literature, and assisting with research design challenge established understandings of authorship, originality, and scholarly contribution. Watermeyer et al. (2024) describe this shift as part of the broader "automating of academia," where academic labor is increasingly mediated by algorithmic systems. While such tools offer efficiency and productivity gains, they also raise concerns about the erosion of academic expertise and the redistribution of responsibility between humans and machines.

Responsibility is, in fact, a central concern in discussions of AI integration. McGrath et al. (2023) explore how university teachers perceive responsibility when AI systems are involved in educational decision-making. Their findings reveal significant ambiguity regarding accountability, particularly when AI-generated outputs influence assessment, feedback, or learning outcomes. This uncertainty extends beyond teaching into research and institutional governance, where questions arise about who is responsible for errors, bias, or unintended consequences produced by AI systems.

From the perspective of academic staff, AI adoption is often experienced as both an opportunity and a source of concern. Pisica et al. (2023) report that academics recognize the potential benefits of AI, including efficiency gains and enhanced analytical capabilities, but simultaneously express apprehension about loss of control, ethical risks, and increased surveillance. These mixed perceptions highlight the importance of involving faculty members in decision-making processes related to AI adoption, rather than imposing technologies through top-down managerial approaches. At the institutional level, AI is increasingly framed as a strategic and organizational issue. George and Wooden (2023) argue that AI-driven transformation in higher education requires deliberate leadership, clear governance structures, and alignment with institutional missions. AI adoption is not simply a matter of acquiring new tools; it involves rethinking workflows, professional roles, and evaluation mechanisms. Gering et al. (2025) demonstrate that leading universities responding to generative AI are developing comprehensive strategies that integrate technological innovation with organizational change, policy development, and cultural adaptation.

This strategic framing of AI aligns with broader discussions of digital transformation and innovation in universities. Yordanova (2024) emphasizes that technological innovation in higher education is most effective when embedded within coherent innovation processes that connect digital tools with institutional culture and governance. Similarly, El Din and Al Harrasi (2024) highlight how AI-driven transformation in administration and management reshapes institutional efficiency, decision-making, and accountability. These changes reflect a shift toward data-driven governance models, which, while offering potential benefits, also raise questions about transparency and ethical oversight.

The influence of AI extends into curriculum design and faculty development, particularly in developing and transitioning higher education systems. Hadi and AlShaikh-Hasan (2025) note that AI-driven curriculum transformation requires significant investment in faculty capacity building to ensure meaningful and responsible use of emerging technologies. Without adequate training and institutional support, AI risks becoming a superficial addition rather than a catalyst for pedagogical and research innovation. Insights from automation research outside higher education further illuminate these dynamics. Myers et al. (2023) argue that intelligent automation does not simply replace human labor but reconfigures professional roles and organizational structures. Studies in industrial automation, such as the work by Azamfirei et al. (2023), demonstrate how automation introduces new standards of efficiency and quality control, often accompanied by shifts in responsibility and oversight. When similar logics are applied to higher education, they can conflict with academic norms that value discretion, creativity, and critical judgment.

Underlying many of these developments is the broader trend of datafication in education. Williamson et al. (2023) caution that AI systems are part of a wider ecosystem of data-driven technologies that reshape how educational activities are measured, evaluated, and governed. This raises concerns about the long-term implications for academic freedom, equity, and institutional autonomy. At the same time, advances in AI-based modeling and intelligent systems continue to expand the technical possibilities for research and analysis (Sarker, 2022), reinforcing the need for robust ethical and policy frameworks. Taken together, the literature suggests that AI in higher education represents a complex and contested transformation rather than a straightforward technological upgrade. AI offers significant opportunities to enhance teaching, research, and institutional management, but it also introduces ethical, professional, and governance challenges that cannot be ignored. The lack of clear policies, shared norms, and institutional coordination risks fragmented adoption and unintended consequences for academic integrity and trust.

Artificial intelligence is increasingly embedded in teaching, research, and institutional operations; however, higher education institutions frequently adopt these technologies without coherent governance frameworks that address ethical responsibility, academic integrity, and institutional accountability simultaneously. Existing discussions tend to examine AI applications within isolated domains such as teaching, research productivity, or administrative automation, which leads to fragmented institutional strategies and inconsistent policy responses. As a result, universities face growing uncertainty regarding how AI should be integrated in ways that preserve academic values while enabling technological innovation.

Although a substantial body of literature examines AI-enabled learning environments, generative AI in academic writing, and AI-driven institutional analytics, there remains limited integrative analysis that connects these developments with institutional governance and policy development in higher education. In particular, there is insufficient attention to how universities can coordinate AI adoption across teaching, research, and administrative functions while ensuring transparency, accountability, and ethical oversight. Addressing this gap requires examining AI integration as an institutional and socio-technical transformation rather than merely a technological innovation.

This chapter examines the role of artificial intelligence in higher education through four interconnected dimensions. First, it analyzes AI-enabled teaching and the associated pedagogical and ethical implications. Second, it evaluates the opportunities and risks associated with AI integration in academic research, particularly in relation to authorship, originality, and research integrity. Third, it explores the growing role of AI in academic service and institutional management, including administrative decision-making and governance processes. Fourth, it discusses the importance of strategic collaboration and policy development for responsible AI adoption. Together, these sections provide an integrated perspective on how higher education institutions can navigate the opportunities and challenges of AI while maintaining academic values and institutional trust.

AI IN TEACHING: TRANSFORMATION AND PEDAGOGICAL ETHICS

The integration of artificial intelligence into teaching and learning environments marks one of the most visible and contested dimensions of AI adoption in higher education. Unlike administrative or back-end research applications, AI in teaching directly affects daily interactions between educators, students, and knowledge. As a result, its adoption has prompted both enthusiasm for pedagogical innovation and concern over ethical, professional, and relational consequences. Contemporary scholarship increasingly recognizes that AI-enabled teaching is not simply about introducing new tools but about reshaping pedagogical practices, instructional roles, and ethical responsibilities. Figure 1 presents the AI in Education Ethics Framework, emphasizing agency, inclusivity, fairness, and safety as foundational principles for ethical AI integration in educational systems.

The ethical principles illustrated in Figure 1 provide a practical framework for evaluating how AI technologies are integrated into educational environments. Agency refers to maintaining the decision-making authority of educators and learners when interacting with AI systems. Inclusivity emphasizes the importance of designing AI-supported learning environments that accommodate diverse learners and avoid reinforcing structural inequalities. Fairness highlights the need to identify and mitigate algorithmic bias that may affect student assessment or learning opportunities. Safety addresses issues related to data privacy, psychological well-being, and responsible system design. Together, these principles illustrate that effective AI adoption in education must balance technological capability with ethical responsibility and institutional oversight.

AI-Enabled Teaching: From Support Tools to Pedagogical Partners

AI-enabled technologies are increasingly positioned as partners in the teaching process rather than passive instructional aids. Adaptive learning systems, intelligent tutoring platforms, and AI-driven analytics support content delivery, assessment, and personalized feedback across disciplines. AI-driven platforms can dynamically adjust instructional content based on learner behavior, performance, and preferences, enabling instruction that responds to individual learning trajectories (Kabudi et al., 2021). Such personalization has been shown to improve learner engagement and academic outcomes (Ellikkal & Rajamohan, 2025). In addition to AI-supported personalization, collaborative pedagogical strategies such as structured discussion forums and effective group division also enhance student participation and engagement in the teaching–learning process (Manojkumar & Krishnan, 2025), reinforcing the broader potential of technology-supported learner-centered pedagogy.

Figure 1. AI in education ethics framework

However, AI's pedagogical role is not limited to personalization. Karumbaiah et al. (2023) provide a spatiotemporal analysis of teacher practices in AI-enabled classrooms, highlighting how educators adapt their instructional strategies when AI systems mediate student engagement. Their work suggests that effective AI integration often depends on teachers' ability to interpret system-generated insights and respond pedagogically rather than deferring decision-making entirely to algorithms.

In this sense, AI reshapes teaching not by replacing educators, but by altering how instructional judgment is exercised.

Educator Perspectives and Professional Agency

Educators' perceptions play a decisive role in determining whether AI enhances or undermines teaching practice. Avci et al. (2025), examining STEM educators' perspectives, reveal a nuanced landscape of attitudes toward AI-enabled technologies. While many educators acknowledge AI's potential to improve instructional efficiency and learner engagement, they also express concern about loss of pedagogical autonomy, over-reliance on automated systems, and insufficient institutional support for meaningful integration. These concerns reflect deeper questions about professional agency. When AI systems recommend instructional actions, identify "at-risk" students, or generate automated feedback, educators may feel pressure to conform to algorithmic outputs even when these conflict with professional judgment. Avci et al. (2025) note that educators are more likely to adopt AI tools when they retain control over instructional decisions and when AI outputs are transparent and interpretable.

The reconfiguration of teaching roles becomes particularly evident in AI-enabled classrooms. Karumbaiah et al. (2023) show that teachers increasingly act as facilitators, sense-makers, and ethical gatekeepers, interpreting AI-generated insights rather than directly delivering content. This shift demands new competencies, including data literacy, critical interpretation of AI recommendations, and the ability to explain AI-supported decisions to students.

Adaptive Learning Systems and Pedagogical Implications

Adaptive learning systems represent one of the most mature applications of AI in education. These systems rely on learner data to tailor instructional pathways, assessment difficulty, and feedback timing. Kabudi et al. (2021) observe that most adaptive systems prioritize cognitive performance metrics, such as accuracy and response time, while fewer systems account for affective or motivational factors. This imbalance raises important pedagogical questions about what dimensions of learning are valued and measured within AI-driven environments.

While adaptive systems can enhance efficiency and scalability, they also risk narrowing pedagogical focus. When learning is reduced to measurable indicators, deeper aspects such as critical thinking, creativity, and collaborative learning may receive less attention. Ellikkal and Rajamohan (2025) caution that personalization should not equate to isolation, emphasizing the need to balance individualized learning with opportunities for peer interaction and collective meaning-making.

Furthermore, adaptive systems may inadvertently reinforce existing inequalities if underlying data reflect biased assumptions or incomplete representations of learners. Kabudi et al. (2021) note that many adaptive learning platforms rely on historical data that may privilege certain learning behaviors or cultural norms, thereby disadvantaging students who do not conform to these patterns.

Ethical Dimensions of AI in Teaching

Ethical considerations are central to discussions of AI in teaching, particularly as systems become more autonomous and pervasive. Córdova and Vicari (2022) identify practical ethical challenges in AI-enabled education, including transparency, accountability, data privacy, and informed consent. When students interact with AI-driven systems, they are often unaware of how their data are collected, processed, and used to shape learning experiences.

Chu et al. (2022) further highlight concerns related to algorithmic bias and fairness. AI systems trained on limited or skewed datasets may produce recommendations that systematically disadvantage certain groups of learners. In educational contexts, such biases can have long-term consequences for student progression, assessment outcomes, and self-perception.

Mobile and app-based AI tools introduce additional ethical complexities. Klimova et al. (2023) examine AI-driven educational mobile applications and identify risks related to surveillance, data security, and psychological dependence. These tools often blur the boundary between learning support and behavioral monitoring, raising questions about students' autonomy and well-being.

Salloum (2024) situates these concerns within the broader debate surrounding generative AI in classrooms. While tools such as conversational agents can support explanation and revision, they also create opportunities for misuse, dependency, and erosion of independent learning skills. Ethical teaching practices must therefore address not only what AI can do, but also what students should be encouraged to do without AI assistance.

Academic Integrity, Assessment, and Trust

One of the most contentious areas of AI integration in teaching relates to assessment and academic integrity. As AI tools become capable of generating essays, solving problems, and answering examination questions, traditional assessment methods face increasing strain. Surahman and Wang (2022), in their systematic review, document widespread concerns about academic dishonesty in online learning environments, emphasizing that technological solutions alone cannot fully address integrity challenges.

AI-centered proctoring systems have been introduced as one response to these concerns. Fidas et al. (2023), through a longitudinal study, examine the use of AI-driven proctoring in tertiary institutions and find that such systems can enhance perceptions of assessment integrity over time. However, they also report student concerns related to privacy, surveillance, and algorithmic decision-making, particularly when systems flag behavior without clear explanation.

The tension between integrity and trust is further complicated by accessibility considerations. Kavitha et al. (2025) argue that learning management systems enhanced with AI must balance integrity enforcement with inclusivity and personalization. Overly rigid monitoring systems may disadvantage students with disabilities, unstable internet access, or culturally different communication behaviors. Rather than relying solely on surveillance-based solutions, scholars increasingly advocate for assessment redesign. Surahman and Wang (2022) emphasize the importance of authentic assessment strategies that prioritize process, reflection, and application over rote reproduction. In such contexts, AI can be reframed as a learning support tool rather than a threat to integrity.

Assessment redesign has therefore emerged as a critical response to AI-enabled academic misconduct. Institutions are increasingly shifting toward authentic assessment models that emphasize analytical reasoning, project-based learning, and reflective assignments that require contextual interpretation rather than reproduction of information. These approaches reduce the effectiveness of AI-generated responses while reinforcing higher-order learning outcomes. At the same time, such strategies require institutional support, including faculty training and revised evaluation frameworks, to ensure that assessment practices remain aligned with evolving technological capabilities.

AI Literacy as a Pedagogical Imperative

A recurring theme in the literature is the need for AI literacy among both students and educators. Ng et al. (2021) define AI literacy as encompassing not only technical understanding but also ethical awareness, critical evaluation skills, and the ability to make informed decisions about AI use. Without such literacy, students may either misuse AI tools or accept AI outputs uncritically. AI literacy is particularly important in contexts where AI systems influence learning pathways, assessment outcomes, or feedback. Ng et al. (2021) argue that students should understand how AI systems function, what their limitations are, and how their data are used. Similarly, educators require professional development opportunities that go beyond tool training to include ethical reasoning and pedagogical integration.

In developing and transitioning education systems, these challenges are even more pronounced. Kumar et al. (2025) note that adaptive learning environments integrated with emerging technologies such as blockchain require coordinated capacity building to ensure that educators can meaningfully engage with AI-driven pedagogical models. Without adequate support, AI risks becoming an externally imposed solution rather than an internally owned educational innovation.

Accessibility, Inclusion, and Equity

AI in teaching holds significant promise for enhancing accessibility, particularly for learners with diverse needs. Advanced technologies integrated into learning management systems can support personalized interfaces, adaptive pacing, and flexible assessment formats, helping reduce barriers for students with disabilities or non-traditional learning backgrounds (Kavitha et al., 2025). Inclusive instructional design supported by digital pedagogies and active learning approaches further strengthens accessibility by promoting equitable participation and engagement among diverse learners (Manojkumar et al., 2026). However, accessibility gains are not automatic. Poorly designed AI-driven applications may exacerbate digital divides when access to devices, connectivity, or digital skills is uneven (Klimova et al., 2023). In addition, AI systems trained predominantly on limited datasets may inadequately represent diverse languages, cultures, and knowledge traditions, potentially reinforcing existing inequalities (Chu et al., 2022).

Reframing Pedagogical Ethics in AI-Enabled Education

Taken together, the literature suggests that AI in teaching represents a profound pedagogical and ethical shift rather than a simple technological enhancement. AI-enabled tools can support personalization, efficiency, and engagement, but they also reconfigure power relations, professional responsibilities, and student agency. Ethical teaching in AI-enabled environments requires continuous reflection on transparency, accountability, and human oversight. Rather than asking whether AI should be used in teaching, the more productive question is how it can be integrated in ways that respect educational values. This involves designing pedagogies that foreground human judgment, foster AI literacy, and promote trust rather than surveillance. It also requires institutional support structures that empower educators to experiment, reflect, and adapt without fear of professional displacement.

Ultimately, AI in teaching should be understood as a sociotechnical practice shaped by human choices, institutional priorities, and ethical commitments. When guided by thoughtful pedagogical frameworks and robust ethical principles, AI has the potential to enhance learning experiences while preserving the relational and reflective foundations of higher education.

AI IN RESEARCH: OPPORTUNITIES, THREATS, AND POLICY IMPLICATIONS

The integration of artificial intelligence into academic research has progressed rapidly from peripheral experimentation to routine practice. Unlike earlier digital tools that primarily supported data storage or retrieval, contemporary AI systems actively participate in knowledge production by assisting with literature discovery, data analysis, hypothesis generation, and scholarly writing. This shift has fundamentally altered how researchers work, raising questions not only about productivity and efficiency but also about authorship, responsibility, and the ethical foundations of research practice. As AI becomes increasingly embedded in research workflows, higher education institutions face the challenge of harnessing its benefits while safeguarding academic integrity and epistemic trust. Figure 2 illustrates the opportunities and challenges associated with the use of AI in research, showing how AI-enabled support in literature review, data analysis, and writing can enhance productivity, while simultaneously raising concerns related to research ethics, authorship, transparency, and governance.

As shown in Figure 2, AI technologies simultaneously expand research capabilities while introducing new ethical and governance challenges. AI-enabled tools facilitate literature discovery, automated summarization, and large-scale data analysis, allowing researchers to process complex information more efficiently. However, these capabilities also create uncertainties regarding authorship attribution, originality of scholarly work, and transparency in research workflows. The figure highlights that the integration of AI into research practice requires institutional mechanisms that ensure accountability and maintain trust in scholarly knowledge production.

Figure 2. AI in research: Opportunities and challenges

AI as a Research Productivity Enabler

A growing body of literature positions AI as a powerful productivity tool in academic research. Khalifa and Albadawy (2024) describe AI-enabled applications as essential aids that streamline repetitive and time-intensive tasks, such as literature screening, reference management, language editing, and data preprocessing. By reducing the cognitive and administrative burden on researchers, AI tools allow greater focus on conceptual thinking, interpretation, and theory development. This productivity-oriented framing has contributed significantly to the rapid uptake of AI tools across disciplines. Similarly, Oyelude (2024) highlights the expanding ecosystem of AI tools available to researchers, ranging from semantic search engines and citation recommendation systems to automated summarization and data visualization platforms. From the perspective of research support services, these tools represent an evolution in scholarly infrastructure, enabling faster access to relevant knowledge and more efficient navigation of increasingly complex academic literature.

Student engagement with AI in research-related writing further underscores its perceived utility. Malik et al. (2023), examining higher education students' perspectives, report that many students view AI-assisted tools as supportive rather than deceptive, particularly when used for brainstorming, structuring arguments, or refining language. These findings suggest that, at least from the learner's perspective, AI is often understood as a legitimate extension of existing academic support mechanisms rather than a violation of scholarly norms.

However, the productivity gains associated with AI are not evenly distributed. Researchers with higher digital literacy, better access to institutional resources, and stronger methodological foundations are more likely to benefit meaningfully from

AI-assisted tools. This raises concerns about the emergence of new inequalities in research capacity, particularly between well-resourced institutions and those operating under constraints.

Generative AI and the Transformation of Academic Writing

Generative AI has introduced a qualitative shift in academic writing practices. Unlike earlier tools that supported editing or formatting, generative models can produce coherent drafts, synthesize arguments, and paraphrase complex texts. Schlagwein and Willcocks (2023) argue that this capability challenges traditional boundaries between assistance and authorship, particularly when AI-generated text becomes indistinguishable from human writing. Rodrigues (2025) conceptualizes this phenomenon as “distant writing,” where intellectual labor is partially delegated to machines. From this perspective, AI-mediated writing complicates established epistemologies of authorship by dispersing creativity across human–machine assemblages. While delegation has always been part of scholarly practice—through peer feedback, editorial assistance, and collaborative authorship—generative AI intensifies this delegation to an unprecedented degree.

Empirical evidence suggests that researchers experience ambivalence toward these tools. Farangi et al. (2025) document a range of emotional responses among researchers using generative AI, including relief, anxiety, guilt, and uncertainty. While some researchers appreciate the efficiency and linguistic support AI provides, others express discomfort about relying on systems that obscure the origin of ideas and phrasing. These emotional dimensions highlight that ethical concerns about AI in research are not merely abstract principles but lived experiences that shape scholarly identity and confidence.

Authorship, Originality, and Epistemic Responsibility

One of the most contentious issues surrounding AI in research concerns authorship and originality. Traditional academic norms assume a clear link between intellectual contribution and authorship attribution. Generative AI disrupts this link by producing text and ideas without intentionality or accountability. Schlagwein and Willcocks (2023) emphasize that AI systems cannot assume moral or epistemic responsibility, yet their outputs increasingly influence scholarly claims. Qadhi et al. (2024), through a scientometric analysis of rcsearch ethics literature, identify authorship ambiguity as a central concern in discussions of generative AI. Questions arise regarding whether AI contributions should be disclosed, how such disclosures should be framed, and whether extensive AI assistance undermines claims of originality. These concerns are particularly acute in fields where writing is closely tied to intellectual contribution, such as the humanities and social sciences.

Rodrigues (2025) further argues that plagiarism in the age of AI cannot be understood solely as textual duplication. When AI generates original text based on probabilistic patterns, traditional definitions of plagiarism become insufficient. Instead, the ethical issue shifts toward transparency and delegation: how much intellectual labor can be delegated before authorship claims become misleading?

Student Use of AI and Emerging Research Norms

The normalization of AI use among students signals broader changes in research culture. Malik et al. (2023) find that students often perceive AI tools as legitimate aids for academic writing, particularly when institutional guidelines are unclear or permissive. This normalization challenges educators and institutions to articulate clearer expectations regarding acceptable AI use in research-related tasks.

While student use of AI is often framed in terms of misconduct, such framing may obscure deeper pedagogical and policy issues. If AI tools are widely accessible and increasingly embedded in academic workflows, outright prohibition may be neither feasible nor desirable. Instead, institutions face the task of redefining research competencies to include ethical AI use, critical evaluation of AI outputs, and responsible disclosure practices.

Detection Technologies and the Limits of Policing

In response to concerns about AI-assisted writing, institutions and publishers have increasingly turned to AI-based detection tools. Ibrahim (2023) critically examines the use of AI detectors in ESL writing contexts, highlighting significant limitations in accuracy and fairness. Detection systems often struggle to distinguish between AI-generated text and legitimate linguistic variation, placing multilingual and non-native English writers at disproportionate risk. Similar challenges are evident in disciplinary publishing contexts. Jairoun et al. (2024), studying AI detection in pharmacy practice manuscripts, report variability in detection outcomes across tools and document types. These inconsistencies raise questions about the reliability of detection-based enforcement and the potential for false accusations to undermine trust in peer review and academic evaluation.

Collectively, these findings suggest that surveillance-oriented responses to AI use may exacerbate existing inequities without effectively addressing underlying ethical issues. Rather than relying solely on detection, institutions may need to shift toward transparency-based approaches that emphasize disclosure and responsible use.

Responsible Integration of AI in Research Practice

Responsible integration of AI in research requires a combination of transparency, verification, and accountability. Researchers must remain responsible for the accuracy and originality of scholarly outputs, regardless of whether AI tools assist in drafting, analysis, or data interpretation. Transparent disclosure of AI assistance in research workflows can help maintain trust in scholarly communication while allowing institutions to monitor emerging practices. In addition, AI-generated outputs must be critically evaluated and validated through established research methodologies. These practices reinforce the principle that AI should function as a supportive tool within research processes rather than a substitute for scholarly responsibility.

Institutional Guidance and Policy Fragmentation

Higher education institutions have begun issuing guidance on generative AI use in research, but these efforts remain fragmented. Ganguly et al. (2025), analyzing institutional guidance across the United States, find considerable variation in how universities address AI-assisted research. While some institutions provide detailed frameworks for disclosure, acceptable use, and authorship responsibility, others offer vague or aspirational statements that leave researchers uncertain.

This policy fragmentation reflects broader tensions between innovation and regulation. Institutions seek to encourage research productivity and competitiveness while avoiding reputational and ethical risks. However, the absence of harmonized standards creates uncertainty for researchers working across institutions, disciplines, and publication venues. Jeon et al. (2025) argue for institutionally grounded AI research ethics that account for disciplinary norms, research contexts, and social impact. Rather than adopting generic ethical principles, they advocate for participatory policy development that involves researchers, ethics committees, and research support units. Such an approach recognizes that ethical AI use is context-dependent and cannot be reduced to universal rules.

Research Ethics Beyond Compliance

A recurring theme in the literature is the need to move beyond compliance-based ethics toward reflexive ethical practice. Qadhi et al. (2024) observe that much of the current discourse on AI ethics focuses on risk mitigation rather than epistemic integrity. While concerns about misconduct are valid, an overemphasis on policing may distract from deeper questions about how AI reshapes knowledge production.

Farangi et al. (2025) highlight that researchers' ethical judgments about AI use are shaped by disciplinary culture, career stage, and institutional expectations.

Early-career researchers, in particular, may feel pressure to adopt AI tools to remain competitive, even when ethical guidelines are unclear. This underscores the importance of institutional support structures that foster ethical reflection rather than fear-driven compliance.

Reframing AI in Research: Toward Responsible Integration

Taken together, the literature suggests that AI in research represents neither a simple productivity solution nor an existential threat to academia. Instead, it constitutes a profound reconfiguration of research practice that demands thoughtful institutional response. AI tools offer significant opportunities to enhance efficiency, inclusivity, and analytical capacity, but they also challenge foundational assumptions about authorship, originality, and responsibility.

Rather than asking whether AI should be used in research, institutions must address how it should be used, disclosed, and governed. This requires coherent policies that balance innovation with integrity, as well as research cultures that value transparency and critical engagement with AI outputs. Detection technologies may play a limited role, but they cannot substitute for ethical education, clear guidelines, and trust-based academic communities. Ultimately, responsible AI integration in research depends on aligning technological capability with institutional values. By foregrounding ethical reflection, participatory governance, and contextual sensitivity, higher education institutions can navigate the opportunities and threats of AI while preserving the credibility and social legitimacy of academic research.

AI IN ACADEMIC SERVICE AND INSTITUTIONAL MANAGEMENT

While discussions of artificial intelligence in higher education often focus on teaching and research, some of the most immediate and far-reaching impacts of AI are occurring in the domain of academic service and institutional management. Administrative systems form the operational backbone of universities, shaping how decisions are made, resources are allocated, and services are delivered to students and staff. As AI-driven technologies become embedded in these systems, they are transforming institutional processes in ways that are less visible than classroom applications but arguably more consequential for governance, accountability, and organizational culture. Figure 3 presents the application of AI in academic service and institutional management, demonstrating its role in automating admissions, supporting student retention analytics, enabling performance and financial planning, and improving institutional productivity, alongside emerging ethical and governance concerns.

Figure 3 illustrates how AI technologies are increasingly integrated into administrative and governance functions within universities. These applications include automated admissions processing, predictive analytics for student retention, performance monitoring, and financial planning systems. While such tools improve operational efficiency and enable data-driven decision-making, they also introduce governance challenges related to algorithmic transparency, accountability, and bias. The figure therefore highlights the dual role of AI as both an efficiency-enhancing technology and a governance challenge that institutions must address through appropriate oversight mechanisms.

Figure 3. AI in academic service and institutional management

AI and the Reconfiguration of Academic and Administrative Work

AI has increasingly been adopted to support a wide range of academic and administrative functions, including admissions processing, student retention analytics, scheduling, performance monitoring, and financial planning. Ahmad et al. (2022) describe AI as a catalyst for enhancing efficiency and responsiveness in both academic and administrative roles, particularly in data-intensive tasks that exceed human processing capacity. From this perspective, AI is framed as an enabler of evidence-based management, capable of improving institutional effectiveness and service quality.

El Din and Al Harrasi (2024) extend this argument by situating AI adoption within broader administrative transformation agendas. They note that AI systems are not merely automating existing workflows but reshaping how decisions are conceptualized and justified. Predictive analytics, for example, allow administrators to anticipate enrollment trends or identify students at risk of attrition, thereby shifting management practices from reactive to anticipatory modes. While such capabilities offer clear benefits, they also redefine institutional priorities by privileging measurable indicators over qualitative judgment. This reconfiguration of work has implications for professional roles within universities. Administrative staff increasingly interact with AI-generated dashboards, alerts, and recommendations, which may influence decision-making authority and accountability. Rather than replacing staff, AI often redistributes responsibility, requiring administrators to interpret and validate algorithmic outputs while remaining accountable for outcomes.

Strategic Leadership and Responsible AI Adoption

The effectiveness of AI in academic service and management depends heavily on leadership and governance. Khairullah et al. (2025) emphasize that responsible AI implementation requires strategic leadership capable of aligning technological innovation with institutional values. Their work highlights that AI adoption should not be driven solely by efficiency gains or competitive pressure but guided by ethical considerations, stakeholder engagement, and long-term institutional vision.

Strategic leadership plays a critical role in determining whether AI systems enhance institutional capacity or exacerbate existing challenges. When AI is introduced without clear governance structures, institutions risk fragmented implementation, resistance from staff, and unintended ethical consequences. Khairullah et al. (2025) argue that leadership must foster transparency, provide clear communication about AI objectives, and ensure that decision-making authority remains accountable to human oversight. This perspective aligns with broader organizational research on AI-driven decision-making. Rajagopal et al. (2022) suggest that AI-enabled frameworks can support organizational culture by improving consistency and rationality in decisions, but only when integrated thoughtfully into existing governance structures. Without such integration, AI risks becoming an opaque authority that undermines trust among institutional stakeholders.

Decision-Making, Automation, and Institutional Culture

AI-driven decision-support systems are increasingly used to inform strategic planning and operational management. These systems aggregate and analyze large datasets, offering insights that would be difficult for human decision-makers to generate independently. While such systems promise objectivity and efficiency, they also raise questions about how decisions are framed and justified within institutional cultures.

Rajagopal et al. (2022) note that AI-driven decision-making frameworks tend to privilege quantifiable outcomes, potentially marginalizing contextual knowledge and professional discretion. In higher education, where decisions often involve competing values—such as access versus selectivity or efficiency versus equity—this privileging of data-driven logic can reshape institutional priorities in subtle but significant ways. Moreover, reliance on AI-generated insights may influence how accountability is distributed. When decisions are justified through algorithmic recommendations, it may become unclear whether responsibility lies with human decision-makers or the systems they rely upon. This ambiguity underscores the need for explicit governance mechanisms that clarify roles, responsibilities, and lines of accountability.

Monitoring, Surveillance, and Student Engagement

One area where AI has been particularly influential is the monitoring of student engagement and behavior. Pabba and Kumar (2022) describe intelligent systems that use facial expression recognition to assess student engagement in large classrooms. Such systems promise real-time feedback for instructors and administrators, potentially enabling timely interventions to support learning.

However, the use of AI-driven monitoring systems raises profound ethical and governance concerns. While engagement analytics can inform pedagogical and administrative decisions, they also introduce elements of surveillance into academic environments. Students may feel constantly observed, leading to anxiety, self-censorship, or resistance. Moreover, the interpretation of behavioral data—such as facial expressions—may be culturally biased or contextually misleading.

These concerns highlight the tension between efficiency and trust in AI-enabled institutional management. While AI systems can generate actionable insights, their deployment must be balanced against respect for privacy, autonomy, and dignity within academic communities.

Bias, Fairness, and Institutional Risk

Bias remains one of the most significant challenges in AI-driven academic service systems. Varsha (2023), in a systematic review, documents how biases can emerge at multiple stages of AI system development, including data collection, model training, and deployment. In higher education, biased AI systems can have serious consequences, influencing admissions decisions, scholarship allocations, or performance evaluations.

Managing bias is not solely a technical challenge but an institutional responsibility. Varsha (2023) emphasizes the importance of continuous monitoring, diverse training datasets, and inclusive design processes. However, these measures require organizational commitment and resources, which may be unevenly distributed across institutions.

Failure to address bias effectively exposes institutions to reputational, legal, and ethical risks. As AI systems increasingly inform high-stakes decisions, institutions must ensure that fairness and equity are embedded into governance frameworks rather than treated as afterthoughts.

Legal and Intellectual Property Challenges

The use of generative AI in institutional contexts introduces complex legal questions, particularly regarding copyright and intellectual property. Lucchi (2024), through a case study of ChatGPT, highlights unresolved challenges related to ownership of AI-generated content and liability for copyright infringement. In academic institutions, these issues arise in administrative communications, policy drafting, marketing materials, and knowledge management systems.

Universities must navigate a complex legal landscape where responsibility for AI-generated outputs remains ambiguous. If AI systems produce content that infringes on copyright or disseminates inaccurate information, determining liability becomes challenging. Lucchi (2024) argues that existing legal frameworks are ill-equipped to address these issues, underscoring the need for institutional policies that clarify acceptable use and responsibility.

Ethical Governance and Institutional Accountability

Ethical governance has emerged as a central theme in discussions of AI in institutional management. Camilleri (2024) argues that AI governance should be grounded in principles of transparency, accountability, and social responsibility.

In higher education, this means ensuring that AI systems align with institutional missions related to equity, inclusion, and public trust.

Frameworks for ethical AI governance increasingly emphasize the translation of abstract principles into operational practice. Xue and Pang (2022) propose an integrated analytical framework that connects ethical values with governance mechanisms, emphasizing the importance of oversight bodies, stakeholder participation, and continuous evaluation. Similarly, Auld et al. (2022) highlight the role of ethical standards and voluntary governance initiatives in shaping responsible AI adoption across sectors.

Blanchard et al. (2025), although focused on defense applications, offer insights relevant to higher education by examining the normative trade-offs involved in translating ethical principles into practice. Their work underscores that ethical governance often involves balancing competing values rather than enforcing rigid rules. In academic institutions, such trade-offs may involve reconciling efficiency with fairness or innovation with accountability.

From Principles to Practice: Institutional Implementation Challenges

Despite growing consensus on the importance of ethical AI governance, implementing these principles remains challenging. Many institutions lack the expertise, resources, or organizational structures needed to operationalize ethical frameworks effectively. Camilleri (2024) notes that ethical governance requires more than policy statements; it demands institutional capacity for auditing, training, and enforcement.

Khairullah et al. (2025) emphasize that responsible AI adoption must be embedded within broader institutional strategies rather than treated as a standalone initiative. This includes aligning AI governance with existing quality assurance mechanisms, risk management processes, and institutional review structures. Without such integration, ethical guidelines risk remaining symbolic rather than impactful.

Reimagining Academic Service in an AI-Enabled Institution

Taken together, the literature suggests that AI in academic service and institutional management represents a profound shift in how universities operate and govern themselves. AI-driven systems offer opportunities to enhance efficiency, consistency, and strategic insight, but they also introduce risks related to bias, surveillance, legal uncertainty, and erosion of trust. Rather than viewing AI as a neutral administrative tool, institutions must recognize it as a socio-technical system that reflects and reshapes organizational values. Responsible integration requires strategic leadership, robust governance frameworks, and ongoing dialogue with academic and administrative stakeholders. By foregrounding ethical considerations and human oversight, universities can leverage AI to strengthen institutional capacity while preserving accountability and public trust. In this sense, AI in academic service is not merely about doing existing tasks faster or cheaper; it is about redefining how institutions understand responsibility, decision-making, and service in an increasingly automated academic environment.

STRATEGIC COLLABORATION AND POLICY DEVELOPMENT FOR RESPONSIBLE AI ADOPTION

As artificial intelligence becomes embedded across teaching, research, and institutional management, higher education institutions face a growing imperative to move beyond ad hoc adoption toward coordinated, responsible governance. While earlier sections have examined how AI reshapes academic practice at operational levels, the sustainability of these changes ultimately depends on strategic collaboration and coherent policy development. AI governance in academia is not simply a technical or legal exercise; it is a socio-institutional process that requires alignment among diverse stakeholders, regulatory frameworks, and ethical principles.

The Global Policy Context for AI in Higher Education

AI governance in higher education is increasingly shaped by global regulatory and policy developments. Mahrishi et al. (2025) document a growing number of international initiatives aimed at establishing regulatory frameworks for AI use in higher education, reflecting concerns about academic integrity, data protection, and ethical accountability. These initiatives vary significantly in scope and enforceability, ranging from high-level ethical guidelines to legally binding regulations. Despite this growing attention, there remains a gap between global policy aspirations and institutional realities. Many universities operate within overlapping regulatory environments that include national laws, accreditation requirements, and disciplinary norms. Mahrishi et al. (2025) note that higher education institutions often struggle to translate broad regulatory principles into actionable institutional policies, particularly when AI technologies evolve faster than regulatory mechanisms. This fragmentation underscores the need for institutional policies that are both globally informed and locally responsive. Rather than adopting external frameworks wholesale, universities must contextualize AI governance within their own missions, values, and operational constraints.

From Guidelines to Governance: Institutional Challenges

The distinction between AI guidelines and AI governance is critical. Ghimire and Edwards (2024) argue that many educational institutions remain at the level of issuing non-binding guidelines that articulate ethical aspirations without establishing enforcement mechanisms or accountability structures. While such guidelines are valuable for signaling institutional intent, they often lack the operational clarity needed to guide everyday practice.

True governance, by contrast, requires formal structures, decision-making authority, and continuous oversight. Batool et al. (2025), in their systematic review of AI governance literature, emphasize that effective governance frameworks integrate ethical principles with organizational processes such as risk assessment, auditing, and stakeholder engagement. In the absence of such integration, AI policies risk becoming symbolic documents that have little impact on practice. Universities face particular challenges in this regard due to their decentralized governance structures. Academic autonomy, disciplinary diversity, and collegial decision-making—hallmarks of higher education—can complicate centralized policy enforcement. Ghimire and Edwards (2024) suggest that successful AI governance in education must balance institutional coherence with disciplinary flexibility, allowing for contextual adaptation while maintaining shared ethical standards.

Policy Development for Teaching and Learning

Teaching and learning represent one of the most visible domains of AI policy development. Chan (2023) proposes a comprehensive AI policy education framework that integrates policy awareness into teaching and learning practices. Rather than treating AI policy as an administrative concern, Chan argues that students and educators should actively engage with policy principles as part of their academic development. Such an approach reframes AI policy from a restrictive mechanism into a pedagogical tool. By embedding policy literacy into curricula, institutions can foster informed and responsible AI use among students while supporting faculty in navigating ethical and regulatory expectations. This aligns with broader calls for AI literacy that encompasses not only technical competence but also ethical reasoning and policy awareness. However, implementing such frameworks requires institutional coordination. Teaching-focused AI policies must align with assessment practices, academic integrity regulations, and faculty development initiatives. Without such alignment, policy messages risk becoming fragmented or contradictory.

Research Governance and Academic Freedom

AI governance in research contexts raises distinct challenges related to academic freedom, intellectual autonomy, and scholarly responsibility. Gao et al. (2025) examine legal regulation of AI-assisted academic writing and highlight tensions between regulatory oversight and researchers' autonomy. While legal frameworks aim to prevent misconduct and protect intellectual property, overly rigid regulation may stifle innovation or discourage legitimate AI-assisted practices.

Haber et al. (2025) argue that navigating this regulatory landscape requires a nuanced understanding of disciplinary norms and research cultures. Rather than imposing uniform rules, institutions should develop research-specific AI policies that clarify expectations around disclosure, authorship, and accountability while preserving space for methodological experimentation.

Academic governance structures play a key role in mediating these tensions. Wang et al. (2021) demonstrate how AI techniques are increasingly integrated into academic governance processes in research universities, influencing evaluation, funding allocation, and strategic planning. While such integration can enhance transparency and consistency, it also raises concerns about algorithmic influence over scholarly priorities. Effective research governance must therefore ensure that AI serves as a decision-support tool rather than a decision-maker, preserving human judgment and academic deliberation at the core of scholarly evaluation.

The Role of Academic Librarians and Support Units

Policy development for responsible AI adoption is not solely the responsibility of senior leadership or legal offices. Michalak (2023) highlights the critical role of academic librarians in AI policy-making, particularly in areas related to information ethics, scholarly communication, and digital literacy. Librarians are uniquely positioned at the intersection of teaching, research, and information governance, enabling them to act as mediators between policy principles and academic practice.

By supporting policy development, offering training on ethical AI use, and advising on data governance and intellectual property issues, librarians contribute to the operationalization of AI governance. Michalak (2023) emphasizes that inclusive policy-making processes that involve support units foster greater institutional buy-in and practical relevance. This collaborative approach reflects a broader shift toward distributed governance models, where responsibility for AI ethics is shared across institutional roles rather than centralized within administrative hierarchies.

Multi-Stakeholder Collaboration as a Governance Principle

A recurring theme in contemporary AI governance literature is the importance of multi-stakeholder collaboration. Deshpande and Sharp (2022) argue that responsible AI systems involve a diverse array of stakeholders, including developers, users, regulators, and affected communities. In higher education, this stakeholder ecosystem includes leadership, faculty, students, administrative staff, librarians, publishers, and policymakers. Insights from other domains reinforce the value of this approach. Rozenblit et al. (2025), examining AI governance in healthcare, demonstrate that balancing multi-stakeholder perspectives leads to more robust and socially responsive governance frameworks. While the contexts differ, the underlying principles—transparency, inclusivity, and shared accountability—are directly applicable to academia.

Multi-stakeholder processes also help address power asymmetries. When AI policies are developed exclusively by leadership or technical experts, they may overlook the concerns of those most affected by AI systems. Inclusive governance processes create opportunities for dialogue, negotiation, and mutual learning, strengthening institutional trust.

Ethics Principles and Cultural Contexts

Ethical principles form the normative foundation of AI governance, but their interpretation and application vary across cultural and regional contexts. Younas and Zeng (2025) propose a multilevel approach to AI ethics that accounts for global norms, regional values, and institutional practices. Their work underscores that responsible AI governance cannot rely on universal principles alone; it must engage with local ethical traditions and socio-political realities. In higher education, this cultural sensitivity is particularly important for international institutions and collaborative research environments. Policies that ignore cultural variation risk alienating stakeholders or imposing inappropriate norms. Conversely, context-aware ethics frameworks can enhance legitimacy and compliance.

Batool et al. (2025) similarly emphasize that effective AI governance integrates ethical principles with contextual factors such as organizational culture, legal systems, and technological maturity. This integration enables institutions to move from abstract ethics statements toward actionable governance practices.

Legal, Ethical, and Regulatory Alignment

One of the central challenges in AI policy development is aligning ethical aspirations with legal and regulatory requirements. Gao et al. (2025) highlight gaps between existing copyright laws and the realities of AI-assisted academic writing. These gaps create uncertainty for institutions seeking to develop compliant yet flexible policies.

Haber et al. (2025) argue that institutions must adopt adaptive policy frameworks capable of evolving alongside technological and regulatory change. Static policies risk becoming obsolete, while overly reactive policies may create confusion. Regular policy review, stakeholder consultation, and alignment with external standards are therefore essential components of responsible governance.

From Policy Documents to Institutional Practice

Despite growing awareness of AI ethics and governance, a persistent challenge lies in translating policy documents into everyday practice. Chan (2023) notes that policy effectiveness depends on communication, training, and reinforcement. Policies that are inaccessible or poorly communicated are unlikely to influence behavior.

Capacity building is therefore a critical component of policy implementation. Training programs, workshops, and advisory services can help faculty, students, and administrators understand policy expectations and apply them in context. Michalak (2023) emphasizes that such initiatives are most effective when they are collaborative and responsive to disciplinary needs.

Institutional Strategies for Responsible AI Governance

Higher education institutions can strengthen responsible AI adoption through coordinated governance strategies. Establishing institutional AI ethics committees can provide oversight for AI-related decision-making across teaching, research, and administration. Universities should also develop clear policy guidelines regarding acceptable AI use in academic writing, research processes, and assessment practices. Faculty development programs focused on AI literacy can help educators critically evaluate AI-generated outputs and integrate AI tools responsibly into their professional activities. In addition, institutions should implement regular auditing mechanisms to monitor AI systems used in decision-support processes, ensuring that issues related to bias, transparency, and accountability are systematically addressed.

Toward a Collaborative Model of Responsible AI Adoption

Taken together, the literature suggests that responsible AI adoption in higher education depends on strategic collaboration and adaptive policy development. AI governance cannot be reduced to compliance checklists or isolated guidelines; it must be understood as an ongoing institutional practice shaped by dialogue, reflection, and shared responsibility. Effective governance frameworks balance innovation with accountability, autonomy with oversight, and global standards with local context. By engaging multiple stakeholders, integrating ethical principles into operational processes, and fostering policy literacy across the academic community, institutions can navigate the complexities of AI adoption more effectively.

Ultimately, strategic collaboration and policy development provide the foundation for aligning AI technologies with the educational mission of universities. When governance structures support transparency, inclusivity, and ethical reflection, AI can be harnessed not only as a tool for efficiency but as a means of strengthening academic integrity, institutional trust, and social responsibility in an increasingly automated academic landscape.

CONCLUSION AND FUTURE DIRECTIONS

The rapid integration of artificial intelligence across teaching, research, academic service, and institutional governance represents a significant transformation in how higher education operates and defines its core responsibilities. AI is no longer a peripheral technological innovation; it has become an influential force shaping academic work, knowledge production, and institutional decision-making. Its impact extends beyond operational efficiency to affect pedagogical practices, research ethics, professional roles, and governance structures within universities.

In teaching and learning, AI technologies provide opportunities to support personalized instruction, improve accessibility, and enhance learner engagement. Adaptive learning systems, intelligent tutoring platforms, and learning analytics tools can strengthen instructional effectiveness when used within carefully designed pedagogical frameworks. At the same time, these technologies introduce ethical concerns related to surveillance, algorithmic bias, and the redistribution of decision-making authority between educators and automated systems. Responsible integration therefore requires preserving educator judgment, strengthening AI literacy among students and faculty, and ensuring that technology supports rather than replaces pedagogical responsibility.

AI is also reshaping academic research practices. AI-enabled tools assist researchers in literature discovery, data analysis, and academic writing, improving efficiency and expanding analytical capabilities. However, generative AI systems challenge long-standing assumptions about authorship, originality, and epistemic responsibility. These developments expose limitations in existing research ethics frameworks, particularly regarding transparency, accountability, and intellectual property. Addressing these challenges requires research cultures that encourage responsible disclosure and critical evaluation of AI-assisted outputs while maintaining scholarly integrity.

Within academic service and institutional management, AI-driven systems are transforming administrative operations and strategic planning processes. Predictive analytics, automated decision-support systems, and monitoring tools can enhance institutional responsiveness and operational efficiency. Nevertheless, these technologies also introduce governance challenges related to data privacy, algorithmic bias, and accountability. Effective implementation therefore depends on strong leadership, transparent governance structures, and continuous oversight to ensure that automated systems support institutional decision-making without undermining professional responsibility or public trust.

Across these domains, the integration of AI highlights the need for coordinated institutional strategies that align technological adoption with ethical governance. Responsible AI use in higher education requires collaboration among institutional leadership, faculty, students, administrators, librarians, and policymakers to ensure that technological innovation is guided by shared academic values and supported by appropriate governance mechanisms.

Recommendations

Several institutional priorities emerge for responsible AI adoption in higher education. Universities should develop comprehensive AI governance policies that address teaching, research, and administrative applications in an integrated manner. These policies should clarify expectations regarding AI use, transparency in AI-assisted research practices, and accountability in data-driven decision-making.

Strengthening AI literacy is also essential. Faculty development initiatives and student training programs should promote critical understanding of AI technologies, their capabilities, and their limitations. In addition, institutions should establish oversight mechanisms, such as AI ethics committees or review structures, to evaluate the ethical implications of AI deployment across academic functions. These measures can help institutions harness the benefits of AI while minimizing risks associated with bias, misuse, or loss of academic autonomy.

Future Directions and Research

This chapter presents a conceptual analysis of AI integration in higher education based primarily on existing literature and emerging institutional practices. As such, it does not include empirical case studies examining how universities implement AI governance frameworks in practice.

Future work should investigate how higher education institutions operationalize AI governance policies across teaching, research, and administrative functions. Empirical studies examining institutional experiences with AI adoption can provide insights into the effectiveness of different governance models and the practical challenges encountered during implementation. Further research may also explore how institutional culture, regulatory environments, and technological maturity influence responsible AI integration in universities.

Additionally, future studies could examine the development of collaborative frameworks involving universities, policymakers, and technology developers to establish shared standards for ethical AI use in higher education. Such research would contribute to building governance models that support innovation while preserving academic integrity, transparency, and institutional accountability.

REFERENCES

Ahmad, S. F., Alam, M. M., Rahmat, M. K., Mubarik, M. S., & Hyder, S. I. (2022). Academic and administrative role of artificial intelligence in education. *Sustainability (Basel)*, *14*(3), 1101. DOI: 10.3390/su14031101

Auld, G., Casovan, A., Clarke, A., & Faveri, B. (2022). Governing AI through ethical standards: Learning from the experiences of other private governance initiatives. *Journal of European Public Policy*, *29*(11), 1822–1844. DOI: 10.1080/13501763.2022.2099449

Avci, H., Lunn, S. J., & Hazari, Z. (2025). Exploring STEM educators' perspectives on the integration of AI-enabled technologies in teaching and learning. *Computers and Education Open*, *9*, 100304. DOI: 10.1016/j.caeo.2025.100304

Azamfirei, V., Psarommatis, F., & Lagrosen, Y. (2023). Application of automation for in-line quality inspection, a zero-defect manufacturing approach. *Journal of Manufacturing Systems*, *67*, 1–22. DOI: 10.1016/j.jmsy.2022.12.010

Bates, T., Cobo, C., Mariño, O., & Wheeler, S. (2020). Can artificial intelligence transform higher education? *International Journal of Educational Technology in Higher Education*, *17*(1), 42. DOI: 10.1186/s41239-020-00218-x

Batool, A., Zowghi, D., & Bano, M. (2025). AI governance: A systematic literature review. *AI and Ethics*, 1–15.

Bearman, M., Ryan, J., & Ajjawi, R. (2023). Discourses of artificial intelligence in higher education: A critical literature review. *Higher Education*, *86*(2), 369–385. DOI: 10.1007/s10734-022-00937-2

Blanchard, A., Thomas, C., & Taddeo, M. (2025). Ethical governance of artificial intelligence for defence: Normative tradeoffs for principle to practice guidance. *AI & Society*, *40*(1), 185–198. DOI: 10.1007/s00146-024-01866-7 PMID: 41640455

Camilleri, M. A. (2024). Artificial intelligence governance: Ethical considerations and implications for social responsibility. *Expert Systems: International Journal of Knowledge Engineering and Neural Networks*, *41*(7), e13406. DOI: 10.1111/exsy.13406

Chan, C. K. Y. (2023). A comprehensive AI policy education framework for university teaching and learning. *International Journal of Educational Technology in Higher Education*, *20*(1), 38. DOI: 10.1186/s41239-023-00408-3

Chu, J., Xi, L., Zhang, Q., & Lin, R. (2022, August). Research on ethical issues of artificial intelligence in education. In International conference on smart learning environments (pp. 101-108). Singapore: Springer Nature Singapore. DOI: 10.1007/978-981-19-5967-7_12

Córdova, P. R., & Vicari, R. M. (2022, August). Practical ethical issues for artificial intelligence in education. In International Conference on Technology and Innovation in Learning, Teaching and Education (pp. 437-445). Cham: Springer Nature Switzerland. DOI: 10.1007/978-3-031-22918-3_34

Crompton, H., & Burke, D. (2023). Artificial intelligence in higher education: The state of the field. *International Journal of Educational Technology in Higher Education*, *20*(1), 22. DOI: 10.1186/s41239-023-00392-8

Deshpande, A., & Sharp, H. (2022, July). Responsible ai systems: who are the stakeholders? In Proceedings of the 2022 AAAI/ACM Conference on AI, Ethics, and Society (pp. 227-236).

El Din, M. S., & Al Harrasi, N. H. (2024). Ai-Driven Transformation in Higher Education: New Frontiers in Administration and Management. In Utilizing AI for Assessment, Grading, and Feedback in Higher Education (pp. 135-161). IGI Global.

Ellikkal, A., & Rajamohan, S. (2025). AI-enabled personalized learning: Empowering management students for improving engagement and academic performance. *Vilakshan-XIMB Journal of Management*, *22*(1), 28–44. DOI: 10.1108/XJM-02-2024-0023

Farangi, M. R., Nejadghanbar, H., & Hu, G. (2025). Use of generative AI in research: Ethical considerations and emotional experiences. *Ethics & Behavior*, *35*(7), 527–543. DOI: 10.1080/10508422.2024.2420133

Fidas, C. A., Belk, M., Constantinides, A., Portugal, D., Martins, P., Pietron, A. M., Pitsillides, A., & Avouris, N. (2023). Ensuring academic integrity and trust in online learning environments: A longitudinal study of an ai-centered proctoring system in tertiary educational institutions. *Education Sciences*, *13*(6), 566. DOI: 10.3390/educsci13060566

Ganguly, A., Johri, A., Ali, A., & McDonald, N. (2025). Generative artificial intelligence for academic research: Evidence from guidance issued for researchers by higher education institutions in the United States. *AI and Ethics*, *5*(4), 1–17. DOI: 10.1007/s43681-025-00688-7

Gao, R., Yu, D., Gao, B., Hua, H., Hui, Z., Gao, J., & Yin, C. (2025). Legal regulation of AI-assisted academic writing: Challenges, frameworks, and pathways. *Frontiers in Artificial Intelligence*, *8*, 1546064. DOI: 10.3389/frai.2025.1546064 PMID: 40260414

George, B., & Wooden, O. (2023). Managing the strategic transformation of higher education through artificial intelligence. *Administrative Sciences*, *13*(9), 196. DOI: 10.3390/admsci13090196

Gering, Z., Feher, K., Harmat, V., & Tamassy, R. (2025). Strategic organisational responses to generative AI-driven digital transformation in leading higher education institutions. *The International Journal of Organizational Analysis*, *33*(12), 132–152. DOI: 10.1108/IJOA-09-2024-4850

Ghimire, A., & Edwards, J. (2024, July). From guidelines to governance: A study of ai policies in education. In International Conference on Artificial Intelligence in Education (pp. 299-307). Cham: Springer Nature Switzerland. DOI: 10.1007/978-3-031-64312-5_36

Haber, E., Jemielniak, D., Kurasiński, A., & Przegalińska, A. (2025). Navigating the Regulatory and Ethical Landscape of AI in Academia. In *Using AI in Academic Writing and Research: A Complete Guide to Effective and Ethical Academic AI* (pp. 119–137). Springer Nature Switzerland. DOI: 10.1007/978-3-031-91705-9_9

Hadi, W., & AlShaikh-Hasan, M. N. (2025). AI-Driven Curriculum Transformation and Faculty Development in Developing Universities. In Revolutionizing Urban Development and Governance With Emerging Technologies (pp. 289-322). IGI Global Scientific Publishing.

Ibrahim, K. (2023). Using AI-based detectors to control AI-assisted plagiarism in ESL writing:"The Terminator Versus the Machines". *Language Testing in Asia*, *13*(1), 46. DOI: 10.1186/s40468-023-00260-2

Jairoun, A. A., El-Dahiyat, F., ElRefae, G. A., Al-Hemyari, S. S., Shahwan, M., Zyoud, S. H., Hammour, K. A., & Babar, Z. U. D. (2024). Detecting manuscripts written by generative AI and AI-assisted technologies in the field of pharmacy practice. *Journal of Pharmaceutical Policy and Practice*, *17*(1), 2303759. DOI: 10.1080/20523211.2024.2303759 PMID: 38229951

Jeon, J., Kim, L., & Park, J. (2025). The ethics of generative AI in social science research: A qualitative approach for institutionally grounded AI research ethics. *Technology in Society*, *81*, 102836. DOI: 10.1016/j.techsoc.2025.102836

Kabudi, T., Pappas, I., & Olsen, D. H. (2021). AI-enabled adaptive learning systems: A systematic mapping of the literature. Computers and education. *Artificial Intelligence*, *2*, 100017.

Karumbaiah, S., Borchers, C., Shou, T., Falhs, A. C., Liu, P., Nagashima, T., . . . Aleven, V. (2023, June). A spatiotemporal analysis of teacher practices in supporting student learning and engagement in an AI-enabled classroom. In International conference on artificial intelligence in education (pp. 450-462). Cham: Springer Nature Switzerland.

Kavitha, S., Anchitaalagammai, J. V., Murali, S., & Annapoorani, S. (2025, March). Enhancing Learning Management Systems with Accessibility, Integrity, and Personalization Through Advanced Technologies. In *2025 International Conference on Data Science, Agents & Artificial Intelligence (ICDSAAI)* (pp. 1-6). IEEE. DOI: 10.1109/ICDSAAI65575.2025.11011537

Khairullah, S. A., Harris, S., Hadi, H. J., Sandhu, R. A., Ahmad, N., & Alshara, M. A. (2025, February). Implementing artificial intelligence in academic and administrative processes through responsible strategic leadership in the higher education institutions. [). Frontiers Media SA.]. *Frontiers in Education*, *10*, 1548104. DOI: 10.3389/feduc.2025.1548104

Khalifa, M., & Albadawy, M. (2024). Using artificial intelligence in academic writing and research: An essential productivity tool. *Computer Methods and Programs in Biomedicine Update*, *5*, 100145. DOI: 10.1016/j.cmpbup.2024.100145

Klimova, B., Pikhart, M., & Kacetl, J. (2023). Ethical issues of the use of AI-driven mobile apps for education. *Frontiers in Public Health*, *10*, 1118116. DOI: 10.3389/fpubh.2022.1118116 PMID: 36711343

Kumar, S., Kameswari, Y. L., Moram, V., & Pasha, M. (2025). Adaptive Learning in Modern Education Systems Leveraged by AI and Blockchain. In Blockchain and AI in Shaping the Modern Education System (pp. 44-71). CRC Press. DOI: 10.1201/9781003502739-3

Lucchi, N. (2024). ChatGPT: A case study on copyright challenges for generative artificial intelligence systems. *European Journal of Risk Regulation*, *15*(3), 602–624. DOI: 10.1017/err.2023.59

Mahrishi, M., Abbas, A., & Siddiqui, M. K. (2025). Global initiatives towards regulatory frameworks for artificial intelligence (AI) in higher education. *Digital Government: Research and Practice*, *6*(2), 1–9. DOI: 10.1145/3672462

Malik, A. R., Pratiwi, Y., Andajani, K., Numertayasa, I. W., Suharti, S., Darwis, A., & Marzuki, . (2023). Exploring artificial intelligence in academic essay: Higher education student's perspective. *International Journal of Educational Research Open*, *5*, 100296. DOI: 10.1016/j.ijedro.2023.100296

Manojkumar, R., & Krishnan, S. (2025). Open Discussion Forums and Effective Group Division for Improved Student Engagement in Teaching Learning Process. Journal of Engineering Education Transformations, 488-494.

Manojkumar, R., Srinivas, T. A. S., & Mekala, V. (2026). Inclusive Instructional Design Through Digital Pedagogies and Active Learning Approaches. In Practical Perspectives on Inclusive and Immersive Learning Environments (pp. 147-180). IGI Global Scientific Publishing. DOI: 10.4018/979-8-3373-5188-9.ch006

McGrath, C., Pargman, T. C., Juth, N., & Palmgren, P. J. (2023). University teachers' perceptions of responsibility and artificial intelligence in higher education-An experimental philosophical study. *Computers and Education: Artificial Intelligence*, *4*, 100139. DOI: 10.1016/j.caeai.2023.100139

Michalak, R. (2023). From ethics to execution: The role of academic librarians in artificial intelligence (AI) policy-making at colleges and universities. *Journal of Library Administration*, *63*(7), 928–938. DOI: 10.1080/01930826.2023.2262367

Myers, M., Brace, C., & Carden, L. (2023). *Intelligent Automation: Bridging the Gap Between Business and Academia*. Chapman and Hall/CRC. DOI: 10.1201/9781003276128

Ng, D. T. K., Leung, J. K. L., Chu, K. W. S., & Qiao, M. S. (2021). AI literacy: Definition, teaching, evaluation and ethical issues. *Proceedings of the Association for Information Science and Technology*, *58*(1), 504–509. DOI: 10.1002/pra2.487

Oyelude, A. A. (2024). Artificial intelligence (AI) tools for academic research. *Library Hi Tech News*, *41*(8), 18–20. DOI: 10.1108/LHTN-08-2024-0131

Pabba, C., & Kumar, P. (2022). An intelligent system for monitoring students' engagement in large classroom teaching through facial expression recognition. *Expert Systems: International Journal of Knowledge Engineering and Neural Networks*, *39*(1), e12839. DOI: 10.1111/exsy.12839

Pisica, A. I., Edu, T., Zaharia, R. M., & Zaharia, R. (2023). Implementing artificial intelligence in higher education: Pros and cons from the perspectives of academics. *Societies (Basel, Switzerland)*, *13*(5), 118. DOI: 10.3390/soc13050118

Qadhi, S. M., Alduais, A., Chaaban, Y., & Khraisheh, M. (2024). Generative AI, research ethics, and higher education research: Insights from a scientometric analysis. *Information (Basel), 15*(6), 325. DOI: 10.3390/info15060325

Rajagopal, N. K., Qureshi, N. I., Durga, S., Ramirez Asis, E. H., Huerta Soto, R. M., Gupta, S. K., & Deepak, S. (2022). Future of business culture: An artificial intelligence-driven digital framework for organization decision-making process. *Complexity, 2022*(1), 7796507. DOI: 10.1155/2022/7796507

Rodrigues, T. V. (2025). *Distant Writing and The Epistemology of Authorship: On Creativity*. Delegation, And Plagiarism in The Age Of AI.

Rozenblit, L., Price, A., Solomonides, A., Joseph, A. L., Koski, E., Srivastava, G., Labkoff, S., Bray, D., Lopez-Gonzalez, M., Singh, R., deBronkart, D., Barr, P. J., Szolovits, P., Dattani, K., Jaffe, C., Fridsma, D., Baris, R., Leftwich, R., Stolper, R., & Quintana, Y. (2025). Toward responsible AI governance: Balancing multi-stakeholder perspectives on AI in healthcare. *International Journal of Medical Informatics, 203*, 106015. DOI: 10.1016/j.ijmedinf.2025.106015 PMID: 40680319

Rozenblit, L., Price, A., Solomonides, A., Joseph, A. L., Srivastava, G., Labkoff, S., deBronkart, D., Singh, R., Dattani, K., Lopez-Gonzalez, M., Barr, P. J., Koski, E., Lin, B., Cheung, E., Weiner, M. G., Williams, T., Thuy Bui, T. T., & Quintana, Y. (2025). Towards a multi-stakeholder process for developing responsible AI governance in consumer health. *International Journal of Medical Informatics, 195*, 105713. DOI: 10.1016/j.ijmedinf.2024.105713 PMID: 39642592

Salloum, S. A. (2024). AI perils in education: Exploring ethical concerns. Artificial intelligence in education: The power and dangers of ChatGPT in the classroom, 669-675.

Sarker, I. H. (2022). AI-based modeling: Techniques, applications and research issues towards automation, intelligent and smart systems. *SN Computer Science, 3*(2), 158. DOI: 10.1007/s42979-022-01043-x PMID: 35194580

Schlagwein, D., & Willcocks, L. (2023). 'ChatGPT et al.': The ethics of using (generative) artificial intelligence in research and science. *Journal of Information Technology, 38*(3), 232–238. DOI: 10.1177/02683962231200411

Surahman, E., & Wang, T. H. (2022). Academic dishonesty and trustworthy assessment in online learning: A systematic literature review. *Journal of Computer Assisted Learning, 38*(6), 1535–1553. DOI: 10.1111/jcal.12708

Varsha, P. S. (2023). How can we manage biases in artificial intelligence systems–A systematic literature review. *International Journal of Information Management Data Insights*, *3*(1), 100165. DOI: 10.1016/j.jjimei.2023.100165

Wang, R., Li, J., Shi, W., & Li, X. (2021). Application of artificial intelligence techniques in operating mode of professors' academic governance in american research universities. *Wireless Communications and Mobile Computing*, *2021*(1), 3415125. DOI: 10.1155/2021/3415125

Watermeyer, R., Phipps, L., Lanclos, D., & Knight, C. (2024). Generative AI and the automating of academia. *Postdigital Science and Education*, *6*(2), 446–466. DOI: 10.1007/s42438-023-00440-6

Williamson, B., Macgilchrist, F., & Potter, J. (2023). Re-examining AI, automation and datafication in education. *Learning, Media and Technology*, *48*(1), 1–5. DOI: 10.1080/17439884.2023.2167830

Xue, L., & Pang, Z. (2022). Ethical governance of artificial intelligence: An integrated analytical framework. *Journal of Digital Economy*, *1*(1), 44–52. DOI: 10.1016/j.jdec.2022.08.003

Yordanova, Z. (2024, October). Innovation Processes in Universities: A Conceptual Model Incorporating Digital Transformation and Technological Innovations. In International Conference on Advanced Research in Technologies, Information, Innovation and Sustainability (pp. 105-117). Cham: Springer Nature Switzerland.

Younas, A., & Zeng, Y. (2025). Proposing Central Asian AI ethics principles: A multilevel approach for responsible AI. *AI and Ethics*, *5*(2), 1629–1637. DOI: 10.1007/s43681-024-00505-7

Section 2
AI Impact Upon Areas of Specialization

Chapter 5
AI in Software Engineering:
Overview, Tools, Limitations, Risks, and Strengths

Sharon K. Andrews
http://orcid.org/0000-0003-1451-2894
University of Houston-Clear Lake, USA

ABSTRACT

The paper presents the results of exploration of the use of AI within the field of software engineering with particular attention to AI support for the tasks of requirements engineering, coding, code reviews, testing and debugging, deployment and maintenance, and software project management. Within this broader topic, the paper discusses current AI tools for software development, the limitations, risks, and strengths of AI in software development, as well as issues of bias, hallucinations, error injection and the juxtaposition of these risks versus productivity gain. The paper and its references together provide an introduction to the current state of AI for assisting with software engineering educators and researchers.

INTRODUCTION

Artificial Intelligence (AI) has been an essential component of computer science for many decades both in the research of the methods and techniques that enable artificial intelligence and in the creation of software that utilizes this research. Early AI work gained traction in the sixties with rule-based expert systems and from there the field of AI matured slowly through the eighties when AI algorithms succeeded in the development of software systems that could beat champion chess players.

DOI: 10.4018/979-8-2600-2811-7.ch005

Fast forward to 2022 when the generative AI Chatbot named ChatGPT (OpenAI, n.d.) was made publicly available (Ooi et al., 2025). Since 2022 the ability of AI systems to perform as increasingly insightful virtual assistants and AI agents has grown tremendously.

Current AI platforms, through the use of Deep Learning, Large Language Models and genetic algorithms, have harnessed the ability to process, model and understand massive data sets resulting in a flurry of interest in integrating AI within every field including industry and academia, all seeking the productivity increases it offers (Andrews & Crawford, 2025; Ooi et al., 2025). Hatzius (2023) predicted that wide scale generative AI adoption could increase global GDP by 7% and raise US labor productivity growth by 1.5 pp over a 10 year period; which translates to a 1.5 acceleration annually in the rate of output produced per hour, pointing to the possibility of a significantly higher standard of living and strong wage growth over these ten years.

In addition to productivity gains that may be seen with the use of AI, there has also been trepidation regarding the loss of jobs that could result from AI replacing human workers across nearly every industry. For example, McKinsey & Company (2018) predicted eight hundred million workers worldwide could lose their jobs due to AI by 2030, while a more recent and less staggering prediction by Hatzius (2023) suggests the number replaced would be three hundred million. However things are adjusting and early 2026 predictions are much less dire and are now predicting software employers are shifting workers into newer higher-value roles rather than downsizing, reflecting an increasing need for AI-savvy developers (Forbes Business Council, 2026; Forrester, 2025; Morgan Stanley, 2025; Morgan Stanley Research, 2026).

AI platforms, tools, and assistive agents currently exist that support the development and maintenance of software. Examples include tools such as OpenAI's (n.d.) ChatGPT and its GPT series, GitHub Copilot (n.d.), and Anthropic's (2026) Claude Code series to mention a few. Generative AI tools make use of Large Language Models (LLMs) that rely upon pattern recognition, machine learning, and natural language processing to enable artificial intelligence abilities. Recent improvements to these models have increasingly taking the form of the use of task specific AI agents working together to solve tasks in specialized domains (DiCuffa et al., 2025).

The end goal for the development and use of these agents is to increase productivity. For example, with respect to maintenance of software systems, an underlying LLM's pattern recognition ability helps with the identification of highly-cohesive and highly-coupled code snippets. This reduces the effort of manual identification of these code segments types. The machine learning techniques within the AI tool analyze the functionality of these snippets by comparison to code the LLM was trained on (Barenkamp et al., 2025). AI's pattern recognition ability is also used to identify sections of redundant code and refactor it, which is essentially rewriting the code without the redundancies, thereby improving code structure (Barenkamp et al., 2025). While generative and assistive AI is revolutionizing how developers approach coding and maintenance tasks, the use of AI for code generation has suffered from error insertion and security violations that often requires extensive error correction interaction by developers (Barenkamp et al., 2020; DiCuffa et al., 2025).

In the software development world, DevOPs is the set of practices, tools and philosophy that integrate and automate the process tasks associated with the software build, test and release phases used to develop, test and maintain software (Hemon-Hildgen & Rowe, 2022). The core principles and practices of the DevOPs philosophy is Continuous Integration and Continuous Delivery (CI/CD). Continuous Integration and Continuous Delivery refers to the development philosophy of regularly integrating new code segments into the system and deploying it into production as a continuous ongoing cycle rather than production of one large final build, test and deliver cycle. Generative AI tools that support CI/CD include Jenkins (Arbat, 2024) and GitHub Copilot (GitHub, n.d.). The integration of AI into DevOps practices has resulted in significant productivity improvements in the development of small-scale code in well-defined, well-known domains (Ghantous, 2024). Ghantous reported that use of AI-assisted software development environments have enhanced traditional development methods.

Indeed many of the prominent generative tools now assist in the areas of source code management, continuous integration/continuous delivery, automated testing, logging, monitoring, data analysis, communication, bug fixing, and automated deployment as this paper will discuss. AI assistance in such tasks were reported to have increased the efficiency of the management of source code from a score of 4 to 8 (Ghantous, 2024). Such increases stemming from automation of repetitive tasks and automation of coding solutions for well known problems. However, human software developers are not replaceable as automated code generation can be quite error-prone and falls short in the face of solving complex problems as will be discussed in coming sections.

The paper presents an overview of the use and ability of AI tools within the field of software engineering and reports the results of study and comparison of AI-assisted requirements engineering, coding and code reviews, testing and debugging, deployment and maintenance, and software project management as well as presents a discussion of the current limitations, risks, and strengths of these tools. The research was conducted by review of literature and associated analysis and comparison of AI tools. The reader is introduced to a set of current AI platforms used within Software Engineering in the following section to familiarize the reader with the major tools before proceeding to the main sections of the paper discussing the use of AI in the various main phases of software development, problems and limitations, risks, and strengths.

BACKGROUND

In this section, we present a group of AI platforms used to assist with one or more aspects of software development as a precursor to the discussion of the use of these tools to support specific tasks required of software development such as requirements engineering, coding, testing, maintenance and project management. Following this introduction of tools we will discuss these and others in the section Use of AI in Software Development.

Table 1 presents AI platforms used to support software development.

Table 1. AI platforms to assist with software development

Name	Software Development Support	Description
GitHub Copilot	Coding Phase	Microsoft's coding assistant tool. Provides real-time code suggestions, intelligent auto completion, and the ability to generate entire functions or substantial code snippets from natural language prompts (Alenezi & Akour, 2025; Barke et al., 2023; Nguyen & Nadi, 2022; Pandey et al., 2024; Peng et al., 2023; Vaithilingam et al., 2022).It integrates as an extension into Integrated Development Environments (IDEs) (Nguyen & Nadi, 2022).
GPT-4 / GPT-4o / GPT 5.2	Coding Phase	GPT-4o is Open AI's flagship Large Language Model designed to generate code from textual prompts. Generates code and is capable of refactoring existing code to improve readability and adherence to coding standards (Poldrack et al., 2023). Gpt-4o matches GPT-4 performance but is faster and better at vision and audio understand (Hurst et al., 2024). GPT 5.2 is OpenAI's flagship model for coding and agentic tasks (OpenAI platform, n.d.-a)
Jenkins	CI/CD	Open-source CI/CD tool that integrates with GitHub Copilot to assist with automated build, test and delivery.
DeepSeek-V2, DeepSeek-V3	Large range of applications	Open-source Mixture-of-Experts Large Language Model is particularly suited for applications in healthcare, finance and security since it incorporates real-time retrieval of information external to the model (Dandage, 2025; DeepSeek, 2026; Liu et al., 2024).
ChatGPT	General AI Chatbot / Code, Testing and others	OpenAI's Large Language Model based on GPT architecture, developed by Open AI. General AI chatbot used for a wide range of applications to generate content and text. Includes code generation and test generation ability.
AlphaCodium	Code Generation	AlphaCodium is used for code generation. GitHub repository is the source location for this tool. The tool reflects a move away from prompt-based methods to flow engineering. It continuously refines LLM-generated code against test cases, improving performance on complex coding problems by identifying and removing errors (Ridnik et al., 2024). Resides in GitHub.

continued on following page

Table 1. Continued

Name	Software Development Support	Description
Jenkins	Continuous Integration and Continuous Delivery support	Jenkins is fundamentally an automation engine for CI/CD tasks. Its primary function is to serve as an open-source automation server for continuous integration and continuous deployment in software development.
Claude, Claude 3.5 Sonnet, Claude Opus 4.6	Code Generation	Anthropic's Claude generates code snippets. Claude 3.5 advanced coding, rapid software prototyping, data visualization, and nuanced content generation
Gemini, Gemini 1.5 Pro	Coding, Testing	Gemini is a general AI model for everyday tasks, including software development. Gemini 1.5 Pro supports more advanced code generation, and code refactoring across multiple languages and assists with visual understanding of diagrams.
AutoCommenter	Code Documentation Google in house tool, not publicly available	Google's research tool to help developers adhere to best code practices for different programming languages, applies best practices across code changes (Vijayvergiya et al., 2024).

A summary description of these AI platforms from Table 1 is provided.

ChatGPT (OpenAi, n.d.) is a conversational chatbot developed by OpenAI. It excels at assistance with general purpose tasks. ChatGPT is the interface to the underlying models of GPT such as GPT 3.5, GPT 4, and GPT 4o. Both ChatGPT and GPT 4 are AI based models that use deep learning to understand natural language. They are two of the most advanced AI models that use cutting edge AI technology. GPT-4's ability exceeds, and is more versatile, than ChatGPT and GPT 3.5. ChatGPT supports software development by generating code snippets, explaining programming concepts, suggesting algorithms, and helping debug. It assists with writing documentation, creating unit tests, and brainstorming. Developers frequently use it for learning new languages or frameworks and for rapid prototyping of small scripts or functions.

GPT-4o (OpenAi, 2024) is OpenAI's flagship model powering advanced versions of ChatGPT. It processes and generates text, audio, images, and video in real time. It supports software development with superior reasoning, multimodal input including code and images and voice and fast response time. It claims to excel at complex debugging, architectural design discussions, generating comprehensive test suites, and producing production-ready code across languages (Hurst et al., 2024). Developers use it for code review simulations, explaining legacy systems, and creating detailed technical documentation or tutorials.

GPT-3.5 (OpenAI Platform, n.d.) is the earlier large language model family from OpenAI, powering the free version of ChatGPT. It is a single model LLM (text-only) whose primary function is to handle general conversational tasks, answer questions, summarize text, draft content, and assist with simple coding or reasoning. It serves as a cost-efficient, fast option for everyday AI assistance but lacks multimodal capabilities.

Gemini 1.5 Pro (Google, n.d.) is Google's conversational chatbot that assists with everyday tasks, especially those integrated with Google apps. It is Google's advanced multimodal model in the Gemini 1.5 family. It supports tasks like question answering, summarization, and multimodal understanding which processes text, code, images, audio, and video via deep reasoning over large datasets. It supports software development by analyzing documents, videos, and codebases as well as code generation, and code refactoring across multiple languages and assists with visual understanding of diagrams.

Jenkins (Jenkins Project, n.d.) is an open-source CI/CD tool used in software development. Its primary function is to automate building, testing, and deploying code changes through customizable pipelines. It integrates with version control systems and testing and deployment frameworks such as GitHub Copilot, supporting the delivery of software.

GitHub Copilot (GitHub, n.d.) is essentially an AI-powered coding assistant. Developed by GitHub in partnership with OpenAI, it integrates directly into IDEs such as VS Code and Visual Studio. Its primary function is to provide real-time code suggestions, auto completions, as well as generation of code blocks. As such, it helps developers write code, particularly boilerplate code, helps navigate unfamiliar languages or frameworks, which allows more focus upon problem-solving than syntax. It also assists with learning APIs, and converting comments to code, which can also reduce time spent on related repetitive tasks.

AutoCommenter (Vijayvergiya et al., 2024) is an internal Google tool for providing automated code reviews and enforcement of software best-practices such reviews strive for. It draws upon large language models during its automated review to generate comments and correction suggestions to meet a set of coding standards. It essentially assists software developers by identifying issues, suggesting improvements, and ensuring coding standards in large-scale codebases. It is not publicly available.

Claude 3.5 Sonnet (Anthropic, 2024) is Anthropic's mid-tier large language model in the Claude 3.5 family. It excels in reasoning, coding, and multimodal tasks consisting of text and images, for example. Its primary function is to provide support for complex tasks like writing, coding, data analysis, and workflows. Anthropic claims it is able to emphasize safety, provide nuanced understanding, and offers agentic capabilities such as code execution. Claude Opus 4.6 (Anthropic, 2026) is the flagship of the Claude family of models as of this writing. It offers significant improvements in handling larger code bases over previous versions, claiming to excel at code reviews and debugging, and offers a one million token context window enabling reasoning over extremely large inputs.

DeepSeek-V2 (DeepSeek, n.d.) is an open-source Mixture-of-Experts (MoE) large language model from DeepSeek-AI. Its primary function is to deliver strong performance in language understanding, reasoning, coding, and multilingual tasks at low cost. It claims to excel in efficiency and cost-effectiveness compared to dense models of similar size.

AlphaCodium (AlphaCodium, n.d.) is a research method/tool developed by CodiumAI for improving code generation by large language models. It represents a shift from traditional prompt engineering to "flow engineering" with an iterative, test-driven generation process. Its primary function is to generate more accurate, reliable, code solutions through iterations of test generation and associated code repair iteration (Ridnik et al., 2024). The official GitHub repository is the primary source for this tool.

These AI platforms and tools each assist with software development to varying degrees depending on the tool's specific ability. To assist with software development tasks, the underlying Large Language Models the platforms rely upon are pre-trained on massive datasets of programming code (Kokol, 2024; Poldrack et al., 2023). The Natural Language Processing ability of these tools play a crucial role by allowing developers to interact with these tools using natural language prompts to articulate their coding requirements to obtain the desired output.

The tools' ability to understand context is important since the tools' ability to effectively generate code aligns with the context and prompt instructions (Negri-Ribalta et al., 2024; Poldrack et al., 2023). Currently, being able to prompt a given tool with clearly written and precisely structured prompts is important for guiding these tools to produce optimal generated results (Medepalli, 2025). For example, effectively utilizing a LLM, such as those in the GPT series, has been determined to be dependent upon precise prompting (DiCuffa et al., 2025; Ridnik et al., 2024). These prompts are natural language prompts that specify what is required of the model. A series of structured well-defined prompts can lead to significant improvements in performance over poorly specified prompts.

Recently, LLMs such as GPT-4 have shown marked improvement over previous LLMs in assisting with the software development tasks such as unit testing (Koubaa, 2023; Mao et al., 2024; Yuan et al., 2024). However current LLM coding and testing models are by no means perfect as they remain unable to produce error-free automated testing and code generation due to hallucinations and error injection (Sabo, et al., 2025; Yuan et al., 2024).

USE OF AI IN SOFTWARE DEVELOPMENT

This section presents how AI is being used to assist with the major software life cycle tasks common to software development. These tasks include requirements engineering, coding, testing, deployment, maintenance as well as the task of management of these tasks. Each of these, and the use of AI to support them, follows in a subsection specific to the various aforementioned tasks.

AI Within Requirements Engineering

Requirements engineering is the phase of software engineering which determines the system modules and requirements of a needed system. It defines what the system is to do. Early AI techniques were used to support the traceability of requirements. Having requirements that are traceable means requirements are specified in such a way that systems goals can be mapped, traced, to requirements that meet those goals as well as mapped to downstream products such as design, tests and code segments. Early tools to assist with these tasks resulted in improved accuracy in linking requirements to the other software artifacts (Cheng et al., 2025). Cheng et al. conducted a survey of requirements engineering tools, the results of which reported that 67% of the efforts of AI in requirement engineering were assistive efforts stemming from the use of ChatGPT.

This suggests that ChatGPT is one of the more frequently used tools to assist with the requirements engineering tasks, particularly with support for requirements elicitation. Requirements elicitation is the task that determines the set of user requirements for a system. The elicitation task is followed by the requirements analysis task where requirements are analyzed with respect to requirements completeness, consistency, verification, priority, classification, risk, and ambiguities found and corrections made. AI assistance to each of these tasks can reduce the effort required.

The of AI to assist with requirements engineering has been illustrated by tools that assist in capturing domain concepts within a requirements description (Arulmohan et al., 2023; Vahabi & Hozhabri, 2024), in finding traceability links within a requirements description (Wang et al., 2023), in the classification of requirements into categories and priorities(Alhoshan et al., 2023; Apte et al., 2023; Hey et al., 2020) and in the assistance with requirement elicitation (Apte et al., 2023; Calle Gallego et al., 2023; Cheng et al., 2025;) and with extraction of features, goals and domain models (Ezzini et al., 2021; Wang et al., 2023). This ability of AI tools to assist with requirements engineering relies on natural language processing, reasoning power and training data of an underlying large language model (Ezzini et al., 2021; Wang et al., 2023).

Despite the flurry of AI tools to assist humans in requirements engineering related tasks, including those tools in Table 1, current tools have not yet risen to a level of automation that can totally remove manual effort from the requirements engineering task. This is supported by an extensive survey of AI in Requirements Engineering by Cheng et al. (2025) that reported 90.3% of studies of AI within Requirements Engineering were conceptual or vision studies, 8.4% were experimental and only 1.3% were production level; suggesting reliable fully generative AI solutions for Requirements Engineering are not yet available.

AI in Coding and Code Reviews

GitHub Copilot is a prominent code generation tool powered by an ultra-large language model. Vaithilingam et al. (2022) performed a study of GitHub Copilot and concluded that Copilot did not reduce the task completion time nor increase the success rate of solving programming tasks in a real world setting due to the errors it created in the generated code. These inserted errors required the developers to read and debug the code (Vaithilingam et al., 2022) negating time saved by generating code. However, participants in the GitHub Copilot study still reported preferring using Copilot in their programming workflows because it eliminated repetitive tasks associated with testing and debugging and helped with project planning (Vaithilingam et al., 2022).

The performance of three prominent LLMs, Claude 3.5 Sonnet, Gemini 1.5 Pro and ChatGPT 3.5, was evaluated by Sabo et al. (2025). Sabo reported Claude 3.5 Sonnet to score a 95% success rate in generating accurate and efficient code for an abstract robot class. This demonstrated potential for increased performance and accuracy over past LLMS used for prototype generation. Much lower scores were reported to be earned by Gemini 1.5 Pro and ChatGPT 3.5. This difference in performance among these three platforms was seen by Sabo as highlighting the complexity of the task of generating precise, error-free code and the need for improvement overall (Sabo, et al., 2025). The 95% success rate of Claude 3.5 Sonnet suggests that code generation can be effective in limited cases for well understood domains, such as code for an abstract robot class implementation, while the lower scoring platforms suggest code generation in general is not yet effective.

To determine the value of AI code generators, a study by Yetiştiren et al. (2023) was undertaken to assess the quality of code generated by GitHub Copilot, Amazon CodeWhisperer and ChatGPT. This study reported that these tools generated correct code 65.2%, 46.3%, and 31.1% of the time, respectively. The study concluded ChatGPT to be the most successful and surmised that providing a clear and accurate problem description was essential. This leaves error rates of 34.8, 68.9 and 68.9, which are quite high. Ramler et al. (2024) concluded from interviews conducted from five software developers regarding AI assistance, that ChatGPT and Copilot were useful for many code-related tasks but the support for the software development workflow in general was shallow.

Since errors are have been demonstrated to be injected by AI code generation platforms, humans are still essential in the coding process and code reviews are taking on increasing importance. Manual code reviews involve human code readers who look for logic errors in code and review code documentation. Code reviews take place when code is being written and after major modifications, the frequency of these is dependent on the project management process being followed. As part of a manual coding process, documentation is added to code, and improved during code reviews, to explain the code segment functionality in natural language comments.

AI tools assist with the task of code documentation. These tools work by scanning the code and auto generating coding comments. One such tool is Google's internal tool AutoCommenter (Vijayvergiya et al., 2024) which generates comments in code based on coding standards for comment formation. These standards applied by an AI will reflect the documentation and coding style guides the LLM was trained on including standards for things such as line limits, use of white space, code formatting and structure, parenthesis, brackets, use of code idioms to improve clarity, code structure modularity and maintainability, and naming standards such as capitalization and descriptiveness.

The code review process used at Google is described by Vijayvergiya et al. (2024) as a well-established process that is labor intensive and time consuming; thus, automation of the process would be significant. Vijayvergiya et al. (2024) describes the development, deployment and evaluation of AutoCommenter, an LLM-backed code-review tool for automating much of the code review process that currently used by Google. The results of an evaluation of AutoCommenter by Vijayvergiya et al. (2024) revealed its auto documentation and code review capabilities exceeded those of traditional static code analysis tools such as linters, as well as displayed a high level of precision and demonstrated a high degree of end-user acceptance.

AI in Testing and Debugging

Some of the more successful functions of AI-assisted software development are those that assist in the testing and debugging phase of Software Engineering which demonstrated varying levels of effectiveness at repairing both human generated code and AI generated code (Gu et al., 2024). TestART, RepairAgent and Testim are AI methods described by Gu et al., (2024) that have been used to automate the testing process by generating test cases and by changing test case assertions based on changes to the code ensuring the tests generated reflect any code changes made. This reduced the effort of developers in the testing and maintenance phases of software development. TestART works by scaning source code and generating test cases to test the scanned code, then compiles and executes the test cases. It then uses the test case output to determine why the tests failed as a prompt to an LLM which iteratively refactors the code and performs retests until a satisfactory solution is found. This type of automation can dramatically reduce the time spent on testing (Gu et al., 2024).

Bouzenia et al. (2024), in their study on AI effectiveness at supporting testing, found that test generation and code repair tools have varying levels of accuracy and often produce complicated solutions to simple problems. One problem reported was that coding solutions an AI platform generates can be non-deterministic (Bouzenia et al., 2024); meaning that the same input can lead to different outputs. This can result in different solutions for the same input so that the solution is non-repeatable. However, the results of this study by Bouzenia et al. (2024) were based on the use of GPT3.5 and the later version, GPT-4, is a much-improved version of GPT in both correctness and efficiency of solution output (Koubbaa, 2023). For instance, GPT-4 is reported by Koubaa (2023) to have a significantly higher accuracy than previous versions of GPT, better reasoning capability, and significantly less hallucination making it more reliable than version 3.5. There are newer improved versions of GPT being released as of this writing, as is the case of most AI platforms.

AI in Deployment and Maintenance

AI use within the deployment and maintenance phase of software engineering targets helping development teams provide faster delivery of software. AI powered tools can help streamline deployment workflows and reduce issues that arise from human error. For example, tools like GitLab's Auto DevOps can automate code analysis, test case generation and execution, and anomaly detection (Ghantous, 2024). Microsoft's (n.d.) Azure DevOps is an AI assisted tool that can help facilitate managing and developing applications in the Azure development environment. These tools provide support for quicker troubleshooting during deployment and maintenance.

AI in Software Project Management

Software Project Management is the process followed to plan and manage the software life cycle activities that direct the development of a software project from its inception to its delivery and maintenance. There arc many software development process models, but any one model will fall into the category of a highly planned waterfall type model or a highly iterative agile model or somewhere in between. The exact steps required of the process will depend on the process model followed. This will depend on the nature of the product. For example, a rigid documentation-heavy project management process would typically be used to manage a strict waterfall development process model. The waterfall model is typically followed for life critical software projects whereas many business applications use a more flexible, documentation-light, agile process and thus require a management process that reflects the agile process. The project management steps of any of these processes can be well supported by AI assistive software. As such, AI platforms for project management exist to aid in these tasks. Bieliajey (2025) characterizes the use of AI in project management as follows:

> *The use of AI in project management has significantly transformed traditional approaches to planning, controlling, and implementing tasks. Its implementation has automated routine operations, improved the accuracy of risk forecasting, allocated resources more efficiently, and adapted to changing conditions. This minimized the impact of the human factor, accelerated decision-making, and increased the overall efficiency of project activities. As a result, AI has become not only an auxiliary tool but also a key factor in the transformation of modern project management. (p. 64)*

Bielieajev's (2025) review of AI to assist with project management concluded that such assistance typically includes support for tasks such as automation of task timelines, schedule creation, task selection, sprint reviews, scrum meeting results, and task completion tracking. AI has demonstrated significant potential in enhancing agility, efficiency, and overall project success within agile project management (Zadeh et al., 2023). In general, the current selection of AI tools for software project management is ample. General Chatbot assistants such as ChatGPT and Gemini have been used extensively to support project management. Airtable's ProductCentral, ChapGPT and Gemini have been ranked among the top three AI project management tools (Airtable, n.d.). In addition to general Chatbot tools, there are also specialized project management AI tools. Some of these are:

ClickUp AI Assistant. ClickUp (ClickUp, n.d.-a*)* is an AI platform that was designed to connect project documents and people. It is an AI heavy platform which asks questions about your project, auto generates tasks and subtasks, writes and updates project status reports, suggests priorities, and can summarize conversation threads. It provides customizable fields, whiteboards, and integration with GitHub and other similar DevOPs platforms. The platform has been praised on various projenct management blogs for the depth of features provided as well as the value provided. ClickUp (n.d.-c) provides a 'What is ClickUp' article that describes the features of its AI project management.

Asana. Asana (2026b) provides an AI driven smart editor, productivity recommendations, progress summaries, and workflow automation suggestions. It is touted as good for teams who need status reporting without the burden of heavy configuration of the system (Asana, 2026a). Some of its core features include those described by Asana (2026c) as 'smart status', 'smart fields', 'smart summaries', 'smart rule creator' and 'smart goals'.

Jira. Jira (Atlassian, 2026) can be used for pure software project management especially agile project management, along with the use of DevOps. Jira visualizes Scrum processes and Kanban boards and uses AI to help with task prioritization, summarizing work, and activity tracking (Pangan, 2026). It can automate routine actions within project management tasks. It uses deep integration to link code activity such as commits, branches, and pull requests to project tasks in real time which allows team members to easily track progress.

Wrike. Wrike (n.d.-d) is an AI-based tool to support risk management which is highly integrated with Microsoft 365. Its features include predicting project delays, issuing early alerts, and action recommendations surrounding project tasks. It describes itself as being good for predicting project risks, spotting bottlenecks, suggesting resource adjustments, and automating status updates. It provides risk-based project management assistance via task scheduling, risk identification, risk prioritization, and more (Wrike, n.d.-a, -b, -c). Wrike claims to be good for teams that need workload views and good reporting with Wrike Copilot being able to interact with Microsoft Copilot, Claude and Google Gemini.

monday. monday.com (n.d.) is an AI driven project management tool that can be accessed at Monday.com. Monday supports project workflow setup and management. It makes use of visual boards that can illustrate workflows, summarize updates, and predict project and task timelines. It has been praised for being good with project tracking within sprints. Mondays AI workflow support including automation, progress visualization, progress predictions and more (O'Connor, 2025).

Other project management tools include Notion (Nation, n.d.), Motion (Motion, n.d.), and Teamwork (Teamwork, n.d.).

PROBLEMS AND LIMITATIONS WITH AI

While AI has contributed vastly to the improvement and automation of tasks associated with software development there exist problems with inaccuracies stemming from bias, hallucinations, lack of deep reasoning and understanding ability in novel or new domains. Such problems can result in security risks, loss of productivity, as well as loss of innovation and creativity. Each of these issues are discussed in turn in the following subsections of this section.

Biases and Hallucinations

Current AI models have been shown to reflect biases and incorrect information in producing solutions (Mao et al., 2024). Biases occur because they are embedded within the training data that is used to train the underlying LLM. Biases typically result in output that is incorrect because they reflect a subjective one-sided view of a problem and its solutions; a view that may be false or that ignores important facts that should be considered. Another concerning phenomenon of AI is hallucinations: a hallucination means the LLM may generate output that is incorrect but sounds plausible (Ooi et al., 2025). Hallucinations can reflect inaccurate, subjective, or missing training data that the tools generate output from. AI tools have been known to make up goals and requirements to justify the Hallucinations. Future work on AI is needed that can remove hallucination or at least recognize the faulty reasoning and flag the output. As for biased output, AI tools need to be able to recognize biased solutions and resolve or remove it or at least warn that bias exists in the case of a solution generated based on bias. However, detection and removal of bias is a non-trivial problem as it relies on the resolution of what has already been noted earlier in this paper as a foundational limitation of AI: a lack of understanding of constraints and lack of deep reasoning ability. Deep reasoning is hindered in the face of biased training models as this automatically limits analysis of a problem from all sides and in the context of the problem.

Intellectual Property & Privacy

AI's underlying LLMs are trained on billions of sets of data gleaned from across the internet. There is an ever-increasing array of AI Tools for everyday tasks which scan and collect data reflecting intellectual property during their use. The LLMs and resulting AI Tools are fundamentally based on harvesting the products produced by millions of individuals and companies; products that have long been treated as protected intellectual property but are now fodder to be collected and used as data to train AI systems. This is pervasive across all domains such as music, art, literature, science, and software engineering. This has resulted in copyright infringement cases that highlight the use of copyrighted content without attribution or license and has raised privacy concerns and legal challenges (Maini, et al., 2024). In addition, tools such as ChatGPT can involve the collection and integration of public and private data such that private financial data may be exposed or movement tracking collected without informed consent (Ooi et al., 2025).

Lack of Deep Reasoning and Understanding

Current AI struggles with understanding constraints and the associated deep logical reasoning needed for problem solving, especially tasks that require tradeoffs, and can result in generating code that reflects inaccuracies and hallucinations. AI failed at understanding basic logic tasks even when the solutions existed and sometimes provided nonsensical justifications for its decisions (Valmeekam et al., 2024). Vaithilingam et al. (2022) reports that most generated code results in less than 30% accuracy, though well-designed prompts may improve this rate somewhat (Ridnick et al., 2024). . Gu et al. (2024) and Pandey et al. (2024) assert that the limitations to AI-generated code exhibits with code that is full of inaccuracies, erroneous output, and hallucinations. Hallucination is the term used to express the phenomenon where the AI fabricates requirements or presents wrong information as fact, and as a result, produces non-sensical output. In software, this can result in the AI generating creating code that executes, but that ignores the reality of the actual requirements of the system. The fact that runnable code is generated quickly can create the illusion of an increase in the velocity of output, but if the system does not meet the actual requirements, maintenance will be heavy and costly and velocity tanks. These issues of inaccuracies and hallucinations support the observation that current generative AI lacks in deep reasoning and understanding of solutions to problems particularly complex problems. This is further illustrated by its tendency to generate unnecessarily complex code, even for simple tasks and its inability to deal effectively with legacy cod as discussed below.

Generates Unnecessarily Complex Code

Using AI to generate code is typically characterized by large blocks of difficult to understand and difficult to debug code: code that is essentially overly complex from what a human coder would produce (Vaithilingam et al., 2022). Vaithilingam observed this can occur even when the solution can be quite simple, demonstrating a tendency for over complexity. However, when LLMs are directed to divide generated code into an iteration of smaller functions or segments, rather than a comprehensive solution, the error rate is reduced. (Ridnik et el., 2024).

AIs tendency to produce unnecessarily complex code demonstrates the LLMs lack of understanding and deep reasoning ability as well as trouble understanding the context of a non-trivial problem; that it truly is not yet "intelligent" and is pattern matching and copying past solutions and creating wrong or hallucinated solutions in the face of uncertainty and complexity. This complexity combined with its errors can lead to frustration and wasted correction and rework time for developers.

Lacking Ability to Deal With Legacy Code

AI struggles with being able to modify, correct, improve, or scale up existing legacy code in large code bases due to the high complexity of this code stemming from intricate dependencies present, lack of patterns in the code, and domain specific logic embedding in millions of lines of code. Current AI models struggle with understanding this type of complex code. As such, the code reviews and prompting required of the human to guide and correct AI code output when dealing with legacy code can negate the use of the AI. This assessment is supported by the productivity study by Becker et al., (2025) which took place as a controlled trial on experienced developers using AI tools to work on legacy code over one million lines and over 10 years old where developers took 19% longer to complete tasks when using the AI.

Generates Code with Security Vulnerability

Cybersecurity vulnerabilities of AI generated code have been highlighted by Medepalli (2025), Vaithilingam et al. (2022), Negri-Ribalta et al., (2024) and others. Vaithilingam et al. (2022) reported that AI generated code can be prone to generating insecure code. This requires the generated code to be analyzed for detection of security issues and these issues fixed by human intervention which can result in no productivity improvement from the auto generation. The level of security vulnerability in generated code can vary wildly depending on the language. For example, generated C code was less secure than Python generated code, while Verilog was the worst in security quality (Negri-Ribalta et al., 2024). Neural networks, another type of AI approach, has been successfully used to identify patterns in code that reflect security attack patterns, thus providing an approach to possibly improve identifying security issues in generated code (Barenkamp et al., 2020).

Lack of Innovation and Creativity

AI fundamentally operates by relying on what has been done already. It does not create new and novel software solutions since it relies heavily on repetition of what has been done before (Becker et al., 2025). If a similar well-known and well-understood problem has been solved before, it can assist with the repetition of that solution or slight variants, but creating new solutions to novel software problems is currently out of reach.

The limitations currently associated with generative AI solutions such as insertion of security vulnerabilities, bias, hallucinations and a tendency for error and over complexity of solutions highlight that human involvement and oversight in the use of AI to assist with software development remains essential for software developments tasks beyond simple repetitive tasks. It also highlights the limitations of the current Large Language Modules behind these tools.

RISKS ASSOCIATED WITH USE OF AI IN SOFTWARE ENGINEERING

The risks associated with the use of AI to assist with software engineering are primarily associated with tasks that involve the generation of code. These risks include a loss of productivity, rather than gain, skill atrophy, and a reduction in the ability of engineers to produce innovative solutions. Each of these risks are a byproduct of over reliance on AI. Another is the risk of end user mistrust of using AI-backed software due to fear of privacy violations and security concerns. Developer trust can become eroded also in the fact of constant error injections with require extensive manual rework. Each of these is discussed in this section.

Loss of Productivity From Over-Reliance

The errors and complexity in code introduced by AI can negate the time savings gained as the finding, understanding and correcting requires human intervention which can take longer than if the AI tool had not been used (Vaithilingam et al., 2022). In short, AI generated code suffers from being error prone (Vaithilingam et al., 2022) and such errors can negate time savings gained from the use of AI (Bouzenia et al., 2024). This loss of productivity occurs when using AI to solve more complex large problems. Over time, continued use of AI with an increased use of generated code could result in the production of large amounts of hard-to-understand code which can dominate developer's time in analyzing, checking and correcting code. This overreliance on generative AI for coding can result in large amounts of hard-to-understand code which in turn results in more time spent analyzing, checking, and correcting than writing.

These limitations and risks are tied to using AI to generating code that is does not truly understand. In smaller, well-defined domains, the generation process can be more accurate. Despite these limitations AI has proven valuable in the assistance of software engineers with the many mundane and repetitive tasks associated with software development tasks throughout the software life cycle as well as with software project management tasks. The future holds promise for the development of better tools with hopefully more complex problem-solving skills, no errors, no hallucinations and no security vulnerably.

Skill Atrophy From Over Reliance

Skill Atrophy is a byproduct of over reliance. Over reliance on AI by junior software engineers to generate code or to automate tasks such a testing and debugging can erode the domain knowledge that is gained by the honing of the foundational programming and problem-solving skills imparted by the practice of manual coding, testing, and debugging. Skills that are learned by doing and that provide the foundation for the deep reasoning and problem-solving skills required to solve more complex problems that AI systems are not able to solve. Such acquired domain knowledge is only obtained through manual practice over years. Junior software engineers deprived of such experience will not progress to the level of expert. The risk over time is a loss of high performing engineers who can detect and correct the inaccuracies and hallucinations currently inherent in AI code generation within complex problem domains. A significant risk.

Reduced Innovation From Overreliance

A reduction in the ability of engineers to produce innovative solutions is also a byproduct of an engineer's overreliance on the use of AI to generate a solution. Creativity is not the mainstay of AI generative systems since they are based on solving problems based on past solutions not design for creative software solutions to novel problems. Thus, overuse of AI, with its inherent reliance on the use of past solutions, can lead to a significant reduction in producing innovative and better solutions to both old and new problems. This can be mitigated by ensuring AI workflows are human-AI hybrids with experienced human engineers interacting in the workflow to actively monitor, correct, advance and improve all output and to direct creativity.

Mistrust of Software Resulting From Data Breach Exposure

Security risks arise from data leaks stemming from an LLMs capture and use of training data from protected and private sources. This harvested data can expose government, industry and private organizations and persons to risks of exposure of many types of protected data: financial, medical, political, educational, military and so forth. Certainly, the possibility of such breach and misuse is of significant concern. A level of mistrust by users of AI surrounding this concern is seen as prudent. Examples include data breaches due to AI embedded in the use of software such as the 2026 breech alerts related to Gmail and Microsoft Autopilot. News of these types of breaches affect an end users trust of software embedded with AI. A software developers trust in AI to generate correct code can suffer from errors injected by AI software development tools since such errors negate the time savings gained sometimes to the extent all times savings is lost in the extensive correction required (Bouzenia et al., 2024). Due to the risk of error injection, and to the still maturing nature of the AI field, the software industry currently tends towards use of AI for partial code or function generation, not whole systems (Bouzenia et al., 2024). Small code segments of less complex code requiring simple logic is better handled by AI with better precision. However, this is expected to improve as the ability of AI continues to improve at an extremely fast rate.

STRENGTHS OF AI IN SOFTWARE DEVELOPMENT

Productivity Gains

Gains reported in productivity from the use of AI in software development have been attributed to its ability to reuse boilerplate code and to identity repeatable patterns in code that can take human much longer to locate (Cui et al., 2025). Gains have also been seen in the increased productivity of less experienced developers. This was attributed to the use of AI to assist with learning new programming languages and new software development frameworks. With AI's ability to refactor code to improve it for maintainability, gains in production have been seen in well-known application domains. Overall, the tasks involved in the coding and testing phase of software development have seen the largest productivity gains from the use of AI in software development. GitHub claims that the use of Copilot showed developers completed tasks 20-55% faster on average on simple tasks (Peng et al., 2023). MIT Microsoft Accenture found that a 27-39% increase in coding output for junior developers and only 8-13% increase for senior developers (Cui et al., 2025). A controlled experiment on the productivity impact of GitHub Copilot found developers often completing tasks faster such as speed gains in the ranges of 20–55% gains in simpler setups, with gains varying by task (Peng et al., 2023). Interestingly, Becker et al. (2025) reported on a randomized controlled trial on experienced developers working on their own mature open-source repositories using 2025 era AI tools which found, despite developers believing the tools made them ~20% faster, that the use of AI made them 19% slower overall on task completion. This actual loss in productivity was attributed to over-trust in the tools, correction overhead, and complexity of legacy code. This suggests the most productivity gains are seen in low complexity work in routine or entry level tasks for junior developers. The strength of AI, especially Agentic-AI is evolving rapidly and becoming more accurate and efficient (Dandage, 2025; Rahman et al., 2025).

Automation of Repetitive Mundane Tasks

AI excels at the automation of repetitive tasks. Certainly, the automation of repetitive mundane tasks contributes substantially to the advantages of using AI to assist in the development of software.

Users Learn New Solutions and New Environments Quickly

The LLMs behind GitHub CoPilot, DeekSeek and similar tools are trained and learn on software repositories with billions of lines of open-source code. From the mined training data, the models learn common solutions, best practices, and project structure such as how to set up a Spring Boot service or handle authentication in Node.js or other such coding tasks (Cui et al., 2025). Using an LLM such as GitHub CoPilot that understands common solutions to coding problems can provide the user of the tool with the ability to learn common solutions faster and can assist with leaning how to use new software environments. This in effect turns the AI into a type of programming partner that has read and understands similar code which can lead to higher productivity, especially for junior developers.

CONCLUSION

AI is touted as being transformative to coding and fundamentally altering traditional software development techniques and workflows (Alenezi & Akour, 2025). AI code generation tools such as GitHub Copilot and GPT-4 and testing tools such as TestART and RepairAgent and Code Review Assistants such as AutoCommenter have demonstrated significant benefits in enhancing developer productivity by automating repetitive tasks associated with coding and testing, assisting with regression testing and library function use (Alenezi & Akour, 2025; Bouzenia et al., 2024; Gu et al., 2023) and code reviews (Vijayvergiya et al., 2024). While AI can assist junior developers in following software practices AI platforms cannot currently generate creative or innovation solutions to new and novel problems, such remains the purview of software engineers (Barenkamp et al., 2020).

AI generative tools have demonstrated a tendency to generate code that is error prone, rife with hallucinations and overly complex (Gu et al., 2024; Pandey et al., 2024); problems that are time intensive for developers to resolve. However, this problem is greatly reduced if the AI is limited to the generation of small sets of simple well know solutions (Ridnik et el. 2024). Thus, generated code has proved most successful for solving small scale simple coding problems while large scale complex problem solving is still very much in need of a human software engineer.

Another challenge is that generated code can inject security vulnerabilities; vulnerabilities which will require detection and removal by software engineers (Jarrahi et al., 2023; Medepalli, 2025). A concerning problem with AI use is the tendency of junior developers to over rely on AI which can result in a false sense of understanding how to program and problem solve. Such over reliance can result in a loss of fundamental programming skill and critical problem solving skills necessary for growth from novice to expert software engineer.

FUTURE DIRECTIONS

AI within software engineering will continue to expand relative to the improvement of the accuracy of code generation and removal of hallucinations, bias, and security vulnerabilities. In addition, improvement in the scope of LLMs deep reasoning, context understanding, constraint handling and associated improvement in ability to perform complex design tasks will continue to provide every increasing gains in the ability of AI to produce complex high quality code. Current AI systems are evolving rapidly and are expected to become much more accurate and efficient especially with the development of small domain-specific agentic models that can operate with high performance, high efficiency and accuracy. Certainly, academic programs will need to teach students to be able to use and apply AI in software development, as well in most other industry areas, as the market now demands those who are competitive and competent in AI.

REFERENCES

Airtable. (n.d.). *Best AI tools for product managers.* https://www.airtable.com/articles/best-ai-tools-for-product-managers

Alenezi, M., & Akour, M. (2025). AI-driven innovations in software engineering: A review of current practices and future directions. *Applied Sciences (Basel, Switzerland), 15*(3), 1344. Advance online publication. DOI: 10.3390/app15031344

Alhoshan, W., Ferrari, A., & Zhao, L. (2023). Zero-shot learning for requirements classification: An exploratory study. *Information and Software Technology, 159,* 107202. DOI: 10.1016/j.infsof.2023.107202

AlphaCodium. (n.d.). *AlphaCodium: From prompt engineering to flow engineering.* GitHub. https://github.com/Codium-ai/AlphaCodium

Andrews, S. K., & Crawford, C. M. (2025). Higher Education Instructor Perceptions of Student Experience Through Artificial Intelligence Agents: Shift From Information Age to the Reasoning Age. In M*otivating Engagement, Belonging, and Success in Higher Education Student Experience* (pp. 305-330). IGI Global Scientific Publishing.

Anthropic. (2024, June 21). *Claude 3.5 Sonnet.* https://www.anthropic.com/news/claude-3-5-sonnet

Anthropic. (2026). *Claude Opus 4.6.* https://www.anthropic.com/claude/opus

Apte, S., Honrao, Y., Shinde, R., Talele, P., & Phalnikar, R. (2023, April). Automatic Extraction of Software Requirements Using Machine Learning. In *International Conference on Information and Communication Technology for Intelligent Systems* (pp. 361-370). Singapore: Springer Nature Singapore. DOI: 10.1007/978-981-99-3758-5_33

Arbat, R. P. (2024). Exploring the effectiveness of Jenkins CI/CD pipelines: A comprehensive survey. *Journal of Emerging Technologies and Innovative Research, 11*(2), 590–595. https://www.jetir.org/papers/JETIR2402090.pdf

Arulmohan, S., Meurs, M. J., & Mosser, S. (2023, October). Extracting domain models from textual requirements in the era of large language models. In 2023 ACM/IEEE International Conference on Model Driven Engineering Languages and Systems Companion (MODELS-C) (pp. 580-587). IEEE. DOI: 10.1109/MODELS-C59198.2023.00096

Asana Inc. (2026a). Human + AI collaboration that moves work forward. https://asana.com/product/ai

Asana Inc. (2026b). For Developers and Teams. https://asana.com/developers

Asana Inc. (2026c). *Get started with Asana AI.* https://help.asana.com/s/article/get-started-with-asana-ai

Atlassian. (2026). *Jira.* https://www.atlassian.com/software/jira

Barenkamp, M., Rebstadt, J., & Thomas, O. (2020). Applications of AI in classical software engineering. *AI Perspectives*, *2*(1), 1. Advance online publication. DOI: 10.1186/s42467-020-00005-4

Barke, S., James, M. B., & Polikarpova, N. (2023). Grounded Copilot: How Programmers Interact with Code-Generating Models. *Proceedings of the ACM on Programming Languages, 7* (OOPSLA1), 85–111. DOI: 10.1145/3586030

Becker, J., Rush, N., Barnes, E., & Rein, D. (2025). Measuring the impact of early-2025 AI on experienced open-source developer productivity *arXiv preprint arXiv:2507.09089.* https://doi.org//arXiv.2507.09089DOI: 10.48550

Bieliaiev, O. (2025). Overview of artificial intelligence-based project management tools for business representatives. *Development Management*, *24*(3), 57–67. DOI: 10.63341/devt/3.2025.57

Bouzenia, I., Devanbu, P., & Pradel, M. (2024). *RepairAgent: An autonomous, LLM-based agent for program repair* (arXiv No. 2403.17134). arXiv. https://doi.org//arXiv.2403.17134DOI: 10.48550

Calle Gallego, J. M., & Zapata Jaramillo, C. M. (2023). QUARE: Towards a question-answering model for requirements elicitation. *Automated Software Engineering*, *30*(2), 25. DOI: 10.1007/s10515-023-00386-w

Cheng, H., Husen, J. H., Lu, Y., Racharak, T., Yoshioka, N., Ubayashi, N., & Washizaki, H. (2025). Generative AI for requirements engineering: A systematic literature review. *Software, Practice & Experience*, *56*(2), 141–170. DOI: 10.1002/spe.70029

ClickUp. (n.d.-a). *ClickUp Brain.* https://clickup.com/brain

ClickUp. (n.d.-c). *What is ClickUp AI?* https://help.clickup.com/hc/en-us/articles/12578085238039-What-is-ClickUp-AI

Cui, Z., Demirer, M., Jaffe, S., Musolff, L., Peng, S., & Salz, T. (2025). *The effects of generative AI on high-skilled work: Evidence from three field experiments with software developers.* Microsoft Research. https://www.microsoft.com/en-us/research/publication/the-effects-of-generative-ai-on-high-skilled-work-evidence-from-three-field-experiments-with-software-developers

Dandage, R. V. (2025). A Comparative Analysis of ChatGPT and DeepSeek: Capabilities, Applications, and Future Directions ChatGPT &DeepSeek. [IJISRT]. *International Journal of Innovative Science and Research Technology, 10*(2), 207–211. DOI: 10.5281/zenodo.14899162

DeepSeek. (2026). *Deepseek Into the unknown.* https://www.deepseek.com/en/

DiCuffa, S., Zambrana, A., Yadav, P., Madiraju, S., Suman, K., & AlOmar, E. A. (2025). *Exploring prompt patterns in AI-assisted code generation: Towards faster and more effective developer-AI collaboration* (arXiv No. 2506.01604). arXiv. / arXiv.2506.01604DOI: 10.1109/ICMI65310.2025.11141320

Ezzini, S., Abualhaija, S., Arora, C., Sabetzadeh, M., & Briand, L. C. (2021). Using domain-specific corpora for improved handling of ambiguity in requirements. In *2021 IEEE/ACM 43rd International Conference on Software Engineering* (ICSE) (pp. 1485–1497). IEEE. DOI: 10.1109/ICSE43902.2021.00133

Forbes Business Council. (2026, March 18). *As AI coding boosts productivity, is cutting software budgets smart or risky?* https://www.forbes.com/councils/forbesbusinesscouncil/2026/03/18/as-ai-coding-boosts-productivity-is-cutting-software-budgets-smart-or-risky/

Forrester. (2025, November 11). *AI is rewriting software work: What it means for your team.* https://www.forrester.com/blogs/ai-is-rewriting-software-work-what-it-means-for-your-team/

Ghantous, G. B. (2024, January). Enhancing devops using ai. In *CEUR Workshop Proceedings.* CEUR-WS.

GitHub. (n.d.). GitHub Copilot. https://github.com/features/copilot

Google. (n.d.). *Gemini 1.5 Pro.* https://ai.google.dev/gemini-api/docs/models

Gu, S., Fang, C., Zhang, Q., Tian, F., Zhou, J., & Chen, Z. (2024). *Improving LLM-based unit test generation via template-based repair* (arXiv No. 2408.03095). arXiv. https://doi.org//arXiv.2408.03095DOI: 10.48550

Hatzius, J. (2023). The potentially large effects of artificial intelligence on economic growth (briggs/kodnani). *Goldman Sachs, 1*(5), 268–296.

Hemon-Hildgen, A., & Rowe, F. (2022). Conceptualising and defining DevOps: A review for understanding, not a framework for practitioners. *European Journal of Information Systems*, *31*(5), 568–574. DOI: 10.1080/0960085X.2022.2100061

Hey, T., Keim, J., Koziolek, A., & Tichy, W. F. (2020, August). Norbert: Transfer learning for requirements classification. In *2020 IEEE 28th international requirements engineering conference (RE)* (pp. 169-179). IEEE.

Hurst, A., Lerer, A., Goucher, A. P., Perelman, A., Ramesh, A., Clark, A., . . . Kivlichan, I. (2024). Gpt-4o system card. *arXiv preprint arXiv:2410.21276.*

Jarrahi, M. H., Lutz, C., Boyd, K., Østerlund, C., & Willis, M. (2023). Artificial intelligence in the work context. *Journal of the Association for Information Science and Technology*, *74*(3), 303–310. DOI: 10.1002/asi.24730

Jenkins Project. (n.d.). *Jenkins.* https://www.jenkins.io

Kokol, P. (2024). The use of AI in software engineering: A synthetic knowledge synthesis of the recent research literature. *Information (Basel)*, *15*(6), 354. Advance online publication. DOI: 10.3390/info15060354

Koubaa, A. (2023). GPT-4 vs. GPT-3.5: A concise showdown.

Liu, A., Feng, B., Wang, B., Wang, B., Liu, B., Zhao, C., ... & Sun, X. (2024). DeepSeek-V2: A Strong, Economical, and Efficient Mixture-of-Experts Language Model. *CoRR.*

Maini, P., Jia, H., Papernot, N., & Dziedzic, A. (2024). LLM dataset inference: Did you train on my dataset? In *Advances in Neural Information Processing Systems*, 37 (pp. 124069–124092).

Mao, R., Chen, G., Zhang, X., Guerin, F., & Cambria, E. (2024, May). GPTEval: A survey on assessments of ChatGPT and GPT-4. In *Proceedings of the 2024 Joint International Conference on Computational Linguistics, Language Resources and Evaluation* (LREC-COLING 2024) (pp. 7844–7866). DOI: 10.63317/3dhqzf3tvt2z

McKinsey & Company. (2018, June 1). *AI, automation, and the future of work: Ten things to solve for.* https://www.mckinsey.com/featured-insights/future-of-work/ai-automation-and-the-future-of-work-ten-things-to-solve-for

Medepalli, S. (2025). AI In Modern Software Development: Current Practices, Challenges and Future Possibilities. [JOIREM]. *Journal Publication of International Research for Engineering and Management*, *10*(01).

Microsoft. (n.d.). *Azure DevOps.* https://learn.microsoft.com/en-us/azure/devops/?view=azure-devops

monday.com. (n.d.). *monday dev | Develop with precision and speed.* https://monday.com/w/dev

Morgan Stanley. (2025, October 29). *AI in software development: Creating jobs and redefining roles.* https://www.morganstanley.com/insights/articles/ai-software-development-industry-growth

Morgan Stanley Research. (2026, February 5). *AI adoption surges driving productivity gains and job shifts.* https://www.morganstanley.com/insights/articles/ai-adoption-accelerates-survey-find

Motion. (n.d.). *Motion.* https://www.usemotion.com/

Negri-Ribalta, C., Geraud-Stewart, R., Sergeeva, A., & Lenzini, G. (2024). A systematic literature review on the impact of AI models on the security of code generation. *Frontiers in Big Data, 7,* 1386720. DOI: 10.3389/fdata.2024.1386720 PMID: 38803522

Nguyen, N., & Nadi, S. (2022, May). An empirical evaluation of GitHub copilot's code suggestions. In *Proceedings of the 19th International Conference on Mining Software Repositories* (pp. 1-5). DOI: 10.1145/3524842.3528470

Notion. (2026). *Notion Labs, Inc.* https://notion.com/product/ai

O'Connor, S. (2025). Best AI workflow software for project managers in tech 2026. monday.com. https://monday.com/blog/project-management/best-ai-workflow-software-project-manager-tech-cm

Ooi, K. B., Tan, G. W. H., Al-Emran, M., Al-Sharafi, M. A., Capatina, A., Chakraborty, A., Dwivedi, Y. K., Huang, T.-L., Kar, A. K., Lee, V.-H., Loh, X.-M., Micu, A., Mikalef, P., Mogaji, E., Pandey, N., Raman, R., Rana, N. P., Sarker, P., Sharma, A., & Wong, L. W. (2025). The potential of generative artificial intelligence across disciplines: Perspectives and future directions. *Journal of Computer Information Systems, 65*(1), 76–107. DOI: 10.1080/08874417.2023.2261010

Open, A. I. (2024, May 13). *Hello GPT-4o.* https://openai.com/index/hello-gpt-4o

Open, A. I. (n.d.). *ChatGPT.* https://chatgpt.com

Open, A. I. Platform. (n.d.). *GPT-3.5 Turbo.* https://platform.openai.com/docs/models/gpt-3.5-turbo

Open Ai Platform. (n.d.-a). GPT 5.2. https://platform.openai.com/docs/models/gpt-5.2

Pandey, R., Singh, P., Wei, R., & Shankar, S. (2024). Transforming Software Development: Evaluating the Efficiency and Challenges of GitHub Copilot in Real-World Projects. ArXiv (Cornell University). https://doi.org//arxiv.2406.17910DOI: 10.48550

Pangan, K. (2026, January 16). *A practical guide to Jira AI automation features in 2026*. Eesel AI. https://www.eesel.ai/blog/jira-ai-automation-features

Peng, S., Kalliamvakou, E., Cihon, P., & Demirer, M. (2023). *The impact of AI on developer productivity: Evidence from GitHub Copilot* (arXiv preprint No. 2302.06590). arXiv. https://arxiv.org/abs/2302.06590

Poldrack, R. A., Lu, T., & Beguš, G. (2023). *AI-assisted coding: Experiments with GPT-4*. arXiv preprint arXiv:2304.13187.

Rahman, A., Mahir, S. H., Tashrif, M. T. A., Karim, M. A., Aishi, A. A., Kundu, D., ... & Karim, H. A. (2025). Comparative analysis based on deepseek, chatgpt, and google gemini: Features, techniques, performance, future prospects. *Systems and Soft Computing*, 200396.

Ramler, R., Moser, M., Fischer, L., Nissl, M., & Heinzl, R. (2024, April). Industrial experience report on ai-assisted coding in professional software development. *In Proceedings of the 1st International Workshop on Large Language Models for Code* (pp. 1-7). DOI: 10.1145/3643795.3648377

Ridnik, T., Kredo, D., & Friedman, I. (2024). *Code generation with alphacodium: From prompt engineering to flow engineering. arXiv preprint arXiv:2401.08500.* https://doi.org//arXiv.2401.08500DOI: 10.48550

Sabo, I. C., Maurmann, A. S. V., de Brito Santos, G., Junior, M. M., Vieira, M. F., Mohr, J. G., ... & Rover11, A. J. (2025). AVANÇOS INICIAIS DO PROJETO CONCIL-IA: desafios e potenciais impactos1 PRELIMINARY PROGRESS OF THE CONCIL-IA PROJECT: challenges and potential impacts.

Teamwork. (n.d.). *AI features*. https://www.teamwork.com/features/ai/

Vahabi, S., & Hozhabri, A. (2024). Automatic use case classification based on topic grouping for requirements engineering. *Innovations in Systems and Software Engineering*, *20*(1), 85–96. DOI: 10.1007/s11334-023-00535-0

Vaithilingam, P., Zhang, T., & Glassman, E. L. (2022). Expectation vs. Experience: Evaluating the Usability of Code Generation Tools Powered by Large Language Models. In *CHI Conference on Human Factors in Computing Systems Extended Abstracts (CHI '22 Extended Abstracts)*, (pp. 1–7). ACM. DOI: 10.1145/3491101.3519665

Valmeekam, K., Stechly, K., & Kambhampati, S. (2024). *LLMs Still Can't Plan; Can LRMs? A Preliminary Evaluation of OpenAI's o1 on PlanB*ench. *a*rXiv preprint arXiv:2409.13373. https://arxiv.org/pdf/2409.13373?

Vijayvergiya, M., Salawa, M., Budiselić, I., Zheng, D., Lamblin, P., Ivanković, M., & Just, R. (2024, July). Ai-assisted assessment of coding practices in modern code review. In *Proceedings of the 1st ACM International Conference on AI-Powered Software* (pp. 85-93). DOI: 10.1145/3664646.3665664

Wang, Y., Hu, K., Jiang, B., Xia, X., & Tang, X. S. (2023). A Systematic Literature Review of Software Traceability Links Automation Techniques. Jisuanji Xuebao. *Chin. J. Comput*, *46*, 1919–1946.

Wrike. (n.d.-a). *AI.* https://www.wrike.com/ai

Wrike. (n.d.-b). *AI project risk prediction.* https://help.wrike.com/hc/en-us/articles/360055046934-AI-Project-Risk-Prediction

Wrike. (n.d.-c). *Project risk management.* https://www.wrike.com/use-cases/project-risk-management

Wrike. (n.d.-d). *Develop your own integration on the Wrike API.* https://developers.wrike.com/

Yetiştiren, B., Özsoy, I., Ayerdem, M., & Tüzün, E. (2023). *Evaluating the code quality of ai-assisted code generation tools: An empirical study on github copilot, amazon codewhisperer, and chatgp*t. arXiv preprint arXiv:2304.10778. https://arxiv.org/pdf/2304.10778

Yuan, Z., Liu, M., Ding, S., Wang, K., Chen, Y., Peng, X., & Lou, Y. (2024). Evaluating and improving chatgpt for unit test generation. *Proceedings of the ACM on Software Engineering, 1*(FSE), 1703-1726. DOI: 10.1145/3660783

Zadeh, E. K., Khoulenjani, A. B., & Safaei, M. (2023). Integrating AI for Agile Project Management: Innovations, Challenges, and Benefits. [IJIECM]. *International Journal of Industrial Engineering and Construction Management*, *1*(1), 1–10.

KEY TERMS AND DEFINITIONS

Agentic AI: are smaller highly efficient task-specific tools than general Chabot's. They are not a general use AI tool. They can execute domain-specific tasks efficiently in their trained area of expertise and make decisions about what tasks to perform, and perform them, with little to no human interference.

Bias: Biased output can result in generative AI when the solution generated reflects opinions rather than facts in its training which injects errors in the solution.

Chatbot: A type of AI tool that understands natural language text prompts which a person can prompt and receive answers to questions or solutions to problem from the chatbot. ChatGPT is an example.

Continuous Integration / Continuous Delivery: CI/CD is a set of practices and tools designed to improve the software development process by automating builds, testing, and deployment, enabling developers to continuously integrate new changed code into and existing system and to ship code changes faster and reliably.

Deep Learning.: Deep Learning is a function of Machine Learning that relies on artificial neural networks to analyze complex data.

Generative AI: Artificial Intelligence in the general sense is software that makes a machine operate as if can make decisions and perform tasks like a human such as smart assistants like Alexa or Siri and self-driving cars. Generative AI is capable of creating new content like generating a new software game or art or music.

Hallucinations: An AI hallucination is an output generated that is presented as truth based on fact and sounds plausible but in fact is a fabrication. Examples include fake citations, invented references, fake news stories.

Large Language Models: Very large deep learning models that are pre-trained on massive amounts of data. It relies of the use of neural networks to extract meaning from the data mined and to understand relationships between words and phrases.

Machine Learning: A subfield of AI that enables systems to learn from data that is mined for training purposes.

Mixture-of-Experts (MOE) LLM: A large language model that is made up of multiple sub-model experts. This divides an AI model into sub-networks or experts that specialize in subsets of the input data. This reduces cost and increases speed.

Chapter 6
Trustworthy AI and Nursing Education

Emine Ela Küçük
Faculty of Health Sciences, Giresun University, Turkey

Dilek Küçük
http://orcid.org/0000-0003-2656-1300
TÜBİTAK Marmara Research Center, Turkey

ABSTRACT

AI use in education is becoming more prevalent every day and the particular research subfield of AI in education is commonly abbreviated as AIEd. AI in higher education is particularly getting research attention; there are several survey papers published on this topic. On the other hand, trustworthy AI is an important research problem that emerged due to the need to address the topics of fairness, privacy, accountability, explainability, bias, and ethics when deploying and using AI applications and tools. In this book chapter, we focus on trustworthy AI and nursing education, based on recent related papers. First, we cover those studies on AI use in higher education, and next we analyze research papers and review papers on the use of AI systems in nursing education, with a particular emphasis on trustworthy AI concepts and principles. We conclude our chapter with a compilation of relevant insights on the topic and also outline future research directions.

INTRODUCTION

Recent developments in AI have made sea changes in many different application domains, including professional and higher education. Nursing education also faces important opportunities and obstacles when it comes to AI incorporation into this

DOI: 10.4018/979-8-2600-2811-7.ch006

education domain. Related research emphasizes that AI-based virtual learning environments and tutors, as well as AI-based prediction tools for clinical diagnoses and interventions are among the opportunities offered by AI, and particularly, generative AI tools. For instance, AI-based virtual simulation environments are deemed effective for the interprofessional training of nurses and physicians (Liaw et al., 2023).

On the other hand, recent AI-related research also highlights the concept of trustworthiness when AI-based tools are increasingly being deployed in different application domains. As highlighted in related research, the concept of trustworthy AI has emerged because of the vulnerabilities of recent AI systems due to potential bias in such systems in addition to the lack of robustness and privacy protection commonly observed in such tools, among others. Hence, different aspects of trustworthy AI include robustness, fairness, accountability, privacy, safety, security, generalizability, explainability, and transparency.

In this book chapter, we will consider common implications of using AI, and particularly generative AI in nursing education, also considering the principles of trustworthy AI. Based on the related literature, we first provide definitions for trustworthy AI and also for the other closely-related basic concepts. Next, we cover those studies on the use of AI in higher education, highlighting findings related to trustworthy AI. Then we present a review of the studies particularly on AI in nursing education, again with an emphasis on trustworthy AI. Finally, we present the main findings of the related work together with future research directions, and conclude this chapter with a summary of the main points covered.

This book chapter will provide an elaborate discussion on trustworthy AI principles and related practices for the particular domain of nursing education. Important future research directions will also be outlined which can help related researchers interested in the topics considered.

TRUSTWORTHY AI AND RELATED CONCEPTS

As a by-product of the latest developments in AI, numerous important related concepts have emerged and they are commonly employed in the related studies. Apart from those concepts related to trustworthy and responsible AI, **generative AI** refers to the subset of AI that targets the automatic generation of content such as texts or images.

Trustworthy AI is also a very important and contemporary topic related to AI and generative AI. It is usually reported to be associated with the requirements of accountability, reliability, explainability, integrity and data privacy, transparency, and fairness, among others (Larsson, 2020; Kaur et al., 2022; Li et al., 2023). Trustworthy AI is used as a term to denote AI frameworks and systems that ensure trust among their users based on verifiable evidence (Kaur et al., 2022).

A closely related term is **responsible AI** which aims to achieve AI tools that are developed and later deployed considering the ethical issues as well as the aspects of bias, fairness, transparency, and accountability (Rhem, 2023; Dunlap & Michalowski, 2024). Hence, trustworthy AI and responsible AI have many intersecting aspects.

Building trustworthy and responsible AI systems is of particular importance for the healthcare domain, and for the education of health-related professionals. On the other hand, the set of principles and structures regarding the development, deployment, and use of AI systems is usually termed **AI governance**. This term refers to ethical and legal frameworks that guide AI systems toward alignment with the norms of society and public interests (Larsson, 2020). AI governance necessitates the incorporation of ethical guidelines, especially for AI systems proposed and built for the healthcare domain.

AI AND HIGHER EDUCATION

In this section, we cover those studies that analyze the deployment of AI systems in higher education in general. As clarified below, there are several review papers on this topic, in addition to standalone research papers. In the systematic review study dated 2019, the researchers present an overview of the studies (published between 2007 and 2018) on AI applications for higher education (Zawacki-Richter et al., 2019) and recommend that ethical, social, and pedagogical aspects should be well-assessed as part of future work. In (Kuleto et al., 2021), the authors explore the potential of AI use in higher education both using literature review and also through a survey conducted on 103 students. It is concluded that AI technologies are necessary to improve both the skills of students and collaborative learning in higher education (Kuleto et al., 2021). In the survey paper (Crompton & Burke, 2023), studies on the effects of AI systems in higher education that have been published between 2016 and 2022 are considered. It is concluded in the paper that the related usage codes include AI assistants, intelligent teaching systems, and learning management.

The research presented in (Zhou, 2023) aims to assess the impact of AI technologies on higher education in China. The author performs related experiments to determine the effectiveness of an AI-based personalized learning platform for higher education. It is argued that there is a need for the integration of modern technologies like AI in higher education (Zhou, 2023).

In another related study, the author analyzes the perspectives of the students towards emerging AI tools like ChatGPT (Johnston et al., 2024). The study concludes that clear policies should be provided to the students regarding AI use in education, and that educational institutions should ensure that their students have equal access to the related AI systems. Another related study explores the effects of AI employment in higher education through an online questionnaire, filled by 1,113 participants (Al-Zahrani & Alasmari, 2024). Their results suggest that the attitude towards AI utilization is a positive one, yet, issues like bias, privacy, and security should be addressed accordingly.

In (Cordero et al., 2024), the researchers study the use of generative AI tools such as ChatGPT and Gemini in higher education, focusing on improved teaching performance while ensuring ethical and responsible AI concerns are addressed. Possible effects of AI integration into college curricula on the creativity and emotions of students are analyzed in (Lin & Chen, 2024), both from the perspectives of students and educators. Data analysis demonstrates that both groups have positive attitudes regarding the benefits of AI systems in education (Lin & Chen, 2024). Finally, a review of systematic review papers on the topic of AI utilization in higher education is presented in (Bond et al., 2024), where considered review papers are those indexed in IEEE Xplore, Scopus, and Web of Science, among others.

IMPACT OF AI AND TRUSTWORTHY AI ON NURSING EDUCATION

In this section, we highlight the findings of the studies specifically on the existing and potential effects of AI and trustworthy AI on nursing education. Similar to the case of the previous section, a high percentage of the considered related papers are survey papers on the topic.

In (Castonguay et al., 2023), it is emphasized that nursing education is important for the establishment of healthcare systems with technology integration, and that new AI applications such as ChatGPT offer valuable opportunities, in addition to the related challenges. The authors of the paper highlight the potential bias of these AI tools, yet they recommend that nurse educators should integrate ChatGPT into their curriculum.

Several current AI applications in the healthcare domain are analyzed in (Montejo et al., 2024) and the lack of principles and frameworks for AI integration into the nursing education is emphasized. It is reported that simulation-based AI applications constitute one of the important opportunities for practical training, yet ethical and clinical evaluations of these applications are required (Montejo et al., 2024).

A related study in (Jallad et al., 2024) focuses on the sustainability and usefulness of AI applications in the nursing education. It is argued that teaching strategies should be adapted to work with the integration of AI tools as utilizing such tools is gradually being essential for students (Jallad et al., 2024).

A survey of research articles on the AI-integrated nursing education is presented in (Hwang et al., 2024). The authors of the survey paper claim that AI is effective in profiling and prediction in related research and that intelligent agents are the most common AI systems used in nursing.

Trustworthy AI aspects of the use of AI in clinical nursing are studied in (Higgins et al., 2024). It is recommended that nurses should work together with AI researchers and developers to build responsible and reliable AI applications (Higgins et al., 2024).

In (Božić, 2024), integration of AI concepts and tools in the nursing curriculum is considered. In addition to different aspects such as simulations and clinical decision support tools based on AI, the authors also focus on AI ethics as well as responsible AI, as related to trustworthy AI (Božić, 2024).

Data ethics concerns that emerged from using AI in nursing are considered in (Dunlap & Michalowski, 2024). The recommendations of this study to achieve data ethics engagement are significant. For instance, it is recommended that data literacy of nurses should be improved and the domain expertise of nurses should be utilized during the development of AI systems and tools for nurses (Dunlap & Michalowski, 2024).

Ethical issues that should be considered when integrating generative AI in nursing education are also explored in (De Gagne et al., 2024). It is suggested that ethical principles should be integrated into nursing curricula and also related ethical guidelines should be prepared and employed.

In (Simms, 2025), the author emphasizes the need for the integration of generative AI literacy in nursing education, with the necessary changes in the curricula and teaching methods. It is pointed out that generative AI literacy covers the capabilities to understand the features of the generative AI tools employed, assess the validity of the content generated by such tools, and use the outputs of these tools responsibly (Simms, 2025).

In the related literature review (Borromeo et al., 2025), the authors explore the current state-of-the-art on generative AI use in nursing education. They highlight the growing trend of AI use in nursing education, and the need for ethical integration of such intelligent systems in this specific domain. Again, in the related review paper in (Wei et al., 2025), a critical evaluation of AI integration in nursing is presented. The authors claim that limitations against successful integration include ethical issues such as the lack of ethical frameworks and guidelines specifically created for the nursing education, technical constraints, insufficient impact assessment.

The focus of a related paper (Allana & Ali, 2025) is the use of AI in nursing education, where the opportunities with the issues related to trustworthy AI including data privacy, accountability, and bias are explored. The researchers claim that education needs empathy and concern for ethical issues, and therefore AI should help traditional nursing education by complementing the human educators.

The study presented in (Sajja et al., 2025) suggests that ethical concerns should be considered when utilizing AI in nursing education. The authors indicate that related AI guidelines should be supplied to the nursing students by the educators.

The systematic review study in (Alnawafleh et al., 2025) focuses on the ethical dimensions of using AI tools and related applications in nursing education. The researchers claim that ethical education, transparency in AI governance, and nurse-centered system design and development are necessary to address the related ethical implications.

In another related survey paper (El Arab et al., 2025), it is stated that widespread adoption of AI by nurses will be affected by the readiness and literacy of the practicing nurses. AI adoption in nursing curricula; hands-on iterative training, and robust governance and ethics are listed as important priorities during AI adoption in nursing education (El Arab et al., 2025).

Another related survey (Cucci et al., 2025) emphasizes the utility of virtual simulators and AI chatbots like ChatGPT in order to improve the learning rates, communication skills, as well as the clinical preparedness of nursing students. Yet, the authors also indicate that topics including data quality, privacy, and ethics can be identified and addressed, as part of future studies (Cucci et al., 2025).

Ethical guidelines and responsible AI integration are also highlighted in (Zgambo et al., 2025). This study is conducted through an online survey on nursing students. The authors claim that the lack of the related guidelines leads to uncertainties in widespread adoption of AI tools and applications in nursing education. Additionally, it is argued that the adoption of AI tools during nursing education should not compromise academic integrity (Zgambo et al., 2025).

It is pointed out in the related systematic review paper (Ma et al., 2025) that AI employment in nursing education has a positive effect on nursing students from three different aspects including learning attitude, effectiveness, and clinical nursing proficiency. Yet, the authors emphasize the need for upcoming research on privacy and long-term effectiveness of AI deployment (Ma et al., 2025).

In the related review paper on AI and nursing research (Ruksakulpiwat et al., 2025), three main themes are pinpointed: AI applications in nursing research, issues related to ethics and bias, and benefits of AI integration. The paper is concluded with the observation that AI provides transformative opportunities for related researchers.

The review paper in (Labrague et al., 2025) groups AI-based teaching models in nursing education into three groups, namely, AI-based simulations, AI-augmented instruction, AI-based content generation. It is claimed that these three approaches have positive effects on different capabilities of the students. For instance, the authors argue that AI-based simulations improve the clinical understanding of the students. It is concluded that

AI-based approaches can lead to transformative effects on nursing education (Labrague et al., 2025).

In (Evans et al., 2025), the incorporation of AI-based systems in nursing curricula is analyzed. It is emphasized in the paper that nurses need novel skills to make use of the corresponding AI applications safely, ethically, and responsibly.

In the scoping review paper in (Amankwaa et al., 2025), the researchers cover the use of generative AI applications like ChatGPT particularly, in nursing education and training. It is pointed out that employing such tools leads to improvements in content creation, assessment, and generation of clinical scenarios. The researchers argue that AI literacy should be improved, AI governance protocols should be standardized, and infrastructures should be created in low-income settings (Amankwaa et al., 2025).

Another scoping review focuses on the use of generative AI tools by nurse academics during nursing education and point out that these tools are mostly used to improve student learning as well as time management (Hamilton et al., 2025). It is suggested that AI tools used during education can enhance the clinical reasoning of nursing students and may help them build confidence. Yet, issues such as limited data literacy of the students and educators, and the lack of related ethical frameworks to be employed during curricula generation need to be appropriately addressed (Hamilton et al., 2025).

A related study takes an existing *Health Informatics* course for health administration students and customizes it for nursing students by incorporating AI-generated lecture notes, contextualized assignments, and tools for improved accessibility (Avramovic & Mobahi, 2025). Most of the nursing students agreed that AI-based content was useful and that AI tools led to improved learning. It is reported that AI-enhanced courses can lead to improved engagement and learning for students (Avramovic & Mobahi, 2025).

Bahari et al. (2025) carried out cross-sectional research to determine possible relationships between the AI perception in nursing students and their self-efficacy and distress. It is reported that AI perceptions of nursing students cannot be considered a significant indicator of the self-efficacy and distress of these students (Bahari et al., 2025).

A review of seven review papers that are published on the AI employment in nursing education between 2019 and 2023 is presented in (Kovalainen et al., 2025). The researchers report that utilizing machine learning improves the diagnostic skills of the students and it enables personalization of learning experiences. Similarly, the use of robotics has enhancing effects on the training of nursing, dental, and medical students (Kovalainen et al., 2025).

Threats towards the use of generative AI in healthcare education are explored in (Rodger et al., 2025). The authors claim that AI integration can lead to overdependence on AI and can degrade critical thinking and related clinical skills of the students. It is pointed out that AI literacy of the healthcare professionals and educators should be improved to better comprehend the possible limitations and biases AI tools to be used in clinical settings (Rodger et al., 2025).

The study by Prosen & Ličen (2025) focuses on the perceptions as well as the experiences of the students of health sciences regarding the utilization of generative AI during learning. It is emphasized that issues of ethics, AI literacy, and accessibility should be conveniently addressed in related applications. Trustworthy AI principles should be considered to attain sustainable and effective integration of AI tools and applications to health education (Prosen & Ličen, 2025).

In their study, Ghimire & Qiu (2025) determine that nursing students are using AI tools during their personal learning activities, and international students are particularly utilizing AI tools to bridge the cultural and linguistic gaps during training. The researchers highlight the fact that algorithmic bias in AI tools is an important issue to be tackled, because the data used for training these AI tools may not be diverse enough to cover the health disparities, i.e., the health-related differences among populations originating from ethnic, geographical, socio-demographic, and cultural features (Ghimire & Qiu, 2025). Also emphasized in the paper is the need to address issues related to data privacy, security, ethical implications, and academic integrity, when AI tools are used by nursing students and during nursing education.

The use of AI tools by nursing students to automatically create care plans is investigated in (Shen et al., 2025). Iterative prompt engineering is also employed to improve the care plans generated. It is concluded that employed generative AI tools improve efficiency as well as conceptual clarity during care plan generation. The limited emotional understanding and empathy of AI tools, as well as trustworthy AI issues such as data privacy are yet to be addressed (Shen et al., 2025).

A related study handles the topic from the perspective of undergraduate nursing students using semi-structured interviews for data collection (Lei et al., 2025). It is pointed out that for effective integration of AI tools in nursing education, their being supplementary tools should be acknowledged, and issues arising from overreliance on AI tools should be properly addressed. Additionally, related ethical issues should also be considered to ensure academic integrity (Lei et al., 2025).

In a related review paper (Sengul et al., 2025), the ethical challenges regarding the use of AI in nursing education are considered. As commonly pointed out in related literature, the authors emphasize the transformative effects of AI adoption in nursing education, and suggest that ethical guidelines should be created and adopted and nursing educators should be trained to acquire the necessary skills to better help their students (Sengul et al., 2025).

A recent scoping review study (Almagharbeh et al., 2026) emphasizes that clinical reasoning and decision-making can be supported by AI-enabled simulations. This review study also points out that learners usually report high levels of satisfaction and engagement under AI-based learning settings. Hence, the study concludes that AI-enhanced simulations facilitate learning for nursing students (Almagharbeh et al., 2026).

Another recent scoping review by Rahman (2026) particularly targets studies on algorithmic bias and transparency of AI systems used in nursing education. It is emphasized that automated tutoring and grading systems, virtual simulations like virtual patients are among common AI applications used during nursing education. Joint efforts from nursing educators, developers, and institutions are recommended to cope with the algorithmic bias, ethical issues, and transparency so that employed AI systems can be aligned with the values of nursing education (Rahman, 2026).

The use of generative AI during teaching, learning, and assessment stages of nursing education is considered in another relevant scoping review (Hardie et al., 2026). It is argued that simulations and personalized learning are among the common educational purposes during content creation using such AI tools. It is also emphasized that ethical policies and guidelines are required before widespread employment of AI tools in nursing education (Hardie et al., 2026).

In their related recent study (Aziz et al., 2026), the authors emphasize the importance of AI-based virtual simulation environments during the education of health professionals including nurses. They indicate the fact that the AI-based virtual simulation environments are particularly useful for improved interprofessional training and also for cultural responsiveness (Aziz et al., 2026), where the concept of cultural responsiveness (within the context of healthcare) is commonly defined as the level of healthcare professionals' consideration of the values, beliefs, and cultural backgrounds of the patients (Minnican & O'Toole, 2020).

In (Nacer et al., 2026), it is claimed that AI integration in nursing education aims to improve critical thinking, learning, and confidence of these students, through AI-based virtual simulations, among others. Yet, responsible use of such AI tools during nursing education is also recommended to gain sufficient benefits from the technology without compromising the values of nursing education.

Another related study is conducted in the Philippines on nursing educators to determine their experiences of using AI tools during nursing education (Kulintang et al., 2026). It is found that nurse educators perceive AI tools as transformative and innovative, and that AI tools improve efficiency and personalized learning of nursing students. Yet, as also indicated commonly in related research, it is reported that clear policies and guidelines are necessary before the integration of AI tools to nursing education (Kulintang et al., 2026).

Kubota et al. (2026) propose a framework for integrating AI into nursing Objective Structured Clinical Examinations (OSCEs) through a 5-role model. This model is applied across the different stages of the OSCE process, keeping human judgment as the final decision-maker. Based on the agile development approach of Taiwan and standards-driven approach of Japan, the authors outline an AI governance framework and roadmap to ensure reliability, fairness, and transparency in AI-augmented assessments, to be used as a reference model (Kubota et al., 2026).

In (Paloma & Paloma, 2026), a framework called SAFE-GenAI is proposed for the integration of generative AI tools into nursing education in an accountable fashion. It is argued that the proposed framework ensures academic integrity, critical thinking, and AI literacy, and it can be readily used during the generation of related nursing curricula and other decision-making stages by the related nursing faculties (Paloma & Paloma, 2026).

We conclude this section with the schematic summary of the main trustworthy AI concepts and other closely-related concepts encountered in the studies reviewed in this section, as given in Figure 1 below.

Figure 1. Trustworthy AI and related concepts in studies on AI adoption in nursing education

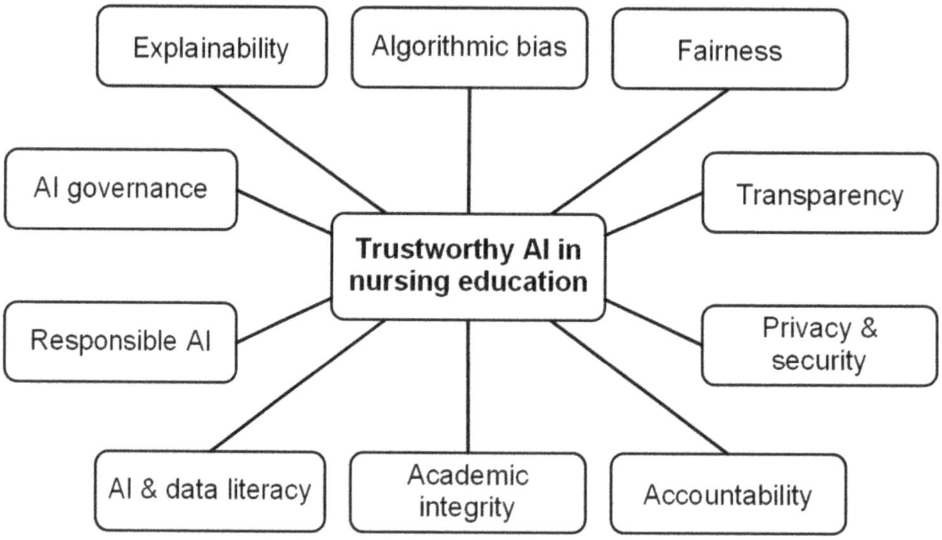

INSIGHTS FROM THE RELATED WORK AND FUTURE RESEARCH DIRECTIONS

In this section, we compile the insights related to the use of trustworthy AI in nursing education, as derived from the related work reviewed in the previous sections.

Since these insights also highlight important open research challenges on the topic, they are presented together with the related pointers to future research directions.

In most of the related work, it is pointed out that AI tools and systems have increasingly innovative and transformative effects on nursing education and research (Ruksakulpiwat et al., 2025; Labrague et al., 2025; Kulintang et al., 2026). As such, AI-based or AI-enabled simulations constitute one of the main research directions considering the AI applications in the education of health-related domains including nursing education, where trustworthy AI principles should be followed (Minnican & O'Toole, 2020; Montejo et al., 2024; Božić, 2024; Labrague et al., 2025; Almagharbeh et al., 2026; Rahman, 2026; Hardie et al., 2026). Some studies demonstrated that AI-based simulations improve the clinical understanding and critical thinking of the nursing students, in addition to boosting their professional confidence (Hamilton et al., 2025; Nacer et al., 2026). On the other hand, some other studies claim that overdependence on AI tools may instead degrade critical thinking and clinical understanding skills of the students (Rodger et al., 2025). Other common purposes of AI tools in higher education of nursing and other related professions are reported to be personalized learning (Zhou, 2023; Shen et al., 2025; Hardie et al., 2026) and academic tutoring (Rahman, 2026). Related studies also indicate that, instead of completely replacing human educators, AI-based tools and applications are valuable as complementary or supplementary means during nursing education (Allana & Ali, 2025; Lei et al., 2025). On the other hand, as previously pointed out, issues that may arise from overreliance or overdependence on such AI tools are also emphasized in related work (Lei et al., 2025; Rodger et al., 2025).

While some studies investigate the topic from the perspectives of nurse educators (Kulintang et al., 2026), other studies consider the perspectives of the nursing students (Lei et al., 2025; Zgambo et al., 2025). Yet, there exist studies considering the perspectives of both educators and students alike (Lin & Chen, 2024). From the viewpoint of the students, it is reported that students of higher education institutions consider AI-integration in their curricula positively (Almagharbeh et al., 2026).

One of the common recommendations is the need for the improvement of the data literacy and AI literacy of nurses and educators (Dunlap & Michalowski, 2024; Hamilton et al., 2025; Simms, 2025). Similarly, other studies also indicate that nursing educators should gain the necessary technical and other relevant skills to better help their students during AI adoption in nursing education so that the outputs of these tools can be used responsibly (Sengul et al., 2025; Simms, 2025). It is argued in several related studies that nurses should be partnered with AI developers and AI researchers in order to achieve nurse-centered AI system design and development for better AI integration in nursing education (Higgins et al., 2024; Alnawafleh et al., 2025). Ensuring or maintaining academic integrity while integrating AI tools in nursing education is a common concern highlighted in several related studies (Lei et al., 2025; Zgambo et al., 2025; Paloma & Paloma, 2026). A related framework to ensure academic integrity during the adoption of AI in nursing education is proposed in (Paloma & Paloma, 2026). Similarly, in (Kubota et al., 2026) an AI governance framework for nursing examinations is proposed as a result of joint efforts from researchers from Japan and Taiwan.

Algorithmic bias and cultural bias existing in many generative AI tools and applications used during nursing and other health-related education stand as significant issues to be dealt with (Rahman, 2026). These tools are generally trained on skewed datasets generated from populations of certain and limited geographical and cultural characteristics. Therefore, their use during the education of other populations may not be equally effective if not harmful at all, as pointed out by related studies (Ghimire & Qiu, 2025; Rahman, 2026). Hence, solutions to cope with the inherent bias in AI tools should be elaborated and considered during the employment of such AI tools during nursing education, as part of future work.

It is highlighted in various studies that ethical aspects and considerations should be well-assessed before widespread deployment of these applications in the nursing education (Bond et al., 2024; Montejo et al., 2024; De Gagne et al., 2024; Alnawafleh et al., 2025; Cucci et al., 2025; El Arab et al., 2025; Ruksakulpiwat et al., 2025; Sajja et al., 2025; Hamilton et al., 2025). These studies suggest that related ethical and responsible AI guidelines should be provided to the nursing students for better and ethical student engagement (Sajja et al., 2025). Additionally, some authors highlight the need for the development and deployment of related ethical policies and frameworks (Wei et al., 2025; Hamilton et al., 2025; Hardie et al., 2026).

Previous studies also emphasize that students should have equal access to AI tools during their education (Johnston et al., 2024). Several studies also emphasize the need to provide the necessary technical infrastructures for low-income settings (Amankwaa et al., 2025). Existing literature also focuses on the need for related interdisciplinary research, as part of future work (Bond et al., 2024).

Related work suggests that clear guidelines and principles should be compiled and provided to the students, and that transparency should be ensured (Rahman, 2026). Researchers emphasize that with active involvement of the nurses, sociotechnical risks of such AI employment in the nursing education should be addressed (Ruksakulpiwat et al., 2025). When considering the impact of AI on nursing education, the issues of privacy protection and security are equally important and should be considered, as pointed out in different related studies (Ma et al., 2025; Al-Zahrani & Alasmari, 2024). Additionally, the long-term effectiveness of AI applications should also be addressed within the course of future research (Ma et al., 2025).

In general, other trustworthy AI concepts including (but not limited to) transparency, robustness, fairness, data quality, explainability, and accountability are also highlighted in related work as promising lines for future work (Al-Zahrani & Alasmari, 2024; Cucci et al., 2025).

Based on our above summary of the related studies, the prominent applications and benefits of AI adoption in nursing education are listed in Table 1. The table provides a structured synthesis of the key applications and benefits, with representative references given in the last column. Notably, a significant number of studies emphasize AI-based virtual simulations and personalized learning as specific applications of AI in nursing education, as indicated in the first two rows of Table 1.

Table 1. Applications and benefits of AI integration in nursing education

	Applications & benefits	References
1	AI-based virtual simulations	Minnican & O'Toole (2020) Montejo et al. (2024) Labrague et al. (2025) Nacer et al. (2026)
2	Personalized learning	Zhou (2023) Shen et al. (2025) Hardie et al. (2026)
3	Academic tutoring support	Rahman (2026)
4	Complementary or supplementary to human educators	Allana & Ali (2025) Lei et al. (2025)
5	Improved critical thinking & confidence	Hamilton et al. (2025) Nacer et al. (2026)
6	Transformative educational effects	Ruksakulpiwat et al. (2025) Labrague et al. (2025) Kulintang et al. (2026)

Similarly, common related challenges and concerns based on the reviewed literature are summarized in Table 2. These findings suggest that the related concerns are not limited to a particular aspect such as privacy and security, but rather, there is a wide range of issues to be addressed including algorithmic and cultural bias, and disadvantages of overreliance on AI tools. Again, representative references are provided in the last column of Table 2, for further reading.

Table 2. Challenges and concerns related to AI in nursing education

	Challenges & concerns	References
1	Overreliance on AI tools	Lei et al. (2025) Rodger et al. (2025)
2	Algorithmic & cultural bias	Ghimire & Qiu (2025) Rahman (2026)
3	Academic integrity risks	Lei et al. (2025) Zgambo et al. (2025) Paloma & Paloma (2026)
4	Privacy & data security	Ma et al. (2025) Al-Zahrani & Alasmari (2024)
5	Unclear long-term effectiveness	Ma et al. (2025)
6	Sociotechnical risks	Ruksakulpiwat et al. (2025)
7	Lack of transparency	Rahman (2026)

Building on the findings presented in Tables 1 and 2, actionable recommendations for the effective AI adoption in nursing education are presented in Table 3, again with related references in the last column. The recommendations in Table 3 are compiled from the related literature and they constitute a roadmap for the related stakeholders such as nurse educators, policy makers, and AI developers.

Table 3. Recommendations for AI integration in nursing education

	Recommendations	References
1	Improve AI & data literacy	Dunlap & Michalowski (2024) Hamilton et al. (2025) Simms (2025)
2	Develop ethical AI guidelines & policies	De Gagne et al. (2024) Wei et al. (2025) Hamilton et al. (2025) Sajja et al. (2025) Hardie et al. (2026)
3	Apply trustworthy AI principles	Montejo et al. (2024) Bozic (2024) Kubota et al. (2026)
4	Ensure equal access to AI tools	Johnston et al. (2024)
5	Develop infrastructures for low-income settings	Amankwaa et al. (2025)
6	Promote interdisciplinary research	Bond et al. (2024)

Overall, Tables 1 through 3 provide an integrated synthesis of the main findings of the reviewed literature on trustworthy AI and nursing education. Hence, they serve as useful and compact references for interested readers. Additionally, they cover important future work directions for related researchers, educators, and students.

CONCLUSION

This book chapter focuses on implications of using AI and particularly generative AI in nursing education, considering the aspects of trustworthy AI. There is a rise in research conducted regarding AI use in higher education, and programs for health-related professions such as nursing programs are also affected by the recent developments in AI. Several studies point out that AI-based simulations, AI-based clinical decision support tools, and AI-based virtual tutors are among plausible AI applications and tools in nursing education. Related studies report that AI-based applications can considerably help traditional nursing education as complementary tools. Additionally, related studies also report that students in higher education perceive AI-integration into their curricula positively. However, many studies indicate that trustworthy AI topics of fairness, transparency, privacy, security, accountability, and explainability should be considered when incorporating AI in nursing education. Due to the particular nature of nursing education, ethical aspects should also be well assessed prior to incorporating AI tools into the nursing curricula. Further and interdisciplinary research is necessary to better analyze corresponding opportunities and issues of AI integration into nursing education, particularly considering the principles and concepts of trustworthy and responsible AI.

REFERENCES

Al-Zahrani, A. M., & Alasmari, T. M. (2024). Exploring the impact of artificial intelligence on higher education: The dynamics of ethical, social, and educational implications. *Humanities & Social Sciences Communications, 11*(1), 1–12. DOI: 10.1057/s41599-024-03432-4

Allana, H., & Ali, S. (2025). Artificial intelligence in nursing education: balancing reluctance and embracing innovation. *Pedagogical Inquiry and Practice*, 1(1).

Almagharbeh, W. T., Ahmed, W. R., Alfanash, H. A., Alnawafleh, K. A., & Tajoury, O. H. (2026). Touching the future: How haptic technology and AI are revolutionizing nursing simulations: A systematic scoping review. *Journal of Professional Nursing : Official Journal of the American Association of Colleges of Nursing*, *63*, 18–25. DOI: 10.1016/j.profnurs.2025.12.010 PMID: 41796557

Alnawafleh, K. A., Almagharbeh, W. T., Alfanash, H. A., Alasmari, A. A., Alharbi, A. A., Alamrani, M. H., Alkubati, S. A., Altayar, M. A., & Rezq, K. A. (2025). Exploring the ethical dimensions of AI integration in nursing practice: A systematic review. *Journal of Nursing Regulation*, *16*(3), 228–237. DOI: 10.1016/j.jnr.2025.08.001

Amankwaa, I., Ekpor, E., Cudjoe, D., Kobiah, E., Fuseini, A. K. J., Diebieri, M., Gyamfi, S., & Brownie, S. (2025). Patterns, advances, and gaps in using ChatGPT and similar technologies in nursing education: A PAGER scoping review. *Nurse Education Today*, *153*, 106822. DOI: 10.1016/j.nedt.2025.106822 PMID: 40644844

Avramovic, S., & Mobahi, H. (2025). Redesigning a health informatics course for nursing students through AI-driven instruction and clinically contextualized assignments. *Canadian Journal of Nursing Informatics*, *20*(4).

Aziz, Z., Mazeh, A. C., Ilic, D., Ciardulli, M., El Hadi, S. N., Camuccio, A., Moore, J., & Kiegaldie, D. (2026). Leveraging AI simulations for enhancing cultural responsiveness and interprofessional collaboration in health professions education. *Nurse Education in Practice*, *91*, 104711. DOI: 10.1016/j.nepr.2026.104711 PMID: 41520588

Bahari, G., Alenazi, L., & Alkathiri, A. M. (2025). The implementation of artificial intelligence in nursing education and its psychological impact on nursing students: A cross-sectional study. *Nurse Education Today*, *153*, 106816. DOI: 10.1016/j.nedt.2025.106816 PMID: 40544672

Bond, M., Khosravi, H., De Laat, M., Bergdahl, N., Negrea, V., Oxley, E., Pham, P., Chong, S. W., & Siemens, G. (2024). A meta systematic review of artificial intelligence in higher education: A call for increased ethics, collaboration, and rigour. *International Journal of Educational Technology in Higher Education, 21*(1), 4. DOI: 10.1186/s41239-023-00436-z

Borromeo, A. S., Manaloto, A. M., Santos, M. J. M. D., Antonio, R. P., Soyosa, M. D., & Wider, W. (2025). Harnessing generative AI in nursing education: A bibliometric review. *Teaching and Learning in Nursing, 20*(4), e1002–e1011. DOI: 10.1016/j.teln.2025.04.014

Božić, V. (2024). Artificial Intelligence in nurse education. In *Engineering Applications of Artificial Intelligence* (pp. 143–172). Springer Nature Switzerland. DOI: 10.1007/978-3-031-50300-9_9

Castonguay, A., Farthing, P., Davies, S., Vogelsang, L., Kleib, M., Risling, T., & Green, N. (2023). Revolutionizing nursing education through AI integration: A reflection on the disruptive impact of ChatGPT. *Nurse Education Today, 129*, 105916. DOI: 10.1016/j.nedt.2023.105916 PMID: 37515957

Cordero, J., Torres-Zambrano, J., & Cordero-Castillo, A. (2024). Integration of generative artificial intelligence in higher education: Best practices. *Education Sciences, 15*(1), 32. DOI: 10.3390/educsci15010032

Crompton, H., & Burke, D. (2023). Artificial intelligence in higher education: The state of the field. *International Journal of Educational Technology in Higher Education, 20*(1), 22. DOI: 10.1186/s41239-023-00392-8

Cucci, F., Marasciulo, D., Romani, M., Soldano, G., Cascio, D., De Nunzio, G., Caldararo, C., Rubbi, I., Vitale, E., Lupo, R., & Conte, L. (2025). The contribution of artificial intelligence in nursing education: A scoping review of the literature. *Nursing Reports, 15*(8), 283. DOI: 10.3390/nursrep15080283 PMID: 40863670

De Gagne, J. C., Hwang, H., & Jung, D. (2024). Cyberethics in nursing education: Ethical implications of artificial intelligence. *Nursing Ethics, 31*(6), 1021–1030. DOI: 10.1177/09697330231201901 PMID: 37803810

Dunlap, P. A. B., & Michalowski, M. (2024). Advancing AI data ethics in nursing: Future directions for nursing practice, research, and education. *JMIR Nursing, 7*(1), e62678. DOI: 10.2196/62678 PMID: 39453630

El Arab, R. A., Alshakihs, A. H., Alabdulwahab, S. H., Almubarak, Y. S., Alkhalifah, S. S., Abdrbo, A., Hassanein, S., & Sagbakken, M. (2025). Artificial intelligence in nursing: A systematic review of attitudes, literacy, readiness, and adoption intentions among nursing students and practicing nurses. *Frontiers in Digital Health*, *7*, 1666005. DOI: 10.3389/fdgth.2025.1666005 PMID: 41079691

Evans, W., Baker, N., & Farrelly, T. (2025). Artificial Intelligence considerations in nursing curricula: Embracing with care, its potential in transforming learning. *Journal of Nursing Education and Practice*, *15*(7), 37–52. DOI: 10.63564/jnep.v15n7p37

Ghimire, A., & Qiu, Y. (2025). Redefining pedagogy with artificial intelligence: How nursing students are shaping the future of learning. *Nurse Education in Practice*, *84*, 104330. DOI: 10.1016/j.nepr.2025.104330 PMID: 40090205

Hamilton, J., Costello, M., Barr, L., Cooper, S., & Jones, M. (2025). Application of generative artificial intelligence by nurse academics in higher education: A scoping review. *Nurse Education in Practice*, 104669. PMID: 41353944

Hardie, P., Darley, A., Derwin, R., Eustace-Cook, J., Kearns, S., Mc Brien, B., Siddiquee, A., Zheng, D., & Mooney, M. (2026). Applications, attitudes and ethical considerations of Generative Artificial Intelligence (Gen AI) in nursing education: A scoping review. *BMC Nursing*, *25*(148), 148. Advance online publication. DOI: 10.1186/s12912-025-04253-9 PMID: 41545825

Higgins, O., Chalup, S. K., & Wilson, R. L. (2024). Artificial Intelligence in nursing: Trustworthy or reliable? *Journal of Research in Nursing : JRN*, *29*(2), 143–153. DOI: 10.1177/17449871231215696 PMID: 39070561

Hwang, G. J., Tang, K. Y., & Tu, Y. F. (2024). How artificial intelligence (AI) supports nursing education: Profiling the roles, applications, and trends of AI in nursing education research (1993–2020). *Interactive Learning Environments*, *32*(1), 373–392. DOI: 10.1080/10494820.2022.2086579

Jallad, S. T., Alsaqer, K., Albadareen, B. I., & Al-Maghaireh, D. (2024). Artificial intelligence tools utilized in nursing education: Incidence and associated factors. *Nurse Education Today*, *142*, 106355. DOI: 10.1016/j.nedt.2024.106355 PMID: 39163690

Johnston, H., Wells, R. F., Shanks, E. M., Boey, T., & Parsons, B. N. (2024). Student perspectives on the use of generative artificial intelligence technologies in higher education. *International Journal for Educational Integrity*, *20*(1), 2. DOI: 10.1007/s40979-024-00149-4

Kaur, D., Uslu, S., Rittichier, K. J., & Durresi, A. (2022). Trustworthy artificial intelligence: A review. *ACM Computing Surveys*, *55*(2), 1–38. DOI: 10.1145/3491209

Kovalainen, T., Pramila-Savukoski, S., Kuivila, H. M., Juntunen, J., Jarva, E., Rasi, M., & Mikkonen, K. (2025). Utilising artificial intelligence in developing education of health sciences higher education: An umbrella review of reviews. *Nurse Education Today*, *147*, 106600. DOI: 10.1016/j.nedt.2025.106600 PMID: 39904286

Kubota, K., Nishimura, A., Seto, R., & Li, L. (2026). Trustworthy AI-augmented objective structured clinical examinations in nursing education: Taiwan-Japan viewpoint on 5 AI roles, governance, and cross-border implementation. *JMIR Formative Research*, *10*, e87830. DOI: 10.2196/87830 PMID: 41818744

Kuleto, V., Ilić, M., Dumangiu, M., Ranković, M., Martins, O. M., Păun, D., & Mihoreanu, L. (2021). Exploring opportunities and challenges of artificial intelligence and machine learning in higher education institutions. *Sustainability (Basel)*, *13*(18), 10424. DOI: 10.3390/su131810424

Kulintang, M. B. M., Ngo, A. D., Salas, C. J. C., Sumaoy, K., & Alquwez, N. A. (2026). Nurse educators' experiences integrating artificial intelligence in teaching and practice: A descriptive phenomenological study. *Nurse Education Today*, *162*, 107050. DOI: 10.1016/j.nedt.2026.107050 PMID: 41747322

Labrague, L. J., Sabei, S. A., & Yahyaei, A. A. (2025). Artificial intelligence in nursing education: A review of AI-based teaching pedagogies. *Teaching and Learning in Nursing*, *20*(3), 210–221. DOI: 10.1016/j.teln.2025.01.019

Larsson, S. (2020). On the governance of artificial intelligence through ethics guidelines. *Asian Journal of Law and Society*, *7*(3), 437–451. DOI: 10.1017/als.2020.19

Lei, P., Duo, E. N., Gao, Y., & Zhu, X. (2025). Research on the experience of utilizing artificial intelligence in nursing learning from the perspective of nursing students–a qualitative study. *BMC Nursing*, *24*(1), 1062. DOI: 10.1186/s12912-025-03704-7 PMID: 40797323

Li, B., Qi, P., Liu, B., Di, S., Liu, J., Pei, J., Yi, J., & Zhou, B. (2023). Trustworthy AI: From principles to practices. *ACM Computing Surveys*, *55*(9), 1–46. DOI: 10.1145/3555803

Liaw, S. Y., Tan, J. Z., Lim, S., Zhou, W., Yap, J., Ratan, R., Ooi, S. L., Wong, S. J., Seah, B., & Chua, W. L. (2023). Artificial intelligence in virtual reality simulation for interprofessional communication training: Mixed method study. *Nurse Education Today*, *122*, 105718. DOI: 10.1016/j.nedt.2023.105718 PMID: 36669304

Lin, H., & Chen, Q. (2024). Artificial intelligence (AI)-integrated educational applications and college students' creativity and academic emotions: Students and teachers' perceptions and attitudes. *BMC Psychology*, *12*(1), 487. DOI: 10.1186/s40359-024-01979-0 PMID: 39285268

Ma, J., Wen, J., Qiu, Y., Wang, Y., Xiao, Q., Liu, T., Zhang, D., Zhao, Y., Lu, Z., & Sun, Z. (2025). The role of artificial intelligence in shaping nursing education: A comprehensive systematic review. *Nurse Education in Practice*, *84*, 104345. DOI: 10.1016/j.nepr.2025.104345 PMID: 40168750

Minnican, C., & O'Toole, G. (2020). Exploring the incidence of culturally responsive communication in Australian healthcare: The first rapid review on this concept. *BMC Health Services Research*, *20*(1), 20. DOI: 10.1186/s12913-019-4859-6 PMID: 31910837

Montejo, L., Fenton, A., & Davis, G. (2024). Artificial intelligence (AI) applications in healthcare and considerations for nursing education. *Nurse Education in Practice*, *80*, 104158. DOI: 10.1016/j.nepr.2024.104158 PMID: 39388757

Nacer, N., Chouikh, J., & Nacer, K. (2026). Artificial intelligence and nursing education: Enhancing teaching, learning, and critical thinking. In *Transforming Humanities and Social Sciences Through AI* (pp. 129–158). IGI Global Scientific Publishing.

Paloma, Z. B., & Paloma, J. R. S. (2026). From adoption to accountable integration in nursing higher education: A SAFE-GenAI framework for nurse academics. *Nurse Education in Practice*, *93*, 104796. DOI: 10.1016/j.nepr.2026.104796 PMID: 41887953

Prosen, M., & Ličen, S. (2025). Perceptions, ethical challenges and sustainable integration of generative AI in health science education: A cross-sectional study. *Sustainability (Basel)*, *17*(14), 6546. DOI: 10.3390/su17146546

Rahman, M. I. (2026). Algorithmic bias and transparency in artificial intelligence tools for nursing education: A scoping review. *Nurse Education in Practice*, *92*, 104756. DOI: 10.1016/j.nepr.2026.104756 PMID: 41653525

Rhem, A. J. (2023). Ethical use of data in AI Applications. In *Ethics-Scientific Research, Ethical Issues, Artificial Intelligence and Education*. IntechOpen.

Rodger, D., Mann, S. P., Earp, B., Savulescu, J., Bobier, C., & Blackshaw, B. P. (2025). Generative AI in healthcare education: How AI literacy gaps could compromise learning and patient safety. *Nurse Education in Practice*, *87*, 104461. DOI: 10.1016/j.nepr.2025.104461 PMID: 40633198

Ruksakulpiwat, S., Phianhasin, L., Benjasirisan, C., Su, T., Riangkam, C., Thorngthip, S., Aldossary, H. M., Ahmed, B., Pongsuwun, K., & Angkaew, N. (2025). Artificial intelligence in nursing research: A systematic review of applications, benefits, and challenges. *International Nursing Review*, *72*(3), e70080. DOI: 10.1111/inr.70080 PMID: 40714821

Sajja, R., Sermet, Y., Chi, N. C., & Demir, I. (2025). Evaluating artificial intelligence assisted nursing education: Student perceptions, ethical concerns, and pedagogical implications. *Teaching and Learning in Nursing*.

Sengul, T., Sariköse, S., & Gul, A. (2025). Ethical decision-making and artificial intelligence in nursing education: An integrative review. *Nursing Ethics*, *32*(8), 2490–2515. DOI: 10.1177/09697330251366600 PMID: 40865964

Shen, M., Shen, Y., Liu, F., & Jin, J. (2025). Prompts, privacy, and personalized learning: Integrating AI into nursing education—a qualitative study. *BMC Nursing*, *24*(1), 470. DOI: 10.1186/s12912-025-03115-8 PMID: 40301862

Simms, R. C. (2025). Generative artificial intelligence (AI) literacy in nursing education: A crucial call to action. *Nurse Education Today*, *146*, 106544. DOI: 10.1016/j.nedt.2024.106544 PMID: 39708405

Wei, Q., Pan, S., Liu, X., Hong, M., Nong, C., & Zhang, W. (2025). The integration of AI in nursing: Addressing current applications, challenges, and future directions. *Frontiers in Medicine*, *12*, 1545420. DOI: 10.3389/fmed.2025.1545420 PMID: 40007584

Zawacki-Richter, O., Marín, V. I., Bond, M., & Gouverneur, F. (2019). Systematic review of research on artificial intelligence applications in higher education–where are the educators? *International Journal of Educational Technology in Higher Education*, *16*(1), 1–27. DOI: 10.1186/s41239-019-0171-0

Zgambo, M., Costello, M., Buhlmann, M., Maldon, J., Anyango, E., & Adama, E. (2025). Artificial intelligence and academic integrity in nursing education: A mixed methods study on usage, perceptions, and institutional implications. *Nurse Education Today*, *153*, 106796. DOI: 10.1016/j.nedt.2025.106796 PMID: 40517666

Zhou, C. (2023). Integration of modern technologies in higher education on the example of artificial intelligence use. *Education and Information Technologies*, *28*(4), 3893–3910. DOI: 10.1007/s10639-022-11309-9

Chapter 7
Teaching, Research, and Service Through Smart Aquaculture in the Age of AI-Powered Automation:
An IoT System for Automatic Feeding and Monitoring

Balkis Tej
http://orcid.org/0000-0002-4688-4599
National Engineering School of Monastir, University of Monastir, Tunisia

Soulef Bouaafia
Higher Institute of Applied Sciences and Technology of Kairouan, University of Kairouan, Tunisia

Mohamed Ali Hajjaji
Higher Institute of Applied Sciences and Technology of Sousse, University of Sousse, Tunisia

Abdellatif Mtibaa
National Engineering School of Sfax, University of Sfax, Tunisia

ABSTRACT

A strength of higher education is the ability to engage teaching, research, and service for greater good. With the growing worldwide demand for seafood, aquaculture has emerged as an essential element of nutritional security and sustainability. In this context, automatic monitoring and feeding have become indispensable tools for im-

DOI: 10.4018/979-8-2600-2811-7.ch007

proving aquaculture performance. In this paper, we developed an intelligent system for real-time monitoring and automatic food distribution in aquaculture. The system combines sensors, electronic devices, and data processing algorithms to monitor fish health, analyze environmental conditions, and distribute feed in a precise and controlled way. The main goal is to increase productivity and profitability while ensuring the welfare of the fish. By detecting signs of disease, stress, or abnormal behavior, the system enables rapid intervention to prevent health issues and reduce losses. Furthermore, by adjusting the amount and frequency of feed according to the specific needs of the fish, the system minimizes food waste and supports healthy, consistent growth.

I. INTRODUCTION

Aquaculture has become one of the fastest-growing food production sectors worldwide and plays an important role in global food security and economic development by providing a reliable and sustainable source of aquatic products (Adimulam et al., 2024; Tina et al., 2025; Wu et al., 2025). As the global population continues to grow and the demand for seafood increases, aquaculture producers face increasing pressure to improve production efficiency while maintaining sustainable farming practices. In this context, the optimization of aquaculture management processes has become a key challenge for fish farmers and researchers. Among the various operational aspects of aquaculture, feeding management remains one of the most decisive factors influencing fish growth, health, and farm profitability (Luna et al., 2022) (Ilahy et al., n.d.). Feed represents a significant portion of the operational costs in aquaculture, often accounting for more than half of total production expenses. Inefficient feeding practices can therefore lead to substantial economic losses. Overfeeding may result in feed wastage and deterioration of water quality, while underfeeding can slow fish growth and reduce overall productivity. In addition to economic implications, improper feeding strategies may negatively affect the aquatic environment by increasing organic waste accumulation in water systems. Traditionally, feeding operations in many aquaculture farms rely on manual labor, where farmers distribute feed at specific times based on observation and experience. Although this method is widely used, it is often time-consuming, labor-intensive, and prone to human error. Manual feeding also makes it difficult to control the precise quantity of feed distributed and to adapt feeding schedules according to fish behavior or environmental conditions (Choudhury et al., 2025). As aquaculture production scales up, these limitations become increasingly significant and highlight the need for more automated and intelligent feeding solutions.

Recent technological advances have opened new opportunities for improving aquaculture management through the integration of digital technologies. In particular, the Internet of Things (IoT) has enabled the development of connected monitoring systems capable of collecting environmental data in real time through distributed sensors. Parameters such as water temperature, dissolved oxygen, pH levels, and water turbidity can be continuously monitored to ensure optimal living conditions for aquatic organisms (Yue & Shen, 2022) (Ubina et al., 2023) These technologies allow farmers to better understand environmental dynamics and make informed decisions regarding feeding and farm management. At the same time, artificial intelligence (AI) techniques, especially computer vision and machine learning, are increasingly being applied in aquaculture to analyze fish behavior and detect patterns that are difficult to observe manually. By using cameras and image processing algorithms, AI-based systems can monitor fish activity, detect abnormal behavior, and assist in optimizing feeding strategies. Such intelligent monitoring systems can significantly reduce feed wastage, improve fish welfare, and increase overall production efficiency.

In this chapter, we propose an intelligent aquaculture monitoring and feeding system that integrates IoT technologies with artificial intelligence techniques. The proposed system combines an Arduino-based automatic feeding mechanism with a Raspberry Pi platform responsible for image acquisition and processing. A Convolutional Neural Network (CNN) model is employed to detect fish presence and activity in real time using images captured by a camera installed above the tank. By combining automated feed scheduling with computer vision-based monitoring, the system aims to improve feeding management and reduce unnecessary feed distribution. The proposed architecture also integrates an IoT monitoring interface through the Cayenne platform, allowing remote supervision of the system and providing alerts in case of abnormal conditions. This combination of embedded systems, IoT connectivity, and artificial intelligence contributes to the development of smart aquaculture solutions capable of supporting more efficient and sustainable fish farming practices.

Beyond its direct application in aquaculture, the proposed system can also serve as a practical educational platform for students and researchers working in the fields of embedded systems, artificial intelligence, and IoT-based monitoring systems. By integrating hardware and software components within a real-world application, the system offers valuable opportunities for experimentation and interdisciplinary learning in modern AIoT technologies.

II. LITERATURE REVIEW

Several studies have explored the use of IoT and AI technologies to improve aquaculture monitoring and feeding management.

The authors in (Divya et al., 2023) propose an IoT-based smart fish monitoring system built on an ESP32 with connected sensors to track water temperature, level, and basic water quality, while also enabling remote control of feeding, aeration, and heating through a mobile application and Arduino IoT Cloud. Kedhareswari et al. (2025) present an AI-driven IoT framework that integrates underwater cameras, sensors, and machine learning to monitor fish behavior and water quality in real time, enabling early detection of stress, disease, and abnormal feeding patterns. (Adegboye et al., 2020) introduce an intelligent feeding system that uses computer vision to assess fish feeding intensity in real time and adjust the quantity of feed accordingly. By linking fish behavior with automated dispensing, the system reduces feed wastage, avoids underfeeding, and ensures more balanced growth across the fish population. The study of (Daru et al., 2023) presents an IoT-based automatic koi fish feeder that applies fuzzy logic to optimize feeding decisions. Using NodeMCU, ultrasonic sensors, and a servo motor, the system monitors feed levels and dispenses food with precision, while the Mamdani fuzzy method adjusts distribution based on real-time conditions. Table 1 presents a comparison of several representative smart aquaculture systems reported in the literature.

Table 1. Comparison of existing smart aquaculture monitoring systems

Study	Main Technologies	Automated Feeding	Fish Behavior Monitoring	AI Technique
Divya et al. (2023)	ESP32 + environmental sensors + IoT platform	Yes (remote control)	No	None
Kedhareswari et al. (2025)	Cameras + sensors + IoT	Not specified	Yes	Machine Learning
Adegboye et al. (2020)	Camera-based monitoring system	Adaptive feeding	Yes	Computer Vision
Daru et al. (2023)	NodeMCU + ultrasonic sensor + fuzzy logic + servo motor	Yes	No	Fuzzy Logic
Proposed system	**Arduino + Raspberry Pi + camera + IoT**	**Yes**	**Yes**	**CNN (MobileNetV2)**

Previous studies have explored either automated feeding mechanisms or fish behavior monitoring using sensors or computer vision techniques. However, many systems focus on a single functionality and do not combine intelligent fish detection with automated feed distribution. The proposed system integrates both aspects by combining an Arduino-based automatic feeding mechanism with a CNN-based fish detection module implemented on a Raspberry Pi platform. The use of the MobileNetV2 model enables efficient real-time fish identification while maintaining low computational cost, making the system suitable for embedded IoT environments.

III. PROPOSED SYSTEM FOR AQUACULTURE FEEDING MONITORING

This work presents an intelligent system designed for the automatic feeding and real-time monitoring of aquaculture. The proposed system, illustrated in Figure 1, is composed of three interconnected subsystems. The first subsystem is responsible for automatic feeding and is controlled by an Arduino board. This board communicates with a Real-Time Clock (RTC) module to schedule feeding times and with an LCD display to present relevant information to the user. The second subsystem includes a servo motor that manages the opening of the food reservoir. The motor receives control signals from the Arduino, allowing it to rotate and release feed in the appropriate quantity at the scheduled times. This mechanism ensures a controlled and consistent distribution of feed, which contributes to improving feeding efficiency and reducing feed waste. The third subsystem is built around a Raspberry Pi connected to a camera. This unit analyzes the captured images in real time using a convolutional neural network (CNN), enabling the detection and tracking of fish activity in the tank. Through this configuration, the system can feed the fish according to predefined schedules, monitor the state of the reservoir, and detect the presence and behavior of fish, providing a more reliable and automated approach to aquaculture management.

In modern aquaculture systems, environmental monitoring plays a critical role in maintaining optimal conditions for fish growth and health. Parameters such as water temperature, dissolved oxygen (DO), and pH significantly influence fish metabolism, feeding behavior, and overall productivity. As a result, many smart aquaculture platforms integrate water quality sensors to continuously monitor these environmental conditions. By combining automated feeding mechanisms with environmental sensing technologies, aquaculture farms can achieve more precise management of both feeding strategies and habitat conditions.

IV. PROTOTYPE IMPLEMENTATION

A. Automatic Feeding System

The automatic feeding system integrates a Real-Time Clock (RTC) module and an LCD display, as shown in Figure 2. The RTC module is responsible for keeping accurate time through its internal clock and backup battery. It is connected to the Arduino (or microcontroller) to provide the current date and time needed for scheduling. The LCD display, usually an alphanumeric type, shows the main timing information, including the current hour and other details related to the programmed feeding schedule.

Figure 1. Flowchart of the proposed system

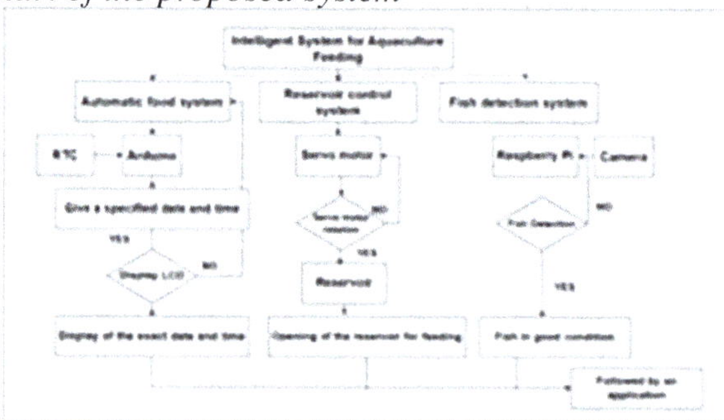

Figure 2. Automatic feeding system

B. Control Reservoir System

The automatic fish feeding system, shown in Figure. 3 consists of a servo motor and a reservoir. The servo motor provides precise control of its output shaft rotation, which is used to drive the food distribution mechanism inside the aquarium. The reservoir, specifically designed for this purpose, stores the fish feed and ensures a steady flow towards the distribution unit. The distribution mechanism, coupled to the servo motor, can take the form of a lever, a hopper, or a similar device that allows food to be released in a controlled way into the aquarium. When the servo motor rotates in a specific direction, the mechanism dispenses a predetermined quantity of feed into the water, ensuring accurate and adequate nourishment for the fish. The quantity of feed distributed can be adjusted by controlling the rotation angle and activation duration of the servo motor. This mechanism allows the system to dispense feed in a controlled and repeatable manner during each scheduled feeding cycle. This programmed feeding system helps maintain an optimal diet by delivering the right amount of food at scheduled times. By combining the servo motor and reservoir, the system achieves reliable and precise feeding, which contributes directly to the health and well-being of the fish.

Figure 3. Control reservoir system

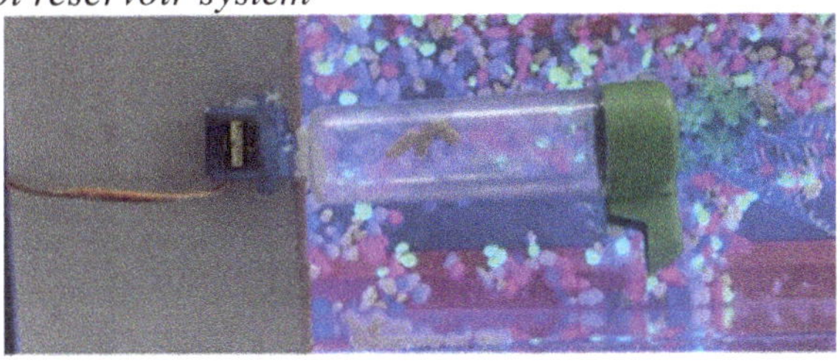

C. Fish Detection System

The fish detection subsystem provides continuous real-time monitoring of the aquarium environment. The system is built around a Raspberry Pi board connected to a camera module that continuously captures images of the fish during feeding periods and normal activity. The captured images are transmitted to an image processing module where they are analyzed using a deep learning model. To perform fish recognition, a convolutional neural network based on MobileNetV2 is employed. MobileNetV2 is a lightweight deep learning architecture specifically designed for embedded and resource-constrained devices. Its efficient structure makes it particularly suitable for deployment on edge computing platforms such as Raspberry Pi, enabling real-time inference while maintaining a good balance between computational efficiency and classification accuracy. The model processes the captured images and extracts visual features that allow the identification of different fish classes. Based on these extracted patterns, the system can monitor fish activity and potentially detect abnormal behaviors during feeding or swimming periods. Figure 4 illustrates the architecture of the MobileNetV2 model(Seidaliyeva et al., 2020). The network receives an input image of size 224×224×3, which first passes through a standard convolution layer responsible for extracting low-level visual features such as edges and textures. After this initial stage, the network is composed of a sequence of bottleneck residual blocks, which represent the core component of the MobileNetV2 architecture and implement the concept of inverted residual connections. Each bottleneck block consists of three main operations. First, a 1×1 convolution layer expands the number of feature channels, allowing the network to learn richer feature representations. This expansion layer is followed by a ReLU6 activation function, which introduces non-linearity while limiting activation values to a maximum of six. The use of ReLU6 improves numerical stability and is particularly suitable for low-precision computations in embedded systems. Next, a depthwise convolution with a 3×3 kernel is applied to perform spatial filtering independently on each feature channel. This operation is also followed by a ReLU6 activation function, enabling the network to capture more complex spatial patterns in the input image. Finally, a 1×1 convolution layer projects the expanded features back into a lower-dimensional space, forming what is known as a linear bottleneck. Unlike the previous layers, this projection layer does not use an activation function in order to preserve the information contained in the feature representation. When the input and output dimensions are compatible, a residual connection is added between the input and output of the block, which improves gradient propagation and facilitates the training of deeper networks. Through the stacking of multiple bottleneck blocks, the network progressively extracts higher-level semantic features from the input images. After the final convolution layer, the extracted features are passed to a fully connected layer, which performs the final classification of the fish species.

Figure 4. MobileNetV2 architecture

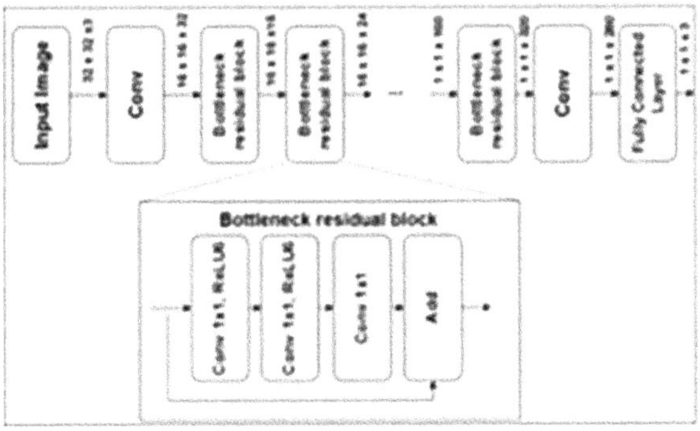

The proposed model was trained using the A Large-Scale Fish Dataset (Ulucan et al., 2020), which was developed to support research in fish species classification and segmentation tasks. This dataset contains images of nine seafood species. For most fish categories, approximately fifty original images were collected for each class. To increase the diversity of the dataset and improve the generalization capability of the learning model, several data augmentation techniques were applied, including image rotations, reflections, and other geometric transformations. Unlike many datasets that rely on uniform white backgrounds, this dataset was intentionally created with a blue and slightly noisy background in order to better simulate real-world conditions. All images were resized to a resolution of 590 × 445 pixels while preserving their original aspect ratio. Through the application of augmentation techniques, each fish category was expanded to approximately 1000 images, resulting in a dataset of nearly 9000 images in total. This large and diverse dataset provides a suitable foundation for training deep learning models capable of accurately recognizing different fish species.

The performance of the MobileNetV2 model was evaluated using the accuracy and loss curves obtained during the training process. Figure 5-a illustrates the evolution of the training and validation accuracy, while Figure 5-b presents the corresponding training and validation loss curves. Accuracy represents the proportion of correctly classified samples, whereas the loss function measures the difference between the predicted outputs and the true class labels. As shown in Figure 5-a, the training accuracy increases rapidly during the first epochs, rising from approximately 78% to more than 98% after only a few epochs. The validation accuracy follows a similar trend and quickly approaches the training accuracy, reaching values close to 100%. The close alignment between the two curves indicates that the model generalizes well to unseen data and does not suffer from significant overfitting. Figure 5-b presents the evolution of the training and validation loss. At the beginning of the training process, the loss values are relatively high, reflecting the initial difficulty of the model in correctly classifying the images. However, both the training and validation losses decrease rapidly during the first epochs and progressively stabilize at very low values. This consistent reduction in loss confirms that the model parameters are effectively optimized during the learning process. Furthermore, the small gap between the training and validation curves demonstrates that the model maintains stable learning behavior and achieves good generalization performance. The final evaluation on the test dataset yielded a test loss of 0.00198 and a test accuracy of 99.89%, indicating that the proposed MobileNetV2-based model is highly effective for fish species classification.

Figure 5. MobileNet performance evaluation

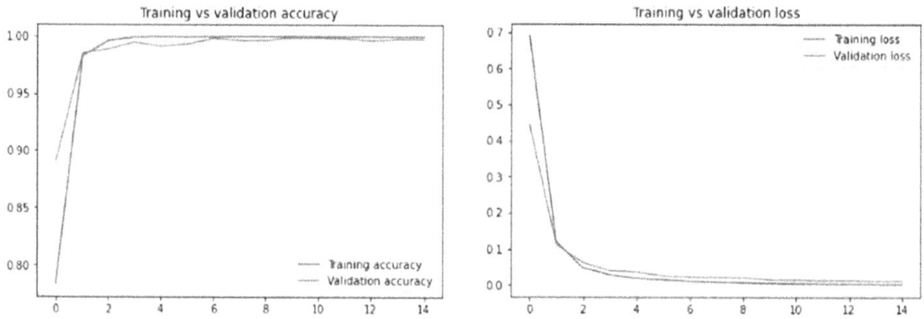

D. Complete Aquaculture Feeding and Monitoring System Implementation

Figure 6 shows the integration of the three subsystems together to build our final prototype. The hardware modules, including the Arduino with the RTC and LCD for time scheduling, the servo motor with the food reservoir to handle automatic feeding, and the Raspberry Pi with a camera for monitoring the fish. All these parts were connected to work as one system, giving us a functional prototype that joins feeding and monitoring in the same platform.

Figure 6. Proposed system implementation

V. RESULTS AND DISCUSSION

In this section, we present the results obtained from our proposed system. Several tests and experiments were carried out to evaluate the performance and effectiveness of the automatic aquaculture feeding and monitoring system. In this setup, a Raspberry Pi is used for data acquisition, analysis, and processing from a USB webcam. The webcam captures real-time images of the aquarium and is connected directly to the Raspberry Pi. To ensure proper coverage of the tank, the camera is placed in a strategic position to focus on the area where fish detection is required, as shown in Figure 7. The combination of the Raspberry Pi and the webcam allows continuous and automated monitoring of the aquarium as illustrated in Figure 8.

Figure 7. Test results of the system fish detection

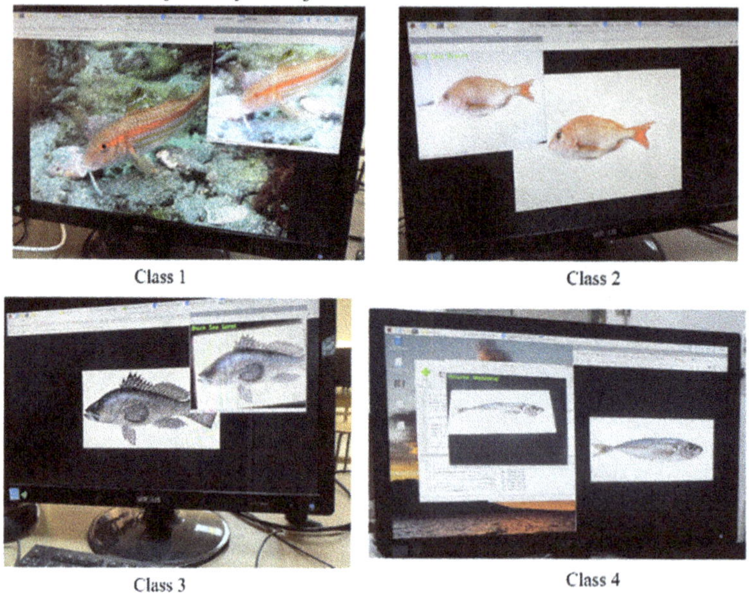

By analyzing the captured images, the system can detect the presence of fish and react accordingly. This functionality is particularly useful for monitoring the aquarium environment, automating tasks such as adjusting feeding according to fish activity, and sending alerts to users in case of abnormal behavior or potential problems in the tank.

Figure 8. Real-time fish detection

The connectivity testing phase of our system was carried out using the IoT platform Cayenne. This platform allowed us to monitor and visualize data from three key events. First, the system was programmed to automatically restart whenever a high temperature or RAM saturation was detected by the Raspberry Pi status interface. This automatic restart is important to maintain proper system operation and to prevent potential malfunctions, as shown in Figure 9.

Through Cayenne, these events could be monitored in real time, making it possible to take timely actions to ensure the stability and reliability of the proposed system. In addition, the Raspberry Pi plays a key role in supervising the feeding action carried out by the automatic distribution system. It continuously monitors this process to ensure that it is executed correctly. If no fish are detected in the aquarium during feeding, the Raspberry Pi triggers an alert and displays a warning message on the Cayenne application, as shown in Figure 10. This functionality ensures that the user is immediately informed of any potential problem with the detection system or in the case of fish absence, allowing corrective measures to be taken without delay.

Figure 9. Automatic system restart in case of problem

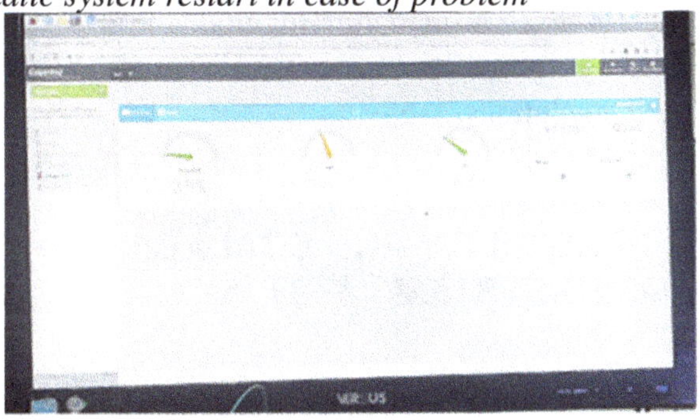

Figure 10. Fish non-detection alert during feeding on the cayenne IoT application

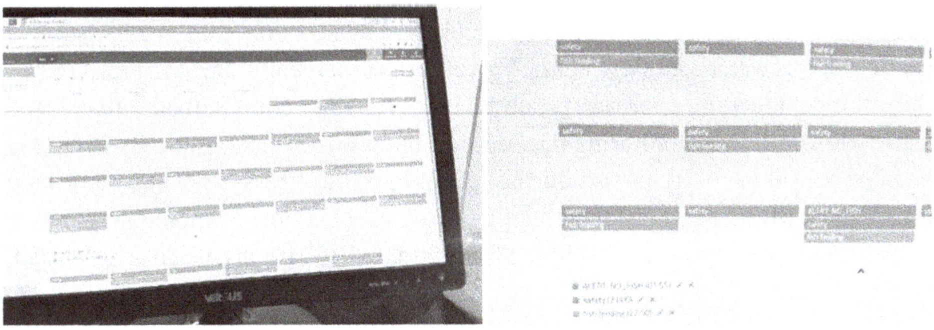

The automatic feeding system is programmed to operate at predefined times. This feature guarantees a regular and consistent feeding routine for the fish, helping to maintain an adequate diet. Feeding times can be easily adjusted and customized according to the specific needs of the fish and the conditions of the aquarium. Moreover, the image-based fish monitoring system produced promising results. The detection and tracking algorithm was able to accurately identify the fish in the aquarium, making it possible to follow their movement and behavior. This capability provides a way to monitor the health and well-being of the fish and to detect abnormal behaviors or potential health problems at an early stage.

In practical aquaculture environments, monitoring systems must operate under challenging conditions characterized by humidity, water splashes, and variable environmental parameters. Therefore, beyond algorithmic performance, the reliability of hardware components and environmental sensing capabilities becomes essential for real farm deployment. Smart aquaculture systems must be designed to operate continuously in wet environments while maintaining accurate monitoring and feeding operations. These considerations highlight the importance of combining intelligent data processing with robust hardware design when developing practical aquaculture monitoring solutions.

VI. ECONOMIC FEASIBILITY AND SCALABILITY OF THE PROPOSED SYSTEM

Beyond technical performance, the practical adoption of smart aquaculture technologies depends on their economic feasibility and their ability to operate in real aquaculture environments. Automated monitoring and feeding systems are increasingly being explored as a way to improve farm productivity while reducing operational costs and labor requirements. In aquaculture production, feed represents one of the most significant expenses, often accounting for a large proportion of total production costs. Inefficient feeding practices can lead to overfeeding, feed waste, and deterioration of water quality, which negatively affect fish health and farm profitability. The intelligent feeding approach proposed in this chapter combines automated feed distribution with fish monitoring through computer vision techniques. By detecting the presence and activity of fish during feeding periods, the system can contribute to a more controlled and efficient feeding process. This type of monitoring makes it possible to avoid unnecessary feed distribution when fish are inactive or absent, thereby reducing feed losses and improving feeding management. In aquaculture, feeding efficiency is commonly evaluated using the Feed Conversion Ratio (FCR), which represents the amount of feed required to produce a given quantity of fish biomass. Lower FCR values indicate more efficient feed utilization. Intelligent feeding systems that distribute feed according to fish behavior and activity therefore have the potential to improve FCR and contribute to more sustainable aquaculture production. From an economic perspective, the proposed system relies on commonly available Internet of Things (IoT) technologies such as microcontrollers, embedded processing units, camera modules, and electromechanical actuators. These technologies are widely used in embedded and monitoring applications and are relatively accessible for research and prototype development. The integration of such components allows the creation of flexible and modular aquaculture monitoring platforms that can be adapted to different operational requirements. Although the current implementation was validated as a prototype in an aquarium environment, the proposed architecture provides a foundation for the development of larger-scale smart aquaculture systems. For deployment in commercial aquaculture farms or outdoor ponds, several engineering considerations must be taken into account. Electronic components would need to be protected using waterproof enclosures, and sensors should be designed using corrosion-resistant materials suitable for humid or saltwater environments. In addition, more robust camera systems and communication infrastructures may be required to ensure reliable monitoring in outdoor conditions.

VII. CONCLUSION

In this paper, an intelligent aquaculture system that combines automatic feeding with real-time fish monitoring is developed. The proposed system integrates an Arduino with RTC and LCD for scheduling, a servo motor with a food reservoir for feeding, and a Raspberry Pi with a camera for fish detection. Tests showed that the system can reliably dispense food at predefined times and monitor fish activity through image analysis. The CNN-based detection achieved promising accuracy, while the Cayenne IoT platform enabled remote alerts and supervision. As a result, the system improves feeding efficiency, reduces manual effort, and supports healthier aquaculture management. Future work will focus on improving the accuracy and robustness of the fish detection algorithm by training the CNN with larger and more diverse datasets. In addition, integrating water quality sensors and automating environmental parameters such as temperature, oxygen, and pH will allow for a more complete monitoring and management solution. Finally, exploring cloud connectivity would open the way to advanced features and extended remote control of the system.

VIII. FUTURE WORK AND RESEARCH DIRECTIONS

Although the proposed system demonstrates promising results for automated feeding and fish monitoring, several improvements can be explored in future developments. The current implementation was designed as a prototype and validated in a controlled aquarium environment. While this configuration allows the evaluation of the system architecture and its main functionalities, additional developments are required to extend the solution to real aquaculture farming conditions. One important direction for future work is the integration of water quality monitoring sensors. Environmental parameters such as water temperature, dissolved oxygen, and pH play a crucial role in fish health and aquaculture productivity. By incorporating sensors capable of measuring these parameters, the system could provide a more comprehensive monitoring platform that combines environmental supervision with intelligent feeding management. Another potential improvement concerns the enhancement of the fish detection and behavior analysis model. Training the convolutional neural network with larger and more diverse datasets could improve detection accuracy and enable the identification of more complex behavioral patterns such as stress, abnormal swimming activity, or feeding response. In addition, future developments may focus on improving the scalability of the system for deployment in larger aquaculture environments.

REFERENCES

Adegboye, M. A., Aibinu, A. M., Kolo, J. G., Aliyu, I., Folorunso, T. A., & Lee, S.-H. (2020). Incorporating Intelligence in Fish Feeding System for Dispensing Feed Based on Fish Feeding Intensity. *IEEE Access : Practical Innovations, Open Solutions*, *8*, 91948–91960. DOI: 10.1109/ACCESS.2020.2994442

Adimulam, R. P., Kokkiligadda, V., & Polagani, A. (2024). Automatic Feed Dispenser for Aquaculture using Arduino Technology. *2024 3rd International Conference for Advancement in Technology (ICONAT)*, 1–5. DOI: 10.1109/ICONAT61936.2024.10774929

Choudhury, M. E., Sathvin, C. S., Akash, M., & Sundar, S. (2025). Smart Fish Feeding and Monitoring System. *2025 International Conference on Sensors and Related Networks (SENNET) Special Focus on Digital Healthcare(64220)*, 1–6. DOI: 10.1109/SENNET64220.2025.11136052

Daru, A. F., Hirzan, A. M., Susanto, S., & Adhiwibowo, W. (2023). Automatic Koi Fish Feeding Device with Internet of Things Concept Using Fuzzy Control Logic. *2023 International Conference on Technology, Engineering, and Computing Applications (ICTECA)*, 1–6. DOI: 10.1109/ICTECA60133.2023.10490906

Divya, T., Ramyadevi, R., & Vijaya Chamundeeswari, V. (2023). Smart fish monitoring system using IoT. In A. Dagur, K. Singh, P. S. Mehra, & D. K. Shukla, *Artificial Intelligence, Blockchain, Computing and Security Volume 2* (1st ed., pp. 270–273). CRC Press. DOI: 10.1201/9781032684994-42

Ilahy, R., R'him, T., Tlili, I., & Jebari, H. (n.d.). *Effect of Different Shading Levels on Growth and Yield Parameters of a Hot Pepper (Capsicum annuum L.) Cultivar 'Beldi' Grown in Tunisia*. (1).

Kedhareswari, B., Indu, S., Kumar, P. V., Meenakshi Srivani, N., & Saikeerthana, T. (2025). AI-Driven IoT System for Real-Time Fish Behaviour Monitoring and Automated Feeding in Smart Aquaculture. *2025 5th International Conference on Trends in Material Science and Inventive Materials (ICTMIM)*, 1236–1242. DOI: 10.1109/ICTMIM65579.2025.10988280

Luna, M., Llorente, I., & Cobo, A. (2022). Determination of feeding strategies in aquaculture farms using a multiple-criteria approach and genetic algorithms. *Annals of Operations Research*, *314*(2), 551–576. DOI: 10.1007/s10479-019-03227-w

Seidaliyeva, U., Akhmetov, D., Ilipbayeva, L., & Matson, E. T. (2020). Real-Time and Accurate Drone Detection in a Video with a Static Background. *Sensors (Basel)*, *20*(14), 3856. Advance online publication. DOI: 10.3390/s20143856 PMID: 32664365

Tina, F. W., Afsarimanesh, N., Nag, A., & Alahi, M. E. E. (2025). Integrating AIoT Technologies in Aquaculture: A Systematic Review. *Future Internet*, *17*(5), 199. DOI: 10.3390/fi17050199

Ubina, N. A., Lan, H.-Y., Cheng, S.-C., Chang, C.-C., Lin, S.-S., Zhang, K.-X., Lu, H.-Y., Cheng, C.-Y., & Hsieh, Y.-Z. (2023). Digital twin-based intelligent fish farming with Artificial Intelligence Internet of Things (AIoT). *Smart Agricultural Technology*, *5*, 100285. DOI: 10.1016/j.atech.2023.100285

Ulucan, O., Karakaya, D., & Turkan, M. (2020). A Large-Scale Dataset for Fish Segmentation and Classification. *2020 Innovations in Intelligent Systems and Applications Conference (ASYU)*, 1–5. DOI: 10.1109/ASYU50717.2020.9259867

Wu, A.-Q., Li, K.-L., Song, Z.-Y., Lou, X., Hu, P., Yang, W., & Wang, R.-F. (2025). Deep Learning for Sustainable Aquaculture: Opportunities and Challenges. *Sustainability (Basel)*, *17*(11), 5084. DOI: 10.3390/su17115084

Yue, K., & Shen, Y. (2022). An overview of disruptive technologies for aquaculture. *Aquaculture and Fisheries. Aquaculture and Fisheries*, *7*(2), 111–120. DOI: 10.1016/j.aaf.2021.04.009

Chapter 8

Higher Education Instruction Through AI-Powered Automation With Machine Learning in Financial Market Prediction:

Algorithmic Trading, Structural Limits, and Economic Realities

Mohammad Irfan
http://orcid.org/0000-0002-4956-1170
Chandigarh University, India

Bhanu Pratap Singh
http://orcid.org/0009-0002-5233-1170
Chandigarh University, India

Saurabh Kumar
SRM University, India

Rashi Malik
SRM University, India

DOI: 10.4018/979-8-2600-2811-7.ch008

ABSTRACT

AI-powered teaching support has reshaped financial market prediction by capturing non-linear relationships, complex features, and hidden structures in data. Improved computing power and advanced algorithms have raised hopes of overcoming earlier forecasting limits. Yet, financial markets tend to absorb information quickly, reducing the scope for consistent predictability. Although these models can detect patterns, their stability over time remains doubtful. Market data often show non-stationarity, volatility clustering, and structural changes, making predictions less reliable. In addition, as market participants adapt, widely known patterns lose their advantage. Challenges such as overfitting, data leakage, and weak signal strength further affect model outcomes. Studies also show that better statistical results do not always lead to real economic benefits once costs and risks are considered. Therefore, the limits of prediction are largely economic in nature, and machine learning is better viewed as a support tool for decision-making rather than a guaranteed source of excess returns.

1. INTRODUCTION

Movement prediction in financial markets has been at the forefront of intersections of economics, statistics, and applied mathematics. The attempt to model the movement of asset prices is an intellectual activity as well as a practical necessity, because it has the implication of capital allocation, portfolio management and risk avoidance. The classical financial theory, embodied by the Efficient Market Hypothesis, has introduced a background of scepticism on systematic predictability. Consistent with financial theory, markets incorporate information efficiently (Fama, 1970). Later empirical studies have strengthened these theoretical limitations and have shown that it is very hard to forecast with consistency superior benchmark models in long horizons (Goyal, 2007).

Nevertheless, theoretical work in data processing and computational learning has made a resurgence in the belief in algorithmic forecasting as a means of discovering non-linear high dimensional structures never reachable through the traditional econometric models (Hastie, 2009). Predictive frameworks have become more advanced, starting with support-vector machines and ensemble learning and changing to deep neural architecture (Vapnik, 1998; Goodfellow, Bengio, & Courville, 2016).

There is one major question up till now: does increased computational capability yield economically viable predictive power? The proposed research aims to address that question and dwells upon the structural constraints of machine learning in the competitive, adaptive financial ecosystem.

1.1 Historical Underpinnings of Predictability of Markets

The initial empirical studies of financial economics focused on the stochastic nature of asset prices and the feasibility of profitability of patterns of returns. According to theoretical assertions, the prices that are correctly predicted are supposed to change erratically in reaction to new information (Samuelson, 1965). These challenges formed the basis of formal statements of informational efficiency, according to which surplus returns are possible to be produced not systematically using data accessible in the market (Fama, 1991). Patterns into predictability in empirical studies of the predictability of returns, weak, context-dependent results were often found.

Studies of equity risk premia showed that lots of candidate predictors failed to satisfy robustness in out of sample. Furthermore, econometric tests revealed deep-seated structural instability and drift in parameters over the years and made it difficult to determine the long- term forecasting correlations (Pesaran & Timmermann, 1995). Such results set a reserved standard upon which modern algorithmic methods have to be evaluated.

1.2 History of Machine Learning on Financial Models

The spread of high frequency data and alternative sources of data and stream of text-based information transformed the analytical landscape of finance. Machine learning became a toolbox of flexible models that could model nonlinear interactions without any strict parametric assumptions (Breiman, 2001). Initial users of neural networks used artificial neural networks to model complex time-dependence of time-series that went beyond linear autoregressive models (Zhang, 2003).

Similar progress in transformer-based models of natural-language-processing has made it possible to extract sentiment evidence on news and corporate disclosures (Devlin et al., 2019). Though these breakthroughs both massively increased the capacity of modelling, they are also the sources that raised an issue about generalisation and interpretability, which have become central methodological challenges (Bishop, 2006).

1.3 Structure Complexity and Adaptation of the Market

Financial markets are essentially different to the setting of prediction which is fixed and static since they are constituted of learning agents interacting. In case of algorithmic strategies, the capital flows modify the prices and may eliminate the patterns to which the strategies rely (Farmer & Lo, 1999). This adaptive feedback implies that predictive success is often short-lived. The views of Adaptive Markets represents markets as evolutionary systems whereby efficiency varies based on the periods and competition levels (Lo, 2004).

In this context, algorithmic prediction at a profit depends on conditions related to regimes and behaviour of participants. Evidence of empirical studies on regime shifts indicate that, structural discontinuities occur frequently and shift the nature of returns thus diminishing the stability of learned parameters (Bai, 2003). Therefore, an increase in algorithmic sophistication does not cut predictive models off the environmental weakness.

1.4 Financial Machine Learning Methodological Vulnerabilities

Despite the high in-sample performance of machine learning algorithms, financial data is the worst to work with due to its low signal-to-noise ratio and a significant risk of over-fitting. The fact that modern models are intrinsically flexible also seeks to increase the probability of picking up stochastic noise as opposed to structure of economic significance (López de Prado, 2018). The multiple hypothesis testing and data mining activities may get statistically significant but economically spurious results (Diebold & Mariano, 1995).

In addition, financial time series have volatility clusters and heteroskedasticity making it harder to validate a model (Pagan & Schwert, 1990). Most statistically promising strategies do not lead to risk-adjusted profitability when the transaction costs, liquidity constraints and market impact are taken into consideration (Jensen, 1978). Such realities of methodology necessitate the assessment strategies that transcend the issue of predictive soundness to the issue of economic soundness.

1.5 Research Gap and Study Contributions

The available body of literature generally tests machine learning models using statistical metrics or momentary forecasting results. There is a dearth of literature incorporating the computational performance with the structural economic constraints, adaptive competition, and behavioural instability in a single analysis (Mullainathan & Spiess, 2017).

Furthermore, appropriate attention is given to algorithmic innovation with an underestimation of systemic consequences of embracing a large-scale adoption of the models (Bouchaud, Farmer, & Lillo, 2009). This paper aims to re-brand machine learning as part of the large institutional and competitive structure of financial markets. It states that the frontiers of predictive performance are mostly economic, and not computational. The paper combines the information provided by financial theory, econometrics, behavioural finance, and computational learning theory to suggest that algorithmic forecasting can be interpreted as a conditional, regime dependent decision support mechanism, but not as a universally accurate prediction engine (Ang & Timmermann, 2012).

1.6 Repackaging Predictability, Economic Feasibility and Computational Capability

The fast development of computational intelligence has spawned the unspoken belief that any improvement in the algorithm architecture would result in better forecasting performance. Emerging technical capabilities of detecting complicated patterns in financial data have grown in recent years with advances in ensemble learning, deep neural networks and high-dimensional optimisation (Hastie et al., 2009; Goodfellow et al., 2016; Irfan et al., 2023). However, the capability of computation cannot be equated to economic feasibility. Financial markets are sharply distinct to the traditional prediction tasks in that price formation is self-inflicted upon participant behaviour and strategic interaction; successful prediction may in turn change the environment with which it is based (Brock & Hommes, 1998).

As discussed earlier, financial returns exhibit a low signal-to-noise ratio. Competitive dynamics and the arbitrage of opportunities tend to squeeze exploitable opportunities even in cases where machine learning systems have shown marginal statistical gains (Farmer, Patelli, & Zovko, 2005). This fact highlights a formidable conceptual difference between modern study: the cutting edge of machine learning is characterized by the efficiency of optimisation, the cutting edge of financial forecasting characterised by economic competition and structural uncertainty. According to recent interdisciplinary studies in economics, predictive algorithms are currently to be assessed in institutional and incentive contexts, in which they are implemented (Mullainathan & Spiess, 2017), (Singh et al., 2024).

Competitive capital markets yield their profits based not only on the accuracy of their forecast but also on timing, scalability, exposure to risk and crowding effects. With more institutions implementing such like data driven strategy, divergent benefit of diversification may be reduced and systemic vulnerability heightened through correlation between algorithmic behaviours (Bouchaud, Farmer, & Lillo, 2009). As a result, the revision of the boundaries of machine learning requires the reconsideration of the segregated model accuracy in the context of expanded economic sustainability and a system-wide effect.

1.7 Market Microstructure and Short Term Predictability

Although the presence of long-horizon predictability has been an issue of contention, short-term predictability of financial markets has been a topic of interest as per market microstructure. Transient predictive opportunities can be generated during an order-flow imbalance, bid-ask spread, and liquidity shock (Bouchaud, Farmer, & Lillo, 2009). These inefficiencies in the microstructure are in the form of trading frictions and not macroeconomic mispricing. Limit order book data has also been the target of machine learning models because of the high-frequency data, short-lived patterns can be identified (Kearns & Nevmyvaka, 2013).

However, predictive benefits tend to diminish when there is an increase in the level of algorithmic competition, which supports the perspective of predictability in the field of financial market as being conditional and arbitraged out (Farmer, Patelli, & Zovko, 2005).

1.8 Behavioral Dynamics and Market Irrationality

The market is irrational and exhibits behavioral dynamics. Along with the structural and informational factors, certain literature of behavioural finance helps to clarify the impact of cognitive biases on the formation of prices. Investors are often guilty of overconfidence, loss aversion and herding behaviour that can create temporary anomalies in the market (Kahneman, 2011). The betting is recorded in empirical research of over-reactions and momentum effects that test pure versions of market efficiency (De Bondt & Thaler, 1985). The latest development in the natural language processing offers machine learning to include sentiment signals of news and social media platforms (Tetlock, 2007). Though such methods show short-term predictable value, behavioural indicators are unpredictable and specific to situations, which makes them unreliable in the long run.

1.9 Stability of the Economic Multilinear Model

One of the features of financial time series is non-stationarity. Distribution of returns, regime of volatility and structure of correlation change with time as a result of macroeconomic changes, policy changes as well as innovation in technology (Hamilton, 1989). Multiple structural breaks can be detected through various formal statistical process that show high variability in the parameters of financial data (Bai & Perron, 2003). Such instability makes the prediction modelling difficult since the results of learning relationships in one regime are not guaranteed to be the same as in the following environment. Therefore, the prediction of performance ought to be measured in terms of regime-conscious constructs instead of homogeneous past samples (Ang & Timmermann, 2012).

1.10 Model Risk, Overfitting, Data Mining

The adaptability of the modern machine learning architectures increases the threat of over-fitting especially in signal-to-noise-ratio-characterised datasets. Financial returns are not only highly random but also highly vulnerable to being subjected to spurious patterns detection considering the fact that the returns accommodate a high level of randomness as opposed to exploitable form. The frequency of hypothesis testing and the heavy engineering of features may over inflate back-testing performance that has no real economic content (López de Prado, 2018).

The theory of statistical learning underlines the trade-off and postulates that over the complexity of model the high-level of the generalisation capacity, and so, alerting that the over-parameterisation of a model can lead to the deterioration of out-of-sample quality (Bishop, 2006). These risks to methods are important to highlight the need of strong validation procedures and financial interpretability.

1.11 Practice Learning and Multistage Decision-Making

Unlike the supervised classification models, the reinforcement learning structures view financial prediction as a stepwise decision-making process. The interaction between agents and an environment and reward-feedback mechanisms obtain optimal trading policies (Sutton & Barto, 2018). The deep reinforcement learning has already been applied to complex control settings such as strategic games (Mnih et al., 2015).

However, in financial markets, transaction costs, market impact and adaptive competition are determinants of the reward structure. The factors break the assumption of Markov in the stationary (Lo, 2004). As such, as much as reinforcement learning is dynamically adaptable, its use in finance is limited by environmental uncertainty.

1.12 Objectives and Study Contribution Research Objectives

It is on this theoretical and empirical background that the current study is aimed at re-evaluating the limits of machine learning in predicting financial markets using an integrated conceptual and empirical framework. The predictive capacity in both static and adaptive contexts are determined by fusing correlation analysis, Support Vector Machine prediction and reinforcement learning modeling in the research.

The main aim is not just to measure the accurateness of forecasting, but it aims to find out whether the sophistication of the algorithms has the power to surmount structural limitations inherent in competitive markets. The available studies tend to focus on gradual statistical progress with an omnipresent inclusion of economic feasibility and regime sensitivity (Mullainathan & Spiess, 2017). This article helps to bridge the research gap by validating machine learning performance in a systematic relationship with structural instability, adaptive competition, and economic evaluation statements. By doing so, this will promote a more realistic view of algorithmic trading as a conditional decision-support system, not as a continuing source of abnormal returns (Fama, 1991).

2. LITERATURE REVIEW

2.1 Background of Financial Predictability

Since the existing financial system operates under complete predictability, it follows that the foundations of financial predictability are established. The discussion of predictability in financial markets has derivatives in the fundamental economic theories of informational efficiency and rational expectation. This was discussed by the early theoretical arguments theorizing that the available information is nearly reflected by the price of an asset such that similar abnormal returns cannot be found with consistency (Fama, 1970). To augment this argument, formal stochastic models postulated that the expected prices do change in forms of randomness and it therefore constrained the possibilities of systematic forecasting (Samuelson, 1965). All these arguments formed a theoretical standard with which future predictive methodologies would have to be judged.

Empirical studies of predictability of returns have had inconclusive results. Some studies reported insignificant but statistically significant pattern of returns with the use of macroeconomic variables and value ratio (Pesaran & Timmermann, 1995). However, extensive testing established that a high number of predictors are unable to be maintained in out of sample situations most especially when they are tested over extended horizons (Welch & Goyal, 2007). These contradictions strengthened the doubts about the existence of exploitable signals in the competitive stock markets.

2.2 Limits of Econometric Evolution and Forecasting

Earlier, financial forecasting strongly depended on econometric models, including autoregressions, the vector autoregression, and factor-based regressions. These procedures presented systematic explanations of dynamics of returns but were limited by the assumptions of linearity and stabilized parameter formulation (Campbell, Lo, & MacKinlay, 1997). Heteroskedasticity and volatility clustering in the returns of assets were resolved through introduction of conditional volatility models including ARCH and GARCH (Pagan & Schwert, 1990).

These models helped a lot in estimating the risk but did not significantly address the question of predictability of returns. The literature on structural break also revealed that in the case with financial time series the assumption of parameters constancy is often violated (Bai & Perron, 2003). Regime switching models emphasized the switch of economic environment between the state of different volatility and returns (Hamilton, 1989). These results suggest that predictive relations can be non-persistent but episodic, and thus it is difficult to predict across time periods.

2.3 Emerging Finance Machine Learning

The growing access to massive datasets and computing power enhanced the introduction of machine learning methods in financial modeling (Irfan et al., 2023). In contrast to the classical econometric models, ML methods focus on predictive accuracy instead of a focus on parameters (Breiman, 2001). The tree-based ensembles and support machine (SVM) proved to have the ability to shape the non-linear relationships in the financial data (Vapnik, 1998). The initial applications of the neural networks attempted to represent the sophisticated correlation in the stock market price changes and among financial macro-factors (Zhang, 2003).

Later comparative computations indicated that ML procedures tend to surpass the benchmarks in short-term classification, especially in direction-forecasting drawbacks (Yen & Lee, 2008). The opponents however claim that financial datasets are not like traditional domains of supervised learning since the signal is weak and the noise overrides the structure. This small signal to noise space makes it more likely that the flexible models pick up spurious correlations.

2.4 Multimodal Architectures and Deep Learning

However, over the recent years we have seen a change toward much deeper architectures that are able to extract features in a hierarchical manner. Recurrent neural networks (RNNs) and long short-term memory (LSTM) systems have been extensively used as mechanisms of modeling sequential relationships of stock returns (Nelson, Pereira, & Oliveira, 2017). Additionally, convolutional neural networks are transformed to extract structure patterns in the limit order book data (Hoseinzade & Haratizadeh, 2019). Models based on transformers proposed the mechanisms of attention that enhanced the processing of financial text information in a context (Devlin et al., 2019).

Intermodal models that combine price, text-based sentiment, and relational graph information have documented a higher level of performance compared to unimodal systems (Li et al., 2020). In spite of these improvements, issues on interpretability and generalization are a major concern. Deep architectures can be used as high-capacity approximators of functions, but they do not have economic interpretability (Goodfellow, Bengio, & Courville, 2016). The fact that there are no clear rules of decision making makes it rather hard to assess the possibility of predictive gains as manifestations of significant economic structure.

2.5 Behavioural Finance and Anomalies in the Market

Behavioral finance literature criticizes the realistic assumption of fully rational agents by highlighting the cognitive bias and decision-making as a heuristic. The empirical data follow investor overreaction and underreaction to the information, which produce short-term anomalies (De Bondt & Thaler, 1985). Psychological models place emphasis on overconfidence, representativeness bias and loss aversion as the factors that influence the dynamics of pricing assets (Kahneman, 2011).

Story-based market changes have also been demonstrated to shape the valuation cycles and speculative bubbles (Shiller, 2017). Algorithms are being used in machine learning to include sentiment indicators based on textual analysis and social media indicators (Tetlock, 2007). Even though these models can show some short-term predictive gains, behavioral consequences may be regime-specific and unstable.

2.6 Microstructure and High-Frequency Evidence of the Market

Predictability of short-horizon price fluctuations has been an active topic of research in the literature of market -microstructure. Disorder in order flow, startling liquidity outsider shocks, and the rearrangements in the bid-ask spread will provide momentary chances of forecasting (Bouchaud, Farmer, & Lillo, 2009). The use of machine-learn algorithms on limit-order book information has discovered patterns in prices at the level of a few microseconds (Kearns & Nevmyvaka, 2013)

However, the implementation of these strategies depends on highly complex, low-latency infrastructure. It has been shown empirically that the benefit of high-frequency predictability is swiftly arbitraged as the competition between algorithms grows (Farmer & Zovko, 2005). Based on this, the microstructure literature confirms the perception that any predictive advantage is short lived and reliant on technological asymmetry.

2.7 Evaluation Metrics: Statistical and Economic Significance

The non-correlations present between statistical improvements and economic benefits frequently occur in the literature on predictive finance. Comparative forecast-evaluation tends generally to measure the decrease in the error of prediction but not necessarily profitability (Diebold & Mariano, 1995). Strict research of equity-premium forecasting demonstrates that even complex predictors at best have only a marginal impact over simple one-point averages at real-time settings (Goyal & Welch,

2008). When transaction costs, turnover and risk-adjusted measures are taken into consideration, many algorithmic schemes lose their attractiveness (Jensen, 1978). Such observations are important in terms of embedding economic constraints in model-evaluation schemes.

2.8 Raising Concerns: Interpretability and Systemic Concerns

Financial instability: Due to the rapidly rising rate of adoption of machine-learning systems in financial institutions, the question of transparency and the stability of systems become important. The black-box models blur causal reasoning strategies, thus making it difficult to govern the problem and regulate it (Bishop, 2006). Synchronised trading might increase stress volatility when a number of institutions operate a similar predictive architecture (Farmer & Lo, 1999). The study of the complex adaptive systems suggests an increased systemic vulnerability caused by the homogeneity of technology (LeBaron, 2006). Therefore, the literature suggests that machine learning can be limited in performance only to a certain degree where it entails institution and systemic factors.

3. RESEARCH METHODOLOGY

3.1 Research and Analytical Framework

In the current research, an integrated methodological research design is implemented, which will combine conceptual synthesis and empirical modeling to question the shortcomings of machine learning in predicting the financial-market. Its theoretical part provides the economical background, and the empirical one can assess the predicting behavior under the conditions of realities (Campbell, Lo, & MacKinlay, 1997).

The study model includes three and supportive analytical layers: 1) statistical analysis and dependency mapping through heatmap correlations; 2) supervised classification, using Support-vector-Machines (SVM) and adaptive decision-making, based on the Reinforcement Learning (RL). This multilayer method allows considering the case of both Detection of the static pattern and dynamic learning aspect of financial conditions, which is becoming the trend of the applied machine-learning literature in economics (Mullainathan & Spiess, 2017).

3.2 Data Preprocessing and Data Structure

The characteristic features of financial time - series data are non- stationarity, clustering of volatility and undispersed return distribution. To counter such features, daily log returns are normally computed to cinch variance and normalize scale across assets. The methods of feature engineering involved lagged returns, moving averages, volatility measures, relative strength index (RSI) and volume-based measurements.

Time-series splitting is done through rolling-window validation as opposed to random cross-validation to preserve time to avoid leakage of information (Hyndman & Athanasopoulos, 2018). Normalization is conducted using standard scaling to ensure model convergence, particularly for margin-based classifiers such as SVM (Vapnik, 1998).

3.3 HeatMap Correlation and Dependency Using HeatMaps.

Table 1. Correlation matrix (heatmap data)

Returns	1	-0.08296	0.444836	-0.05779	0.016979
Volatility	-0.08296	1	-0.05709	0.074446	-0.05104
Momentum	0.444836	-0.05709	1	-0.04219	0.358282
Volume	-0.05779	0.074446	-0.04219	1	-0.02535
Target	0.016979	-0.05104	0.358282	-0.02535	1

Exploratory data analysis facilitates visualization of linear dependencies between engineered features using heatmaps of correlation prior to the use of predictive models. Heatmaps give a graphical expression of Pearson or Spearman correlation coefficients and therefore clarify the multicollinearity structures and predictors that may be redundant (Zhang, 2003).

Various features interacting in a financial context can confound real predictive information because of the overlap between information structures; strong correlations can be used to refine the dimensions and select features (Breiman, 2001). It should however be pointed out that correlation does not imply predictive causality especially in markets that have regime changes and structural volatility (Bai & Perron, 2003). On this note, the usefulness of heatmaps in diagnostic purposes cannot be considered conclusive tests of predictive power.

3.4 Support Vector Machine (SVM) Modeling

SVM offers a trained classification system to forecast the directional market trends. SVM develops an ideal hyperplane that splits the classes with the highest margin, which makes it particularly functional in high-dimensional systems (Vapnik, 1998). Nonlinear nonlinearity of the input space is provided by specific kernel functions, including radial basis function (RBF), and therefore, the complex boundaries in financial data can be identified (Hastie, Tibshirani, & Friedman, 2009).

Evidence also indicates that SVM is relatively robust with relation to the existing linear models in financial classification tasks (Yen & Lee, 2008). Hyperparameters such as the regularisation parameter C and kernel parameters were optimized using grid search to prevent overfitting. In spite of its successes, SVM is susceptible to the variance in regimes and the composition of classes, common in the aspects of financial returns distributions (Ang & Timmermann, 2012). Therefore, its performance has to be approached cautiously in adaptive-market contexts.

3.5 Reinforcement Learning Framework of Adaptive Trading

Figure 1. RL reward per episode

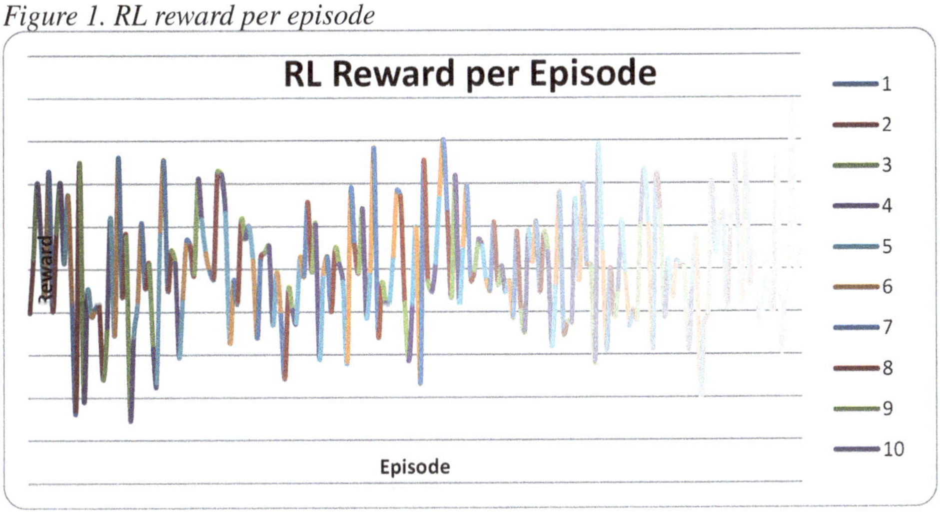

In order to capture the concept of dynamic adaptation, a reinforcement learning (RL) framework is included in this study. As opposed to paradigms of the supervised learning, RL evolves through the active exploration of the environment and taking actions that maximize the total cumulative reward, which is described by Sutton and Barto (2018).

In finance, the environment is characterized by market states based on engineered characteristics; the agent chooses an action, e.g. to Buy, Sell or Hold, and gets rewards depending on risk-adjusted returns. Deep Q - networks (DQN) approximate value functions operate in high dimensional state space. Sequential decision-making activities that would fit with the portfolio-rebalancing strategies are especially suited to RL. However, financial markets do not satisfy the stationary Markov hypotheses of classical RL models; These challenges reflect the non-stationarity and regime dynamics discussed earlier, trading costs, and competitor adaptation and hence the issue of convergence stability (Lo, 2004), (Irfan et al., 2026).

Based on this, the structural economic constraints are used in the evaluation of RL outcomes as opposed to the maximisation of pure rewards.

3.6 Evaluation and Validation Plan of the Model

Statistical diagnostics and economic performance metrics are used to evaluate the performance of the proposed models. Statistical diagnostics are Accuracy, Precision, Recall, F1 -Score and ROC-AUC, and economic diagnostics are cumulative returns, Sharpe ratio, maximum drawdown, and turnover adjusted profitability. The tests of forecast comparison by Diebold and Mariano (1995) are used to prove the statistical superiority of one model over another. Moreover, transaction costs which were retrieved out of Jensen (1978) are included to make sure that the analysis is based on practical trading conditions.

The out of sample performance is also examined in various market regimes to examine the time-permanence of the strategy, which is following regime conscious validation paradigms of Ang and Timmermann (2012). Combining a fixed classification algorithm (SVM) with a method of adaptive decision-making through reinforcement learning, the approach enables a more subtle assessment of the possibility of algorithmic sophistication to overcome natural market limitations.

3.7 Checking Robustness and Sensitivity

In order to reflect the idea that predictive results are not just products of the specific choice of parameters or sample arrangements, strict robustness tests are put within the methodological framework. As discussed earlier, financial datasets are highly prone to overfitting, sensitivity is evaluated across model specifications (López de Prado, 2018). With the SVM, sensitivity of hyperparameters is explored through changing the values of kernel parameters, and strength of regularisation, thus, by evaluating the robustness of classification results.

The reinforcement-learning element has rates of exploration and discount factors that are adjusted in a systematic manner to experiment convergence dynamics when reward structures are varied (Sutton & Barto, 2018). It also rolls back testing using windows so as to evaluates the stability of information with respect to time in subperiods as the process is considered necessary in cases where structural breaks could alter relationships with prediction over time (Bai & Perron, 2003). The empirical validity of such findings is therefore enhanced, by such robustness analyses, as one is able to differentiate genuine predictive data, which cut across samples, and merely noise associated with the sample.

3.8 Economic Backtesting and Adjustment of the transaction cost.

Although statistical measures shed light on predictive correctness, economic authentication requires simulation in realistic trading borders. It follows that the methodology includes techniques of back-testing, which are used in converting the model projections into a hypothetical trade strategy, where the position size has been adjusted to directional predictions and returns realized over investment period.

Predominantly stated by the explicit presence of transaction costs, both in form of bid-ask spreads and expenses associated with the turnover, makes the profitability estimates inflated unnaturally (Jensen, 1978). It has been empirically proved that the failure to consider the cost of implementation can overstate the performance of algorithms (Goyal & Welch, 2008). Risk-adjusted measures like the Sharpe ratio and the maximum drawdown are then calculated in order to evaluate economical feasibility in excess of crude cumulative returns (Campbell & MacKinlay, 1997). The framework ensures that findings made based on machine-learning models are based on practical trading constraints and not on statistical optimisation.

4. FINDINGS AND ANALYSIS

4.1 Signal Strength and Feature Dependency

The heat map of correlation shows linear moderate relationships between the engineered financial indicators with stronger relationships being known between the lagged returns and short-term momentum variables. However, the size of the correlation coefficients is rather low, which indicates the lack of linear predictability in the dataset. This observation is consistent with earlier findings that financial returns are dominated by noise.

Although some of the volatility-related variables exhibit the clustering behaviour, their predictive ability seems to be unsteady when considered between the subperiods. According to structural-break literature, these relationships are likely to be vivid periods, as opposed to lasting relationships, especially in a setting that experiences macroeconomic migration of regimes (Bai & Perron, 2003). As a result, the heatmap contributes to the idea that the financial data are not organized into a consistent and definitive design.

4.2 Support Vector Machine Performance Appraisal

The SVM classifier exhibits moderate predictive performance in forecasting directional prices. Out of sample results in the short-term indicate that the nonlinear kernel functions attain some boundary separation of positive and negative return states. This result aligns with literature which states that margin-based classifiers are able to avert linear benchmarks on high dimensional financial situations (Yen & Lee, 2008).

Although the statistical measures are acceptable, though, model performance changes with rolling windows, suggesting that it is sensitive to changes in the dynamism of returns over time. This finding is consistent with evidence of regime switches which predicts that the correlation between the predictors and relationship declines as there is a shift in the environmental conditions (Hamilton, 1989). The confusion chart also indicates that false positives are not the trivial ones, which means that predictive gains are retained instead of radical, which serves as an indication of the argument of consistency in that predictive gains do not imply the steady economic benefit.

4.3 Adaptation Behaviour Referred to as Reinforcement Learning

In the reinforcement-learning context, signal reinforcement is progressively augmented throughout the initial training sessions depicting adaptive optimisation of action policy. The result corresponds to the conceptual background of Q-learning, whereby the convergence of the value functions is achieved due to the maximisation of the rewards in an iterative manner (Sutton & Barto, 2018). However, trajectories of rewards are not smooth convergences, but are instead volatile and unstable, implying that the monetary environment in question does not satisfy the Markov stationarity usually assumed in stable performance of reinforcement-learning (Irfan, 2024), (Irfan & George, 2022).

The financial markets are defined by dynamic state distributions and strategic interactions of the agents and might upset the stability of a policy (Lo, 2004). Further, the accumulation of rewards may not always be deciphered into the higher cumulative returns when transaction costs are factored which reiterates the arguments that optimising reward functions do not necessarily translate into economic profitability (Jensen, 1978).

4.4 Statistical Accuracy Versus Economic Profitability

Figure 2. Cumulative returns

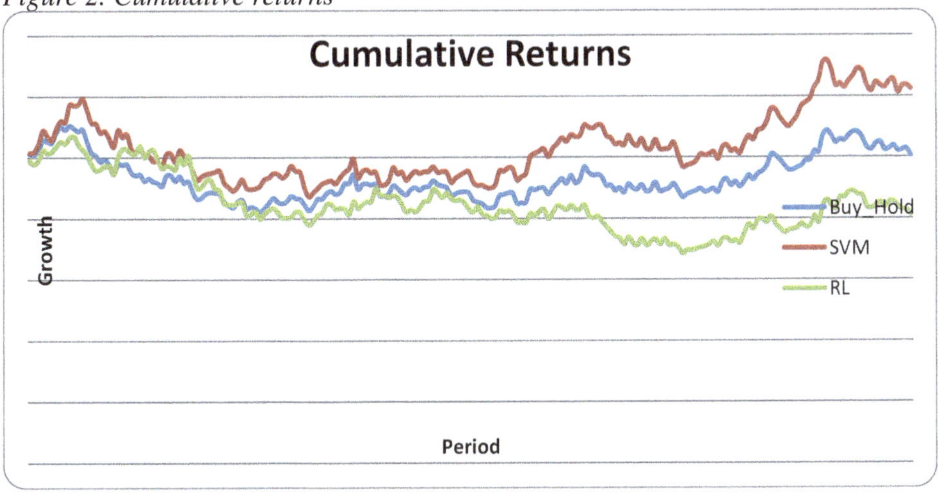

On the comparative basis of statistical performance measures and economic returns, onc can notc thc undcrperformance of the classification and risk-adjusted profitability. Although the SVM produces a reasonable accuracy levels, the Sharpe ratios are low hence justifying commentaries that forecast assessment using evaluation of error reduction alone can exaggerate practical application (Diebold & Mariano, 1995).

Equally, in spite of the adaptive improvement, reinforcement-learning strategies are sensitive to turnover and exposure to drawdown. Realistic transaction costs minimize cumulative returns, as have been widely done in equity-premium predictability studies (Goyal & Welch, 2008). All these findings affirm the main topic which is that statistical improvement in financial prediction should be applied within the scope of the economy.

Figure 3. Performance metrics

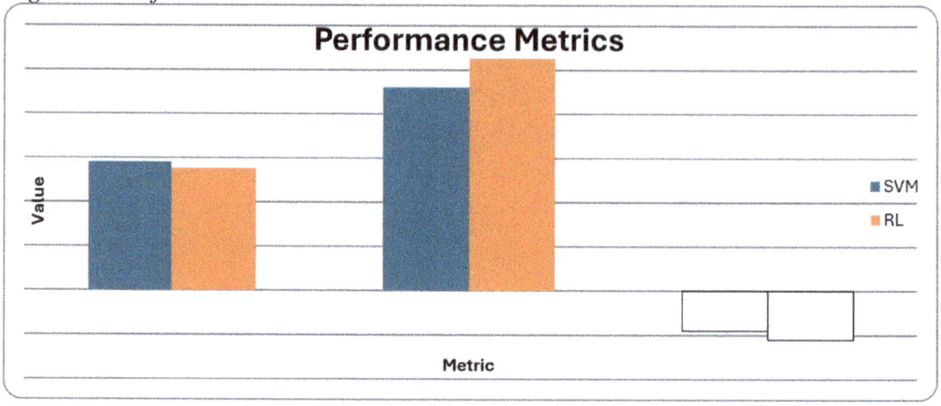

4.5 Regime Sensitivity and Structural Instability

Figure 4. Market regime distribution

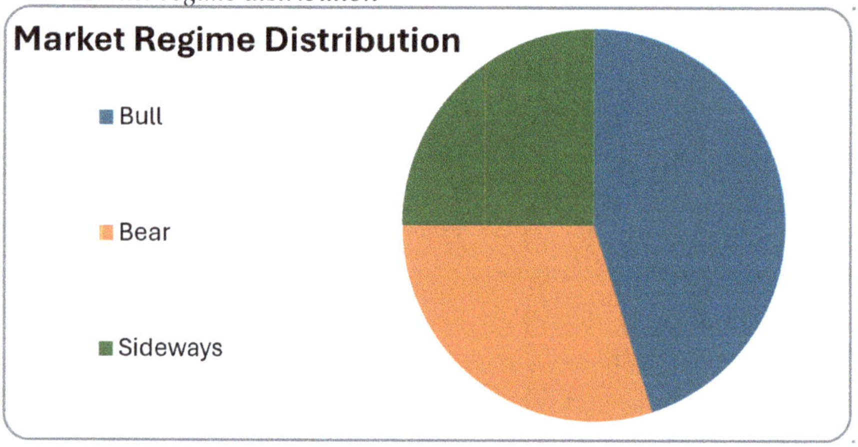

The comparison of the predictive power of the models in different market conditions, using rolling-window evaluation, indicates a significant variation in the predictive performance. Consistent with earlier discussion on regime shifts, predictive performance varies across market conditions, whilst high-volatility periods exhibit unstable predictive behavior. Empirical studies of regime dependence argue that the process of asset-return is often switching between structural regimes (Ang & Timmermann, 2012).

As discussed earlier, adaptive competition reduces the persistence of predictive advantages. Complex-system theory research indicates that technological homogeneity have the potential to increase the synchronised behaviour, which minimizes the benefits of diversification (Bouchaud, Farmer, & Lillo, 2009).

The sporadic deviations of the observed performance are therefore the result of machine-learning models being used in adaptive ecosystems, which are characterised by either conditional or transient predictive edges. This is an observation which can be extended to argue further that financial prediction boundaries are based on both structural and competitive factors, and not computational inadequacy. Model complexity and overfitting risk remain central limitations of machine learning in financial prediction.

4.6 Complexity of the Models and Risk of Overfitting

As discussed earlier, model complexity increases the risk of overfitting in financial markets. The boundaries in which non-linear classifiers as well as reinforcement-learning agents decide are astonishingly complicated; however, their effectiveness is extremely dependent on careful hyper-parameter tuning and training window arrangement. This sensitivity indicates the general threat of over-fitting in low-signal-to-noise financial markets (López de Prado, 2018). Consistent with earlier discussion, financial returns are highly stochastic in nature.

Empirical-research in the theories of statistical-learning underlines that higher model capacity minimises bias to the expense of increase in variance, hence, generalisation is weakened in volatile datasets (Bishop, 2006). Out of sample tests during rolling-validation tests show that out-of-sample workings decrease the performance of the model. This result supports the theoretical conclusion that financial forecasting is structurally (and not computationally) constrained since even sophisticated architectures do not always manage to cope with environmental instabilities (Ang & Timmermann, 2012).

4.7 Implication to Systematics and Interpretability

In addition to predictive performance, interpretability is also a clustering aspect of financial machine learning that is essential. Support -Vector Machines offer little transparency on feature contribution, and reinforcement -learning policies evolve opaque approximations on value functions. There is no explicit economic explanation available to make it difficult to understand the issue of structural relationships or statistical coincidence in predictions (Breiman, 2001). When there are numerous agents, dependent on similar signals, liquidity shocks can be intensified as a result of concomitant portfolio changes (Bouchaud, Farmer, & Lillo, 2009).

These issues imply that machine learning is not only limited to the correctness of the forecast but also applies potentially to the governance and control of risks as well as the stability of the system as a whole. Predictive innovation should then be considered at the portfolio level, but in the larger context of financial markets.

5. RECOMMENDATIONS

5.1 Machine Learning Research in Finance

The results suggest that future studies on financial machine learning must focus on regime-sensitive validation systems other than cross-sectional performance comparisons in validation. The standards of assessing predictive stability should switch to rolling-window evaluation, structural-break testing and multi-regime back-testing. In addition, the economic contribution of predictive models, both with and without transaction cost and risk adjusted models should also be clearly reported by the researcher. It is possible that forecasting gains by classification alone can be exaggerated in their practical superiority (Diebold & Mariano, 1995). Since asset returns exhibit low-signal-to-noise properties, one should not blindly neglect model simplicity and adopt architectural complexity. Parsimonious structures can be generalised more effectively during structural instability (Bishop, 2006).

5.2 Institutional Investors

To investment professionals, machine-learning systems are to be viewed as probabilistic decision-aids as opposed to autonomous predictive devices. The empirical findings indicate that predictive edges are conditional and they are prone to regime shifts therefore suggesting that discretionary oversight has not gone away (Lo, 2004). Turnover limits and liquidity should be used to implement a portfolio in order to avoid the loss of statistical gains by means of transaction costs (Jensen, 1978).

Crowding risk can be reduced in diversification when modelling strategies are not duplicated in many institutions, particularly when there are different architectures used in banks (Bouchaud, Farmer, & Lillo, 2009). Stress-testing of algorithmic strategies to simulated volatility shocks should also be carried out by investors in order to determine its resilience than historical conditions (Campbell & MacKinlay, 1997).

5.3 Model Development and Design

Financial model development should be more focused on interpretability and even grounded in economics besides quality predictive capability. Black-box architectures can yield short-term performance benefits, however without any analysis of feature-election it is unclear whether these buildings are structurally reliable (Breiman, 2001). Reward functions used in reinforcement-learning systems must utilize the risk-adjusted measures instead of the direct maximisation of returns to avoid over-exposing to drawdown (Sutton & Barto, 2018). Hybrid modelling approaches that incorporate both the econometric understanding as well as the machine-learning adaptability can present a trade-off solution, in order to have both nonlinear structure and theoretical integrity (Mullainathan & Spiess, 2017).

5.4 Systemic and Regulatory Supervision

The growing use of algorithmic trading approaches is an issue of concern through the amplification of systemic risk. By resulting in the institutions all predicting the same signals, the congruence in trading will in turn enhance volatility in stress events (Farmer & Lo, 1999). Regulators are likely to take into account transparency conditions of implementing algorithms in large financial institutions especially in terms of risk-management procedures and stress-testing procedures (LeBaron, 2006).

Moreover, algorithmic concentration risk might have to be used as a unique aspect of the financial stability analysis in macroprudential frameworks. Machine learning systemic implication is not limited to the analytics of the performance of individual portfolios but to the structure of financial ecosystem.

5.5 Governance and Information Integrity

The growing need to access alternative sources of data, high-frequency signals, and nonstructured textual data requires a greater system of data-governance. Financial machine-learning models are both sensitive to the quality of input, and all biases present in training are prone to bias the predictive results (Goodfellow, Bengio, & Courville, 2016). The institutions are advised to adopt strict data-audit testing policies to guarantee that the preprocessing pipelines do not cause look-ahead bias or survivorship bias, which would artificially enhance the performance of the back-testing method (López de Prado, 2018).

5.6 Future Research Patterns in Financial Machine Learning

The relevant research results should be addressed in the future by examining adaptive validation frameworks that can monitor performance deterioration in real-time. Constant monitoring systems can be used to detect the instances of predictive signs worsening by regime changes or crowding out (Ang & Timmermann, 2012). Also, financial economics, behavioral science and machine learning theory can be interdisciplinarily integrated to produce more robust modeling paradigms.

Although hard to encode, behavioral anomalies are also important factors of explanation of market fluctuations (Kahneman, 2011). New studies in explainable artificial intelligence (XAI) provide promising solutions to enhancing the interpretability of financial models (Bishop, 2006). Inclusion of both explainability and performance optimization has the potential in improving trust, regulatory compliance and system resilience. Lastly, the consequences of just-like-origins at a macro-level and its effect on financial stability when subjected to stress should be explored in future work (Farmer & Lo, 1999). Such broader impacts will be important to realize as machine learning keeps defining the world capitalism markets.

5.7 Integration of Risk Management

The empirical evidence allows proposing that machine learning classifications need to be incorporated into the larger risk management procedures but not used as single all-powerful predictive engines. Although the efficiency of SVM and reinforcement learning models can be used in short-term directional variations, the variability of their performance across regimes means that they are susceptible to structural instability (Ang & Timmermann, 2012). The institutions are advised to integrate the algorithmic trading systems into the dynamic risk control systems involving a volatility targeting, limit constraints on drawdown, and scenario stress tests (Campbell & MacKinlay, 1997).

To avoid delicate policy behaviour, reinforcement learning reward is supposed to explicitly discourage high turnover and excessive exposure to tail-risk exposure (Sutton & Barto, 2018). Besides, model-risk governance systems must consider parameter drifting as well as frequency of recalibration especially in an environment that showed structural breaks (Bai & Perron, 2003). Constant delivery monitoring is necessary to discourage a predictive degradation prior to a considerable amount of capital exposure is involved.

5.8 Elucidable Financial AI and Transparency

The increased use of machine learning in the framework of algorithmic trading highlights why the field of financial decision systems requires explainability and transparency. Trading decisions are not always understood whether using complex models like nonlinear SVM kernels and deep reinforcement learning architectures as interplays are black-box even in the black-box case (Breiman, 2001). Accountability may be improved with explainable artificial intelligence (XAI) frameworks that determine the feature importance, decision boundaries as well as policy drivers in predictive models (Bishop, 2006).

Open practices in modelling enhance institutional trust and compliance with the regulations, especially in highly regulated financial markets. Moreover, greater openness could minimize system risk because it can take away the blind faith in opaque algorithmic results. The institutions are well placed to assess robustness when faced with any stress situation when they have known the structural premises of model decisions (Farmer & Lo, 1999). Therefore, explainability cannot be considered as a technical addition only, but a prerequisite to making machine learning deployment in financial markets sustainable.

5.9 Competitive and Ethical Considerations in Financial Markets

The fact that machine learning is being quickly integrated into algorithmic trading highlights ethical and competition issues that may not be limited to the predictive accuracy. Informational asymmetries can also be broadened with the larger, more technologically developed institutions against smaller market players as the institutions use more sophisticated models to play with. According to research studies about adaptive markets, competition is a dynamic phenomenon, and technological capabilities can change the distribution of market power (Lo, 2004). Market domination by algorithms as well can help to increase market concentration, in which the visible predictive advantages may be averted by a few well-endowed institutions.

This concentration may affect the process of providing liquidity and price-discovery (Bouchaud, Farmer, & Lillo, 2009). Policymakers and exchanges might hence have to keep track of the competitive effect of substantial AI exploitation in financial markets. Furthermore, ethical deployment needs protection against manipulative artifices, undesired feedback loops and automation that amplifies market stress. The incidences of flash crashes in the past indicate the ability of the interaction among algorithms to create systemic instabilities when conditions are extreme (Farmer & Lo, 1999). It is necessary to balance market integrity and technological progress to guarantee responsible innovation. Finally, financial machine learning should be developed sustainably, which could involve a balance between predictive performance, fairness, competition, and resilience of the systems.

CONCLUSION

The accelerated development of machine learning has greatly widened the methodological horizon of financial market. Algorithms in the category of robotized nonlinear classification include Support Vector Machines, adaptive reinforcement learning systems; each is showing more and more ability to jump up the hierarchy of such methodologies at the high-dimensionality level of perceiving intricate structure in financial data. Nevertheless, the results of this research indicate that it is not computational sophistication that would be able to beat the structural limitations inherent with competitive capital markets. These findings reinforce earlier discussions on market efficiency that companies have always considered prices to be a fast way to incorporate information thus avoiding always high arbitrage (Fama, 1970).

Empirical findings support the idea that predictive gains remain conditional and, in most cases, weak. Empirical results further indicate that engineered features exhibit weak linear dependence, which would argue the point that financial returns have weak signal strength relative to noise. Even though SVM models show modest classification performance, there is a variation in their performance over rolling windows that suggests that the models are sensitive to the regime, as well as environmental, volatility. This is in line with the empirical evidence that predictive relationships often deteriorate due to alteration of the underlying economic conditions (Ang & Timmermann, 2012).

Equally, adaptive reward optimisation is exhibited in reinforcement learning structures but convergent stability is lacking, so financial markets fail to satisfy stationary assumptions in learning policies (Lo, 2004). There comes to the fore a fundamental difference between statistical performance and economic profitability. An increase in classification or push-up of rewards may not be matched with the higher quality of the risk-adjusted returns when the transaction costs and drawdown risks are added (Diebold & Mariano, 1995; Jensen, 1978).

This deviation highlights the need to test machine learning models within economic viable parameters as opposed to just making use of predictive measures. Besides, the systemic impact of the mass adoption of algorithms should be given due attention. Correlated strategies can also increase market volatility when stress occurs, as more institutions adopt these types of machine learning architectures (Farmer & Lo, 1999). Machine learning should not be regarded as a deterministic forecasting engine that is apt to invariably deliver alpha because it serves as a conditional decision-making aid functioning in adaptive, competitive, and structurally unstable settings (Mullainathan & Spiess, 2017).

REFERENCES

Ang, A., & Timmermann, A. (2012). Regime changes and financial markets. *Annual Review of Financial Economics, 4*, 313–337.

Bai, J., & Perron, P. (2003). Computation and analysis of multiple structural change models. *Journal of Applied Econometrics, 18*(1), 1–22.

Bishop, C. M. (2006). *Pattern recognition and machine learning*. Springer.

Bouchaud, J. P., Farmer, J. D., & Lillo, F. (2009). How markets slowly digest changes in supply and demand. In Hens, T., & Schenk-Hoppé, K. R. (Eds.), *Handbook of financial markets: Dynamics and evolution*. Elsevier. DOI: 10.1016/B978-012374258-2.50006-3

Breiman, L. (2001). Statistical modeling: The two cultures. *Statistical Science, 16*(3), 199–231.

Campbell, J. Y., Lo, A. W., & MacKinlay, A. C. (1997). *The econometrics of financial markets*. Princeton University Press. DOI: 10.1515/9781400830213

De Bondt, W., & Thaler, R. (1985). Does the stock market overreact? *Journal of Finance, 40*(3), 793–805.

Diebold, F. X., & Mariano, R. S. (1995). Comparing predictive accuracy. *Journal of Business & Economic Statistics, 13*(3), 253–263.

Fama, E. F. (1970). Efficient capital markets: A review of theory and empirical work. *Journal of Finance, 25*(2), 383–417.

Fama, E. F. (1991). Efficient capital markets II. *Journal of Finance, 46*(5), 1575–1617.

Farmer, J. D., & Lo, A. W. (1999). Frontiers of finance: Evolution and efficient markets. *Proceedings of the National Academy of Sciences*, 96(18), 9991–9992. DOI: 10.1073/pnas.96.18.9991

Farmer, J. D., Patelli, P., & Zovko, I. (2005). The predictive power of zero intelligence in financial markets. *Proceedings of the National Academy of Sciences*, 102(6), 2254–2259. DOI: 10.1073/pnas.0409157102

Goodfellow, I., Bengio, Y., & Courville, A. (2016). *Deep learning*. MIT Press.

Goyal, A., & Welch, I. (2008). A comprehensive look at the empirical performance of equity premium prediction. *Review of Financial Studies, 21*(4), 1455–1508.

Hamilton, J. D. (1989). A new approach to the economic analysis of nonstationary time series and the business cycle. *Econometrica, 57*(2), 357–384.

Hastie, T., Tibshirani, R., & Friedman, J. (2009). *The elements of statistical learning* (2nd ed.). Springer. DOI: 10.1007/978-0-387-84858-7

Irfan, M. (2024). Delving into the exchange-traded funds (ETFs) market: Understanding market efficiency. *Journal of Ecohumanism, 3*(4), 2670–2681. DOI: 10.62754/joe.v3i4.3787

Irfan, M., Elhoseny, M., Kassim, S., & Metawa, N. (2023). *Advanced machine learning algorithms for complex financial applications*. IGI Global., DOI: 10.4018/978-1-6684-4483-2

Irfan, M., & George, J. P. (2022). A systematic review of challenges, tools, and myths of big data ingestion. In *Lecture Notes in Networks and Systems*. Springer., DOI: 10.1007/978-981-19-2211-4_43

Jensen, M. C. (1978). Some anomalous evidence regarding market efficiency. *Journal of Financial Economics, 6*(2–3), 95–101.

Kahneman, D. (2011). *Thinking, fast and slow*. Farrar, Straus and Giroux.

Kearns, M., & Nevmyvaka, Y. (2013). Machine learning for market microstructure and high-frequency trading. In Kearns, M., & Nevmyvaka, Y. (Eds.), *High frequency trading**.

LeBaron, B. (2006). Agent-based computational finance. In Tesfatsion, L., & Judd, K. L. (Eds.), *Handbook of computational economics* (Vol. 2). Elsevier.

Lo, A. W. (2004). The adaptive markets hypothesis. *Journal of Portfolio Management, 30*(5), 15–29.

López de Prado, M. (2018). *Advances in financial machine learning*. Wiley.

Mnih, V., Kavukcuoglu, K., Silver, D., et al. (2015). Human-level control through deep reinforcement learning. *Nature, 518*, 529–533.

Mullainathan, S., & Spiess, J. (2017). Machine learning: An applied econometric approach. *Journal of Economic Perspectives, 31*(2), 87–106.

Pesaran, M. H., & Timmermann, A. (1995). Predictability of stock returns: Robustness and economic significance. *Journal of Finance, 50*(4), 1201–1228.

Samuelson, P. A. (1965). Proof that properly anticipated prices fluctuate randomly. *Industrial Management Review, 6*(2), 41–49.

Shiller, R. J. (2017). Narrative economics. *American Economic Review, 107*(4), 967–1004.

Singh, S., Dias, R., Irfan, M., Galvão, R., Alexandre, P., & Gonçalves, S. (2024). The role of perceived organisational support in predicting organisational commitment and organizational citizenship behavior in professional organizations. *Journal of Ecohumanism, 3*(6), 239–249. DOI: 10.62754/joe.v3i6.4000

Sutton, R. S., & Barto, A. G. (2018). *Reinforcement learning: An introduction* (2nd ed.). MIT Press.

Tetlock, P. C. (2007). Giving content to investor sentiment: The role of media in the stock market. *Journal of Finance, 62*(3), 1139–1168.

Vapnik, V. (1998). *Statistical learning theory*. Wiley.

Welch, I., & Goyal, A. (2007). A comprehensive look at the empirical performance of equity premium prediction. *Review of Financial Studies, 21*(4), 1455–1508.

Yen, G., & Lee, C. (2008). Efficient market hypothesis (EMH): Past, present and future. *Review of Pacific Basin Financial Markets and Policies, 11*(2), 305–329.

Zhang, G. P. (2003). Time series forecasting using a hybrid ARIMA and neural network model. *Neurocomputing, 50*, 159–175.

Section 3
Technology as an Innovation

Chapter 9
The AI-Enhanced Classroom:
A Blueprint for Collaborative Intelligence

Seema Mishra
http://orcid.org/0000-0001-9102-0522
Lovely Professional University, India

Devender Kumar
Lovely Professional University, India

ABSTRACT

The widespread release of the generative AI towards the end of 2022 has not only been a technological disruption, but it has triggered a major epistemological crisis in the field of higher education. Schools of higher education all over the world have reacted in a fairly familiar pattern of panic, reactive policymaking, and existential panic that revolves around detection, banning, and policing of academic honesty. This chapter claims that this kind of defensive posture, though it may be explainable, is a misdiagnostic of the situation that we are in. It is not whether artificial intelligence will be present in our classrooms but whether we have the vision to help make it so, with the purpose of humanistic educational goals.

DOI: 10.4018/979-8-2600-2811-7.ch009

1. INTRODUCTION: FROM THREAT TO PARTNERSHIP

1.1 The Revenant Spectre: Educational Technology and the Historiography of the Moral Panic

The generative artificial intelligence has not entered the academy in a historical vacuum on a seismic basis in late 2022 and is publicly available. Rapidly made task forces, the near-panic amendments made in academic integrity policies, the tense faculty gatherings, all of this will have to be placed in a chronicle of a history of anxious and revelatory responses to educational technology panics. The interaction of higher education and technological innovation has been repetitively defined in terms of a cyclic process of euphoric adoption, institutional anxiety, and the resultant integration of new technologies, which is negotiated and usually at a reduced scale.

This tendency, which experts in the sociology of education and media studies have consistently noticed, is not an incidental finding; it is a structural characteristic of the process by which the conservative institutions are incorporating the disruptive tools. The archetype is familiar. The inception of the pocket calculator in the 1970s was passionately debated as a sign of the death of mental arithmetic and the loss of numerical literacy. Ten years after that the word processor was charged with rotting the drafting skills and encouraging a slapdash approach to writing. The internet and wikipedia raised the spectre of a lower level of research rigour and blind adherence to uncredible sources. The language was exceptionally uniform with each successive wave: a new technology is created, it is first taken in by the educational establishment with some little regard, students start using it in a manner that undermines the concept of traditional testing, and it is eventually condemned as something that is threatening the very existence of core cognitive processes and education quality.

As one of the media academics Buckingham (2003) declared in his critique of media education, these episodes tend to become a moral panic, whereby a condition or group is justified as a challenge to the values of society, the nature of this is represented in stylized and stereotypical ways by the mass media, moral barricades are staffed by editors, bishops, politicians and other right-thinking persons. The present AI hype is entirely accurate to this model. It is the generative AI that is stereotypically depicted as an infallible, all-knowing cheat-engine. The threat is to its fundamental values of originality, critical thinking, and academic integrity. Faculty senates and educational traditionalists man the so-called moral barricades. However, the AI moment is what is different in comparison with the other instances, not the form of the panic but its extent and condition. Other technologies in the past posed a threat to certain forms of competence (calculation, spelling, source-checking). Generative AI, in its turn, is seen as a threat to the very process of cognition- the internal, tacit process of journey between the question and the insight that has been the final aim of education.

It does not merely facilitate counting or display, it imitates the synthetic and analytic processes of the intellectual mind. It is this felt attack upon the temple of thought, which is the reason of the great, almost existential, character of the present crisis. A critical analysis of this historiography does however, point out the second act which is critical and ignored. After the panic, there is the process of pedagogical accommodation that happens. The calculator was later used to investigate more advanced mathematical ideas with the loss of emphasis on rote calculation. The facilitation of revision provided by the word processor ultimately facilitated more and more intricate writing pedagogies. Internet compelled a needed and desirable development in information literacy programs.

In retrospect, the panic itself does not seem like a prophecy of the inevitable downfall. The technology did not contain it, instead, it was the educational model that moved around the technology, which in most cases resulted in a more advanced learning outcome. The study conducted by Sun and Zhou(2024) experimented 28 findings involving 1909 students, demonstrated that G-AI is beneficial for the students in improving their academics, proven by the statistical values of Hedges's $g = 0.533$, $p < 0.05$ The acknowledgment of this trend is not to reject the existing issues as simple hysteria, but it is important to look at them as the first stage of a deep-rooted change that does not require the reactionary policing, but the strategic and philosophical leadership.

1.2 The Focal Thesis: Teaching in Collaborative Intelligence as Educational Necessity

Teaching in Collaborative Intelligence as Educational Necessity. The main idea developed in this chapter is the future of higher education is neither what students can do without AI, but what they, along with their educators, can do with it, and do it in a deliberate cooperation to address more intricate, real, and significant issues than could be previously handled in the context of the traditional classroom. We call this relationship Collaborative Intelligence, the cooperative combination of human and artificial intelligence in which both have their unique strengths in the common cognitive objectives. Human intelligence offers what AI has in most cases lacks: intentionality, moral judgment, situational wisdom, emotional intelligence and meaning-making ability.

AI, in its turn, provides humanity with what it cannot afford to maintain but requires in the form of instant access to large information spaces, pattern recognition, multilingual abilities, and the capability to produce more than one view or solution in a large scale. According to a systematic review by Ogunleye et al. (2024), among

355 studies, there are critical gaps in research: whereas much of the research has focused on AI detection, there is not enough research on how GenAI can be applied to curriculum design to examine assessment and learning delivery. In particular, the authors request more interdisciplinary, multidimensional research in higher education to provide information to guidelines and frameworks The educational necessity is obvious: The world in which our graduates will live in, both professional and civic as well as personal, will be the world of inevitable human-AI cooperation. We need to train them to become advanced coordinators of collaborative intelligence, people who are capable of using the capabilities of AIs tactically and preserve the critical, ethical, and creative agency that characterizes fully-fledged human judgment.

1.3 Chapter Mission

This chapter mission is to take a decisive step beyond theoretical discussions as to whether AI is part of education or not, but give a wide-ranging, empirical, and philosophical-based Blueprint of Collaborative Intelligence in higher education teaching and learning, Bang et al. (2023). This is a blueprint that is visionary and actionable, which means that it bridges the gap between general educational principles and specific classroom practices in any field. Precisely, this chapter will seek to:

- Develop a coherent philosophy of education of the AI-enhanced classroom that comes to terms with technological capability and humanistic values.
- Tackle legitimate anxieties over academic honesty, equity, discrimination, and intellectual deskilling not as a way of shirking, but rather as a design constraint that should be effectively considered within a responsible integration model.
- Offer an elaborate pedagogical model- the five-stage Collaborative Intelligence Blueprint, which will help teachers refine their assignments, assessments, and classroom engagements to be better adapted to a world of human-AI collaboration.
- Show other cross-disciplinary applicability by using detailed case studies where the blueprint is applied in humanities, STEM, social sciences and professional education settings.
- Rediscover evaluation to this new paradigm, shifting the emphasis in evaluation on products to processes in the form of documentation of collaborative thinking.
- Rethink the role of the educator as a knowledge-deliverer or a plagiarism-detection unit instead as the designer of learning experience, facilitator of human- machine communication and advisor of moral co-creation.

1.4 Chapter Navigation

In this chapter, the action takes place in six parts. Part 2, which forms the basis of the paper after this introduction, gives the core mission and the need to adopt collaborative intelligence, basing its thesis on four pillars, which are workforce preparation, raising the learning goals, metacognitive development, and equity considerations. Part 3 tackles the essential issues that must be handled by any responsible framework; academic integrity, bias, privacy, and the digital divide, and does not see them as a hindrance to them, but a crucial design parameter. Part 4 is the core of the chapter that introduces the Collaborative Intelligence Blueprint, a five-stage framework of designing the learning experience, where human-guided problem framing is followed by AI collaboration and then critical synthesis and reflection. Part 5 implements this blueprint by cross-disciplinary case studies in great detail, showing how it can be used throughout the curriculum. Part 6 is the last part that deals with the critical problem of assessment in this new paradigm and includes new models of assessment that critique the process of collaboration and its products. The chapter is finished with a vision of the change of the role of the educator and the significant repercussions of such change of the role of the educator as related to the future of the university itself. We maintain that by thoughtful, moral, and imaginative interaction with AI, higher education can not only fail in its humanistic purpose, but can also be enhanced by it--by producing graduates possessing inimitable talent, due to their command of collaborative intelligence.

1.5 The Stakes: Why This Moment Matters

We are writing at what some of us may come to think of as an inflection point in the history of education like the advent of the printing press or the emergence of the research university. Our decisions in years ahead as faculty, administrators, and educational designers would determine not just how AI is applied to classes, but eventually what an educated person will be in the 21 st century. It is the road to prohibition, which has resulted in what sociologist Sherry Turkle has cautioned against: a society of surveillance that erodes the trust and intellectual risk-taking that education demands. This is the route of blind following that ends in commodification of human judgment as predicted by philosopher Michael Sandel and degradation of agency. The direction that can be offered here, i.e., the active development of collaborative intelligence, is a third way, the one that takes into consideration the disruptive potential of AI at the same time and yet at the same time, does not impose its solution on the educational enterprise, but even, conversely, belongs to it.

It is a journey that requires increased efforts by the students and the teachers not less. It asks us to learn and to teach new literacies as we become more committed to the oldest educational values: wisdom, character, the examined life. This chapter can provide the map of the journey. It starts by the belief that the classroom of the future does not have to be a place of human replacement but can be a place of human amplification - a place where the unique powers of human and machine intelligence are combined to form new structures of understanding, creativity and problem-solving, neither of which could do alone. The plan below is a proposal to create that future, collectively.

2. THE CENTRAL MISSION AND RATIONALE

The key idea behind this chapter is to provide teachers with a background framework and tangible pedagogical approaches to the introduction of AI as a cooperative learning and teaching tool. This is motivated by some of the following beliefs:

(a) Teaching Students the Future Workforce: The future professional environment our students will be introduced to will be that of human-AI collaboration. It is the role of higher education to empower them with the knowledge required to prompt, criticize, control, and exploit AI tools.
(b) Higher Learning Objective: When we leave offloading lower-order cognitive tasks (e.g. summarization, initial research, grammar checking) to AI, we can free up the cognitive resource of students to higher-order thinking: critical thinking, ethical thinking, synthesis via creativity, and complex problem solving.
(c) Ensuring Equity and Access: AI can serve as an effective personal tutor, 24/7 support, scaffolding students with learning disabilities, and extension students will provide an opportunity to design a more form-focused and inclusive educational environment.

3. CRITICAL FRAMEWORK: MANAGING AN ETHICAL AND PEDAGOGICAL MINEFIELD OF AI INTEGRATION

3.1 Concerns to Design Constraints

The Collaborative Intelligence interest should be restrained by stiff critical scrutiny. Artificial intelligence integration into higher education is not just a pedagogical option, it is an ethical, legal, and social intervention that has been associated with risks, which have been documented. These concerns cannot be accepted by a responsible framework as panic. Rather, it needs to make them the key design constraints- parameters that cannot be compromised and which are used to define and constrain any implementation of the Collaborative Intelligence Blueprint.

This chapter does not just pay lip service to this but offers a deeper analysis of five areas of concern which are 1) redefined academic integrity, 2) cognitive and epistemic risks of automation bias, 3) the ubiquitous audience of algorithmic bias, 4) the legal and ethical nightmare of data privacy and intellectual property, and 5) the reinforcement of structural inequities by the digital divide. The analysis based on recent research, case law, and research findings can offer the necessary checkpoints to ethical implementation.

3.2 Academic Honesty Rediscovered

This is the nearest institutional problem and the academic integrity is perceived to be eroded. Traditional codes of honor and plagiarism are formulated on a dichotomous authorship platform: the work is either original or is a creation of the student or the student has robbed it by the hands of another (human) writer. Such ambiguity renders the application of the traditional plagiarism detection application (e.g., Turnitin) virtually futile, as these are designed to detect the string match, but not probable originality. The academic response, led by academics like Sarah Eaton (2022) and Cath Ellis (2023), argues that it is time to shift the paradigm not to the product-oriented integrity, but to process-oriented one. The instruction goal becomes regulation of provenance of a final artifact to the evaluation of the critical and ethical process in which the artifact was created. This is through re-conceptualization of assignments as a kind of cognitive apprenticeship (Collins, Brown, and Holum, 1991) whereby the process of thinking is also exposed. The usage of AI is not barred in this model but has to be reported and justified.

The evaluation will take a form of portfolios which will include: The initial prompts and the way the AI later refined them; The uncritical AI output; the critical commentary made by the student to the output which will contain advantages, disadvantages, and biases; and a final conclusion which will elaborate on the way human judgment came into play in achieving the final outcome. This solution is accompanied by overall tendencies towards genuine assessment. It does not lean towards high-stakes, AI-generated, and easily-disposable the assignment (Wiley, 2013), but instead leans towards tasks situated, requiring them to think and they are intrinsically hard to outsource, as they are valuable in the unique mental activity of the student themselves. The integrity breach, in its turn, prevents or precludes the use of AI and becomes the inability to clearly document and be able to contribute to the collaborative process critically.

3.3 Cognitive and Epistemic Risks: the Automation Bias, Deskilling, and the Illusion of Infallibility

Another, more insidious challenge to the cognitive functions of education is that of automation bias and intellectual deskilling, which is an outside threat. Automation bias is also the recorded tendency of human beings to believe decision-support systems, implying that a person trusts the results of their automated processes regardless of whether the results are discrepant or not, or even whether it is common sense (Parasuraman and Manzey, 2010). It is observable within an educational context, where the students (and potentially faculty) would simply trust AI-generated text, code or analysis. The study by Bang et al. (2023) empirically established that users rated GPT-3.5 higher than human-written text at all times, which was the case despite the content of the AI being false. This constitutes a simple epistemic threat: it can destroy even the habit of critical questioning that is the goal of education. The risk that comes with it is cognitive deskilling. Similarly to the overreliance of GPS as a matter of de-training spatial navigation abilities, overreliance on AI in the drafting, summarizing and simple problem-solving can also worsen the underlying academic muscles.

History has a few points in common: Socrates in the Phaedrus of Plato had posed a warning that writing would kill memory. Though this was an overstatement, it was partly true on the issue of redistribution of cognitive labor. This is a critical structure which will therefore demand conscious unplugged practice. Similar to mathematics curricula the necessity of still teaching manual calculation and calculators, one must as well teach writing instruction exercises of unaided drafting and revision, research instruction manual literature navigation to equip students with the skills as to how to evaluate and direct the AI effectively. The pedagogical design ought to make the rule that AI is an augmenting, as opposed to a substituting partner, impose itself.

3.4 The Algorithmic Bias Pervasiveness

The most socially important outcome, arguably, is the instilling of the algorithmic bias. The AI models cannot be described as neutral, as they are trained using massive amounts of human-generated data, which are biased by the historical and contemporary biases. This is supported by some groundbreaking research: in their article, Gender Shades, Buolamwini and Gebru (2018) established that the precision of facial recognition software regarding gender and skin color differed radically. The language models exhibited by Bolukbasi et al. (2016) showed that gender stereotypes are modeled in the word embeddings (e.g. it is a male-word, so doctor; it is a female-word, so nurse). These biases do not happen as glitches, they are systemic reproductions of inequality. When an AI receives most of its training on Western and English-language content, it will create its own form of worldview grounded on it- a form of digital colonialism (Couldry and Mejias, 2019).

3.5 Structural Inequality and the Digital Divide

More than Access to Critical Empowerment. The hope of AI to bring about an egalitarian approach in education is contrastingly met by the digital divide that is multi-level. The access to hardware and stable internet remains as the first-level divide. The introduction of AI, which involves strong-powered gadgets or high-speed Internet to perform more complicated tasks, will automatically put students with low-income backgrounds at a disadvantage. Nevertheless, the second-level divide, which is less obvious but no less dangerous, is the differences in the quality of use, skills, and social support (van Dijk, 2020).

3.6.1 Student Perceptions and Patterns of Usage

Having insights into the actual perception and utilisation of GenAI by students is an essential part of the responsible design of a framework. The survey conducted by Johnston et al. (2024) on 2,555 students of the university presented important results:

Awareness and adoption: GenAI technologies were not heard of by only 7 percent of the students; more than half of students had used or thought of using them in school.

Soft opinions about the correct usage: 54.1% did not mind the usage of AI in editing tools (e.g., Grammarly) but 70.4% opposed the idea of using ChatGPT to compose whole essays.

Confidence correlation: The more confident students were of their academic writing, the less likely they were to use GenAI or promote the use of GenAI by others.

Policy demand: 41.1% specifically desired university-wide policies regarding the proper AI use.

The implications of these findings to Collaborative Intelligence framework are:

Confidence-building as defense: Because less confident writers use AI, the metacognitive reflection of the Blueprint (Phase 5) must directly develop the writing self-efficacy.

Clarity of policy as need of students: The framework should be entrenched in clear institutional policy as demanded by the students.

4. THE COLLABORATIVE INTELLIGENCE BLUEPRINT: 5-PHASE PEDAGOGICAL FRAMEWORK OF HUMAN-AI SYNERGY

Architecturing Cognitive Partnership. The reasons behind the Collaborative Intelligence conceptual rationale and the main guardrails are used to draw the line of why and what should not be or can be done. This chapter provides the most crucial how of a pedagogical framework. The Five-Phase Collaborative Intelligence Blueprint is not a prescriptive model, however, it is a loose, recursive, plan of how to design learning experiences that make strategic use of AI to augment, and not replace, human thought. It is grounded on the constructivist theory of learning, the cognitive load theory and metacognitive studies and implements philosophical principles into the classroom practice.

All the phases are variants of thinking and shift the burden of responsibility to both human and machine to maximize the strengths of either. The framework has strength in its straightforward form allowing the collaborative process to be visible, teachable, and also assessable. It applies AI as a black box shortcut to a transparent device of cognitive apprenticeship.

4.1 Phase 1: Issue Framing and Timely Crafting (The Human Domain) Cognitive Focus: Intentionality, Epistemic Cognition and Precision

It is an initial stage that is purely human. It is aimed at defining intellectual purpose and strategic focus prior to any AI involvement, which is a response to the risk of delegating the thought process to the machine. It is at this that learning objectives are converted into an organized cognitive mission.

Sub-Strategies and Theoretical Underpinnings: In accordance with a theory of problem-solving presented by Jonassen (1997), educators ought to present problems, which do not have clear paths of solution, demand integration of various knowledge spheres, and need attention to values and constraints. Examples: "Develop a community-based intervention to address vaccine hesitancy in a particular socio-cultural setting, which takes ethical communication and historical mistrust into account and has certain resource constraints, not: List the causes of vaccine hesitancy.

Cognitive Task Analysis (CTA) Pre-Prompting: It involves breaking down the overall problem into the individual cognitive tasks. Without problem-solving, a CTA may find the need to synthesize the literature, find the major stakeholders, assess the ethical risk, brainstorm creative messaging ideas, and measure the outcomes. This sense of meta-awareness is what makes sure that AI is implemented in specific subtasks instead of being an oracle of the entire. The Pedagogy of Prompt designing, making it beyond basic questions, this is the teaching of prompt architectures based on the principles of human-computer interaction:

- Role-Persona Prompting: "You are a community-oriented research expert in the field of bioethics. An examination of the following situation.
- Chain-of-Thought (CoT) Solicitation: This problem has to be solved step-by-step and the reasoning is to be demonstrated at each step.
- Iterative Refinement Protocols: Train the procedure of first prompt - output analysis - prompt refinement (e.g., add constraint such as, 2020 peer-reviewed studies only, or in a decolonial perspective).
- Example-In-Context (Few-Shot) Prompting: Giving the AI examples of the desired format of output and style of reasoning in the prompt.

Cognitive Theory: This stage involves much use of the epistemic cognition- the way students frame knowledge and the knowing process (Hofer and Pintrich, 1997). They shift their passive perception of knowledge as something received to an active perception of knowledge as something created through disciplined investigation by compelling them to specify each other, the scope, constraints and approach of a problem.

4.2 Phase 2: AI Ideation and Drafting (The Collaborative Domain) Cognitive Focus Ideation fluency, Divergent Thinking and Information Synthesis

AI is a cognitive developmental strategy in this instance. It is supposed to generate a breadth of ideas of raw materials, outlines, data interpretations, draft text, which would have been time-prohibitive had a human been required to do so manually. The student position is transformed into the curator and strategic director.

Sub-Strategies and Theoretical Foundations: With human problem-solvers they traditionally possess a problem with functional fixedness (Duncker, 1945). AI can overcome this within a short time and mashing unusual associations and solutions that may not be within the original set of mentality of the student. Evaluate AI in the form of a committee of professionals. A student can perform sequential prompts, each prompt possesses a specific role/persona: Run the analysis of the urban structure like a Marxist geographer, a feminist urban planncr, and an cnvironmental economist, give the measurements of sustainability. The student is responsible for the role of synthesizing these views.

The Intermediate Artifacts: It is neither an AI-generated end product, nor the generation of useful intermediates: annotated bibliographies, concept maps, multi-thesis statements, procedural algorithms, or opposing literature reviews. This coincides with the cognitive offloading theory (Risko & Gilbert, 2016), at which external artifacts unload the working memory to the higher-order analysis.

Cognitive theory: It is the level that develops on AI to increase ideational fluency which is one of the key components of creativity. It is also an actualisation of Cognitive Load Theory (Sweller, 1988).

4.3 Phase 3: Critical Analysis and Human Judgment

It is the crucial stage, and human intelligence reinvests dominance. Learners need to shift generative collaboration to critical evaluation and see AI deliverables as hypotheses to be verified and products to be disambiguated.

Sub-Strategies and Theoretical Bases: Source Verification and "Hallucination" Hunting Protocols: The students are required to verify all of the substantive claims, citation, and data that the AI produces. This is information literacy in its most most extreme way. Strategy: The so-called lateral reading technique (Wineburg and McGrew, 2019) leave the AI text and confirm claims with the help of credible databases and the primary sources.

Logical and Argumentative Deconstruction: The students will deconstruct the argument structure of the AI, determining the premises used, identifying logical fallacies, assessing the credibility of the evidence used, and identifying non-sequitures. This is the application of formal critical schools of thought to a specific text.

Gap and Silence Identification: students pose the question: What is missing? What were the questions that the AI was not asking? What are other arguments it had not taken into consideration? This acquires negative capability- the art of thinking about the non-existent.

Cognitive Theory: This stage involves putting practical use to critical thinking and epistemic vigilance (Sperber et al., 2010). It artificially causes a sense of cognitive dissonance when students are presented with believable yet erroneous or skewed AI materials, which they have to actively resolve and enhance their evaluation abilities. It also develops the metacognitive judgment since students learn to gauge their trust on the tool.

Sample (Social Sciences - Public Policy): Following the utilization of AI to create a Policy brief proposing a pilot of basic income (UBI) throughout a mid-sized city in the US, the critical analysis of the student would include:

- Fact-Checking: Checking the economic research and pilot outcomes presented by the AI.

- Bias Audit: Indicating whether the brief either implicitly presumes a heteronormative nuclear family in its analysis of impact or it does not take into account the wealth gap of racism.
- Logical Analysis: Business Analysis of the logical consistency of the cost projections based on the parameters of the described implementation.
- Gap Identification: It is worth noting that there was nothing said about the process of political coalition-building that is required to pass or effects on the informal economy. The student generates an "AI Output Audit Report including the findings, flaws, and unsolved questions.

4.4 Phase 4: Refining, Synthesising and Refining (The Synergistic Domain) Cognitive Focus

Integration, Creative Transformation, and Authorial Voice. In this case, the student will be integrating the raw material of Phase 2 with the critical insights of Phase 3 in order to build new and authoritative work. AI returns to a subservient, instrument-like position (e.g. to edit, format or translate polished human ideas). Integrative synthesis is the main mental activity.

Sub-Strategies and Theoretical Bases: The Sandwich Model of Composition: The end composition must possess a definite human throughline. Strategy: The students will compose their intro and thesis, use the chosen and adapted AI generated material (now corrected and reviewed during Phase 3) to fill in parts and compose their own analytical commentary, conclusion and synthesis.

Human framing and human analysis are put between the AI content. Transformative vs. Derivative Use: Show students the way to go beyond putting together AI snippets. This is aimed at transformative use, in which AI-generated ideas are put together, re-contextualized and argued with in manners unexpected by the AI itself. It is the implementation of the Remix concept (Lessig, 2008) to cognition so that what is produced is a rare intellectual mix. Developing Authorial Voice and Rhetorical Purpose Students are strongly encouraged to edit any AI-generated prose to match their own academic voice, conventions of their discipline, and the rhetorical purposes of their readers. This is done at the sentence level, to rewrite in a tone, to make it clear and to make it argumentative. **Iterative Human-AI Refinement Loops: At this stage, AI may be applied to particular sub-tasks:** "Make this paragraph more readable," "Propose transitions between these two parts," syntax-check this code, or generate a graph based on this cleaned dataset that I give. The human reserves the right to complete creativity.

Cognitive Theory: This stage marks constructivist integration as knowledge is constructed by the learner by bringing together and balancing various bits of knowledge (Bruner, 1966). It also symbolizes the utmost degree of Bloom Taxonomy: Creation. The student not only analyzes or evaluates but creates a new whole out of unrelated parts. The focus on voice and change is linked to the sociocultural theory of learning where the control of the discourse of a discipline is of concern to be integrated into the community of practice within the discipline.

Example (Natural Sciences - Biology): A student conducting research on CRISPR gene drives may, at Phases 2 and 3, produce a literature review. They would:

- Explain their own structured argument concerning the trade off between the elimination of the vectors caused diseases and the risk of ecological chain.
- Infuse correctly abstracted ideas in AI-generated descriptions of the various drive mechanisms of which they have now been proven right.
- Integrate their critical assessment of regulatory frameworks, possibly with an AI doing the formatting of their duly referenced sources.
- Write original conclusion sections offering a prioritized research agenda by synthesizing them.

4.5 Phase 5: Reflection/Metacognitive Documentation (The Learning Domain) Cognitive Focus: Metacognition, Self-regulated learning and Process Awareness

In the given cycle, structured reflection is a final step that entails solidifying the learning not only on the topics covered, but on the process of AI-based thinking. Process-oriented assessment generates the evidence in this phase.

Sub-Strategies and Theoretical Underpinnings: The Collaborative Intelligence Portfolio: Students prepare a Portfolio with their Phase 1 problem frame and prompts; the Phase 2 AI output they choose; their Phase 3 audit reports; and the drafts and final work of Phase 4. This portfolio brings thinking to the fore.

Guided Metacognitive Prompts: The students accentuate to structured questions: o Strategic Knowledge: Which triggers produced the most and least helpful results? Why?"

- Cognitive Knowledge: When did I know the subject the best? Was it during the time I was generating, critiquing or synthesizing?
- Task Knowledge: How did my application of AI differ the way I would have done this task without it? What would I do myself that I would not have trusted to AI?
- Ethical Reflection: Where was I likely to find bias? How did I address it?

Comparative Self-Assessment: The students are going to submit their final product and a 300-word statement that describes their working process, the most important decision-making moments, and the overall impact of their critical judgment on the final product. This resembles the statement of the artist in the arts.

Cognitive Theory: It is a stage that is clearly defined to build metacognitive skills (Flavell, 1979) and facilitate self-directed learning (Zimmerman, 2002). The students acquire control over their mental strategies by considering how they plan, monitor, and evaluate the collaborative process. This learning about learning is the final barrier to automation bias and deskilling as it leads to a conscious, deliberate relationship with technology.

Show (Across Disciplines): A concluding reflective note could look as follows: My early prompts were too wide and generated generic AI results. I got to learn how to confine them with disciplinary prism (e.g., as a behavioral economist...). My critical evaluation showed the AI has to downplay ethical issues regularly in the quest to advance arguments of efficiency. I thus made a special effort to reinforce that part with my own research. The synthesis was most difficult; I had to make several drafts to combine the structural sketch of the AI with my critical voice. In the future, I will rely on AI to do the first scoping and generate ideas, yet I will dedicate more time to the most important processes verification and original synthesis.

The Blueprint in Action: Collaborative Intelligence Cross-Disciplinary Case Studies.

5. INTRODUCTION: THEORY TO PRACTICE IN SITU

The practicality of the Five-Phase Blueprint is no longer a theory but a practice that may be used at the different epistemological levels of higher education. The chapter provides four large, repeatable case studies that make the framework come to life into particular assignments in the STEM, Humanities, Social Sciences, and Professional Education. In both case studies, the specified learning goals, a sample assignment prompt, a stepwise working procedure, which can be tracked and traced following the Five Phases, and a candid account of the potential traps and avoidance techniques are presented. These are studies that are supposed to be templates by offering a specific example and a methodology that can be used by the instructors to their respective field.

To successfully implement the Collaborative Intelligence Blueprint, the five phases of the framework must be modified to fit specific disciplinary cultures since the way the faculty uses AI is vastly different across different disciplines. Based on the classification of Becher, the hard pure sciences, such as physics, gain more benefits by placing an emphasis on computational help (Phase 2) and verification (Phase 3), whereas the hard applied sciences, such as engineering, gain advantages by placing an emphasis on constraint specification (Phase 1) and an iterative refinement (Phase 4). Soft pure disciplines such as history must emphasize bias-detection (Phase 3) and authorial voice formation (Phase 5) whereas the soft applied disciplines, like education, are productively involved in all the phases with a focus on the real-world application. This theory of disciplinary differentiation is based on the theory of academic tribes, and it proves the fact that the main cognitive principles of the Blueprint are always constant, and only the scaffolding of its expression needs flexibility in relation to the way other disciplines create knowledge, utilize instruments, and define authorial authenticity.

5.1 Case Study 1: STEM -Computational Ethics and Algorithmic Design. Degree: Computer Science / Software Engineering / Data Science. Level of Study: Graduate or Advanced Undergraduate. Central issue

How to incorporate the elements of moral reasoning and practical constraint analysis in technical design.

Learning Objectives: Create an effective algorithm or data processing pipeline to address a specified problem. Proactively find and examine ethical, social, and practical failure modes of a computational system. Refine a technical design iteratively on a multi-stakeholder impact assessment basis. Translate technical decisions and trade-offs with ethics into non-technical language.

Sample Assignment: The Ethical Algorithmic Design Sprint. In the same team, students will create a draft of a core algorithm or data model of a socially-embedded system (e.g., a resume-screening system, a predictive policing hotspot algorithm, a dynamic pricing model of utility subsidies) using an LLM and/or code-generation AI (e.g., GitHub Copilot). The ultimate output is no longer the code, but a complete Design Ethics Dossier comprising: the code produced by the AI, a failure mode and effects analysis (FMEA), a revised technical specification with explanations of why it is revised, and a brief on how to communicate with the stakeholders.

Step-by-Step Workflow: Phase 1 - Problem Framing & Prompt Crafting:

Task: Teams specify a given computational problem having precise social consequences. They provide specification, context-based prompts to the code-generation AI, such as desired programming language, desired predictive model (e.g., logistic regression, etc.), intended datasets to use (X, Y, Z), and desired functions within the code (e.g., data cleaning, feature weighting, probability output).

Deliverable: A problem definition statement and the technical prompt. Phase 2 - AI Ideation & Drafting:

Task: Teams produce first code out of the AI. The users are advised to repeat prompts to enhance functionality. They also cause an LLM to become a consultative ethicist and make an initial list of possible risks that such a system has to the society.

Product: AI-generated code files and the first ethics risk list. Phase 3: Critical Analysis and Human Judgment:

Task: Teams perform systematic FMEA. They diagram the parts of the system and processes, and against each, pose the question: How can this fail? How could this be misused? What prejudice might be brought in here? They troubleshoot the code using different synthetic or actual data to seek discriminatory results. They screen the list of ethics of the AI through academic sources about algorithmic fairness (e.g. by Buolamwini, Gebru, O'Neil).

Deliverable: A complete FMEA table and bias audit report. Phase 4 -Synthesis, Refinement and Creation:

Task: According to the FMEA, teams come up with a new technical design document. In this document, it should be stated how the AI-generated prototype should be changed (e.g., fairness restrictions, audit logs, transparency features) and why this change should be made in connection with an ethical risk. After that, they prepare a 2-page non-technical report to a hypothetical city council, describing the purpose of the system, its major security measures, and what limitations it has received.

Deliverable: Technical specification and stakeholder communication brief revised. Phase 5 - Reflection and Metacognitive Documentation:

Task: Each team member individually considers: the conflict between optimization and ethical constraint in design; the way the AI supported and inhibited the process; how a responsible software development lifecycle would look.

Deliverable: Personal reflection accounts. Potential Pitfalls & Mitigations: Pitfall 1: Excessive Relying on AI-Generated Code. The students can treat AI code as a black box and be unaware of the logic.

Mitigation: In the final specification, have line-by-line comments on the purpose of major sections of the key code, and relate them to design decisions. Add a code walk through on team presentation. **Pitfall 2: Theoretical Ethical Discussion.** Ethics can be a general term of communication distinct of the specifics.

Mitigation: The FMEA drives down to component analysis of ethics. The rubric should recognize the points related to direct response to certain identified ethical risks, namely, specific technical changes. **Pitfall 3: The Deus ex Machina Solution.** Students may argue that the problem of bias can be resolved by introducing one measure of fairness.

Mitigation: Base the assignment on critical data studies literature that makes it hard to fix simple technical problems, thus a student must explain inherent trade-offs and value judgments in his/her design.

5.2 Case Study 3: Social Sciences - Policy Analysis and Simulated Stakeholder Negotiation. Education

PhD in Political Science, Public Policy, Sociology. Course Type: Undergraduate or Graduate. Riddle: How to cope with multi-stakeholder, value-based problems where information is missing and views are disputed. Learning Objectives: Think about a complex policy issue in the lenses of several, conflicting stakeholder positions. Combine quantitative and qualitative data into convincing policy means. Assess the policy alternatives in terms of political plausibility and ethics. Partake in deliberation and negotiation to develop the compromise positions.

Sample Assignment: The AI-Stakeholder Simulation: Climate Adaptation Policy. In a simulated policy negotiation on climate adaptation (e.g. managed retreat from coastline), students will be given a particular stakeholder role (e.g. coastal city mayor, EPA regulator, fossil fuel industry lobbyist, environmental justice NGO advocate). They will apply AI to do research on the fundamental interests of their stakeholder; create first policy positions and points to make; simulate discussions with other stakeholders; and create compromise proposals. Their research, simulated dialogues, a final negotiated policy memo and a personal analysis of the process are the final product which is a Negotiation Portfolio.

Step-by-Step Workflow: Phase 1 - Problem Framing & Prompt Crafting:

Activity: Every student conducts a research on his or her stakeholder. To ensure that the AI always represents that stakeholder, they design a persona prompt that the AI will follow (e.g., you are the mayor of a seashore city with a declining tax base and exposed infrastructure). The issues that concern you the most are property prices, city budgets and safety. You do not believe in top-down dictates.

Deliverable A persona and stakeholder profile prompt. Phase 2 - AI Ideation & Drafting:

Task: Students should prompt the AI to create: a list of key policy requests, a 2-minute introductory statement to the negotiations, and possible trade-offs they can make with the help of their persona prompt. Then, they make the AI simulates bilateral conversations with the rest of the types of the stakeholders (Simulate a conversation between the Mayor and the NGO advocate...).

Deliverable: simulated transcripts of a dialogue and position papers that are generated by AI.

Phase 3 - Critical Analysis and Human Judgment:

Job: The students critically evaluate the AI-generated roles in the example of their stakeholder. Are they in line with the real-world interests? Do they know their politics or are they unsophisticated? They interpret the simulated conversations as well: in which areas has the AI taken common ground too far? In which areas was it lacking in fundamental areas of conflict? They supplement this with practical information on expenses, demography and case laws.

Deliverable: The strengths and weaknesses of the AI-simulated stakeholder behavior. Phase 4 - Synthesis, Refinement and Creation:

Task: The students engage in live in-class negotiation with other students (in character). They operate using their ready materials but need to make changes. Once the negotiations are completed, they write a collaborative, multi-party policy memo that describes the compromise that has been agreed upon and have the AI as an editor and formatter to the final document.

Deliverable: A signed policy memo and individual notes of the live negotiation that has been delivered as negotiated. Phase 5 - Reflection and Metacognitive Documentation:

Task: The students consider the distinction between the AI based negotiation and the human based one. What was more challenging? What was the impact of strategy preparation with the AI? Would the AI have expanded or limited the range of their knowledge of the positions of their stakeholder?

Deliverable: A comparative reflection essay. Possible Pitsfalls and mitigations: **Pitfall 1: Stereotyped Caricatures.** The AI can create superficial, stereotypical positions of stakeholders.

Mitigation: It is necessary to have Phase 1 research that has real-life examples (e.g., a quote of a real pool of a mayor, an NGO with its published manifesto), to anchor the AI persona and ensure that stereotypes are compensated.

Pitfall 2: The Fallacy of the Bandwagon. The AI-generated conversations can solve conflict too well.

Mitigation: This is a major instruction. The Phase 3 analysis should pinpoint where AI levelled over intractable conflict to get the students accustomed to the increased reality in the live negotiation.

Pitfall 3: Role Confusion. Learners can mix their own opinions with the interests of the stakeholder that they are assigned.

Mitigation: The assignment evaluates their faithfulness toward the stakeholder role. The reflection is where they can make peace or compare the personal perceptions with the role they had.

5.3 Case Study 4: Professional education- Strategic communication and Crisis simulation

Degree: Business, Communications, Journalism, Public Relations. Level of Course: MBA or Professional Master. Third-Level Issue: Developing subtle, audience-focused communication within the limits of time, reputation, and legal responsibility. Learning Objectives: Dissect a complex organizational crisis through the lenses of diverse audiences (media, investors, employees, public). Create draft strategic communication materials which are channel and stakeholder specific. Consider the possible social impact and moral consequences of communication decisions. Quickly re-strategize according to simulated changing situations. Sample Assignment: The AI-Powered Crisis Communication Lab. A student is introduced to a vivid, changing crisis situation (e.g., a data breach in one of the healthcare firms, a product malfunction in one of the technology firms). They will have to utilize AI to produce quick templates of communication content (press releases, internal memos, social media statements, CEO talking points). The AI will also replicate the reaction of the people as well as the media. Based on this feedback, students need to continuously improve their communications. The end product is a Crisis Communication Playbook of the situation, with chronological manuscripts, a breakdown of important changes, and a post-mortem explanation.

Step-by-Step Workflow: Phase 1 - Problem Framing & Prompt Crafting:

Task: The first crisis alert is given to the students. They carry out a rapid stakeholder mapping. They create specificities of the prompts of the AI according to the communication genres and the target audience (e.g., "Write a 300-word email that is compassionate and legally accurate, to explain to the deeply affected customers that there was a data breach," vs. "Write a bullet-pointed internal FAQ to the employees to clarify rumors).

Output: Stakeholder map and a series of genre specific prompt templates.

Phase 2 - AI Ideation & Drafting:

Task: The students perform their prompts by generating first drafts of all the necessary materials. Then, they apply the AI to imitate the critical responses (e.g., You are a suspicious technological reporter. Write three hard follow-up questions to this press release, or "Simulate the top 10 negative Twitter comments in reaction to this statement).

Deliverable: First-draft communications package and response report simulated by AI. Phase 3 - Critical Analysis and Human Judgment:

Task: Students act as their own crisis comms board and assess each of their drafts critically using the following criteria: clarity, tone, legal exposure, empathy, and cross-channel consistency. They examine the simulated negative reactions so as to find weaknesses in their messages.

Deliverable: Red lined mark-up of the drafts with a vulnerability assessment.

Phase 4 - Synthesis, Refinement and Creation:

Task: The teacher adds a second-wave crisis twist (e.g., leaks of new potentially damaging information). The students are required to redesign their major materials with the AI, with references to the lessons learned during the Phase 3 examination. They create an end product, unified communication package that is fit to be published.

Deliverable Final version of crisis communication package (v2.0). Phase 5 - Reflection and Metacognitive Documentation:

Task: Students compose a post-mortem memo addressed to the CEO, which defines the strategic principles of communication, and provides an explanation of the major changes introduced according to the simulated feedback and direction of advice to use AI in crisis cases in the future.

Deliverable: Strategic after-mortem memo. Possible Pitsfalls and mitigations: Pitfall 1: Formless, soulless Messaging. Artificially intelligent drafts may be grammatically correct, but they will lack the empathy of a real person, which is a critical weakness in a crisis.

Mitigation: Construct "tone audits" into Phase 3. Apply rubrics that put significant emphasis on authenticity, compassion, and consistency in brand voice. Make force students rewrite important empathetic passages manually.

Pitfall 2: Not paying attention to Simulated Feedback. The students can reject the criticism created by AI as not realistic.

Mitigation: The instructor must certify that the responses made by the AI are realistic. The grade on the assignment can be partially associated with the effectiveness with which the final materials are used when it comes to dealing with the vulnerabilities that were identified in the simulated feedback.

Pitfall 3: Speed Over Strategy. The breakneck speed can favor expedient AI scripts as opposed to the considered plan.

Mitigation: Design the assignment to require clear points of strategic alignment (Phase 1 and 3) before and after the rapid drafting phases. The last Playbook should be able to describe the overall strategy and illustrate that the work was not only a quick generation.

5.4 Evidence of Early Implementation

The first stage application of team intelligence pedagogies shows quantifiable results. A study of pre-service teachers based on project-based learning (Nam, 2024) reported that students who were generating educational resources with the help of generative AI showed not only a greater engagement and immersion, but also "positive shifts in their capability in using the generative AI and their awareness of the necessity of AI convergence education" . According to the participants, they were able to continue learning outside of formal classroom settings and do problem-solving independently. Nonetheless, there are some illogical refutations. Wecks et al. (2024) established that students who used GenAI tools obtained a lower average grade of 6.71 which is worse than students that did not use the tools and the effects were especially negatively impacting students with high learning capabilities indicating that use of GenAI tools impairs learning, the reverse, is true. The given finding highlights the necessity of uncontrolled AI access being inadequate a notch above the importance of having structured schemes, such as the Five-Phase Blueprint, which requires critical thinking and the involvement of humans (Phase 3) to avoid cognitive deskilling. The discipline-specific researches also confirm the necessity of differentiated approaches. The survey of computing students in 59 courses by Kiesler et al. (2024) revealed that the correct GenAI use is greatly dependent on the courses learning objectives and policies, which supports the flexibility of the Blueprint.

5.5 Conclusion

The Adaptive Framework. These case studies illustrate the applicability of the Five-Phase Blueprint. The basic frame or outline is always Frame, Generate, Critique, Synthesize and Reflect, but it will be applied variably according to the requirements of the individual epistemology of a discipline. The similarity lies in the fact that AI is rebranded to stop being the answer and rather the stimulus to more critical, profound, and creative interactions between humans. The chapter equips educators with a sense of confidence in taking up the role of the orchestrator, as it offers detailed roadmaps in an effort to create learning experiences that will equip students not just to live in a world without AI, but to live in a world where human judgment is more essential than ever through the use of such frameworks.

6. RECONCEPTUALIZING EVALUATION TO COLLABORATIVE INTELLIGENCE: PRODUCT TO PROCESS. THE ASSESSMENT IMPERATIVE OF AN AI-INFUSED ACADEMY

Should pedagogy be retracted to accommodate Collaborative Intelligence, assessment which is the driving force behind student behavior and credibility of the institution must also be radically changed. The paradigms of traditional assessment that revolve around the evaluation of fixed, end-point products, as to individual authorship and the correct answers are not just challenged by AI but are obsolesced. Trying to retrofit AI-detection software or proctoring is an appropriate and ultimately losing fight that is incongruent with the educational aims of critique, synthesis, and ethical tool usage. It is proposed in this chapter that the paradigm shift towards formative process assessment, rather than summative product assessment, is necessary, with specific suggestions of the models that could be used to evaluate the quality of the human-AI collaboration as such. We outline comprehensive rubrics structures, the portfolio structures and we deliberate on the institutional policy changes that will be required to authenticate and normalize this new method of learning measurement.

6.1 Foundational Principles

What Do we mean by assessing it? The object of assessment needs to be redefined before designing instruments. There are three domains that are interrelated that we evaluate in a Collaborative Intelligence model:

- Quality of Cognitive Process: The strategy, rigor, and criticality of interaction with AI throughout the Five Phases.
- Ethical and Disciplinary Integrity: The transparency, mitigation of prejudice and discipline of AI use.
- Synthetic Output Quality: The originality, richness and convincing nature of the ultimate human synthesis, assessed with the knowledge that it was produced through a technologically enhanced procedure. The evaluation will have to bring the process of thinking with AI to light and hence assessable. This is in line with the educative adage: We judge what we appreciate. When we appreciate collaborative effort where critical work is done, rather than individual production, then an evaluation should be done to reflect that.

6.2 Model 1: The Collaborative Intelligence Process Rubric

This formative assessment grading rubric judges the work of the student within the five phases blueprint. It would be applicable to the entire portfolio or to individual assignments. Phase (Criterion) Exemplary (4) Proficient (3) Developing (2) Unsatisfactory (1) Problem Structuring & Timely Fashioning Identifies a multifaceted nuanced issue. Prompts are advanced in nature, and they include role, context and constraint to aid AI in a strategic manner. Defines a clear problem. Prompts are operational and have key parameters to get the appropriate AI output. Issue is oversimplified or abstract. Prompts are simplistic, and they are likely to produce generic or off-target AI responses. Problem is not defined or absent. Prompts are either not recorded or the ones that are recorded are ineffective. Employs AI to create suitable content. Documents are very responsive and give clear outputs. The use of AI is less or insufficiently reported. Outputs are mindlessly accepted or ineffective. Critical Analysis & Judgment Carries out a thorough and multi-faceted audit of AI outputs: Fact-checks in-depth, finds bias/logical fallacies, interprets gaps/silences wisely. Audits AI reports cohesiveness and biasness, and a number of issues concerning evidence are found.

6.3 The Critical AI Literacy Competency Rubric

The rubric evaluates the acquisition of particular skills that are necessary in ethical and productive collaboration and can be used during assignments. Immediate Design Similar to refinement Prompt sequences are designed iteratively to improve outputs, with sophisticated methods (chain-of-thought, few-shot).

Ethical Integration & Synthesis: Always makes AI a subservient tool; the end result shows a strong bidirectional intellectual leadership of the human and the transformative use of AI material. Augments through AI; completed work contains recognisable human structures and analysis over AI-generated foundation.

Practice: This competency model is used to endorse a mastery-based grading strategy. The level of development in these competencies can be evaluated during a course, and the final grade is the manifestation of accordance with the mastery of the Collaborative Intelligence skills.

6.4 The Collaborative Intelligence Dossier

The process rubric also requires a different form of submission a structured portfolio or dossier which is a summary of the whole process of collaboration.

There are four things that should be paid attention to:

- Re-Conceptualizing Academic Integrity Policies: University honor codes need to be revised to ensure that bans on unauthorized assistance are substituted with mandates to engage in open cooperation. The new standard must be: Permitted use of generative AI tools, and, on some occasions, encouraged. Any such use should be clearly noted down and all the work turned in should be the ultimate synthesis, analysis and voice of the student. The way of failing to record transparently the use of AI is an academic misconduct. This reverses the presupposition of prohibition to a compulsory disclosure.
- Grading Policy and Credit Allocation: Departments should approve grading schemes which put much emphasis on process. This might involve changing course description templates by adding such language as, Assessment in this course focuses on the process of inquiry and critical collaboration with digital tools, assessed using portfolios and process rubrics. Institutional research offices might be required to confirm that such assessments are reliable in measuring course learning outcomes.
- Transcripts and Credentialing: Co-curricular transcripts or competency badges are one of the opportunities that institutions need to think about as a formal credentialing of these skills as Collaborative Intelligence becomes a core learning outcome. A learner might graduate with a certified Critical AI

Literacy badge on top of his or her degree, indicating a confirmed skill set outside of the major.

- Faculty Development and Support: This change must not be penal. It involves high investments in faculty development. Faculty should be trained in centers of teaching and learning in:
  - Designing process-oriented tasks.
  - Calibration and use of the new rubrics.
  - Effectively evaluating portfolios (which may take more time in the first instance).
  - Creation of institutional models and common repositories of successful tests.

6.5. Implementation The challenges of implementing an action plan. The Workload grading

Although grading portfolios is more laborious at first, it is an improvement to the exhausting game of AI detective. Rubrics make assessment easier. Besides, process evaluation can be more objective and less subjective than deliberation of the originality of a final product. Resistance by students: the students who have been used to grades based on correct answers may not easily understand process assessment. This requires an explicit unpacking of the rubric, and examples of exemplary portfolios, and a clear pedagogical rationale that is established at the beginning of the course.

6.6 Institutional Implementation Realities

The key to successfully introducing the Collaborative Intelligence Blueprint at the institutional level is the strategic investment in the faculty development and equal resource allocation, along with the effective data management and accreditation alignment. This movement to process-based evaluation requires teaching and learning institutions to educate faculty on how to create tasks that AI cannot solve, scale rubrics and run portfolios, and institutions should make premium AI resources widely accessible on campus to avoid digital divide differences. In order to shift classroom innovation to systemic change, leaders need to find ways of addressing faculty workload issues based on incentives and not mandate, create a clear data policy to safeguard student privacy, and implement a structure that fits the Global South context where language and bandwidth remains a barrier. Although the initial implementation adds an average of 57 minutes per faculty, more mature implementation shifts the cost of academic integrity resources of AI monitoring to more genuine assessment development, which places institutions in a strategic stance of using collaborative intelligence, as opposed to responding to AI abuse

7. CONCLUSION

Evaluation as the Agent of Change

The evaluation models suggested in this paper are not simply techno solutions; they are the key to the promise of Collaborative Intelligence becoming a reality. We can make our evaluation corresponding to the multi-faceted, tool-rich world our students live in by creating assessment that embraces the interrogative interaction with AI, the detective technique of corroboration, and the creative process of synthesis. This change eventually bridges the gap in terms of our teaching, our assessment and our future preparation of the students. It brings the academy out of a defensive attitude of mistrust, to an offensive attitude of organisation, when we produce not merely learned men, but traditionally sound, ethically skilled, critically versatile, orchestrators of intelligence. The final trial of our system of education will be its ability to produce graduates who can find their way through this new world with prudence and our system of assessment should be the first and most definite step in that direction.

Orchestrating the Future of Learning

The emergence of AI generation is not something to control, but a paradigm shift that must be accepted. The argument presented in this chapter is that the decision in front of higher education is not one between tradition and obsolescence, but between two futures, one where we pointlessly police a new intelligence, the other where we explicitly collaborate with it. The blueprint to this voyage can be found in "The AI-Enhanced Classroom: A Blueprint for Collaborative Intelligence," which offers the path to follow in the world of apps and apps. We are able to take the opportunity to rise our mission to a new level by doing more than simply detecting plagiarism, and by actively planning the creation of synergistic learning experiences. This roadmap enables teachers to turn their classrooms into the incubators of a new type of intelligence, one that is a combination of human creativity, morale, and critical thinking and the ability of AI to compute, scale, and analyse. It will not just result in a more efficient classroom, but it will result in a deeper one; we will be training a generation of students who are not just replaceable by AI, but are actually indispensable to it and are ready to solve the most intricate tasks in the world in a new and powerful way of thought that will be collaborative.

REFERENCES

Bang, Y., Cahyawijaya, S., Lee, N., Dai, W., Su, D., Wilie, B., & Fung, P. (2023, November). A multitask, multilingual, multimodal evaluation of chatgpt on reasoning, hallucination, and interactivity. In *Proceedings of the 13th international joint conference on natural language processing and the 3rd conference of the asia-pacific chapter of the association for computational linguistics* (volume 1*: Long papers)* (pp. 675-718). DOI: 10.18653/v1/2023.ijcnlp-main.45

Bolukbasi, T., Chang, K. W., Zou, J. Y., Saligrama, V., & Kalai, A. T. (2016). Man is to computer programmer as woman is to homemaker? debiasing word embeddings. *Advances in Neural Information Processing Systems*, 29.

Buckingham, D. (2003). Media education: Literacy, learning and contemporary culture. *Polity*.

Buolamwini, J., & Gebru, T. (2018). Gender shades: Intersectional accuracy disparities in commercial gender classification. *Proceedings of the 1st Conference on Fairness, Accountability and Transparency*.

Buolamwini, J., & Gebru, T. (2018). Gender shades: Intersectional accuracy disparities in commercial gender classification. *Proceedings of the 1st Conference on Fairness, Accountability and Transparency*.

Collins, A., Brown, J. S., & Holum, A. (1991). Cognitive apprenticeship: Making thinking visible. *American Educator*, *15*(3), 6–11.

Couldry, N., & Mejias, U. A. (2019). *The costs of connection: How data is colonizing human life and appropriating it for capitalism*. Stanford University Press.

Duncker, K. (1945). On problem-solving. *Psychological Monographs*, *58*(5), i-113. DOI: 10.1037/h0093599

Eaton, S. E. (2022). *Postplagiarism: Transdisciplinary ethics and integrity in the age of artificial intelligence and neurotechnology*. University of Calgary. DOI: 10.4135/9781071892992

Ellis, C. (2023). *The end of authenticity: Artificial intelligence and the future of assessment*. Routledge.

Flavell, J. H. (1979). Metacognition and cognitive monitoring: A new area of cognitive–developmental inquiry. *The American Psychologist*, *34*(10), 906–911. DOI: 10.1037/0003-066X.34.10.906

Hofer, B. K., & Pintrich, P. R. (1997). The development of epistemological theories: Beliefs about knowledge and knowing and their relation to learning. *Review of Educational Research*, *67*(1), 88–140. DOI: 10.3102/00346543067001088

Johnston, H., Wells, R. F., Shanks, E. M., Boey, T., & Parsons, B. N. (2024). Student Perspectives on the Use of Generative Artificial Intelligence Technologies in Higher Education. *International Journal for Educational Integrity*, *20*(2), 2. DOI: 10.1007/s40979-024-00149-4

Jonassen, D. H. (1997). Instructional design models for well-structured and ill-structured problem-solving learning outcomes. *Educational Technology Research and Development*, *45*(1), 65–94. DOI: 10.1007/BF02299613

Lessig, L. (2008). *Remix: Making art and commerce thrive in the hybrid economy.* Penguin. DOI: 10.5040/9781849662505

Nam, S. W. (2024). Case Study on Teaching with Project-Based Generative AI. *Journal of Internet of Things and Convergence*, *10*(6), 43–48.

O'Neil, C. (2016). *Weapons of math destruction: How big data increases inequality and threatens democracy*. Crown Publishing Group.

Ogunleye, B., Zakariyyah, K. I., Ajao, O., Olayinka, O., & Sharma, H. (2024). A systematic review of generative AI for teaching and learning practice. *Education Sciences*, *14*(6), 636. DOI: 10.3390/educsci14060636

Parasuraman, R., & Manzey, D. H. (2010). Complacency and bias in human use of automation: An attentional integration. *Human Factors*, *52*(3), 381–410. DOI: 10.1177/0018720810376055 PMID: 21077562

Risko, E. F., & Gilbert, S. J. (2016). Cognitive Offloading. *Trends in Cognitive Sciences*, *20*(9), 676–688. DOI: 10.1016/j.tics.2016.07.002 PMID: 27542527

Sperber, D., Clément, F., Heintz, C., Mascaro, O., Mercier, H., Origgi, G., & Wilson, D. (2010). Epistemic vigilance. *Mind & Language*, *25*(4), 359–393. DOI: 10.1111/j.1468-0017.2010.01394.x

Sun, L., & Zhou, L. (2024). Does Generative Artificial Intelligence Improve the Academic Achievement of College Students? A Meta-Analysis. *Journal of Educational Computing Research*, *62*(7), 1896–1933. DOI: 10.1177/07356331241277937

Sweller, J. (1988). Cognitive load during problem solving: Effects on learning. *Cognitive Science*, *12*(2), 257–285. DOI: 10.1207/s15516709cog1202_4

van Dijk, J. A. (2020). *The digital divide*. John Wiley & Sons.

Wecks, J. O., Voshaar, J., Plate, B. J., & Zimmermann, J. (2024). Generative AI usage and exam performance. *arXiv preprint arXiv:2404.19699.*

Wiley, D. (2013). *What is Open Pedagogy?* iterating toward openness. [Blog]. Bruner, J. S. (1966). *Toward a theory of instruction.* Harvard University Press.

Wineburg, S., & McGrew, S. (2019). Lateral reading and the nature of expertise: Reading less and learning more when evaluating digital information. *Teachers College Record*, *121*(11), 1–40. DOI: 10.1177/016146811912101102

Zimmerman, B. J. (2002). Becoming a self-regulated learner: An overview. *Theory into Practice*, *41*(2), 64–70. DOI: 10.1207/s15430421tip4102_2

Chapter 10
Large Language Models (LLMs)

Nizirwan Anwar
http://orcid.org/0000-0003-1189-9093
Universitas Esa Unggul, Indonesia

Abdul Rakhim Nanda
Muhammadiyah University of Makassar, Indonesia

Muhammad Faisal
http://orcid.org/0000-0003-1469-9468
Muhammadiyah University of Makassar, Indonesia

Irmawati Irmawati
Politeknik Negeri Ujung Pandang, Indonesia

Muhammad Syafaat S. Kuba
Muhammadiyah University of Makassar, Indonesia

Muh. Fajri Raharjo
http://orcid.org/0009-0009-8286-6345
Politeknik Negeri Ujung Pandang, Indonesia

Nurnawaty Nurnawaty
Muhammadiyah University of Makassar, Indonesia

Alex Gufron
http://orcid.org/0009-0008-9293-3022
Universitas Negeri Semarang, Indonesia

Ida Lestari
Indonesia Open University, Indonesia

Nina Nurhasanah
http://orcid.org/0000-0001-8130-752X
Universitas Esa Unggul, Indonesia

ABSTRACT

This chapter examines the transformative role of Large Language Models (LLMs) in AI-powered automation within higher education, highlighting strategic opportunities and emerging risks across teaching, research, and academic service. The purpose of this chapter per the authors is to evaluate how LLMs support pedagogical innovation, personalised learning, curriculum design, research productivity, and administrative efficiency, while addressing challenges related to academic integrity,

DOI: 10.4018/979-8-2600-2811-7.ch010

bias, data governance, epistemic reliability, and potential deskilling. Drawing on recent theoretical and empirical developments, the discussion situates LLM adoption within ethical AI, quality assurance, and institutional governance frameworks. Emphasis is placed on human-centred integration that balances automation with academic oversight. The chapter concludes by proposing a governance-oriented model to guide responsible and sustainable LLM deployment in higher education ecosystems.

INTRODUCTION

The emergence of Large Language Models (LLMs) and other generative Artificial Intelligence (AI) tools marks a watershed moment for higher education, raising both transformative possibilities and substantive challenges for teaching, research, and service. LLMs such as ChatGPT have demonstrated capabilities in natural language understanding and generation, enabling personalized feedback, writing assistance, drafting support, and automated routine communications. In this sense, AI-powered automation anchored by LLMs promises to augment instructional design, accelerate scholarly workflows, and streamline administrative processes, thereby contributing to more scalable and efficient university operations while preserving the central role of human expertise and judgment (Ahme et al., 2024; Bobula, 2024; Lytras et al., 2024; Sarker et al., 2023). At the same time, the rapid proliferation of generative AI raises critical questions about reliability, biases, privacy, academic integrity, and the potential disruption of established pedagogies and governance structures that underpin higher education's mission (Ahme et al., 2024; Popenici et al., 2023; Sarker et al., 2023).

A central motivation for this chapter is to articulate a balanced, evidence-informed understanding of how LLMs can meaningfully contribute to three core domains of the higher education enterprise. In teaching and learning, LLMs offer opportunities for adaptive guidance, real-time formative feedback, and scalable support for diverse and multilingual learners, while challenging educators to design assessments and curricula that preserve higher-order thinking and academic integrity in an AI-enabled environment (Ahme et al., 2024; El Fougour & Erradi, 2025; Sarker et al., 2023). In research and scholarly activity, LLMs can assist with literature synthesis, drafting and editing, and grant-writing workflows, but they also introduce concerns about authorship clarity, data privacy, and the potential for biased outputs or misinterpretation if not carefully validated and supervised (Ahme et al., 2024; Bobula, 2024; Phillipson, 2013; Popenici et al., 2023). In service and administration, AI-powered automation can handle routine inquiries, admissions processes, scheduling, and knowledge-management tasks, potentially freeing staff to focus on higher-value activities; however, institutions must establish transparent governance, data-handling policies, and interoperability standards to maintain accountability and trust (Bobula, 2024; Popenici et al., 2023; Sarker et al., 2023).

This chapter adopts a multi-faceted frame that foregrounds ethical considerations, policy implications, and implementation challenges alongside practical deployment patterns and theoretical foundations. It acknowledges a spectrum of positions found in the literature: some scholars emphasize augmentation and human-in-the-loop design as the prudent path forward, while others highlight domain-specific adaptations and the need for rigorous evaluation to avoid over-reliance on automated processes (Bobula, 2024; Denny et al., 2024; Sarker et al., 2023). By weaving together perspectives from empirical studies, theoretical analyses, and cross-domain syntheses, the introduction clarifies the scope of inquiry - how LLMs intersect with teaching, research, and service in higher education - and outlines the structure of the chapter as a guide for stakeholders seeking to navigate opportunities and mitigate threats in AI-powered automation.

Figure 1. Opportunities and threats of LLMs in teaching, research, and service

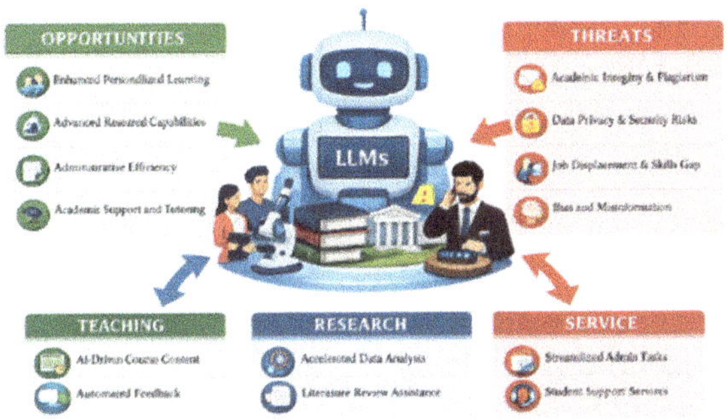

he image presents a balanced conceptual overview of how LLMs influence the core missions of higher education - teaching, research, and service - while simultaneously highlighting associated opportunities and threats. At the center, LLMs are depicted as a transformative technological agent interacting with academic stakeholders and institutional structures. On the opportunity side, the framework illustrates enhanced personalized learning, advanced research capabilities, improved administrative efficiency, and strengthened academic support. These benefits are operationalized across teaching (AI-driven course content and automated feedback), research (accelerated data analysis and literature review assistance), and service (streamlined administrative tasks and student support services). Conversely, the image also emphasizes key threats and challenges, including academic integrity concerns, data privacy and security risks, job displacement and skills gaps, and bias or misinformation. These risks underscore the necessity for governance frameworks, ethical safeguards, and institutional oversight.

Overall, the visual functions as a strategic reflection model, demonstrating that LLM integration in higher education requires a careful balance between innovation and responsibility, ensuring that institutional benefits are maximized while risks are systematically managed.

Notes on evidence and nuance;

- The discussion of opportunities in teaching and learning aligns with literature emphasizing personalized feedback, adaptive learning, and scalable instructional support provided by LLMs, as well as the importance of inclusive design and multilingual capabilities when context and pedagogy are carefully considered (Ahme et al., 2024; El Fougour & Erradi, 2025; Sarker et al., 2023).
- The concerns about reliability, bias, privacy, and integrity reflect ongoing debates in higher education literature regarding model hallucinations, data governance, and the need for robust validation, accountability, and policy frameworks (Bobula, 2024; Popenici et al., 2023; Sarker et al., 2023).
- The framing of implementation as augmentation rather than replacement is supported by discussions on human-AI collaboration and the necessity of professional development to foster AI literacy among faculty and staff (Dubey & Crevar, 2025; Em et al., 2025; Sarker et al., 2023).

The integration of artificial intelligence (AI) within complex socio-technical systems has significantly transformed decision-making processes, operational efficiency, and cross-organizational collaboration. Recent studies emphasise that machine learning models enhance predictive accuracy and adaptive optimisation across dynamic environments, particularly when supported by robust data governance and interoperable architectures (Jordan & Mitchell, 2015; Wagner, 2017). In parallel, the adoption of environmentally sustainable and data-driven technologies demonstrates how intelligent systems can simultaneously improve performance and sustainability outcomes, reinforcing the strategic value of AI-enabled innovation (Zuo et al., 2023). However, the expansion of AI also necessitates careful consideration of transparency, accountability, and trust, as opaque algorithmic processes may undermine stakeholder confidence and governance integrity (Jobin et al., 2019). Collectively, these findings indicate that sustainable and trustworthy AI deployment requires a balanced framework integrating technical robustness, interoperability standards, and ethical oversight to ensure long-term organisational and societal value.

THEORETICAL AND PRACTICAL FOUNDATIONS OF LLMS IN HIGHER EDUCATION

The theoretical and practical foundations of LLMs in higher education rest at the intersection of advanced NLP capabilities and the distinctive goals of teaching, research, and service. On the theory side, LLMs are grounded in probabilistic language modeling, deep learning architectures, and emergent behaviors that enable context-aware dialogue, content generation, and automated reasoning. This theoretical base informs how higher education scholars conceptualize the potential roles of LLMs in instructional design, formative assessment, and scholarly writing. The literature emphasizes that LLMs should be understood as powerful tools for augmentation rather than autonomous replacement, with human oversight, domain-specific validation, and rigorous quality assurance as central design principles (Ladehoff et al., 2023; Neubauer et al., 2022). In this sense, the theoretical lens foregrounds issues of reliability, epistemic authority, and the need for principled governance to preserve academic integrity while leveraging AI-enabled capabilities (Bobula, 2024; Denny et al., 2024; Popenici et al., 2023).

Practically, deployment patterns for LLMs in higher education include integration into learning management systems, deployment of chatbots and virtual tutors, automated feedback and drafting assistance, and support for scholarship workflows such as literature synthesis and manuscript editing. The practical literature consistently notes that successful adoption hinges on human-AI collaboration, with clear delineations of responsibilities, professional development for educators, and thoughtfully designed workflows that maintain critical thinking and scholarly rigor. Evidence from multiple domains indicates that LLMs can scale personalized feedback, generate scaffolding for diverse learners, and assist with routine administrative or research tasks, while also presenting risks such as hallucinations, data privacy concerns, and potential biases in outputs that require validation and monitoring (Ahme et al., 2024; Bobula, 2024; El Fougour & Erradi, 2025; Phillipson, 2013; Ravikumar et al., 2025). This dual emphasis on capability and guardrails shapes implementation strategies that favor augmentation, interoperability with existing institutional ecosystems, and ongoing evaluation to refine models and prompts over time (Dubey & Crevar, 2025; Lytras et al., 2024; van Rensburg & van der Westhuizen, 2024).

A core practical implication is the need for governance, policy, and infrastructure to realize responsible LLM use in higher education. Institutions should establish explicit guidelines on data handling, model provenance, authorship attribution, and transparency of AI-assisted work, alongside investment in data pipelines, accessibility, and security. The literature argues for aligned policy ecosystems, with governance mechanisms tailored to disciplinary contexts and regional considerations to ensure equitable access and ethical use across teaching, research, and service activities (Ferreira-Meyers, 2025; Lomachinska et al., 2026; Lytras et al., 2024; van Rensburg & van der Westhuizen, 2024). Moreover, given the rapid evolution of AI tools, change management that engages faculty, students, and administrators through professional development, communities of practice, and sandbox environments is essential for sustainable adoption and continuous learning about best practices in AI-enhanced pedagogy and scholarship (Dubey & Crevar, 2025; Em et al., 2025; Uysal & Yüksel, 2024).

Nuances across sources deserve explicit acknowledgement. Some scholars emphasize domain-adaptation and prompt engineering as critical for domain-specific effectiveness, while others stress the importance of robust evaluation designs to distinguish genuine learning gains from superficial automation. There is ongoing debate about detection and authenticity in AI-generated content, and about how to balance the benefits of automation with the preservation of higher-order thinking and intellectual independence. When comparing regional contexts, issues such as digital infrastructure, equity of access, and cultural considerations influence both theoretical adoption frameworks and practical deployment decisions. These nuances highlight the need for a plural, context-aware approach to the theoretical and practical foundations of LLMs in higher education, integrating insights from multiple disciplinary and geographic perspectives to guide responsible, effective use (Popenici et al., 2023; Rao & Al-Obaidi, 2024; van Rensburg & van der Westhuizen, 2024; Vetrivel et al., 2025; Zhai & Krajcik, 2024).

In sum, the theoretical foundations provide a map of what LLMs can do and what they should not replace, while the practical foundations translate that map into deployment patterns, governance structures, and implementation roadmaps that enable teaching, research, and service to benefit from AI-enabled automation without compromising core educational values. The synthesis across the cited literature underlines the imperative for augmentation-friendly designs, rigorous validation, and ethically grounded, evidence-based policies as the compass guiding AI-enabled transformation in higher education (Ahme et al., 2024; Bobula, 2024; Denny et al., 2024; Dubey & Crevar, 2025; El Fougour & Erradi, 2025; Lytras et al., 2024; Ravikumar et al., 2025).

Figure 2. Core functional architecture of LLMs

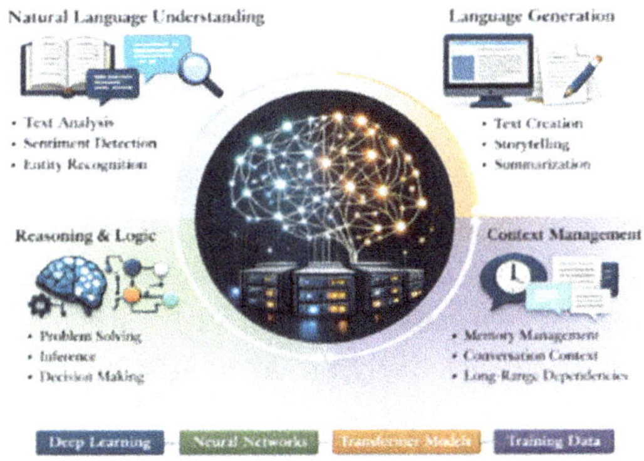

The image presents a conceptual (Figure 2) overview of the foundational architecture and functional capabilities of LLMs. It visually integrates four primary cognitive domains - Natural Language Understanding, Language Generation, Reasoning and Logic, and Context Management - around a central representation of a neural network powered by computational infrastructure.

The diagram illustrates how LLMs perform key language processing tasks such as text analysis, sentiment detection, entity recognition, text creation, storytelling, summarisation, inference, and decision-making. It further highlights context management mechanisms, including memory handling and long-range dependency modelling, which enable coherent multi-turn interactions.

At the foundational layer, the image identifies enabling technologies - Deep Learning, Neural Networks, Transformer Models, and Training Data - emphasising the technical backbone that supports these advanced linguistic and reasoning capabilities.

Overall, the visual functions as an explanatory framework for understanding how LLMs combine architectural design, large-scale training data, and transformer-based deep learning to simulate language comprehension, contextual reasoning, and generative intelligence within modern AI systems.

Artificial neural networks constitute the computational foundation of LLMs, enabling the representation and transformation of linguistic information through layered, parameterised functions. Contemporary LLMs are primarily based on deep neural network architectures, particularly the Transformer model, which employs self-attention mechanisms to capture contextual dependencies across long sequences without relying on recurrent structures (Patro et al., 2022). Through distributed vector representations (embeddings), neural networks support natural language understanding tasks such as entity recognition and sentiment classification, as well as language generation functions including summarisation and structured text creation. The attention mechanism enables reasoning-like behaviour by dynamically weighting relevant tokens, facilitating inference across long-range dependencies (Devlin et al., 2019). Moreover, scaling neural network parameters and training data has been empirically associated with improved reasoning capacity and broader contextual generalisation, highlighting the decisive role of deep learning architectures in enhancing LLM performance (Ruan et al., 2022). Empirical evidence indicates that larger transformer-based models exhibit more coherent long-range dependency modelling and more consistent multi-step inference, particularly when trained on diverse, large-scale corpora. Collectively, these neural architectures underpin the four principal aspects of LLMs: natural language understanding, text generation, reasoning through attention-based inference, and context handling via high-dimensional representation learning, all of which rely on scalable parameterisation and optimised training regimes (Devlin et al., 2019; Patro et al., 2022).

The layered conceptual framework of LLMs in higher education illustrates a structured integration of technological infrastructure, pedagogical application, institutional governance, and systemic impact within a unified architecture. At its core, LLM technology is grounded in transformer-based neural architectures that employ self-attention mechanisms to capture contextual dependencies across large-scale textual data (Devlin et al., 2019). Empirical research indicates that increasing model parameters and training data scale significantly enhances representation learning capacity, transfer performance, and generalisation across complex tasks, thereby enabling LLMs to undertake advanced analytical and reasoning-oriented academic functions. Through large-scale pre-training followed by domain adaptation and alignment optimisation strategies, including reinforcement learning from human feedback, LLMs can be calibrated to follow instructions and conform more closely to human evaluative standards. Within higher education contexts, such adaptability facilitates integration across teaching design, research augmentation, and administrative automation, positioning LLMs as foundational enablers of AI-driven institutional transformation (Devlin et al., 2019; Kasneci et al., 2023).

Built upon this technological layer, the application layer encompasses three primary academic domains: Teaching and Learning, Research and Innovation, and Administration and Services. In teaching contexts, LLMs support adaptive tutoring, automated formative feedback, and multilingual scaffolding, contributing to more personalised and scalable instruction (Kasneci et al., 2023). In research workflows, they assist with literature synthesis, code generation, and knowledge extraction, accelerating scholarly productivity while raising important questions regarding epistemic reliability. Administratively, conversational agents and document-generation systems enhance operational efficiency and student support services, reflecting broader trends in AI-enabled organisational transformation (Dwivedi et al., 2023).

Figure 3. Integrated ecosystem model for LLMs

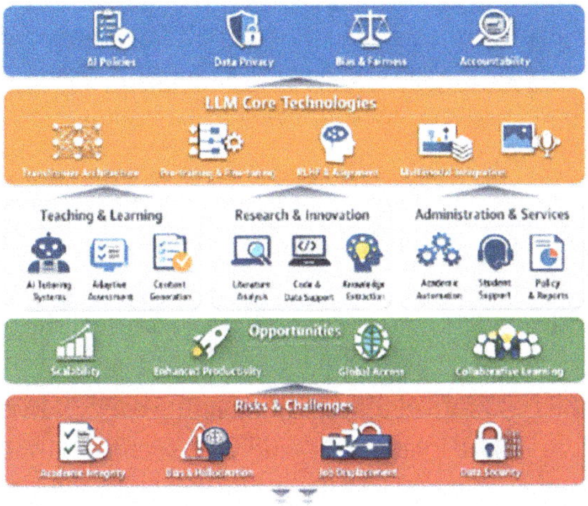

Above the application layer, the governance and ethical oversight layer functions as a critical regulatory mechanism. This layer includes AI policy frameworks, data privacy protections, bias mitigation strategies, and accountability mechanisms. Responsible AI principles emphasise transparency, fairness, explainability, and human oversight as essential conditions for trustworthy deployment in education (Floridi et al., 2018). Without structured governance, risks such as algorithmic bias, hallucination, academic integrity violations, and data security vulnerabilities may undermine institutional credibility and social trust.

At the systemic level, the framework recognises a dual dynamic of opportunities and risks. Opportunities include scalability, enhanced research productivity, global accessibility of academic support, and collaborative human–AI learning environments. Conversely, risks encompass cognitive dependency, potential deskilling, labour displacement, and privacy exposure. Empirical analyses of generative AI adoption highlight that the impact of LLMs is not deterministic but contingent upon governance maturity, digital literacy, and institutional readiness (Dwivedi et al., 2023). Overall, the layered architecture model conceptualises LLM integration in higher education as a socio-technical system rather than a purely technological intervention. It demonstrates that technological capability, pedagogical innovation, governance structure, and institutional strategy must operate in alignment to ensure that AI-powered automation strengthens academic integrity, inclusivity, and sustainable knowledge production.

The image presents (Figure 3), a layered ecosystem framework illustrating how LLMs function within a comprehensive higher education environment. It visually organises AI integration into interconnected layers: governance foundations, core technologies, application domains, opportunities, and associated risks.

At the top layer, governance principles - AI policies, data privacy, bias and fairness, and accountability - establish ethical and regulatory oversight. The central layer highlights core LLM technologies, including transformer architectures, pre-training and fine-tuning processes, reinforcement learning from human feedback (RLHF), and multimodal integration. These technologies enable applications across three primary institutional domains: teaching and learning, research and innovation, and administration and services.

The framework further identifies strategic opportunities such as scalability, enhanced productivity, global access, and collaborative learning. At the same time, it acknowledges critical risks and challenges, including academic integrity concerns, bias and hallucination, job displacement, and data security vulnerabilities.

Overall, the visual serves as a holistic conceptual model demonstrating that LLM implementation in higher education operates as a dynamic ecosystem where governance, technology, institutional functions, benefits, and risks must be carefully aligned to ensure responsible, sustainable, and value-driven AI adoption.

TEACHING, LEARNING, AND STUDENT EXPERIENCE

The integration of LLMs into higher education represents a transformative development in teaching, learning, and student experience, particularly in relation to personalisation and scalable instruction. LLM-driven systems enable adaptive feedback mechanisms that respond to individual learner profiles, prior knowledge, and real-time performance indicators. Through natural language interaction, students can receive scaffolded explanations, contextualised examples, and iterative clarification tailored to their cognitive needs. Such adaptive scaffolding aligns with long-standing principles of formative pedagogy and learner-centred design, enhancing engagement while mitigating cognitive overload. Furthermore, multilingual support embedded within LLM architectures expands accessibility for international and linguistically diverse student populations, thereby reinforcing inclusive educational practices consistent with universal design for learning frameworks (Zawacki-Richter et al., 2019). Empirical research indicates that AI-enabled adaptive systems can enhance learning efficiency and foster self-regulated learning behaviours when strategically aligned with pedagogical objectives (Kulik & Fletcher, 2016). Consequently, personalisation through LLMs does not merely automate instruction but reconfigures instructional delivery towards responsive and data-informed engagement at scale.

In the domain of assessment and formative feedback, LLMs introduce new possibilities for real-time analytic insight and adaptive evaluation. AI-supported tools can generate immediate formative comments, propose targeted revision strategies, and construct adaptive quizzes that dynamically adjust difficulty based on learner responses. This capacity enhances feedback timeliness, a factor widely recognised as central to effective learning progression (Hattie & Timperley, 2007). By analysing linguistic patterns and conceptual coherence, LLM-based systems can support rubric-aligned feedback that encourages reflective practice and metacognitive awareness (Zhai & Krajcik, 2024). However, reliability and validity considerations remain critical. Algorithmic bias, probabilistic inaccuracies, and fabricated outputs necessitate structured human oversight and transparent evaluation frameworks (Williamson & Eynon, 2020). Moreover, the widespread availability of generative AI tools raises concerns regarding academic integrity, authenticity of student work, and assessment security, thereby requiring the redesign of assessments toward authentic, process-oriented, and higher-order tasks. Institutional responses, therefore, demand robust governance structures and explicit disclosure policies to ensure responsible and pedagogically aligned AI integration.

The pedagogical implications of LLM adoption extend beyond student-facing applications to fundamentally reshape faculty roles and professional identity. Academic staff are increasingly positioned as designers of AI-augmented learning environments rather than sole transmitters of disciplinary knowledge (Williamson & Eynon, 2020; Zawacki-Richter et al., 2019). This shift necessitates structured professional development initiatives aimed at cultivating AI literacy, ethical evaluation competencies, and critical awareness of algorithmic limitations (Holmes et al., 2022). Research in AI in education consistently emphasises that human judgement remains indispensable in ensuring alignment between technological affordances and meaningful learning outcomes (Development, 2016). Importantly, evidence suggests that AI integration operates as a systemic transformation affecting pedagogy, assessment, and governance simultaneously rather than functioning as an isolated technological enhancement (Zawacki-Richter et al., 2019). Institutional strategies must therefore address data privacy, algorithmic transparency, digital equity, and sustainability to ensure responsible deployment (Williamson & Eynon, 2020).

Figure 4. Pedagogical transformation framework for AI-enabled higher education

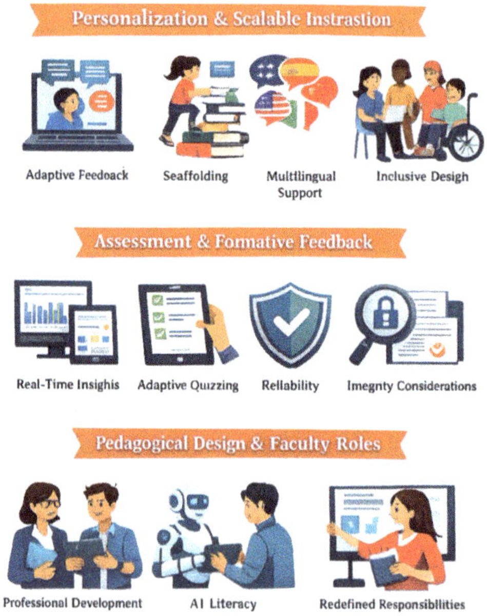

The image presents (Figure 4), a comprehensive conceptual framework illustrating how LLMs and AI-powered automation can transform teaching and learning in higher education. It is structured around three interrelated domains: Personalization and Scalable Instruction, Assessment and Formative Feedback, and Pedagogical Design and Faculty Roles. The first section highlights AI's capacity to support adaptive feedback, scaffolding strategies, multilingual assistance, and inclusive design to accommodate diverse learner needs. The second section focuses on assessment innovation, including real-time insights, adaptive quizzing, reliability measures, and integrity considerations to ensure valid and ethical evaluation practices. The third section addresses the evolving role of faculty, emphasising professional development, AI literacy, and redefined instructional responsibilities in technology-enhanced environments. Overall, the visual functions as a strategic and pedagogical guide, demonstrating that AI integration in higher education extends beyond automation to encompass personalised learning, responsible assessment practices, and the professional evolution of educators within digitally mediated academic ecosystems.

RESEARCH AND SCHOLARLY ACTIVITY

Research and scholarly activity within the context of LLMs represents a paradigmatic shift in how knowledge is discovered, synthesised, produced, and evaluated in higher education. LLMs enable accelerated literature mapping, automated summarisation, hypothesis generation, and structured drafting, thereby augmenting researchers' cognitive capacity in managing large-scale and interdisciplinary corpora. As generative AI systems become embedded in academic workflows, they function as assistive technologies that support ideation, linguistic refinement, and preliminary data interpretation rather than autonomous knowledge producers. Empirical analyses highlight that such systems can enhance productivity and research efficiency when combined with critical human oversight and domain expertise (Dwivedi et al., 2023). In educational and research environments, LLMs have demonstrated potential to scaffold analytical reasoning and academic writing processes, while also raising questions about epistemic reliability and responsible integration (Kasneci et al., 2023).

Despite these opportunities, the scholarly deployment of LLMs introduces significant concerns regarding validity, authorship, and academic integrity. The probabilistic architecture of LLMs can produce confident but inaccurate outputs, including fabricated references and misleading claims - commonly described as "hallucinations." Such limitations underscore the necessity of verification, transparency in AI-assisted writing, and explicit disclosure policies within research institutions (Bender et al., 2021). Ethical analyses further emphasise that AI systems must adhere to principles of accountability, transparency, fairness, and non-maleficence, particularly when used in high-stakes scholarly contexts (Floridi et al., 2018). These principles are directly relevant to authorship clarity, prevention of plagiarism, bias mitigation in generated content, and protection of sensitive research data.

Moreover, the integration of LLMs into research ecosystems intersects with broader issues of data governance and digital scholarship. As LLM-assisted analytics increasingly inform research evaluation, funding proposals, and institutional decision-making, concerns emerge regarding data privacy, algorithmic bias, and responsible data stewardship. Critical scholarship on digital governance in education warns that AI-driven infrastructures may inadvertently reinforce inequities unless guided by transparent regulatory frameworks and participatory oversight (Williamson & Eynon, 2020). Consequently, the responsible incorporation of LLMs into research and scholarly activity requires a balanced framework that integrates technological innovation with ethical safeguards, institutional governance, and advanced AI literacy. When strategically managed, LLMs can serve as transformative tools for knowledge production while preserving the integrity, credibility, and trustworthiness of academic scholarship.

Figure 5. Framework for AI-supported research workflows, ethics, and data governance

The three interrelated domains (Figure 5) illustrated - research workflow enhancements, research integrity and ethics, and data governance and analytics - reflect a comprehensive transformation of contemporary scholarly practice in the era of artificial intelligence (AI). Research workflow enhancements encompass literature synthesis, drafting and editing, grant-writing support, and data interpretation. AI-powered tools can accelerate systematic literature reviews through semantic search and automated clustering, improve linguistic clarity in manuscript preparation, and assist in structuring competitive funding proposals. Empirical studies indicate that generative AI can enhance productivity and reduce cognitive load in academic writing when used as a decision-support system rather than a replacement for scholarly judgement (Dwivedi et al., 2023; Kasneci et al., 2023). Furthermore, AI-supported data interpretation, including pattern recognition and predictive modelling, strengthens analytical rigour, particularly in large and heterogeneous datasets.

However, these efficiencies must be balanced with robust research integrity and ethical safeguards. Clear authorship attribution, transparency regarding AI assistance, and mitigation of algorithmic hallucinations are essential to maintain academic credibility. Concerns regarding fabricated citations and inaccurate outputs highlight the necessity of human verification and methodological accountability

(Bender et al., 2021). In parallel, data privacy and bias mitigation require systematic governance mechanisms, especially where sensitive educational or research data are processed. Bias embedded in training data may reproduce structural inequalities unless proactively audited and corrected (Floridi et al., 2018).

The third domain, data governance and analytics, extends these principles into institutional practice. Learning analytics and student success signals can provide early identification of academic risk, enabling timely intervention and personalised support. Nevertheless, responsible data use demands compliance with privacy regulations, proportional data collection, and transparent analytical frameworks (Williamson & Eynon, 2020). Effective governance integrates technical controls, ethical oversight, and institutional policy alignment to ensure that analytics serve pedagogical improvement rather than surveillance. Collectively, these domains demonstrate that AI integration in research and higher education must be guided by a balanced framework that combines productivity gains with ethical responsibility, methodological transparency, and accountable data stewardship.

SERVICE, ADMINISTRATION, AND STUDENT SUPPORT

Within higher education, the integration of LLMs into service, administration, and student support functions signals a structural evolution in institutional management and learner engagement. LLM-powered conversational agents and decision-support systems are increasingly deployed for automated academic advising, enrolment guidance, financial aid clarification, multilingual communication, and 24/7 virtual helpdesk services. Such systems enhance scalability and responsiveness, particularly in large or resource-constrained institutions. Empirical and policy-oriented analyses suggest that generative AI can improve organisational efficiency and service delivery when embedded within structured oversight and quality assurance mechanisms (Dwivedi et al., 2023). Broader examinations of ChatGPT and similar systems in educational contexts further indicate their potential to streamline administrative communication and personalise student-facing support.

Nevertheless, the adoption of LLMs in administrative and student support domains raises critical concerns regarding transparency, bias, reliability, and data protection. The probabilistic architecture of LLMs may generate inaccurate or misleading outputs, requiring robust human-in-the-loop supervision and validation processes (Bender et al., 2021). Ethical governance frameworks emphasise accountability, fairness, explicability, and respect for human autonomy - principles that must underpin AI-enabled student services (Floridi et al., 2018). Furthermore, institutional reliance on AI-mediated decision systems intersects with regulatory obligations concerning personal data protection and algorithmic transparency. Research on trustworthy

AI governance highlights the importance of risk assessment, documentation, and continuous monitoring to mitigate unintended discriminatory effects.

From a data governance and analytics perspective, LLM-supported student services often operate in conjunction with learning analytics and predictive modelling systems designed to identify student success signals and at-risk profiles. While such analytics can facilitate early intervention and targeted support, they also introduce concerns related to surveillance, consent, and proportionality in data use. Critical scholarship on digital education governance warns that data-intensive infrastructures may reshape institutional power relations unless grounded in participatory oversight and transparent policy frameworks (Williamson & Eynon, 2020). Complementary research on AI in higher education governance stresses that institutional readiness, digital literacy among staff, and clear accountability structures are essential for responsible implementation (Zawacki-Richter et al., 2019).

Collectively, these perspectives demonstrate that while LLMs offer transformative potential to enhance service quality, administrative agility, and inclusive student support, their sustainable adoption depends on rigorous ethical safeguards, transparent governance mechanisms, and continuous institutional evaluation.

Figure 6. Governance and infrastructure framework for responsible AI integration in higher education

The image presents (Figure 6), a structured framework outlining the foundational components required for the responsible integration of LLMs and AI systems within higher education institutions. It is organised into three interconnected domains: Administrative Automation, Policy, Governance, and Accountability, and Infrastructure and Accessibility. The first section highlights operational efficiency through AI-enabled automation in admissions, scheduling, routine inquiries, and knowledge management systems. The second section emphasises governance mechanisms, including AI usage policies, attribution norms for AI-assisted work, and transparency requirements to ensure accountability and ethical compliance. The third section focuses on the technical and organisational infrastructure necessary to sustain AI adoption, including robust data pipelines, interoperability standards, and scalable, accessible service design.

Overall, the visual functions as a strategic blueprint, illustrating that effective AI implementation requires coordinated alignment between operational innovation, governance oversight, and resilient infrastructure to ensure transparency, accountability, and long-term institutional sustainability.

EQUITY, INCLUSION, AND GLOBAL CONTEXT

The integration of LLMs into higher education must be examined through the lens of equity, inclusion, and global context, as these systems both expand access to knowledge and risk reinforcing structural inequalities. On one hand, LLMs offer multilingual support, real-time translation, adaptive feedback, and assistive communication tools that can benefit students from diverse linguistic, cultural, and socio-economic backgrounds. In global higher education systems, such capabilities may reduce barriers to academic participation and enhance inclusive learning environments. Research on AI in education indicates that intelligent systems can personalise support and widen access when designed with pedagogical and cultural sensitivity (Zawacki-Richter et al., 2019). Similarly, analyses of generative AI in educational contexts highlight its potential to democratise information access while simultaneously requiring careful contextual adaptation.

However, LLMs are trained on large-scale datasets that often reflect dominant linguistic, cultural, and geopolitical perspectives, raising concerns about representational bias and epistemic inequality. Foundational critiques of large language models argue that embedded biases in training corpora can reproduce stereotypes, marginalise underrepresented communities, and privilege Global North knowledge systems (Bender et al., 2021). Broader examinations of algorithmic bias demonstrate how automated systems may amplify social inequities if fairness auditing and bias mitigation strategies are not systematically implemented (Mehrabi et al., 2021). From a global governance perspective, the ethical deployment of AI requires adherence to principles of justice, inclusivity, and human rights, particularly in cross-border educational ecosystems (Floridi et al., 2018).

In addition, the digital divide remains a critical determinant of equitable AI adoption. Unequal access to computational infrastructure, high-speed internet, and

AI literacy training may widen disparities between institutions in high-resource and low-resource contexts. Global analyses of AI governance emphasise that inclusive policy frameworks and capacity-building initiatives are necessary to prevent technological colonialism and ensure that AI systems serve diverse educational communities (Jobin et al., 2019). Within higher education, equity-oriented implementation therefore requires participatory design, culturally responsive datasets, multilingual evaluation benchmarks, and transparent accountability structures.

Collectively, the discussion of LLMs in relation to equity, inclusion, and global context underscores a dual reality: these technologies can enhance accessibility and global knowledge exchange, yet they also carry the risk of entrenching systemic biases. Responsible adoption demands not only technical optimisation but also sustained ethical reflection, inclusive governance, and international collaboration to ensure that AI-powered automation advances social justice rather than reproducing inequality.

Figure 7. Equitable and context-sensitive AI integration framework

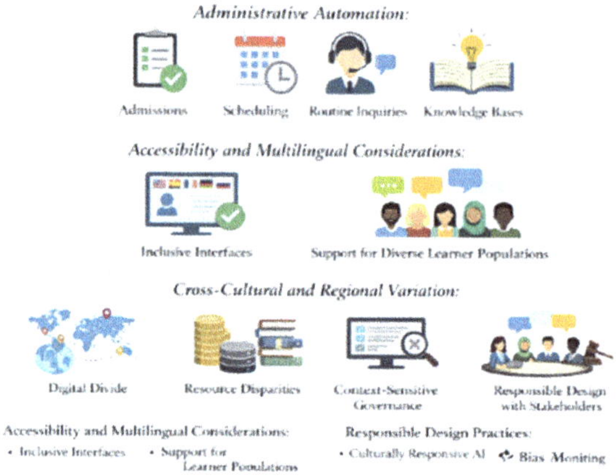

The image presents (Figure 7), a structured framework illustrating how LLMs and AI systems can be integrated into higher education while prioritising equity, accessibility, and contextual governance. It is organised into three interconnected dimensions: Administrative Automation, Accessibility and Multilingual Considerations, and Cross-Cultural and Regional Variation.

The first section highlights how AI can streamline institutional functions such as admissions, scheduling, routine inquiries, and knowledge management to improve operational efficiency. The second section emphasises inclusive design principles, including multilingual support and interfaces that accommodate diverse learner populations. The third section addresses global and regional disparities, drawing attention to the digital divide, resource inequalities, context-sensitive governance, and stakeholder-informed responsible design practices.

Overall, the visual serves as a strategic and ethical guidance model, demonstrating that AI-enabled automation in higher education must extend beyond efficiency gains to include inclusive access, cultural responsiveness, participatory governance, and equitable technological deployment across diverse institutional and regional contexts.

ETHICAL, LEGAL, AND SOCIAL IMPLICATIONS

Ethical, legal, and social implications (ELSI) of LLMs in higher education arise from their growing role in knowledge production, assessment support, administrative decision-making, and student-facing services. Ethically, LLMs can improve access through scalable tutoring and multilingual support, yet they also introduce risks of *epistemic harm* when outputs appear authoritative but contain inaccuracies or fabricated claims ("hallucinations"), requiring robust human oversight and verification practices to protect academic standards (Bender et al., 2021; Kasneci et al., 2023). Socially, LLMs can reproduce and amplify existing inequities because training data often reflect historical and institutional biases; fairness auditing and bias mitigation are therefore essential to prevent disproportionate harms to underrepresented student groups and marginalised knowledge traditions (Mehrabi et al., 2021; Williamson & Eynon, 2020). Legally and institutionally, LLM adoption raises questions about data protection (e.g., handling sensitive student data), consent, and governance accountability, particularly where LLMs integrate with learning analytics and student success monitoring; ethical dilemmas intensify when analytics infrastructures increase surveillance capacity without clear proportionality, transparency, and participatory oversight. ELSI also includes intellectual property and authorship norms: as AI-assisted drafting becomes routine, institutions must clarify attribution and disclosure expectations to preserve scholarly integrity and trust (Dwivedi et al., 2023). At a governance level, widely cited principles for "trustworthy" AI - such as accountability, transparency, fairness, and human oversight - offer a structured basis for policy design, but implementation requires context-sensitive standards and continuous review because global AI governance approaches remain heterogeneous (Floridi et al., 2018; Jobin et al., 2019). Consequently, responsible LLM integration in higher education depends on aligning technical deployment with ELSI safeguards, including documented use policies, privacy-by-design controls, bias monitoring, and evidence-based evaluation of impacts on learning, equity, and institutional legitimacy (Zawacki-Richter et al., 2019).

Figure 8. Safeguarding academic integrity and responsible AI governance in higher education

The image presents an integrated (Figure 8) governance and responsibility framework for the adoption of LLMs in higher education. It organises critical safeguards into three interrelated domains: Academic Integrity and Authenticity; Privacy, Security, and Governance; and Information and Digital Literacy.

The first domain emphasises mechanisms that preserve authenticity in AI-enabled environments, including detectability tools, policy alignment, and process-focused assessment models that prioritise learning development over product-based evaluation. The second domain highlights institutional responsibilities in protecting data, ensuring model privacy, and implementing structured risk management to address bias, misuse, and security vulnerabilities. The third domain underscores the importance of fostering critical AI literacy and responsible information evaluation, equipping students and educators to engage with AI systems thoughtfully, ethically, and analytically.

Overall, the visual functions as a strategic safeguard model, demonstrating that sustainable LLM integration depends not only on technological capability but on institutional accountability, ethical governance, and the cultivation of informed and responsible AI users across academic communities.

QUALITY, EVALUATION, AND EVIDENCE

The integration of LLMs into higher education necessitates rigorous attention to quality, evaluation, and evidence to ensure that technological innovation aligns with academic standards and measurable learning outcomes. As generative AI systems increasingly support teaching, research, and administrative processes, institutions must adopt systematic evaluation frameworks that assess accuracy, reliability, pedagogical effectiveness, and impact on scholarly performance. Empirical studies examining generative AI in educational contexts highlight both performance gains and variability in output quality, underscoring the importance of benchmarking, validation protocols, and human oversight (Kasneci et al., 2023). Broader analyses of AI integration in education similarly emphasise the need for evidence-based implementation rather than speculative adoption (Zawacki-Richter et al., 2019).

From a technical perspective, evaluation of LLMs involves assessing robustness, generalisability, transparency, and alignment with intended tasks. Foundational work on large language models demonstrates that scale improves performance but does not eliminate risks related to bias, misinformation, or contextual misunderstanding. Complementary critiques argue that stochastic text generation systems can produce plausible yet inaccurate content, thereby challenging traditional notions of validity and evidentiary reliability in academic environments (Bender et al., 2021). Concerns highlight the necessity of multi-layered evaluation strategies that combine quantitative performance metrics with qualitative expert review.

Quality assurance in higher education also demands alignment with ethical and governance standards. Frameworks for trustworthy AI stress the importance of accountability, explicability, technical robustness, and continuous monitoring in high-stakes contexts (Floridi et al., 2018). In parallel, global surveys of AI governance reveal substantial variation in regulatory approaches, reinforcing the need for institutional policies that integrate ethical review, data protection safeguards, and transparent reporting mechanisms (Jobin et al., 2019). Within educational systems, evaluation must therefore extend beyond algorithmic accuracy to include impact assessments on academic integrity, student equity, and institutional trust.

Collectively, discussions of quality, evaluation, and evidence in relation to LLMs underscore that responsible adoption requires structured validation frameworks, empirical performance studies, and ongoing institutional review. When embedded within comprehensive quality assurance mechanisms, LLMs can contribute to enhanced efficiency and innovation; however, without systematic evaluation and evidentiary scrutiny, their deployment risks undermining academic credibility and educational standards.

Figure 9. Evaluation, evidence, and risk governance framework for LLMs

The image presents a structured framework (Figure 9) designed to guide the responsible evaluation and continuous improvement of LLMs in higher education. It integrates three core dimensions: Evaluation Frameworks, Case Studies and Empirical Evidence, and Risk Assessment and Mitigation. The first dimension focuses on performance measurement, including how to assess learning impact, research productivity, and service efficiency to ensure that AI adoption aligns with institutional objectives and educational outcomes. The second dimension highlights the importance of empirical validation through illustrative case studies across disciplines and modalities, reinforcing evidence-based implementation rather than speculative deployment. The third dimension addresses risk governance by identifying potential challenges such as bias, hallucinations, and over-reliance, alongside structured mitigation strategies to safeguard academic integrity and institutional credibility. Overall, the visual functions as a quality assurance model, demonstrating that sustainable LLM integration requires systematic evaluation, empirical grounding, and proactive risk management to balance innovation with accountability in higher education ecosystems.

IMPLEMENTATION STRATEGY AND CHANGE MANAGEMENT

The implementation of LLMs in higher education requires a structured strategy and comprehensive change management approach to ensure alignment with institutional missions, academic values, and governance standards. Beyond technical deployment, successful integration depends on organisational readiness, leadership commitment, stakeholder engagement, and capacity-building initiatives. Research on digital transformation in higher education emphasises that technological innovation must be accompanied by cultural adaptation, professional development, and policy reform to achieve sustainable impact (Zawacki-Richter et al., 2019). In the context of generative AI, institutions must define clear objectives - whether enhancing research productivity, improving student services, or augmenting teaching practices - while establishing measurable performance indicators and risk assessment mechanisms (Dwivedi et al., 2023). Change management frameworks provide a critical lens for understanding AI adoption dynamics. Organisational transformation literature underscores that resistance to innovation often emerges from uncertainty, skill gaps, and perceived threats to professional identity (Vial, 2019). Within academic environments, concerns regarding academic integrity, workload redistribution, and authorship transparency must be addressed through participatory governance and transparent communication. Empirical analyses of emerging technologies in education indicate that professional learning communities and AI literacy programmes significantly enhance institutional preparedness and reduce adoption barriers (Kasneci et al., 2023). Consequently, implementation strategies should integrate continuous training, pilot testing phases, and feedback loops that enable iterative refinement.

Equally important is the establishment of governance structures that ensure responsible AI deployment. Frameworks for trustworthy AI highlight the necessity of accountability, human oversight, technical robustness, and compliance with data protection standards (Floridi et al., 2018). Global analyses of AI policy further demonstrate that institutional alignment with regulatory principles strengthens stakeholder trust and mitigates reputational risks (Jobin et al., 2019). In higher education, this translates into clear disclosure guidelines for AI-assisted work, ethical review processes, procurement standards, and impact assessment protocols.

Collectively, an effective implementation strategy for LLMs must balance innovation with institutional resilience. Strategic planning, inclusive leadership, structured change management, and ethical governance mechanisms are mutually reinforcing components of sustainable AI integration. When institutions adopt a phased, evidence-informed, and participatory approach, LLM deployment can enhance organisational agility and academic excellence while safeguarding integrity, equity, and long-term institutional trust.

Figure 10. Strategic implementation and governance framework for LLMs

The image presents (Figure 10) a comprehensive implementation framework for integrating LLMs into higher education institutions. It is structured around three interconnected pillars: Strategic Planning, Stakeholder Engagement, and Infrastructure Needs.

The first pillar emphasises alignment with institutional goals and the development of a phased adoption roadmap to ensure that AI integration supports long-term academic and organisational objectives. The second pillar highlights the importance of inclusive stakeholder engagement, involving faculty, students, administrators, policymakers, and governance structures to foster transparency, shared responsibility, and institutional trust. The third pillar focuses on infrastructure readiness, including platform integration, data governance mechanisms, cybersecurity protections, and adaptive model governance as AI systems evolve.

Overall, the visual functions as a strategic implementation blueprint, illustrating that successful and sustainable LLM adoption requires coordinated planning, participatory governance, and resilient technological infrastructure rather than isolated technological deployment.

POLICY AND GOVERNANCE LANDSCAPE

The policy and governance landscape surrounding LLMs in higher education is rapidly evolving, reflecting broader global debates on artificial intelligence regulation, accountability, and ethical oversight. As LLMs become embedded in teaching, research, administration, and student services, institutions must navigate complex regulatory environments that address transparency, data protection, intellectual property, and algorithmic fairness. Foundational analyses of AI governance emphasise that trustworthy AI systems require principled frameworks grounded in accountability, explicability, justice, and human oversight (Floridi et al., 2018). These normative principles provide a basis for institutional policy design, particularly in contexts where automated systems influence academic assessment, research outputs, or student decision-making processes.

Globally, comparative policy studies reveal substantial variation in national AI governance approaches, ranging from innovation-driven strategies to rights-based regulatory frameworks (Jobin et al., 2019). In higher education, this diversity translates into differing institutional responses to generative AI, including disclosure mandates, AI usage guidelines, academic integrity revisions, and procurement standards. Research examining the integration of AI in educational settings underscores the importance of aligning institutional policies with broader digital governance frameworks to ensure coherence and legal compliance (Zawacki-Richter et al., 2019). Without clear governance structures, the deployment of LLMs risks generating inconsistencies in authorship attribution, data handling, and evaluation practices.

Moreover, the probabilistic architecture and scale of LLMs introduce governance challenges related to misinformation, bias amplification, and opacity. Critical scholarship on large language models highlights structural risks, including the generation of plausible yet inaccurate content and the embedding of historical biases within training datasets (Bender et al., 2021). Complementary research on algorithmic fairness and bias mitigation stresses the need for systematic auditing, documentation, and impact assessments in AI-enabled systems (Mehrabi et al., 2021). These concerns reinforce the necessity for higher education institutions to adopt governance instruments such as AI ethics committees, model evaluation protocols, transparency reporting requirements, and continuous risk monitoring mechanisms.

In addition, the increasing use of LLMs intersects with data governance obligations concerning privacy, consent, and cross-border data flows. Educational institutions operating in global contexts must reconcile local regulatory requirements with international standards for digital rights and responsible innovation. Digital governance research in education warns that AI-driven infrastructures may reshape institutional authority and knowledge production processes unless guided by participatory oversight and inclusive policymaking (Williamson & Eynon, 2020).

Collectively, the policy and governance landscape for LLMs in higher education demands a multi-layered approach that integrates ethical principles, regulatory compliance, institutional accountability, and stakeholder engagement. Effective governance does not merely constrain technological adoption; rather, it enables sustainable innovation by fostering trust, protecting academic integrity, and ensuring that AI-powered automation advances educational values within an increasingly complex global ecosystem.

Figure 11. AI policy, intellectual property, and compliance framework in higher education

The image presents (Figure 11) a structured governance model outlining the key policy and regulatory components required for the responsible use of LLMs in higher education. It is organised into three principal domains: AI Usage Policies, Intellectual Property and Authorship Norms, and Compliance and Standards. The first domain emphasises foundational governance elements, including transparency in AI deployment, informed consent mechanisms, and responsible data handling practices to ensure ethical and lawful use. The second domain addresses intellectual property and academic authorship norms, highlighting the importance of clear attribution in AI-assisted work to preserve scholarly integrity and accountability. The third domain focuses on compliance and standards, including interoperability requirements, accessibility standards, and regulatory alignment to ensure that AI systems operate within established legal and institutional frameworks. Overall, the visual functions as a policy-oriented blueprint, demonstrating that sustainable LLM integration depends not only on technological advancement but also on structured governance, ethical attribution practices, and adherence to institutional, national, and international standards.

ROADMAP AND PRACTICAL GUIDANCE

A practical roadmap for implementing LLMs in higher education should progress from institutional purpose to controlled deployment and continuous evidence-based improvement, ensuring that innovation remains aligned with academic values and regulatory obligations. The first phase is strategic scoping, where institutions prioritise high-impact use cases (e.g., student support, academic writing assistance, staff knowledge services) and define success criteria such as service responsiveness, learning support quality, and integrity risk thresholds; this framing helps avoid "tool-first" adoption and anchors LLM use in measurable organisational outcomes (Dwivedi et al., 2023; Vial, 2019). The second phase is governance-by-design, establishing policies for acceptable use, disclosure, authorship attribution, and auditability, supported by a cross-functional committee spanning academic leadership, IT, legal, and quality assurance; this phase should explicitly address known LLM risks - plausible but incorrect outputs, embedded bias, and opacity - through review workflows, documentation standards, and human oversight (Bender et al., 2021; Floridi et al., 2018). Third phase is data and risk readiness, including privacy and security controls, role-based access, retention limits, and bias/fairness assessment plans, recognising that algorithmic bias can be amplified at scale if not systematically evaluated and mitigated (Mehrabi et al., 2021; Williamson & Eynon, 2020). The fourth phase is piloting and evaluation, using limited-scope deployments with representative user groups and rigorous quality metrics - accuracy, harmful error rates, equity impacts, and user experience - combined with disciplinary expert review; evidence from education-focused analyses of generative AI supports the need for structured evaluation and AI literacy development to ensure that benefits are realised without weakening standards (Kasneci et al., 2023; Zawacki-Richter et al., 2019). The final phase is scaling with continuous monitoring, where institutions operationalise feedback loops, incident reporting, model and prompt governance, and periodic policy updates to respond to evolving risks, regulatory interpretations, and user practices - treating LLM integration as an ongoing socio-technical transformation rather than a one-time system rollout (Dwivedi et al., 2023; Vial, 2019).

Figure 12. Phased roadmap for sustainable Large Language Model (LLM)

The image presents (Figure 12) a structured, time-based implementation roadmap for integrating LLMs into higher education institutions. It organises institutional actions into three progressive phases: short-term, mid-term, and long-term strategies. The short-term phase focuses on initiating pilot programs, investing in faculty development, and establishing governance pilots to test feasibility and build institutional readiness. The mid-term phase emphasises scaling successful initiatives, developing reusable templates and operational frameworks, and forming communities of practice to support shared learning and cross-departmental collaboration. The long-term phase highlights the establishment of sustainable AI ecosystems supported by continuous evaluation, systematic monitoring, and ongoing research to ensure adaptive governance and long-term institutional resilience. Overall, the visual functions as a strategic transformation guide, illustrating that responsible LLM adoption requires phased planning, capacity building, governance alignment, and continuous institutional learning rather than isolated or short-term technological implementation.

FUTURE DIRECTIONS, GAPS, AND RESEARCH AGENDA

Future directions for LLMs in higher education (Fig. 14) point toward a research agenda that is simultaneously technically rigorous, pedagogically grounded, and governance-aware. A primary gap concerns quality and evidence: much current adoption is opportunistic, while robust studies linking LLM use to learning outcomes, research productivity, and service quality remain uneven across disciplines and institutional types (Kasneci et al., 2023; Zawacki-Richter et al., 2019). This implies a need for validated evaluation protocols that go beyond accuracy to include epistemic reliability, harmful error rates, calibration, and equity impacts, especially given persistent risks of plausible-but-incorrect generation and the broader concerns about scaling language models without sufficient accountability (Bender et al., 2021). A second gap is academic integrity and attribution in LLM-assisted scholarship: future work should develop auditable disclosure norms, contribution taxonomies, and reproducibility practices suitable for AI-assisted drafting and analysis, coupled with institutional policy alignment and field-specific standards (Dwivedi et al., 2023; Floridi et al., 2018). A third priority is equity and inclusion at scale, where research must address multilingual performance gaps, cultural representational bias, and differential access (infrastructure, bandwidth, and AI literacy), so that LLM-enabled support does not intensify global and local disparities (Jobin et al., 2019; Mehrabi et al., 2021). A fourth agenda area concerns data governance and learning analytics integration: as LLMs increasingly mediate student support and institutional decision-making, research should test governance designs that protect privacy, minimise surveillance, and ensure proportional, consent-aware data use

- building on established ethical debates in learning analytics (Heemskerk et al., 2014; Williamson & Eynon, 2020). Finally, practical research should focus on implementation science for LLMs - comparative studies of change management, capability-building, and policy effectiveness across different national and regulatory contexts - so institutions can move from fragmented experimentation to sustainable, accountable deployment (Dwivedi et al., 2023; Vial, 2019).

Figure 13. Future trajectories and research agenda for LLMs

The image presents (Figure 13 and Table 1) a forward-looking framework that outlines the evolving landscape of LLMs in higher education. It is organised into three interconnected dimensions: Emerging Capabilities and Evolving Risks, Open Questions, and Suggested Research Directions and Collaboration Opportunities. The first dimension highlights the dynamic balance between expanding technical capabilities and associated risks, emphasising the need for adaptive governance as AI systems mature. The second dimension identifies critical open questions, including pedagogy optimisation, the development of reusable implementation frameworks, and cross-institutional collaboration to ensure scalable and context-sensitive adoption. The third dimension proposes structured research directions and partnership opportunities to foster interdisciplinary inquiry, shared standards, and collective learning. Overall, the visual functions as a strategic foresight model, demonstrating that the sustainable integration of LLMs depends on continuous research, collaborative governance, and proactive engagement with both technological advancements and emerging institutional challenges.

Figure 14. LLMs impact in higher education matrix

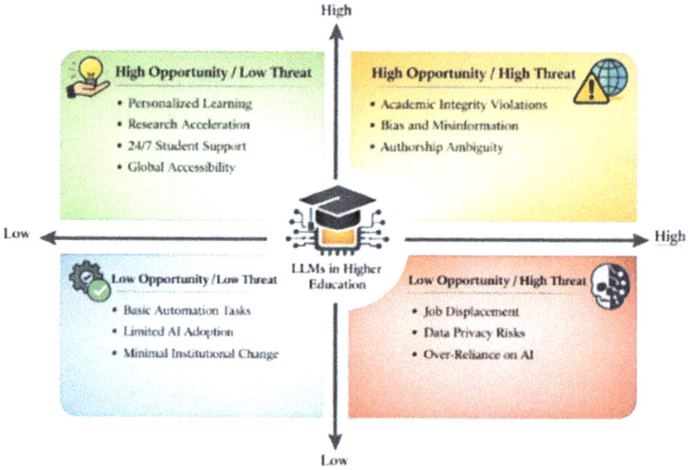

Table 1. Qualitative comparison of opportunities and threats of LLMs in higher education

Domain	Functional Role of LLMs	Opportunities (Value Creation)	Threats (Risks & Limitations)	Governance & Mitigation Strategies	References
Teaching & Learning	Adaptive tutoring, content generation, feedback automation	Personalised learning, scalable support, multilingual access	Academic integrity violations, over-reliance, hallucinations	AI literacy, assessment redesign, disclosure policies	(Kasneci et al., 2023; Zawacki-Richter et al., 2019).
Assessment & Evaluation	Automated grading, adaptive testing	Fast feedback, workload reduction, analytics insights	Bias in grading, lack of transparency	Human-in-the-loop, explainable AI	(Holmes et al., 2022).
Research & Innovation	Literature synthesis, coding, hypothesis generation	Accelerated research, interdisciplinary discovery	Hallucinated citations, epistemic bias	Verification protocols, AI disclosure	(Dwivedi et al., 2023; van Dis et al., 2023).
Academic Writing & Publication	Drafting, editing, summarisation	Writing support, productivity, accessibility	Authorship ambiguity, fabricated content	Journal AI policies, plagiarism detection	(Editorial, 2023).

continued on following page

Table 1. Continued

Domain	Functional Role of LLMs	Opportunities (Value Creation)	Threats (Risks & Limitations)	Governance & Mitigation Strategies	References
Administration & Services	Chatbots, automation, decision support	Efficiency, 24/7 services, cost reduction	Job displacement, data privacy risks	Data governance, human oversight	(Dwivedi et al., 2023).
Institutional Governance	Policy analytics, institutional intelligence	Evidence-based decisions, strategic planning	Algorithmic bias, opacity	Ethical AI frameworks, audits	(Floridi et al., 2018).
Student Experience	AI advising, learning assistants	Personalised guidance, retention support	Misguidance, reduced human interaction	Hybrid human–AI systems	(Holmes et al., 2022; Kasneci et al., 2023).
Systemic Impact	Global access, knowledge dissemination	Democratisation of education, inclusion	Digital divide, environmental cost	Sustainable AI, equity policies	(Crawford, 2021; Dwivedi et al., 2023).

CONCLUSION

The integration of LLMs into higher education represents not merely a technological shift but a systemic transformation across teaching, research, and service. As discussed throughout this chapter, LLMs operate within a layered socio-technical ecosystem that connects core transformer-based architectures with pedagogical applications, research augmentation, administrative automation, and governance frameworks. In teaching and learning, LLMs enable adaptive scaffolding, real-time formative feedback, and multilingual accessibility, supporting more inclusive and scalable instructional models. In research, they accelerate literature synthesis, drafting, and analytical workflows while necessitating rigorous validation, authorship clarity, and methodological accountability. In service and administration, AI-powered automation enhances operational efficiency and student support, yet requires structured oversight to ensure transparency, privacy, and fairness. Across these domains, the evidence consistently indicates that LLMs function most effectively as augmentation tools embedded within human-centred design principles rather than as autonomous replacements for academic expertise.

At the same time, the chapter underscores that technological capability alone does not guarantee institutional benefit. ELSI - including academic integrity risks, bias amplification, data privacy vulnerabilities, and equity disparities - demand robust governance, policy alignment, and continuous evaluation. Responsible AI integration therefore depends on coordinated implementation strategies, participatory change management, infrastructure readiness, and sustained professional development to cultivate AI literacy among faculty and students. The roadmap articulated herein highlights phased adoption, governance-by-design, rigorous evaluation frameworks, and long-term monitoring as essential mechanisms for balancing innovation with institutional resilience.

Looking forward, the future of LLMs in higher education will be shaped by the quality of evidence, inclusivity of design, and maturity of governance ecosystems. Research gaps remain in measuring learning impact, developing reproducible attribution standards, mitigating multilingual and cultural bias, and aligning cross-institutional regulatory approaches. The transformative potential of LLMs lies not in automation alone but in their capacity to enhance human creativity, critical inquiry, and collaborative knowledge production when embedded within ethically grounded, transparent, and context-sensitive institutional frameworks. Ultimately, sustainable AI-powered automation in higher education will depend on aligning technological advancement with academic integrity, social responsibility, and the enduring mission of universities to advance equitable and trustworthy knowledge.

REFERENCES

Ahme, Z., Shanto, S. S., & Jony, A. I. (2024). Potentiality of generative AI tools in higher education: Evaluating ChatGPT's viability as a teaching assistant for introductory programming courses. *STEM Education*, *4*(3), 165–182. DOI: 10.3934/steme.2024011

Bender, E. M., Gebru, T., McMillan-Major, A., & Shmitchell, S. (2021). On the Dangers of Stochastic Parrots: Can Language Models Be Too Big?? *Proceedings of the 2021 ACM Conference on Fairness, Accountability, and Transparency*, 610–623. DOI: 10.1145/3442188.3445922

Bobula, M. (2024). Generative artificial intelligence (AI) in higher education: A comprehensive review of challenges, opportunities, and implications. *Journal of Learning Development in Higher Education*, *30*(30). Advance online publication. DOI: 10.47408/jldhe.vi30.1137

Crawford, K. (2021). Atlas of AI. In *Yale University Press*. Yale University Press., DOI: 10.2307/j.ctv1ghv45t

Denny, P., Prather, J., Becker, B. A., Finnie-Ansley, J., Hellas, A., Leinonen, J., Luxton-Reilly, A., Reeves, B. N., Santos, E. A., & Sarsa, S. (2024). Computing Education in the Era of Generative AI. *Communications of the ACM*, *67*(2), 56–67. DOI: 10.1145/3624720

Development, O. for E. C. and. (2016). Innovating Education and Educating for Innovation: The Power of Digital Technologies and Skills. In *Educational Research and Innovation*. OECD Publishing. DOI: 10.1787/9789264265097-en

Devlin, J., Chang, M. W., Lee, K., & Toutanova, K. (2019). BERT: Pre-training of deep bidirectional transformers for language understanding. *NAACL HLT 2019 - 2019 Conference of the North American Chapter of the Association for Computational Linguistics: Human Language Technologies - Proceedings of the Conference, 1*, 4171–4186. https://aclanthology.org/N19-1423/

Dubey, P. K., & Crevar, A. R. (2025). Integrating artificial intelligence in higher education: Enhancing pedagogy, instruction, and administration. *AI Integration Into Andragogical Education*, 181–208. DOI: 10.4018/979-8-3373-0502-8.ch008

Dwivedi, Y. K., Kshetri, N., Hughes, L., Slade, E. L., Jeyaraj, A., Kar, A. K., Baabdullah, A. M., Koohang, A., Raghavan, V., Ahuja, M., Albanna, H., Albashrawi, M. A., Al-Busaidi, A. S., Balakrishnan, J., Barlette, Y., Basu, S., Bose, I., Brooks, L., Buhalis, D., & Wright, R. (2023). "So what if ChatGPT wrote it?" Multidisciplinary perspectives on opportunities, challenges and implications of generative conversational AI for research, practice and policy. *International Journal of Information Management*, *71*, 102642. DOI: 10.1016/j.ijinfomgt.2023.102642

Editorial, N. (2023). Tools such as ChatGPT threaten transparent science. *Nature*, *613*(7945), 612. DOI: 10.1038/d41586-023-00191-1 PMID: 36694020

El Fougour, W., & Erradi, M. (2025). Enhancing Formative Assessment With AI: Supporting Cognitive Development Through Adaptive Feedback. In *Reimagining Curriculum and Assessment in the Age of Generative AI* (pp. 307–332). DOI: 10.4018/979-8-3373-7579-3.ch010

Em, S., Mok, S., Sam, R., Pen, D., & Serey, M. (2025). Implications and Considerations of AI-Generative Tools for Higher Education Practices: Opportunities, Challenges, and Future Directions. *Examining AI Disruption in Educational Settings: Challenges and Opportunities*, 297–332. DOI: 10.4018/979-8-3693-7873-1.ch011

Ferreira-Meyers, K. (2025). Augmented or Automated. *Artificial Intelligence Transforming Higher Education*, *1*, 129–152. DOI: 10.64449/9780906785959-05

Floridi, L., Cowls, J., Beltrametti, M., Chatila, R., Chazerand, P., Dignum, V., Luetge, C., Madelin, R., Pagallo, U., Rossi, F., Schafer, B., Valcke, P., & Vayena, E. (2018). AI4People—An Ethical Framework for a Good AI Society: Opportunities, Risks, Principles, and Recommendations. *Minds and Machines*, *28*(4), 689–707. DOI: 10.1007/s11023-018-9482-5 PMID: 30930541

Hattie, J., & Timperley, H. (2007). The Power of Feedback. *Review of Educational Research*, *77*(1), 81–112. DOI: 10.3102/003465430298487

Heemskerk, I., Kuiper, E., & Meijer, J. (2014). Interactive whiteboard and virtual learning environment combined: Effects on mathematics education. *Journal of Computer Assisted Learning*, *30*(5), 465–478. https://doi.org/https://doi.org/10.1111/jcal.12060. DOI: 10.1111/jcal.12060

Holmes, W., Bialik, M., & Fadel, C. (2022). Artificial intelligence in education: Promise and implications for teaching and learning. *Humanities & Social Sciences Communications*, *9*, 120. DOI: 10.1057/s41599-022-01041-0

Jobin, A., Ienca, M., & Vayena, E. (2019). The global landscape of AI ethics guidelines. *Nature Machine Intelligence*, *1*(9), 389–399. DOI: 10.1038/s42256-019-0088-2

Jordan, M. I., & Mitchell, T. M. (2015). Machine learning: Trends, perspectives, and prospects. *Science, 349*(6245), 255–260. DOI: 10.1126/science.aaa8415 PMID: 26185243

Kasneci, E., Sessler, K., Küchemann, S., Bannert, M., Dementieva, D., Fischer, F., Gasser, U., Groh, G., Günnemann, S., Hüllermeier, E., Krusche, S., Kutyniok, G., Michaeli, T., Nerdel, C., Pfeffer, J., Poquet, O., Sailer, M., Schmidt, A., Seidel, T., & Kasneci, G. (2023). ChatGPT for good? On opportunities and challenges of large language models for education. *Learning and Individual Differences, 103*, 102274. DOI: 10.1016/j.lindif.2023.102274

Kulik, J. A., & Fletcher, J. D. (2016). Effectiveness of Intelligent Tutoring Systems: A Meta-Analytic Review. *Review of Educational Research, 86*(1), 42–78. DOI: 10.3102/0034654315581420

Ladehoff, C., Pfetsch, J., & Ophardt, D. (2023). How university teachers can support the linking of theory and practice in lesson debriefings with student teachers. *International Conference on Higher Education Advances*, 91–98. DOI: 10.4995/HEAd23.2023.16325

Lomachinska, I., Ishchuk, A., Yakovenko, O., Rykhlitska, O., Patlaichuk, O., Pasko, K., Lobanchuk, O., & Lomachinskiy, B. (2026). Opportunities and Challenges of AI Language Models in Higher Education for Sustainable Development. *European Journal of Sustainable Development, 15*(1), 331. Advance online publication. DOI: 10.14207/ejsd.2026.v15n1p331

Lytras, M. D., Serban, A. C., Alkhaldi, A., Aldosemani, T., & Malik, S. (2024). What's Next in Higher Education: The AI Revolution 2030. *Digital Transformation in Higher Education, Part A: Best Practices and Challenges*, 155–172. DOI: 10.1108/978-1-83549-480-620241008

Mehrabi, N., Morstatter, F., Saxena, N., Lerman, K., & Galstyan, A. (2021). A Survey on Bias and Fairness in Machine Learning. *ACM Computing Surveys, 54*(6), 1–35. DOI: 10.1145/3457607

Neubauer, L. C., Merzel, C., Weist, E. M., Corvin, J. A., Forsman, A., Fraser, J., Henderson, H. L., Hinyard, L. J., Opacich, K. J., & Runnerstrom, M. G. (2022). Realizing Promising Educational Practices in Academic Public Health: A Model for the Scholarship of Teaching and Learning. *Frontiers in Public Health, 9*, 750682. Advance online publication. DOI: 10.3389/fpubh.2021.750682 PMID: 35174129

Patro, G. K., Porcaro, L., Mitchell, L., Zhang, Q., Zehlike, M., & Garg, N. (2022). Fair ranking: a critical review, challenges, and future directions. *ACM International Conference Proceeding Series*, 1929–1942. DOI: 10.1145/3531146.3533238

Phillipson, R. (2013). Response to a book review in World Englishes, 30(2), 283–6. *World Englishes*, *32*(3), 453–456. DOI: 10.1111/weng.12047

Popenici, S., Catalano, H., Mestic, G., & Ani-Rus, A. (2023). A Systematic Review of the Artificial Intelligence Implications in Shaping the Future of Higher Education. *Educatia, 21*(26), 92–107. DOI: 10.24193/ed21.2023.26.11

Rao, M. N., & Al-Obaidi, J. A. (2024). Embracing how AI responsibly empowers students and faculty in higher education: Theoretical perspectives. *Emerging Technologies Transforming Higher Education: Instructional Design and Student Success*, 1–32. DOI: 10.4018/979-8-3693-3904-6.ch001

Ravikumar, R. N., Aarthi, S., Sapaeva, B., Jumaniyozov, Y., Manoj Praveen, V., & Siddheswaran, V. (2025). Revolutionizing Education With NLP and ML: Innovations, Challenges, and Future Directions. *Educational Applications of Natural Language Processing, Chatbots, and AI*, 293–324. DOI: 10.4018/979-8-3373-6791-0.ch011

Ruan, B. K., Lo, L., Shuai, H. H., & Cheng, W. H. (2022). Mimicking the Annotation Process for Recognizing the Micro Expressions. *MM 2022 - Proceedings of the 30th ACM International Conference on Multimedia*, 228–236. DOI: 10.1145/3503161.3548185

Sarker, D., Eiaz-Ur-Rahman, A. F. M., Sakib, A. R., Terano, H. J. R., & Rahman, M. M. (2023). ChatGPT's Applications in Higher Education: Unmasking Opportunities and Challenges. *Journal of Education. Management and Development Studies*, *3*(4), 37–47. DOI: 10.52631/jemds.v3i4.250

Uysal, B. Ç. B., & Yüksel, I. (2024). AI-powered lesson planning: Insights from future EFL teachers. *AI in Language Teaching, Learning, and Assessment*, 101–132. DOI: 10.4018/979-8-3693-0872-1.ch006

van Dis, E. A. M., Bollen, J., Zuidema, W., van Rooij, R., & Bockting, C. L. (2023). ChatGPT: Five priorities for research. *Nature*, *614*(7947), 224–226. DOI: 10.1038/d41586-023-00288-7 PMID: 36737653

van Rensburg, Z. J., & van der Westhuizen, S. (2024). Ethical AI Integration in Academia: Developing a Literacy-Driven Framework for LLMs in South African Higher Education. *AI Approaches to Literacy in Higher Education*, 23–48. DOI: 10.4018/979-8-3693-1054-0.ch002

Vetrivel, S. C., Vidhyapriya, P., Gunasekar, T., & Arun, V. P. (2025). Cross-Cultural and Inclusive Strategies for AI in Language Education. In *Human-Centered Approaches to AI-Enhanced English Language Learning and Teaching* (pp. 309–338). DOI: 10.4018/979-8-3373-3561-2.ch011

Vial, G. (2019). Understanding digital transformation: A review and a research agenda. *The Journal of Strategic Information Systems*, *28*(2), 118–144. https://doi.org/https://doi.org/10.1016/j.jsis.2019.01.003. DOI: 10.1016/j.jsis.2019.01.003

Wagner, A. J. (2017). Essential or extravagant: Considering FOIA budgets, costs and fees. *Government Information Quarterly*, *34*(3), 388–395. DOI: 10.1016/j.giq.2017.09.001

Williamson, B., & Eynon, R. (2020). Historical threads, missing links, and future directions in AI in education. *Learning, Media and Technology*, *45*(3), 223–235. DOI: 10.1080/17439884.2020.1798995

Zawacki-Richter, O., Marín, V. I., Bond, M., & Gouverneur, F. (2019). Systematic review of research on artificial intelligence applications in higher education – where are the educators? *International Journal of Educational Technology in Higher Education*, *16*(1), 1–27. DOI: 10.1186/s41239-019-0171-0

Zhai, X., & Krajcik, J. (2024). Uses of artificial intelligence in STEM education. *Uses of Artificial Intelligence in STEM Education*, 1–625. DOI: 10.1093/oso/9780198882077.001.0001

Zuo, S., Liang, Y., Wu, Y., Ge, S., Shi, J., Ma, X., Cai, L., Li, J., Lam, S. S., & Xia, C. (2023). Using environmentally friendly technology for fabricating special plywood with ultra-high strength. *Journal of Cleaner Production*, *396*, 136462. DOI: 10.1016/j.jclepro.2023.136462

Chapter 11
Navigating Artificial Intelligence Policy and Governance Frontiers:
Applying Established Policy Frameworks

Anand R. Navaratna
http://orcid.org/0009-0009-7199-259X
Indian Institute of Technology, Jodhpur, India

Deepak Saxena
http://orcid.org/0000-0002-9331-3799
Indian Institute of Technology, Jodhpur, India

ABSTRACT

Artificial Intelligence has emerged as a lifestyle adaptation technology posing novel challenges to existing legal and ethical frameworks. Such frameworks are required to ensure that AI systems are developed with safety, transparency, and alignment with human values and ethics in mind. The evolving and ever-changing characteristics of AI make it difficult to regulate or govern. This chapter focuses on three broad aspects. Firstly, we try to define characteristics that make AI governance a unique endeavour. Secondly, we examine prevalent frameworks that are adopted worldwide by various organisations/ nations. Thereafter, we concentrate on five policy frameworks that can be used by academics, policymakers, and practitioners to design, govern, and regulate AI in the education field. Finally, we apply one of the frameworks, multiple streams framework to the application of AI in education

DOI: 10.4018/979-8-2600-2811-7.ch011

1. INTRODUCTION

Artificial Intelligence (AI) has emerged as a lifestyle adaptation technology posing novel challenges to existing legal and ethical frameworks. AI governance is a challenging and distinct field, primarily due to its speed, complexity, breadth across disciplines, and data-driven learning capabilities. Most traditional technologies are relatively static and have a clear purpose guided by rules and control. In contrast, AI is dynamic, highly adaptive, and difficult to explain. In this chapter, we first explore five unique characteristics of AI that present significant governance challenges. Subsequently, we investigate five foundational principles of AI policy. Then we get on to the approaches to AI governance in vogue across the globe. In the next section, we get into five major policy design frameworks, namely, the Advocacy Coalition Framework (ACF), Institutional Analysis and Development (IAD), Innovation Diffusion and Adoption (IDD), Punctuated Equilibrium Theory (PET), and Multiple Streams Framework (MSF), through the lens of their relevance to AI. Each of these frameworks is given a brief overview, with identification of major areas of application and their relevance to AI (strengths and limitations). As an application use case, the MSF frameworks are applied in higher education and research. Let us first try to understand the unique characteristics and foundational principles of AI that make its governance challenging.

2. UNIQUE CHARACTERISTICS OF AI

This section discusses five unique characteristics of AI that pose governance and policy-related challenges.

Fluid definition of 'AI': The term AI is broad, encompassing a range of technologies, from simple algorithms to complex machine learning models and large language models. Alan Turing, through his famous Turing Test, proposed that a machine is deemed "intelligent" if a human cannot distinguish its conversation from that of another human (Turing, 1950). Similarly, John McCarthy defined AI as 'the science and engineering of making intelligent machines. Conceptually, expert systems, which were the initial avatar of AI, are systems that can think and act rationally. With the evolution of computer algorithms and computing power, Artificial Narrow Intelligence (ANI) refers to AI systems designed and trained for a specific task, which constitutes the vast majority of AI in use today (Russel & Norvig, 2021). Artificial General Intelligence is a theoretical type of AI that could understand, learn, and apply its intelligence to solve any problem, much like a human being.

Furthermore, the definitions of Machine Learning, Deep Learning, and Transformer models further complicate the definition of AI. As the fundamental field itself is not constant, the governing and regulating mechanisms cannot be universal or one-size-fits-all. For instance, the governance mechanism for self-driving cars will focus on safety-critical trajectories, while chatbot governance centres on content integrity, misinformation, and intellectual property (Taeihang, 2025; Zhou et al., 2024). In addition, applications to specific domains add a layer of complexity.

The speed of development: Traditional policy design mechanisms are struggling to keep pace with the rapid evolution of AI. By the time policymakers acknowledge the need for regulation and design it, the AI technology would have evolved, rendering the regulation obsolete. The time policymakers have lost has led to 'governance lag'.

Data dependency and bias: AI model accuracy depends on the data they are trained on. If the data reflects historical biases or is over- or under-fitting, the knowledge derived from the data will be amplified in AI outcomes (Jones, 2025). It is observed that the biases are perpetuating and even scaling basic human values, such as gender biases, discrimination, racial discrimination, and ethical values (Saxena et al., 2021). An interesting case study, as revealed by Apple co-founder Steve Wozniak, is relevant to quote: his wife was given a credit limit 10 times lower than his on the Apple Card. The resulting investigation found that while the algorithm did not directly use gender, it was likely trained on historical data that reflected and reinforced pre-existing societal biases, leading to discriminatory outcomes (Ukanwa & Rust, 2020).

The Black Box problem and lack of explainability: AI and its algorithms are often referred to as 'black boxes' because they lack explainability. Certain studies have also shown that AI fails to generate the same outcome when the problem is executed repeatedly. The decision-making process is driven by a complex model, which sometimes leaves its developers perplexed. This is a fundamental challenge to accountability. In traditional legal systems, there is a need to prove a causal link between an action and an outcome to assign responsibility. With AI, that link is often obscured. In a well-documented case, the Correctional Offender Management Profiling for Alternative Sanctions (COMPAS) algorithm was used in US courts to predict a defendant's likelihood of reoffending (Dressel & Farid, 2018; Van Woerkom et al., 2024). In 2016, it was observed that black defendants were assigned a much higher risk score than white defendants (Angwin et al., 2016).

Responsibility and accountability: As the fundamental definition of AI says, 'think like humans', legally, who is to be blamed if AI makes a mistake- the developer, the user, or the company or firm that has deployed it? There have been instances in which financial repercussions have resulted from errors in AI chatbots or applications. In 2024, Air Canada's AI chatbot offered bereavement fares at a discount to customers, which contradicted the airline's policy. The customer legally challenged the issue, and the tribunal ruled that 'the holding company is responsible' for the actions of the AI chatbot, which set a precedent (Fung & Lo, 2025; St-Hilaire, 2025).

These instances suggest a need to delve deeper into the 'foundational principles' of AI for its governance.

3. THE FOUNDATIONAL PRINCIPLES OF AI GOVERNANCE

Having explored the core challenges of AI governance, it is pertinent to define its guiding principles before addressing AI policy design frameworks. These principles must form the core of governance, regardless of the approach used to design the policy. Various academic studies and organisational findings have benchmarked certain core principles, which are listed below:

Inclusive growth, sustainable development and well-being: AI must be used as a tool for positive societal impact. It must not spread inequality, biases and misinformation. Further, it must foster growth and development (OECD, 2019).

Human-centred values and fairness: AI and its systems must respect human rights, dignity and democratic values. The algorithms and policies must mitigate biases and discrimination (Floridi et al., 2020).

Transparency and explainability: The level of transparency of AI-based systems and policies must be commensurate with the potential risks of the application (Weller, 2019). The developers must be able to understand and explain the means and logic behind the application's decision process.

Robustness, security and safety: The systems akin to AI must be reliable and secure. As AI-based systems are data-intensive, aspects like privacy, security, and safety become paramount. GDPR across countries and unions place strong emphasis on data in general. As AI-based systems run on the internet, they must also be resilient to misuse, attack and sabotage.

Accountability: The responsibility and accountability must be clearly defined throughout the life cycle of an AI system, from design to development and beyond.

4. AI POLICY PRACTICES APPROACH IN VOGUE

With advances in computing power and the development of complex algorithms and high-performance chipsets, the field of AI and its applications has advanced significantly. To mitigate the challenges of AI and its unique characteristics, various policy approaches are employed. A few popular policy approaches in vogue are discussed in this section.

4.1 Risk-Based Framework

This model is adopted by the European Union AI Act 2024 (EU, 2024). The model categorises AI applications based on their potential to cause harm. The level of regulation and oversight is commensurate with its level of risk. Various levels under the risk-based framework are:

Unacceptable Risk - This category includes AI systems that pose a clear threat to human rights and safety. These include systems that manipulate human behaviour in harmful ways. These kinds of systems are banned in the interest of humanity and the greater good of society.

High Risk – Certain AI models are subject to stringent regulatory requirements before market launch. They include AI used in critical infrastructure, law enforcement and medical devices. Due to its field of application, the policy requires a comprehensive risk assessment, high-quality data, human oversight, and detailed documentation. This will enable transparency and standards.

Limited to minimal to no risk - The vast majority of AI applications fall into this category and are subject to voluntary codes of conduct and self-regulation. Certain voluntary declarations and compliance standards are set for developers. Users can review the declaration and decide on the risk involved, as well as whether to proceed with wilful onboarding.

Although this framework is effective and avoids a one-size-fits-all approach, critics argue that classifying risk can be complex and that the rapid pace of AI development may render these classifications obsolete (Smuha, 2021). Also, classifying models/ systems under these headings can be subjective.

4.2 Adaptive and Collaborative Governance Approaches

This section discusses various governance approaches suggested by entities worldwide, primarily outside EU.

Regulatory Sandboxes: Regulations are often viewed as tools to stifle innovation. Under the sandbox approach, controlled environments are established where developers can test new AI products under regulatory supervision, enabling regulators to collect data and learn about potential risks without stifling innovation (Lippoldt, 2024).

Multi-stakeholder Engagement: Policymaking involves not just governments but also civil society, academia and the private sector. Multi-stakeholder engagement ensures that a diversity of perspectives is considered from ethical concerns to technical feasibility (Taeihagh, 2025; Navaratna & Saxena, 2025a).

Principles-Based Regulation: Instead of prescriptive rules, this framework often relies on high-level principles that guide the development and use of AI.

Organisations are then deemed responsible for demonstrating how their systems adhere to these principles, such as through internal audits and ethical committees (Accenture, 2024; Navaratna & Saxena, 2025b). This model is particularly well-suited to managing the uncertainty and complexity of AI, enabling a more responsive and nuanced approach (Janssen, 2025). However, it may lack the legal certainty and enforcement power of more traditional regulatory models.

Rights-based Framework: Evolving from UNESCO's recommendation on the Ethics of AI, the rights-based framework centres governance on the protection of fundamental human rights. Aspects like privacy, non-discrimination, freedom of expression and societal good form cornerstones that developers must follow and abide by. This framework emphasises:

Human oversight and determination- AI must never overcome humans in the middle. This policy ensures that human responsibility and accountability are not displaced (UNESCO, 2021).

Fairness and non-discrimination- Policies must actively promote social justice and address biases in AI systems that could lead to discriminatory outcomes (Saxena et al., 2021), and

Privacy and Data protection – The data that underlies AI modelling and machine learning must be protected. The right to privacy and data protection is a fundamental right in many countries. Compromising on these will undermine the rights and ethics of users in general and civilisation at large. However, this raises a complex question about the appropriate level of human intervention in light of the growing prevalence of autonomous systems. This approach is typically referred to as rights-compliant AI (Olariu & Zeleznikow, 2025).

Through the policy in practice, as listed above, the broad classification of approaches to AI Governance and regulation can be grouped into the following categories:

The choice between control by government-instituted regulation or self-regulation by stakeholders (Katzenbach & Ulbricht, 2019; Yeung & Bygrave, 2022; Navaratna & Saxena, 2025b). Due to a lack of a reliable compliance framework, governments are forced to issue soft law, with diverse arguments for the centralisation or decentralisation of AI regulation among public, private, and other institutions (Gutierrez et al., 2021). The interrelation between types of regulatory regimes and responsibility (May, 2007; Djeffala et al., 2022) results in a hybrid model of regulation, with no standardisation across the globe. It is in this context that the next section situates AI policy design with reference to various theoretical frameworks.

5. AI POLICY DESIGN

As stated above, to date, no standard or global framework has been established for the governance and regulation of AI. Policy makers, practitioners, and academics are often forced to choose between government-instituted regulation and self-regulation, as well as between soft law and shared regulatory regimes. Thus, it is both imperative and interesting to explore the relevance and suitability of well-established social science policy design frameworks for AI policy, given its unique characteristics. In the subsequent paragraphs, we explore five well-established frameworks, including the Advocacy Coalition Framework (ACF), Institutional Analysis and Development (IAD), Innovation Diffusion and Adoption (IDD), Punctuated Equilibrium Theory (PET), and Multiple Streams Framework (MSF), through the lens of their relevance to AI. Each framework offers a unique lens, illuminating different aspects of the policymaking process, from the role of beliefs and power to the dynamics of change and the influence of technology adoption. Though these are independent and full-fledged frameworks with strong foundations, we intend to highlight their relevance to AI policy design. However, an effort is made to provide a brief overview of each framework, starting with its history, evolution, key terms, and popular fields of application. We then highlight its relevance to AI policymaking.

5.1 Advocacy Coalition Framework (ACF)

Paul Sabatier and Hank Jenkins-Smith, in the 1980s, developed the **Advocacy Coalition Framework** (ACF) that emerged as a response to the limitations of the traditional "policy cycle" model. The framework views policymaking not as a simple, linear process but as a competition between groups of actors who share a common belief system. The framework coins certain key concepts:

Policy Subsystem: A policy subsystem is a collection of actors involved in a specific policy issue operating within a particular jurisdiction. There can be multiple stakeholders, including government officials, interest groups, researchers, and journalists (Kim & Roh, 2008).

Advocacy Coalition: The set or group of people who share a set of common belief systems and undertake a certain degree of coordinated activity over time to influence policy. The common belief system is the framework's core concept. These coalitions are key players in the policy subsystem.

Belief System: Each actor in the ACF is treated to have behaviour largely motivated by their beliefs. Depending on the degree of belief, the levels are classified as deep core beliefs, policy core beliefs, and secondary beliefs. Deep core beliefs are more fundamental, normative and ontological axioms that are resistant to change. Policy core beliefs, on the other hand, are more specific to a particular policy subsystem but remain remarkably stable (Olsson, 2009). They include an actor's basic causal assumptions and policy positions for achieving their deep core beliefs within that subsystem. Secondary beliefs are the most specific and least resistant to change. They concern the details of policy implementation, such as administrative rules, budget allocations, and programmatic decisions.

Policy-oriented learning: This refers to a change in an individual's or a coalition's beliefs or behavioural intentions resulting from new information or experiences. ACF argues that policy-oriented learning may occur on secondary beliefs but is less likely to change core beliefs.

External System Shocks: These are significant changes outside the policy subsystem that can disrupt the status quo and lead to major policy change. A notable concept in ACF is 'devil shift', which describes the tendency of policy actors to demonise opponents who hold differing goals or beliefs (Gabehart & Weible, 2023).

5.1.1 Popular Fields of Application

ACF that had initial applications predominantly surrounding environmental issues in the USA (Paul Cairney, 2019). Soon, by late 1990, its applications included domains of climate change and public health (Gabehart & Weible, 2023). Due to aspects surrounding the 'belief system' and 'advocacy framework', its applications soon expanded to carnivore management in Sweden, Swiss climate policy, and transportation policy in California, USA (Weible et al., 2011). The policy subsystem approach, which focuses on interactions and motivations among stakeholders, helped Bangladesh develop a 'Detailed Area Plan'. The inherent flexibility of the framework enables its application across various disciplines of the social sciences. Studies have examined ACF alongside other theoretical approaches, making it a robust framework for diverse policy inquiries. Further, John, P. (2003), while deliberating on evolutionary theory to explain policy change, uses ACF to argue that evolutionary theory may usefully uncover the micro-level processes at work, particularly as some of the three frameworks refer to dynamic models and methods. Sabatier, P. A. (1998), suggesting revisions to ACF in the context of its relevance for Europe, summarises some of the more important findings and changes to the ACF since the last major revision in 1993. The article also briefly addresses the ACF's applicability to parliamentary systems, to the countries of Eastern Europe, and to the dynamic politics of the European Union. More recently, Jun Park, H., & Han, J. (2025) analysed the Digital Transformation of Legal Services and the Role of Policy Brokers in Korea, in which the intersection of traditional legal services and technological innovation was examined using the Advocacy Coalition Framework. Also, Ydersbond, I. M. (2025) underscores the importance of theoretical approaches to liberal intergovernmentalism (LI) and the advocacy coalition framework (ACF) and examines their complementary interconnections to achieve several important EU climate and energy targets.

5.1.2 Strengths of the ACF in AI Policy Analysis

Various strengths can enhance the application of the ACF framework in AI analysis and policy design. They can be listed as:

Multi-stakeholder Engagement: Due to the evolving nature and complexity of AI, the domain is largely multi-stakeholder and multi-disciplinary. Government bodies, legal institutions, the technology industry, civil society organisations, academic institutions, think tanks, and international forums, among others. ACF's core strength lies in its ability to recognise and analyse the complex network of diverse coalitions (Gabehart & Weible, 2023). Designing and studying the AI policy process provides an effective conceptual tool.

Belief Systems and Conflict Analysis: AI concepts and policies are deeply rooted in each country's beliefs about societal norms, legal systems, ethical considerations, and inherent risks. Some belief systems are contradictory, in some cases counterproductive, and in others conflicting. Governmental regulation versus self-regulation, AI innovation versus AI safety, and human control versus AI automation or AGI are a few to name (Gabehart & Weible, 2023). ACF's 'shared belief system' is especially relevant in cases of coalition formation and inter-coalition conflict resolution. The polarising views on AI, with its inherent characteristics, make it an ideal fit for ACF's 'devil shift' concept.

Policy Dynamics: As AI evolves, there may be a need to revisit policy status and design repeatedly. The ACF's structure for accommodating internal and external 'shocks' is valuable for understanding the AI policy shift. These shifts can be technical (bias, new algorithms, computing power, new methods, etc.) or policy (governmental policy, regulation, new legislation, or executive order). ACF can effectively analyse disruption to existing policy equilibria and new policy directions/opportunities.

5.1.3 Limitations

Temporal Mismatch: ACF is more suited for a long-term perspective. The application timelines vary from a decade or more to adequately understand policy processes (Gabehart & Weible, 2023). Due to the rapid evolution and revolution surrounding AI, the need for policy change is occurring at an unprecedented pace (Sieweke, 2025). This temporal mismatch may significantly limit the efficacy of ACF in capturing and explaining the need for fast-paced policy adaptation in AI.

Complexity of Belief Systems: AI has features such as 'black boxes' that are opaque and complex. These features are contradictory to the 'belief system', including 'policy core beliefs' and 'secondary beliefs', which form the core foundation of ACF. 'Black Boxes' presents a hurdle in forming a coalition based on shared technical understanding.

Focus on Adversarial Subsystem: ACF's success is attributed to theoretical arguments around policy conflicts with mature, adversarial policy subsystems featuring two or more competing coalitions (Gabehart & Weible, 2023). On the other hand, AI is not limited to adversarial features but also encompasses cross-coalition collaboration and consensus, given its pervasive nature and profound global implications.

Limited Generalizability: ACF's success is attributed to an established and robust policy subsystem. In the case of AI, its emerging, ever-changing nature often results in subsystems that are either nascent or form weak coalitions (Gabehart & Weible, 2023). With evolving actors, relationships, and a lack of a mature policy subsystem, it challenges the strong adversarial model that ACF usually relies on (Gabehart & Weible, 2023).

5.2 The Institutional Analysis and Development (IAD)

IAD was originally conceived in the 1980s by Elinor Ostrom and her colleagues at a workshop in Political Theory and Policy Analysis at Indiana University (Cole, 2017). IAD is a systematic method for policy analysis and design that explains and predicts outcomes by formally exploring and documenting governance structures and the positions of actors, utilising both formal and informal rules. It is envisaged as a 'multi-level conceptual map' that allows researchers to zoom in and out of different hierarchical parts of governance structures within a social system (Cole, 2017). A complex problem is dissected into 'action areas'. Within these action arenas, actors equipped with cognitive capacities, information, preferences and strategies interact in positions framed by existing rules (Cole, 2017). 'Rules in use' is a central concept of IAD, referring to the actual norms and behaviours that individuals learn and apply in practice, which sometimes differ from formal written rules (Ostrom, 2011). Rules are classified into seven categories: position, boundary, choice, aggression, information, payoff and scope. These rules also collectively govern interdependencies among actors in an action situation (Cole, 2017). 'Multi-level' analysis includes Operational (day-to-day activities), Collective choice (defining interdependencies) and constitutional choice (rule-defining individual or body) (Carter & Christopher, 2015).

5.2.1 Popular Fields of Application

IAD was initially applied to the study of common-pool resources. Over the decades, its applications have expanded to sectors such as forest governance, water allocation (Cole, 2017), climate adaptation (Roggero et al., 2017), and fisheries (*The IAD Framework*, 2014). Some even argue that IAD can be applied to diverse social settings, including markets, courtrooms, corporate boardrooms, clubs, faculty meetings, religious synods and even family dinner tables (Cole, 2017). More recently, IAD has been applied to analyse data governance and data policy design within the context of smart cities (Filgueiras & Silva, 2022). The framework allows for integration of heterogeneous variables from multi-disciplinary perspectives, making it suitable for comparative analysis across different contexts (*The IAD Framework*, 2014). In a short introduction, Ostrom, E. (2011) addresses the relationship of IAD to a more complex framework for analysing social-ecological systems and concludes with a brief discussion of future challenges facing IAD scholars. Balani, K., Sharma, B., & Agrawal, S. (2025) indicate a complex layering of institutional rules that shape the decisions of local actors and various agents of the distribution company (discom) using IAD. Zhang, J., Busck, A. G., & Kristensen, S. B. P. (2025) employ the IAD framework to examine the rule configuration and dynamics surrounding contract forming in rural China. Bakhanova et al. (2025) use IAD to understand how institutional factors influence integrative outcomes by examining operational-level rules that guide actions and interactions among various actors.

5.2.2 Strengths of the IAD in AI Policy Analysis

Structured analysis of complex interactions: The strength of IAD lies in dissecting complex interactions among institutions, decision-making processes and resource management (Ostrom, 2010). On the same lines, the basic AI tenants also involve multiple actors, formal, informal, and soft rules/laws, and diverse outcomes. IAD can provide a systematic lens for understanding the interplay among various stakeholders in the AI ecosystem (Ostrom, 2011), particularly in terms of actor interactions, decision-making, cooperation, and conflict. These are effective in AI governance.

Rules in use and Institutions: Due to the evolutionary nature of AI, the rules are raw, formative, and, in some cases, already legislated. Furthermore, it is also evolving, incorporating industry standards and formal practices. The IAD aspects of 'rules in form' and 'rules in use' are highly pertinent, enabling an analysis of how actual behaviours and formal agreements influence AI governance, especially in areas where formal regulations are lacking (Ostrom, 2011). IAD helps diagnose institutional agreements to understand the theory driving specific outcomes (Ostrom, 2010).

Multi-level analysis: AI policy operates at various levels – national AI strategy, executive orders, federal legislation, organisational policies, and individual developer practices - making it a multi-level approach. Multi-level analysis enables the analysis of constitutional, collective, and operational levels of decision-making, making it comprehensive for understanding how rules at different tiers influence AI governance and how design adaptations occur over time (Cole, 2017).

Collective action problem: AI governance often grapples with collective action problems, such as ensuring data privacy across jurisdictions or coordinating efforts to mitigate global AI risks (Roggero et al., 2017). IAD helps to understand how institutions address such problems by shaping individual behaviour to foster coordination and cooperation. This makes IAD suitable for designing mechanisms that encourage responsible AI development and deployment, particularly in areas such as data sharing for the public good or the establishment of common ethical standards.

5.2.3 Limitations

Potential for being too general: IAD is often treated as over-fitting or being 'too general' in certain contexts due to its broad applicability (Ostrom, 2010). AI is continuously and rapidly evolving. Further, AI is a highly technical domain with an inherent 'black box' paradox. This might make IAD's applicability to AI nuanced and complex. Extensive and intricate work will be required to define relevant 'action situations' and 'rules in use' for AI systems.

Explicit Inclusions: Some authors argue that IAD poses a 'limited inclusion of ecological processes' (Ostrom, 2010). This can also be superimposed on the AI domain. Although IAD is dynamic, it may not fully capture the self-modifying nature of AI algorithms or the emergent properties of complex AI systems. Its focus on short-term fixed-action situations might struggle to account for the ongoing, often unpredictable evolution of AI capabilities and their societal impacts.

Tackling the Opacity: IAD has inherent hindrance in identifying the 'invisible institutions' that are treated as shared-implicit knowledge (Clinio, 2016). The 'black box' nature of AI makes it difficult to clearly distinguish between 'rules in form' and 'rules in use', thereby complicating the structuring of institutional arrangements.

5.3 Institutional Design and Development (IDD)

IDD is a conceptual approach or a field of study that draws heavily from institutional analysis, particularly the IAD framework. It is centred on conscious creation and the evolution of institutions. IAD emphasises the deliberate construction and revision of institutional mechanisms, structures, and processes (Lee, 2025a). IDD, on the other hand, stems from the belief that the sustenance of institutional mechanisms, structure and processes is as important as their creation. It believes that institutions are not static entities but are systems of dynamic rules, norms and agreements that collectively shape behaviour and actions (Klijn & Koppenjan, 2006).

The key objective of IDD is to align policy instruments with overarching public policy objectives, promoting efficiency, coherence, transparency, and adaptability.

5.3.1 Popular Fields of Application

IDD is widely used in educational training and development to improve human performance across sectors such as business, healthcare, government, and education (Mancilla & Frey, 2020). From curriculum design to performance analysis and program effectiveness, IDD is an ideal application. IDD has been used for evolving the 'institutional framework' of the AI industry (Nikitaeva & Salem, 2022). Narain, V., & Ranjan, P. (2024) examine how scholars' study collective action institutions in relation to natural resource management in peri-urban spaces, with a regional focus on South Asia, and present the implications for institutional design and development in these contexts. Lee & Yeung (2017) use IAD to study the Principal Officials Accountability System (POAS), which marked the beginning of a Hong Kong-style system of ministerial government. Bolan, R. S. (1992) used IAD to study implications of the Polish experience in the context of the country's policy of sustainable development.

5.3.2 Strengths

Proactive: IDD, due to its ability to address the conscious creation and revision of governance mechanisms, is more proactive, extending beyond existing policy dynamics. This proactive nature suits the AI domain well, as this framework is expected to be more accommodating of the fact that the domain is technologically advancing. This also helps keep tabs on potential areas of risk in the design of regulatory frameworks.

Rules and Structure: IDD has a structured approach that provides detailed attention to rules; its typologies and hierarchical nesting are well-suited to AI. This hierarchical approach defines aspects of AI operation, its accountability, and oversight mechanisms. This structuring can be applied to data governance, ethical considerations, human-in-the-middle interventions, and AI-generated content (WitnessAI, 2025).

Adaptability and Resilience: IDD helps design institutions that can adapt to policy failures or address emerging challenges (Lee, 2025b). Given the rapid pace of AI development and unpredictable nature of its impacts (Sieweke, 2025), this capacity for iterative design and revision is invaluable. This makes AI adaptation with strong governance mechanisms and robust feedback mechanisms more practically oriented.

5.3.3 Limitations

Opacity: Effectiveness of IDD relies on a clear understanding of 'elements, linkages and foundational logic' designs (Carter & Christopher, 2015). The complex, 'black box' nature of many AI systems makes it difficult to comprehend their internal workings fully and potential consequences (Sieweke, 2025).

Resource Allocation: The effectiveness of IDD, especially in domains like AI, will be complex given the significant expertise across legal, technical, ethical, and sociological dimensions. The absence of standardised legal, technical, and ethical standards constitutes a hurdle (Sieweke, 2025).

5.4 Policy Evolution Theory (PET)

PET emerged in the 1960s in the United States of America as a means to explain the results of public action and its effect on society (El Dessouky, 2016). It is a mechanism for determining the success or failure of public policy and for providing effective feedback. PET is considered generational in its evolution. Its three primary generations are measurement, description and judgement (El Dessouky, 2016). Peter Rossi proposed a five-stage evolution process of PET, viz., problem definition, feasibility review, causal model development, research design and results valorisation. At its core, PET involves systematic research to examine the outcomes, intended impacts and unintended consequences of government policies. Key evaluative criteria often include efficiency, effectiveness and equity (Lee, 2025a). In recent times, PET has incorporated various frameworks, including the Logic Model Framework, the Theory of Change, cost-benefit analysis, and performance management. PET also recognises the highly political nature of policy analysis, emphasising the need for technical and political feasibility solutions (Palgrave Pivot, n.d.).

5.4.1 Popular Fields of Application

Policy Evaluation Theory is a pervasive discipline that can be applied across various sectors of public policy, enabling the assessment of the impact and efficacy of interventions. PET has a wide range of applications in public health, including predicting disease outbreaks, assessing preventive measures, and improving medical diagnosis and treatment (Yar et al., 2024). Another domain where PET is effectively used to forecast the effects of climate change and to inform scenarios, aiding the development of mitigation and adaptation policy measures (Yar et al., 2024). Other fields of application include social services – assessing the impact of social programs, such as homelessness initiatives (Hoefer, 2022)- and law enforcement and urban planning – using predictive tools and ML to counter crime (Hoefer, 2022).

5.4.2 Strengths

Data-driven Assessment: PET decisions and outcomes are informed by data, aligning with AI system requirements. PET's emphasis on systematic research to examine outcomes, intended impacts, and unintended consequences aligns well with the need for evidence-based AI policy (Lee, 2025a; Navaratna & Saxena, 2023). This can help build capacity for data-driven policy evaluation and improve decision-making outcomes.

Identification of Consequences: PET's core function of identifying unintended consequences can help assess the transformative nature of AI. This can prove vital for addressing issues such as algorithmic discrimination, its societal impact, and energy consumption.

Policy Improvement: The ability to undertake developmental evaluation within PET, designed for innovative and evolving policies, is vital for fostering real-time learning and adjusting programs to improve policy.

5.4.3 Limitations

Black Box and Explainability: Like many frameworks proposed above, PET's complexity and opacity make it challenging for AI policymaking. This hindered the causal link between policy interventions and specific AI-driven outcomes. Lack of explainability makes it challenging to conduct a thorough evaluation of an AI policy's effectiveness.

Subjectivity and Political Pressure: Policy interventions are always, in a way, affected by subjective interpretations and political pressures. PET does not cater for this type of policy design. Thus, in a highly contested and politicised domain of AI, the intersection of powerful industry and national interest becomes crucial. This aspect of political impact on policy can impact the effectiveness of PET.

5.5 Multiple Streams Framework (MSF)

The Multiple Streams Framework (MSF), developed by Kingdon (2003), posits that the policy process comprises three parallel and independent streams: the problem stream, the policy stream, and the politics stream. This tool has emerged as a major tool for analysing the policy process in a wide variety of issue areas, countries, and levels of government (Herweg et al., 2015). Kingdon describes the gap between policymakers' attention to a problem and their adaptation of a meaningful solution. He also rejects the linear understanding of policymaking, which holds that policymakers identify a problem to solve, the bureaucracy produces a wide range of possible solutions, and policymakers select the best choice. Instead, MSF proposes that these three streams come together during a 'window of opportunity' in which people pay attention to a problem, a viable solution is determined with policymakers' motives in mind, and administrators roll out the policy. In this paper, we have used MSF and its three pillars to determine and set the agenda for AI governance. The theoretical framework used is MSF, while the analytical framework is an algorithmic application to the policy domain.

5.5.1 Popular Fields of Application

MSF is one of the most widely used policy design frameworks with extensive applications across domains. Key fields of application include, but are not limited to, environmental policy, public health, labour market policy, national security, and policy research. Zahariadis (2019) provides a comprehensive overview of MSF's assumptions and guiding principles. It outlines the framework's main structural elements. Knaggård (2015) suggests that it is crucial to study policy actors, as problem framing affects the work of policy entrepreneurs, agenda-setting, and decision-making. Herweg et al (2018) outline the main assumptions of the MSF before presenting several structural elements of the framework. It discusses how MSF is applied to other stages of the policy process.

5.5.2 Strengths

Policy Change Explainability: MSF can excel at explaining policymaking under conditions of ambiguity and political pressure. This is in accordance with the AI policy definition. This MSF ability facilitates goal maximisation and rationality.

Window of Opportunity – AI Governance: The unique ability to define a window of opportunity enables AI adaptation triggered by technological breakthroughs, shifts in public mood, national perspectives, and public perception, thereby accommodating policy design.

Policy Entrepreneurs: MSF defines the role of 'policy entrepreneurs' in coupling streams and advocating for policy change. AI involves a multi-verse of stakeholders, ranging from governmental institutions to academicians to corporate developers. So, a change in AI policy can be triggered by any of these institutions. The ability to frame problems, propose solutions and leverage political timing is central to shaping the AI policy agenda.

5.5.3 Limitations

Stream Interaction: The framework does not establish or identify causal relations among the various streams. This affects the policy analysis of the AI ecosystem, which is highly interconnected and dynamic. Understanding how a technical problem in AI directly translates into a political problem and then designing a policy solution can affect the governance framework.

AI Evolution: MSF focuses on a discrete instance of development – 'window of opportunity'. However, AI development is multi-spectral and multi-stakeholder. This makes AI development more continuous. Thus, defining a single instance as a window of opportunity shortens development cycles.

6. AI GOVERNANCE CHARACTERISTICS AND POLICY FRAMEWORK

The various frameworks analysed in the above texts can be summed up in Table 1 below. The table lays emphasis on the core focus of each framework, the key concept defining each framework, the relevance of the framework to AI and finally the limitations of each framework in the context of AI policy design.

Table 1. Summary of the AI governance framework in a nutshell

Framework	Core Focus	Key Concept	AI Relevance	Limitation
ACF	Policy Change with time within subsystem and competing coalitions (beliefs, resources, strategies)	Policy Learning, Belief Systems, External Shocks	AI institutions and coalitions' interactions. Eg: study risk, innovation coalitions	Stresses the ongoing process of AI policy change. Establishing optimal policy content may be challenging.
IAD	Analyse how a set of rules/ institutions affects the outcome in Action Arena.	Action Arena, Rules-in-use, Physical world attributes	Design specific governance rules like data, algorithms, bias, etc	Difficult to define 'Action Arena' or 'rules in use' in the evolving AI paradigm
IDD	Focuses on information surrounding change opinions/ behaviour	Communication, Public awareness, campaigns	Can address areas like addressing public scepticism surrounding AI.	Has the ability to neglect political, institutional and economic barriers to AI policy design.
PET	Policy to Goal Achievement Analysis	Metrics and indicators, counterfactuals, cost-benefit analysis	Has the ability to undertake an audit of AI policy impact by establishing feedback loops.	It requires reliable, measurable data and clear policy objectives, which may not always be possible in the context of AI.
MSF	Ability to look at policy in various sub-streams, which have societal and technological breadth	Policy, Problem, Politics, Policy Window and entrepreneurs.	Undertake AI policy impact in depth and through various sub-streams	More apt for discrete developments than for a continuous nature.

Can these frameworks be effective in tackling the unique characteristics of AI discussed earlier? A general comparison of features v/s framework can be summed up as indicated in Table 2.

Table 2. AI features v/s framework comparison

Framework	Defining AI	Speed of development	Data Dependency/ Bias	Black Box Problem	Responsibility/ Accountability
ACF	It can be defined based on the rival coalition comparison	Speed/ pace will be treated as an external shock. It will bring in a belief shift and realignment	Data/ bias can be treated as a coalition's deep core belief	Could be a limitation in defining, but will process for transparency as a policy instrument	Actors in the dominant policy coalition will be considered for responsibility/ accountability
IAD	Requires clear rules in use (algorithms, ethics, goals) to define the action arena	Formal rules may become obsolete, and operational rules may be defined to keep pace with development.	Data dependency will be a prerequisite for developing operational rules	Will pose a challenge due to the lack of visibility in defining information rules, payoff rules and finally operational rules	Define position, authority and payoffs
IDD	The definition can depend on the technical literacy of policymakers	It will emphasise the diffusion of accurate information based on capabilities to policymakers	Bias/ data dependency will be viewed as aspects that need an educational campaign/ awareness	It will be addressed as a knowledge gap through mandated communication.	Policy for legal accountability while raising awareness to set responsibility in development or usage
PET	Need for a predefined, measurable definition with AI-appropriate indicators	Set forward-looking metrics to adapt to the agility of the AI system	crucial aspect that quantitative metrics and the adoption of bias mitigation techniques can tackle	Difficult to access effectiveness/ transparency via measurable indicators	It can be tackled through accountability mechanisms.
MSF	It can be defined through a basic stream network.	Speed can be arrested through problem stream definition, which includes the policy entrepreneur and the policy window.	Data dependency/ bias is part of the problem stream	Black box is a problem stream that must be addressed through a policy solution	The said problem stream can be addressed through policy entrepreneurs at the policy window through the political stream.

7. APPLICATION OF AI-POWERED AUTOMATION IN HIGHER EDUCATION: THREATS AND OPPORTUNITIES

The integration of AI in higher education has shifted from a speculative technological trend to a disruptive reality that demands an urgent policy response. As institutes grapple with generative models and automated systems, the landscape of academia is undergoing a fundamental transformation across teaching, research and service. By applying the broad AI policy frameworks outlined above, we aim to understand the opportunities and threats to education through a tripartite analysis of teaching, research, and service/administration. While not all frameworks can be discussed in this context due to space constraints, we use the MSF framework as an illustration in Table 3 below. The table brings in the opportunities provided by AI and the threats it poses to each of the educational parameters.

Table 3. MSF in the context of AI-powered higher education

Educational Parameter	AI Opportunity	AI Threat
Teaching/ Learning	● Provides for unprecedented potential for personalised learning (Holmes et al., 2019). ● Can provide tailored feedback to each student to address learning gaps (Baker, 2021) ● Manual/time-consuming processes, such as evaluation, grading, and repetitive assignments, can be automated. This time can be used for high-impact mentorship (Luckin et al., 2016)	● The automation of thought poses a significant threat to academic integrity (Cotton et al., 2023). ● The ease of AI-generated content can lead to 'student cognitive disengagement'. Where the student bypasses the learning process (Qadir, 2023) ● Assessment tools, if unfairly trained, can lead to historical prejudices (Compilatio, 2025)
Research/ Scholarship	● AI can accelerate the pace of discovery through data synthesis, literature review and predictive modelling (Wang et al, 2023). ● LLMs can enhance drafting complex reports and translate findings to a global audience, enhancing research productivity (Kitamura, 2023)	● The quality of research can be compromised through 'hallucinated data' (Alkaissi & McFarlane, 2023). ● Ethical considerations in research, such as 'erosion of authorship' and 'ethical research', get eroded (O'Connor, 2023) ● Due to a lack of transparency and 'black box' algorithms, the outcome cannot be reproduced or verified, thereby eroding the credibility of research (O'Connor, 2023).
Service/ Administration	● Streamlines through automation aspects like enrolment management, forms/ application management, 24*7 student/ faculty support, and counsellor support through micro bots or chatbots (Hyland, 2025) ● Scarce resources can be optimised for better student facilities through automation (Popenici & Kerr, 2017).	● All the processes are data-driven. This poses a grave threat to data privacy (Zeide, 2019). ● Risk of student/ faculty/institutional surveillance and third-party access (Saidakhror, 2024).

To the above scenario, let us now apply the Multiple Streams Framework. Kingdon suggests that policy change occurs when three independent streams converge during a 'window of opportunity'.

7.1 The Problem Stream

This stream consists of conditions identified as 'problematic' and requiring action. In the context of higher education, these include:

Focusing Event: Launch of LLMs and their use by students in academic work, leading to mass academic misconduct. Use of LLMs served as a 'critical juncture', sparking a crisis in academic integrity as students began using it for critical academic assessments (Sullivan et al., 2023)

Feedback from Faculty: Complaints about the inadequacy of the current honour codes due to student violations are flagged by academic staff. They suggest that traditional honour codes and definitions of plagiarism are insufficient to address the nuances of AI-generated content (Bearman & Ajjawi, 2023).

Indicators: Declining student performance in proctored vs. unproctored settings, resulting in a performance gap. Further, students' knowledge of the fundamentals of the subjects is shallow, suggesting evidence of surface-level learning that lacks the foundational depth required for critical synthesis (Susnjak, 2022).

7.2 The Policy Stream

This 'primaeval policy soup' contains ideas/ solutions generated by the specialists and researchers to address the identified problems, which include:

Technical Feasibility: Develop AI detection software, the related ecosystem, and the transition towards 'authentic assessment' before each submission, and conduct a 'digitally locked' environment exam to ensure the validity of students' work (Dawson, 2020).

Acceptability: Debate over AI prohibition vs. AI integration through digital literacy is ongoing. Researchers argue that AI literacy is a core 21st-century competency (Selwyn, 2024)

Proposals: Develop a 'Human-in—the-loop' (HIL) framework that mandates human oversight in research and all steps of academics to maintain ethical accountability and cognitive engagement (Bond et al., 2024).

7.3 The Policy Stream

This stream reflects the institutional and social environment surrounding AI in higher education through:

Institutional Mood: Use AI as a mechanism to transform from an AI-sceptic campus to an AI-forward campus. This mandates an organisational or institutional shift in ethos towards AI adaptation. This transition is often driven by the need to remain competitive and relevant in a digital-first labour market (Zawacki-Richter et al., 2019). Further, pressure from accreditation bodies and industry stakeholders compels institutions to formalise an AI governance stance.

7.4 The Policy Window and Policy Entrepreneur

When the 'Problem' in the form of cheating or inefficiency comes to light, the institute administration, acting as Policy Entrepreneur, brings in the Institute AI framework through a 'Political' stream, i.e., Academic Council/ Senate of the institute, by providing requisite budget/ manpower/and infrastructure, thereby opening a window of opportunity. Breaking this down further, Dean and Pro Vice Chancellor act as policy entrepreneurs, leveraging the crisis of academic misconduct (Problem) and the availability of the HITL framework (Policy) during a period of institutional readiness (politics) to advocate for formal change (Mintrom, 2019). The academic Council/Senate of the institute, coupled with entrepreneurs, contributed to the institutional AI policy framework (Zahariadis, 2019).

8. CONCLUSION

As the preceding text indicates, each policy design framework has a distinctive approach to AI policy. Each framework also provides context for the policy process, actor interactions, and institutional dynamics. At the outset, it is clear that no one policy framework emerges as the best fit for AI policy design. The AI domain poses a dual challenge: continuous evolution, aided by the 'black box' syndrome. This makes it unique and complex, taking into account societal good and ethical considerations. AI policy governance is not only required to maintain compliance with societal good, but also serves as a prerequisite for economic development, employment generation, AI intellectual property creation, and good governance. The accelerated pace of AI development poses a considerable 'governance gap'. The policy governance at all levels, namely government, corporate, and academia, is finding it equally hard to adopt. This calls for an adaptive, iterative, and responsible governance model that can operate effectively in an evolving, uncertain environment.

Thus, the chapter highlights fundamental challenges and uniqueness surrounding AI policy design. It then discusses each well-established policy design framework, its key concepts, core strengths for AI policy design, and limitations. Further, the chapter provides a summary of the use of each framework in defining AI policy design and tackling its uniqueness. The chapter shows that there is no best-fit module; however, it would be interesting to study AI in depth using a single framework. MSF has three basic streams, namely, policy, political, and problem streams, coupled with a window of opportunity for policy entrepreneurs. The use of MSF in higher education is illustrated in section 7 as a step toward furthering the impact of AI in education. One such policy can be the 'National AI Policy for Education' of various countries. Thus, studying it through the lens of MSF can highlight the relevance of AI policy through an established practical perspective.

REFERENCES

Accenture. (2024). (2024). AI and the Next Era of Personalisation: Customer Experience 2030 Report. *Accenture Strategy Insights.* https://www.accenture.com. Accenture.

Alkaissi, H., & McFarlane, S. I. (2023). Artificial intelligence in medical writing: A friend or a foe? *Cureus, 15*(2), e35224. Advance online publication. DOI: 10.7759/cureus.35224 PMID: 36968855

Angwin, J., Larson, J., Mattu, S., & Kirchner, L. (2016). *Machine bias: There's software used across the country to predict future criminals. And it's biased against blacks*. ProPublica.

Baker, J. A. (2021). The impact of adaptive learning environments on student self-efficacy. *Journal of Educational Technology.*

Bakhanova, E., Vinke-de Kruijf, J., Wöhler, L., Warbroek, B., & Arentsen, M. (2025). Integrative Approaches to Interconnected Environmental Challenges: How Institutional Factors Influence Cross-Sector Integration in Dutch Rural Areas. *Environmental Management, 75*(5), 1308–1321. DOI: 10.1007/s00267-025-02140-2 PMID: 40053119

Balani, K., Sharma, B., & Agrawal, S. (2025). From linesmen to local leaders: How does informal governance influence India's electricity policy outcomes? *Energy Research & Social Science, 124*, 104056. DOI: 10.1016/j.erss.2025.104056

Bearman, M., & Ajjawi, R. (2023). Learning to work with the black box: Pedagogy for a world with generative AI. *British Journal of Educational Technology, 54*(5), 1160–1173. DOI: 10.1111/bjet.13337

Bolan, R. S. (1992). Organising for Sustainable Growth in Poland. *Journal of the American Planning Association, 58*(3), 301–311. DOI: 10.1080/01944369208975809

Bond, M., Passy, R., & Agnew, S. (2024). A systematic review of generative AI in higher education: The need for ethical frameworks. *Educational Technology Research and Development.* Advance online publication. DOI: 10.1007/s11423-024-10351-w

Carter, D. P., & Christopher, M. (2015). Integrating core concepts from the institutional analysis and development framework for the systematic analysis of policy designs: An illustration from the US National Organic Program regulation—. *Journal of Theoretical Politics, 28*(1), 159–185. DOI: 10.1177/0951629815603494

Clinio, A. (2016). *Reflections on the Application of the IAD Framework to analyse the Ubatuba Open Science Platform | OCSDNET*. Ocsdnet.org. https://ocsdnet.org/reflections-on-the-application-of-the-institutional-analysis-and-development-iad-framework-to-analyze-the-ubatuba-open-science-platform/

Cole, D. H. (2017). Laws, norms, and the Institutional Analysis and Development framework. *Journal of Institutional Economics, 13*(4), 829–847. DOI: 10.1017/S1744137417000030

Compilatio. (2025). *Artificial intelligence in education: Opportunities and challenges in 2025*. https://www.compilatio.net/en/blog/ai-in-education

Cotton, D. R. E., Cotton, P. A., & Shipway, J. R. (2023). Chatting and cheating: Ensuring academic integrity in the era of ChatGPT. *Innovations in Education and Teaching International, 61*(2), 228–239. DOI: 10.1080/14703297.2023.2190148

Dawson, P. (2020). *Defending Assessment Security in a Digital World: Preventing E-Cheating and Supporting Academic Integrity in Higher Education* (1st ed.). Routledge., DOI: 10.4324/9780429324178

Djeffal, C., Siewert, M. B., & Wurster, S. (2022). Role of the state and responsibility in governing artificial intelligence: A comparative analysis of AI strategies. *Journal of European Public Policy, 29*(11), 1–23. DOI: 10.1080/13501763.2022.2094987

Dressel, J., & Farid, H. (2018). The accuracy, fairness, and limits of predicting recidivism. *Science Advances, 4*(1), eaao5580. Advance online publication. DOI: 10.1126/sciadv.aao5580 PMID: 29376122

El Dessouky, N.F (2016). PUBLIC POLICY EVALUATION THEORY: FROM FIRST TO FIFTH GENERATION. *EPRA International Journal of Economic and Business Review(JEBR), 4*(4).

Elinor Ostrom. (2011). UNESCO – EOLSS SAMPLE CHAPTERS HISTORICAL DEVELOPMENTS AND THEORETICAL APPROACHES IN SOCIOLOGY – Vol. II - Institutional Analysis and Development: Elements of The Framework in Historical Perspective. *Encyclopedia of Life Support Systems (EOLSS).*

Filgueiras, F., & Silva, B. (2022). Designing data policy and governance for smart cities: Theoretical essay using the IAD framework to analyse data-driven policy. *Revista de Administração Pública, 56*(4), 508–528. DOI: 10.1590/0034-761220220078x

Fung, C., & Lo, A. (2025). *The Air Canada chatbot lawsuit and its implications for AI in customer service*. PolyU Institutional Research Archive. https://ira.lib.polyu.edu.hk/handle/10397/114706

Gabehart, K. M., & Weible, C. M. (2023). Advocacy Coalition Framework. *Springer EBooks*, 1–10. DOI: 10.1007/978-3-030-90434-0_5-2

Gutierrez, C. I., Marchant, G. E., & Michael, K. (2021). Effective and Trustworthy Implementation of AI Soft Law Governance. SSRN *Electronic Journal*. DOI: 10.2139/ssrn.4031992

Herweg, N., Huß, C., & Zohlnhöfer, R. (2015). Straightening the three streams: Theorising extensions of the multiple streams framework. *European Journal of Political Research*, *54*(3), 435–449. DOI: 10.1111/1475-6765.12089

Herweg, N., Zahariadis, N., & Zohlnhöfer, R. (2018). The Multiple Streams Framework: Foundations, Refinements, and Empirical Applications. In Weible, C. M., & Sabatier, P. A. (Eds.), *Theories of the Policy Process* (4th ed., pp. 17–53). Routledge., DOI: 10.4324/9780429494284-2

Hoefer, R. (2022). The multiple streams framework: Understanding and applying the problems, policies, and politics approach. *Journal of Policy Practice and Research*, *3*(1), 1–5. DOI: 10.1007/s42972-022-00049-2

Holmes, W., Bialik, M., & Fadel, C. (2019). *Artificial intelligence in education: Promises and implications for teaching and learning*. Centre for Curriculum Redesign.

Hyland. (2025). *AI use cases in higher education*. https://www.hyland.com/en/resources/articles/ai-higher-education

Janssen, M. (2025). Responsible governance of generative AI: Conceptualising GenAI as complex adaptive systems. *Policy and Society*, *44*(1), 38–51. DOI: 10.1093/polsoc/puae040

John, P. (2003). Is There Life After Policy Streams, Advocacy Coalitions, and Punctuations: Using Evolutionary Theory to Explain Policy Change? *Policy Studies Journal: The Journal of the Policy Studies Organization*, *31*(4), 481–498. DOI: 10.1111/1541-0072.00039

Jones, J. (2025). *AI-Driven Demand Forecasting in Supply Chains: A Qualitative Analysis of Adoption and Impact*. DOI: 10.20944/preprints202501.1349.v1

Jun Park, H., & Han, J. (2025). Analysis of the Digital Transformation of Legal Services and the Role of Policy Brokers in KOREA through the Advocacy Coalition Framework. *Policy & Governance Review*, *9*(1), 30. DOI: 10.30589/pgr.v9i1.1171

Katzenbach, C., & Ulbricht, L. (2019). Algorithmic governance. *Internet Policy Review*, *8*(4), 1–18. DOI: 10.14763/2019.4.1424

Kim, Y.-J., & Roh, C.-Y. (2008). Beyond the Advocacy Coalition Framework in Policy Process. *International Journal of Public Administration, 31*(6), 668–689. DOI: 10.1080/01900690701465384

Kingdon, J. W. (2003). *(2003). Agendas, alternatives and public policies* (2nd ed.). Longman.

Kitamura, Y. (2023). Generative AI in research: Productivity and pitfalls. *Journal of Scholarly Publishing*.

Klijn, E.-H., & Koppenjan, J. F. M. (2006). Institutional design. *Public Management Review*, *8*(1), 141–160. DOI: 10.1080/14719030500518915

Knaggård, Å. (2015). The Multiple Streams Framework and the problem broker. *European Journal of Political Research*, *54*(3), 450–465. DOI: 10.1111/1475-6765.12097

Lee, E. W. Y., & Yeung, R. L. K. (2017). The "Principal Officials Accountability System": It is under development as a system of ministerial government. *Asia Pacific Journal of Public Administration*, *39*(2), 120–134. DOI: 10.1080/23276665.2017.1325623

Lee, S. (2025a). *A Quick Look at Top Policy Evaluation Frameworks*. Numberanalytics.com. https://www.numberanalytics.com/blog/quick-look-top-policy-evaluation-frameworks

Lee, S. (2025b). *Key Steps to Institutional Design in Public Policy*. Numberanalytics.com. https://www.numberanalytics.com/blog/key-steps-institutional-design-public-policy

Lippoldt, D. (2024). AI Innovation Concentration and the Governance Challenge. *Centre for International Governance Innovation*. https://www.cigionline.org/static/documents/no.292.pdf

Luckin, R., Holmes, W., Griffiths, M., & Forcier, L. B. (2016). *Intelligence unleashed: An argument for AI in education*. Pearson.

Mancilla, R., & Frey, B. (2020). A Model for Developing Instructional Design Professionals for Higher Education Through Apprenticeship: Blending Theory and Practice. *Journal of Applied Instructional Design*, *9*(2). Advance online publication. DOI: 10.51869/92rmbf

May, P. J. (2007). Regulatory regimes and accountability. *Regulation & Governance*, *1*(1), 8–26. DOI: 10.1111/j.1748-5991.2007.00002.x

Mintrom, M. (2019). *Public policy: Investing for a better world*. Oxford University Press.

Narain, V., & Ranjan, P. (2024). Belling the cat: Designing collective action institutions for natural resource management in the peri-urban interface. *Urban Studies (Edinburgh, Scotland)*, *61*(8), 1604–1614. DOI: 10.1177/00420980231211681

Navaratna, A. R., & Saxena, D. (2023). An Indian approach to AI policy: A comparative study between three sectors. In *Handbook of Evidence-Based Management Practices in Business* (pp. 440–452). Routledge. DOI: 10.4324/9781003415725-55

Navaratna, A. R., & Saxena, D. (2025a). From policy to practice in digital governance: A three-level analysis of citizen-centric applications. *JeDEM-eJournal of eDemocracy and Open Government, 17*(1), 33–64.

Navaratna, A. R., & Saxena, D. (2025b). Digital Governance Through Self-Regulation: A user-developer perspective of AI chatbots. *Journal of Telecommunications and the Digital Economy, 13*(3), 1–29. DOI: 10.18080/jtde.v13n3.1077

Nikitaeva, A. Y., & Salem, A.-B. M. (2022). Institutional Framework for The Development of Artificial Intelligence in The Industry. *Journal of International Students, 14*(1), 108–126. DOI: 10.17835/2076-6297.2022.14.1.108-126

O'Connor, S.ChatGPT. (2023). Open artificial intelligence platforms in nursing education: Tools for academic progress or abuse? *Nurse Education in Practice, 66*, 103537. Advance online publication. DOI: 10.1016/j.nepr.2022.103537 PMID: 36549229

OECD. (2019). *Artificial Intelligence in Society*. OECD., DOI: 10.1787/eedfee77-

Olariu, O., & Zeleznikow, J. (2025). Human Rights-Compliant Artificial Intelligence. *Digitalisation and Artificial Intelligence in Courts: Opportunities and Challenges, 259*, 275.

Olsson, J. (2009). The Power of the Inside Activist: Understanding Policy Change by Empowering the Advocacy Coalition Framework (ACF). *Planning Theory & Practice, 10*(2), 167–187. DOI: 10.1080/14649350902884425

Ostrom, E. (2010). Response: The Institutional Analysis and Development Framework and the Commons. SSRN *Electronic Journal, 95*(4). DOI: 10.2139/ssrn.1615582

Ostrom, E. (2011). Background on the Institutional Analysis and Development Framework. *Policy Studies Journal: The Journal of the Policy Studies Organization, 39*(1), 7–27. DOI: 10.1111/j.1541-0072.2010.00394.x

Palgrave Pivot. (n.d.). *The Politics of Policy Analysis 100-word description*. https://paulcairney.wordpress.com/wp-content/uploads/2020/02/paul-cairney-the-politics-of-policy-analysis-palgrave-pivot-full-draft-27.2.20.pdf

Paul Cairney. (2019, February 11). *Policy in 500 Words: The advocacy coalition framework*. Paul Cairney: Politics & Public Policy. https://paulcairney.wordpress.com/2019/02/11/policy-in-500-words-the-advocacy-coalition-framework/

Popenici, S. A. D., & Kerr, S. (2017). Exploring the impact of artificial intelligence on teaching and learning in higher education. *Research and Practice in Technology Enhanced Learning*, *12*(1), 22. Advance online publication. DOI: 10.1186/s41039-017-0062-8 PMID: 30595727

Qadir, J. (2023). Generative AI and academic integrity: A risk assessment. *International Journal for Educational Integrity*.

Roggero, M., Bisaro, A., & Villamayor-Tomas, S. (2017). Institutions in the climate adaptation literature: A systematic literature review through the lens of the Institutional Analysis and Development framework. *Journal of Institutional Economics*, *14*(3), 423–448. DOI: 10.1017/S1744137417000376

Sabatier, P. A. (1998). The advocacy coalition framework: Revisions and relevance for Europe. *Journal of European Public Policy*, *5*(1), 98–130. DOI: 10.1080/13501768880000051

Saidakhror, G. (2024). *Economic effects and infrastructure requirements for AI in universities*. Educational Finance Review.

Saxena, D., Lamest, M., & Bansal, V. (2021). Responsible machine learning for ethical artificial intelligence in business and industry. In *Handbook of Research on Applied Data Science and Artificial Intelligence in Business and Industry* (pp. 639–653). IGI Global. DOI: 10.4018/978-1-7998-6985-6.ch030

Selwyn, N. (2024). On the limits of artificial intelligence (AI) in education. *Nordisk Tidsskrift for Pedagogikk og Kritikk*, *10*(1), 3–14. DOI: 10.23865/ntpk.v10.6062

Sieweke, D. (2025, July 25). *AI Policy and Governance: Shaping the Future of Artificial Intelligence*. Scytale. https://scytale.ai/center/grc/ai-policy-and-governance-shaping-the-future-of-artificial-intelligence/

Smuha, N. A. (2021). Beyond the individual: Governing AI's societal harm. *Internet Policy Review*, *10*(3). Advance online publication. DOI: 10.14763/2021.3.1574

St-Hilaire, I. (2025). Lying chatbot makes airline liable: Negligent misrepresentation in Moffatt v Air Canada. *UBC Law Review*, *58*(2), 591–612. https://commons.allard.ubc.ca/ubclawreview/vol58/iss2/8

Sullivan, M., Kelly, A., & McLaughlan, P. (2023). ChatGPT in higher education: Considerations for academic integrity and student learning. *Journal of Applied Learning and Teaching*, *6*(1), 31–40. DOI: 10.37074/jalt.2023.6.1.17

Susnjak, T. (2022). ChatGPT: The End of Online Exam Integrity? arXiv:2212.09292. https://doi.org//arXiv.2212.09292DOI: 10.48550

Taeihagh, A. (2025). Governance of Generative AI. *Policy and Society*, *44*(1), 1–22. Advance online publication. DOI: 10.1093/polsoc/puaf001

The IAD Framework. (2014, October 8). OCSDNET. https://ocsdnet.org/about-ocsdnet/about-ocs/iad-framework/

Turing, A. (1950). Computing Machinery and Intelligence. *Mind; A Quarterly Review of Psychology and Philosophy*, *59*(236), 433–460. DOI: 10.1093/mind/LIX.236.433

Ukanwa, K., & Rust, R. T. (2020). Algorithmic discrimination in service. SSRN *Electronic Journal*. DOI: 10.2139/ssrn.3654943

UNESCO. (2021). *Recommendation on the Ethics of Artificial Intelligence | UNESCO*. Www.unesco.org. https://www.unesco.org/en/articles/recommendation-ethics-artificial-intelligence

Van Woerkom, W., Grossi, D., Prakken, H., & Verheij, B. (2024). A fortiori case-based reasoning: From theory to data. *Journal of Artificial Intelligence Research*, *81*, 401–441. DOI: 10.1613/jair.1.15178

Wang, H., Fu, T., Du, Y., Gao, W., Huang, K., Liu, Z., Chandak, P., Liu, S., Van Katwyk, P., Deac, A., Anandkumar, A., Pande, V. S., & Zitnik, M. (2023). Scientific discovery in the age of artificial intelligence. *Nature*, *620*(7972), 47–60. DOI: 10.1038/s41586-023-06221-2 PMID: 37532811

Weible, C. M., Sabatier, P. A., Jenkins-Smith, H. C., Nohrstedt, D., Henry, A. D., & deLeon, P. (2011). A Quarter Century of the Advocacy Coalition Framework: An Introduction to the Special Issue. *Policy Studies Journal: The Journal of the Policy Studies Organization*, *39*(3), 349–360. DOI: 10.1111/j.1541-0072.2011.00412.x

Weller, A. (2019). Transparency: Motivations and Challenges. *Explainable AI: Interpreting, Explaining and Visualising Deep Learning*, 23–40. DOI: 10.1007/978-3-030-28954-6_2

Witness, A. I. (2025, May 30). *AI Policy: How to Build a Responsible Framework for AI Use*. WitnessAI. https://witness.ai/blog/ai-policy/

Yar, M. A., Hamdan, M., Anshari, M., Fitriyani, N. L., & Syafrudin, M. (2024). Governing with Intelligence: The Impact of Artificial Intelligence on Policy Development. *Information (Basel)*, *15*(9), 556. DOI: 10.3390/info15090556

Ydersbond, I. M. (2025). Power Through Pressure: How Interconnection Became Part of the EU's Overarching Climate and Energy Policy. *Journal of Common Market Studies*, *63*(2), 624–644. DOI: 10.1111/jcms.13642

Yeung, K., & Bygrave, L. A. (2022). Demystifying the modernised European data protection regime: Cross-disciplinary insights from legal and regulatory governance scholarship., 16(1), 137–155. *Regulation & Governance*, *16*(1), 137–155. DOI: 10.1111/rego.12401

Zahariadis, N. (2019). The Multiple Streams Framework. In Sabatier, P. A. (Ed.), *Theories of the Policy Process* (1st ed., pp. 65–92). Routledge., DOI: 10.4324/9780367274689-3

Zawacki-Richter, O., Marín, V. I., Bond, M., & Gouverneur, F. (2019). Systematic review of research on artificial intelligence applications in higher education – where are the educators? *International Journal of Educational Technology in Higher Education*, *16*(1), 39. DOI: 10.1186/s41239-019-0171-0

Zhang, J., Busck, A. G., & Kristensen, S. B. P. (2025). Integrating Farmers into Contract Farming in Peripheral Rural Areas in China. *Land (Basel)*, *14*(5), 976. DOI: 10.3390/land14050976

Zhou, X., Liu, M., Yurtsever, E., Zagar, B. L., Zimmer, W., Cao, H., & Knoll, A. C. (2024). Vision language models in autonomous driving: A survey and outlook. *IEEE Transactions on Intelligent Vehicles*, 1–20. DOI: 10.1109/TIV.2024.3402136

Chapter 12

Navigating Job Displacement in the Circular Economy:
Ethical AI and the Future of Work

Sharad Kumar
http://orcid.org/0000-0002-0037-3785
Karnavati University, India

Aditya Jadeja
http://orcid.org/0009-0008-9238-9741
Karnavati University, India

Supriya Singh
http://orcid.org/0000-0002-9650-235X
Karnavati University, India

ABSTRACT

The chapter starts from risk identification and proceeds to analyse the strategic and ethical and policy-based solutions that US and Asian and African case studies offer. The analysis considers various critical levers which encompass ethical AI development practices and workforce reskilling and algorithmic transparency and inclusive labour policy frameworks. The multi-stakeholder ethical model agenda requires involvement from policymakers and businesses and technologists and educators to achieve equitable transitions in the AI-driven economy. The chapter investigates how human people and intelligent technologies exchange "agreement" about controlling human agency and maintaining human dignity and providing human access to an AI-driven environment.

DOI: 10.4018/979-8-2600-2811-7.ch012

1. INTRODUCTION

Artificial intelligence and automation are increasingly changing worldwide labour markets. These technologies are no longer limited to experimental applications. They are progressively integrated in core economic activities across manufacturing, services, education, healthcare, and public administration. Advances in machine learning, data analytics, robotics, and generative systems have broadened the range of tasks that can be executed by intelligent machines. Consequently, work processes are being reorganized at a faster rate than ever. This shift has fuelled debates on productivity, employment, and the future of work in both the advanced and developing economies. Artificial intelligence and automation are increasingly changing the worldwide labour market. (Acemoglu & Restrepo, 2020; Brynjolfsson, Rock, & Syverson, 2021; World Economic Forum, 2023).

Spread of AI-based automation has been closely linked to productivity gains. Organizations apply AI technology to increase efficiency, enhance decision-making, and decrease operational expenses. There is evidence that AI could improve the quality of outputs, foster innovation, and enable novel business models (Brynjolfsson, Rock, & Syverson, 2021; Agrawal, Gans, & Goldfarb, 2019). However, these gains are also uneven across the board. Productivity increases are frequently accompanied by work force polarization, skill mismatches, and job insecurity. High-skilled workers are expected to benefit from augmentation opportunities enabled by AI, while low- and medium-skilled workers are exposed to an increasing risk of displacement (Marguerit, 2025; IOE, 2024). This are tension between economic efficiency and social stability is central to modern AI debates.

Ethics are now intertwined with the discussion of AI and automation. Implications for fairness, transparency, accountability and human agency (Floridi et al., 2021) in decisions are raised with the use of agent-based systems. Predictive decision-making might reinforce existing inequalities, or introduce novel forms of exclusion. Labour relations are increasingly affecpted by workplace surveillance, the commodification of labour data and opaque automated system (Zuboff, 2019; Kellogg, Valentine, & Christin, 2020). The ethical risks are not collateral. These are not bugs to be fixed but are inscribed in the very ways AI systems are designed and governed and used within and across in and organisational contexts (Machucho & Ortiz, 2025; Bashynska, 2024). Addressing these risks requires moving beyond technical measures of performance toward more comprehensive socio-economic and ethical evaluation.

In order to effectively mitigate these issues, it is essential to have well- defined understandings. Artificial intelligence refers to the area of study focused on systems that can independently analyse data, learn from it, and generate outputs capable of affecting enviroments or decisions. Modern AI systems adopt the model of goal-oriented agents (IOE, 2024), they observe the world in their own way – perceive, infer, and act in a specific context to achieve given goals. In labor markets, AI appears mainly through two currently separate but likely converging channels: labour automation and labour augmentation. AI-based process automation aims to eliminate human labor by doing the work on its own. This logic is typically applied in routine, predictable and data-heavy jobs. Conversely, augmentation AI works along with human competency, enhancing decision making, creativity and problem solving. Augmentation supports the interaction of man with machine, it does not intend to replace the man (Marguerit, 2025).

Job displacement is a significant consequence of automation-driven AI adoption. Displacement relates to more than just job loss. It also involves the erosion of tasks, the restructuring of occupations and the degradation of jobs. Workers can lose autonomy, take a pay cut or have a stifled career without losing their job. The technological change does not equally cause job losses. Certain industries as well as places and individuals are affected more than others. The vulnerable workers are more susceptible to the negative impact of the changes, maybe because they have poor computer skills or have access to training. Such developments imply that we must have solutions to regulate AI in a manner that accounts for both the knock- on and direct consequences on employment (IOE, 2024; Larsson andamp; Hatzigeorgiou, 2025).

The argument will become even more difficult when the transformation of labour described in AI will be placed within the framework of the circular economy. Circular economy promotes sustainable production and consumption by increased efficiency of resources and by use of reuse, recycling and prevention of waste. Digital technologies and especially AI is often mentioned as the most important technology enabler of the circular systems. AI enables predictive maintenance, smart supply chains, resource management, and circular business models. However, the evaluation of the circular economy transitions can be deemed to be more attuned in nature to the environmental and less to the social outcomes. The social aspects in particular labour, are completely under-researched (Roberts et al., 2024; Bashynska, 2024).

This disproportionality represents a important gap in research. The environmental benefits linked with AI- enabled circularity are extensively discussed, but the ethical issues of the AI-induced labour displacement in the circular economies are underdeveloped. Circular shifts have the perversely increase labour precarity in case automation, instead of social protection, is a priority. Discourse of sustainability is able to co-opt dispossession in the name of ecological modernization. In the absence of ethical grounding, circular-economic pathways can reproduce inequalities rather than promote inclusive development (Roberts et al., 2024; Larsson & Hatzigeorgiou, 2025). This disjuncture highlights the need for a normative perspective that combines environmental sustainability and social justice.

The aim of this chapter is to contribute to filling that gap by analyzing AI-driven job displacement through an ethics of care perspective in a circular economy context. The chapter makes three core contributions. First, it clearly differentiates automation from substitution routes and assesses their respective impacts in terms of jobs. Second, it brings ethical AI principles into circularity thinking to highlight social, rather than only environmental, sustainability. Third, it suggests governance responses that promote just transition, workforce resilience, and inclusive innovation. It builds on insights from labour economics, AI ethics and the studies on sustainability and provides an interdisciplinary outlook on future of work in AI-driven circular systems.

The structure of this chapter is as follows. Background on the circular economy, and its confluence with digital transformation, is provided in the next section. The subsequent sections explore the AI labour disruptive effect, occupational inequalities, and automation versus augmentation. Once ethical and policy issues have been brought up, the attention shifts to response and multi-stakeholder governance approaches. The chapter concludes with the discussion of the road toward a just and inclusive AI-enabled circular economy and the future research agendas.

2. UNDERSTANDING THE CIRCULAR ECONOMY FRAMEWORK

The circular economy has already taken a central place in the global environmental framework. It covers the structure limitations of the linear economics based on extraction design, production, consumption, and disposal. The outcome of this linear thinking has caused an incredible destruction of the environment, loss of resources and society instability. In the circular economy, the objective is, on the contrary, to model the economies that operate within the ecological parameters. It is a matter of renewal not consumption. The system celebrates long-term resilience instead of short-term effectiveness (Roberts et al., 2024).

Principles when you reduce it to the bare bones, there are few principles that do not entirely conflict that inform the circular economy. These are; resources efficiency, minimizing wastages, prolongation of the product life and closed material circulation loo. Value is stored within the system when goods, parts and materials are used as long as it is possible. They are encouraged to repair, reuse, remanufacture, and recycle instead of disposing. They also use systematic strategies in that they realize that production and consumption are not individual processes but components of a system (Bashynska, 2024). These values shift sustainability to more than incremental improvement and to radical change.

Circular economy models are not merely a technical solution to the shift in linear ones. It constitutes a total re-engineering of the way companies conduct their business, the mode of operation of supply chains and the way institutions are run. Linear models assign environmental and social costs to the periphery. Circular models attempt to take them in. Alterations necessary to this change involve changes in product design, organizational strategy, regulatory regimes and consumer behavior. It is also necessary that firms should move beyond value creation models that are based on ownership to service-based and performance-based models. These shifts are complex and can even be disturbing, and this is particularly true of industries that require workers (Roberts et al., 2024).

Digital technology is a very important facilitator of this change. The coming data analytics, sensor and digital platforms offer more transparency either on the value chain or on the consumers. They help companies trace the material movement, monitor the use of products and enhance the efficiency of resources. The most salient of these technologies is that of artificial intelligence.AI systems are used for predictions on maintenance, demand, intelligent sorting, and dynamic resource allocation. These functionalities contribute to expanding the operational viability of circular initiatives in scale (Machucho & Ortiz, 2025).

Artificial intelligence facilitates circular systems by enabling decision making in complexity. VA Circular value chains Unlike VA linear value chains, circular value chains comprise several agents, feedback loops and uncertainty. AI can analyse massive amounts of data to find inefficiencies and maximize the system performance. In production, AI facilitates circular manufacturing, by detecting defects, optimizing procedures and assessing life cycles. Standard applications of AI in production include defect detection, process optimization and life cycle assessment, which facilitate circular manufacturing. AI also supports circular goals in supply chains by providing adaptive logistics and inventory management that take circular principles into consideration. These cases show that AI may be a technology and organizational ground breaker for circular transformation (Roberts et al., 2024).

Nevertheless, the implication of AI in circular systems also poses new socio-economic dilemmas. Digitalisation contributes to resource efficiency but changes the structure of labour demand and the organisation of work. The demand for routine work may be reduced through automation of such work as sorting, monitoring and optimizing. In the meantime, there are also new skills requirements in such areas as data analysis, system management and digital coordination. This shift brings about a split labour production on both job and area of workforce. The presence of the well-intended but accidental circular transitions may enhance labour disparities (Larsson and Hatzigeorgiou, 2025).

Thus the labour implications of circular economy transitions are immense. Circular business models emphasize on efficiency, flexibility, and technology intensity. These emphases may also privilege capital over labour if the social moments are ignored. Labor in more traditional production positions may be subject to displacement or deskilling. Informal workers who repair, recycle, or handle waste may be put at further risk of exploitation if circular systems grow more automated. These vulnerabilities support the urgency of ensuring labor and circular economy accountability.

We thus argue that the social sustainability aspect must be included along with the environmental sustainability aspect in circular systems. Environmental performance is therefore not a good proxy for sustainability. A circular economy which cuts emissions at the cost of weakening job quality would not be sustainable morally. Social sustainability refers to aspects such as decent work, inclusion, equity and the well-being of people. It means that workers share in and benefit from economic transformation. Ethical circularity requires attention to quality job, access to reskilling, and equitable distribution of value gained through technological innovation (Bashynska, 2024).

The invisibilization of social aspects ties back to a more general constraint in circular economy science and policy- making. Many of the frameworks aim to optimize material and energy use, let treatment of labor be an adaptive variable. The danger here is that we wind up endorsing the destruction of jobs as the price of environmental responsibility. Such logic obscures the moral duty of corporations and governments. Circular transitions are influenced by design decisions. They are not technology determined. The confluence of circularity, ethical AI governance and labor protections has the potential to angle circular strategies in the direction of inclusive models (Roberts et al., 2024).

The growing integration of artificial intelligence (AI), job displacement, and the circular economy (CE) has required a substantial body of scholarship since 2022. Researchers have found this integration from various angles- empirical labour market studies, ethical analyses, and the transition of the workforce, and sustainability-related views- all together indicating a relationship that is both transformative and deeply debated.

Chen et al. (2022) give a fundamental empirical input through an occupational-level analysis of 701 detailed occupations in US, finding how AI -induced displacement risk impacts wages and unemployment and whether digital skills can regulate this impact. Using fixed-effects modelling and heterogeneity analysis, the study found that AI displacement risk has a considerably negative effect on occupational wages and employment, that Varied impacts across occupational features are significant, and that digital skills have a meaningful moderating effect in safeguarding workers against the displacement risk. The study's core policy implication – that digital skills must be incorporated in education and training systems-is directly relevant to the circular economy context, where new green and data-oriented roles increasingly require competencies that the existing workforce may lack.

Expanding this individual-level insight to the organisational aspect, Morandini et al. (2023) investigate the effect of AI on workers' skills through the lens of upskilling and reskilling within the organisation. The research proposes that reskilling is an important process for organisations introducing AI systems, as it supports employees in adjusting to technology-related changes, helping them formulate the knowledge and skills required to work effectively with the technology. This finding is specifically applicable to the circular economy transitions, where AI-enabled automation of tasks in areas such as waste sorting, predictive maintenance, and supply chain enhancement in restructuring current job roles. The authors stressed that the pace and effectiveness of reskilling programmes will determine factor in whether AI adoption broadens or narrows labour market inequalities.

From a sustainability governance point of view, Roberts et al. (2024) published a critical analysis in AI & society examining the ethical dimensions of AI Execution in support of the circular economy. This research argues that AI is an important enabler for the circular economy, aiding in the design of sustainable products, supporting new circular business models, and supporting the broader infrastructure needed to scale circularity. Adding to this author's emphasis, the workforce implications are integrated in the transition. The authors note that the present reskilling measures are left mainly to individual organisations, that these measures can help manage prompt business needs but are inadequate for managing longer-term professional shifts due to their recurring disconnect and limited focus, and that sector-wide skills councils could give a stronger base for addressing the structural change needed by the circular economy. The institutional evaluation draws attention to the governance gap between AI's technical promise and the social infrastructure required to assure an inclusive circular change.

Olawade et al. (2025) present a narrative review investigating the role of AI in enhancing the circular economy within the waste management sector, examining peer-reviewed literature from 2015 to 2025. The review highlights ethical issues around the potential displacement of workers due to automation in material recovery facilities, which may decrease the demand for manual labour and result in losses of jobs, specifically impacting low-skilled and vulnerable populations. The authors propose a just transition framework that promotes the importance of retraining and upskilling programs to support displaced workers in adapting to new positions related to AI system management, maintenance, or data analysis, while also supporting social safety nets and fair distribution of efficiency improvements during these transitions.

To sum up, circular economy presents a good road to sustainable development. Its success shows just how well environmental, technical and social systems can integrate. Digital technologies and AI are strong enablers for circularity, but they are also reshaping the labour market. To ignore these facts is to undermine normative sustainability. Social sustainability is essential in the transition to circular economy.

For only in this way can we make sure that ecological progress and human progress go hand in hand.

2.1 Sustainability and Circular Economy Perspective

From the lens (perspective) of the circular economy, AI plays a critical role in improving resource efficiency, reducing waste, and enabling sustainable production systems. Technologies such as data-driven maintenance, smart logistics, and automated recycling systems assist in minimizing environmental impact while enhancing resource utilization (Roberts et al., 2024).

However, sustainability in the circular economy must extend beyond environmental outcomes to consider social dimensions, specifically labour. An AI-driven circular economy that enhances efficiency at the cost of job quality or employee well-being cannot be considered truly sustainable.

Hence, integrating ethical AI fundamentals with circular economy strategies is crucial to ensure that technological advancements lead to equitable development. This requires equilibrating productivity gains with social protection and fair distribution of benefits

3. AI DISRUPTION IN THE LABOR MARKET

AI is redefining job roles in global labor markets. Unlike previous types of mechanization, artificial intelligence is as much about hands as brains. And it is not limited to any particular industry or community. Instead, it is a general-purpose technology with systemic labour consequences. Advances in machine learning, robotics and generative software have extended the range of what can be automated or augmented. This growth has amplified concerns with job security and quality as well as workforce restructuring (International Organisation of Employers [IOE], 2024).

The AI-induced automation trend has created visible effects which already affect various industrial sectors. Organizations need to apply AI technology for cost automation because it helps them achieve better operational speed and consistent performance. Automated decision-making systems now perform human judgment functions to handle scheduling operations, logistics management, customer service, and quality control for standard tasks. The current market trends demonstrate that capitalist organizations follow a basic system to boost their market competition efficiency. But automation adoption also varies. The system operates differently depending on the business sector, company scale, and established institutional systems. The implementation of AI technology progresses more swiftly in large businesses because they possess both financial resources and established data systems than small to medium-sized businesses (Machucho & Ortiz, 2025).

To analyze AI-driven labor upheaval, we need to go beyond occupation-level assessment. Conventional labor market analyses assume entire occupations are destroyed or emergence. AI challenges this approach. Most athletes knuckle down on a daunting number of tasks, each of which can be automated at differing degrees. Task-based analysis therefore offers a better lens. Rather than whole jobs, AI systems tend to automate tasks. The most vulnerable tasks are those that are routine, repetitive, and rule-bound. Non-routine work that involves social interaction, creativity, or contextual situational judgment such as R&D or performing arts is not (Marguerit, 2025).

Part of the task-based nature of displacement that occupational-based displacement has is consequences. Statistics on the level of occupations may conceal the extent of disruption, if tasks within occupations are being eroded. Workers, who may be employed, but change where they work within the task, skill, and quality of work space spheres of this are of their jobs or of their work objects. This kind of displacement is slow and usually unseen. It is wages, autonomy, and career trajectories who are displaced, not the employed per se. Task-level displacement thus stands as a substantial but underappreciated arena of AI-enhanced workforce transformation (IOE, 2024).

In manufacturing, the rise of AI-based automation is amplifying long-established trends. Intelligent robots, computer vision and predictive maintenance are now part of the production processes. These techniques and tools minimize manual labor associated with assembly, inspection and material handling (3). Manufacturing work has become more divided. Demand increases for highly skilled technicians, engineers and system operators. And low-skilled production jobs are going the way of the dodo at the same time. This reshaping exacerbates skill intensification and spatial disparities – particularly so in the industrial economies facing circular and digital transformations (Larsson & Hatzigeorgiou, 2025).

Retail has seen a different type of disruption. AI is deployed for inventory management, demand prediction, dynamic pricing, and customer data analysis. Automated checkout and online systems have reduced the need for on-the-floor sales staff. Concurrently, new positions arise in logistics, platform management and data-enriched marketing. So the impact on employment is mixed. Retail employees are increasingly subjected to greater performance monitoring, and job insecurity. Algorithmic management also changes the intensity of work and scheduling methods, and has raised ethical issues regarding worker autonomy (Akwiri, 2024).

The broadest reach of AI disruption is shown in the services sector. AI-driven chatbots, virtual assistants, and recommendation systems have redefined customer service, finance, healthcare, and hospitality. Routine service interactions are automated more and more. Human employees are reskilled and redeployed to tackle more complex or emotionally draining jobs. Although the emerging habit can enhance service quality, it also brings expectations for multitasking and emotional labor. Service work may be intensified rather than eliminated. These trends complicate simple narratives of jobs lost or created (Brandao, 2025).

Science was once thought to be largely impervious to mechanization. That premise no longer holds true. Generative AI systems are taking on roles in content creation, data analysis, legal drafting, and financial reporting. The AI-induced automation trend has created visible effects that already affect various industrial sectors. Organizations need to apply AI technology for cost automation because it helps them achieve better operational speed and consistent performance. Automated decision-making systems now perform human judgment functions to handle scheduling operations, logistics management, customer service, and quality control for standard tasks. The current market trends demonstrate that capitalist organizations follow a basic system to boost their market competition efficiency. But automation adoption also varies. The system operates differently depending on the business sector, company scale, and established institutional systems. The implementation of AI technology progresses more swiftly in large businesses because they possess both financial resources and established data systems than small to medium-sized businesses (Machucho & Ortiz, 2025).

The research evidence demonstrates that artificial intelligence produces various effects on working population members who possess different levels of skills. The research evidence shows that automation-based AI systems produce their largest effects on workers who operate in low-skill and medium-skill positions. The financial benefits from Augmentation activities appear to flow directly toward employees who possess advanced expertise and show additional complementary capabilities. The growing wage gap between workers results from AI technology delivering better returns to workers who understand how to operate these systems. In fact, these patterns exacerbate existing inequalities rather than turning into efficiency-equalizing ones. Labor market institutions are also important in mediating these effects through education, training, and social protection systems (IOE, 2024).

Short-run labour market impacts of AI adoption often are job displacements, task reallocations, and transitional unemployment. Firms focus on getting quick efficiency gains and let go of people in the impacted roles. Adjustment costs are borne by workers, who lose income and whose skills may become obsolete. These are the most significant effects on places that have minimal infrastructure for reskilling. Thus, short-period disturbances call for appropriate governmental interventions in order to prevent permanent withdrawal from labor markets (Akwiri, 2024).

The effects on the labor market over longer periods are less straightforward. There is no a priori reason to believe that technological change should not lead to other types of jobs historically. System, software, and platform developers, overseers, and integrators, AI drives demand for new jobs in... But these jobs require a high level of skill; not a lot of displaced workers are likely to be able to make a direct transition to them. Otherwise, the long-run effects could include structural unemployment and entrenched inequality if people do not invest in education and lifelong learning. So, benefits in the long run are contingent rather than automatic (Larsson & Hatzigeorgiou, 2025).

Governance choices shape the interaction between AI and labour markets. There is no technological imperative for AI-driven disruption. Design choices, regulatory environments and business strategies all shape job results. Substitution is the highest potential impact of automation-related deployment. Deployment for bulking up supports human–AI collaboration. The relative strength of these pathways controls whether AI aggravates or attenuates labor market disruption. Ethics considerations are thus core to employment outcomes, rather than secondary concerns (Machucho & Ortíz, 2025).

In sum, AI is reshaping labour markets through multifaceted, uneven processes. This effect is not consistent for all tasks, occupation and industries. Manufacturing, retail, services and knowledge work have all displayed different patterns of disruption. There is growing empirical evidence suggesting the increasing inequality between those workers who benefit from AI and those who bear its costs. There are short-term disruptions and long-term structural changes. Grasping these dynamics will be crucial to building ethical, inclusive, sustainable AI-powered economic systems.

Case Study 1: Amazon Warehousing and AI-Driven Automation (left)

One of the prominent and widely cited real-world cases of AI-driven labour transformation is Amazon's use of robotics and artificial intelligence in its warehousing functions. Amazon has implemented over 750,000 robotic systems throughout its global fulfilment centres, notably rising functional efficiency and reducing processing time (Amazon, 2023). These AI- backed robots conduct tasks such as sorting, packaging, and inventory management, which were manually carried out by employees.

While this automation has improved productivity, it has resulted to significant changes in labour demand. Reports show that warehouse automation has decreased the need for regular manual roles, which simultaneously raises the demand for higher-skilled positions such as robotics technicians, data analysts, and system engineers (International Federation of Robotics, 2023). For example, Amazon has invested over 41.2 billion in workforce upskilling programs, targeting to train employees for advanced technical roles (Amazon, 2023).

This case emphasizes the dual nature of AI adoption -while automation displaces low-skilled labour, it also creates opportunities for skill enhancement and new job roles. Additionally, the change is not always equitable, as employees lacking access to reskilling initiatives may face job uncertainty and income loss. This indicates broader concerns about workplace inequality and the uneven distribution of AI gains across the workforce.

Case Study 2: AI in Agriculture in India (Precision Farming)

In developing countries such as India, the adoption of AI in agriculture offers a clear case of improvement rather than automation. AI-based precision farming technologies, such as crop monitoring systems, predictive analytics, and mechanized irrigation, are increasingly being used to enhance productivity and use resources efficiently.

As per the report by NITI Aayog (2021), AI applications in Indian agriculture can increase crop yields by up to 20-30% while decreasing input costs such as water and fertilizers. Organisations and startups are using AI tools to give farmers real-time insights on weather patterns, the health of soil, and pest control

However, the adoption of such technologies also bypasses labour dynamics. While AI reduces dependency on manual labour for routine agricultural work, it simultaneously creates demand for digitally skilled employees who have the potential to function and manage these systems. The challenge lies in assuring that small and marginal farmers have access to digital infrastructure and training, without which AI adoption may intensify rural inequality.

This case indicates how AI can back circular economy goals by improving resource efficiency and reducing waste, while also emphasizing the need for inclusive policies to assure equitable labour outcomes.

3.1 Long-Term Labour Market Transformations

AI is projected to fundamentally reshape labour markets over the long term, moving forward, with short-term job displacement towards structural transition. Unlike previous technological revolution's, AI impacts both manual and cognitive work, resulting in reconfiguration of job roles instead of complete job elimination (Acemoglu & Restrepo, 2020).

Over time, labour markets tend to experience three important and major transitions. First, there will be a shift from routine to non-routine work, where task-demanding creativity, problem-solving, and emotional intelligence will be more needed. Second, hybrid jobs roles integrating technical and human skills will become more common.

Third. Lifelong learning will become vital, as employees constantly adapt to evolving technological environments (World Economic Forum, 2023).

These transitions propose that the future of work will not be specified solely by jobs loss, but by the evolution of job. However, without adequate institutional support, such change my lead to structural unemployment and expanding inequality.

3.2 Emerging Job Roles in the AI Economy

The expansion of AI technologies is also generating new employment opportunities across various sectors. Emerging job roles include:

The expansion of artificial intelligence is generating a range of latest service opportunities that need both technical expertise and multidisciplinary abilities. Among the most notable roles are AI and machine learning experts, who are accountable for designing, developing, and improving intelligent systems that assist automation and decision-making processes. These experts play a significant role in shaping how AI technologies are positioned across industries.

Adding to this, data scientists and analysts are moreover in demand, as organizations depend on large-scale data to train to AI models and extract actionable findings. Their role Expands beyond technical analysis to strategy-based decision making, making them crucial in AI-driven business environments.

In addition, AI ethics and governance experts are acquiring importance as organizations and governments strive to address issues of fairness, transparency, and accountability in AI applications. These professionals support to policy development, risk assessment, and ethical auditing of AI systems.

Finally, robotics engineers and technical personnel are important in supporting the physical implementation of AI technologies, specifically in manufacturing and logistics. Their role consists of system design, monitoring, and maintenance of automated systems, assuring operational efficiency and safety.

According to the World Economic Forum (2023), roles related to artificial intelligence, data, and sustainability are among the fastest-growing job categories globally, highlighting the transformative impact of AI on employment structures.

As per the World Economic Forum (2023), roles related to data, artificial intelligence, and sustainability are among the rapidly growing job categories worldwide. These roles needs advanced technical skills as well as interdisciplinary knowledge, emphasizing the significance of education and reskilling measures.

However, access to these emergent opportunitics rcmains uneven, with high-skilled employees gaining more benefits than low-skilled employees, thereby reinforcing current inequalities.

4. OCCUPATIONAL INEQUALITY AND VULNERABLE GROUPS

Transformations in the labor market driven by AI have brought with them the deepening of occupational inequality. Change brought about by technology does not influence all labor in the same way. Rather, it is a matter of reshuffling risk and opportunity along pre-existing socio-economic cleavage lines. Artificial intelligence escalates these discriminations by awarding value to a particular set of skills, roles and types of capital and devaluing others. Hence, the extent of technological feasibility and structural vulnerability in labour markets is also reflected in occupational inequality (Larsson & Hatzigeorgiou, 2025).

Occupational disparities in risk of labour market exclusion have been termed 'occupational inequality'. Such threats include job elimination, task encroachment, wage compression, and weakened bargaining power. Automating with AI exacerbates those threats by enabling automation of tasks that are routine, predictable, and codifiable. These are the jobs that are most vulnerable to being generalized. By contrast, activities that required complex judgment, creativity, and social interaction were subject to some degree of insulation or amplification (Marguerit, 2025). The distinction reshuffles rather than does away with existing occupational hierarchies.

There are more low-skilled working roles at risk due to disruption caused by AI. Several low-skilled positions are dependent on repetitive manual or mental effort-based tasks. These are jobs that can be readily automated with robotics, machine learning and algorithmic management platforms. As AI displaces such work, demand for low-skilled labor is falling. Workers are losing jobs or moving down the employment ladder. Transitions are challenging due to limited educational opportunities and pathways for reskilling. This interplay is compounding cycles of precarity and exclusion (International Organisation of Employers [IOE], 2024).

Women are uniquely vulnerable to the changing dynamics of labor markets predicted by AI. Gender segregation within employment means that women are more likely than men to work in administration, clerical or service positions. The following work positions face the highest risk of being automated. Women face barriers that prevent them from learning digital skills and getting technical training opportunities. The historical data that supports algorithmic systems contains gender biases that these systems will perpetuate. As a result, the implementation of AI technology threatens to make existing workplace gender discrimination problems between men and women more severe when it comes to job quality, salary differences and career development opportunities (Akwiri, 2024; Brandao, 2025).

Older workers face a rising risk that threatens their ability to continue working in their current positions. The digital literacy and training attendance patterns of different age groups create obstacles which prevent them from maintaining their essential skills for AI-driven transformation. Older workers face discrimination through the false belief which states they will resist change and require more expensive training than others. Older employees develop greater risk of losing their jobs and face permanent employment loss when they reach higher age levels. More people start to leave their jobs before they reach retirement age. The developing trend creates problems for elderly citizens because it threatens their financial stability and their social participation in countries that experience fast technological development (Larsson & Hatzigeorgiou, 2025).

The lower-income groups experience the most severe occupational discrimination because of their economic status. People who earn different amounts can access education and technology and social security benefits according to their financial situation. People who work at jobs of low-income families face higher dangers of their positions becoming automated for replacement. The group experiences two main obstacles because they face tough income shocks and they struggle to get funding for their retraining programs. The combination of AI work interruptions and rising economic differences creates two major problems which affect the workforce and people's monetary stability. The interaction between these elements creates problems for the idea that technological development automatically leads to economic growth which benefits everyone (IOE, 2024). The digital divide is a key factor shaping job-related disparity. Availability of digital infrastructure, training courses and learning environments differ significantly between rural and urban areas as well as among different groups of people. Disconnected workers are being locked out of new AI-augmented jobs. Even if there are training programs, barriers to participation remain: cost, time commitments and institutional constraints. The digital divide thus turns technological change into a means of social stratification rather than mobility (Machucho & Ortiz, 2025).

Reskilling is often touted as the fix for AI-driven inequality. However, reskilling is not evenly accessible. The highly skilled participate in employer-sponsored training and ongoing education. At-risk employees tend to depend on public programs, which are typically underfunded or mismatched with the needs of the labor market. Reskilling efforts also assume the individual responsibility for adaptation by transferring risk away from institutions. This is a framing that erases systemic barriers and moral duties toward displaced workers (Akwiri, 2024).

The intersection of Vulnerabilities under the gender, age, and income categories appears in tandem. Low-income women or older women are twice as oppressed. Intersectionality exacerbates where and how someone can be displaced and in recovery. AI systems developed in the absence of diverse perspectives will likely have the unintended consequence of reinforcing those intersecting inequalities. Therefore, ethical AI governance has to be seen in terms of differentiated implications on its body of relations among social groups-specific rather than universal solutions to the governance question the possibility of universal solutions to the governance question (Brandao, 2025).

The ethics of disproportionate displacement are compelling. Differential risk exposure in technology raises issues of fairness, justice, and liability. Gains in efficiency from AI favor firms and high-skilled workers, while the costs are socialized and borne by vulnerable populations. This kind of asymmetry challenges the moral justification for AI deployment. Its ethical evaluation needs to go beyond the aggregate matter of productivity to the matter of distribution and human dignity (Bashynska, 2024).

The social bonds between people face danger because of differential displacement which also blocks their ability to move through social ranks. Mcgregor identified that occupational discrimination functions as the base that supports both institutional trust and technological trust. The lack of assistance for displaced workers makes them likely to oppose technological changes. The resistance shown in this situation will create obstacles that will prevent social stability from achieving permanent success with innovative solutions. The solution to control social inequalities requires ethical governance systems that should protect workers and include all people in design processes and establish democratic decision-making structures according to IOE 2024.

The final analysis shows that AI-based labour conversion systems do not create occupational segregation as an unplanned outcome. The main results emerge from how society distributes its workforce abilities between different work environments and social circles and institutional power structures. The risks create an unfair distribution of harm because they primarily affect defenceless people who include unskilled labourers and women and senior citizens and members of economically disadvantaged groups. To solve these social disparities, need to create AI and circular economy policies that operate through ethical decision-making systems. Sociological knowledge needs to integrate with technological progress because society will continue to experience the same social inequalities that have existed throughout history.

5. AUTOMATION VS. AUGMENTATION: A COMPARATIVE LENS

Two logics, distinct yet related, drive how artificial intelligence is changing work. These logics are augmented and autonomous. They need to be distinguished to adequately evaluate their effects on the labor market. The distinction also explains why the employment effects of AI penetration are so variable across industries and social groups. It also shows how design and governance decisions can determine whether AI displaces or supports workers (Marguerit, 2025).

AI focused on automation is on a substitution logic. It is intended to substitute human work in certain established activities or procedures. This logic embodies the pursuit of efficiency, velocity, and uniformity. Tasks are performed by automated systems, which do not need human intervention after they are installed for any step in the process. Human intervention is reduced to none. The best performing Automation AIs in the world are realized in environments where the future is known, real-world experience programming rules have been developed, and the rules can be commanded. These include robotic assembly, automated customer service, algorithmic scheduling, and data-driven decision-making systems (International Organisation of Employers [IOE], 2024).

The logic of replacement that underpins automation AI carries some important implications for jobs and employment. If tasks are automated, too, human labor will be in even less demand. Adoption is driven by the desire to reduce costs. Companies might downsize their workforces or restructure work around the monitoring of machines. But it comes at a time when the benefits of automation are increasingly are pooled at the organizational level. Workers are laid off, deskilled, or have less control over their work. Those outcomes compound pre-existing labour market disparities (Akwiri, 2024).

Complementarity-based AI-human labour social relation Augmentation – Based AI The complementarity logic Augmentation-Oriented AI According to the complementarity logic, which aims to maximize efficiency, labour and capital (technology) should be combined to utilize their respective advantages. Instead of substituting for the workers, it extends human possibilities. AI-based tools also facilitate decision-making, pattern recognition, and problem-solving. Nonetheless, task implementation and judgments still rely on humans. It's the Contrasting View: Augmentation AI is meant to operate with people. It boosts output but doesn't replace people. It is based on the fact that human and machine intelligence should work together (Marguerit, 2025).

The complementarity logic has different effects on labour. Result quality can be improved through augmentation by reducing cognitive load and repetitive motion. Workers are better equipped with sophisticated analytical tools to perform better. What humans do better (creativity, empathy, context) becomes scarcer. The augmentation, as a skill deepener, is as opposite to skill erosion. However, the access to its augmentation benefits is a privileged one and mostly reserved for the high-skilled workers with digital literacy (Brandao, 2025).

These are benefits that can be measured, and measured quickly. Gains of augmentation are slower Buffered (later) productivity improvements from augmentation More gradual productivity improvements are produced from augmentation. Resulting improvements include higher quality decisions, fewer errors, and increased innovation. Although less immediate, augmentation-enhanced productivity tend to be more enduring and sensitive to time (Machucho & Ortiz, 2025)

Outcomes in terms of quality of work are also heterogeneous. Automation-oriented execution may decrease work complexity The remaining roles are all surveillance or maintenance. Autonomy of workers diminishes with increasing algorithmic control. By contrast, enhancement serves to increase in task diversity and cognitive participation. Workers have agency and accountability. Enhanced positions have a better chance of offering meaningful work and opportunities for long-term career advancement. These are crucial differences in terms of assessing ethical AI implementation (Bashynska, 2024).

Skill acquisition is another major area of divergence. Automation reduces the requirement for people to perform repetitive tasks. People lose their existing skills when organizations fail to provide training programs which enable them to learn new abilities. The demand for advanced technical abilities has created an expanding gap between different types of skills which society needs. The educational method of Augmentation supports students to expand their knowledge base throughout their entire life. Workers develop hybrid skills through their ability to combine professional knowledge from their main field with digital competencies. The system creates flexible skill networks which replace traditional job frameworks according to Larsson and Hatzigeorgiou (2025).

Automation systems generate lower employee payments through their ability to duplicate human work which people do during their daily activities. The distribution of productivity gains between capital owners and top skilled workers has created a rising trend of wage inequality. The research shows that AI-led automation systems create decreasing wage patterns throughout their operational systems. The process of augmentation creates wage effects which produce more inclusive results for all workers. Workers who create direct value through their work receive a portion of productivity improvements which become shared benefits. Research outcomes will produce different results based on how organizations handle their operations and their ability to negotiate with each other according to Marguerit (2025) and IOE (2024).

The latest research studies have validated the current separation between these two fields. Research findings show that automated systems have extended their reach across different employment positions which require either basic or moderate professional expertise. The augmentation effects generate positive outcomes for employees who perform tasks which align with the functions of the AI system. Substitution oriented AI systems create job losses in routine work positions while they drive down wages for existing employees in these roles according to Marguerit (2025). Research studies which support policy development demonstrate that AI affects employment through its deployment methods rather than its actual technological capabilities (IOE, 2024).

The distinction between automation and augmentation creates essential requirements which organizations need to build their future workforce plans. Organizations need to make strategic choices about their AI deployment locations. Automation delivers immediate operational improvements to companies yet it creates potential dangers which impact both public perception and social systems in the long term. Organizations need to show their dedication to employee training and organizational changes when they start their augmentation process. The system operates in agreement with the principles which support both inclusive economic development and strong workforce growth. The strategic coordination between human capital development and AI design needs to become a fundamental element of organizational operations according to Machucho and Ortiz (2025).

These systems are pivotal for determining the result. Automation-adjacent futures call for little worker investment, yet produce pressures for displacement. Futures that are oriented towards augmentation necessitate education systems that can teach digital literacy, critical thinking, and lifelong learning. Conventional teaching is not enough. Reskilling is a continuous process and so is cross-disciplinary learning. Collaboration is needed between higher education institutions and employers to equip the workforce for human-AI collaboration (Larsson & Hatzigeorgiou, 2025).

Ethical issues are relevant throughout this analogy. Automation promotes efficiency, but in doing so, it threatens to degrade our understanding of the worth of people when workers are conceptualized as disposable components. Augmentation is more consistent with ethical AI values, as it ensures agency and involvement. However, augmentation is not innately ethical. Without wider access, it can reproduce elite privilege. Therefore, ethical management should steer AI application in the direction of enhancement that is accessible to all (Bashynska, 2024).

To summarize, automation and augmentation are two very different paths of AI-based labor transformation. Automation is associated with replacement, efficiency, and cost saving. Augmentation focuses on complementarity, enhanced capabilities and collaboration. Their effects differ for productivity, job quality, skill formation and wages. Empirical analysis confirms that these results are driven by design choices and not technological determinism. Separating the two is key to understanding how to build ethical, inclusive, sustainable AI strategies for the future of work.

6. ETHICAL AND POLICY CHALLENGES OF AI-INDUCED DISPLACEMENT

AI-based displacements in the labor market. Contemporary labor market is fraught with uncertainties, challenges and even threats of AI-based displacements in the labor market 3. The spread of smart systems is also transforming the balance of power between firms, workers, and institutions. Such transformations call into question conceptions of what is fair, responsible, and socially protected. Ethical issues are embedded in both outcomes and the processes by which AI systems are developed and implemented. Governance is thus pivotal in assessing the appropriateness of AI-led labour transformation (International Organisation of Employers [IOE], 2024).

Algorithmic bias is a core ethical issue. AI systems are trained on historical data, which include existing social and labor market disparities. When used for hiring, task allocation or performance evaluation, biased models may reproduce discrimination against gender, age, or socio-economic status. These biases work at a very subtle level and are very difficult to discern. Individuals subjected to biased systems may also be disempowered from challenging algorithmic decisions. Bias, then, turns technical efficiency into a mechanism of structural exclusion (Brandao, 2025).

The level of transparency determines how people can detect bias in various situations. AI systems function as black boxes because their decision-making processes remain completely invisible to both users and regulatory bodies. The workers remain unaware about why their work assignments undergo changes while their salaries experience reductions and their positions disappear from existence. The lack of clear information creates obstacles for people to verify things properly which stops them from giving their proper consent. Technical systems lack transparency because it does not exist as a natural characteristic of these systems. The ethical requirement allows people to examine things while they can also challenge decisions and institutions remain under constant monitoring. The lack of transparency prevents accountability systems from working properly according to Machucho and Ortiz in their 2025 study.

Accountability adds another layer of difficulty. Displacement is AI-mediated when algorithms, organizational strategies, and market forces interact in complex ways. Responsibility is spread across the different players. The displacement may be credited to technology by firms. Developers may assert that they are neutral. Innovation imperatives may be appealing to policymakers who are reluctant to interfere. This dispersal of responsibility leads to a 'responsibility gap' so that no one actor 'owns' the risk of poor labour outcomes. To ensure ethical governance, a clear division of responsibilities at each stage of the AI value chain is needed (Bashynska, 2024).

Explainability is a complement to transparency and accountability. Explainable AI makes it possible for stakeholders to know how and why decisions were made. Explainability promotes procedural fairness in employment outcomes. They can challenge results and demand recourse from application outcomes. But believability is often sacrificed to boost performance. Complex models are less interpretable and therefore offer less value in understanding. Such trade-offs raise ethical questions about how much opacity in a system affecting livelihoods is acceptable (IOE, 2024).

The current set of labor protections don't translate well to this challenge. Labor laws were built around humans making decisions and stable employer-employee relations. The research findings demonstrate that the AI system produces results which prove both original hypotheses to be invalid. Algorithmic management has created a situation where employers and technology providers now operate as indistinguishable entities. The employee classification system faces rising complexity because platform-based work arrangements have entered the workforce. The system blocks workers who lost their jobs from receiving standard benefits which include both mandatory termination notices and company payment obligations and union negotiation rights. The existing regulatory frameworks have not managed to match the speed of technological development according to Larsson & Hatzigeorgiou (2025).

The policy toolkit lacks any direct equivalent for task-level displacement which functions as a separate entity. The current labor regulations focus on preventing workers from losing their jobs but they do not protect their work activities or their ability to perform their tasks properly. Employers have the power to terminate employees without any impact on their salary payments or their ability to work independently. The system allows for particular escapes which happen to evade all forms of monitoring. Social welfare systems fail to handle the regular population shifts which occur over time. The present restrictions prevent labor organizations from leading AI transformation solutions because they cannot effectively direct AI system development (Akwiri, 2024). The governance of AI itself is also fraught with gaps. Many national and international rules include exhortations to ethical principles without binding mechanisms. Voluntary code of conduct is non-binding. Regulatory responses commonly emphasize data protection and consumer rights and not labor effects. "Employment issues continue to take a backseat in AI governance discussions." This mismatch mirrors a general inclination to conceptualize labor as an adjustment variable rather than a safeguarded social space (Bashynska, 2024).

Moral responsibility is shared among different actors. Responsibility for deployment decisions and effects on the workforce lies with companies. But having a social obligation and earning a profit aren't mutually exclusive. Productivity gains from which firms benefit, and hence have incentives to mitigate displacement. This means investing in reskilling, retraining, and reliable transition strategies. Labor must feature in ethical AI adoption strategies (Machucho & Ortiz, 2025).

States are pivotal in determining ethical outcomes. Governments create regulatory frameworks that make certain types of AI use more attractive. There is a disincentive to regulate for substitution through automation. Good social policy is cohesive and based on social participation. States have the duty to revise labour standards, to finance retraining and to guarantee social protection. Public policy options, therefore, determine if AI serves to promote inclusive growth or to exacerbate inequality (IOE, 2024).

Developers are also ethically responsible. AI systems are not neutral objects. Values and assumptions are baked in by design decisions. Developers have a say in whether systems should prioritize efficiency over fairness or transparency over opacity. Ethical design is led by interdisciplinary efforts and an understanding of social implications. Addressing labour concerns in system design is part of responsible innovation (Brandao, 2025).

Compounding the difficulties is that many of these are in the 'Global South.' These scenarios are often characterized by combining high rates of AI adoption with low levels of institutional capacity. People frequently perform their duties through informal work arrangements. Social safety nets exist as minimal programs which provide insufficient protection to citizens. The process of workforce retraining has become more difficult because workers now face challenges when trying to acquire new skills. AI-enabled displacement creates an urgent need to protect workers because it leads to job losses which establish permanent social segregation between employed and unemployed people. The present time shows developing nations function as experimental sites which scientists use to study automated systems. The global inequality between countries becomes more complex because researchers must study technological development in different testing environments

Policy coordination faces its most difficult implementation process when operating in these particular environments. The enforcement process encounters obstacles because decentralized authority structure blocks its progress. The international agreements which countries sign fail to produce any impact on how their local communities operate. Transnational companies obtain business advantages through their ability to operate in different countries which have distinct regulatory environments. Developing nations need to create specific laws which will safeguard their communities from AI-based job elimination while they must establish international alliances to fight this problem. Organizations need to develop "Ethical AI" systems which will address worldwide workplace inequalities instead of maintaining the current social gaps (Akwiri, 2024).

So, to conclude, the ethical and public policy implications of displacement due to AI are complex and have converged. Algorithmic bias, opacity, and accountability gaps contribute to unfairness. Labor laws as they stand do not go far enough. Frameworks for the governance of AI ignore its effects on employment. Responsibility is diffused: it covers firms and states and developers. These challenges are magnified in developing countries. Responding to them requires a shift from abstract ethical ideals toward enforceable systems of governance that safeguard workers and support just transitions.

7. STRATEGIC RESPONSE MECHANISMS

The strategic responses to challenge the job market disruption from AI are to be consciously planned and broadly coordinated. To criticize is not enough. Without any countermeasure, inequality in labor markets could be reinforced and become embedded in the structure. Strategic intervention, then, must emphasize adaptability, inclusion, and long-horizon viability. These instruments are to converge technological development with social responsibility and ethical governance (International Organisation of Employers [IOE], 2024).

Workforce reskilling and upskilling is the most common recommendation for responding to AI-related disruption. As AI alters task demands, employees need to develop new skills. Reskilling prepares displaced workers for different jobs. Upskilling deepens skills – but within existing roles. Good programs address both technical and non-technical skills. Digital literacy, data analysis, and human–AI collaboration skills are becoming paramount. Nevertheless, re-skilling needs to be ongoing rather than episodic in order to be effective in rapidly evolving labour markets (Larsson & Hatzigeorgiou, 2025).

What makes upskilling programs more inclusive? Employer-led efforts in this space tend to best serve those who are already privileged. Marginalized communities confront obstacles of expense, time, and accessibility. A publicly funded program is thus needed to provide equal opportunity for everyone to get involved. Reskilling is a collective not individual responsibility. Ethical workforce policies also understand that companies that derive the greatest benefit from AI productivity improvements have the greatest responsibility in supporting workforce transition (Akwiri, 2024).

Lifelong learning is at the heart of employability maintenance. Traditional education is based on the idea that learning can be "bottled up" and consumed in the beginning. Skill renewal throughout life course the economy in the age of AI requires such renewal as a matter of course Universities must transform their educational programs because employment market requirements keep shifting. The interdisciplinary approach of combining technology with ethics and specialized knowledge through academic courses proves to be highly beneficial. The organizations serve as locations which distribute information to people while they also enable community members to move through different social levels. The organizations deliver more than credential awarding because they develop innovation ecosystems which welcome all members according to Larsson and Hatzigeorgiou (2025).

The development of lifelong learning models depends on the strong partnerships which universities establish with industry organizations. The creation of curriculum through co-information methods enables educational programs to maintain their relevant content which responds to present-day requirements. The adaptable educational programs serve two separate groups which include people who work during the day and those who are currently out of work. Micro-credentials along with modular programs allow students to acquire knowledge through hands-on learning activities. These methods remove some barriers that block people from joining the program while they also boost the workforce's ability to adapt. The research by Machucho and Ortiz (2025) demonstrates that higher education institutions play an active role in AI-induced transitions instead of remaining passive participants.

The core principles of Inclusive AI design address the first stage of displacement which occurs at the beginning of the process. The design selection process determines how labour operations will affect the production methods. Systems that focus on efficiency alone will replace human operators with automated control systems. Designers working with human-centered methods receive top priority during the inclusive design process. The system connects three main problems that affect both employee involvement and accessibility and fairness. Organizations that include various stakeholders in system design work to reduce bias while they build a better understanding of their specific context. AI design, which includes all users, unites technical development standards with ethical labour results through Bashynska's 2024 framework.

The design principle known as Humans-in-the-loop demonstrates excellent implementation of inclusive design practices. The core operation of AI systems needs human evaluation together with human decision-making to function correctly. Workers team with AI, they don't answer to it. The current design works best for system expansion instead of complete automation. The system allows users to maintain their responsibility and control which they started with.

The ethics of AI adoption are largely shaped by organisations. A holistic focus on risk management and humans who are managing the risk within the HR framework is critical for the alignment of AI application and HR. Ethical application of these principles to one's own employees requires having transparency into the decision-making and communication with employees. Laborers also need to know how AI is impacting their jobs and futures. The earlier you can get involved, the less resistance you will have and the easier it will be to bring your organization along. Ethical companies treat their workers as stakeholders in the company, and monitor labor effects is to give organizations a way to also reverse course if need be. Responsible application of AI is a development not a destination. Regular assessment ensures ongoing conformance with developing societal expectations and regulatory norms (Machucho & Ortiz, 2025).

Models of public–private collaboration strengthen the strategic response. The challenges of AI pressures on jobs are too complex for governments to address alone. Firms are expert in the technology and in how to implement it. Public bodies bring legitimacy, funding and coordination. Hybrid models leverage these capabilities. Joint investing in training infrastructure and labour market information systems facilitates evidence-based policy making (IOE, 2024).

Sectoral collaborations address distinct challenges pertinent to the context. Varied labor dynamics are evident within manufacturing, services, and digital platforms. This necessitates tailored solutions. Public-private initiatives possess the capacity to align reskilling efforts with sector-specific demands. (Larsson & Hatzigeorgiou, 2025)

Increasingly robust international governance, for its part, comes with strengthened strategic responses. Labor disruption from artificial intelligence exceeds the limits of any single nation-state. Reverberations spread through global supply networks and digital platforms to all corners of the world. Coordination of norms and best practices make the road to ethical convergence go a bit faster. International trade bodies facilitate coordination through the provision of protocols, and thus transferring ideas around. But in the broader sense, it is important to need global systems to be harmonized with local habits of application; otherwise,

Basically, strategic responses are how we turn ethical problems into actual solutions. When folks reskill and keep learning throughout their lives, it really helps the workforce keep up with all the changes happening. When we design AI with everyone in mind, it helps prevent people from getting pushed out of their homes or jobs. Ethics are a core part of how we make choices about putting things into action; they're already built right into our company's policies and procedures. Public–private partnership promotes scaling up and coordination. Collectively, these instruments act as building blocks for creating inclusive and resilient labor markets in AI-powered economies.

8. MULTI-STAKEHOLDER ETHICAL FRAMEWORK FOR AI GOVERNANCE

When AI changes how we work, it really shows us that trying to control things with just one main player in charge doesn't really cut it anymore. Tech systems these days just blow past any lines we draw, whether they're between companies, industries, or even countries. They also mess with people who work there, the local communities, and even nature outside the company itself. So, getting ethical governance right really comes down to a lot of different groups working together. Not a single one of these places has enough say, smarts, or good standing to deal with AI-related job losses all on their own. When it comes to handling really complicated stuff in charge, bringing in different groups to help out means everyone has to share the load and be responsible for what happens, as the International Organisation of Employers pointed out this year.

The reason we need so many different groups involved in governing AI comes down to how AI is built and how it affects people. Technical and design choices really shape AI systems, along with what companies want and what society values. You know, what we get from our work really comes from putting all these pieces together, not just from the tech itself. When governance is broken up, it creates gaps where no one is responsible, and people aren't protected. When you bring in lots of different groups, each with their own ideas and goals, it forces everyone to really talk about what's most important. It also makes things more legitimate because people affected by AI systems get to have a say in how all of that gets put out there.

They legislate on labor, the education system, and the welfare state. It is up to the governments to update regulatory frameworks for task-level displacements and algorithmic management. They have to ensure that AI governance considers employment in addition to data protection and consumer rights. Public policy also plays a role in how the pain- and gain-sharing in technological change works (IOE, 2024).

Coordination is in the purview of the government beyond regulation. They provide a mechanism for cross-sector coordination and alignment of national approaches with global standards. Reskilling infrastructure and digital access investment redress structural inequality. Governments perform a redistributive role by aiding workers in transition. States have an ethical responsibility to ensure that labour protection is taken as a core pillar of the AI strategy and not a token element (Akwiri, 2024).

There are more companies than individuals that own AI systems. Their strategic efforts have a direct bearing on how many jobs are created. Companies decide whether to use AI to replace or augment worker labor. They make choices about worker input and how much they want to allocate it to training or redeployment. Labor impact assessments in AI adoption strategies are a matter of responsible corporate governance. Earning a profit doesn't preclude being socially responsible. Productivity increases accrue to firms, which thus bear a joint responsibility in coping with displacement risks (Machucho & Ortiz, 2025).

The role of technologists is crucial and yet often underappreciated. Labor outcomes are partially shaped by decisions of AI developers. And systems embody values in decisions about model architecture, data selection, and optimization criteria. Technologists are, therefore ethical actors rather than neutral technicians. Successful growth is contingent upon consciousness of its impact on society and theologizing amongst the social nontechnical spheres. Incorporating fairness, transparency, and explainability into the system design in the first place is a key enabler of accountability in deployment (Brandao, 2025).

The ethical-by-design tenets embody this duty. These are accepted standards for incorporating ethical issues into all stages of the engineering process. Human-in-the-loop designs maintain supervision and control. Explainable models are contestability and trust-enabling. Technologists who collaborate with labor specialists and ethicists do so in a manner that is conducive to socially responsive innovation. This cross-disciplinary strategy mitigates potential negative side effects (Machucho & Ortiz, 2025).

Education professionals act as a bridge between technology and the labour market. How people are trained for the AI-work environment is determined by education systems. Skills development and the ethical are shaped by postsecondary organizations. Teaching units that integrate technical knowledge with ethical reflection and social discourse are needed. As they do, they invite practices of lifelong learning across open and plural education route experiences. Their purpose is knowledge (not work, Larsson & Hatzigeorgiou, 2025).

Educational organizations, too, are a form of knowledge broker. They translate research into practice and inform policy debates. Industry collaboration provides relevance. Engagement with civil society adds inclusiveness. Through education, anticipatory governance is strengthened by preparing workers and firms to deal with new challenges, rather than reacting to job loss after the fact (IOE, 2024).

Civil society nonetheless exercises critical oversight and representation. They speak for the workers and other underprivileged classes. Civil society tracks labour impacts and demands responsibility. They also promote transparency and democratic slap pots. There is a risk that without the participation of civil society in governance, it will be dominated by state and corporate as opposed to diverse social interests. With Engagement as a solution for Power Imbalances (Akwiri, 2024).

The duties of these stakeholders were synthesised in the proposed model of ethical governance. The conceptual model is a nested system. At the batter of this is ethical AI use (or augmentation and inclusion), and then there are five different stakeholder index.al The third layer are five stakeholder groups that orbit al. Five stakeholder clusters orbit this core. The governments offer the regulation and the coordination. Business is responsible and to them. Technologists embed ethical design. Teachers facilitate adaptation. Civil society guarantees accountability. Learn and Adjust Constant feedback loops operate Yin these domains, which facilitate Learning and adapting. This is reinforced on further by consistency with principles of circular economy. Circularity concentrates on renewal and resilience and on the production of long-lasting value. These values are reflected in ethical AI governance, which focuses on sustainable labor outcomes. Social sustainability has its place in environmentally friendly organizations. Material regeneration is to workforce replenishment as a fraction is to a whole. Circular value creation is enabled by developing inclusive skills. Labor ethics implications in circular strategies help ensure that sustainability transitions do not become social cost externalizers (Bashynska, 2024).

The framework also supports just transitions. Circular economy reforms tend to be grounded in AI-sensitivities and efficiency. These programmes may exacerbate the issue if there's no ethical governance. Multi-stakeholder governance channels circular innovation towards collective value creation. This ensures that workers participate in and shared in these sustainability transitions. This convergence fosters acceptance at the societal level and sustainability in the long term (Larsson & Hatzigeorgiou, 2025).

In essence, the ethical governance of the evolving work of AI entails a multi-stakeholder governance. Governments, corporations, technologists, educators and civil society all have a part to play. Their joint efforts to fill governance gaps and explicitly pool liability. The suggested model combines ethical AI with circular economy principles. It outlines a path to inclusive, resilient and socially sustainable AI-driven futures of work.

9. GLOBAL CASE STUDIES AND CROSS-REGIONAL INSIGHTS

AI-driven labor transformations look different in different parts of the world. Outcomes are shaped by institutional capacity, economic structure and governance traditions. Global case studies thus offer critical empirical grounding for analyses of AI-enabled job displacement and associated ethical responses. To compare labor impacts of similar technologies in different regional contexts also shows the methods of analysis employed. These variations highlight policy choices rather than technological determinism (International Organisation of Employers [IOE], 2024).

The mature AI adoption context. The U.S. is a mature context for AI adoption, with the latest technological infrastructure and labor market arrangements that are highly flexible in many respects. Manufacturing, services and knowledge firms use AI on a large scale in their day-to-day efforts to become more productive. Logistics, retail and back-office services are particular beneficiaries of automation. Task substitution is also on the rise with routine clerical and customer service jobs. While the AI-driven labour market has acquired a seemingly high proportion of 'wanted' roles (from a demand-side perspective), e.g., in fields such as data science, system design and AI governance (Larsson & Hatzigeorgiou, 2025).

Polarisation effects in the US. Some empirical analyses from the United States find similar results. Highly skilled workers gain disproportionately from AI-enhanced work. Low and medium-skilled workers are either displaced or deskilled. The rally in wage inequality is nothing more than uncoupling of productivity and wage gains. Flexibility in the labor market brings also rapid adjustment but at the same time attenuates employment security. Weak collective bargaining, stagnating social protection as well as economic and financial crisis exacerbate adjustment burdens of people losing work (Marguerit, 2025).

Policy responses in the United States are focused on market-driven adaptation. Companies make selective investments in reskilling, usually in high-potential employees. Public-sector responses are geared toward the development of the workforce and provision of digital skills, but are somewhat patchy. Ethical AI governance is characterized by a reliance on voluntary protocols and not binding law. Innovation remains strong, but gaps in labor protection remain. These results illustrate the trade-off between innovation speed and social inclusiveness (IOE, 2024).

There is more diversity among the Asian economies. Advanced economies such as Japan, South Korea and Singapore have rapidly embraced AI with coordinated industrial policy. AI is used in manufacturing, and logistics, and public services. Automation is complemented by augmentative approaches that focus on the upgrading of the workforce. Displacement risks are reduced by strong vocational training systems and employer–state coordination. Labor transitions are handled via active reskilling and internal redeployment (Larsson & Hatzigeorgiou, 2025).

Comparatively, rising Asian states are fragmented. AI is adopted primarily in export-oriented manufacturing and digital platforms. Automation decreases the need for routine work in factories and services. Informal employment continues to be significant. Social protection is scarce. AI has displaced workers, and those workers have difficulty getting new jobs. Policy capacity differs; hence, responses are piecemeal. These dynamics demonstrate the importance of institutional strength in overseeing technological transitions (International Organisation of Employers, 2024).

Asian policy responses highlight strategic coordination of AI with education and industry development. Governments are investing in skills ecosystems and in public–private partnerships. The national AI policies have more ethical considerations. Yet, gaps p, particularly relating to informal work and platform work. The Asian case suggests that harmonized governance can stem displacement, but is dependent on ongoing (Brandao, 2025).

Distinct challenges and opportunities emerge in African contexts. AI usage is still patchy but expanding in areas including agriculture, finance and public administration. Automation is creeping into clerical and transactional jobs, especially in banking and government work. But at the same time there is also leapfrogging through digital platforms and mobile technologies driven by AI. So, employment impacts are both positive and negative and vary greatly depending on context (Akwiri, 2024).

Vulnerability is prominent in empirical work from Africa. Labour markets are dominated by informal jobs. The social safety net is feeble. Displaced workers fail to get reskilling. The efficiency-enhancing benefits VRF contribute to may therefore exacerbate poverty and inequality without the parallel advancement of social policy measures. Yet specialized AI-enabled (agriculture and health) solutions illustrate potential for augmentation when tailored to local context. These cases illustrate the need for context-conscious implementation (Larsson & Hatzigeorgiou, 2025).

Political response in African economies is also limited by fiscal and institutional constraints. The national AI strategies typically emphasize economic growth over labor protection. International collaborations contribute to capacity building but do not necessarily engage with local labor markets. Ethical systems of governance are emergent. In turn, this leads to workers bearing an uneven share of the costs of adjustment. These developments raise concerns about global inequality and technological asymmetry (Akwiri, 2024).

Cross-regional analysis uncovers patterns of recurrence. Automation-related AI adoption predictably results in short-term displacement. Negative effects are mitigated by augmentation-focused policies. Institutional capacity matters for outcomes more so than the technological capability itself. Good education, coordinated governance and inclusive labour market policies are best able to help regions and communities through the transition, while those without them see deeper inequality and longer-term disruption (IOE, 2024).

Policy results demonstrate these differences even more starkly. Market-led approaches have been celebrated for encouraging faster pace of innovation, if not the social costs. Coordinated models of labour integration, however, tend to involve long-term commitments of public resources. Poor governance contexts find it difficult to mold AI purchase to social purposes. These distinctions show that ethical and inclusive AI governance is a political and institutional choice rather than a natural consequence of technological evolution (Bashynska, 2024).

The comparison offers lessons for the development and emerging economies alike. Among them are early skills investment and early investment in digital infrastructure. Intervention is more costly when it is delayed. AI and circular economy policies, as well as labor issues, must be mainstreamed from the beginning. Third, public–private coordination strengthens effectiveness and legitimacy. Fourth, the ethical governance models developed must not be seen as imported models applied in toto (International Organisation of Employers, 2024).

Emerging economies have also been proven to gain from favoring augmentation paths. AI technologies that support rather than supplant human work are more likely to contribute to inclusive growth. Agriculture, healthcare and education present big opportunities for augmentation. Bringing AI adoption in line with social demand makes it more legitimate and more sustainable. These policies should be based on participatory governance and international cooperation in dealing with resource limitations (Larsson & Hatzigeorgiou, 2025).

Insofar as global case studies are indicative, where AI shocks employment, the nature of labour disruption is largely regional. The United States exemplifies a polarization under market-oriented adaptatoin. Asia shows the strengths and the limitations of coordinated governance. Africa: The Challenge of Inclusive Innovation. The comparative analysis demonstrates that ethical governance, institutional capability and strategic choice matter. These lessons illuminate pathways to fair and inclusive.

10. TOWARD A JUST AI-POWERED CIRCULAR ECONOMY

The intersection of artificial intelligence, Labour transformation, and the circular economy call for a holistic ethical response. These fields tend to be analysed independently. Such division masks between them a relation of symbiotic dependence. AI reshapes work. Production and consumption are reorganised by the circular economy. Ethics is the normative perspective that bridges technological effectiveness with human well-being. Labour-led AI-powered circular economy is in turn just a sustainable labor outcomes-aligned AI-powered circular economy that does not relegate work to an afterthought (Bashynska, 2024).

The convergence of ethics, labor, and sustainability is rooted in considering labor as inherently circular. 6.1 Environmental Sustainability: Material and Energy Flowse Environmental sustainability deals with material and energy flows. People and work: the focus of social sustainability. AI mediates both domains. Sustainability is left incomplete when resources are being used efficiently by AI without considering its impact on jobs. Ethical convergence ensures that ecological gains are not predicated on social losses. This connection reconceives CE transitions as socio-technical, rather than purely environmental, strategies (please see Roberts et al., 2024 for further discussion).

In this sense, human-role AI social contract needs to be redefined. Traditional social contracts are predicated on the assumption of permanent employment relationships, and decisions are made by humans. AI disrupts both assumptions. Algorithms are playing a growing role in hiring, task allocation, and job design. In the era of AI-mediated work, a new social contract will need to define the rights, duties, and expectations of all parties. Workers not be treated as residual inputs to be optimized away. Instead, they should be treated as co-producers of value (Larsson & Hatzigeorgiou, 2025).

Boldly redefining the social contract means focusing on human agency. AI technologies should facilitate rather than replace human decision-making. Trust requires transparency and explainability. Employees need to know how AI will impact their jobs and their future. Decision-making participation increases legitimacy. Hence, ethical governance of AI contributes to the renewed social contract based on dignity, fairness and shared benefits (International Organisation of Employers [IOE], 2024).

Fairly enabling automation depends on conditions. Selective, not wholesale, automation is the first step. Processes that contravene safety or decency can be automated. Tasks that are meaningful and give learning should be augmented. Second, the gains in productivity must be shared. Companies reaping the benefits of AI-enhanced efficiency should also contribute to workforce education and support for transitions. Third, displacement threats should be forecasted rather than handled reactively (Lane, 2019). Intervening early reduces inequality in the long run (Marguerit, uncite).

Education and reskilling are key ingredients to these conditions. Accessible lifelong learning systems are essential to a just transition. Before being displaced, workers should be given a chance to develop new skills. Education should combine technical knowledge with ethical and social knowledge. This strategy trains workers to work with AI and not against it. Both higher education institutions and employers must take responsibility in developing these systems (Larsson & Hatzigeorgiou, 2025).

Policy pathways are a decisive factor in the transformation towards inclusive circular economies. Governments shape the deployment of AI by regulating it, incentivizing it, and investing in the public goods necessary to make it affordable and accessible. Policies that push for further automation without labour protections contribute to greater inequality. Inclusive policies embed labour standards in AI and green transition agendas. These consist of active labour market policies, social protection, and reskilling assistance. A just result requires policy alignment in the spheres of AI, work, and the environment (IOE, 2024).

Public–private partnerships contribute to more effective policies. Firms have technological qualification in turn. Governments provide coordination and legitimacy. Joint efforts coordinate innovation with social concerns. In the circular economy, cooperation facilitates workforce shifts to new production methods. Ethical governance frameworks direct these alliances towards co-creation of value as opposed to cost externalization (Machucho & Ortiz, 2025).

An inclusive circular economy calls for a global outlook as well. AI-based transitions take place in linked value chains. Labor effects cross borders. Developing countries and those with emerging economies are more vulnerable due to the fact that they have weaker institutions. International collaboration facilitates capacity development and knowledge sharing. A responsible AI governance must deal with global inequalities instead of reinforcing such inequalities through technological differing (Akwiri, 2024).

At the end of the day, a fair AI-enabled circular economy is not a natural by-product of innovation. It is a normative endeavor influenced by decisions. These are the decisions about how we build, deploy, and govern AI. They influence whether transitions to sustainability empower or disempower workers. The combination of ethics, labor, and sustainability leads to inclusive resilience. Technological Scrum product development advances in lockstep with human development," not at the expense of it.

In conclusion, the convergence of AI with labor ethics and circular economy models holds significant promise for the future, but also harbors risks. The ethical dimension redefines sustainability to more closely align with social justice. A re-vitalised human–AI social contract puts agency and participation at the forefront. Socially just automation is "done right," which serves as a shorthand for selective deployment, shared benefits, and anticipatory governance. Policy routes based on inclusion and collaboration allow for circular economies that are productive and fair and perceived to be so.

11. CONCLUSION AND FUTURE RESEARCH DIRECTIONS

In this chapter, we analyzed the ethics of artificial intelligence-led job losses in the circular economy. It argued that AI is not just a technological tool, but rather a socio-economic organization that transforms labour markets, organizational routines, and sustainability transitions. The findings indicated that decisions on design and governance, and capacity-building within institutions in recipient countries, have a significant impact on employability. Productivity-related gains driven by AI are at risk of being accompanied by large disparities in job-task- and socio-economic-related outcomes in the absence of due attention to ethics (International Organisation of Employers [IOE], 2024).

A key conclusion is that it matters greatly to differentiate between automation and augmentation. Automation-centric AI is based on substitution and cost minimisation. It has a disproportionate impact on routine and unskilled work. Complementary- (or augmentation-centric AI focuses on complementarity and enhancement of capabilities and skills. It promotes job quality and the development of skills over a long period as long as participation is broad-based. This explanation also explains why AI results in differential labour market effects in different industries and regions. It also reveals the normative importance of deployment decisions as opposed to technological determinism (Marguerit, 2025).

The chapter contributes to theorizing by drawing on ethical AI, labour economics, and circular economy literature. It reframes sustainability as a social technical process that must incorporate labour outcomes. In doing so, the chapter contributes to the critical when where to study circular economics, bridging the concept with occupational inequality. The suggested multi-stakeholder ethical governance model pushes forward thinking by sharing responsibility among governments, corporations, technologists, educators, and civil society. This approach discards firm-centric or state-centric models of AI governance (Larsson & Hatzigeorgiou, 2025).

The policy relevance is evident from the discussion above. Governments need to modernize labor laws to the scale of task-level displacement and algorithmic management. Social protection systems need to be adjusted to enable work transitions and lifelong learning. AI governance models could also consider labor in relation to data protection and innovation interests. Synergistic policy formulation in the areas of AI,labor, and the environment promotes overall policy coherence and AOE 2024 effectiveness.

The implications for managers are also profound. Organizations have a deterministic effect on labor market outcomes in AI adoption. Ethical AI implementation also involves transparency, engaging with workers, and investing in their reskilling. Companies that focus on augmentation routes are more resilient in their workforces and more socially acceptable. Passive ethical governance, accomplished through impact assessments and mechanisms to ensure accountability. These activities represent the convergence of long-term corporate performance and social responsibility (Machucho & Ortiz, 2025).

However, this is not an exhaustive and exhaustive chapter. The analysis is based largely on secondary literature and policy documents. Although they offer applicable breadth and comparative knowledge, they restrict causality interpretation. Empirical heterogeneity between regions also makes extrapolation difficult. Local institutional settings shape labor market processes in ways that cannot be captured fully in one generalized model. These limitations call for empirical work that is context-specific (Akwiri, 2024).

It would be interesting for prospective studies to contribute to the ethical AI scholarship by investigating the way ethical principles are translated into practice in the organisations. Research on transparency, accountability, and explainability and their effects on workers, could examine these processes in practice. Cross-country research on ethical-by-design principles would enhance the understanding of how values are integrated into technical systems (Bashynska, 2024).

Impact in labor economics should be on the task level that captures the long-term career path. Longitudinal research on the effect of AI on skill acquisition and wage elasticity is also called for to investigate the potential for evolving development. And special focus should be on vulnerable populations in the informal work sectors, particularly in the Third World and the emerging economies (Larsson & Hatzigeorgiou, 2025).

Research on digital governance should focus on coordination at multiple levels of local, national, and global institutions. The interplay of corporate governance with public regulation and civil society surveillance remains underexplored. Future research should also consider the convergence of circular economy policies with AI governance work and labor standards. Such evidence-based research would feed into more systemic/just sustainability transitions (IOE, 2024).

In summary, the work of the future in AI-driven circular economies is not foreordained. It is the product of ethical decisions, institutional design, and collective action. AI can be used to deepen inequality or to foster inclusive development. Circular economy transitions can either perpetuate social stifling or regenerate human capability. Shaping these trajectories to converge will require purposeful governance based in ethical responsibility. A fair AI-driven circular economy is thus both a policy challenge and a moral imperative.

REFERENCES

NITI Aayog. (2021). *Artificial intelligence in agriculture: Opportunities and challenges in India.*

Acemoglu, D., & Restrepo, P. (2020). Artificial intelligence, automation, and work. *The Journal of Economic Perspectives*, *34*(1), 3–30. DOI: 10.1257/jep.29.1.3

Agrawal, A., Gans, J., & Goldfarb, A. (2019). *Prediction machines: The simple economics of artificial intelligence.* Harvard Business Review Press. DOI: 10.7208/chicago/9780226613475.001.0001

Akwiri, D. (2024, December 18). *AI's Impact on Employment: Workforce Displacement and Ethical Considerations.* ResearchGate. https://doi.org/DOI: 10.13140/RG.2.2.28346.91841

Bashynska, Y. (2024). ГЛОБАЛЬНІ ЕКОНОМІЧНІ АСПЕКТИ РОЗВИТКУ ВІДНОВЛЮВАНОЇ ЕНЕРГЕТИКИ В УКРАЇНІ ТА ПОЛЬЩІ. *Public Management and Policy*, (3-4), 14–22. DOI: 10.70651/3041-2498/2024.3-4.02

Brandao, P. R. (2025). The impact of artificial intelligence on modern society. *AI*, *6*(8), 190. DOI: 10.3390/ai6080190

Brynjolfsson, E., Rock, D., & Syverson, C. (2021). The productivity J-curve: How intangibles complement general purpose technologies. *American Economic Journal. Macroeconomics*, *13*(1), 333–372. DOI: 10.1257/mac.20180386

Chen, N., Li, Z., Tang, B., Zárate-González, C. A., & Xue, B. (2022). Can digital skill protect against job displacement caused by artificial intelligence? Empirical evidence from 701 detailed occupations. *PLoS One*, *17*(11), e0277280. DOI: 10.1371/journal.pone.0277280 PMID: 36346798

Floridi, L., Cowls, J., Beltrametti, M., Chatila, R., Chazerand, P., Dignum, V., Luetge, C., Madelin, R., Pagallo, U., Rossi, F., Schafer, B., Valcke, P., & Vayena, E. (2021). AI4People—An ethical framework for a good AI society. *AI & Society*, *36*(2), 689–707. DOI: 10.1007/s00146-020-01044-2 PMID: 30930541

International Federation of Robotics. (2023). *World robotics report 2023.*

International Organisation of Employers (IOE). (2024). *The impact of artificial intelligence on work and employment.*

Kellogg, K. C., Valentine, M. A., & Christin, A. (2020). Algorithms at work: The new contested terrain of control. *The Academy of Management Annals*, *14*(1), 366–410. DOI: 10.5465/annals.2018.0174

Larsson, A., & Hatzigeorgiou, A. (2025). Introduction: The Way Disruption, Technology and Practice Will Change the Way We Work in the Future. In *The Future of Labour* (pp. 1-14). Routledge.

Machucho, R., & Ortiz, D. (2025). The impacts of artificial intelligence on business innovation: A comprehensive review of applications, organizational challenges, and ethical considerations. *Systems*, *13*(4), 264. DOI: 10.3390/systems13040264

Morandini, S., Fraboni, F., De Angelis, M., Puzzo, G., Giusino, D., & Pietrantoni, L. (2023). The impact of artificial intelligence on workers' skills: Upskilling and reskilling in organizations. *Informing Science*, *26*, 39–68. DOI: 10.28945/5078

Roberts, H., Zhang, J., Bariach, B., Cowls, J., Gilburt, B., Juneja, P., ... & Floridi, L. (2024). Artificial intelligence in support of the circular economy: ethical considerations and a path forw

World Economic Forum. (2023). *The future of jobs report 2023.* https://www.weforum.org/reports/the-future-of-jobs-report-2023

Zuboff, S. (2019). *The age of surveillance capitalism: The fight for a human future at the new frontier of power.* PublicAffairs. Marguerit, D. (2025). Augmenting or automating labor? The effect of AI development on new work, employment, and wages. *arXiv preprint arXiv:2503.19159.*

Chapter 13
Large Language Models as Adaptive and Context-Aware Partners in Knowledge Creation

Ashutosh Bhardwaj
http://orcid.org/0009-0008-3311-8335
Poornima University, Jaipur, India

ABSTRACT

The concept of Large Language Models (LLMs) has become the innovative technologies that can transform the existing knowledge creation processes due to the capability to act as adaptive and context-sensitive partners instead of passive computational mechanisms. With the use of modern architectures, contextual reasoning, and lifelong learning, LLMs have the ability to dynamically comprehend user intent, domain knowledge and situational context to ideate, analyze and synthesize information. The chapter discusses theoretical principles of LLMs, their use in human-AI collaborative knowledge creation, and their uses in academia, education, industry, and policy making. It also seeks to critically point out with their application to ethical, governance and reliability issues. Placing LLMs as co-producers in a human-centered system of knowledge offers a direction in future research and stresses on the necessity of responsible, transparent, and trustful application of such models into the practice of knowledge-intensive activities.

DOI: 10.4018/979-8-2600-2811-7.ch013

1. INTRODUCTION

1.1 Evolution of Knowledge Creation in the Digital Era

With the development of digital technologies, the knowledge creation has gone through a significant revolution. Conventionally, the creation of knowledge has progressed in linear measures that implied human discovery, cogitation, experimentation and written communication, uninhibited in most cases, by scarcity of information and by tardy shares of distribution. With the advent of computers, databases and the internet, there was a shift in tides as it became possible to store, retrieve and share information that crossed geographical boundaries as well as disciplinary boundaries very quickly. Online journals, online repositories, online collaboration platforms have significantly transformed the way in which individual people and institutions generate and authenticate knowledge.

With the maturity of the digital systems, knowledge creation turned out to be networked and collaborative as opposed to isolated and individualistic. Online systems facilitated collective intelligence, in which knowledge was created through leading to interactions between multiple participants. Search engines, data analytics applications, and the content management systems started to help humans see patterns, synthesize and create insights on levels never seen before. But these systems were mostly the passive devices which relied on the direct instructions of people and direct rules (Brown et al., 2020).

The present generation is another development, in which intelligent systems can also actively take part in the knowledge creation process. AI, especially machine learning and natural language processing have evolved to interpretation and generation of information beyond the information retrieval stage. This transformation is the beginning of a paradigm shift when digital technologies ceased to be facilitators of intellectual labor but became partners. In this context, Large Language Models are a not only significant milestone, which provided the opportunity to interact with knowledge dynamically, contextually, and adaptively.

1.2 Emergence of Large Language Models (LLMs)

The history of the development of Large Language Models is hundreds of years of research in the field of computational linguistics, neural networks, and representation learning. In contrast to previous rule-based or shallow statistical models, the LLMs are trained on large amounts of textual data using the deep learning architecture, especially transformer-based models. Such training allows them to learn complicated syntactic outlines, semantic connections and contextual networks over large areas of expertise. Consequently, the output of coherent content, context-dependent and human-like language can be obtained using LLMs (Kumari et al., 2026).

The noteworthiness of LLMs is founded on their scale as well as the versatility. These models can accomplish many duties, typically summarization, explanation, translation, reasoning, and take inspiringly creative writing, with no task-specific reprogramming. This all-purpose feature enables their use in all fields including scientific research and education, business strategy and policy analysis. More to the point, the interactions with LLMs become more natural and effective because the latter are capable of adapting to the user input, tone, and contextual indicators.

The high rate of uptake of LLMs has changed the anticipations of human-machine interaction. The interaction between the users is not one-way communication with features of strict interfaces or command systems but conversation and dialogue exhibiting collaboration-like interactions. This is transforming LLMs into partners, able to aid sense-making, hypothesis and concept exploration. As a result, their introduction creates a primordial question of what authorship is, what expertise is, and what fallacies between human and machine knowledge additions (Vaswani et al., 2017).

1.3 Motivation and Scope of the Chapter

Recent development of the incorporation of LLMs in knowledge activities prompts a further study of this tool as an adaptive and context-responsive collaborator in the knowledge generation. Although the extant body of literature in detail addresses the technical potential of LLMs, not much consideration has been placed on the epistemic potential of the learning models to influence the manner in which knowledge are created, authenticated, and disseminated. Knowledge about this role is important especially with the growing application of these models in the academic writing, research design, learning process and decision-making in organizations.

The necessity to shift the focus to different approaches than instrumental perspective of LLMs inspires this chapter. The chapter also views the LLM as an agent of collaboration, and not as an automated content generator, integrating humans into the knowledge systems. This approach places interaction, adaptability, and contextual understanding among its key characteristics that make the knowledge creation based on LLM distinctive in comparison to the previous computational techniques. It also admits that there is such a bi-directional relationship where human judgment, expertise in the domain and moral reasoning are dominant.

The chapter has a wide range that includes the theoretical background, practical application, and the most critical problems in relation to the LLM-empowered knowledge creation. It examines this by discussing how context awareness and adaptability can help LLMs make meaningful contributions in fields and it also discusses the ethical, governance, and trust concerns. The chapter also seeks to present a forward-thinking and balanced system of placing the LLM into wider social-technical systems to enlighten researchers, educators, and practising to responsibly and effectively use the system to create knowledge using the LLM as a collaborator.

Figure 1. Large language models as adaptive and context-aware partners in knowledge creation

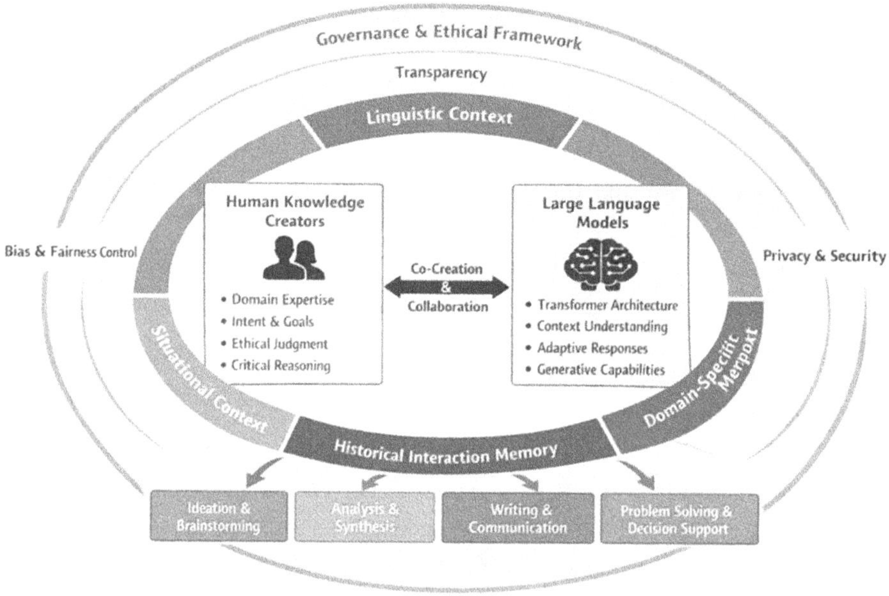

2. FOUNDATIONS OF LARGE LANGUAGE MODELS

2.1 Architecture and Training Paradigms of LLMs

Big Machine The core of LLLMs is based on the models of deep neural networks, where the majority of the modern systems consist of transformers. Self-attention that was presented as part of the transformer architecture enables the model to consider whether each word in the sequence is important or not with respect to other words whether they are close to each other or not. Such an ability allows LLMs to learn long-long-run dependencies and fine-tuning semantic interactions previously hard to learn by earlier recurrent or convolutional models successfully. Consequently, LLMs reveal better performance regarding comprehending the sophisticated structure of a language and the ability to create coherent text (Petroni et al., 2019).

Most of training parameter of LLM is a multi-stage process. The first step involves large-scale pretraining of models using huge amounts of text expressed in the form of books, academic articles, web content, and other text. At this stage, the model acquires general linguistic patterns, grammar, factual associations and contextual representations through prediction of the next token in a sequence. This unsupervised or self-supervised form of learning has allowed the model to learn very general information that is not dependent on its domain of focus without the need to be annotated by humans at scale.

After that, fine-tuning and alignment of LLMs are carried out. Through curated datasets strategy, to fine-tune pretrained models to tasks or domains, as well as to make sure that outputs are useful, safe, and aligned with human expectations, alignment methods, including reinforcement learning based on human feedback, are applied. Combined, these training paradigms make raw language prediction systems adaptive models that can be used to assist in knowledge creation tasks in a variety of real-world tasks (Kumari & Goyal, 2026).

2.2 Context Modeling and Semantic Understanding

One of the strengths of Large Language Models is that at several levels they model the context. Context modeling is not a simple matter of cognition about the immediate linguistic input, but also includes more extensive semantic, pragmatic, and domain-specific hints. LLMs have the ability to change its interpretation dynamically, through a combination of attention-based mechanisms and layered representations, based on the text around, based on past uses of the word, and based on implicit learnings built into language. This allows them to come up with responses that are sensitive to subtlety, will, and contextual release (Wei et al., 2022).

LLM semantic understanding is a manifestation of distributed meaning representations that are acquired throughout training. High-dimensional vectors represent words, phrases and concepts, consisting of high-dimensional vectors representing relationships, including similarity, hierarchy and analogy. This enables the interpretation of meaning in new or ambiguous scenes in LLMs, which are valued in the creation of such activities as description, abstraction, and synthesis. Although these representations is not human-like understanding, they bring in a functional semantic competence which is incredibly effective in areas of application concerning knowledge.

Notably, context modeling is not confined to text only. LLMs can use the history of interactions in interactive environments, user preferences, and goal of a task to achieve consistency in longer interactions. This ability is fundamental to consider

LLMs as knowledge partners combined with non-response generators. LLMs can facilitate step-wise improvement of ideas by incorporating new signals and can aid in multi-faceted reasoning processes and help change the input of ideas based on the changing knowledge requirements (Sharma et al., 2026).

2.3 Adaptability and Continual Learning Capabilities

Adaptability is one of the key features that differentiate Large Language Models and much more traditional rule-based or narrow-trained systems. Prompt based learning where task instructions and contextual constraints are given dynamically during the inference time are examples of adaptive behavior of LLLMs. This enables one to control model behavior without retraining, and thus quickly customize to a different domain, audience, or expertise level (Kaplan et al., 2020).

Besides adaptability in the form of prompt, LLMs can be extended by generation methods with retrieval augmentation and external memory. The methods enable models to make use of up-to-date or domain-specific data when generating responses which somewhat offsets constraints of fixed training data. The combination of external knowledge sources makes LLMs more aware of any context and credible, which increases their usability in research and learning and professional decision-making settings.

Although true continual learning where the internal parameters of a model are automatically updated over time is still an active research problem, existing architectures can support the principles of adaptive interaction on both the user level and the system level. Such a kind of flexibility allows the utilization of LLMs in changing knowledge ecosystems. With the development of research, one can predict that the combination of ongoing learning processes will further empower the role of LLMs as long-term collaborators in knowledge creation that can change according to human knowledge and social needs (Shanahan, 2024).

3. CONTEXT AWARENESS IN KNOWLEDGE CREATION

3.1 Understanding Context: Linguistic, Situational, and Domain Context

One of the key prerequisites to meaningful knowledge creation is context awareness and it has been central to determining the quality of any Large Language Model as a collaborative partner. Linguistic context denotes the contextual words, sentences and discourse structure, which is used to influence the meaning of an utterance. The attention mechanisms are used to analyze this linguistic environment, and the

LLLMs can thus disambiguate terms, make sense in terms of references at scales, and hold continuity mattering to very long-term texts. This is a needed ability to generate explanations, arguments and stories that are logically and semantically consistent (Farooqi et al., 2026).

In addition to semantic factors, the context of a given situation plays a very big role in the creation of knowledge. Situational context includes intent of the user, the intent of the interaction, the amount of formality needed and the phase of a task of a project. LLMs automatically will respond to the prompts and patterns of interaction and infer these cues, and therefore they can alter the tone, depth, and focus. As an example, an adaptive situational awareness would be deemed by similar query drawing a conceptual overview in a school environment and technical analysis in a research one.

Domain context also narrows down the contributions of the model by placing the responses in definite fields of knowledge. In the field of healthcare, engineering, social sciences, and law, LLMs are based on the terms, conventions, and arguments related to the field. Although this domain awareness is trained indirectly, it is also practicalised via prompting and framing of information. The domain context integration allows the effective use of the LLM in the creation of specialized knowledge and minimizes the possibility of irrelevant or misleading results (Bommasani, et al., 2021).

Figure 2. Key contexts and their impact on large language model interactions for knowledge creation

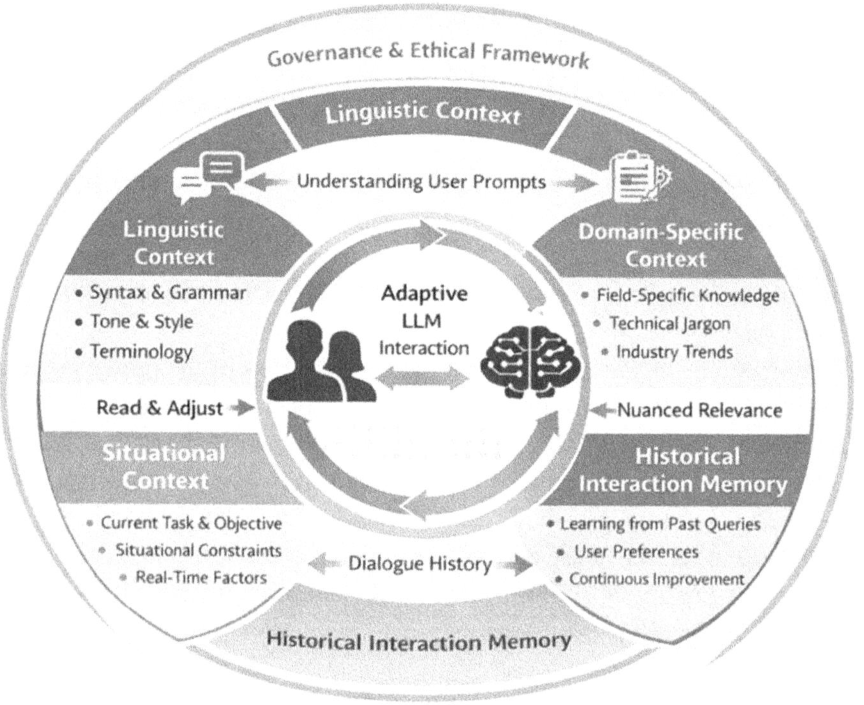

This diagram illustrates how an adaptive Large Language Model (LLM) understands and responds to users by integrating linguistic, situational, and domain-specific contexts along with historical interaction memory.

All these layers work within a **governance and ethical framework** to continuously learn from dialogue history and deliver relevant, accurate, and context-aware responses.

3.2 Prompt Engineering and Contextual Conditioning

The act of promoting engineering has become a top priority to determine the situation-sensitivity of Large Language Models. Using instructions, prompts, and background characteristics allow the user to condition models to produce results in a particular direction as required by certain goals. Effectively, this process is an interface to the context, which then converts human intent into a format which is operationalized by the model. Rightly-constructed prompts increase clarity, decrease the amount of ambiguity, and steer the model to knowledge areas of interest (Goyal et al., 2026).

A contextual conditioning goes beyond individual prompts and involves both iterative and multi turn interactions. By means of constant conversation, the users are able to effectively narrow down context with feedback, clarifications, and other limitations. LLMs integrate this dynamic context to make dynamic outputs to support solving knowledge exploration, and collaborative activities. The interactive conditioning enables models to engage in brainstorming and hypothesis formulation and critical thinking during periods of time.

Nevertheless, timely engineering, as well, raises the issue of the reliance of the performance of LLM on human experience. Bad framing may result in the false or shallow results, whilst well-designed circumstances may elevate the advanced emotional intelligence and amalgamation. This dependency confirms the collaborative characteristic of knowledge creation by the LLMs where human prompts and framing are both relevant in utilizing the model capabilities effectively and responsibly (Ouyang et al., 2022).

3.3 Memory, Retrieval, and Knowledge Grounding Mechanisms

Memory and retrieval systems are other knowledge grounding methods that boost context awareness of LLMs. The concept of memory in this respect is the capability of the model of recalling some relevant information throughout interactions, be it through conversational history, or external memory systems. Maintaining continuity and coherence is a key aspect to complex knowledge generation activities, such as research writing or long-term project support, and by preserving key aspects of past interactions, LLCs can guarantee these understandings (Roberts et al., 2020).

The concept of retrieval-augmented generation is a major development when it comes to basing the results of LLM on credible references. Models can also produce contextually aware and fact-grounded responses by incorporating the information accessed at the inference time like the information retrieved in databases, documents, or knowledge graphs. This strategy will mitigate the constraints of fixed training data and minimize the chances of hallucinations, which helps to increase confidence in AI-assisted knowledge generation.

There is also transparency and accountability through knowledge grounding mechanisms. With the associations of verifiable sources and the LLMs, the users can track the outputs, as they are supported by the underlying evidence, which lends credence to their critical appraisal and validation. Such pragmatic approach helps to align the knowledge creation by LLM with the conventional scholarly and professional standards, and makes such models more responsible and context-conscious, as opposed to opaque and independent authorities (Goyal et al., 2026).

4. LLMS AS COLLABORATIVE PARTNERS IN KNOWLEDGE CREATION

4.1 Human–AI Co-Creation Models

The human-AI co-creation of knowledge has become a more prominent way of understanding the role of Large Language Models in knowledge creation as cognitive work is shared between a human user and intelligent systems. Human plays the role of domain knowledge, moral knowledge and creative intent in this model whereas LLM presents the virtues of scale of computation, establishment of patterns as well as fast synthesis of information. Such a partnership implies that AI is not just the means of support but is an active integral part of intellectual processes and will make the knowledge creation more productive and exploratory (Dong et al., 2024).

The process of human-AI co-creation is defined by the process of iteration, as opposed to unidirectional production of output. Contextual feedback prompts users to ask questions, criticize answers, refine goals and direct the reasoning of the model. The response of LLLM is to adjust language, form and depth and is essentially involved in a dialog process of meaning-making. This dynamic resembles more collaborative practices that exist in a human team where the idea is developed by discussing and revising it.

Notably, co-creation does not mean that the human and machine agency are equal to each other. Intentionality and epistemic responsibility are human qualities that are not found in LLM. Rather, co-creation is based on complementarity, where the capabilities of the human are supplemented by the power of LLMs without the latter taking over the role of the former. Such a moderate approach is needed to sustain responsibility and reliance of AI-assisted knowledge building (Dandotiya et al., 2026).

4.2 Supporting Research, Writing, and Ideation

It has been found that LLLMs can be of great help in sustaining research-oriented processes especially in initial stages of ideation and exploratory analysis. LLMs assist researchers in sifting through the plethora of information by quickly creating summaries of the already existing literature and drawing a service of thematic connections and research questions. This will enable the conceptual stage of research to be executed at a higher rate giving the researchers more time to concentrate on critical analysis and original contribution (Wei et al., 2022).

LLMs also help in argument structuring, refinement, and coherence of complex writing in academic and professional writing. They are able to propose modifications of phrasing, explain technical meanings and modify content in different orders without changing the underlying intellectual meaning. These contributions contribute to clarity and accessibility when used properly and do not distort the voice of the writer and his authority.

LLM generative capabilities also have an advantage in ideation processes. Models provide a way to come across the various views and unconventional associations that can be brought into light through brainstorming and scenario exploration to trigger creative thinking. Instead of substituting human creative power, LLMs play the role of cognitive catalysts, broadening the scope of the options under consideration in creating knowledge and in innovation (Petroni et al., 2020).

4.3 Enhancing Creativity, Critical Thinking, and Problem Solving

Among the most interesting things about LLM cooperation is that it makes them more creative and problem-solving. The recombination of ideas in different fields allows LLMs to present new solutions to hard problems. This cross disciplinary synthesis promotes interdisciplinary thinking which is increasingly becoming very essential in dealing with problems which are scientific, social, and technological in nature.

Another aspect of critical thinking that LLLMs help with is those of counterarguments, alternative readings and structural analysis. Models can be used to assist users to recognize flaws in reasoning and the possibility of bias when asked to either challenge assumptions or test evidence. This reflective capability helps to enhance the rigour of knowledge generation especially when it is incorporated in peer review, policy analysis or even strategic planning (Kumari et al., 2026).

However, regardless of these advantages, active human interaction is crucial to the UAE improvement in creativity and problem-solving. Unless critically supervised, LLM products may contribute to strengthening powerful discourses or making probable but erroneous arguments. Hence, successful collaboration presupposes that users should view LLMs as knowledge collaborators who need to be confronted and put in context, so that human knowledge and machine-generated opportunities can be brought together to create and generate insight (Guu et al., 2020).

5. APPLICATIONS ACROSS DOMAINS

5.1 Academic Research and Scholarly Communication

Largescale Language Models are becoming an inseparable part of the academic research process, transforming the process of creating, communicating and sharing scholarly knowledge. In scholarly settings with high activity in research, LLMs can be used to help researchers perform early literature search through text summarization and detection of conceptual patterns across multiple areas of study. This feature comes in especially handy when one has to work across different fields, and one might get lost in the terminology and different theories of new fields. Recent advances in the field of LLMs have enabled researchers to devote more attention to narrow analysis and original input by decreasing the cognitive load that comes with information overload (Hoffman et al., 2022).

Llams are used in the academic world of writing where they help enhance the clarity, coherence and accessibility of such academic writing. Researchers rely on these models to polish the abstracts, organize the arguments and provide uniformity in terminologies and style. Multilingual scholarly communication that depends on the translation of research output and at the same time maintains technical accuracy can be enabled by LLM as well. The applications allow increased access and inclusivity to academic knowledge, which allows participation in global research communities.

Nevertheless, academia usage of LLMs also creates significant concerns in terms of authorship and originality and academic integrity. Although LLMs can be used to aid in the drafting and revision processes, intellectual content and interpretation is still left to the human writers. Consequently, institutions and publications are putting greater focus on open disclosure and ethical standards of AI-aided research and writing, and strengthening the supportive and not replacementary role of LLMs in knowledge building of academicians Kumari et al., 2026).

5.2 Education and Personalized Learning

In the education field, LLaMs are changing how we teach and learn because they allow learners to have customized, adaptive, and interactive learning experiences on knowledge. LLM-driven systems are able to customize the explanations to suit the background of the individual learners, as well as their learning pace and cognitive preferences. These models facilitate more in-depth conceptual learning and self-guided learning especially in technical or complex topics, through provision of targeted feedback and instructions to the learner (Zhao et al., 2026).

ELLs can also be used as intelligent tutoring systems that can help to make the learning process active and inquiry based. In a low-risk setting, students are able to engage with models, query models, investigate alternative explanation and test their knowledge. Such forms of dialogue make them curious and thoughtful and frame learners as participants in the knowledge generation process and not the recipients of knowledge.

Regarding using LLMs in instruction, teachers employ these technologies to create teaching content, create and generate test questions, and simulate an effect of real-life situations. Although these applications make things more efficient and pedagogically advanced, they also require close supervision and make sure that it is accurate, fair, and aligned with the objectives of learning. When applied in a wise way, the concept of LLM helps to extend human education by enlarging the scope of high-quality and context-driven support of education (Wang et al., 2020).

5.3 Industry, Innovation, and Decision Support

In both industry and organizational contexts, Large Language Models have seen increased use to aid in the process of innovation, strategic planning and decision making. In industries with high levels of knowledge like technology, healthcare, finance and consulting, LPMs help people to synthesize reports, analyze the market trends, and come up with insights in the form of scenarios. The capabilities allow making decisions in dynamic and uncertain environments faster and informed.

LLMs also contribute to the realms of innovation as it assists in the ideation and creation of a product. Teams utilize models to investigate the needs of customers, conceptualize design options as well as assess risk and opportunities. The speed of processing a wide range of data and opinions can assist any organization in uncovering the developing trends and opportunities previously ignored even by the most focused organizations. This advances the innovation processes and increases competitiveness (Sheikh et al., 2026).

Even though these advantages are true, the use of LLMs as decision support can bring about issues of transparency, accountability, and bias. The decisions that an organization may have to make are of great importance both ethically and financially and it is resorted to human judgment and previous contextual understanding which cannot be found in the model generated insights. In turn, the practices of embedding LLMs into decision-support systems that underline the importance of human control, explainability, and accountable application can be the most efficient ones (Le Scao et al., 2022).

5.4 Policy Making and Societal Knowledge Systems

The use of Large Language Models in policy making and other systems of more general knowledge is becoming more relevant, as it involves synthesis of complex information that has to be conveyed to various stakeholders. LLMs are used by the policymakers to support the analysis of documents related to legislation, sum up the opinions of people and investigate the policy scenario. The applications contribute to the development of evidence-based policies since it is possible to analyse the social, economic, and technological factors in a more thorough manner.

LLMs allow retrieving dependable and context-driven information in the knowledge systems of the society, including social information websites and civic engagement software. Models can also close the gap between experts and the public since they involve translating technical policy language into a form that is easy to understand. This will help bring a better-informed civic engagement and democratic decision-making to become more prominent in the sectors where new technologies and regulatory difficulties may arise (Jiang et al., 2020).

However, using LLMs in policies prompts important issues to do with impartiality, expression, and control. Trained models based on historical data can report any existing power structure or bias, which changes the policy. It is clear that the solution to these threats is through open model design, share data practices and well-established governance structures. LLMs can be useful allies in enhancing the knowledge building and informed administration in society when directed by moral ethics and human responsibility (Zhu et al., 2024).

6. ETHICAL, TRUST, AND GOVERNANCE CONSIDERATIONS

6.1 Bias, Fairness, and Transparency

The introduction of Large Language Models into knowledge creation processes creates a number of ethical issues connected to bias, justice, and transparency. The training content of LLMs is based on mass-sized datasets through human created content which can be thought to reflect historical inequalities, cultural failures and perspective bias. Consequently, these models can recreate or even increase the biases in language, representation and reasoning. Within the context of knowledge creation, these biases may create distortions, dismiss other opinions, and damage the validity of AI-supported results.

The technical and organizational interventions needed to ensure a fair knowledge creation in the context of LLCs based on their LLM should be carried out. Bias detection, dataset curation, and model auditing are some of the techniques that can be used to curb negative trends in model behavior. But fairness is not entirely a difficulty in technology, but also includes normative decisions concerning what knowledge should be considered and what different views ought to be voiced. To put model outputs in perspective and to review its outcomes, especially in sensitive areas like education, policy and social research, a human presence is required (Nye et al., 2021).

Transparency is an important decrease in breeding trust in LLCs as knowledge partners. A clear understanding should be made on the capabilities and limitations of the model to the users, as well as information sources. Although even towards explainable AI efforts, and disclosure practices, no explicit reasoning trace is provided by LLPs like in the human conceptualization, this can be better achieved through transparency. The stakeholders may assess the reliability and suitability of AI-assisted knowledge creation by making model behavior more understandable and responsible (Lampinen et al., 2022).

6.2 Intellectual Property and Authorship Issues

The application of LLMs in the creation and polishing of materials raises difficult issues of intellectual property and authorship. Human creativity, willfulness, and responsibility initiatives form the basis of traditional authorship, and they are not immediately applicable to AI systems. In situations where the LLM is incorporated in the research papers, educational materials or even business reports, then establishing ownership and attribution is a delicate affair. Such problems are especially topical in the academic and creative spheres of work, in which the originality and authorship obtained are the key to professional success.

The use of at present methods tends to view LLCs as instruments instead of authors, with the human operators who control and filter the plants bearing the responsibility and custody. Nevertheless, such an attitude needs to be compelled to have precise guidelines about disclosure and citation of AI assistance. The transparency regarding the level of AI engagement will contribute to ethical practice and will assist in preserving trust in the academic and professional circles. Policies that define the reasonable application of LLMs and stress human responsibility are now being formulated by many institutions and publishers (Razniewski et al., 2021).

Training data and reuse of the output also falls under the intellectual property issues. As LLMs are trained on huge and usually black-box data, the question of reproduction of copyrighted content and manipulation of proprietary material emerge. Focusing on these issues should entail the involvement of technologists, legal professionals, and policymakers in designing mechanisms of governance to accommodate innovation without breaching the intellectual property laws and creative work (Han et al., 2023).

6.3 Privacy, Security, and Responsible AI Use

The privacy and security issues have to be the first priority in the use of the LLMs in the knowledge creation setups that entail sensitive or personal information. The communications with the LLM can contain sensitive research information, student-related data, or the organizational knowledge that is considered personal. Unless there are proper precautions, such information may be leaked or abused, which will weaken the trust and adherence to the legal and ethical norms. Stewardly implementation then necessitates stringent data security and implementation policy (Li et al., 2023).

The question of the abuse of LLMs in generating misleading, manipulative or harmful materials also presents security risks. This may be in the form of man-made evidence; convincing yet untrue analyzes, or robotic misinformation in the field of knowledge creation. The reduction of these risks relates to both technical protection (filtering and monitoring of the content) and human governmental frameworks that facilitate the use of such content in critical thinking and ethically.

The ultimate reliance of responsible AI use is the governance structures which are characterized by roles, responsibility, and accountability among stakeholders. The institutions have to develop a set of guidelines that can relate the implementation of the LLM to the ethical values, societal values, and regulations. Through the implementation of ethical discourse and governance in the design and application of LLMs, organizations can develop trust and support the idea that such models act in positive ways as flexible and situational collaborators in knowledge production as opposed to risky and disruptive agents (Zelikman et al., 2022).

7. CHALLENGES AND LIMITATIONS OF LLM-DRIVEN KNOWLEDGE CREATION

7.1 Hallucination and Reliability Concerns

The phenomenon of hallucination is one of the most widely discussed limitations linked to Large Language Models as models produce their outputs, which are linguistically plausible and factually false or not supported by evidence. Knowledge creation situations are the most dangerous ones where these hallucinations may lead to an inaccuracy in academic research, education sources, or even decision-making in the workplace. In contrast to the conventional information retrieval system, LLMs do not distinguish verifiable knowledge and probable text generation inherently, which makes it difficult to evaluate reliability.

There is a high chance of hallucination in specialized or elaborate areas where specific language, empirical evidence and grounding in context are very crucial. Where models are not geographically grounded enough, they can make extrapolations based on the sampled patterns instead of knowledge. The given restriction highlights the significance of the role of a human during a review, validation, and contextualization of the LLM-generated materials, particularly in high-stakes settings (Yu et al., 2024).

To solve the issue of reliability, a mix of a technical and a procedural solution would be needed. Factual grounding can be enhanced by techniques like retrieval-augmented generation, source attribution and confidence estimation. Nevertheless, these mechanisms need to be reinforced with human control as well as institutional practice which focuses on the critical analysis. To incorporate the models into the knowledge creation processes in a responsible manner, it is crucial to identify the probabilistic nature of the outputs that LLM provides (Bills et al., 2023).

7.2 Context Drift and Misalignment

Context drift is the progressive contextual degradation or misrepresentation in a long-term interaction or complicated task. Multi-turn knowledge creation processes can cause Lloyd machines to misunderstand changing objectives, forget previous constraints or give more attention to recent inputs. This drift may introduce inconsistencies, decrease in relevance or not aligned products, which threatens the consistency of collaborative knowledge generation.

Misalignment is also produced within the context of mismatch of the goals of models and human will or morals. They are designed in order to align the responses given by the LLM with helpful and safe behavior, but even in this case, the responses might be contradictory to the domain norms and institutional values, as well as cultural sensitivities. Such misalignment may happen in knowledge generation contexts where the original arguments will be framed, evidence will be understood or opinions shall be represented at fault (Wei et al., 2022).

Context drift and misalignment can be averted through human interaction design and constant human interaction. Coherence can be promoted through structured prompts, periodic context reinforcement as well as express goal restatement. The issues mentioned more generally point to the drawbacks of existing LLM architectures with regards to long-term Maria major aspect of contextual coherence, and the necessity of future research on memory, alignment, and adaptive control strategies.

7.3 Scalability and Resource Constraints

Although Large Language Models are capable of doing quite a bit, they are limited in both their ability to scale by consuming a lot of computational and resource bases. The deployment and formal training of LLMs require huge amounts of energy, hardware and money, which may restrict access to smaller institutions or researchers or organizations in on-resource constrained places. This difference begs the question of equity in the access to high level tools of knowledge creates [39].

The resource constraints also have an impact on the real-time deployment and responsiveness especially when it is used on a large scale or interactive action. The cost of computer computation can limit the frequency or depth of models use, which will affect the way of integrating the use of LLMs into a workflow. Such constraints have the potential to define the extent and viability of knowledge creation programs that are reliant on AI, specifically in the sectors of the public or education.

The solution to the issue of scalability entails being innovative on model efficiency, optimization and governance. Model distillation, edge deployment and sharing infrastructure are all approaches that can be used to decrease resource requirements. Simultaneously, the institutions and policymakers should think about environmental and social effects of massive implementation of AI. Awareness of these limitations is crucial in establishing their inclusion and sustainability strategies that can help maximize the advantages of the knowledge creation enabled by LLM and reduce the costs associated with it [40].

CONCLUSION

Large Language Models have become disruptive actors in the mode of changing knowledge creation, that they are re-inventing how human beings create, process, and share knowledge in the various fields. Contrary to the previous computational tools which acted as passive tools to facilitate an intellectual process, LLMs portray responsive and contextual expectations that make them be active agents in an intellectual process. By enabling modeling of language, capability to integrate contextual input/cues and these models endorsing the interactive processes (iterative) this has placed them in the works of being collaborative partners in human-oriented knowledge systems.

The chapter has demonstrated the versatile nature of the role of LLM in knowledge creation, which covers underlying structures, context sensitivity, joint co-creation, and domain specialization. In all areas of academia, education, industry, and policy making, at best, LLMs are a source of efficiency, creativity, and the depth of analysis when in responsible use. Meanwhile, it has been highlighted during the discussion that significant ethical, trust and governance issues are at stake when underlining that human judgment, accountability and transparency are still essential. LLMs lack epistemic authority, instead having a value in enhancing the human cognition and broadening the range of investigation.

On the other hand, the potential of the LLM-based knowledge creation is limited by the issues of hallucination, drift, misalignment, and resource-consuming implementation. Such constraints further support a careful implementation approach, gradual testing, and still current studies should be done to produce more stable, understandable, and sustainable AI systems. In the ongoing evolution of LLMs, the next steps should be ensuring that such systems are beneficial to humankind, inclusive, and conscientious.

To sum up, Large Language Models are to be seen not as the substitutes of human knowledge creators but as flexible and adaptable collaborators that change the terms under which knowledge is generated. When incorporated into ethical guidelines and under the guidance of informed human control, LLMs can enact more content onto knowledge-making processes, enable interdisciplinary interaction and help make more knowledgeable and mindful decisions in the ever-more complicated world.

REFERENCES

Bills, S., Cammarata, N., Mossing, D., Tillman, H., Gao, L., Goh, G., ... & Saunders, W. (2023). Language models can explain neurons in language models.

Bommasani, R., Hudson, D. A., Adeli, E., Altman, R., Arora, S., von Arx, S., . . . Liang, P. (2021). On the opportunities and risks of foundation models. *arXiv preprint arXiv:2108.07258.*

Brown, T., Mann, B., Ryder, N., Subbiah, M., Kaplan, J. D., Dhariwal, P., & Amodei, D. (2020). Language models are few-shot learners. *Advances in Neural Information Processing Systems*, *33*, 1877–1901.

Dandotiya, M., Goyal, N. K., Yadav, P., Sankhla, K., & Kumari, M. (2026). GENALYTICS: A deep dive into real-time insights via generative AI. In *Generative AI-Powered Data Architectures* (pp. 105–134). IGI Global. DOI: 10.4018/979-8-3373-5616-7.ch005

Dong, Q., Li, L., Dai, D., Zheng, C., Ma, J., Li, R., & Sui, Z. (2024, November). A survey on in-context learning. In *Proceedings of the 2024 conference on empirical methods in natural language processing* (pp. 1107-1128). DOI: 10.18653/v1/2024.emnlp-main.64

Farooqi, A., Das, D., Tripathi, M., Dutta, R., Goyal, N. K., & Sheikh, M. F. (2026). Navigating ethical frontiers in AI-driven geriatric care. In *AI for Geriatric Care in an Aging Society* (pp. 243–266). IGI Global., DOI: 10.4018/979-8-3373-5462-0.ch009

Goyal, N. K., Goyal, N. K., Kumar, S., Dutta, R., Kothari, V., & Sinha, S. K. (2026). Empowering elderly care through artificial intelligence. In *AI for Geriatric Care in an Aging Society* (pp. 1–28). IGI Global., DOI: 10.4018/979-8-3373-5462-0.ch001

Guu, K., Lee, K., Tung, Z., Pasupat, P., & Chang, M. (2020). Retrieval augmented language model pre-training. *Proceedings of ICML*, 3929–3938.

Han, J., Collier, N., Buntine, W., & Shareghi, E. (2023). Prompting with iterative verification improving graph-based generative capability of LLMs. *arXiv preprint arXiv:2305.12392.*

Jiang, Z., Xu, F. F., Araki, J., & Neubig, G. (2020). How can we know what language models know? *Transactions of the ACL, 8*, 423–438. DOI: 10.1162/tacl_a_00324

Kaplan, J., McCandlish, S., Henighan, T., Brown, T. B., Chess, B., Child, R., . . . Amodei, D. (2020). Scaling laws for neural language models. *arXiv preprint arXiv:2001.08361.*

Kumari, M., & Goyal, N. K. (2026). Artificial intelligence in the cryptocurrency ecosystem: Crime mechanisms, detection strategies, and legal perspectives. In *Innovations in Cryptocrime and Financial Fraud* (pp. 245–282). IGI Global., DOI: 10.4018/979-8-3373-0675-9.ch007

Kumari, M., Kumawat, R., Tripathi, M., Suganthi, K., Goyal, N. K., & Sheikh, M. F. (2026). Blockchain for transparency and traceability in supply chains. In *Maximizing Operational Efficiency at the Intersection of Supply Chain Management and Marketing* (pp. 35–64). IGI Global., DOI: 10.4018/979-8-3373-3109-6.ch002

Lampinen, A., Dasgupta, I., Chan, S., Mathewson, K., Tessler, M., Creswell, A., & Hill, F. (2022, December). Can language models learn from explanations in context? In *Findings of the Association for Computational Linguistics* (pp. 537–563). EMNLP. DOI: 10.18653/v1/2022.findings-emnlp.38

Le Scao, T., Wang, T., Hesslow, D., Bekman, S., Bari, M. S., Biderman, S., & Beltagy, I. (2022, December). What language model to train if you have one million gpu hours? In *Findings of the Association for Computational Linguistics* (pp. 765–782). EMNLP. DOI: 10.18653/v1/2022.findings-emnlp.54

Li, L., Zhang, Y., & Chen, L. (2023). Personalized prompt learning for explainable recommendation. *ACM Transactions on Information Systems, 41*(4), 1–26.

Nye, M., Andreassen, A. J., Gur-Ari, G., Michalewski, H., Austin, J., Bieber, D., ... & Odena, A. (2021). Show your work: Scratchpads for intermediate computation with language models.

Ouyang, L., Wu, J., Jiang, X., Almeida, D., Wainwright, C., Mishkin, P., Zhang, C., Agarwal, S., Slama, K., Ray, A., Schulman, J., Hilton, J., Kelton, F., Miller, L., Simens, M., Askell, A., Welinder, P., Christiano, P., Leike, J., & Lowe, R. (2022). Training language models to follow instructions with human feedback. *Advances in Neural Information Processing Systems, 35*, 27730–27744. DOI: 10.52202/068431-2011

Petroni, F., Lewis, P., Piktus, A., Rocktäschel, T., Wu, Y., Miller, A. H., & Riedel, S. (2020). How context affects language models' factual predictions. *arXiv preprint arXiv:2005.04611.*

Petroni, F., Rocktäschel, T., Riedel, S., Lewis, P., Bakhtin, A., Wu, Y., & Miller, A. (2019, November). Language models as knowledge bases? In *Proceedings of the 2019 conference on empirical methods in natural language processing and the 9th international joint conference on natural language processing (EMNLP-IJCNLP)* (pp. 2463-2473). DOI: 10.18653/v1/D19-1250

Razniewski, S., Yates, A., Kassner, N., & Weikum, G. (2021). Language models as or for knowledge bases. *arXiv preprint arXiv:2110.04888.*

Roberts, A., Raffel, C., & Shazeer, N. (2020). How much knowledge can you pack into the parameters of a language model? *arXiv preprint arXiv:2002.08910.* DOI: 10.18653/v1/2020.emnlp-main.437

Shanahan, M. (2024). Talking about large language models. *Communications of the ACM, 67*(2), 68–79. DOI: 10.1145/3624724

Sharma, P., Kumawat, R., Jain, G., Keswani, G., Goyal, N. K., & Sheikh, M. F. (2026). Machine learning-based intrusion detection systems for healthcare IoT. In *Resilient Healthcare Internet of Things Systems* (pp. 185–214). IGI Global., DOI: 10.4018/979-8-3373-7610-3.ch007

Sheikh, M. F. A., Kapoor, S. K., Goyal, N. K., Tuba, E., & Rao, A. (2026). Enhancing healthcare security with fog computing and blockchain technology. In *Recent Advancements in Artificial Intelligence*. Springer., DOI: 10.1007/978-981-96-7760-3_38

Vaswani, A., Shazeer, N., Parmar, N., Uszkoreit, J., Jones, L., Gomez, A. N., & Polosukhin, I. (2017). Attention is all you need. *Advances in Neural Information Processing Systems*, 30.

Wang, C., Liu, X., & Song, D. (2020). Language models are open knowledge graphs. *arXiv preprint arXiv:2010.11967.*

Wei, J., Wang, X., Schuurmans, D., Bosma, M., Xia, F., Chi, E., & Zhou, D. (2022). Chain-of-thought prompting elicits reasoning in large language models. *Advances in Neural Information Processing Systems, 35*, 24824–24837. DOI: 10.52202/068431-1800

Yu, J., Wang, X., Tu, S., Cao, S., Zhang-Li, D., Lv, X., & Li, J. (2024, May). Kola: Carefully benchmarking world knowledge of large language models. In *International Conference on Learning Representations* (Vol. 2024, pp. 44594-44637).

Zelikman, E., Wu, Y., Mu, J., & Goodman, N. (2022). STAR: Bootstrapping reasoning with reasoning. *Advances in Neural Information Processing Systems, 35*, 15476–15488. DOI: 10.52202/068431-1126

Zhao, W. X., Zhou, K., Li, J., Tang, T., Dong, Z., Hou, Y., Zhang, B., Min, Y., Zhang, J., Liu, P., Wang, X., Du, Y., Yang, C., Chen, Y., Chen, Z., Jiang, J., Ren, R., Li, Y., Tang, X., & Wen, J. R. (2026). A survey of large language models. *Frontiers of Computer Science, 20*(12), 2012627. DOI: 10.1007/s11704-026-60308-3 PMID: 41813245

Zhu, Y., Wang, X., Chen, J., Qiao, S., Ou, Y., Yao, Y., . . . Zhang, N. (2024). Llms for knowledge graph construction and reasoning: Recent capabilities and future opportunities. *World Wide Web, 27*(5).

Xi, Y., Liu, W., Lin, J., Cai, X., Zhu, H., Zhu, J., & Yu, Y. (2024, October). Towards open-world recommendation with knowledge augmentation from large language models. In *Proceedings of the 18th ACM Conference on Recommender Systems* (pp. 12-22).

Compilation of References

Abbas, N., Whitfield, J., Atwell, E., Bowman, H., Pickard, T., & Walker, A. (2022). Online chat and chatbots to enhance mature student engagement in higher education. *International Journal of Lifelong Education*, *41*(3), 308–326. DOI: 10.1080/02601370.2022.2066213

Abrar, M., Aboraya, W., Subramanian, K. P., Abdulghafor, R., Al Husaini, Y., & Al Husaini, M. (2025). Adaptive intelligence: AI-powered personalized learning and dynamic assessments. In *Proceedings of the 2025 International Conference on Electrical, Communication and Computer Engineering (ICECCE)* (pp. 1–7). IEEE. DOI: 10.1109/ICECCE67514.2025.11257877

Accenture. (2024). (2024). AI and the Next Era of Personalisation: Customer Experience 2030 Report. *Accenture Strategy Insights.* https://www.accenture.com. Accenture.

Acemoglu, D., & Restrepo, P. (2020). Artificial intelligence, automation, and work. *The Journal of Economic Perspectives*, *34*(1), 3–30. DOI: 10.1257/jep.29.1.3

Adamopoulou, E., & Moussiades, L. (2020). Chatbots: History, technology, and applications. *Machine Learning with Applications*, *2*, 100006. Advance online publication. DOI: 10.1016/j.mlwa.2020.100006

Adegboye, M. A., Aibinu, A. M., Kolo, J. G., Aliyu, I., Folorunso, T. A., & Lee, S.-H. (2020). Incorporating Intelligence in Fish Feeding System for Dispensing Feed Based on Fish Feeding Intensity. *IEEE Access : Practical Innovations, Open Solutions*, *8*, 91948–91960. DOI: 10.1109/ACCESS.2020.2994442

Adimulam, R. P., Kokkiligadda, V., & Polagani, A. (2024). Automatic Feed Dispenser for Aquaculture using Arduino Technology. *2024 3rd International Conference for Advancement in Technology (ICONAT)*, 1–5. DOI: 10.1109/ICONAT61936.2024.10774929

Aghaee, N., Vrågård, J., & Brorsson, F. (2024). Generative AI in Higher Education: Educators' Perspectives on Academic Learning and Integrity. European Conference on E-Learning, 23(1), 406-414. DOI: 10.34190/ecel.23.1.3090

Agrawal, A., Gans, J., & Goldfarb, A. (2019). *Prediction machines: The simple economics of artificial intelligence*. Harvard Business Review Press. DOI: 10.7208/chicago/9780226613475.001.0001

Ahmad, S. F., Alam, M. M., Rahmat, M. K., Mubarik, M. S., & Hyder, S. I. (2022). Academic and administrative role of artificial intelligence in education. *Sustainability (Basel)*, *14*(3), 1101. DOI: 10.3390/su14031101

Ahme, Z., Shanto, S. S., & Jony, A. I. (2024). Potentiality of generative AI tools in higher education: Evaluating ChatGPT's viability as a teaching assistant for introductory programming courses. *STEM Education*, *4*(3), 165–182. DOI: 10.3934/steme.2024011

Airtable. (n.d.). *Best AI tools for product managers*. https://www.airtable.com/articles/best-ai-tools-for-product-managers

Akwiri, D. (2024, December 18). *AI's Impact on Employment: Workforce Displacement and Ethical Considerations*. ResearchGate. https://doi.org/DOI: 10.13140/RG.2.2.28346.91841

Al Hashmi, R. A., Ozturk, I., & Elmehdi, H. M. (2025). Early detection of at-risk health sciences students: A machine learning-based predictive study using midterm grades. *BMC Medical Education*, *25*(1), 1651. DOI: 10.1186/s12909-025-08192-6 PMID: 41299422

Alaidi, A., Yahya, O., & Alrikabi, H. T. H. S. (2020). Using Modern Education Technique in Wasit University. *International Journal of Interactive Mobile Technologies (Ijim)*, *14*(06), 82. DOI: 10.3991/ijim.v14i06.11539

Alenezi, M., & Akour, M. (2025). AI-driven innovations in software engineering: A review of current practices and future directions. *Applied Sciences (Basel, Switzerland)*, *15*(3), 1344. Advance online publication. DOI: 10.3390/app15031344

Aleven, V., McLaughlin, E. A., Glenn, R. A., & Koedinger, K. R. (2017). Instruction based on adaptive learning technologies. In Mayer, R. E., & Alexander, P. A. (Eds.), *Handbook of research on learning and instruction* (pp. 522–560). Routledge.

Alhoshan, W., Ferrari, A., & Zhao, L. (2023). Zero-shot learning for requirements classification: An exploratory study. *Information and Software Technology*, *159*, 107202. DOI: 10.1016/j.infsof.2023.107202

Alkaissi, H., & McFarlane, S. (2023). Artificial hallucinations in ChatGPT: Implications in scientific writing. *Cureus*. Advance online publication. DOI: 10.7759/cureus.35179

Alkaissi, H., & McFarlane, S. I. (2023). Artificial intelligence in medical writing: A friend or a foe? *Cureus*, *15*(2), e35224. Advance online publication. DOI: 10.7759/cureus.35224 PMID: 36968855

Allana, H., & Ali, S. (2025). Artificial intelligence in nursing education: balancing reluctance and embracing innovation. *Pedagogical Inquiry and Practice*, 1(1).

Allouch, M., Azaria, A., & Azoulay, R. (2021). Conversational agents: Goals, technologies, vision and challenges. *Sensors (Basel)*, *21*(24), 8448. Advance online publication. DOI: 10.3390/s21248448

Almagharbeh, W. T., Ahmed, W. R., Alfanash, H. A., Alnawafleh, K. A., & Tajoury, O. H. (2026). Touching the future: How haptic technology and AI are revolutionizing nursing simulations: A systematic scoping review. *Journal of Professional Nursing : Official Journal of the American Association of Colleges of Nursing*, *63*, 18–25. DOI: 10.1016/j.profnurs.2025.12.010 PMID: 41796557

Alnawafleh, K. A., Almagharbeh, W. T., Alfanash, H. A., Alasmari, A. A., Alharbi, A. A., Alamrani, M. H., Alkubati, S. A., Altayar, M. A., & Rezq, K. A. (2025). Exploring the ethical dimensions of AI integration in nursing practice: A systematic review. *Journal of Nursing Regulation*, *16*(3), 228–237. DOI: 10.1016/j.jnr.2025.08.001

AlphaCodium. (n.d.). *AlphaCodium: From prompt engineering to flow engineering*. GitHub. https://github.com/Codium-ai/AlphaCodium

Alrayes, A., Henari, T., & Ahmed, D. (2024). ChatGPT in Education – Understanding the Bahraini Academics Perspective. *Electronic Journal of e-Learning*, *22*(2), 112–134. DOI: 10.34190/ejel.22.2.3250

Al-Saadawi, H., & Daş, R. (2024). Multimodal Emotion Recognition Using Bi-LG-GCN for MELD Dataset. *Balkan Journal of Electrical and Computer Engineering*, *12*(1), 36–46. DOI: 10.17694/bajece.1372107

Al-Shallakh, M. (2024). Embedding Artificial Intelligent Applications in Higher Educational Institutions to Improve Students' Pronunciation Performance. *Theory and Practice in Language Studies*, *14*(6), 1897–1906. DOI: 10.17507/tpls.1406.31

Al-Zahrani, A. M., & Alasmari, T. M. (2024). Exploring the impact of artificial intelligence on higher education: The dynamics of ethical, social, and educational implications. *Humanities & Social Sciences Communications*, *11*(1), 1–12. DOI: 10.1057/s41599-024-03432-4

Amankwaa, I., Ekpor, E., Cudjoe, D., Kobiah, E., Fuseini, A. K. J., Diebieri, M., Gyamfi, S., & Brownie, S. (2025). Patterns, advances, and gaps in using ChatGPT and similar technologies in nursing education: A PAGER scoping review. *Nurse Education Today, 153*, 106822. DOI: 10.1016/j.nedt.2025.106822 PMID: 40644844

American Association of Colleges and Universities (AAC&U). (2025). *Higher education leaders navigate AI disruption: Leading through disruption survey report*. AAC&U & Elon University. https://www.aacu.org/newsroom/higher-education-leaders-navigate-ai-disruption

Andrews, S. K., & Crawford, C. M. (2025). Higher Education Instructor Perceptions of Student Experience Through Artificial Intelligence Agents: Shift From Information Age to the Reasoning Age. In M*otivating Engagement, Belonging, and Success in Higher Education Student Experience* (pp. 305-330). IGI Global Scientific Publishing.

Ang, A., & Timmermann, A. (2012). Regime changes and financial markets. *Annual Review of Financial Economics, 4*, 313–337.

Angwin, J., Larson, J., Mattu, S., & Kirchner, L. (2016). *Machine bias: There's software used across the country to predict future criminals. And it's biased against blacks*. ProPublica.

Anselmo, C., Bete-Liban, A., Ollero, J., Baui, D., Pascua, J., & Sario, Y. (2025). Role of AI in Enhancing Critical Thinking in Science Education: Challenges and Opportunities for Science Instructor. *International Journal of Multidisciplinary Applied Business and Education Research*, *6*(8), 3877–3891. DOI: 10.11594/ijmaber.06.08.12

Anthropic. (2024, June 21). *Claude 3.5 Sonnet*. https://www.anthropic.com/news/claude-3-5-sonnet

Anthropic. (2026). *Claude Opus 4.6*. https://www.anthropic.com/claude/opus

Apte, S., Honrao, Y., Shinde, R., Talele, P., & Phalnikar, R. (2023, April). Automatic Extraction of Software Requirements Using Machine Learning. In *International Conference on Information and Communication Technology for Intelligent Systems* (pp. 361-370). Singapore: Springer Nature Singapore. DOI: 10.1007/978-981-99-3758-5_33

Arbat, R. P. (2024). Exploring the effectiveness of Jenkins CI/CD pipelines: A comprehensive survey. *Journal of Emerging Technologies and Innovative Research, 11*(2), 590–595. https://www.jetir.org/papers/JETIR2402090.pdf

Arulmohan, S., Meurs, M. J., & Mosser, S. (2023, October). Extracting domain models from textual requirements in the era of large language models. In 2023 ACM/IEEE International Conference on Model Driven Engineering Languages and Systems Companion (MODELS-C) (pp. 580-587). IEEE. DOI: 10.1109/MODELS-C59198.2023.00096

Asana Inc. (2026a). Human + AI collaboration that moves work forward. https://asana.com/product/ai

Asana Inc. (2026b). For Developers and Teams. https://asana.com/developers

Asana Inc. (2026c). *Get started with Asana AI.* https://help.asana.com/s/article/get-started-with-asana-ai

Atlassian. (2026). *Jira.* https://www.atlassian.com/software/jira

Auld, G., Casovan, A., Clarke, A., & Faveri, B. (2022). Governing AI through ethical standards: Learning from the experiences of other private governance initiatives. *Journal of European Public Policy*, *29*(11), 1822–1844. DOI: 10.1080/13501763.2022.2099449

Avci, H., Lunn, S. J., & Hazari, Z. (2025). Exploring STEM educators' perspectives on the integration of AI-enabled technologies in teaching and learning. *Computers and Education Open*, *9*, 100304. DOI: 10.1016/j.caeo.2025.100304

Avramovic, S., & Mobahi, H. (2025). Redesigning a health informatics course for nursing students through AI-driven instruction and clinically contextualized assignments. *Canadian Journal of Nursing Informatics*, *20*(4).

Ayedoun, E., Hayashi, Y., & Seta, K. (2019). Adding communicative and affective strategies to an embodied conversational agent to enhance second language learners' willingness to communicate. *International Journal of Artificial Intelligence in Education*, *29*(1), 29–57. DOI: 10.1007/s40593-018-0171-6

Azamfirei, V., Psarommatis, F., & Lagrosen, Y. (2023). Application of automation for in-line quality inspection, a zero-defect manufacturing approach. *Journal of Manufacturing Systems*, *67*, 1–22. DOI: 10.1016/j.jmsy.2022.12.010

Azevedo, L., Robles, P., Best, E., & Mallinson, D. J. (2025). Institutional Policies on Artificial Intelligence in Higher Education: Frameworks and Best Practices for Faculty. *New Directions for Adult and Continuing Education*, *2025*(188), 70–78. DOI: 10.1002/ace.70013

Aziz, Z., Mazeh, A. C., Ilic, D., Ciardulli, M., El Hadi, S. N., Camuccio, A., Moore, J., & Kiegaldie, D. (2026). Leveraging AI simulations for enhancing cultural responsiveness and interprofessional collaboration in health professions education. *Nurse Education in Practice*, *91*, 104711. DOI: 10.1016/j.nepr.2026.104711 PMID: 41520588

Babalola, D., Adedoyin, A., Ogundipe, F., Folorunso, A., & Nwatu, C. (2024). Policy framework for Cloud Computing: AI, governance, compliance and management. *Global Journal of Engineering and Technology Advances*, *21*(2), 114–126. DOI: 10.30574/gjeta.2024.21.2.0212

Bahari, G., Alenazi, L., & Alkathiri, A. M. (2025). The implementation of artificial intelligence in nursing education and its psychological impact on nursing students: A cross-sectional study. *Nurse Education Today*, *153*, 106816. DOI: 10.1016/j.nedt.2025.106816 PMID: 40544672

Bai, J., & Perron, P. (2003). Computation and analysis of multiple structural change models. *Journal of Applied Econometrics, 18*(1), 1–22.

Baker, J. A. (2021). The impact of adaptive learning environments on student self-efficacy. *Journal of Educational Technology.*

Baker, R. S., & Inventado, P. S. (2014). Educational data mining and learning analytics. In Larusson, J. A., & White, B. (Eds.), *Learning analytics: From research to practice* (pp. 61–75). Springer. DOI: 10.1007/978-1-4614-3305-7_4

Bakhanova, E., Vinke-de Kruijf, J., Wöhler, L., Warbroek, B., & Arentsen, M. (2025). Integrative Approaches to Interconnected Environmental Challenges: How Institutional Factors Influence Cross-Sector Integration in Dutch Rural Areas. *Environmental Management*, *75*(5), 1308–1321. DOI: 10.1007/s00267-025-02140-2 PMID: 40053119

Balani, K., Sharma, B., & Agrawal, S. (2025). From linesmen to local leaders: How does informal governance influence India's electricity policy outcomes? *Energy Research & Social Science*, *124*, 104056. DOI: 10.1016/j.erss.2025.104056

Bang, Y., Cahyawijaya, S., Lee, N., Dai, W., Su, D., Wilie, B., & Fung, P. (2023, November). A multitask, multilingual, multimodal evaluation of chatgpt on reasoning, hallucination, and interactivity. In *Proceedings of the 13th international joint conference on natural language processing and the 3rd conference of the asia-pacific chapter of the association for computational linguistics* (volume 1*: Long papers)* (pp. 675-718). DOI: 10.18653/v1/2023.ijcnlp-main.45

Barenkamp, M., Rebstadt, J., & Thomas, O. (2020). Applications of AI in classical software engineering. *AI Perspectives*, *2*(1), 1. Advance online publication. DOI: 10.1186/s42467-020-00005-4

Barke, S., James, M. B., & Polikarpova, N. (2023). Grounded Copilot: How Programmers Interact with Code-Generating Models. *Proceedings of the ACM on Programming Languages, 7* (OOPSLA1), 85–111. DOI: 10.1145/3586030

Ba, S., Stein, D., Liu, Q., Long, T., Xie, K., & Wu, L. (2021). Examining the effects of a pedagogical agent with dual-channel emotional cues on learner emotions, cognitive load, and Knowledge transfer performance. *Journal of Educational Computing Research*, *59*(6), 1114–1134. DOI: 10.1177/0735633121992421

Bashynska, Y. (2024). ГЛОБАЛЬНІ ЕКОНОМІЧНІ АСПЕКТИ РОЗВИТКУ ВІДНОВЛЮВАНОЇ ЕНЕРГЕТИКИ В УКРАЇНІ ТА ПОЛЬЩІ. *Public Management and Policy*, (3-4), 14–22. DOI: 10.70651/3041-2498/2024.3-4.02

Bassner, P., Lottner, A., & Krusche, S. (2025). Towards understanding the impact of context-aware AI tutors and general-purpose AI chatbots on student learning. In *Proceedings of the 25th Koli Calling International Conference on Computing Education Research* (pp. 1–11). ACM. DOI: 10.1145/3769994.3770025

Bates, T., Cobo, C., Mariño, O., & Wheeler, S. (2020). Can artificial intelligence transform higher education? *International Journal of Educational Technology in Higher Education*, *17*(1), 42. DOI: 10.1186/s41239-020-00218-x

Batool, A., Zowghi, D., & Bano, M. (2025). AI governance: A systematic literature review. *AI and Ethics*, 1–15.

Bavaresco, R., Silveira, D., Reis, E., Barbosa, J., Righi, R., Costa, C., Antunes, R., Gomes, M., Gatti, C., Vanzin, M., Junior, S. C., Silva, E., & Moreira, C. (2020). Conversational agents in business: A systematic literature review and future research directions. *Computer Science Review*, *36*, 100239. DOI: 10.1016/j.cosrev.2020.100239

Bearman, M., & Ajjawi, R. (2023). Learning to work with the black box: Pedagogy for a world with generative AI. *British Journal of Educational Technology*, *54*(5), 1160–1173. DOI: 10.1111/bjet.13337

Bearman, M., Ryan, J., & Ajjawi, R. (2023). Discourses of artificial intelligence in higher education: A critical literature review. *Higher Education*, *86*(2), 369–385. DOI: 10.1007/s10734-022-00937-2

Bender, E. M., Gebru, T., McMillan-Major, A., & Shmitchell, S. (2021). On the Dangers of Stochastic Parrots: Can Language Models Be Too Big?? *Proceedings of the 2021 ACM Conference on Fairness, Accountability, and Transparency*, 610–623. DOI: 10.1145/3442188.3445922

Bhat, J., & Jayaram, Y. (2023). Predictive analytics for student retention and success using AI/ML. *International Journal of Artificial Intelligence, Data Science, and Machine Learning*, *4*(4), 121–131. DOI: 10.63282/3050-9262.IJAIDSML-V4I4P114

Bickmore, T., Trinh, H., Hoppmann, M., & Asadi, R. (2016). Virtual agents in the classroom: Experience fielding a co-presenter agent in University courses. [Springer International Publishing.]. *Lecture Notes in Computer Science*, *10011*, 154–163. DOI: 10.1007/978-3-319-47665-0_14

Bieliaiev, O. (2025). Overview of artificial intelligence-based project management tools for business representatives. *Development Management*, *24*(3), 57–67. DOI: 10.63341/devt/3.2025.57

Bills, S., Cammarata, N., Mossing, D., Tillman, H., Gao, L., Goh, G., ... & Saunders, W. (2023). Language models can explain neurons in language models.

Bishop, C. M. (2006). *Pattern recognition and machine learning*. Springer.

Blanchard, A., Thomas, C., & Taddeo, M. (2025). Ethical governance of artificial intelligence for defence: Normative tradeoffs for principle to practice guidance. *AI & Society*, *40*(1), 185–198. DOI: 10.1007/s00146-024-01866-7 PMID: 41640455

Bobula, M. (2024). Generative artificial intelligence (AI) in higher education: A comprehensive review of challenges, opportunities, and implications. *Journal of Learning Development in Higher Education*, *30*(30). Advance online publication. DOI: 10.47408/jldhe.vi30.1137

Bolan, R. S. (1992). Organising for Sustainable Growth in Poland. *Journal of the American Planning Association*, *58*(3), 301–311. DOI: 10.1080/01944369208975809

Bolukbasi, T., Chang, K. W., Zou, J. Y., Saligrama, V., & Kalai, A. T. (2016). Man is to computer programmer as woman is to homemaker? debiasing word embeddings. *Advances in Neural Information Processing Systems*, 29.

Bommasani, R., Hudson, D. A., Adeli, E., Altman, R., Arora, S., von Arx, S., . . . Liang, P. (2021). On the opportunities and risks of foundation models. *arXiv preprint arXiv:2108.07258*.

Bond, M., Khosravi, H., De Laat, M., Bergdahl, N., Negrea, V., Oxley, E., Pham, P., Chong, S. W., & Siemens, G. (2024). A meta systematic review of artificial intelligence in higher education: A call for increased ethics, collaboration, and rigour. *International Journal of Educational Technology in Higher Education, 21*(1), 4. DOI: 10.1186/s41239-023-00436-z

Bond, M., Passy, R., & Agnew, S. (2024). A systematic review of generative AI in higher education: The need for ethical frameworks. *Educational Technology Research and Development*. Advance online publication. DOI: 10.1007/s11423-024-10351-w

Borromeo, A. S., Manaloto, A. M., Santos, M. J. M. D., Antonio, R. P., Soyosa, M. D., & Wider, W. (2025). Harnessing generative AI in nursing education: A bibliometric review. *Teaching and Learning in Nursing, 20*(4), e1002–e1011. DOI: 10.1016/j.teln.2025.04.014

Bouchaud, J. P., Farmer, J. D., & Lillo, F. (2009). How markets slowly digest changes in supply and demand. In Hens, T., & Schenk-Hoppé, K. R. (Eds.), *Handbook of financial markets: Dynamics and evolution*. Elsevier. DOI: 10.1016/B978-012374258-2.50006-3

Božić, V. (2024). Artificial Intelligence in nurse education. In *Engineering Applications of Artificial Intelligence* (pp. 143–172). Springer Nature Switzerland. DOI: 10.1007/978-3-031-50300-9_9

Brandao, P. R. (2025). The impact of artificial intelligence on modern society. *AI, 6*(8), 190. DOI: 10.3390/ai6080190

Breiman, L. (2001). Statistical modeling: The two cultures. *Statistical Science, 16*(3), 199–231.

Briel, A. (2021). Toward an eclectic and malleable multiagent educational assistant. *Computer Applications in Engineering Education*, cae.22449. Advance online publication. DOI: 10.1002/cae.22449

Brown, T., Mann, B., Ryder, N., Subbiah, M., Kaplan, J. D., Dhariwal, P., & Amodei, D. (2020). Language models are few-shot learners. *Advances in Neural Information Processing Systems, 33*, 1877–1901.

Brummelen, J., & Lin, P. (2020). Engaging Teachers to Co-Design Integrated AI Curriculum for K-12 Classrooms. https://doi.org//arxiv.2009.11100DOI: 10.48550

Brynjolfsson, E., Rock, D., & Syverson, C. (2021). The productivity J-curve: How intangibles complement general purpose technologies. *American Economic Journal. Macroeconomics, 13*(1), 333–372. DOI: 10.1257/mac.20180386

Buckingham, D. (2003). Media education: Literacy, learning and contemporary culture. *Polity.*

Buolamwini, J., & Gebru, T. (2018). Gender shades: Intersectional accuracy disparities in commercial gender classification. *Proceedings of the 1st Conference on Fairness, Accountability and Transparency.*

Calle Gallego, J. M., & Zapata Jaramillo, C. M. (2023). QUARE: Towards a question-answering model for requirements elicitation. *Automated Software Engineering, 30*(2), 25. DOI: 10.1007/s10515-023-00386-w

Camilleri, M. A. (2024). Artificial intelligence governance: Ethical considerations and implications for social responsibility. *Expert Systems: International Journal of Knowledge Engineering and Neural Networks, 41*(7), e13406. DOI: 10.1111/exsy.13406

Campbell, J. Y., Lo, A. W., & MacKinlay, A. C. (1997). *The econometrics of financial markets.* Princeton University Press. DOI: 10.1515/9781400830213

Carayannopoulos, S. (2018). Using chatbots to aid transition. *International Journal of Information and Learning Technology, 35*(2), 118–129. DOI: 10.1108/IJILT-10-2017-0097

Carter, D. P., & Christopher, M. (2015). Integrating core concepts from the institutional analysis and development framework for the systematic analysis of policy designs: An illustration from the US National Organic Program regulation—. *Journal of Theoretical Politics, 28*(1), 159–185. DOI: 10.1177/0951629815603494

Castonguay, A., Farthing, P., Davies, S., Vogelsang, L., Kleib, M., Risling, T., & Green, N. (2023). Revolutionizing nursing education through AI integration: A reflection on the disruptive impact of ChatGPT. *Nurse Education Today, 129*, 105916. DOI: 10.1016/j.nedt.2023.105916 PMID: 37515957

Catalano, I. (2025). Rearing condition affects behavioral response to cross-modal expectancy violation paradigm in zebra finches. DOI: 10.1101/2025.10.10.681716

Cervantes, J., Garcia-Lamont, F., Rodríguez-Mazahua, L., & Lopez, A. (2024). Faculty perceptions and adoption of artificial intelligence tools in higher education. *Frontiers in Education, 9*, 1360300. DOI: 10.3389/feduc.2024.1360300

Chan, C. K. Y. (2023). A comprehensive AI policy education framework for university teaching and learning. *International Journal of Educational Technology in Higher Education, 20*(1), 38. DOI: 10.1186/s41239-023-00408-3

Chang, C. Y., Hwang, G. J., & Gau, M. L. (2022). Promoting students' learning achievement and self-efficacy: A mobile chatbot approach for nursing training. *British Journal of Educational Technology*, *53*(1), 171–188. DOI: 10.1111/bjet.13158

Cheng, H., Husen, J. H., Lu, Y., Racharak, T., Yoshioka, N., Ubayashi, N., & Washizaki, H. (2025). Generative AI for requirements engineering: A systematic literature review. *Software, Practice & Experience*, *56*(2), 141–170. DOI: 10.1002/spe.70029

Chen, N., Li, Z., Tang, B., Zárate-González, C. A., & Xue, B. (2022). Can digital skill protect against job displacement caused by artificial intelligence? Empirical evidence from 701 detailed occupations. *PLoS One*, *17*(11), e0277280. DOI: 10.1371/journal.pone.0277280 PMID: 36346798

Chen, Y., Jensen, S., Albert, L. J., Gupta, S., & Lee, T. (2022). Artificial intelligence (AI) student assistants in the classroom: Designing chatbots to support student success. *Information Systems Frontiers*. Advance online publication. DOI: 10.1007/s10796-022-10291-4

Chinta, S. V., Wang, Z., Yin, Z., Hoang, N., Gonzalez, M., Quy, T. L., & Zhang, W. (2024). FairAIED: Navigating fairness, bias, and ethics in educational AI applications. *arXiv*. https://arxiv.org/abs/2407.18745

Choudhury, M. E., Sathvin, C. S., Akash, M., & Sundar, S. (2025). Smart Fish Feeding and Monitoring System. *2025 International Conference on Sensors and Related Networks (SENNET) Special Focus on Digital Healthcare(64220)*, 1–6. DOI: 10.1109/SENNET64220.2025.11136052

Chu, J., Xi, L., Zhang, Q., & Lin, R. (2022, August). Research on ethical issues of artificial intelligence in education. In International conference on smart learning environments (pp. 101-108). Singapore: Springer Nature Singapore. DOI: 10.1007/978-981-19-5967-7_12

ClickUp. (n.d.-a). *ClickUp Brain*. https://clickup.com/brain

ClickUp. (n.d.-c). *What is ClickUp AI?* https://help.clickup.com/hc/en-us/articles/12578085238039-What-is-ClickUp-AI

Clinio, A. (2016). *Reflections on the Application of the IAD Framework to analyse the Ubatuba Open Science Platform | OCSDNET*. Ocsdnet.org. https://ocsdnet.org/reflections-on-the-application-of-the-institutional-analysis-and-development-iad-framework-to-analyze-the-ubatuba-open-science-platform/

Cole, D. H. (2017). Laws, norms, and the Institutional Analysis and Development framework. *Journal of Institutional Economics*, *13*(4), 829–847. DOI: 10.1017/S1744137417000030

Collins, A., Brown, J. S., & Holum, A. (1991). Cognitive apprenticeship: Making thinking visible. *American Educator, 15*(3), 6–11.

Compilatio. (2025). *Artificial intelligence in education: Opportunities and challenges in 2025.* https://www.compilatio.net/en/blog/ai-in-education

Conati, C., & Kardan, S. (2013). Student modeling: Supporting personalized instruction from problem solving to exploratory open-ended activities. *AI Magazine, 34*(3), 13–26. DOI: 10.1609/aimag.v34i3.2483

Cordero, J., Torres-Zambrano, J., & Cordero-Castillo, A. (2024). Integration of generative artificial intelligence in higher education: Best practices. *Education Sciences, 15*(1), 32. DOI: 10.3390/educsci15010032

Córdova, P. R., & Vicari, R. M. (2022, August). Practical ethical issues for artificial intelligence in education. In International Conference on Technology and Innovation in Learning, Teaching and Education (pp. 437-445). Cham: Springer Nature Switzerland. DOI: 10.1007/978-3-031-22918-3_34

Costa, G., Júnior, W., Mombelli, M., & Júnior, G. (2024). Revisiting a Teaching Sequence on the Topic of Electrolysis: A Comparative Study with the Use of Artificial Intelligence. *Journal of Chemical Education, 101*(8), 3255–3263. DOI: 10.1021/acs.jchemed.4c00247

Cotton, D. R. E., Cotton, P. A., & Shipway, J. R. (2023). Chatting and cheating: Ensuring academic integrity in the era of ChatGPT. *Innovations in Education and Teaching International, 61*(2), 228–239. DOI: 10.1080/14703297.2023.2190148

Couldry, N., & Mejias, U. A. (2019). *The costs of connection: How data is colonizing human life and appropriating it for capitalism.* Stanford University Press.

Crawford, K. (2021). Atlas of AI. In *Yale University Press.* Yale University Press., DOI: 10.2307/j.ctv1ghv45t

Crompton, H., & Burke, D. (2023). Artificial intelligence in higher education: The state of the field. *International Journal of Educational Technology in Higher Education, 20*(1), 22. DOI: 10.1186/s41239-023-00392-8

Cucci, F., Marasciulo, D., Romani, M., Soldano, G., Cascio, D., De Nunzio, G., Caldararo, C., Rubbi, I., Vitale, E., Lupo, R., & Conte, L. (2025). The contribution of artificial intelligence in nursing education: A scoping review of the literature. *Nursing Reports, 15*(8), 283. DOI: 10.3390/nursrep15080283 PMID: 40863670

Cui, Z., Demirer, M., Jaffe, S., Musolff, L., Peng, S., & Salz, T. (2025). *The effects of generative AI on high-skilled work: Evidence from three field experiments with software developers.* Microsoft Research. https://www.microsoft.com/en-us/research/publication/the-effects-of-generative-ai-on-high-skilled-work-evidence-from-three-field-experiments-with-software-developers

Dandage, R. V. (2025). A Comparative Analysis of ChatGPT and DeepSeek: Capabilities, Applications, and Future Directions ChatGPT &DeepSeek. [IJISRT]. *International Journal of Innovative Science and Research Technology, 10*(2), 207–211. DOI: 10.5281/zenodo.14899162

Dandotiya, M., Goyal, N. K., Yadav, P., Sankhla, K., & Kumari, M. (2026). GENALYTICS: A Deep Dive Into Real-Time Insights via Generative AI. In Elbaghazaoui, B., Amnai, M., & Gherabi, N. (Eds.), *Generative AI-Powered Data Architectures: From Governance to Autonomous Analytics* (pp. 105–134). IGI Global Scientific Publishing., DOI: 10.4018/979-8-3373-5616-7.ch005

Daru, A. F., Hirzan, A. M., Susanto, S., & Adhiwibowo, W. (2023). Automatic Koi Fish Feeding Device with Internet of Things Concept Using Fuzzy Control Logic. *2023 International Conference on Technology, Engineering, and Computing Applications (ICTECA)*, 1–6. DOI: 10.1109/ICTECA60133.2023.10490906

Dawson, P. (2020). *Defending Assessment Security in a Digital World: Preventing E-Cheating and Supporting Academic Integrity in Higher Education* (1st ed.). Routledge., DOI: 10.4324/9780429324178

De Bondt, W., & Thaler, R. (1985). Does the stock market overreact? *Journal of Finance, 40*(3), 793–805.

De Gagne, J. C., Hwang, H., & Jung, D. (2024). Cyberethics in nursing education: Ethical implications of artificial intelligence. *Nursing Ethics, 31*(6), 1021–1030. DOI: 10.1177/09697330231201901 PMID: 37803810

DeepSeek. (2026). *Deepseek Into the unknown.* https://www.deepseek.com/en/

Denny, P., Prather, J., Becker, B. A., Finnie-Ansley, J., Hellas, A., Leinonen, J., Luxton-Reilly, A., Reeves, B. N., Santos, E. A., & Sarsa, S. (2024). Computing Education in the Era of Generative AI. *Communications of the ACM, 67*(2), 56–67. DOI: 10.1145/3624720

Deshpande, A., & Sharp, H. (2022, July). Responsible ai systems: who are the stakeholders? In Proceedings of the 2022 AAAI/ACM Conference on AI, Ethics, and Society (pp. 227-236).

Development, O. for E. C. and. (2016). Innovating Education and Educating for Innovation: The Power of Digital Technologies and Skills. In *Educational Research and Innovation*. OECD Publishing. DOI: 10.1787/9789264265097-en

Devlin, J., Chang, M. W., Lee, K., & Toutanova, K. (2019). BERT: Pre-training of deep bidirectional transformers for language understanding. *NAACL HLT 2019 - 2019 Conference of the North American Chapter of the Association for Computational Linguistics: Human Language Technologies - Proceedings of the Conference, 1*, 4171–4186. https://aclanthology.org/N19-1423/

DiCuffa, S., Zambrana, A., Yadav, P., Madiraju, S., Suman, K., & AlOmar, E. A. (2025). *Exploring prompt patterns in AI-assisted code generation: Towards faster and more effective developer-AI collaboration* (arXiv No. 2506.01604). arXiv. / arXiv.2506.01604DOI: 10.1109/ICMI65310.2025.11141320

Diebold, F. X., & Mariano, R. S. (1995). Comparing predictive accuracy. *Journal of Business & Economic Statistics, 13*(3), 253–263.

Diederich, S., Brendel, A. B., Morana, S., & Kolbe, L. (2022). On the design of and interaction with conversational agents: An organizing and assessing review of human-computer interaction research. *Journal of the Association for Information Systems*, *23*(1), 96–138. DOI: 10.17705/1jais.00724

Divya, T., Ramyadevi, R., & Vijaya Chamundeeswari, V. (2023). Smart fish monitoring system using IoT. In A. Dagur, K. Singh, P. S. Mehra, & D. K. Shukla, *Artificial Intelligence, Blockchain, Computing and Security Volume 2* (1st ed., pp. 270–273). CRC Press. DOI: 10.1201/9781032684994-42

Djeffal, C., Siewert, M. B., & Wurster, S. (2022). Role of the state and responsibility in governing artificial intelligence: A comparative analysis of AI strategies. *Journal of European Public Policy*, *29*(11), 1–23. DOI: 10.1080/13501763.2022.2094987

Dong, Q., Li, L., Dai, D., Zheng, C., Ma, J., Li, R., & Sui, Z. (2024, November). A survey on in-context learning. In *Proceedings of the 2024 conference on empirical methods in natural language processing* (pp. 1107-1128). DOI: 10.18653/v1/2024.emnlp-main.64

Dressel, J., & Farid, H. (2018). The accuracy, fairness, and limits of predicting recidivism. *Science Advances*, *4*(1), eaao5580. Advance online publication. DOI: 10.1126/sciadv.aao5580 PMID: 29376122

Dubey, P. K., & Crevar, A. R. (2025). Integrating artificial intelligence in higher education: Enhancing pedagogy, instruction, and administration. *AI Integration Into Andragogical Education*, 181–208. DOI: 10.4018/979-8-3373-0502-8.ch008

Duncker, K. (1945). On problem-solving. *Psychological Monographs*, *58*(5), i-113. DOI: 10.1037/h0093599

Dunlap, P. A. B., & Michalowski, M. (2024). Advancing AI data ethics in nursing: Future directions for nursing practice, research, and education. *JMIR Nursing*, *7*(1), e62678. DOI: 10.2196/62678 PMID: 39453630

Dwivedi, Y. K., Kshetri, N., Hughes, L., Slade, E. L., Jeyaraj, A., Kar, A. K., Baabdullah, A. M., Koohang, A., Raghavan, V., Ahuja, M., Albanna, H., Albashrawi, M. A., Al-Busaidi, A. S., Balakrishnan, J., Barlette, Y., Basu, S., Bose, I., Brooks, L., Buhalis, D., & Wright, R. (2023). "So what if ChatGPT wrote it?" Multidisciplinary perspectives on opportunities, challenges and implications of generative conversational AI for research, practice and policy. *International Journal of Information Management*, *71*, 102642. DOI: 10.1016/j.ijinfomgt.2023.102642

Eaton, S. E. (2022). *Postplagiarism: Transdisciplinary ethics and integrity in the age of artificial intelligence and neurotechnology*. University of Calgary. DOI: 10.4135/9781071892992

Editorial, N. (2023). Tools such as ChatGPT threaten transparent science. *Nature*, *613*(7945), 612. DOI: 10.1038/d41586-023-00191-1 PMID: 36694020

El Arab, R. A., Alshakihs, A. H., Alabdulwahab, S. H., Almubarak, Y. S., Alkhalifah, S. S., Abdrbo, A., Hassanein, S., & Sagbakken, M. (2025). Artificial intelligence in nursing: A systematic review of attitudes, literacy, readiness, and adoption intentions among nursing students and practicing nurses. *Frontiers in Digital Health*, *7*, 1666005. DOI: 10.3389/fdgth.2025.1666005 PMID: 41079691

El Dessouky, N.F (2016). PUBLIC POLICY EVALUATION THEORY: FROM FIRST TO FIFTH GENERATION. *EPRA International Journal of Economic and Business Review(JEBR)*, *4*(4).

El Din, M. S., & Al Harrasi, N. H. (2024). Ai-Driven Transformation in Higher Education: New Frontiers in Administration and Management. In Utilizing AI for Assessment, Grading, and Feedback in Higher Education (pp. 135-161). IGI Global.

El Fougour, W., & Erradi, M. (2025). Enhancing Formative Assessment With AI: Supporting Cognitive Development Through Adaptive Feedback. In *Reimagining Curriculum and Assessment in the Age of Generative AI* (pp. 307–332). DOI: 10.4018/979-8-3373-7579-3.ch010

Elinor Ostrom. (2011). UNESCO – EOLSS SAMPLE CHAPTERS HISTORICAL DEVELOPMENTS AND THEORETICAL APPROACHES IN SOCIOLOGY – Vol. II - Institutional Analysis and Development: Elements of The Framework in Historical Perspective. *Encyclopedia of Life Support Systems (EOLSS).*

Ellikkal, A., & Rajamohan, S. (2025). AI-enabled personalized learning: Empowering management students for improving engagement and academic performance. *Vilakshan-XIMB Journal of Management, 22*(1), 28–44. DOI: 10.1108/XJM-02-2024-0023

Ellis, C. (2023). *The end of authenticity: Artificial intelligence and the future of assessment.* Routledge.

Ellucian. (2024). *AI in higher education: Annual survey report* (2nd ed.). Ellucian. https://www.ellucian.com/newsroom/ellucians-ai-survey-higher-education-professionals-reveals-surge-ai-adoption-despite

Ellucian. (2025). *AI in higher education: Annual survey report* (3rd ed.). Ellucian. https://www.ellucian.com/newsroom/ellucians-3rd-annual-higher-education-ai-survey-signals-shift-individual-ai-use

Em, S., Mok, S., Sam, R., Pen, D., & Serey, M. (2025). Implications and Considerations of AI-Generative Tools for Higher Education Practices: Opportunities, Challenges, and Future Directions. *Examining AI Disruption in Educational Settings: Challenges and Opportunities*, 297–332. DOI: 10.4018/979-8-3693-7873-1.ch011

Evans, W., Baker, N., & Farrelly, T. (2025). Artificial Intelligence considerations in nursing curricula: Embracing with care, its potential in transforming learning. *Journal of Nursing Education and Practice, 15*(7), 37–52. DOI: 10.63564/jnep.v15n7p37

Ezzini, S., Abualhaija, S., Arora, C., Sabetzadeh, M., & Briand, L. C. (2021). Using domain-specific corpora for improved handling of ambiguity in requirements. In *2021 IEEE/ACM 43rd International Conference on Software Engineering* (ICSE) (pp. 1485–1497). IEEE. DOI: 10.1109/ICSE43902.2021.00133

Fama, E. F. (1970). Efficient capital markets: A review of theory and empirical work. *Journal of Finance, 25*(2), 383–417.

Fama, E. F. (1991). Efficient capital markets II. *Journal of Finance, 46*(5), 1575–1617.

Farangi, M. R., Nejadghanbar, H., & Hu, G. (2025). Use of generative AI in research: Ethical considerations and emotional experiences. *Ethics & Behavior, 35*(7), 527–543. DOI: 10.1080/10508422.2024.2420133

Farmer, J. D., & Lo, A. W. (1999). Frontiers of finance: Evolution and efficient markets. *Proceedings of the National Academy of Sciences*, 96(18), 9991–9992. DOI: 10.1073/pnas.96.18.9991

Farmer, J. D., Patelli, P., & Zovko, I. (2005). The predictive power of zero intelligence in financial markets. *Proceedings of the National Academy of Sciences*, 102(6), 2254–2259. DOI: 10.1073/pnas.0409157102

Farooqi, A., Das, D., Tripathi, M., Dutta, R., Goyal, N. K., & Sheikh, M. F. (2026). Navigating Ethical Frontiers in AI-Driven Geriatric Care. In Stolakis, K., & Efthymiou, I. (Eds.), *AI for Geriatric Care in an Aging Society: Ethical, Clinical, and Policy Challenges* (pp. 243–266). IGI Global Scientific Publishing., DOI: 10.4018/979-8-3373-5462-0.ch009

Ferreira-Meyers, K. (2025). Augmented or Automated. *Artificial Intelligence Transforming Higher Education, 1*, 129–152. DOI: 10.64449/9780906785959-05

Fidan, M., & Gencel, N. (2022). Supporting the instructional videos with chatbot and peer feedback mechanisms in online learning: The effects on learning performance and intrinsic motivation. *Journal of Educational Computing Research, 60*(7), 1716–1741. Advance online publication. DOI: 10.1177/07356331221077901

Fidas, C. A., Belk, M., Constantinides, A., Portugal, D., Martins, P., Pietron, A. M., Pitsillides, A., & Avouris, N. (2023). Ensuring academic integrity and trust in online learning environments: A longitudinal study of an ai-centered proctoring system in tertiary educational institutions. *Education Sciences, 13*(6), 566. DOI: 10.3390/educsci13060566

Filgueiras, F., & Silva, B. (2022). Designing data policy and governance for smart cities: Theoretical essay using the IAD framework to analyse data-driven policy. *Revista de Administração Pública, 56*(4), 508–528. DOI: 10.1590/0034-761220220078x

Flavell, J. H. (1979). Metacognition and cognitive monitoring: A new area of cognitive–developmental inquiry. *The American Psychologist, 34*(10), 906–911. DOI: 10.1037/0003-066X.34.10.906

Floridi, L., Cowls, J., Beltrametti, M., Chatila, R., Chazerand, P., Dignum, V., Luetge, C., Madelin, R., Pagallo, U., Rossi, F., Schafer, B., Valcke, P., & Vayena, E. (2018). AI4People—An ethical framework for a good AI society: Opportunities, risks, principles, and recommendations. *Minds and Machines, 28*(4), 689–707. DOI: 10.1007/s11023-018-9482-5 PMID: 30930541

Floridi, L., Cowls, J., Beltrametti, M., Chatila, R., Chazerand, P., Dignum, V., Luetge, C., Madelin, R., Pagallo, U., Rossi, F., Schafer, B., Valcke, P., & Vayena, E. (2021). AI4People—An ethical framework for a good AI society. *AI & Society*, *36*(2), 689–707. DOI: 10.1007/s00146-020-01044-2 PMID: 30930541

Forbes Business Council. (2026, March 18). *As AI coding boosts productivity, is cutting software budgets smart or risky?* https://www.forbes.com/councils/forbesbusinesscouncil/2026/03/18/as-ai-coding-boosts-productivity-is-cutting-software-budgets-smart-or-risky/

Forrester. (2025, November 11). *AI is rewriting software work: What it means for your team.* https://www.forrester.com/blogs/ai-is-rewriting-software-work-what-it-means-for-your-team/

Fung, C., & Lo, A. (2025). *The Air Canada chatbot lawsuit and its implications for AI in customer service.* PolyU Institutional Research Archive. https://ira.lib.polyu.edu.hk/handle/10397/114706

Gabehart, K. M., & Weible, C. M. (2023). Advocacy Coalition Framework. *Springer EBooks*, 1–10. DOI: 10.1007/978-3-030-90434-0_5-2

Ganguly, A., Johri, A., Ali, A., & McDonald, N. (2025). Generative artificial intelligence for academic research: Evidence from guidance issued for researchers by higher education institutions in the United States. *AI and Ethics*, *5*(4), 1–17. DOI: 10.1007/s43681-025-00688-7

Gao, R., Yu, D., Gao, B., Hua, H., Hui, Z., Gao, J., & Yin, C. (2025). Legal regulation of AI-assisted academic writing: Challenges, frameworks, and pathways. *Frontiers in Artificial Intelligence*, *8*, 1546064. DOI: 10.3389/frai.2025.1546064 PMID: 40260414

George, B., & Wooden, O. (2023). Managing the strategic transformation of higher education through artificial intelligence. *Administrative Sciences*, *13*(9), 196. DOI: 10.3390/admsci13090196

Gering, Z., Feher, K., Harmat, V., & Tamassy, R. (2025). Strategic organisational responses to generative AI-driven digital transformation in leading higher education institutions. *The International Journal of Organizational Analysis*, *33*(12), 132–152. DOI: 10.1108/IJOA-09-2024-4850

Ghantous, G. B. (2024, January). Enhancing devops using ai. In *CEUR Workshop Proceedings*. CEUR-WS.

Ghimire, A., & Edwards, J. (2024, July). From guidelines to governance: A study of ai policies in education. In International Conference on Artificial Intelligence in Education (pp. 299-307). Cham: Springer Nature Switzerland. DOI: 10.1007/978-3-031-64312-5_36

Ghimire, A., & Qiu, Y. (2025). Redefining pedagogy with artificial intelligence: How nursing students are shaping the future of learning. *Nurse Education in Practice*, *84*, 104330. DOI: 10.1016/j.nepr.2025.104330 PMID: 40090205

GitHub. (n.d.). GitHub Copilot. https://github.com/features/copilot

González, L. A., Neyem, A., Contreras-Mckay, I., & Molina, D. (2022). Improving learning experiences in software engineering capstone courses using artificial intelligence virtual assistants. *Computer Applications in Engineering Education*, *30*(5), 1370–1389. DOI: 10.1002/cae.22526

Goodfellow, I., Bengio, Y., & Courville, A. (2016). *Deep learning*. MIT Press.

Google. (n.d.). *Gemini 1.5 Pro*. https://ai.google.dev/gemini-api/docs/models

Goyal, A. (2025). AI as a Cognitive Partner: A Systematic Review of the Influence of AI on Metacognition and Self-Reflection in Critical Thinking. International Journal of Innovative Science and Research Techno, 1231-1238. DOI: 10.38124/ijisrt/25mar1427

Goyal, A., & Welch, I. (2008). A comprehensive look at the empirical performance of equity premium prediction. *Review of Financial Studies, 21*(4), 1455–1508.

Goyal, N. K., Goyal, N. K., Kumar, S., Dutta, R., Kothari, V., & Sinha, S. K. (2026). Empowering elderly care through artificial intelligence. In *AI for Geriatric Care in an Aging Society* (pp. 1–28). IGI Global. , DOI: 10.4018/979-8-3373-5462-0.ch001

Gupta, S., & Chen, Y. (2022). Supporting inclusive learning using chatbots? A chatbot-led interview study. *Journal of Information Systems Education and Information Technologies*, *33*(1), 98–108.

Gurung, L., & Kc, A. (2023). Considerations of Artificial Intelligence for Higher Education and Implications of ChatGPT for Teaching and Learning. *The Journal of Educational Research*, *13*(1), 1–7. DOI: 10.51474/jer.v13i1.660

Gutierrez, C. I., Marchant, G. E., & Michael, K. (2021). Effective and Trustworthy Implementation of AI Soft Law Governance. SSRN *Electronic Journal*. DOI: 10.2139/ssrn.4031992

Gutiérrez, F., Seipp, K., Ochoa, X., Chiluiza, K., De Laet, T., & Verbert, K. (2020). LADA: A learning analytics dashboard for academic advising. *Computers in Human Behavior, 107*, 105826. DOI: 10.1016/j.chb.2018.12.004

Guu, K., Lee, K., Tung, Z., Pasupat, P., & Chang, M. (2020). Retrieval augmented language model pre-training. *Proceedings of ICML*, 3929–3938.

Haber, E., Jemielniak, D., Kurasiński, A., & Przegalińska, A. (2025). Navigating the Regulatory and Ethical Landscape of AI in Academia. In *Using AI in Academic Writing and Research: A Complete Guide to Effective and Ethical Academic AI* (pp. 119–137). Springer Nature Switzerland. DOI: 10.1007/978-3-031-91705-9_9

Hadi, W., & AlShaikh-Hasan, M. N. (2025). AI-Driven Curriculum Transformation and Faculty Development in Developing Universities. In Revolutionizing Urban Development and Governance With Emerging Technologies (pp. 289-322). IGI Global Scientific Publishing.

Hamilton, J. D. (1989). A new approach to the economic analysis of nonstationary time series and the business cycle. *Econometrica, 57*(2), 357–384.

Hamilton, J., Costello, M., Barr, L., Cooper, S., & Jones, M. (2025). Application of generative artificial intelligence by nurse academics in higher education: A scoping review. *Nurse Education in Practice*, 104669. PMID: 41353944

Hamzah, W. M. A. F. W., Ismail, I., Yusof, M. K., Saany, S. I. M., & Yacob, A. (2021). Using learning analytics to explore responses from student conversations with chatbot for education. [iJEP]. *International Journal of Engineering Pedagogy, 11*(6), 70–84. DOI: 10.3991/ijep.v11i6.23475

Han, J., Collier, N., Buntine, W., & Shareghi, E. (2023). Prompting with iterative verification improving graph-based generative capability of LLMs. *arXiv preprint arXiv:2305.12392*.

Hardie, P., Darley, A., Derwin, R., Eustace-Cook, J., Kearns, S., Mc Brien, B., Siddiquee, A., Zheng, D., & Mooney, M. (2026). Applications, attitudes and ethical considerations of Generative Artificial Intelligence (Gen AI) in nursing education: A scoping review. *BMC Nursing, 25*(148), 148. Advance online publication. DOI: 10.1186/s12912-025-04253-9 PMID: 41545825

Hastie, T., Tibshirani, R., & Friedman, J. (2009). *The elements of statistical learning* (2nd ed.). Springer. DOI: 10.1007/978-0-387-84858-7

Hattie, J., & Timperley, H. (2007). The Power of Feedback. *Review of Educational Research, 77*(1), 81–112. DOI: 10.3102/003465430298487

Hatzius, J. (2023). The potentially large effects of artificial intelligence on economic growth (briggs/kodnani). *Goldman Sachs, 1*(5), 268–296.

Hayashi, Y. (2020). Gaze awareness and metacognitive suggestions by a pedagogical conversational agent. *International Journal of Computer-Supported Collaborative Learning, 15*(4), 469–498. DOI: 10.1007/s11412-020-09333-3

Heemskerk, I., Kuiper, E., & Meijer, J. (2014). Interactive whiteboard and virtual learning environment combined: Effects on mathematics education. *Journal of Computer Assisted Learning, 30*(5), 465–478. https://doi.org/https://doi.org/10.1111/jcal.12060. DOI: 10.1111/jcal.12060

Hemon-Hildgen, A., & Rowe, F. (2022). Conceptualising and defining DevOps: A review for understanding, not a framework for practitioners. *European Journal of Information Systems, 31*(5), 568–574. DOI: 10.1080/0960085X.2022.2100061

Herweg, N., Huß, C., & Zohlnhöfer, R. (2015). Straightening the three streams: Theorising extensions of the multiple streams framework. *European Journal of Political Research, 54*(3), 435–449. DOI: 10.1111/1475-6765.12089

Herweg, N., Zahariadis, N., & Zohlnhöfer, R. (2018). The Multiple Streams Framework: Foundations, Refinements, and Empirical Applications. In Weible, C. M., & Sabatier, P. A. (Eds.), *Theories of the Policy Process* (4th ed., pp. 17–53). Routledge., DOI: 10.4324/9780429494284-2

Hey, T., Keim, J., Koziolek, A., & Tichy, W. F. (2020, August). Norbert: Transfer learning for requirements classification. In *2020 IEEE 28th international requirements engineering conference (RE)* (pp. 169-179). IEEE.

Higgins, O., Chalup, S. K., & Wilson, R. L. (2024). Artificial Intelligence in nursing: Trustworthy or reliable? *Journal of Research in Nursing : JRN, 29*(2), 143–153. DOI: 10.1177/17449871231215696 PMID: 39070561

Hoefer, R. (2022). The multiple streams framework: Understanding and applying the problems, policies, and politics approach. *Journal of Policy Practice and Research, 3*(1), 1–5. DOI: 10.1007/s42972-022-00049-2

Hofer, B. K., & Pintrich, P. R. (1997). The development of epistemological theories: Beliefs about knowledge and knowing and their relation to learning. *Review of Educational Research, 67*(1), 88–140. DOI: 10.3102/00346543067001088

Holmes, W., Bialik, M., & Fadel, C. (2019). *Artificial intelligence in education: Promises and implications for teaching and learning*. Centre for Curriculum Redesign.

Holmes, W., Bialik, M., & Fadel, C. (2022). Artificial intelligence in education: Promise and implications for teaching and learning. *Humanities & Social Sciences Communications, 9*, 120. DOI: 10.1057/s41599-022-01041-0

Hsu, M.-H., Chen, P.-S., & Yu, C.-S. (2021). Proposing a task-oriented chatbot system for EFL learners speaking practice. *Interactive Learning Environments.* Advance online publication. DOI: 10.1080/10494820.2021.1960864

Hurst, A., Lerer, A., Goucher, A. P., Perelman, A., Ramesh, A., Clark, A., . . . Kivlichan, I. (2024). Gpt-4o system card. *arXiv preprint arXiv:2410.21276.*

Hu, X., & Zhang, H. (2025). Exploring AI-Assisted Self-Regulated Learning Profiles and the Predictive Role of Academic Appraisals: A Control-Value Perspective on Chinese EFL University Students. *European Journal of Education, 60*(4), e70249. Advance online publication. DOI: 10.1111/ejed.70249

Hwang, G. J., Tang, K. Y., & Tu, Y. F. (2024). How artificial intelligence (AI) supports nursing education: Profiling the roles, applications, and trends of AI in nursing education research (1993–2020). *Interactive Learning Environments, 32*(1), 373–392. DOI: 10.1080/10494820.2022.2086579

Hyland. (2025). *AI use cases in higher education.* https://www.hyland.com/en/resources/articles/ai-higher-education

Ibrahim, K. (2023). Using AI-based detectors to control AI-assisted plagiarism in ESL writing:"The Terminator Versus the Machines". *Language Testing in Asia, 13*(1), 46. DOI: 10.1186/s40468-023-00260-2

Ilahy, R., R'him, T., Tlili, I., & Jebari, H. (n.d.). *Effect of Different Shading Levels on Growth and Yield Parameters of a Hot Pepper (Capsicum annuum L.) Cultivar 'Beldi' Grown in Tunisia.* (1).

International Federation of Robotics. (2023). *World robotics report 2023.*

International Organisation of Employers (IOE). (2024). *The impact of artificial intelligence on work and employment.*

Irfan, M. (2024). Delving into the exchange-traded funds (ETFs) market: Understanding market efficiency. *Journal of Ecohumanism, 3*(4), 2670–2681. DOI: 10.62754/joe.v3i4.3787

Irfan, M., Elhoseny, M., Kassim, S., & Metawa, N. (2023). *Advanced machine learning algorithms for complex financial applications.* IGI Global., DOI: 10.4018/978-1-6684-4483-2

Irfan, M., & George, J. P. (2022). A systematic review of challenges, tools, and myths of big data ingestion. In *Lecture Notes in Networks and Systems*. Springer., DOI: 10.1007/978-981-19-2211-4_43

Isiaku, L., Muhammad, A., Kefas, H., & Ukaegbu, F. (2024). Enhancing technological sustainability in academia: Leveraging ChatGPT for teaching, learning and evaluation. *QEA*, *1*(1), 385–416. DOI: 10.1108/QEA-07-2024-0055

Ivanytska, N., Vasylivna, K., Kovalevska, T., Matsera, O., & Tetiana, T. (2024). Analyzing the Possibilities of Implementation of AI and Social Networks in Teaching Foreign Language Students: Ukrainian Universities Case Study. https://doi.org/ DOI: 10.31235/osf.io/gn7s8

Jairoun, A. A., El-Dahiyat, F., ElRefae, G. A., Al-Hemyari, S. S., Shahwan, M., Zyoud, S. H., Hammour, K. A., & Babar, Z. U. D. (2024). Detecting manuscripts written by generative AI and AI-assisted technologies in the field of pharmacy practice. *Journal of Pharmaceutical Policy and Practice*, *17*(1), 2303759. DOI: 10.1080/20523211.2024.2303759 PMID: 38229951

Jallad, S. T., Alsaqer, K., Albadareen, B. I., & Al-Maghaireh, D. (2024). Artificial intelligence tools utilized in nursing education: Incidence and associated factors. *Nurse Education Today*, *142*, 106355. DOI: 10.1016/j.nedt.2024.106355 PMID: 39163690

Janssen, M. (2025). Responsible governance of generative AI: Conceptualising GenAI as complex adaptive systems. *Policy and Society*, *44*(1), 38–51. DOI: 10.1093/polsoc/puae040

Jarrahi, M. H., Lutz, C., Boyd, K., Østerlund, C., & Willis, M. (2023). Artificial intelligence in the work context. *Journal of the Association for Information Science and Technology*, *74*(3), 303–310. DOI: 10.1002/asi.24730

Jenkins Project. (n.d.). *Jenkins*. https://www.jenkins.io

Jensen, M. C. (1978). Some anomalous evidence regarding market efficiency. *Journal of Financial Economics, 6*(2–3), 95–101.

Jeon, J., Kim, L., & Park, J. (2025). The ethics of generative AI in social science research: A qualitative approach for institutionally grounded AI research ethics. *Technology in Society*, *81*, 102836. DOI: 10.1016/j.techsoc.2025.102836

Jiang, Z., Xu, F. F., Araki, J., & Neubig, G. (2020). How can we know what language models know? *Transactions of the ACL, 8*, 423–438. DOI: 10.1162/tacl_a_00324

Jia, X., & Tu, J. (2024). Towards a New Conceptual Model of AI-Enhanced Learning for College Students: The Roles of Artificial Intelligence Capabilities, General Self-Efficacy, Learning Motivation, and Critical Thinking Awareness. *Systems*, *12*(3), 74. DOI: 10.3390/systems12030074

Jobin, A., Ienca, M., & Vayena, E. (2019). The global landscape of AI ethics guidelines. *Nature Machine Intelligence*, *1*(9), 389–399. DOI: 10.1038/s42256-019-0088-2

John, P. (2003). Is There Life After Policy Streams, Advocacy Coalitions, and Punctuations: Using Evolutionary Theory to Explain Policy Change? *Policy Studies Journal: The Journal of the Policy Studies Organization*, *31*(4), 481–498. DOI: 10.1111/1541-0072.00039

Johnson, H. L., Cruthirds, D. F., Taylor, L. A., Suszan, L. T., Owen, R. P., Trautmann, J. L., & Seibert, D. C. (2024). Redefining faculty workload metrics: A data-driven approach. *Journal of Professional Nursing : Official Journal of the American Association of Colleges of Nursing*, *55*, 112–118. DOI: 10.1016/j.profnurs.2024.08.006 PMID: 39667876

Johnston, H., Wells, R. F., Shanks, E. M., Boey, T., & Parsons, B. N. (2024). Student perspectives on the use of generative artificial intelligence technologies in higher education. *International Journal for Educational Integrity*, *20*(1), 2. DOI: 10.1007/s40979-024-00149-4

Jonassen, D. H. (1997). Instructional design models for well-structured and ill-structured problem-solving learning outcomes. *Educational Technology Research and Development*, *45*(1), 65–94. DOI: 10.1007/BF02299613

Jones, J. (2025). *AI-Driven Demand Forecasting in Supply Chains: A Qualitative Analysis of Adoption and Impact*. DOI: 10.20944/preprints202501.1349.v1

Jordan, M. I., & Mitchell, T. M. (2015). Machine learning: Trends, perspectives, and prospects. *Science*, *349*(6245), 255–260. DOI: 10.1126/science.aaa8415 PMID: 26185243

Jun Park, H., & Han, J. (2025). Analysis of the Digital Transformation of Legal Services and the Role of Policy Brokers in KOREA through the Advocacy Coalition Framework. *Policy & Governance Review*, *9*(1), 30. DOI: 10.30589/pgr.v9i1.1171

Kabudi, T., Pappas, I., & Olsen, D. H. (2021). AI-enabled adaptive learning systems: A systematic mapping of the literature. Computers and education. *Artificial Intelligence*, *2*, 100017.

Kaddouri, M., Chniete, I., Mhamdi, K., Bouamri, A., & Atmani, K. (2025). Critical Thinking Skills and Artificial Intelligence (AI)., 337-376. DOI: 10.4018/979-8-3373-4576-5.ch010

Kahneman, D. (2011). *Thinking, fast and slow*. Farrar, Straus and Giroux.

Kaplan, J., McCandlish, S., Henighan, T., Brown, T. B., Chess, B., Child, R., . . . Amodei, D. (2020). Scaling laws for neural language models. *arXiv preprint arXiv:2001.08361*.

Karpouzis, K., Pantazatos, D., Taouki, J., & Meli, K. (2024). Tailoring Education with GenAI: A New Horizon in Lesson Planning. DOI: 10.1109/EDUCON60312.2024.10578690

Karumbaiah, S., Borchers, C., Shou, T., Falhs, A. C., Liu, P., Nagashima, T., . . . Aleven, V. (2023, June). A spatiotemporal analysis of teacher practices in supporting student learning and engagement in an AI-enabled classroom. In International conference on artificial intelligence in education (pp. 450-462). Cham: Springer Nature Switzerland.

Kasneci, E., Sessler, K., Küchemann, S., Bannert, M., Dementieva, D., Fischer, F., Gasser, U., Groh, G., Günnemann, S., Hüllermeier, E., Krusche, S., Kutyniok, G., Michaeli, T., Nerdel, C., Pfeffer, J., Poquet, O., Sailer, M., Schmidt, A., Seidel, T., & Kasneci, G. (2023). ChatGPT for good? On opportunities and challenges of large language models for education. *Learning and Individual Differences*, *103*, 102274. DOI: 10.1016/j.lindif.2023.102274

Kasneci, E., Seßler, K., Küchemann, S., Bannert, M., Dementieva, D., Fischer, F., & Kasneci, G. (2023). ChatGPT for Good? On Opportunities and Challenges of Large Language Models for Education. https://doi.org/DOI: 10.35542/osf.io/5er8f

Katzenbach, C., & Ulbricht, L. (2019). Algorithmic governance. *Internet Policy Review*, *8*(4), 1–18. DOI: 10.14763/2019.4.1424

Kaur, D., Uslu, S., Rittichier, K. J., & Durresi, A. (2022). Trustworthy artificial intelligence: A review. *ACM Computing Surveys*, *55*(2), 1–38. DOI: 10.1145/3491209

Kavitha, S., Anchitaalagammai, J. V., Murali, S., & Annapoorani, S. (2025, March). Enhancing Learning Management Systems with Accessibility, Integrity, and Personalization Through Advanced Technologies. In *2025 International Conference on Data Science, Agents & Artificial Intelligence (ICDSAAI)* (pp. 1-6). IEEE. DOI: 10.1109/ICDSAAI65575.2025.11011537

Kearns, M., & Nevmyvaka, Y. (2013). Machine learning for market microstructure and high-frequency trading. In Kearns, M., & Nevmyvaka, Y. (Eds.), *High frequency trading**.

Kedhareswari, B., Indu, S., Kumar, P. V., Meenakshi Srivani, N., & Saikeerthana, T. (2025). AI-Driven IoT System for Real-Time Fish Behaviour Monitoring and Automated Feeding in Smart Aquaculture. *2025 5th International Conference on Trends in Material Science and Inventive Materials (ICTMIM)*, 1236–1242. DOI: 10.1109/ICTMIM65579.2025.10988280

Kellogg, K. C., Valentine, M. A., & Christin, A. (2020). Algorithms at work: The new contested terrain of control. *The Academy of Management Annals*, *14*(1), 366–410. DOI: 10.5465/annals.2018.0174

Khairullah, S. A., Harris, S., Hadi, H. J., Sandhu, R. A., Ahmad, N., & Alshara, M. A. (2025, February). Implementing artificial intelligence in academic and administrative processes through responsible strategic leadership in the higher education institutions. [). Frontiers Media SA.]. *Frontiers in Education*, *10*, 1548104. DOI: 10.3389/feduc.2025.1548104

Khalifa, M., & Albadawy, M. (2024). Using artificial intelligence in academic writing and research: An essential productivity tool. *Computer Methods and Programs in Biomedicine Update*, *5*, 100145. DOI: 10.1016/j.cmpbup.2024.100145

Khoury, Z., Ferguson, A., Price, J., Sultan, A., & Wang, R. (2024). Responsible artificial intelligence for addressing equity in oral healthcare. *Frontiers in Oral Health*, *5*, 1408867. Advance online publication. DOI: 10.3389/froh.2024.1408867 PMID: 39092200

Kim, Y.-J., & Roh, C.-Y. (2008). Beyond the Advocacy Coalition Framework in Policy Process. *International Journal of Public Administration*, *31*(6), 668–689. DOI: 10.1080/01900690701465384

Kingdon, J. W. (2003). *(2003). Agendas, alternatives and public policies* (2nd ed.). Longman.

Kiran, A. (2025). Applications and impact of AI tools in Education. DOI: 10.47716/978-93-92090-38-7

Kitamura, Y. (2023). Generative AI in research: Productivity and pitfalls. *Journal of Scholarly Publishing*.

Klijn, E.-H., & Koppenjan, J. F. M. (2006). Institutional design. *Public Management Review*, *8*(1), 141–160. DOI: 10.1080/14719030500518915

Klimova, B., Pikhart, M., & Kacetl, J. (2023). Ethical issues of the use of AI-driven mobile apps for education. *Frontiers in Public Health, 10*, 1118116. DOI: 10.3389/fpubh.2022.1118116 PMID: 36711343

Knaggård, Å. (2015). The Multiple Streams Framework and the problem broker. *European Journal of Political Research, 54*(3), 450–465. DOI: 10.1111/1475-6765.12097

Knobloch, J., Kaltenbach, J., & Bruegge, B. (2018). Increasing student engagement in higher education using a context-aware Q&A teaching framework. In *Proceedings of the 40th International Conference on Software Engineering: Software Engineering Education and Training* (pp. 136–145). ACM. DOI: 10.1145/3183377.3183389

Koedinger, K. R., Booth, J. L., & Klahr, D. (2013). Instructional complexity and the science to constrain it. *Science, 342*(6161), 935–937. DOI: 10.1126/science.1238056 PMID: 24264979

Kokol, P. (2024). The use of AI in software engineering: A synthetic knowledge synthesis of the recent research literature. *Information (Basel), 15*(6), 354. Advance online publication. DOI: 10.3390/info15060354

Kotsiantis, S., Pierrakeas, C., & Pintelas, P. (2004). PREDICTING STUDENTS'PERFORMANCE IN DISTANCE LEARNING USING MACHINE LEARNING TECHNIQUES. *Applied Artificial Intelligence, 18*(5), 411–426. DOI: 10.1080/08839510490442058

Koubaa, A. (2023). GPT-4 vs. GPT-3.5: A concise showdown.

Kovalainen, T., Pramila-Savukoski, S., Kuivila, H. M., Juntunen, J., Jarva, E., Rasi, M., & Mikkonen, K. (2025). Utilising artificial intelligence in developing education of health sciences higher education: An umbrella review of reviews. *Nurse Education Today, 147*, 106600. DOI: 10.1016/j.nedt.2025.106600 PMID: 39904286

Krueger, L., Clemenson, S., Johnson, E., & Schwarz, L. (2025). ChatGPT in Higher Education: Practical Ideas for Addressing Artificial Intelligence in Nursing Education. *The Journal of Nursing Education, 64*(5), 323–326. DOI: 10.3928/01484834-20240424-02 PMID: 39038826

Kubota, K., Nishimura, A., Seto, R., & Li, L. (2026). Trustworthy AI-augmented objective structured clinical examinations in nursing education: Taiwan-Japan viewpoint on 5 AI roles, governance, and cross-border implementation. *JMIR Formative Research, 10*, e87830. DOI: 10.2196/87830 PMID: 41818744

Kuhail, M. A., Alturki, N., Alramlawi, S., & Alhejori, K. (2023). Interacting with educational chatbots: A systematic review. *Education and Information Technologies*, *28*(1), 973–1018. DOI: 10.1007/s10639-022-11177-3

Kuleto, V., Ilić, M., Dumangiu, M., Ranković, M., Martins, O. M., Păun, D., & Mihoreanu, L. (2021). Exploring opportunities and challenges of artificial intelligence and machine learning in higher education institutions. *Sustainability (Basel)*, *13*(18), 10424. DOI: 10.3390/su131810424

Kulik, J. A., & Fletcher, J. D. (2016). Effectiveness of Intelligent Tutoring Systems: A Meta-Analytic Review. *Review of Educational Research*, *86*(1), 42–78. DOI: 10.3102/0034654315581420

Kulintang, M. B. M., Ngo, A. D., Salas, C. J. C., Sumaoy, K., & Alquwez, N. A. (2026). Nurse educators' experiences integrating artificial intelligence in teaching and practice: A descriptive phenomenological study. *Nurse Education Today*, *162*, 107050. DOI: 10.1016/j.nedt.2026.107050 PMID: 41747322

Kumar, S., Kameswari, Y. L., Moram, V., & Pasha, M. (2025). Adaptive Learning in Modern Education Systems Leveraged by AI and Blockchain. In Blockchain and AI in Shaping the Modern Education System (pp. 44-71). CRC Press. DOI: 10.1201/9781003502739-3

Kumar, H., & Martin, A. (2024). Cross-Modal Harmony: Low-Rank Fusion for Enhanced Artificial Emotion Recognition. *Interantional Journal of Scientific Research in Engineering and Management*, *08*(10), 1–5. DOI: 10.55041/IJSREM37976

Kumari, M., & Goyal, N. K. (2026). Artificial Intelligence in the Cryptocurrency Ecosystem: Crime Mechanisms, Detection Strategies, and Legal Perspectives. In Lin, L. (Ed.), *Innovations in Cryptocrime and Financial Fraud* (pp. 245–282). IGI Global Scientific Publishing., DOI: 10.4018/979-8-3373-0675-9.ch007

Kumari, M., Kumawat, R., Tripathi, M., Suganthi, K., Goyal, N. K., & Sheikh, M. F. (2026). Blockchain for Transparency and Traceability in Supply Chains. In Khan, M., Mehmood, T., & Rao, M. (Eds.), *Maximizing Operational Efficiency at the Intersection of Supply Chain Management and Marketing* (pp. 35–64). IGI Global Scientific Publishing., DOI: 10.4018/979-8-3373-3109-6.ch002

Kumar, J. A. (2021). Educational chatbots for project-based learning. *International Journal of Educational Technology in Higher Education*, *18*(1), 65. Advance online publication. DOI: 10.1186/s41239-021-00302-w

Labrague, L. J., Sabei, S. A., & Yahyaei, A. A. (2025). Artificial intelligence in nursing education: A review of AI-based teaching pedagogies. *Teaching and Learning in Nursing*, *20*(3), 210–221. DOI: 10.1016/j.teln.2025.01.019

Ladehoff, C., Pfetsch, J., & Ophardt, D. (2023). How university teachers can support the linking of theory and practice in lesson debriefings with student teachers. *International Conference on Higher Education Advances*, 91–98. DOI: 10.4995/HEAd23.2023.16325

Lahav, O., Talis, V., Cinamon, R. G., & Rizzo, A. (2020). Virtual interactive consulting agent to support freshman students in transition to higher education. *Journal of Computing in Higher Education*, *32*(2), 330–364. DOI: 10.1007/s12528-019-09237-8

Lāma, G., & Lastovska, A. (2025). AI competence and sentiment: A mixed-methods study of attitudes and open-ended reflections. *Frontiers in Artificial Intelligence*, *8*, 1658791. Advance online publication. DOI: 10.3389/frai.2025.1658791 PMID: 41069933

Lampinen, A., Dasgupta, I., Chan, S., Mathewson, K., Tessler, M., Creswell, A., & Hill, F. (2022, December). Can language models learn from explanations in context? In *Findings of the Association for Computational Linguistics* (pp. 537–563). EMNLP. DOI: 10.18653/v1/2022.findings-emnlp.38

Larsson, A., & Hatzigeorgiou, A. (2025). Introduction: The Way Disruption, Technology and Practice Will Change the Way We Work in the Future. In *The Future of Labour* (pp. 1-14). Routledge.

Larsson, S. (2020). On the governance of artificial intelligence through ethics guidelines. *Asian Journal of Law and Society*, *7*(3), 437–451. DOI: 10.1017/als.2020.19

Latorre-Navarro, E. M., & Harris, J. G. (2015). An intelligent natural language conversational system for academic advising. *International Journal of Advanced Computer Science and Applications*, *6*(1). Advance online publication. DOI: 10.14569/IJACSA.2015.060116

LeBaron, B. (2006). Agent-based computational finance. In Tesfatsion, L., & Judd, K. L. (Eds.), *Handbook of computational economics* (Vol. 2). Elsevier.

Lee, S. (2025a). *A Quick Look at Top Policy Evaluation Frameworks*. Numberanalytics.com. https://www.numberanalytics.com/blog/quick-look-top-policy-evaluation-frameworks

Lee, S. (2025b). *Key Steps to Institutional Design in Public Policy*. Numberanalytics.com. https://www.numberanalytics.com/blog/key-steps-institutional-design-public-policy

Lee, E. W. Y., & Yeung, R. L. K. (2017). The "Principal Officials Accountability System": It is under development as a system of ministerial government. *Asia Pacific Journal of Public Administration, 39*(2), 120–134. DOI: 10.1080/23276665.2017.1325623

Lei, P., Duo, E. N., Gao, Y., & Zhu, X. (2025). Research on the experience of utilizing artificial intelligence in nursing learning from the perspective of nursing students–a qualitative study. *BMC Nursing, 24*(1), 1062. DOI: 10.1186/s12912-025-03704-7 PMID: 40797323

Lessig, L. (2008). *Remix: Making art and commerce thrive in the hybrid economy.* Penguin. DOI: 10.5040/9781849662505

Létourneau, A., Deslandes Martineau, M., Charland, P., Karran, J. A., Boasen, J., & Léger, P. M. (2025). A systematic review of AI-driven intelligent tutoring systems in K–12 education. *npj Science of Learning, 10*(1), 29.

Liaw, S. Y., Tan, J. Z., Lim, S., Zhou, W., Yap, J., Ratan, R., Ooi, S. L., Wong, S. J., Seah, B., & Chua, W. L. (2023). Artificial intelligence in virtual reality simulation for interprofessional communication training: Mixed method study. *Nurse Education Today, 122*, 105718. DOI: 10.1016/j.nedt.2023.105718 PMID: 36669304

Li, B., Qi, P., Liu, B., Di, S., Liu, J., Pei, J., Yi, J., & Zhou, B. (2023). Trustworthy AI: From principles to practices. *ACM Computing Surveys, 55*(9), 1–46. DOI: 10.1145/3555803

Li, L., Zhang, Y., & Chen, L. (2023). Personalized prompt learning for explainable recommendation. *ACM Transactions on Information Systems, 41*(4), 1–26.

Lin, H., & Chen, Q. (2024). Artificial intelligence (AI)-integrated educational applications and college students' creativity and academic emotions: Students and teachers' perceptions and attitudes. *BMC Psychology, 12*(1), 487. DOI: 10.1186/s40359-024-01979-0 PMID: 39285268

Lippoldt, D. (2024). AI Innovation Concentration and the Governance Challenge. *Centre for International Governance Innovation.* https://www.cigionline.org/static/documents/no.292.pdf

Liu, A., Feng, B., Wang, B., Wang, B., Liu, B., Zhao, C., ... & Sun, X. (2024). DeepSeek-V2: A Strong, Economical, and Efficient Mixture-of-Experts Language Model. *CoRR.*

Liu, X., Wei, F., Jiang, W., Zheng, Q., Qiao, Y., Liu, J., Niu, L., Chen, Z., & Dong, H. (2023). MTR-SAM: Visual Multimodal Text Recognition and Sentiment Analysis in Public Opinion Analysis on the Internet. *Applied Sciences (Basel, Switzerland), 13*(12), 7307. DOI: 10.3390/app13127307

Lo, A. W. (2004). The adaptive markets hypothesis. *Journal of Portfolio Management, 30*(5), 15–29.

Lomachinska, I., Ishchuk, A., Yakovenko, O., Rykhlitska, O., Patlaichuk, O., Pasko, K., Lobanchuk, O., & Lomachinskiy, B. (2026). Opportunities and Challenges of AI Language Models in Higher Education for Sustainable Development. *European Journal of Sustainable Development, 15*(1), 331. Advance online publication. DOI: 10.14207/ejsd.2026.v15n1p331

López de Prado, M. (2018). *Advances in financial machine learning*. Wiley.

Lucchi, N. (2024). ChatGPT: A case study on copyright challenges for generative artificial intelligence systems. *European Journal of Risk Regulation, 15*(3), 602–624. DOI: 10.1017/err.2023.59

Luckin, R., Holmes, W., Griffiths, M., & Forcier, L. B. (2016). *Intelligence unleashed: An argument for AI in education*. Pearson.

Luna, M., Llorente, I., & Cobo, A. (2022). Determination of feeding strategies in aquaculture farms using a multiple-criteria approach and genetic algorithms. *Annals of Operations Research, 314*(2), 551–576. DOI: 10.1007/s10479-019-03227-w

Lytras, M. D., Serban, A. C., Alkhaldi, A., Aldosemani, T., & Malik, S. (2024). What's Next in Higher Education: The AI Revolution 2030. *Digital Transformation in Higher Education, Part A: Best Practices and Challenges*, 155–172. DOI: 10.1108/978-1-83549-480-620241008

Machucho, R., & Ortiz, D. (2025). The impacts of artificial intelligence on business innovation: A comprehensive review of applications, organizational challenges, and ethical considerations. *Systems, 13*(4), 264. DOI: 10.3390/systems13040264

Mahrishi, M., Abbas, A., & Siddiqui, M. K. (2025). Global initiatives towards regulatory frameworks for artificial intelligence (AI) in higher education. *Digital Government: Research and Practice, 6*(2), 1–9. DOI: 10.1145/3672462

Maini, P., Jia, H., Papernot, N., & Dziedzic, A. (2024). LLM dataset inference: Did you train on my dataset? In *Advances in Neural Information Processing Systems*, 37 (pp. 124069–124092).

Ma, J., Wen, J., Qiu, Y., Wang, Y., Xiao, Q., Liu, T., Zhang, D., Zhao, Y., Lu, Z., & Sun, Z. (2025). The role of artificial intelligence in shaping nursing education: A comprehensive systematic review. *Nurse Education in Practice, 84*, 104345. DOI: 10.1016/j.nepr.2025.104345 PMID: 40168750

Malik, A. R., Pratiwi, Y., Andajani, K., Numertayasa, I. W., Suharti, S., Darwis, A., & Marzuki, . (2023). Exploring artificial intelligence in academic essay: Higher education student's perspective. *International Journal of Educational Research Open*, *5*, 100296. DOI: 10.1016/j.ijedro.2023.100296

Mancilla, R., & Frey, B. (2020). A Model for Developing Instructional Design Professionals for Higher Education Through Apprenticeship: Blending Theory and Practice. *Journal of Applied Instructional Design*, *9*(2). Advance online publication. DOI: 10.51869/92rmbf

Manojkumar, R., & Krishnan, S. (2025). Open Discussion Forums and Effective Group Division for Improved Student Engagement in Teaching Learning Process. Journal of Engineering Education Transformations, 488-494.

Manojkumar, R., Srinivas, T. A. S., & Mekala, V. (2026). Inclusive Instructional Design Through Digital Pedagogies and Active Learning Approaches. In Practical Perspectives on Inclusive and Immersive Learning Environments (pp. 147-180). IGI Global Scientific Publishing. DOI: 10.4018/979-8-3373-5188-9.ch006

Mao, R., Chen, G., Zhang, X., Guerin, F., & Cambria, E. (2024, May). GPTEval: A survey on assessments of ChatGPT and GPT-4. In *Proceedings of the 2024 Joint International Conference on Computational Linguistics, Language Resources and Evaluation* (LREC-COLING 2024) (pp. 7844–7866). DOI: 10.63317/3dhqzf3tvt2z

May, P. J. (2007). Regulatory regimes and accountability. *Regulation & Governance*, *1*(1), 8–26. DOI: 10.1111/j.1748-5991.2007.00002.x

McGrath, C., Pargman, T. C., Juth, N., & Palmgren, P. J. (2023). University teachers' perceptions of responsibility and artificial intelligence in higher education-An experimental philosophical study. *Computers and Education: Artificial Intelligence*, *4*, 100139. DOI: 10.1016/j.caeai.2023.100139

McKinsey & Company. (2018, June 1). *AI, automation, and the future of work: Ten things to solve for*. https://www.mckinsey.com/featured-insights/future-of-work/ai-automation-and-the-future-of-work-ten-things-to-solve-for

Medepalli, S. (2025). AI In Modern Software Development: Current Practices, Challenges and Future Possibilities. [JOIREM]. *Journal Publication of International Research for Engineering and Management*, *10*(01).

Mehrabi, N., Morstatter, F., Saxena, N., Lerman, K., & Galstyan, A. (2021). A Survey on Bias and Fairness in Machine Learning. *ACM Computing Surveys*, *54*(6), 1–35. DOI: 10.1145/3457607

Mehta, V., Sharma, C., & Thiyagarajan, K. (2025). Large Language Models and 3D Vision for Intelligent Robotic Perception and Autonomy. *Sensors (Basel), 25*(20), 6394. DOI: 10.3390/s25206394 PMID: 41157446

Michalak, R. (2023). From ethics to execution: The role of academic librarians in artificial intelligence (AI) policy-making at colleges and universities. *Journal of Library Administration, 63*(7), 928–938. DOI: 10.1080/01930826.2023.2262367

Michel-Villarreal, R., Vilalta-perdomo, E., Salinas-Navarro, D., Thierry-Aguilera, R., & Gerardou, F. (2023). Challenges and Opportunities of Generative AI for Higher Education as Explained by ChatGPT. *Education Sciences, 13*(9), 856. DOI: 10.3390/educsci13090856

Microsoft. (n.d.). *Azure DevOps.* https://learn.microsoft.com/en-us/azure/devops/?view=azure-devops

Minnican, C., & O'Toole, G. (2020). Exploring the incidence of culturally responsive communication in Australian healthcare: The first rapid review on this concept. *BMC Health Services Research, 20*(1), 20. DOI: 10.1186/s12913-019-4859-6 PMID: 31910837

Mintrom, M. (2019). *Public policy: Investing for a better world.* Oxford University Press.

Mnih, V., Kavukcuoglu, K., Silver, D., et al. (2015). Human-level control through deep reinforcement learning. *Nature, 518*, 529–533.

monday.com. (n.d.). *monday dev | Develop with precision and speed.* https://monday.com/w/dev

Montejo, L., Fenton, A., & Davis, G. (2024). Artificial intelligence (AI) applications in healthcare and considerations for nursing education. *Nurse Education in Practice, 80*, 104158. DOI: 10.1016/j.nepr.2024.104158 PMID: 39388757

Moonsamy, W., & Lotriet, H. (2026). Contextualization, assessment, and generative AI. In *ICT Education: 54th Annual Conference of the Southern African Computer Lecturers' Association (SACLA 2025), Revised Selected Papers* (p. 17). Springer.

Morandini, S., Fraboni, F., De Angelis, M., Puzzo, G., Giusino, D., & Pietrantoni, L. (2023). The impact of artificial intelligence on workers' skills: Upskilling and reskilling in organizations. *Informing Science, 26*, 39–68. DOI: 10.28945/5078

Morgan Stanley Research. (2026, February 5). *AI adoption surges driving productivity gains and job shifts.* https://www.morganstanley.com/insights/articles/ai-adoption-accelerates-survey-find

Morgan Stanley. (2025, October 29). *AI in software development: Creating jobs and redefining roles*. https://www.morganstanley.com/insights/articles/ai-software-development-industry-growth

Motion. (n.d.). *Motion*. https://www.usemotion.com/

Mukooyo, H., & Kasse, J. (2024). Towards Sustainable Education: A Machine Learning Model for Early Student Dropout Prediction in Higher Education Institutions. *UHERJ, 11*(2), 57–68. DOI: 10.58653/nche.v11i2.5

Mullainathan, S., & Spiess, J. (2017). Machine learning: An applied econometric approach. *Journal of Economic Perspectives, 31*(2), 87–106.

Muñoz, A., Lasheras, J., Capel, A., García-Valverde, T., & Caballero, A. (2014). On adapting LMS for recommendation and personalization based on context-aware technologies. In *EDULEARN14 Proceedings* (pp. 5694–5701). IATED.

Myers, M., Brace, C., & Carden, L. (2023). *Intelligent Automation: Bridging the Gap Between Business and Academia*. Chapman and Hall/CRC. DOI: 10.1201/9781003276128

Nacer, N., Chouikh, J., & Nacer, K. (2026). Artificial intelligence and nursing education: Enhancing teaching, learning, and critical thinking. In *Transforming Humanities and Social Sciences Through AI* (pp. 129–158). IGI Global Scientific Publishing.

Nam, S. W. (2024). Case Study on Teaching with Project-Based Generative AI. *Journal of Internet of Things and Convergence, 10*(6), 43–48.

Narain, V., & Ranjan, P. (2024). Belling the cat: Designing collective action institutions for natural resource management in the peri-urban interface. *Urban Studies (Edinburgh, Scotland), 61*(8), 1604–1614. DOI: 10.1177/00420980231211681

Navaratna, A. R., & Saxena, D. (2025a). From policy to practice in digital governance: A three-level analysis of citizen-centric applications. *JeDEM-eJournal of eDemocracy and Open Government, 17*(1), 33–64.

Navaratna, A. R., & Saxena, D. (2023). An Indian approach to AI policy: A comparative study between three sectors. In *Handbook of Evidence-Based Management Practices in Business* (pp. 440–452). Routledge. DOI: 10.4324/9781003415725-55

Navaratna, A. R., & Saxena, D. (2025b). Digital Governance Through Self-Regulation: A user-developer perspective of AI chatbots. *Journal of Telecommunications and the Digital Economy, 13*(3), 1–29. DOI: 10.18080/jtde.v13n3.1077

Navarro, M., Prasetyo, Y., Young, M., Nadlifatin, R., & Redi, A. (2021). The Perceived Satisfaction in Utilizing Learning Management System among Engineering Students during the COVID-19 Pandemic: Integrating Task Technology Fit and Extended Technology Acceptance Model. *Sustainability (Basel), 13*(19), 10669. DOI: 10.3390/su131910669

Negri-Ribalta, C., Geraud-Stewart, R., Sergeeva, A., & Lenzini, G. (2024). A systematic literature review on the impact of AI models on the security of code generation. *Frontiers in Big Data, 7*, 1386720. DOI: 10.3389/fdata.2024.1386720 PMID: 38803522

Neubauer, L. C., Merzel, C., Weist, E. M., Corvin, J. A., Forsman, A., Fraser, J., Henderson, H. L., Hinyard, L. J., Opacich, K. J., & Runnerstrom, M. G. (2022). Realizing Promising Educational Practices in Academic Public Health: A Model for the Scholarship of Teaching and Learning. *Frontiers in Public Health, 9*, 750682. Advance online publication. DOI: 10.3389/fpubh.2021.750682 PMID: 35174129

Neumann, A. T., Arndt, T., Köbis, L., Meissner, R., Martin, A., de Lange, P., Pengel, N., Klamma, R., & Wollersheim, H.-W. (2021). Chatbots as a tool to scale mentoring processes. *Frontiers in Artificial Intelligence, 4*, 668220. Advance online publication. DOI: 10.3389/frai.2021.668220

Ng, D. T. K., Leung, J. K. L., Chu, K. W. S., & Qiao, M. S. (2021). AI literacy: Definition, teaching, evaluation and ethical issues. *Proceedings of the Association for Information Science and Technology, 58*(1), 504–509. DOI: 10.1002/pra2.487

Nguyen, A., Tuunanen, T., Gardner, L., & Sheridan, D. (2021). Design principles for learning analytics information systems in higher education. *European Journal of Information Systems, 30*(5), 541–568. DOI: 10.1080/0960085X.2020.1816144

Nguyen, N., & Nadi, S. (2022, May). An empirical evaluation of GitHub copilot's code suggestions. In *Proceedings of the 19th International Conference on Mining Software Repositories* (pp. 1-5). DOI: 10.1145/3524842.3528470

Nikitaeva, A. Y., & Salem, A.-B. M. (2022). Institutional Framework for The Development of Artificial Intelligence in The Industry. *Journal of International Students, 14*(1), 108–126. DOI: 10.17835/2076-6297.2022.14.1.108-126

NITI Aayog. (2021). *Artificial intelligence in agriculture: Opportunities and challenges in India.*

Notion. (2026). *Notion Labs, Inc.* https://notion.com/product/ai

Noviaristanti, S. and Hanifan, H. (2022). Factor Analysis of Learning Management System Acceptance.. DOI: 10.46254/EU05.20220464

Nye, M., Andreassen, A. J., Gur-Ari, G., Michalewski, H., Austin, J., Bieber, D., ... & Odena, A. (2021). Show your work: Scratchpads for intermediate computation with language models.

O'Connor, S. (2025). Best AI workflow software for project managers in tech 2026. monday.com. https://monday.com/blog/project-management/best-ai-workflow-software-project-manager-tech-cm

O'Connor, S.ChatGPT. (2023). Open artificial intelligence platforms in nursing education: Tools for academic progress or abuse? *Nurse Education in Practice*, *66*, 103537. Advance online publication. DOI: 10.1016/j.nepr.2022.103537 PMID: 36549229

O'Neil, C. (2016). *Weapons of math destruction: How big data increases inequality and threatens democracy*. Crown Publishing Group.

OECD. (2019). *Artificial Intelligence in Society*. OECD., DOI: 10.1787/eedfee77-

Ogunleye, B., Zakariyyah, K. I., Ajao, O., Olayinka, O., & Sharma, H. (2024). A systematic review of generative AI for teaching and learning practice. *Education Sciences*, *14*(6), 636. DOI: 10.3390/educsci14060636

Oh, S., & Sanfilippo, M. (2024). University Governance for Responsible AI. *Proceedings of the Alise Annual Conference*. DOI: 10.21900/j.alise.2024.1706

Olariu, O., & Zeleznikow, J. (2025). Human Rights-Compliant Artificial Intelligence. *Digitalisation and Artificial Intelligence in Courts: Opportunities and Challenges*, *259*, 275.

Olsson, J. (2009). The Power of the Inside Activist: Understanding Policy Change by Empowering the Advocacy Coalition Framework (ACF). *Planning Theory & Practice*, *10*(2), 167–187. DOI: 10.1080/14649350902884425

Ooi, K. B., Tan, G. W. H., Al-Emran, M., Al-Sharafi, M. A., Capatina, A., Chakraborty, A., Dwivedi, Y. K., Huang, T.-L., Kar, A. K., Lee, V.-H., Loh, X.-M., Micu, A., Mikalef, P., Mogaji, E., Pandey, N., Raman, R., Rana, N. P., Sarker, P., Sharma, A., & Wong, L. W. (2025). The potential of generative artificial intelligence across disciplines: Perspectives and future directions. *Journal of Computer Information Systems*, *65*(1), 76–107. DOI: 10.1080/08874417.2023.2261010

Open Ai Platform. (n.d.-a). GPT 5.2. https://platform.openai.com/docs/models/gpt-5.2

Open, A. I. (2024, May 13). *Hello GPT-4o*. https://openai.com/index/hello-gpt-4o

Open, A. I. (n.d.). *ChatGPT*. https://chatgpt.com

Open, A. I. Platform. (n.d.). *GPT-3.5 Turbo.* https://platform.openai.com/docs/models/gpt-3.5-turbo

Ostrom, E. (2010). Response: The Institutional Analysis and Development Framework and the Commons. SSRN *Electronic Journal, 95*(4). DOI: 10.2139/ssrn.1615582

Ostrom, E. (2011). Background on the Institutional Analysis and Development Framework. *Policy Studies Journal: The Journal of the Policy Studies Organization, 39*(1), 7–27. DOI: 10.1111/j.1541-0072.2010.00394.x

Ouyang, L., Wu, J., Jiang, X., Almeida, D., Wainwright, C., Mishkin, P., Zhang, C., Agarwal, S., Slama, K., Ray, A., Schulman, J., Hilton, J., Kelton, F., Miller, L., Simens, M., Askell, A., Welinder, P., Christiano, P., Leike, J., & Lowe, R. (2022). Training language models to follow instructions with human feedback. *Advances in Neural Information Processing Systems, 35*, 27730–27744. DOI: 10.52202/068431-2011

Oyelude, A. A. (2024). Artificial intelligence (AI) tools for academic research. *Library Hi Tech News, 41*(8), 18–20. DOI: 10.1108/LHTN-08-2024-0131

Pabba, C., & Kumar, P. (2022). An intelligent system for monitoring students' engagement in large classroom teaching through facial expression recognition. *Expert Systems: International Journal of Knowledge Engineering and Neural Networks, 39*(1), e12839. DOI: 10.1111/exsy.12839

Palgrave Pivot. (n.d.). *The Politics of Policy Analysis 100-word description.* https://paulcairney.wordpress.com/wp-content/uploads/2020/02/paul-cairney-the-politics-of-policy-analysis-palgrave-pivot-full-draft-27.2.20.pdf

Paloma, Z. B., & Paloma, J. R. S. (2026). From adoption to accountable integration in nursing higher education: A SAFE-GenAI framework for nurse academics. *Nurse Education in Practice, 93*, 104796. DOI: 10.1016/j.nepr.2026.104796 PMID: 41887953

Pangan, K. (2026, January 16). *A practical guide to Jira AI automation features in 2026*. Eesel AI. https://www.eesel.ai/blog/jira-ai-automation-features

Papamitsiou, Z., & Economides, A. A. (2014). Learning analytics and educational data mining in practice: A systematic literature review of empirical evidence. *Journal of Educational Technology & Society, 17*(4), 49–64.

Parasuraman, R., & Manzey, D. H. (2010). Complacency and bias in human use of automation: An attentional integration. *Human Factors, 52*(3), 381–410. DOI: 10.1177/0018720810376055 PMID: 21077562

Parnin, C. (2025). Revolutionizing Education through AI with Tailored Learning Experiences and Dynamic Assessments, 10-18. DOI: 10.34293/ICAICM-25.ch002

Patro, G. K., Porcaro, L., Mitchell, L., Zhang, Q., Zehlike, M., & Garg, N. (2022). Fair ranking: a critical review, challenges, and future directions. *ACM International Conference Proceeding Series*, 1929–1942. DOI: 10.1145/3531146.3533238

Paul Cairney. (2019, February 11). *Policy in 500 Words: The advocacy coalition framework*. Paul Cairney: Politics & Public Policy. https://paulcairney.wordpress.com/2019/02/11/policy-in-500-words-the-advocacy-coalition-framework/

Pecuchova, J., & Drlik, M. (2024). Enhancing the early student dropout prediction model through clustering analysis of students' digital traces. *IEEE Access : Practical Innovations, Open Solutions*, *12*, 159336–159367. DOI: 10.1109/ACCESS.2024.3486762

Pedró, F. (2020). Applications of Artificial Intelligence to higher education: Possibilities, evidence, and challenges. *Iul Research*, *1*(1), 61–76. DOI: 10.57568/iulres.v1i1.43

Peng, S., Kalliamvakou, E., Cihon, P., & Demirer, M. (2023). *The impact of AI on developer productivity: Evidence from GitHub Copilot* (arXiv preprint No. 2302.06590). arXiv. https://arxiv.org/abs/2302.06590

Pérez, J. Q., Daradoumis, T., & Puig, J. M. M. (2020). Rediscovering the use of chatbots in education: A systematic literature review. *Computer Applications in Engineering Education*, *28*(6), 1549–1565. DOI: 10.1002/cae.22326

Perkins, M., & Roe, J. (2023). Decoding Academic Integrity Policies: A Corpus Linguistics Investigation of AI and Other Technological Threats. *Higher Education Policy*, *37*(3), 633–653. DOI: 10.1057/s41307-023-00323-2

Pernaa, J., Ikävalko, T., Takala, A., Vuorio, E., Pesonen, R., & Haatainen, O. (2023). Artificial Intelligence Chatbots in Chemical Information Seeking: Educational Insights through a SWOT analysis. DOI: 10.20944/preprints202312.1066.v1

Pesaran, M. H., & Timmermann, A. (1995). Predictability of stock returns: Robustness and economic significance. *Journal of Finance, 50*(4), 1201–1228.

Petroni, F., Lewis, P., Piktus, A., Rocktäschel, T., Wu, Y., Miller, A. H., & Riedel, S. (2020). How context affects language models' factual predictions. *arXiv preprint arXiv:2005.04611*.

Petroni, F., Rocktäschel, T., Riedel, S., Lewis, P., Bakhtin, A., Wu, Y., & Miller, A. (2019, November). Language models as knowledge bases? In *Proceedings of the 2019 conference on empirical methods in natural language processing and the 9th international joint conference on natural language processing (EMNLP-IJCNLP)* (pp. 2463-2473). DOI: 10.18653/v1/D19-1250

Phillipson, R. (2013). Response to a book review in World Englishes, 30(2), 283–6. *World Englishes, 32*(3), 453–456. DOI: 10.1111/weng.12047

Pisica, A. I., Edu, T., Zaharia, R. M., & Zaharia, R. (2023). Implementing artificial intelligence in higher education: Pros and cons from the perspectives of academics. *Societies (Basel, Switzerland), 13*(5), 118. DOI: 10.3390/soc13050118

Poldrack, R. A., Lu, T., & Beguš, G. (2023). *AI-assisted coding: Experiments with GPT-4.* arXiv preprint arXiv:2304.13187.

Popenici, S. A. D., & Kerr, S. (2017). Exploring the impact of artificial intelligence on teaching and learning in higher education. *Research and Practice in Technology Enhanced Learning, 12*(1), 22. Advance online publication. DOI: 10.1186/s41039-017-0062-8 PMID: 30595727

Popenici, S., Catalano, H., Mestic, G., & Ani-Rus, A. (2023). A Systematic Review of the Artificial Intelligence Implications in Shaping the Future of Higher Education. *Educatia, 21*(26), 92–107. DOI: 10.24193/ed21.2023.26.11

Powell, W., & Courchesne, S. (2024). Opportunities and risks involved in using ChatGPT to create first grade science lesson plans. *PLoS One, 19*(6), e0305337. DOI: 10.1371/journal.pone.0305337 PMID: 38885244

Prosen, M., & Ličen, S. (2025). Perceptions, ethical challenges and sustainable integration of generative AI in health science education: A cross-sectional study. *Sustainability (Basel), 17*(14), 6546. DOI: 10.3390/su17146546

Qadhi, S. M., Alduais, A., Chaaban, Y., & Khraisheh, M. (2024). Generative AI, research ethics, and higher education research: Insights from a scientometric analysis. *Information (Basel), 15*(6), 325. DOI: 10.3390/info15060325

Qadir, J. (2023). Generative AI and academic integrity: A risk assessment. *International Journal for Educational Integrity.*

Rahman, A., Mahir, S. H., Tashrif, M. T. A., Karim, M. A., Aishi, A. A., Kundu, D., ... & Karim, H. A. (2025). Comparative analysis based on deepseek, chatgpt, and google gemini: Features, techniques, performance, future prospects. *Systems and Soft Computing*, 200396.

Rahman, M. I. (2026). Algorithmic bias and transparency in artificial intelligence tools for nursing education: A scoping review. *Nurse Education in Practice, 92*, 104756. DOI: 10.1016/j.nepr.2026.104756 PMID: 41653525

Rajagopal, N. K., Qureshi, N. I., Durga, S., Ramirez Asis, E. H., Huerta Soto, R. M., Gupta, S. K., & Deepak, S. (2022). Future of business culture: An artificial intelligence-driven digital framework for organization decision-making process. *Complexity, 2022*(1), 7796507. DOI: 10.1155/2022/7796507

Ramler, R., Moser, M., Fischer, L., Nissl, M., & Heinzl, R. (2024, April). Industrial experience report on ai-assisted coding in professional software development. *In Proceedings of the 1st International Workshop on Large Language Models for Code* (pp. 1-7). DOI: 10.1145/3643795.3648377

Ranasinghe, A., Gresham, T., Newsome, S., & Wijesinghe, D. (2025). Work in progress: Adaptive learning technologies in higher education—Measuring impact on student engagement and academic performance. In *ICERI2025 Proceedings* (pp. 2103–2109). IATED.

Rao, M. N., & Al-Obaidi, J. A. (2024). Embracing how AI responsibly empowers students and faculty in higher education: Theoretical perspectives. *Emerging Technologies Transforming Higher Education: Instructional Design and Student Success*, 1–32. DOI: 10.4018/979-8-3693-3904-6.ch001

Ravikumar, R. N., Aarthi, S., Sapaeva, B., Jumaniyozov, Y., Manoj Praveen, V., & Siddheswaran, V. (2025). Revolutionizing Education With NLP and ML: Innovations, Challenges, and Future Directions. *Educational Applications of Natural Language Processing, Chatbots, and AI*, 293–324. DOI: 10.4018/979-8-3373-6791-0.ch011

Razniewski, S., Yates, A., Kassner, N., & Weikum, G. (2021). Language models as or for knowledge bases. *arXiv preprint arXiv:2110.04888.*

Rhem, A. J. (2023). Ethical use of data in AI Applications. In *Ethics-Scientific Research, Ethical Issues, Artificial Intelligence and Education*. IntechOpen.

Risko, E. F., & Gilbert, S. J. (2016). Cognitive Offloading. *Trends in Cognitive Sciences, 20*(9), 676–688. DOI: 10.1016/j.tics.2016.07.002 PMID: 27542527

Roberts, A., Raffel, C., & Shazeer, N. (2020). How much knowledge can you pack into the parameters of a language model? *arXiv preprint arXiv:2002.08910*. DOI: 10.18653/v1/2020.emnlp-main.437

Roberts, H., Zhang, J., Bariach, B., Cowls, J., Gilburt, B., Juneja, P., ... & Floridi, L. (2024). Artificial intelligence in support of the circular economy: ethical considerations and a path forw

Rodger, D., Mann, S. P., Earp, B., Savulescu, J., Bobier, C., & Blackshaw, B. P. (2025). Generative AI in healthcare education: How AI literacy gaps could compromise learning and patient safety. *Nurse Education in Practice*, *87*, 104461. DOI: 10.1016/j.nepr.2025.104461 PMID: 40633198

Rodrigues, C., Reis, A., Pereira, R., Martins, P., Sousa, J., & Pinto, T. (2022). *A review of conversational agents in education technology and innovation in learning teaching and education*. Springer.

Rodrigues, T. V. (2025). *Distant Writing and The Epistemology of Authorship: On Creativity*. Delegation, And Plagiarism in The Age Of AI.

Rodríguez, J. A., Santana, M. G., Perera, V. A., & Pulido, J. R. (2021). *Embodied conversational agents: Artificial intelligence for autonomous learning*. Pixel-Bit Revista de Medios y Educación., DOI: 10.12795/pixelbit.86171

Roggero, M., Bisaro, A., & Villamayor-Tomas, S. (2017). Institutions in the climate adaptation literature: A systematic literature review through the lens of the Institutional Analysis and Development framework. *Journal of Institutional Economics*, *14*(3), 423–448. DOI: 10.1017/S1744137417000376

Romero, C., & Ventura, S. (2020). Educational data mining and learning analytics: An updated survey. *Wiley Interdisciplinary Reviews. Data Mining and Knowledge Discovery*, *10*(3), e1355. DOI: 10.1002/widm.1355

Rosmayanti, V. (2025). Eco-Linguistics and Digital Learning: Integrating Environmental Awareness in Language Education. In *Nexus of Environmental Quality and Technology Innovation* (pp. 71-96). IGI Global Scientific Publishing. DOI: 10.4018/979-8-3373-1822-6.ch004

Rozenblit, L., Price, A., Solomonides, A., Joseph, A. L., Koski, E., Srivastava, G., Labkoff, S., Bray, D., Lopez-Gonzalez, M., Singh, R., deBronkart, D., Barr, P. J., Szolovits, P., Dattani, K., Jaffe, C., Fridsma, D., Baris, R., Leftwich, R., Stolper, R., & Quintana, Y. (2025). Toward responsible AI governance: Balancing multi-stakeholder perspectives on AI in healthcare. *International Journal of Medical Informatics*, *203*, 106015. DOI: 10.1016/j.ijmedinf.2025.106015 PMID: 40680319

Rozenblit, L., Price, A., Solomonides, A., Joseph, A. L., Srivastava, G., Labkoff, S., deBronkart, D., Singh, R., Dattani, K., Lopez-Gonzalez, M., Barr, P. J., Koski, E., Lin, B., Cheung, E., Weiner, M. G., Williams, T., Thuy Bui, T. T., & Quintana, Y. (2025). Towards a multi-stakeholder process for developing responsible AI governance in consumer health. *International Journal of Medical Informatics*, *195*, 105713. DOI: 10.1016/j.ijmedinf.2024.105713 PMID: 39642592

Ruan, B. K., Lo, L., Shuai, H. H., & Cheng, W. H. (2022). Mimicking the Annotation Process for Recognizing the Micro Expressions. *MM 2022 - Proceedings of the 30th ACM International Conference on Multimedia*, 228–236. DOI: 10.1145/3503161.3548185

Ruksakulpiwat, S., Phianhasin, L., Benjasirisan, C., Su, T., Riangkam, C., Thorngthip, S., Aldossary, H. M., Ahmed, B., Pongsuwun, K., & Angkaew, N. (2025). Artificial intelligence in nursing research: A systematic review of applications, benefits, and challenges. *International Nursing Review*, *72*(3), e70080. DOI: 10.1111/inr.70080 PMID: 40714821

Sabatier, P. A. (1998). The advocacy coalition framework: Revisions and relevance for Europe. *Journal of European Public Policy*, *5*(1), 98–130. DOI: 10.1080/13501768880000051

Sabo, I. C., Maurmann, A. S. V., de Brito Santos, G., Junior, M. M., Vieira, M. F., Mohr, J. G., ... & Rover11, A. J. (2025). AVANÇOS INICIAIS DO PROJETO CONCIL-IA: desafios e potenciais impactos1 PRELIMINARY PROGRESS OF THE CONCIL-IA PROJECT: challenges and potential impacts.

Saidakhror, G. (2024). *Economic effects and infrastructure requirements for AI in universities*. Educational Finance Review.

Sajja, R., Sermet, Y., Chi, N. C., & Demir, I. (2025). Evaluating artificial intelligence assisted nursing education: Student perceptions, ethical concerns, and pedagogical implications. *Teaching and Learning in Nursing*.

Salloum, S. A. (2024). AI perils in education: Exploring ethical concerns. Artificial intelligence in education: The power and dangers of ChatGPT in the classroom, 669-675.

Samuelson, P. A. (1965). Proof that properly anticipated prices fluctuate randomly. *Industrial Management Review, 6*(2), 41–49.

Sarker, D., Eiaz-Ur-Rahman, A. F. M., Sakib, A. R., Terano, H. J. R., & Rahman, M. M. (2023). ChatGPT's Applications in Higher Education: Unmasking Opportunities and Challenges. *Journal of Education. Management and Development Studies*, *3*(4), 37–47. DOI: 10.52631/jemds.v3i4.250

Sarker, I. H. (2022). AI-based modeling: Techniques, applications and research issues towards automation, intelligent and smart systems. *SN Computer Science*, *3*(2), 158. DOI: 10.1007/s42979-022-01043-x PMID: 35194580

Saxena, D., Lamest, M., & Bansal, V. (2021). Responsible machine learning for ethical artificial intelligence in business and industry. In *Handbook of Research on Applied Data Science and Artificial Intelligence in Business and Industry* (pp. 639–653). IGI Global. DOI: 10.4018/978-1-7998-6985-6.ch030

Schlagwein, D., & Willcocks, L. (2023). 'ChatGPT et al.': The ethics of using (generative) artificial intelligence in research and science. *Journal of Information Technology*, *38*(3), 232–238. DOI: 10.1177/02683962231200411

Seidaliyeva, U., Akhmetov, D., Ilipbayeva, L., & Matson, E. T. (2020). Real-Time and Accurate Drone Detection in a Video with a Static Background. *Sensors (Basel)*, *20*(14), 3856. Advance online publication. DOI: 10.3390/s20143856 PMID: 32664365

Selwyn, N. (2024). On the limits of artificial intelligence (AI) in education. *Nordisk Tidsskrift for Pedagogikk og Kritikk*, *10*(1), 3–14. DOI: 10.23865/ntpk.v10.6062

Sengul, T., Sariköse, S., & Gul, A. (2025). Ethical decision-making and artificial intelligence in nursing education: An integrative review. *Nursing Ethics*, *32*(8), 2490–2515. DOI: 10.1177/09697330251366600 PMID: 40865964

Shanahan, M. (2024). Talking about large language models. *Communications of the ACM*, *67*(2), 68–79. DOI: 10.1145/3624724

Sharma, P., Kumawat, R., Jain, G., Keswani, G., Goyal, N. K., & Sheikh, M. F. (2026). Machine Learning-Based Intrusion Detection Systems for Healthcare Internet of Things (HIoT). In Shieh, C., Goel, P., Horng, M., & Pandey, H. (Eds.), *Resilient Healthcare Internet of Things Systems: Architectures, Security, and Trust* (pp. 185–214). IGI Global Scientific Publishing., DOI: 10.4018/979-8-3373-7610-3.ch007

Sheikh, M. F. A., Kapoor, S. K., Goyal, N. K., & Tuba, E. rao, A. (2026). Enhancing Healthcare Security with Fog Computing and Blockchain Technology. In: Nayak, R., Mittal, N., Khunteta, A., Kumar, M. (eds) Recent Advancements in Artificial Intelligence. ICRAAI 2025. Lecture Notes in Networks and Systems, vol 1468. Springer, Singapore. DOI: 10.1007/978-981-96-7760-3_38

Shen, M., Shen, Y., Liu, F., & Jin, J. (2025). Prompts, privacy, and personalized learning: Integrating AI into nursing education—a qualitative study. *BMC Nursing*, *24*(1), 470. DOI: 10.1186/s12912-025-03115-8 PMID: 40301862

Shiller, R. J. (2017). Narrative economics. *American Economic Review, 107*(4), 967–1004.

Siemens, G. (2013). Learning analytics: The emergence of a discipline. *The American Behavioral Scientist*, *57*(10), 1380–1400. DOI: 10.1177/0002764213498851

Sieweke, D. (2025, July 25). *AI Policy and Governance: Shaping the Future of Artificial Intelligence*. Scytale. https://scytale.ai/center/grc/ai-policy-and-governance-shaping-the-future-of-artificial-intelligence/

Simms, R. C. (2025). Generative artificial intelligence (AI) literacy in nursing education: A crucial call to action. *Nurse Education Today, 146*, 106544. DOI: 10.1016/j.nedt.2024.106544 PMID: 39708405

Singh, S., Dias, R., Irfan, M., Galvão, R., Alexandre, P., & Gonçalves, S. (2024). The role of perceived organisational support in predicting organisational commitment and organizational citizenship behavior in professional organizations. *Journal of Ecohumanism, 3*(6), 239–249. DOI: 10.62754/joe.v3i6.4000

Slade, S., & Prinsloo, P. (2013). Learning analytics: Ethical issues and dilemmas. *The American Behavioral Scientist, 57*(10), 1510–1529. DOI: 10.1177/0002764213479366

Smuha, N. A. (2021). Beyond the individual: Governing AI's societal harm. *Internet Policy Review, 10*(3). Advance online publication. DOI: 10.14763/2021.3.1574

Sperber, D., Clément, F., Heintz, C., Mascaro, O., Mercier, H., Origgi, G., & Wilson, D. (2010). Epistemic vigilance. *Mind & Language, 25*(4), 359–393. DOI: 10.1111/j.1468-0017.2010.01394.x

St-Hilaire, I. (2025). Lying chatbot makes airline liable: Negligent misrepresentation in Moffatt v Air Canada. *UBC Law Review, 58*(2), 591–612. https://commons.allard.ubc.ca/ubclawreview/vol58/iss2/8

Sukmawati, R., Rosmayanti, V., & Amin, S. (2025). Blending Technology and Tradition: PjBL in ELT to Foster Self-Directed Learning. *International Journal of Language Education, 9*(2), 356–376. DOI: 10.26858/ijole.v1i2.75114

Sullivan, M., Kelly, A., & McLaughlan, P. (2023). ChatGPT in higher education: Considerations for academic integrity and student learning. *Journal of Applied Learning and Teaching, 6*(1), 31–40. DOI: 10.37074/jalt.2023.6.1.17

Sun, L., & Zhou, L. (2024). Does Generative Artificial Intelligence Improve the Academic Achievement of College Students? A Meta-Analysis. *Journal of Educational Computing Research, 62*(7), 1896–1933. DOI: 10.1177/07356331241277937

Surahman, E., & Wang, T. H. (2022). Academic dishonesty and trustworthy assessment in online learning: A systematic literature review. *Journal of Computer Assisted Learning, 38*(6), 1535–1553. DOI: 10.1111/jcal.12708

Susnjak, T., Ramaswami, G. S., & Mathrani, A. (2022). Learning analytics dashboard: A tool for providing actionable insights to learners. *International Journal of Educational Technology in Higher Education, 19*(1), 12. DOI: 10.1186/s41239-021-00313-7 PMID: 35194560

Sutton, R. S., & Barto, A. G. (2018). *Reinforcement learning: An introduction* (2nd ed.). MIT Press.

Sweller, J. (1988). Cognitive load during problem solving: Effects on learning. *Cognitive Science, 12*(2), 257–285. DOI: 10.1207/s15516709cog1202_4

Taeihagh, A. (2025). Governance of Generative AI. *Policy and Society, 44*(1), 1–22. Advance online publication. DOI: 10.1093/polsoc/puaf001

Teamwork. (n.d.). *AI features.* https://www.teamwork.com/features/ai/

Tetlock, P. C. (2007). Giving content to investor sentiment: The role of media in the stock market. *Journal of Finance, 62*(3), 1139–1168.

The IAD Framework. (2014, October 8). OCSDNET. https://ocsdnet.org/about-ocsdnet/about-ocs/iad-framework/

Thomas, D. R., Gatz, E., Gupta, S., Lin, J., Tipper, C., & Koedinger, K. R. (2024). Using generative AI to provide feedback to adult tutors in training and assess real-life performance. In *Proceedings of the Learning Ideas Conference* (pp. 204–214). Springer. DOI: 10.1007/978-3-031-73427-4_21

Tina, F. W., Afsarimanesh, N., Nag, A., & Alahi, M. E. E. (2025). Integrating AIoT Technologies in Aquaculture: A Systematic Review. *Future Internet, 17*(5), 199. DOI: 10.3390/fi17050199

Tohir, A., Muslim, S., & Situmorang, R. (2025). Integration of Technology in Learning: Enhancing Higher Order Thinking Skills (HOTS) in Secondary School Students. *International Journal of Computational and Experimental Science and Engineering, 11*(3). Advance online publication. DOI: 10.22399/ijcesen.3474

Turing, A. (1950). Computing Machinery and Intelligence. *Mind; A Quarterly Review of Psychology and Philosophy, 59*(236), 433–460. DOI: 10.1093/mind/LIX.236.433

Tzoneva, I. (2023). Benefits and challenges in using AI-powered educational tools. DOI: 10.36315/2023v2end079

Ubina, N. A., Lan, H.-Y., Cheng, S.-C., Chang, C.-C., Lin, S.-S., Zhang, K.-X., Lu, H.-Y., Cheng, C.-Y., & Hsieh, Y.-Z. (2023). Digital twin-based intelligent fish farming with Artificial Intelligence Internet of Things (AIoT). *Smart Agricultural Technology, 5*, 100285. DOI: 10.1016/j.atech.2023.100285

Ukanwa, K., & Rust, R. T. (2020). Algorithmic discrimination in service. SSRN *Electronic Journal.* DOI: 10.2139/ssrn.3654943

Ulucan, O., Karakaya, D., & Turkan, M. (2020). A Large-Scale Dataset for Fish Segmentation and Classification. *2020 Innovations in Intelligent Systems and Applications Conference (ASYU)*, 1–5. DOI: 10.1109/ASYU50717.2020.9259867

UNESCO. (2021). *Recommendation on the Ethics of Artificial Intelligence | UNESCO.* Www.unesco.org. https://www.unesco.org/en/articles/recommendation-ethics-artificial-intelligence

UNESCO. (2025). *UNESCO survey: Two-thirds of higher education institutions have or are developing guidance on AI use.* UNESCO. https://www.unesco.org/en/articles/unesco-survey-two-thirds-higher-education-institutions-have-or-are-developing-guidance-ai-use

Uysal, B. Ç. B., & Yüksel, I. (2024). AI-powered lesson planning: Insights from future EFL teachers. *AI in Language Teaching, Learning, and Assessment*, 101–132. DOI: 10.4018/979-8-3693-0872-1.ch006

Vahabi, S., & Hozhabri, A. (2024). Automatic use case classification based on topic grouping for requirements engineering. *Innovations in Systems and Software Engineering, 20*(1), 85–96. DOI: 10.1007/s11334-023-00535-0

Vaithilingam, P., Zhang, T., & Glassman, E. L. (2022). Expectation vs. Experience: Evaluating the Usability of Code Generation Tools Powered by Large Language Models. In *CHI Conference on Human Factors in Computing Systems Extended Abstracts (CHI '22 Extended Abstracts)*, (pp. 1–7). ACM. DOI: 10.1145/3491101.3519665

Valmeekam, K., Stechly, K., & Kambhampati, S. (2024). *LLMs Still Can't Plan; Can LRMs? A Preliminary Evaluation of OpenAI's o1 on PlanB*ench. *a*rXiv preprint arXiv:2409.13373. https://arxiv.org/pdf/2409.13373?

van Dijk, J. A. (2020). *The digital divide.* John Wiley & Sons.

van Dis, E. A. M., Bollen, J., Zuidema, W., van Rooij, R., & Bockting, C. L. (2023). ChatGPT: Five priorities for research. *Nature, 614*(7947), 224–226. DOI: 10.1038/d41586-023-00288-7 PMID: 36737653

van Rensburg, Z. J., & van der Westhuizen, S. (2024). Ethical AI Integration in Academia: Developing a Literacy-Driven Framework for LLMs in South African Higher Education. *AI Approaches to Literacy in Higher Education*, 23–48. DOI: 10.4018/979-8-3693-1054-0.ch002

Van Woerkom, W., Grossi, D., Prakken, H., & Verheij, B. (2024). A fortiori case-based reasoning: From theory to data. *Journal of Artificial Intelligence Research, 81*, 401–441. DOI: 10.1613/jair.1.15178

VanLehn, K. (2011). The relative effectiveness of human tutoring, intelligent tutoring systems, and other tutoring systems. *Educational Psychologist, 46*(4), 197–221. DOI: 10.1080/00461520.2011.611369

Vapnik, V. (1998). *Statistical learning theory*. Wiley.

Varsha, P. S. (2023). How can we manage biases in artificial intelligence systems–A systematic literature review. *International Journal of Information Management Data Insights, 3*(1), 100165. DOI: 10.1016/j.jjimei.2023.100165

Vaswani, A., Shazeer, N., Parmar, N., Uszkoreit, J., Jones, L., Gomez, A. N., & Polosukhin, I. (2017). Attention is all you need. *Advances in Neural Information Processing Systems*, 30.

Vetrivel, S. C., Vidhyapriya, P., Gunasekar, T., & Arun, V. P. (2025). Cross-Cultural and Inclusive Strategies for AI in Language Education. In *Human-Centered Approaches to AI-Enhanced English Language Learning and Teaching* (pp. 309–338). DOI: 10.4018/979-8-3373-3561-2.ch011

Vial, G. (2019). Understanding digital transformation: A review and a research agenda. *The Journal of Strategic Information Systems, 28*(2), 118–144. https://doi.org/https://doi.org/10.1016/j.jsis.2019.01.003. DOI: 10.1016/j.jsis.2019.01.003

Vijayvergiya, M., Salawa, M., Budiselić, I., Zheng, D., Lamblin, P., Ivanković, M., & Just, R. (2024, July). Ai-assisted assessment of coding practices in modern code review. In *Proceedings of the 1st ACM International Conference on AI-Powered Software* (pp. 85-93). DOI: 10.1145/3664646.3665664

Vikram, E., Kalaivani, K., Praanesh, M., & Surya, M. (2025). GEN AI Based Personalized AI Tutor. *Interantional Journal of Scientific Research in Engineering and Management, 09*(10), 1–9. DOI: 10.55041/IJSREM52545

Villegas-Ch, W., García-Ortiz, J., Mullo-Ca, K., Sánchez-Viteri, S., & Roman-Cañizares, M. (2021). Implementation of a virtual assistant for the academic management of a university with the use of artificial intelligence. *Future Internet, 13*(4), 97. DOI: 10.3390/fi13040097

Wagner, A. J. (2017). Essential or extravagant: Considering FOIA budgets, costs and fees. *Government Information Quarterly, 34*(3), 388–395. DOI: 10.1016/j.giq.2017.09.001

Wang, C., Liu, X., & Song, D. (2020). Language models are open knowledge graphs. *arXiv preprint arXiv:2010.11967.*

Wang, A., & Wu, X. (2025). Building a triadic model of technology, motivation, and engagement: A mixed-methods study of AI teaching assistants in design theory education. *Frontiers in Psychology, 16,* 1624182. Advance online publication. DOI: 10.3389/fpsyg.2025.1624182 PMID: 40672855

Wang, H., Fu, T., Du, Y., Gao, W., Huang, K., Liu, Z., Chandak, P., Liu, S., Van Katwyk, P., Deac, A., Anandkumar, A., Pande, V. S., & Zitnik, M. (2023). Scientific discovery in the age of artificial intelligence. *Nature, 620*(7972), 47–60. DOI: 10.1038/s41586-023-06221-2 PMID: 37532811

Wang, R., Li, J., Shi, W., & Li, X. (2021). Application of artificial intelligence techniques in operating mode of professors' academic governance in american research universities. *Wireless Communications and Mobile Computing, 2021*(1), 3415125. DOI: 10.1155/2021/3415125

Wang, Y., Hu, K., Jiang, B., Xia, X., & Tang, X. S. (2023). A Systematic Literature Review of Software Traceability Links Automation Techniques. Jisuanji Xuebao. *Chin. J. Comput, 46,* 1919–1946.

Watermeyer, R., Phipps, L., Lanclos, D., & Knight, C. (2024). Generative AI and the automating of academia. *Postdigital Science and Education, 6*(2), 446–466. DOI: 10.1007/s42438-023-00440-6

Weber, C., Truong, H. M., & Vas, R. (2015). Context-aware self-assessment in higher education. In *EDULEARN15 Proceedings* (pp. 5910–5920). IATED.

Wecks, J. O., Voshaar, J., Plate, B. J., & Zimmermann, J. (2024). Generative AI usage and exam performance. *arXiv preprint arXiv:2404.19699.*

Weible, C. M., Sabatier, P. A., Jenkins-Smith, H. C., Nohrstedt, D., Henry, A. D., & deLeon, P. (2011). A Quarter Century of the Advocacy Coalition Framework: An Introduction to the Special Issue. *Policy Studies Journal: The Journal of the Policy Studies Organization, 39*(3), 349–360. DOI: 10.1111/j.1541-0072.2011.00412.x

Wei, J., Wang, X., Schuurmans, D., Bosma, M., Xia, F., Chi, E., & Zhou, D. (2022). Chain-of-thought prompting elicits reasoning in large language models. *Advances in Neural Information Processing Systems, 35,* 24824–24837. DOI: 10.52202/068431-1800

Wei, Q., Pan, S., Liu, X., Hong, M., Nong, C., & Zhang, W. (2025). The integration of AI in nursing: Addressing current applications, challenges, and future directions. *Frontiers in Medicine, 12*, 1545420. DOI: 10.3389/fmed.2025.1545420 PMID: 40007584

Welch, I., & Goyal, A. (2007). A comprehensive look at the empirical performance of equity premium prediction. *Review of Financial Studies, 21*(4), 1455–1508.

Weller, A. (2019). Transparency: Motivations and Challenges. *Explainable AI: Interpreting, Explaining and Visualising Deep Learning*, 23–40. DOI: 10.1007/978-3-030-28954-6_2

Wiley, D. (2013). *What is Open Pedagogy?* iterating toward openness. [Blog]. Bruner, J. S. (1966). *Toward a theory of instruction*. Harvard University Press.

Williamson, B., & Eynon, R. (2020). Historical threads, missing links, and future directions in AI in education. *Learning, Media and Technology, 45*(3), 223–235. DOI: 10.1080/17439884.2020.1798995

Williamson, B., Macgilchrist, F., & Potter, J. (2023). Re-examining AI, automation and datafication in education. *Learning, Media and Technology, 48*(1), 1–5. DOI: 10.1080/17439884.2023.2167830

Wineburg, S., & McGrew, S. (2019). Lateral reading and the nature of expertise: Reading less and learning more when evaluating digital information. *Teachers College Record, 121*(11), 1–40. DOI: 10.1177/016146811912101102

Witness, A. I. (2025, May 30). *AI Policy: How to Build a Responsible Framework for AI Use*. WitnessAI. https://witness.ai/blog/ai-policy/

World Economic Forum. (2023). *The future of jobs report 2023*. https://www.weforum.org/reports/the-future-of-jobs-report-2023

Wrike. (n.d.-a). *AI*. https://www.wrike.com/ai

Wrike. (n.d.-b). *AI project risk prediction*. https://help.wrike.com/hc/en-us/articles/360055046934-AI-Project-Risk-Prediction

Wrike. (n.d.-c). *Project risk management*. https://www.wrike.com/use-cases/project-risk-management

Wrike. (n.d.-d). *Develop your own integration on the Wrike API*. https://developers.wrike.com/

Wu, A.-Q., Li, K.-L., Song, Z.-Y., Lou, X., Hu, P., Yang, W., & Wang, R.-F. (2025). Deep Learning for Sustainable Aquaculture: Opportunities and Challenges. *Sustainability (Basel)*, *17*(11), 5084. DOI: 10.3390/su17115084

Xhafaj, E., Qendraj, D., Xhafaj, A., & Gjikaj, N. (2022). A Hybrid Integration of PLS-SEM, AHP, and FAHP Methods to Evaluate the Factors That Influence the Use of an LMS. *International Journal of Decision Support System Technology*, *14*(1), 1–17. DOI: 10.4018/IJDSST.286697

Xi, Y., Liu, W., Lin, J., Cai, X., Zhu, H., Zhu, J., & Yu, Y. (2024, October). Towards open-world recommendation with knowledge augmentation from large language models. In *Proceedings of the 18th ACM Conference on Recommender Systems* (pp. 12-22).

Xue, L., & Pang, Z. (2022). Ethical governance of artificial intelligence: An integrated analytical framework. *Journal of Digital Economy*, *1*(1), 44–52. DOI: 10.1016/j.jdec.2022.08.003

Yar, M. A., Hamdan, M., Anshari, M., Fitriyani, N. L., & Syafrudin, M. (2024). Governing with Intelligence: The Impact of Artificial Intelligence on Policy Development. *Information (Basel)*, *15*(9), 556. DOI: 10.3390/info15090556

Ydersbond, I. M. (2025). Power Through Pressure: How Interconnection Became Part of the EU's Overarching Climate and Energy Policy. *Journal of Common Market Studies*, *63*(2), 624–644. DOI: 10.1111/jcms.13642

Yekollu, R. K., Bhimraj Ghuge, T., Sunil Biradar, S., Haldikar, S. V., & Farook Mohideen Abdul Kader, O. (2024). AI-driven personalized learning paths: Enhancing education through adaptive systems. In *Proceedings of the International Conference on Smart Data Intelligence* (pp. 507–517). Springer. DOI: 10.1007/978-981-97-3191-6_38

Yen, G., & Lee, C. (2008). Efficient market hypothesis (EMH): Past, present and future. *Review of Pacific Basin Financial Markets and Policies, 11*(2), 305–329.

Yetiştiren, B., Özsoy, I., Ayerdem, M., & Tüzün, E. (2023). *Evaluating the code quality of ai-assisted code generation tools: An empirical study on github copilot, amazon codewhisperer, and chatgp*t. arXiv preprint arXiv:2304.10778. https://arxiv.org/pdf/2304.10778

Yeung, K., & Bygrave, L. A. (2022). Demystifying the modernised European data protection regime: Cross-disciplinary insights from legal and regulatory governance scholarship., 16(1), 137–155. *Regulation & Governance*, *16*(1), 137–155. DOI: 10.1111/rego.12401

Yordanova, Z. (2024, October). Innovation Processes in Universities: A Conceptual Model Incorporating Digital Transformation and Technological Innovations. In International Conference on Advanced Research in Technologies, Information, Innovation and Sustainability (pp. 105-117). Cham: Springer Nature Switzerland.

Younas, A., & Zeng, Y. (2025). Proposing Central Asian AI ethics principles: A multilevel approach for responsible AI. *AI and Ethics*, *5*(2), 1629–1637. DOI: 10.1007/s43681-024-00505-7

Yuan, Z., Liu, M., Ding, S., Wang, K., Chen, Y., Peng, X., & Lou, Y. (2024). Evaluating and improving chatgpt for unit test generation. *Proceedings of the ACM on Software Engineering, 1*(FSE), 1703-1726. DOI: 10.1145/3660783

Yue, K., & Shen, Y. (2022). An overview of disruptive technologies for aquaculture. *Aquaculture and Fisheries. Aquaculture and Fisheries*, *7*(2), 111–120. DOI: 10.1016/j.aaf.2021.04.009

Yu, J., Wang, X., Tu, S., Cao, S., Zhang-Li, D., Lv, X., & Li, J. (2024, May). Kola: Carefully benchmarking world knowledge of large language models. In *International Conference on Learning Representations* (Vol. 2024, pp. 44594-44637).

Zadeh, E. K., Khoulenjani, A. B., & Safaei, M. (2023). Integrating AI for Agile Project Management: Innovations, Challenges, and Benefits. [IJIECM]. *International Journal of Industrial Engineering and Construction Management, 1*(1), 1–10.

Zawacki-Richter, O., Marín, V. I., Bond, M., & Gouverneur, F. (2019). Systematic review of research on artificial intelligence applications in higher education–where are the educators? *International Journal of Educational Technology in Higher Education, 16*(1), 1–27. DOI: 10.1186/s41239-019-0171-0

Zelikman, E., Wu, Y., Mu, J., & Goodman, N. (2022). STAR: Bootstrapping reasoning with reasoning. *Advances in Neural Information Processing Systems, 35*, 15476–15488. DOI: 10.52202/068431-1126

Zgambo, M., Costello, M., Buhlmann, M., Maldon, J., Anyango, E., & Adama, E. (2025). Artificial intelligence and academic integrity in nursing education: A mixed methods study on usage, perceptions, and institutional implications. *Nurse Education Today, 153*, 106796. DOI: 10.1016/j.nedt.2025.106796 PMID: 40517666

Zhai, X., & Krajcik, J. (2024). Uses of artificial intelligence in STEM education. *Uses of Artificial Intelligence in STEM Education*, 1–625. DOI: 10.1093/oso/9780198882077.001.0001

Zhang, G. P. (2003). Time series forecasting using a hybrid ARIMA and neural network model. *Neurocomputing, 50*, 159–175.

Zhang, J., Busck, A. G., & Kristensen, S. B. P. (2025). Integrating Farmers into Contract Farming in Peripheral Rural Areas in China. *Land (Basel), 14*(5), 976. DOI: 10.3390/land14050976

Zhang, S., Yang, Y., Sun, F., & Fang, B. (2023). Application of Image Sensing System in Mineral/Rock Identification: Sensing Mode and Information Process. *Advanced Intelligent Systems*, *5*(11), 2300206. Advance online publication. DOI: 10.1002/aisy.202300206

Zhao, W. X., Zhou, K., Li, J., Tang, T., Dong, Z., Hou, Y., Zhang, B., Min, Y., Zhang, J., Liu, P., Wang, X., Du, Y., Yang, C., Chen, Y., Chen, Z., Jiang, J., Ren, R., Li, Y., Tang, X., & Wen, J. R. (2026). A survey of large language models. *Frontiers of Computer Science*, *20*(12), 2012627. DOI: 10.1007/s11704-026-60308-3 PMID: 41813245

Zhou, C. (2023). Integration of modern technologies in higher education on the example of artificial intelligence use. *Education and Information Technologies*, *28*(4), 3893–3910. DOI: 10.1007/s10639-022-11309-9

Zhou, L., Gao, J., Li, D., & Shum, H.-Y. (2022). The Design and implementation of xiaoice, an empathetic social chatbot. *Computational Linguistics*, *46*(1), 53–93. DOI: 10.1162/coli_a_00368

Zhou, X., Liu, M., Yurtsever, E., Zagar, B. L., Zimmer, W., Cao, H., & Knoll, A. C. (2024). Vision language models in autonomous driving: A survey and outlook. *IEEE Transactions on Intelligent Vehicles*, 1–20. DOI: 10.1109/TIV.2024.3402136

Zhu, Y., Wang, X., Chen, J., Qiao, S., Ou, Y., Yao, Y., . . . Zhang, N. (2024). Llms for knowledge graph construction and reasoning: Recent capabilities and future opportunities. *World Wide Web, 27*(5).

Zimmerman, B. J. (2002). Becoming a self-regulated learner: An overview. *Theory into Practice*, *41*(2), 64–70. DOI: 10.1207/s15430421tip4102_2

Zuboff, S. (2019). *The age of surveillance capitalism: The fight for a human future at the new frontier of power*. PublicAffairs. Marguerit, D. (2025). Augmenting or automating labor? The effect of AI development on new work, employment, and wages. *arXiv preprint arXiv:2503.19159.*

Zuo, S., Liang, Y., Wu, Y., Ge, S., Shi, J., Ma, X., Cai, L., Li, J., Lam, S. S., & Xia, C. (2023). Using environmentally friendly technology for fabricating special plywood with ultra-high strength. *Journal of Cleaner Production*, *396*, 136462. DOI: 10.1016/j.jclepro.2023.136462

About the Contributors

Caroline M. Crawford, Ed.D., is a Professor of Instructional Design and Technology at the University of Houston-Clear Lake in Houston, Texas, United States of America. She earned her doctoral degree from the University of Houston in Houston, Texas, United States of America, in 1998, with specialization areas in Instructional Technology and Curriculum Theory, and began her tenure at the University of Houston-Clear Lake (UHCL) the same year. At this point in Dr. Crawford's professional career, her main areas of interest focus upon student success, engagement, and belonging, within learning environments. Further, Dr. Crawford's areas of expertise extend into communities of learning and the appropriate and successful integration of technologies into the learning environment; the learning environment may be envisioned as face-to-face, blended and online (virtual or text-driven) environments, as well as microlearning and micro-assist deliverables.

***

Sharon Andrews Ph.D. is Professor of Software Engineering at the University of Houston-Clear Lake in Houston, Texas, United States of America. She earned her Doctor of Philosophy in Computer Science from the Center for Advanced Computer Studies of the University of Louisiana in Lafayette, Louisiana, United States of America. Dr. Andrews is the designer, developer, and implementer of the Software Engineering MS curriculum, and she serves as Director of Software Engineering. She currently teaches and conducts research in the areas of Software Reuse and Reengineering; Software Architecture; Software Process, and AI in Engineering.

Nizirwan Anwar, MT, IPM, ASEAN.Eng, APEC.Eng is a Lecturer in the Department of Informatics Engineering, Faculty of Computer Science, Universitas Esa Unggul, under the auspices of the Kemala Bangsa Education Foundation (YPKB). The author was born in the city of Bandung on July 24 1964, completed his bachelor's degree from the Physics Study Program, Faculty of Mathematics and Natural Sciences, Padjadjaran University, Bandung in 1989 and continued the Electrical Engineering Study Program, Faculty of Engineering (dh. Postgraduate Study Program) University of Indonesia, Jakarta, completing his studies in 1995, obtaining a Bachelor of Engineering Intermediate Professional (IPM) and ASEAN Engineer (ASEAN.Eng). Alhamdulillah has produced several reputable and indexed published scientific papers at national and international levels (research categories: Internet of Things, Cryptography, Bibliometrics and Data Science). To date, he is registered as active in several professional organisations, National Lecturer BKD assessor (NIRA), as a reviewer in Arjuna accredited journals (Kemendikbud Saintek), Scientific Committee, Central Executive of the Vocational Agency BKI PII,

Soulef Bouaafia is currently Assistant Professor in Electronics at Electrical Engineering Department of the Higher Institute of Applied Sciences and Technology of Kairouan (ISSATKr). She received her master's degree in micro and nano-electronics from the Faculty of Science of Monastir, in 2018, and the Ph.D. degree in the electronics and microelectronics from the Faculty of Sciences of Monastir, University of Monastir, Tunisia. Her current research interests include image and video processing, HEVC, VVC standards, embedded systems, artificial intelligence, deep learning, SoC design, and the IoT.

Yamuna Devi E is a final year postgraduate student in M. Tech in Computer science with specialization in Data science at Vellore Institute of Technology, Vellore. Her work spans Agentic AI, Large Learning Models, GenAI, Machine Learning, Natural Language Processing, and other large language model–based applications. She has worked on academic and applied projects focusing on speech-to-ISL translation, sentiment analysis and computer-vision. Her current research focus lies in technologies such as agentic AI, context-aware AI, advanced reasoning.

Muhammad Faisal his Bachelor of Information Systems (S.SI) in Information Systems Department from STMIK Profesional, Makassar, Indonesia, in 2011, and his Master of Computer Science (M.Kom) in Informatics Engineering Department from Universitas Hasanuddin, Gowa, Indonesia, in 2014. He holds Ph.D degree from the School of Science and Technology, Doctoral Programme, Asia E University Malaysia. He is currently a lecturer and researcher at the Department of Informatics, Universitas Muhammadiyah Makassar, Indonesia. His research interests include Artificial Intelligence, Data Mining, Decision Support Systems, Image Processing, Deep Learning, and Machine Learning

Alex Gufron was born in Pati on 11 July 1994 and is currently based in East Jakarta, Indonesia. He earned his Bachelor's degree in Informatics Engineering from Universitas Esa Unggul in 2017 and is presently pursuing a Master's degree in Informatics at Universitas Negeri Semarang, commencing in 2026. His academic background reflects a strong foundation in computer science and information technology, with continued advancement at the postgraduate level. Alex maintains active academic and professional communication through his institutional email (alexgufron@students.unnes.ac.id) and personal contact (agufronan@gmail.com), demonstrating his ongoing engagement in higher education and professional development within the field of informatics.

Mohamed Ali Hajjaji is a Professor of Electronics specializing in multimedia security, secure embedded systems, and advanced electronic architectures. His research focuses on multimedia cryptography, secure processing and protection of digital content, and hardware implementation of security algorithms on reconfigurable platforms, particularly FPGAs. He also investigates the integration of artificial intelligence techniques in secure electronic and embedded systems. In addition, his research interests include renewable energy systems, with emphasis on the design, control, and optimization of intelligent electronic platforms for renewable energy integration. He has contributed to several research projects and published numerous scientific articles in peer-reviewed international journals. His current work addresses hardware-efficient security, lightweight cryptography, and intelligent electronic system design.

Hasnawati is a dedicated lecturer at Sekolah Tinggi Ilmu Kesehatan (STIKES) Datu Kamanre in Belopa, Kabupaten Luwu, where she has been shaping the future of public health education since 2020. She holds both her Bachelor's and Doctoral degrees in Public Health from Universitas Indonesia Timur. With a strong passion for advancing health education, Hasnawati continues to inspire and mentor students while contributing to the development of public health in her community.

Mohammad Irfan is a Professor at the School of Business and Commerce, Chandigarh University, Lucknow (Unnao), India, with over eighteen years of teaching and research experience. He has published more than 112 Scopus-indexed research papers, accumulating 781+ citations with an H-index of 15. He has authored 14 books with leading international publishers, including Springer and IGI Global, and is recognized among the World's Top 2% Scientists. His research expertise covers Security Analysis and Portfolio Management, Artificial Intelligence, Machine Learning, Blockchain, Cryptocurrency, Financial Engineering, FinTech, Green Finance, and Alternative Finance. He earned his Ph.D. from the Central University of Haryana and holds an MBA in Finance, an M.Com in Accounts and Law, and an

MA in Economics. A UGC-JRF/SRF/NET qualifier in Management and Commerce, he also holds professional certifications from NSE (NCFM) and BSE.

Irmawati is a bachelor of engineering in Electrical Engineering, Hasanuddin University, and an M.T. degree from the master in Information Technology, Postgraduate School of Hasanuddin University. She is currently a lecturer and researcher at Politeknik Negeri Ujung Pandang, Department of Computer and Network Engineering. Her current research interestsinclude data engineer, big data, integration system, and digital supply chain management.

Aditya Jadeja is currently pursuing a Master of Business Administration (MBA) at Karnavati University, India. He holds a Bachelor of Business Administration (Honours) degree and has a strong academic interest in Human Resource Management, Artificial Intelligence, Sustainability, and Organizational Studies. He has actively engaged in scholarly research and has presented his work at five national academic conferences, contributing to discussions on contemporary management and emerging business challenges. His involvement in research publications and book chapters reflects his commitment to academic excellence and knowledge creation. Driven by a passion for learning and inquiry, Aditya aspires to pursue doctoral studies in the future and contribute to the advancement of management research through meaningful scholarly contributions.

Muhammad Syafaat S. Kuba, ST., MT. is a lecturer in Civil Engineering at Universitas Muhammadiyah Makassar with the academic rank of Lektor. His expertise includes hydraulics, drainage systems, sediment transport, and the application of computational and machine learning methods in civil engineering analysis. He completed his undergraduate studies at Universitas Muhammadiyah Makassar and earned his master's degree from Hasanuddin University. In recent years, he has been actively involved in applied research, scientific publications, and community service projects related to sustainable water resources and flood mitigation.

Dilek Küçük, Ph.D, is an associate professor and principal chief researcher at TÜBİTAK Marmara Research Center (MRC). She has obtained her B.S., M.S. and Ph.D. degrees all from Middle East Technical University in Ankara (Turkey), in 2003, 2005, and 2011, respectively. Between May 2013 and May 2014, she has studied as a post-doctoral researcher at European Commission's Joint Research Centre in Italy. Her research interests include energy informatics, data mining, social media analysis, natural language processing, and database applications in engineering domains. She is the author or co-author of 17 papers published at SCI-indexed journals, in addition to 50 papers presented at international conferences.

Emine Ela Küçük, Ph.D., is a full professor at the Faculty of Health Sciences, Giresun University. She received her B.Sc. degree from Giresun Health School of Karadeniz Technical University and her M.Sc. degree from the Public Health Department of the Faculty of Medicine in Karadeniz Technical University. She received her Ph.D. degree from the Public Health Department of the Faculty of Medicine in Erciyes University. Her research topics include public health, public health surveillance, women health, and adolescent health.

Rampelli Manojkumar received his Ph.D. in Power Engineering from the Indian Institute of Technology Guwahati in 2023. He obtained his Master of Technology in Power and Energy Systems from the National Institute of Technology Karnataka, Surathkal, India, in 2015. He is currently an Assistant Professor in the Department of Electrical and Electronics Engineering at BVRIT Hyderabad College of Engineering for Women. He is currently the Editorial Board Member of Scientific Reports, Early Career Editor for the International Journal of Ambient Energy and the Guest Editor for PLOS ONE. He has been a speaker at the IEEE Smart Grid webinar series and has contributed to multiple funded research projects on smart transformer-based microgrid systems and distributed generation management. He has published 10 Q1 journal papers, including articles in IEEE Transactions on Power Systems, IEEE Transactions on Industrial Informatics, and Sustainable Cities and Society. His research expertise spans energy management, hybrid AC/DC distribution systems, energy storage, and power electronics applications in modern distribution systems. Additionally, he is an active reviewer for around 30 SCI journals, including IEEE Transactions on Industrial Informatics, IEEE Systems Journal, Journal of Energy Storage, Applied Energy, etc. He has also been actively involved in faculty training programs focused on teaching and learning enhancement, including instructional design, formative assessment, and teaching analytics, thereby strengthening his interdisciplinary expertise in education and technology integration.

Abdellatif Mtibaa is currently Professor in MicroElectronics and Hardware Design with Electrical department at the National School of Engineering of Monastir and Head of Circuits Systems Reconfigurable Group at Electronic and Microelectronic Laboratory. He holds a Diploma in Electrical Engineering in 1985 and received his PhD degree in Electrical Engineering in 2000. His current research interests include System on Programmable Chip, high level synthesis, rapid prototyping and reconfigurable architecture for real-time multimedia applications. Dr. Abdellatif Mtibaa has authored/co-authored over 100 papers in international journals and conferences. He served on the technical program committees for several international conferences. He also served as a co-organizer of several international conferences.

Abdul Nanda has a Bachelor of Engineering (S.T) in Department of Water Resources Engineering from Universitas Muhammadiyah Makassar, Makassar, Indonesia, in 1994, and his Master of Engineering (M.T) from Universitas Brawijaya, Malang, Indonesia, in 1998. He holds a Doctoral degree from Universitas Hasanuddin, Makassar, Indonesia. He is currently a lecturer and researcher at the Department of Water Resources Engineering, Universitas Muhammadiyah Makassar, Indonesia. His research interests include Civil Engineering and Water Resources Engineering.

Anand R Navaratna is a Research Scholar at the School of Management and Entrepreneurship, Indian Institute of Technology, Jodhpur, in the domain of Digital Transformation. He has over 15 years of industry experience in the field of Aviation Technology Management and Policy design. His area of interest is AI Governance, Policy and Regulation.

NurnaNurnawaty earned her Bachelor of Engineering (S.T.) in Water Resources Engineering from Universitas Muhammadiyah Makassar, Indonesia, in 1994. She subsequently completed her Master of Engineering (M.T.) at Universitas Brawijaya, Malang, Indonesia, in 1998. She later obtained her Doctoral degree from Universitas Hasanuddin, Makassar, Indonesia. She currently serves as a lecturer and researcher in the Department of Water Resources Engineering at Universitas Muhammadiyah Makassar. Her academic and research interests focus on Civil Engineering and Water Resources Engineering, with particular emphasis on sustainable water resource management, hydraulic systems, and infrastructure development. Through her teaching, research, and scholarly contributions, she actively supports the advancement of engineering education and applied research in Indonesia.

Muh Raharjo, Lecturer of Ujung Pantai State Polytechnic, earned a Bachelor of Engineering (S.T.) in Telecommunication Engineering in the Department of Electrical Engineering, Hasanuddin University and earned a Master of Engineering (M.T.) in Telecommunication and Informatics Engineering in the Postgraduate Program in Electrical Engineering, Hasanuddin University. Research fields include telecommunications, information technology, and information systems.

Vivit Rosmayanti, S.Pd.I., M.Pd was born in Botta on June 26, 1987. She has over 10 years of experience teaching at the University. She obtained a bachelor's degree in English Education from Alauddin State Islamic University. She completed her master's and doctoral degrees in English Education from Makassar State University. She is currently a lecturer in the Post Graduate Program, Department of English Education at Makassar State University, South Sulawesi, Indonesia. She is also actively writing research articles to be published in nationally and internationally accredited journals. She has written in some chapter books, monographs, and reference books. She is interested in teaching methods for teaching English. Her research interests include language teaching methodology, ICT instruction, and ESP teaching.

Deepak Saxena is a Head and faculty in the School of Management and Entrepreneurship, IIT Jodhpur. He holds a PhD in Management Information Systems from Trinity College Dublin (Ireland). After obtaining his PhD, he worked with Trinity College Dublin (Postdoctoral Research Fellow), Dublin Institute of Technology (Lecturer), and Birla Institute of Technology & Science Pilani (Assistant Professor). His area of interest includes digital transformation and responsible AI.

Archana Tamizharasan is a Professor in the School of Computer Science and Engineering at VIT University, Vellore, India, with over 18 years of academic experience. She has published several research articles and holds a few Indian patents. Her research interests include Artificial Intelligence, Machine Learning, Internet of Things, and Data Analytics, with a strong focus on applied and industrial AI solutions. She has executed several consultancy projects and actively collaborates with industry to design and deliver problem-driven AI solutions. Dr. Archana mentors students in innovation-oriented research, patents, and startup initiatives and has demonstrated expertise in translating research outcomes into deployable systems. She is engaged in interdisciplinary research addressing real-world engineering challenges and regularly delivers invited talks, workshops, and faculty development programs on emerging AI technologies.

Index

A

C

D

P

R

S

T

www.ingramcontent.com/pod-product-compliance
Lightning Source LLC
LaVergne TN
LVHW062328300926
849161LV00007B/1614
* 9 7 9 8 2 6 0 0 2 8 1 1 7 *